CAMBRI  TION

Cambridge

The city of Cambridge received its royal charter in 1201, having already been home to Britons, Romans and Anglo-Saxons for many centuries. Cambridge University was founded soon afterwards and celebrated its octocentenary in 2009. This series explores the history and influence of Cambridge as a centre of science, learning, and discovery, its contributions to national and global politics and culture, and its inevitable controversies and scandals.

The Archaeology of the Cambridge Region

Sir Cyril Fox (1882–1967) was an archaeologist and later Director of the National Museum of Wales and President of the Museums Association. Having entered Magdalene College, Cambridge as a mature student, his first year dissertation was judged to be more suitable as a PhD thesis, which resulted in him progressing straight to his PhD. His doctoral thesis, reissued here, transformed archaeological thought when it was first published in 1923. In it Fox pioneered the geographical approach to analysing ancient settlement patterns, linking the expansion of human settlement in the Cambridge area from the Neolithic era to the Anglo-Saxon period with favourable environmental conditions. His thesis emphasised the importance of treating archaeological finds as clues to past human settlement instead of being the main focus for archaeological analysis. This approach became the methodological framework for later environmental and landscape archaeology.

Cambridge University Press has long been a pioneer in the reissuing of out-of-print titles from its own backlist, producing digital reprints of books that are still sought after by scholars and students but could not be reprinted economically using traditional technology. The Cambridge Library Collection extends this activity to a wider range of books which are still of importance to researchers and professionals, either for the source material they contain, or as landmarks in the history of their academic discipline.

Drawing from the world-renowned collections in the Cambridge University Library, and guided by the advice of experts in each subject area, Cambridge University Press is using state-of-the-art scanning machines in its own Printing House to capture the content of each book selected for inclusion. The files are processed to give a consistently clear, crisp image, and the books finished to the high quality standard for which the Press is recognised around the world. The latest print-on-demand technology ensures that the books will remain available indefinitely, and that orders for single or multiple copies can quickly be supplied.

The Cambridge Library Collection will bring back to life books of enduring scholarly value (including out-of-copyright works originally issued by other publishers) across a wide range of disciplines in the humanities and social sciences and in science and technology.

The Archaeology of the Cambridge Region

A Topographical Study of the Bronze, Early Iron, Roman and Anglo-Saxon Ages, with an Introductory Note on the Neolithic Age

CYRIL FOX

CAMBRIDGE UNIVERSITY PRESS

Cambridge, New York, Melbourne, Madrid, Cape Town, Singapore,
São Paolo, Delhi, Dubai, Tokyo, Mexico City

Published in the United States of America by Cambridge University Press, New York

www.cambridge.org
Information on this title: www.cambridge.org/9781108011693

© in this compilation Cambridge University Press 2010

This edition first published 1923
This digitally printed version 2010

ISBN 978-1-108-01169-3 Paperback

This book reproduces the text of the original edition. The content and language reflect
the beliefs, practices and terminology of their time, and have not been updated.

Cambridge University Press wishes to make clear that the book, unless originally published
by Cambridge, is not being republished by, in association or collaboration with, or
with the endorsement or approval of, the original publisher or its successors in title.

THE ARCHAEOLOGY
of the
CAMBRIDGE REGION

CAMBRIDGE UNIVERSITY PRESS
C. F. CLAY, Manager
LONDON : FETTER LANE, E.C. 4

NEW YORK : THE MACMILLAN CO.
BOMBAY
CALCUTTA } MACMILLAN AND CO., Ltd.
MADRAS
TORONTO : THE MACMILLAN CO. OF
CANADA, Ltd.
TOKYO : MARUZEN-KABUSHIKI-KAISHA

ALL RIGHTS RESERVED

FRONTISPIECE (PL. XXVIII)

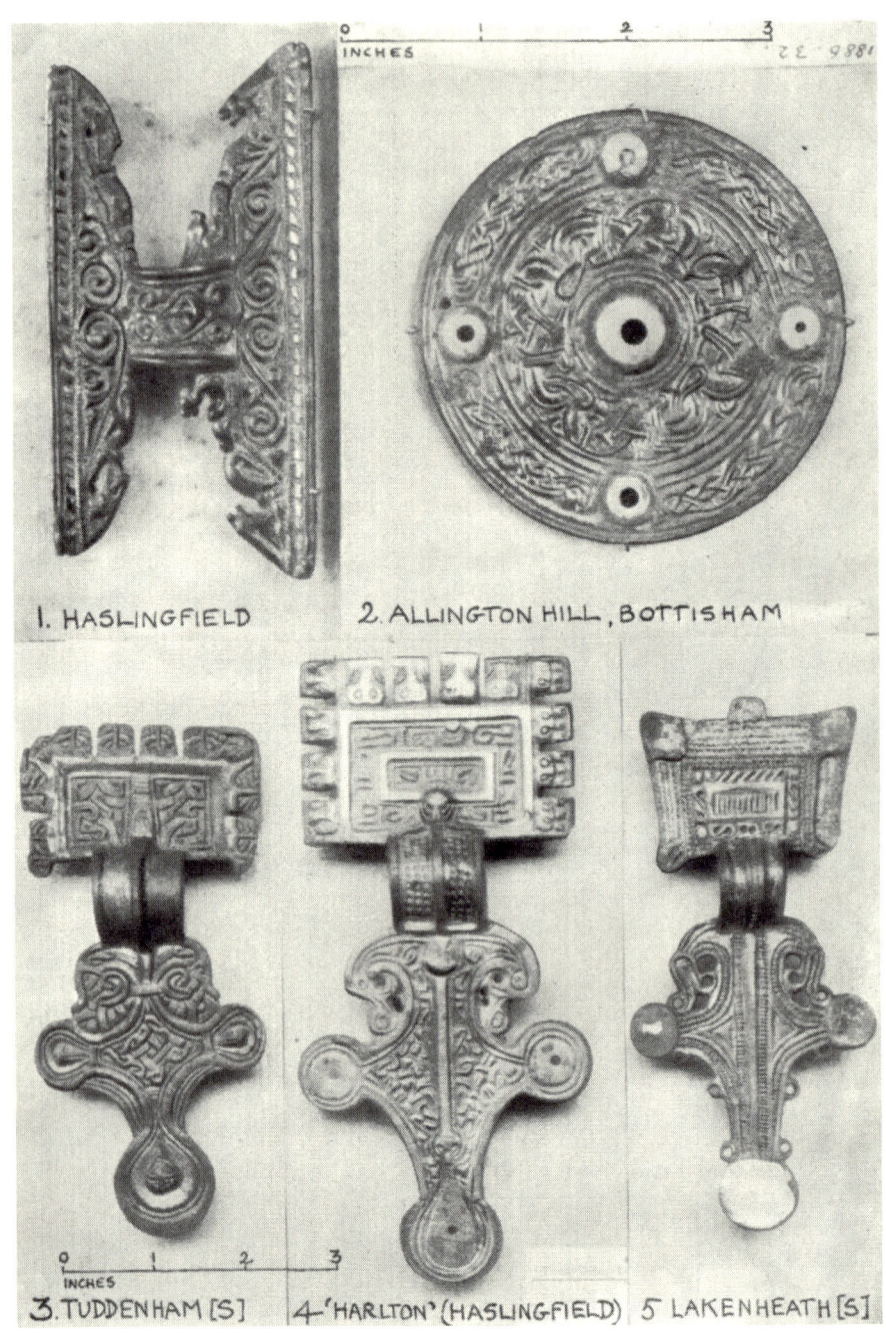

1. HASLINGFIELD 2. ALLINGTON HILL, BOTTISHAM 3. TUDDENHAM [S] 4. 'HARLTON' (HASLINGFIELD) 5. LAKENHEATH [S]

ANGLO-SAXON AGE. GRAVE-FURNITURE OF THE PAGAN PERIOD
No 1, pp. 256, 258, 276; No. 2 pp. 258, 264; Nos. 3, 4, 5, p. 258.

THE ARCHAEOLOGY
of the
CAMBRIDGE REGION

A Topographical Study of the Bronze,
Early Iron, Roman and Anglo-Saxon
Ages, *with an* Introductory Note
on the Neolithic Age

By

CYRIL FOX, Ph.D., F.S.A.

∴

CAMBRIDGE
AT THE UNIVERSITY PRESS
1923

PRINTED IN GREAT BRITAIN

PREFATORY NOTE

THE character and scope of the book are indicated in the Introduction; this prefatory note enables me to acknowledge my indebtedness to the work of others, and the help, both personal and financial, which I have received in connection with it.

A tribute is first due to Cambridge antiquaries, past and present, on whose work this study of mine has been built up, and but for whose labours it would have been impossible to complete it. I wish specially to mention the late Professor C. C. Babington, author of *Ancient Cambridgeshire*, and the late Professor T. McKenny Hughes; Baron Anatole von Hügel also, during whose tenure of the Curatorship of the Museum of Archaeology and of Ethnology (1883–1921) much material of vital importance for the pre-history and early history of the Cambridge Region has been secured for the benefit of my own and future generations.

To the Hon. Richard C. Neville, afterwards fourth Lord Braybrooke, a debt of gratitude is owed by all archaeologists; lacking his researches in connection with Bronze Age barrows, Roman sites and Anglo-Saxon cemeteries our knowledge of the Cambridge Region in past times would be still more limited than it is. That most of the objects found in the course of his investigations have been preserved in the Museum at Audley End House enhances the value of his work. To the present Lord Braybrooke, Visitor of my own College, I am indebted for permission to utilize the evidence available in that Museum.

The use made of the researches of students and investigators referred to directly and indirectly in the preceding paragraphs, and of the labours of others in the field of British archaeology in general, is I hope adequately acknowledged in the text. Here I may record my especial indebtedness to the writings of Professor G. Baldwin Brown and Mr Reginald A. Smith.

To the President and Council of the Cambridge Antiquarian Society special thanks are due; under the Society's auspices, and partly with the aid of its funds, the field work which formed part of my research has been carried through. My indebtedness to Dr W. M. Palmer, member of the Council, who collaborated with me in that work and largely financed it, I have elsewhere acknowledged.

For valued help and encouragement during the four years in which I have been engaged on this work I wish especially to thank Professor H. M. Chadwick and Professor Sir William Ridgeway; I have taken advantage of the permission given me by the latter to describe and refer to important objects in his collection of local antiquities.

For advice and information on special points I am grateful to Mr Miles Burkitt, Mr A. B. Cook, Mr W. J. Corbett, Dr W. H. L. Duckworth, Dr A. C. Haddon, and Mr F. J. H. Jenkinson[1], all of Cambridge; to Professor J. L. Myres and Mr E. Thurlow Leeds of Oxford, to Mr Harold Peake, Mr Bruce Dickins, Mr A. F. Griffith, Mr Guy Maynard and Mr George Morris; to Mr O. G. S. Crawford of the Ordnance Survey; to Mr R. A. Smith and Mr T. D. Kendrick of the British Museum; to the Rev. F. G. Walker, sometime Secretary of the C.A.S., and to Mr W. G. Clarke of Norwich. The latter has freely placed at my disposal his intimate knowledge of the archaeology of N.W. Suffolk, and has revised my Neolithic map of this area.

I am obliged to Mr H. Peake for enabling me to make additions to my list of Bronze Age Implements from the Card Index of such implements now being prepared by him on behalf of the British Association. I have also to thank Miss M. V. Taylor, of the Haverfield Library, Oxford, for access to MS. records bearing on the Roman occupation of my district.

I wish also to acknowledge the courtesy and help which I have received from Mr L. C. G. Clarke, Curator of the Museum of Archaeology and of Ethnology, Cambridge, and from the Curators or owners of the several public or private Museums referred to in the text.

I am indebted to Mr H. Barker, the Curator of Moyses Hall Museum, Bury St Edmunds, for permitting me to obtain the photographs reproduced on Plates I, 4; II, 3, and XV, 1; to Mr J. W. Bodger, Hon. Secretary of the Peterborough Archaeological Society, for permission to reproduce objects in Fig. 1; and to Miss B. S. Phillpotts, Mistress of Girton College, for allowing me to reproduce on Plates XXXI, 1, 2, and XXXV, 1, 2, objects in Girton College Library. The Girton photographs were kindly supplied to me by Miss E. S. Fegan, Librarian of the College.

These excepted, all the objects illustrated are in the Museum of Archaeology and Ethnology, Cambridge; and my thanks are due to the Board of Archaeological and Ethnological Studies for allowing me to reproduce them. The photographs used for the half-tone plates of these objects were taken for me by Mr W. Tams of Cambridge, whose skill and care deserve special recognition here.

I am much indebted to the Syndics of the University Press for undertaking, without hope of financial profit, the publication of this

---

[1] Mr Jenkinson, University Librarian, kindly permitted me to make use of his MS. notes on the Anglo-Saxon Cemetery at Girton, explored by him.

PREFATORY NOTE

book. The high cost of its production, in particular of the series of coloured maps which are essential to my scheme, made it necessary for me to find the sum of one hundred pounds additional to that which the Press was prepared to expend. It is with grateful pleasure that I here record the names of the Society and the personal friends and relations by whom this sum was generously provided.

	£	s.	d.
The Cambridge Antiquarian Society	20	0	0
A. C. Benson, LL.D., C.V.O., Master of Magdalene College	3	3	0
C. G. Brocklebank, M.A., M.C.	25	0	0
Professor H. M. Chadwick, M.A.	10	10	0
L. Cobbett, M.A., M.D., F.R.C.S.	20	0	0
C. F. Fox	5	0	0
Mrs Bernard Gotch	2	7	0
A. Stanley Griffith, M.D., D.P.H.	5	0	0
Professor G. H. F. Nuttall, Sc.D., F.R.S.	2	0	0
W. M. Palmer, M.D., F.S.A.	5	0	0
Miss C. E. Parsons	2	0	0

For the care and skill shown in the production of the coloured maps my best thanks are due to the Director-General and the Staff of the Ordnance Survey. I also wish to thank Mr S. C. Roberts, Secretary to the Syndics of the Press, and the Manager and Staff of the Press for the courtesy and help afforded me in connection with the book.

Miss E. S. Fegan, Librarian of Girton College, generously undertook the thankless task of proof-reading; Mr Miles Burkitt read the proof of Chapter I, Professor H. M. Chadwick the proofs of Chapters I, II, III, VI and VII; Dr W. H. L. Duckworth the proofs of the paragraphs dealing with the ethnology of the district. I have been glad to adopt suggestions made by these friends. I have also received valued help in connection with the proofs from Mr W. J. Corbett, Dr L. Cobbett, and my father, Mr C. F. Fox.

Communications of finds which may in the future be made in the district covered by this survey, or of past discoveries which I may have omitted, will be gratefully received and acknowledged. Such communications should be addressed to me, c/o The Curator, the Museum of Archaeology and of Ethnology, Cambridge.

CYRIL FOX.

RED GABLES,
MILTON, CAMBS.
July, 1923.

CONTENTS

	PAGE
LIST OF ILLUSTRATIONS AND MAPS	xiii
CONTRACTIONS	xix
INTRODUCTION	xxi

Chapter I. THE NEOLITHIC AGE. Duration Unknown. (Metal
    was introduced about 2000 B.C.) 1
  Introduction 1
    The Grimes Graves industry 1
    Stone Implements probably of post-Neolithic date . . . 2
  Topographical Distribution of Finds 5
  The value of the Map Record 8
  The stone axe 9
  Interments: Long Barrows 11
  General considerations 14

Chapter II. THE BRONZE AGE (including the Transition Period
    from Stone to Metal). Circa 2000 B.C. to 500–400 B.C. 16
  Chronological and other problems 16
  System of Classification adopted 20
  The Beaker-Folk and their Pottery 22
    Local Distribution of the Beaker 23
    Typology of the Beaker 25
    Interments associated with Beakers 27
  Interments not associated with Beakers 28
    Topographical Distribution of Round Barrows, etc. . . . 30
    Details of representative burials 31
    Sepulchral pottery other than Beakers 38
  Analysis of Bronze Age Interments 42
  Bronze Age Interments: Summary 44
  Settlements 47
  Finds and Hoards of the Bronze Age 49
    Chronological Analysis 49
  Consideration of the Finds and Hoards as illustrating two Culture
    Phases (subdivided into four Periods):
  The First Phase ending circa 1000 B.C.:
    I. The Transition Period 53
    II. The Early Bronze Period 53
    III. The Middle Bronze Period 55
  The Second Phase, 1000 B.C.—500–400 B.C.:
    IV. The Late Bronze Period 57
  Topographical Distribution of Finds and Hoards 62
  Ethnology 65
  Summary 67

CONTENTS

	PAGE
Chapter III. THE EARLY IRON AGE. From 500–400 B.C. to the middle of I Century A.D.	70
Introduction	70
The First Phase: Centuries V–IV to I B.C.	
Fibulae of early types	72
Interments	76
Weapons	82
Pottery	82
General considerations	84
The Second Phase: I Century B.C.–I Century A.D.	
Coins	87
Pottery	90
(i) Of Aylesford (Belgic) types	90
(ii) Of other types	93
Shale vases and bowls	96
Interments:	
A. By inhumation	97
B. By cremation	97
Associated with fire-dogs, with Italo-Greek amphorae, or with Arretine ware	99
Topographical range of the Aylesford cremation culture	102
Hoard	104
Buckets, bronze vessels, fibulae, weapons, etc.	104
Earthworks, Settlements and Communications of the Early Iron Age	109
Dykes	109
Settlements	109
At Trumpington and Grantchester	111
Communications	113
Racial type or types in the Early Iron Age	114
Topographical Distribution of Finds and Remains of the Age	115
Summary	117
Chapter IV. EARTHWORKS AND TRACKWAYS POSSIBLY OR CERTAINLY PREHISTORIC	121
Introduction	121
The Cambridgeshire Dykes[1]	123
Archaeological evidence bearing on the date of the Dykes	127
Excavations in 1921–22. Worstead Street and Fleam Dyke	129
General considerations bearing on the date of dykes not yet excavated	131
Hill-top fortresses[1]	134
Forts and camps on less lofty ground[1]	137
General considerations bearing on the date of the fortresses	138
Pits or subterranean chambers	141

[1] Listed on p. 122 of text.

CONTENTS

	PAGE
Trackways	141
Icknield Way	143
Ashwell Street: Street Way	147
Mare Way	150
Other routes possibly prehistoric	152
Summary	156

Chapter V. THE ROMAN AGE. From 43 A.D. to early V century A.D. 159
Introduction 159
Roads[1] 161
Towns, Earthworks, etc.[2] 173
   Civil engineering works 179
   Summary of the above analyses 181
Houses in rural districts 183
Interments:
   (A) In flat cemeteries 188
   (B) In barrows 191
   Barrow burial in the Roman Age: general considerations . . 198
Pottery and bronzes, etc., associated with interments; or chance finds 200
   (I) Pottery: Terra Nigra 201
             Terra Sigillata 202
             Other wares 208
   (II) Vessels and objects of bronze and iron, silver, pewter and glass 213
Topographical analysis of the remains of the Age 217
   Absence of evidence of settlement along the highways . . 219
   The new towns, Cambridge and Godmanchester . . . 220
   Traffic and Settlement in the Fens 222
   Were the Forest areas cleared and inhabited? 224
Duration of the Age in the Cambridge Region 225
   (*a*) Area South of the Fens 226
   (*b*) The Southern Fens and North-west Suffolk . . . 229
Evidence illustrating the vicissitudes of the Roman occupation . 231
Note on the Ethnology of the Age 233
Summary 233

Chapter VI. THE ANGLO-SAXON AGE 237
Introduction 237
A. *The Pagan Period: mid-V century to mid-VII century* . . 238
Cemeteries and Isolated Finds:
   I. In Southern Cambridgeshire 241
      Cemeteries at or near Cambridge 242
      Chapel Hill group: Barrington A and B, Haslingfield . . 250
      Sawston, Linton, Wilbraham and others 259
      Burial in a barrow on the chalk escarpment 264

[1] Listed on p. 164 of text.   [2] Listed on p. 173 of text.

CONTENTS

	PAGE
II. In the Border Counties:	
S.W. Norfolk and W. Suffolk	264
N.W. Essex	265
N. Hertfordshire	266
E. Bedfordshire and E. Huntingdonshire	267
Notes on certain grave-goods specially characteristic of the Cambridge Region	268
Topographical distribution of the cemeteries and finds	274
The date and mode of the Anglo-Saxon settlement	276
Cremation and Inhumation	277
Influence of the Roman civilization on the Anglo-Saxon settlers	280
Recurrence of La Tène art	283
Saxons and Angles	284
(A) West Saxons and Middle Angles	286
(B) Middle Angles and East Saxons	288
(C) The boundary between Middle and East Anglia	291
Note on the Anglian culture area	295
Summary	296
B. *The Christian Period, mid-VII century to* 1066 A.D.	297
(I) Remains dated in the period prior to 866 A.D.	297
(II) Remains dated in the heathen interlude 866–950 A.D.	298
(III) Remains dated in the period 950–1066 A.D.	299
Earthworks assignable to the period	301
Homestead Moats considered	303
Dyke at Childerley	305
Non-military earthwork: balks and lynchets	305
Distribution of Settlements at the close of the Age, as recorded in Domesday Book	306
Village Structure in open and forest areas contrasted	310
Expansion of Settlement in the Roman and Anglo-Saxon Ages compared	311
Chapter VII. CONCLUSIONS	313
APPENDICES. (Finds and Remains of the Bronze Age.)	
I. List of Beakers of the Transition Period	322
II. A. List of Hoards, other than Founders'; and small groups of associated objects, some (?) votive	323
B. List of Hoards, probably or certainly Founders' (all of the Late Bronze Period)	324
III. List of sixty-one Barrows in the Cambridge Region, excavated and considered to be of the Bronze Age	325
List of twenty excavated Barrows, probably or possibly of the Bronze Age	329
REFERENCES TO AUTHORS QUOTED	330
INDEX	336

ILLUSTRATIONS[1]

All the objects illustrated, unless otherwise noted, are in the Museum of Archaeology and of Ethnology, Cambridge.

PLATES

XXVIII. ANGLO-SAXON AGE. GRAVE-FURNITURE OF THE PAGAN PERIOD . . . . . . FRONTISPIECE
1. Equal-armed fibula of silver: *Haslingfield*. 2. Disc of gilt bronze, inlaid with shell and garnets: *Allington Hill, Bottisham*. 3, 4, 5. Square-headed fibulae of gilt bronze; No. 5 has the terminals plated with silver: *Tuddenham* [S], *Haslingfield, and Lakenheath* [S].

TO FACE PAGE

I. BRONZE AGE. BEAKER POTTERY OF THE "TRANSITION PERIOD" 24
1. Beaker, zonal rouletted decoration: *Wilburton Fen*. 2. Handled mug, scratched decoration: *March*. 3. Beaker, "coil" decoration: *Lakenheath* [S]. 4. Beaker, stab decoration: *near Bury* [S] (Bury Mus.).

II. BRONZE AGE. BEAKER POTTERY OF THE "TRANSITION PERIOD" 26
1, 1A. Handled mug, decorated with the finger-nail and a pointed tool: *Fordham*. 2. Beaker, zonal rouletted decoration: (?) *Eriswell* [S]. 3. Beaker fragment, ribbed, with stab decoration: *Great Barton* [S] (Bury Mus.).

III. BRONZE AGE. CINERARY URNS 38
1. Biconical urn: *Fen Ditton*. 2. Overhanging-rim urn: *Soham*. 3. Overhanging-rim urn, with accessory vessel: *Mepal Fen*. 4. Overhanging-rim urn: *Therfield Heath* [H].

IV. BRONZE AGE. CINERARY URNS AND OTHER SEPULCHRAL POTTERY 40
1 A, 1 B. Associated vessels: *Midsummer Common, Cambridge*. 2, 3. Cinerary urns, one with lugs: *Upper Hare Park, Swaffham Bulbeck*. 4. Food-vessel (?); *Midsummer Common, Cambridge*. 5. Cinerary urn (?): *Upper Hare Park, Swaffham Bulbeck*. 6 A, 6 B. Bowl and overhanging-rim urn: *Therfield Heath* [H].

V. NEOLITHIC AGE, AXE; BRONZE AGE, IMPLEMENTS ATTRIBUTED TO THE "TRANSITION PERIOD". 52
1. Polished axe of jade-like stone: *Histon*. 2. Perforated axe of deer horn: *Burwell Fen*. 3. Perforated axehammer of stone: *Swaffham Fen*. 4, 5. Perforated "maceheads" of deer horn and stone: *Burwell Fen*. 6. Perforated axehammer of stone: *Bottisham*. 7, 8. Arrowheads of flint: *Santon Downham* [S]; *Aldreth*. 9, 10. Daggers of flint: *Prickwillow;* "*Cambridge Fens.*" 11. Dagger of bone: *Burwell Fen*. 12, 13. Axes of copper or poor bronze: "*near Fordham.*" 14. Tanged knife or dagger of bronze: *The Cardle, Icklingham* [S].

[1] In a few of the Plates [Nos. III 2 and 4, VI B, VIII and XXIV] the details of the scale, photographed with the objects, are partially lost in the process of reproduction. In each of these cases the black lines of the upper portion of the scale represent inches, of the lower portion, centimetres.

xiv ILLUSTRATIONS

TO FACE PAGE

VI. BRONZE AGE. FOOD-VESSELS; AND IMPLEMENTS ATTRIBUTED TO THE "EARLY BRONZE PERIOD"   54
A, B. Food-vessels: *Rothwell* [*Northants.*]; *Wereham* [N]. 1, 2, 3. Axes; flat, or with slight flanges, hammered: *Bottisham Lode; Fordham* (?); *and Quy.* 4, 5, 6. Axes, with flanges, cast: *Stuntney;* "*near*" *Ely;* and *Burwell Fen.* 7. Spearhead (?), tanged: *Saffron Walden* [E]. 8. Dagger, riveted: *Lakenheath* [S]. 9. Bodkin: *Lakenheath* [S]. 10. Halberd: *Manea.* 11. Dagger, tanged: *Swaffham.*

VII. BRONZE AGE. IMPLEMENTS ATTRIBUTED TO THE "MIDDLE BRONZE PERIOD"   56
1–9. Palstaves, arranged in morphological sequence: *Wicken Fen; Reach; Chatteris* (?); *Bassingbourn; Quaveney; Burwell* (two); *Lakenheath Fen* [S]; *Undley* [S]. 10. Chisel, of "palstave" type: *Cambridge.* 11, 12. Spearheads, socketed, looped: *Burnt Fen* (*Lakenheath*) [S]; *Cambridge Common.* 13. Spearhead, socketed, with protected loops: *Isleham Fen.* 14. Rapier, reeded blade: *Isleham Fen.* 15. Dagger, rapier-like: *Quaveney.* 16. Dagger: *Soham Fen.* 17. Rapier: *Feltwell* [N].

VIII. BRONZE AGE. TWO GROUPS OF ASSOCIATED OBJECTS   58
1 A, B. Spearhead with protected loops, and shield: *Langwood Fen, Chatteris.* 2 A, B, C. Palstave, rapier, and socketed sickle: *Downham Fen* [N].

IX. BRONZE AGE. IMPLEMENTS ATTRIBUTED TO THE "LATE BRONZE PERIOD"   60
1, 2. Swords, leaf-shaped: *Aldreth; Coveney.* 3. Sword, hilt-plate flanged with terminal knob: *Coveney.* 4. Sword, leaf-shaped, socketed: "*near*" *Royston* [H]. 5, 6. Palstaves, debased types; No. 6 from *Teversham.* 7, 8. Axes socketed, wing decoration: *Cambridge; Chesterton.* 9, 10. Axes, socketed, rib and pellet decoration: *Barrington; Horningsea.* 11, 12. Axes, socketed, plain: *Quy;* "*Cambridge Fens.*" 13. Gouge, socketed: *Bottisham Lode.* 14. Ring, of V section: *Burwell.* 15. Axe, diminutive, of Gaulish type: *Royston Heath* [H]. 16. Chisel, tanged and shouldered: *Cavenham* [S]. 17. Mould for socketed axe: *New St, Cambridge.*

X. BRONZE AGE. PORTION OF HOARD OF THE "LATE BRONZE PERIOD." From *Wilburton Fen*   62
1. Palstave. 2. Axe, socketed, with indented sides. 3. Axe, socketed, plain. 4, 5. Scabbard chapes for sword and dagger. 6–11. Spearheads, socketed, without loops. 12, 13. Ferules for spear shafts. 14. Scabbard chape for sword. 15. Sword, leaf-shaped.

XI. EARLY IRON AGE. POTTERY OF HALLSTATT TYPES   82
A 1. Pot, handmade, probably sepulchral: *Lakenheath* [S]. A 2–A 6. Beakers and wide-mouthed pots, handmade, fragmentary: *Grantchester and Hauxton Mill.*

XII. EARLY IRON AGE. POTTERY, MAINLY SEPULCHRAL AND OF AYLESFORD TYPES (EXCEPT No. 6, OF THE ROMAN AGE)   90
1. Tazza, wheelmade: *Haslingfield.* 2. Ovoid urn, handmade: *Stourbridge Common, Cambridge.* 3. Pedestalled urn: *Chesterton.* 4. Wide-mouthed pot, wheelmade, with pierced base: *Barrington.* 5. Globular pot, handmade, with pierced base: *Ashwell* or *Guilden Morden.* 6. Beaker, wheelmade, of "Belgic" (Upchurch) ware: *Stourbridge Common, Cambridge.*

ILLUSTRATIONS

TO FACE PAGE

XIII. EARLY IRON AGE. POTTERY, MAINLY SEPULCHRAL AND OF AYLESFORD TYPES 92
    1, 1 A, 1 B. Associated objects; "barrel" urns, wheelmade, and one bronze fibula: *Hauxton Mill*[1]. 2, 3. Urns, wheelmade, with constricted waist: *Barnwell, Cambridge; near Royston* [H].

XIV. EARLY IRON AGE. DOMESTIC POTTERY . . 94
    C 1, C 2. Early forms, handmade: *Arbury Banks, Ashwell* [H]; *Chesterford* [E]. D 1, D 2. Later forms, handmade: *Royston* [H]. C 3. "Hammer" rim: *Lakenheath* [S]. A 7. "Indented" rim: *Trumpington*.

XV. EARLY IRON AGE. POTTERY, SHALE VASE, AND BRONZES 96
    1. Vase, wheelmade, showing bosses and circular depressions: *Icklingham* [S] (Bury Mus.). 2. Vase, ovoid, wheelmade, with cordons: *Odsey, Ashwell* [H]. 3. Vase, of Kimmeridge Shale, turned: *Old Warden* [B]. 4. Fibula, of bronze: *Bottisham Fen*. 5. Objects associated with an interment: *Newnham Croft, Cambridge*.

XVI. EARLY IRON AGE. POTTERY PROBABLY DOMESTIC (EXCEPT No 14. ROMANO-BELGIC) 98
    1–13. Fragmentary vessels of various shapes, the majority handmade: *Trumpington* (three); *Newnham* (two); *Hauxton Mill* (three); *Mutlow Hill, Wilbraham; Lakenheath* [S]; *Brandon* [S]; *War Ditches, Cherryhinton; Great Chesterford* [E]. 14. Tazza, wheelmade: *Great Chesterford* [E].

XVII. EARLY IRON AGE. OBJECTS ASSOCIATED WITH A BURIAL BY CREMATION 100
    "Fire-dogs," tripod and hooks, "spit," and amphora: *Stanfordbury, Southill* [B].

XVIII. EARLY IRON AGE. OBJECTS OF BRONZE AND IRON (EXCEPT No. 10, OF COPPER, BRONZE AGE) . . 106
    1. Sword scabbard, bronze, containing remains of iron sword: *Lakenheath* [S]. 2, 3. Fibulae of bronze: *Trumpington; Barrington*. 2 x. Fibula of bronze, with plaques of shell (?): *Newnham*. 4. Bronze mounts of casket: *Stanfordbury, Southill* [B]. 5–9. Fibulae of bronze: *Santon Downham* [S]. 10. Copper bars: *Money Hill Barrow, Therfield Heath* [H].

XIX. SECTIONS, (A) WORSTEAD STREET, AND (B) FLEAM DYKE, CAMBS. 130

XX. ROMAN AND ROMANO-BELGIC POTTERY . . . 200
    1, 2, 3. "*Terra sigillata*" cups: *Stanfordbury, Southill* [B]. 4–7. "*Terra nigra*" platters: *Foxton* (two); *Shefford* [B]; *Litlington*.

XXI. ROMAN AGE. POTTERY 204
    1. "*Terra sigillata*" platter with *graffito* on basal exterior: (?) *Henlow* [B]. 2. "*Terra sigillata*" bowl, Form 37: *Shefford* [B]. 3, 3 A. "Incense burner," biscuit ware, inscribed: *Litlington*.

XXII. ROMANO-BELGIC POTTERY; ROMAN AND ROMANO-BRITISH POTTERY AND FIBULAE 206
    1. Romano-Belgic bowl, Form 37: *War Ditches, Cherryhinton*. 2. Olla of "British gritted ware"[1]: *Litlington*. 3, 3 A. Arretine *crater* and Belgic platter, associated: *Foxton*. 4–6. Fibulae, bronze, various types: *Barrington; Mildenhall* [S]; "near Cambridge."

---

[1] The lower fibula on the plate was not included in this find.

xvi   ILLUSTRATIONS

                                                           TO FACE PAGE
XXIII. ROMAN AGE. POTTERY   208
       1, 2. Globular *ollae*, showing *La Tène* influence: *Castle St., Cambridge; Great Chesterford* [E]. 3. Amphora, used as a cremation urn: *Haslingfield*. 4. Amphora of colour-coated ware with scroll decoration: *Isleham Fen*.

XXIV. ROMAN AGE. POTTERY   210
       1. Wares made locally: *Horningsea*. 2. Beakers with slip decoration, and mouthpiece of a flagon: *War Ditches, Cherryhinton*. 3. Wares probably made locally: *Jesus Lane, Cambridge*.

XXV. ROMAN AGE. POTTERY AND GLASS VESSELS: PEWTER DISH   214
       1, 2, 3. Beakers, and flagon, of colour-coated wares: *Water Newton* [Hunts.]; "*near*" *Royston* [H]; *Great Chesterford* [E]. 4, 6. Vessels of glass: *Litlington; Wicken Fen*. 5. Dish of pewter, with beaded rim: *Sutton*.

XXVI. ROMAN AGE. BRONZE, GLASS AND POTTERY VESSELS   216
       1. Trefoil-lipped jug, and skillet, of bronze: *Stanfordbury, Southill* [B]. 2. Jug of glass, and two-handled pan of bronze: *Shefford* [B]. 3, 4, 5. Indented beakers of pottery: *Birdbrook* [E]; *Cambridge; Litlington*.

XXVII. ANGLO-SAXON AGE. GRAVE-FURNITURE OF THE PAGAN PERIOD   242
       1. Grave-group, including bronze ring, cruciform and annular fibulae, and silver disc: *St John's, Cambridge*. 2. Grave-group, ncluding cruciform and plate fibulae, tweezers, girdle-hanger, and clasps, all of bronze: *Girton*. 3, 4, 5. Cruciform fibulae of bronze: *St John's, Cambridge; Haslingfield, and Newnham*.

XXIX. ANGLO-SAXON AGE. GRAVE-FURNITURE OF THE PAGAN PERIOD   252
       1. Grave-group, including cruciform and "small long" fibulae, key handle, and clasps, all of bronze: *Barrington "B."* 2–6. Cruciform fibulae of bronze, of various types: *Exning* [S]; *Lakenheath* [S] (two); *Trumpington; Haslingfield*.

XXX. ANGLO-SAXON AGE. GRAVE-FURNITURE OF THE PAGAN PERIOD   254
       1 A, B, C. Grave group, including saucer and square-headed fibulae of bronze gilt, and armlet of silver: *Barrington "A."* 2. Plate of buckle(?), bronze gilt: *Rose Crescent, Cambridge*. 3. Fibula of bronze with enamel inlays, late provincial-Roman: *Girton* (Girton College). 4. Grave-group, including applied fibulae and wrist-clasps of bronze, gilt: *Barrington "B."* 5. Grave-group, including glass beads and "small long" fibulae of bronze: *Girton*. 6–8. "Small long" fibulae of bronze: *Barrington "B"; Hauxton*.

XXXI. ANGLO-SAXON AGE. CINERARY URNS OF THE PAGAN PERIOD: WEAPON OF THE CHRISTIAN PERIOD   260
       1, 2. Cinerary urns, handmade: *Girton* (Girton College Library). 4. Cinerary urn, handmade: *Sandy* [B]. 3. Axe of iron: *Fens near Ely*.

XXXII. ANGLO-SAXON AGE. SEPULCHRAL POTTERY, AND SHIELD BOSSES, OF THE PAGAN PERIOD . .   266
       1, 3. Pots, handmade, with neck cordons: *St John's, Cambridge*. 2. Pot, handmade, with narrow neck: *Eynesbury* [Hunts.].

ILLUSTRATIONS

TO FACE PAGE

4 A. Pot, handmade with glass in the base: *Haslingfield*. 4 B. Piece of glass from base of a pot: *Girton*. 5. Beaker, wheelmade, of Frankish type: *Lakenheath* [S]. 6. Beaker, handmade, showing Frankish influence: *Barrington "B."* 7–8. Shield bosses of iron, one with silvered rivet-heads: *"at" the Fleam Dyke*.

XXXIII. ANGLO-SAXON AGE. GRAVE-FURNITURE OF THE PAGAN PERIOD (EXCEPT No. 7, LATE PROVINCIAL-ROMAN) 268

1, 2, 3. Early fibulae of bronze; proto-cruciform and cruciform: *Mildenhall* [S]; *St John's, Cambridge*; *Lakenheath* [S]. 4. Fibula of iron with bronze pin: *Barrington "B."* 5. Girdle-hanger of bronze: *Little Wilbraham*. 6. Cruciform fibula of bronze with hinged plate: *Trumpington* (?). 7. Belt ornament of bronze: *Willbury Hill, Norton* [H].

XXXIV. ANGLO-SAXON AGE. GRAVE-FURNITURE OF THE PAGAN PERIOD (EXCEPT No. 6, CHRISTIAN PERIOD) 272

1, 1 A; 2, 2 A. Cruciform fibulae and wrist-clasps of bronze: *Girton, and Newnham, Cambridge*. 3, 4. "Small long" fibulae of bronze: *Girton*. 5. Disc of bronze with C scrolls, formerly enamelled: *Barrington "A."* 6. Disc of gilt bronze, the head of a pin: *Cambridge*. 7. Wrist-clasp of bronze with embossed decoration: *Cambridge*. 8. Embossed disc and toilet implements of silver: *Burwell*. 9. Plate of buckle, bronze gilt, formerly inlaid with glass or garnets: *St John's, Cambridge*. 10. Belt-plate of bronze, with garnet centre: *Haslingfield*.

XXXV. ANGLO-SAXON AGE. GRAVE-FURNITURE OF THE PAGAN PERIOD (EXCEPT No. 3, OF THE CHRISTIAN PERIOD) 278

1. Belt suite in bronze gilt with silver plaques: *Girton* (Girton College Library). 2. Fragments of square-headed and saucer fibulae: *Girton* (Girton College Library). 3. Vessel of lead, iron handled, with moulded interlacing ornament: *Westley Waterless*. 4. Fibula of bronze with ring at head: *West Stow* [S].

XXXVI. ANGLO-SAXON AGE. IRON WEAPONS AND TOOLS; ALL PROBABLY OF THE PAGAN PERIOD (EXCEPT No. 13, OF THE CHRISTIAN PERIOD) . . . 292

1. Knives: *Barrington*. 2. Spearheads (and ferule of bronze): *Exning* [S]. 3. Guards for long knives (?): *Hauxton*. 4. Shears: *Girton*. 5. Key, ring, and knife: *St John's, Cambridge*. 6. Sword: *Barrington "B."* 7, 8 A, 11. Axes: *Devil's Dyke, Newmarket*; *Tuddenham* [S]; *Hauxton*. 8, 9. Spearheads: *Barrington "B."* 10. Shield boss with bronze button: *Barrington "B."* 12. Curved knife: *Barrington "A."* 13. Scramasax: *Barrington*.

XXXVII. ANGLO-SAXON AGE. BALKS AND LYNCHETS; SURVIVING TRACES OF THE "OPEN FIELD" SYSTEM OF CULTIVATION 306

1. Terraces (Lynchets): *Coploe Hill, Ickleton*. 2. Terraces (Lynchets): *Clothall* [H]. 3. Lynchets and balks: *Clothall*. 4. Lynchets: *Chishall Down, Chishall*.

xviii ILLUSTRATIONS

TEXT FIGURE

PAGE

1. Hallstatt Fibulae 75
    (a) Bronze fibula of "horned" type: *Castor* [Northants.], Peterborough Mus.
    (b) Bronze wire fibula with flat pin catch: *Castor* [Northants.], Peterborough Mus.
    (c) Bronze fibula, "La Certosa" type: *Ixworth* [S].

TEXT MAPS

A. Eastern Britain in the Late Neolithic and Early Bronze Ages. (The distribution of beakers is based on Abercromby (1912).) . . 13
B. Eastern Britain in the Early Iron Age 73
C. The Dykes of West Norfolk and North-west Suffolk 133
D. The Icknield Way and Ashwell Street in the Heydon Ditch—Brent Ditch sector 144
E. The Mare Way 150
F. Eastern Britain in the Roman Age 163
G. Cambridge; illustrating the relation between the Roman town and the pagan Anglo-Saxon cemeteries, etc. 246
H. The Eastern Counties in the Pagan Anglo-Saxon period. (The distribution of cemeteries is based on Baldwin Brown (1915).) . . 285
J. Portions of Parishes in Cambridgeshire and North Essex . . . 310

MAPS IN POCKET*

A series of five coloured Maps of the Region included in the Survey, on the scale of ¼ inch to one mile.

I. Finds and Remains attributed to the Neolithic Age.
II. ,, ,, ,, Bronze Age.
III. ,, ,, ,, Early Iron Age.
IV. ,, ,, ,, Roman Age.
V. The Anglo-Saxon Age, showing:
   (i) Finds and Remains attributed to the Pagan Period.
   (ii) Roman Roads, probably in use in the Pagan Period.
   (iii) Domesday vills.
   (iv) Trackways, dykes, and other earthworks, the majority of unknown date.

*This map is available as a download from www.cambridge.org/9781108011693

COVER DESIGN

The design on the cover is a full size reproduction of one of the enamelled bronze harness plates of the La Tène IV period, included in the *Santon Downham* hoard.

CONTRACTIONS

The following contractions are frequently used:

I, II etc.	Preceding the words century, millennium; read First, Second etc. In some cases where chronological references are frequent, and where the context permits, Roman numerals alone are used for the centuries.
A.-S.	Anglo-Saxon.
A.S.C.	Anglo-Saxon Chronicle.
[B]	Bedfordshire[1].
B.A.	Bronze Age.
B.M.	Bench Mark.
B.M.G.	British Museum Guide.
[C]	Cambridgeshire.
C.A.S.	Cambridge Antiquarian Society.
C.A.S. Rep. XI, etc.	Reports presented at the Annual General Meetings (No. XI to No. XLVIII) of the Society, from 1851 to 1888; usually bound up with Volumes I to VI of the Communications.
C.I.L.	Corpus Inscriptionum Latinarum.
C.M.	(See under Museums.)
[E]	Essex[1].
E.I.A.	Early Iron Age.
[H]	Hertfordshire[1].
Museums:	
Audley End Mus.	Lord Braybrooke's Museum in Audley End House, Saffron Walden.
Brit. Mus.	British Museum, London.
Bury Mus.	Moyses Hall Museum, Bury St Edmunds.
Camb. Mus. or C.M.	Museum of Archaeology and of Ethnology, Cambridge.
Huntingdon Mus.	Huntingdon Institute and Museum.
St Albans Mus.	Hertfordshire County Museum, St Albans.
Walden Mus.	Saffron Walden Museum.
[N]	Norfolk[1].
N.A.	Neolithic Age.
Num. Chron.	Numismatic Chronicle.
O.D.	Ordnance Survey datum level.
O.S.	Ordnance Survey.
P.S.E.A.	Prehistoric Society of East Anglia.
R.	Roman.
R.C.H.M.	Royal Commission on Historical Monuments (England).
[S]	Suffolk[1].
S.I.	Suffolk Institute; afterwards
S.I.A.	Suffolk Institute of Archaeology.
Soc. Antiq.	Society of Antiquaries of London.
V.C.H.	Victoria County History.

Other abbreviations used, are, it is hoped, self-explanatory.

[1] Places mentioned in the text which, though within the area covered by the survey, are situated in counties other than Cambridgeshire, are when necessary distinguished by the addition of the County letter [B], [E], [H], [N], [S], or abbreviation [Hunts.]. This affords a rough guide to the position of such places on the $\frac{1}{4}$-inch Maps of the Cambridge Region. The exact position of these and all other sites referred to in the text can more easily be found by reference to the Map-Square given in the Index.

INTRODUCTION

Object of the Research

IN this book, the archaeological data available for the study of the prehistory and early history of the Cambridge Region from the Neolithic Age onwards, are arranged and analysed. The work was undertaken in order to provide a basis—which does not at present exist—for the future detailed study, period by period, of the archaeological remains of the district and of the many problems connected therewith. The MS. was submitted in 1922 as a thesis for the Ph.D. degree of the University of Cambridge, and approved.

Boundaries of Area dealt with

The district dealt with is approximately a square with sides 44 miles in length, Cambridge being at the centre. A larger area would have been too extensive for detailed treatment, while the geographical features of the countryside rendered limitation to a smaller area undesirable. The area chosen includes a large extent of fenland, the catchment basin of the Cam, and part of the basins of other fen rivers—the Great and Little Ouse and the Lark—as well as the upper waters of streams flowing southward and eastward away from our area, the valleys of which provide convenient routes into the Cambridge plain. Thus small portions of Norfolk, Suffolk, Essex, Hertfordshire, Bedfordshire, and Huntingdonshire are included in the survey, as well as the greater part of the county of Cambridge.

Physiography of the Region

The district thus defined consisted in early times mainly of four distinct types of country. (i) In the north the fens; readily traversed by water, but by land impassable, save to those locally acquainted with its drier patches and hidden fords. (ii) To the south and east of the fens a continuous belt of dry chalk downland (open, for the most part, but here and there covered with groves of beech and patches of scrub) extending from the extreme south-west of our Region (Hitchin [H][1]) to the River Kennett in the east. (iii) From the Kennett to our northern boundary and beyond stretches the East Anglian heath country, where the chalk or clay is overlaid by sands and other deposits producing a light dry well-drained soil. (iv) To the south and

[1] See List of Contractions, p. xix.

east of the open country oak-ash forest with dense undergrowth extended beyond the limits of our Region, the subsoil being boulder-clay; similar forest, moreover, may be held to have covered the whole upland between the Cam and the Great Ouse Valleys with the exception of the southern border of the fens, certain spurs adjacent to the Cam Valley where the chalk is exposed, and the patch of dry heathy country in the neighbourhood of Sandy [B] and Gamlingay. North of Huntingdon again, the fen-bordered upland on the left bank of the Ouse was until recent times forest.

That my estimate of the extent of forest in our district in primitive times is conservative is shown by the following quotation from Tansley (1911, p. 65): "There is no doubt that by far the greater part of the British Isles was originally covered with forest: in England the whole of the East, South and Midlands, except perhaps some of the Chalk Downs and some of the poorer sands." From the very beginning, however, man's activities tended to reduce the area under forest in districts otherwise suitable for his occupation.

Much confirmatory evidence bearing on the extent and character of the ancient forests is to be found in Domesday Book.

The ready means of access from neighbouring regions by land and water which the belt of open chalk downland and heathland, and the fen rivers respectively afford, and the barriers on the south-east and north-west which the forests present, are the main geographical factors governing the prehistory and early history of our district. The survey will indicate the nature and extent of their influence.

A more detailed discussion of the conditions of specially important areas in primitive times will be better deferred until occasion arises for their consideration. It should here, however, be noted that there is evidence which suggests that subsidence took place in the eastern fens during the Neolithic Age—the III millennium B.C.—and it is probable that the greater part of that area was in subsequent centuries a mere or meres which were only gradually replaced by peat. It is hardly to be doubted that the topography of the fenlands must in pre-Roman times have differed greatly from that indicated on the maps, the difference being such as to increase the range of movement by water and to curtail that by land.

Topographical description of the Cam river system is rendered difficult by the lack of ancient names for the several branches of the river. The main stream, rising at Ashwell [H] and flowing through Cambridge, is throughout the book referred to as the Cam. Its chief tributary, rising near Henham [E] and flowing past Chesterford [E], I call the Essex Cam.

INTRODUCTION

The small tributary from the west which joins the main stream at Grantchester has always been known as the Bourn Brook, and it will so be referred to in my text. The stream which rises in the forest country near Castle Camps and which flows through Linton, joining the Essex Cam at Shelford, is called the Granta on the Ordnance Maps. It is well known that this name is loosely used as a synonym for the Cam, and there is, I think, no authority for applying it, or any other name, to the stream in question. Since, however, the bridge where the London-Newmarket road crosses the latter has always been known as Bourn Bridge this generic river name seems the most suitable, and I therefore follow Hughes (1909, p. 37) in describing the stream as the Bourn River, which I hope distinguishes it sufficiently clearly.

A portion only of the Great Ouse river system is within our district. The main river enters it near Roxton [B], being at the point of entry joined by its tributary the Ivel; a large part of the basin of the latter river is included.

Maps

(A) *Large Scale*

The principal map of the district used for the work is the quarter-inch to one mile Ordnance Survey map, printed in faint grey. This is overprinted in colours in accordance with the description given above, green being used to represent areas probably densely afforested, and brown for fen and marsh, the portions left uncoloured being considered to have been open, or, at most, lightly afforested. The river system is emphasized in blue, the courses of the rivers within the fens being such as early maps and records show, and existing traces confirm. For the physiographical reconstruction in general I have relied on geological data available in the publications of the *Geological Survey* and on personal knowledge of the countryside.

The courses of the fen rivers were no doubt frequently altered in prehistoric as in historic times owing to the blocking of the outfalls by sandbanks, etc. The Great Ouse no doubt sometimes followed the course of the "West Water" northward from Earith to Benwick, and joined the River Nene (when the channel of the "Old West River" would be a swampy morass); sometimes it flowed in an easterly direction, by the latter channel, joining the Cam near Stretham. Both routes are indicated. The Cam (or Great Ouse, which is the usual designation of the combined streams of the Cam and the Old West River below Stretham) would appear to have flowed sometimes in an ancient channel past Stuntney Hall and village, sometimes by Ely. Both courses are indicated. North of Ely the river originally passed by Littleport and up the "Old Croft" and "Welney" rivers to Upwell (outside our area) where it received the waters of the Nene, and so flowed through Wisbech. The Great Ouse was thus probably unconnected with the Little Ouse until recent times. The chief meres are shown; and certain of the lodes also, for although they cannot be prehistoric, yet they represent the outfalls of streams from the uplands, the original course of which must approximately have coincided with their alignments. See Skertchly (1877), Cunningham (1909), and maps of the fens by Hondius and others.

(B) *Small Scale*

The four small-scale maps of Eastern England which will be found in the text are designed to illustrate the relation between the Cambridge Region and Eastern England generally in successive culture periods; those marked (A) and (B) also indicate areas probably densely afforested; they show how important at times our countryside must have been commercially and militarily. The chalk belt is a natural highway, and is the only route by which East Anglia could be reached from the Midlands, the upper Thames Valley and Salisbury Plain.

METHOD OF PRESENTATION OF MATERIAL

(I) *Text* and (II) *Maps*

Five Periods or Ages are included in the survey, the Neolithic, Bronze, Early Iron, Roman and Anglo-Saxon. The finds and remains of each Age are entered on one of the quarter-inch Regional Maps already referred to. Since these show the modern topography, the relation between ancient trackways, settlements, etc., and the roads, villages and towns of the present day can conveniently be studied on them. The small-scale maps previously mentioned, and maps of certain portions of the Cambridge Region which will also be found in the text, present information relevant to the enquiry.

In Chapter I of the text the Neolithic Age is briefly dealt with, mainly as an introduction to the succeeding Ages. In Chapters II and III the Bronze and Early Iron Ages are considered; in Chapter IV Earthwork possibly or certainly prehistoric is discussed. Chapters V and VI deal with the Roman and Anglo-Saxon Ages respectively, the survey closing at the Norman Conquest. In Chapter VII the main results are coördinated, and their general bearing discussed.

In order that the greatest possible amount of information may be given on the Regional Maps certain symbols have been employed[1]; these are fully explained on the maps themselves. The method of recording finds the exact provenance of which is unknown is detailed on pp. 9 and 217 of the text. The Index gives the map-square of

[1] It is important for the reader to note that the scale of the map is such that when remains and finds from a given site are numerous, the group of symbols can only approximately represent the true position.

INTRODUCTION

every place in our Region mentioned in the text. Places and sites in our Region not marked on the ¼-inch Ordnance map are distinguished by a star in the Index, and the position of most of them is described in detail therein.

Remains of a given Age have been sought for in connection with the whole area included on the Regional Map. The material thus gathered together has been embodied in a topographical index, which forms the basis on which this study of the archaeology of the district has been built up. It has not been found possible to include the index in the book; but all the important material dealt with in the text is fully referenced and its present provenance indicated. A list of authors quoted will be found at the end of the book, where also are appendices containing lists of beakers, hoards and round barrows attributed to the Bronze Age.

A disappointing result of an examination of the literature and of museum collections is the scarcity of information which would give clues to the age of the hill-forts and dykes. Few of these have been excavated, and the proof of age and date or period of construction lies, doubtless, in their banks or ditches[1]; but one might expect that finds of the period to which a given fort or dyke belongs would occur more frequently in its neighbourhood than elsewhere. Recorded finds, however, of any sort in or near such are rare. Roman coins, it is true, have been found in or adjacent to practically every earthwork in the district, but this is certainly no evidence of origin.

(III) *Illustrations and Diagrams*

The argument is, with unavoidable exceptions, throughout verbally illustrated by reference to objects of local provenance preserved in the Museum of Archaeology and of Ethnology, Cambridge. The objects illustrated pictorially and diagrammatically, too, are almost all in the local museum[2]. The basic importance of pottery in a study of this character will be found to have been fully recognized; for the rest, my endeavour has been to cover as wide a range as possible in my illustrations of finds attributed to each Age, from the Bronze Age onward.

Certain important objects and group finds in the Cambridge Museum are not illustrated. This is because adequate reproductions are available in accessible publications, to which references are given.

[1] An attempt to determine the age of the Fleam Dyke was carried out by Fox and Palmer in 1921–2.
[2] I hope, therefore, that the book may be found useful as a Museum Guide to the collection of local antiquities.

CHAPTER I

THE NEOLITHIC AGE

"That is clever," said Puck. "How truly you shape it!" KIPLING.

INTRODUCTION

THE study of the Neolithic Age in this book is almost entirely confined to an examination of the distribution of the remains referable to it, in order that a topographical basis may be available for comparison when the evidence relating to subsequent periods is reviewed. Unless the range of Neolithic man in the district be determined, the significance of the distribution of finds attributable to his successors cannot be correctly appreciated. Had this not been evident, I should have commenced my survey in the first Age of Metal, as being, in the present state of our knowledge, a more convenient starting point.

The chief problem that arises for consideration, in preparing a topographical survey of the Neolithic Age, is what to include. Numerous stone implements occur as surface finds in the Cambridge Region, such as axes—chipped, ground, or polished; adzes; maces, holed axes, and axehammers; hammerstones; chisels, picks and fabricators; awls, scrapers and trimmed flakes; slugs, leaf-shaped tools and daggers; arrows—leaf-shaped, tanged, winged or barbed; gouges, and chipped or polished discs. The majority of these forms are recognized as being of the Neolithic Age, but others, which must be discussed in detail, are known to occur in deposits dating in the Bronze and later Ages.

Some of the flint used for making implements was mined at the well-known site at Grimes Graves, Weeting [N], and it is necessary to determine whether the industry centred here comes within the scope of my survey.

THE GRIMES GRAVES INDUSTRY

The mines at Grimes Graves, Weeting, three miles north of Brandon on the Little Ouse, are of especial importance, equalled perhaps only by those of Cissbury in this country and Spiennes in Belgium. The area covers over 20 acres; and the number of pits is estimated at 346.

Important excavations on the site have been carried out on two occasions—in 1870 by Greenwell and in 1914 by the Prehistoric Society of East Anglia, which published an elaborate report (*P.S.E.A. Rep.* 1915) on the work[1].

In the former excavations a ground basalt axe was discovered, but its association with the mines is open to doubt; in the latter case no trace of polished stone or of metal was found in the galleries. Hammerstones of quartzite and flint, rough chipped axes and other implements of flint, flakes innumerable, and picks of deerhorn were found in both series of excavations, and the culture picture resembled that at Cissbury in Sussex explored by Pitt-Rivers. The miners lived on the spot, their hearths being found in the cone-shaped hollows formed by deserted and half-filled pits, and piles of their chippings and rejects occur on the lips of their shafts.

Some authorities (R. A. Smith (1915 *a*) and A. E. Peake, the director of the 1914 excavations (1917), may be cited) consider that *the forms of the implements* indicate an early Upper Palaeolithic date. The recent discovery by A. L. Armstrong (1921) on a living floor at the Graves of naturalistic engravings upon flint crust, seems to provide an additional argument in favour of this view. On the other hand, the only skull found in the 1914 excavations was "not markedly Palaeolithic," "the shells and fauna generally point to Early Neolithic times," and that pottery was used by the miners also suggests Neolithic date.

The view that the mines present a survival of Palaeolithic culture into the Early Neolithic Age seems best to fit the facts, and finds of Grimes Graves type are therefore marked on the map. It may be noted that apart from the Weeting area these forms are rare in surface finds in the Cambridge Region, and their exclusion would not result in any modification of importance in the distribution picture here presented.

Stone Implements probably of post-Neolithic date

We must now consider the implements which are probably post-Neolithic, and which ought therefore to be excluded from our map of finds of the Neolithic Age.

Holed Axeheads. Numerous examples of holed implements and weapons of simple form—perforated pebbles (maceheads) and

---

[1] This report contains an account of previous work on the site. Accounts of further work in 1916 and subsequent years will be found in the *Proceedings, P.S.E.A.*

THE NEOLITHIC AGE

celt-like tools, the latter probably used as adzes—occur in the district. That most of these are of Neolithic date is probable[1]. The elaborately wrought axes and axehammers, sometimes with upper and lower faces parallel, sometimes with expanding blade, such as the fine example from Chesterford [E] in Walden Museum and those figured on Plate V, 3 and 6, are, however, in a different category. The drilled hole is usually a perfect cylinder (which is not the case with the simpler forms mentioned above), and the type belongs in Scandinavia to the cist-grave period—the beginning of the II millennium, according to Montelius. Such weapons have in Britain frequently been met with in Bronze Age burials (though rarely in this district) and the type certainly here belongs to the early Age of Metal.

Maceheads and hammers of deerhorn with cylindrical perforations have been found in the fens, and perforated maceheads of stone of a form natural to the former material are known. These doubtless all belong to the early Age of Metal. Examples from Burwell Fen are on Plate V, 4, 5. See also R. A. Smith (1920, pp. 6–8). J. Evans (1897, p. 193) records a quartzite axehammer found with an "urn" on Wilton Heath [N].

Daggers. Thin finely-chipped pointed-oval blades of flint, some of which show lateral notches (presumably to assist in fixing the weapon to a handle), occur not infrequently in the district. Typical specimens from Prickwillow near Ely, Haslingfield, Quy Fen and other sites are in the local collection and two are figured on Plate V, 9, 10. Dr Lucas of Burwell has a similar blade of black flint with deep side notches, derived from Burwell Fen.

Evidence of date for these local examples is entirely lacking; but identical forms have elsewhere been found associated with beakers and with jet buttons with V perforations and the whole series may belong to the beginning of the II millennium—the transition stone-bronze period. R. A. Smith (1920, p. 5) points out that the thickening at the butt-end, well marked in some of our examples, suggests connection with Scandinavia, where similar blades are of the passage-grave phase of the later Neolithic.

The doubt that may exist as to whether all these blades are of as late date as is here suggested, does not affect the group next to be considered, of which we have some dozen fragmentary examples, all from N.W. Suffolk, the majority from North Stow in West Stow parish (W. G. Clarke, 1918, p. 546).

[1] It should, however, be noted that in the Late Bronze Age midden-trench at Swaffham Prior, referred to on p. 47, a water-worn pebble partially drilled in hour-glass fashion was found. There was no reason to doubt its contemporaneity with the other finds.

These are finely chipped handles of daggers—thrown away, doubtless, when the blade was broken off—of the developed Danish type, influenced by metal forms, and in Scandinavia associated with the cist-grave culture and the latest phase of the Neolithic. Attribution to the transition period in Britain may be regarded as certain.

Arrowheads. Both the leaf-shaped and the tanged types commonly occur in the district. They are found together in Neolithic deposits (Warren, 1912 a, pp. 110 and 114), but the tanged forms appear to have been in frequent use in the Bronze Age, and I have not marked isolated finds of such on the map.

Hammerstones. These are met with locally in inhumation burials of the Bronze and Early Iron Ages, and cannot be held indicative of Neolithic settlement unless associated with objects manifestly of that Age.

Scrapers and Trimmed Flakes. The rougher forms of flint implements such as scrapers and trimmed flakes were, it is certain, commonly in domestic use all through the Bronze and even in the Early Iron Age, and records of their presence cannot alone be used as evidence of the use by Neolithic man of any given site.

Such, for example, occurred in the late Bronze Age trench at Swaffham Prior (see p. 47); they were found by A. J. Evans (1890, p. 319) in the La Tène cemetery at Aylesford; and by the writer in a Romano-British deposit at the Fleam Dyke. Finds of these implements are therefore excluded from the map, unless their character and associations mark them as definitely of Neolithic date.

There are a few other (rare) types, such as gouges, long narrow chisels of flint, axes and adzes with expanding blades, which, one may suppose, are unlikely to have been produced independently of metal exemplars. I have, however, included these, since we have no definite evidence that they are of the Metal Age. And, in any event, error in dealing with exceptional forms is relatively unimportant. On the other hand, while fully admitting the difficulty of dating surface finds of stone implements I consider that with the reservations already made, we may safely refer the great majority of implements of "Neolithic" types found in the district to a period prior to the introduction of metal.

We may now proceed to examine the topographical distribution of "Neolithic" implements as thus defined, commencing in the north-east.

THE NEOLITHIC AGE

TOPOGRAPHICAL DISTRIBUTION OF FINDS

Immense numbers of implements of all types are found on the sandy heaths and warrens in the River Lark—Little Ouse area[1]. Chipped axes of flint, lanceheads, knives, borers, scrapers, fabricators, etc., are here especially common, in addition to the more highly finished (polished and partially polished) types; and arrowheads also are frequently met with. Sturge (1911, p. 253) remarked that almost every type of implement described by Evans was to be found in Suffolk; and he wrote with special reference to the district under review. W. A. Dutt (1911, pp. 259, 261) emphasizes moreover the striking abundance of all forms of Neolithic implements in this area. "Thousands of implements," he says, "have been found in the two Icklingham parishes"; "Santon Downham has been very prolific of neolithic implements many of which are of very finished workmanship"; "Mildenhall has produced an immense number of implements," including arrowheads and polished and unpolished axes; "a very great number of implements," especially arrowheads, have been found at Lakenheath, and on the warrens round Thetford. Moreover, there is not a parish in the district from which a number of such implements has not been obtained, and numerous implements have been found in the adjacent fens, especially in Burnt Fen.

This abundance implies a prolonged period of occupation, as well as a considerable population. The range of types found suggests that occupation has been unbroken from Palaeolithic times onwards; and it is probable that a certain number of surface finds recorded from this area as Neolithic are of earlier date. The number of implements undoubtedly Neolithic is, however, large enough to justify the estimates given above as to the richness of the locality.

Forms which on various grounds are thought to belong to the earliest phase of the Neolithic occur less frequently elsewhere in our district; and the following reason has been offered for this. In a note to Tansley's *Types of British Vegetation* (p. 97) J. E. Marr remarks that the East Anglian Heath Region "exhibits the nearest approach to steppe conditions to be found within the British Isles." "It is doubtful," he continues, "if this area ever bore natural woodland"; while, as has already been pointed out, even the chalk escarpment may be held to have borne in parts natural forest. W. G. Clarke

---

[1] Until the XIX century this was for the most part a treeless unenclosed waste of heath; the surface soil being a layer of sand, in some parts covering boulder clay of no great thickness, in others resting directly on the chalk.

(1912) concludes that "Breckland" therefore was perhaps better suited to the mode of life of Early Neolithic peoples than any other part of England.

Though exact quantitative analysis of the products of so rich an area is impossible, an examination parish by parish of such of the finds from the district as are on record discloses interesting variations, and an attempt is made to indicate graphically on the map the results thus obtained. The Icklingham-Mildenhall-Lakenheath area and the fens adjacent are undoubtedly the richest, while the Weeting–Santon–Santon Downham–Brandon district is second only to it in productivity. Finds rapidly become less numerous as one proceeds eastward and the soil becomes less sandy (producing a modification of steppe conditions); they diminish also in the district south of the River Lark, doubtless for the same reason.

Labelled specimens in museums give little help in determining the most prolific areas within a given parish in this district; but it is generally agreed that implements are most numerous nearest the rivers and the fens, and least numerous on sites most distant from a water supply. The well-head known as Hunwell Spring doubtless accounts for a number of finds near Elveden[1].

The only area which can in our district compare with the warrens in productivity and in range of types is the fen and its borders east of the River Cam between Quy and Wicken. The chalk upland here, suitable for pasture and settlement, with perennial springs of pure water issuing from its lower slopes, forms the shore-line of the fen teeming with fish and fowl; and the number and variety of the implements derived hence, especially from Burwell (which has yielded axes of Cissbury type), may indicate occupation all through the Neolithic Age. In these eastern fens lanceheads, arrowheads, knives, saws, daggers, etc., of the most delicate workmanship are preserved as nowhere else in the district, save on the unploughed sandy warrens.

The only important hoard in our district comes from the fen borders. On a site adjacent to the Temple Springs at Wilbraham was found, in a nest, a group of four partially ground flint axes 5–6 inches in length, apparently unused, and all of the same type. These are preserved at Wilbraham Temple; the rarity of such finds makes the discovery worthy of special mention. Two chisels and an axe of flint, found together on Newmarket Heath and now in Dr Lucas' collection, also deserve record here.

[1] See Sturge (1911), Dutt (1911), W. G. Clarke (1905 and 1907, p. 397), and Clinch (1901); J. Evans (1897, Index), Clarke and Hewitt (1914, p. 432) also give useful information. The collections in the British Museum and in the Norwich, Ipswich, Cambridge and other local museums are representative. The *Proceedings, P.S.E.A.*, contain much detailed and general information.

THE NEOLITHIC AGE

Dr Lucas of Burwell informs me that in Burwell Fen the stone (and bronze) implements are found lying on the clay below the peat, and it is on record that finds in other fens have been similarly situated. How is this to be accounted for? The probability that subsidence took place in the fenlands as elsewhere in Britain in Neolithic times has been referred to in the introduction. Reid (1913) holds that this downward movement ceased early in the II millennium. Warren (1912 *a* and 1919) has established the fact of subsidence of the Essex coast before and during occupation by the beaker folk.

A subsidence of the Fen Basin contemporary with that described by Warren would readily explain the occurrence of scattered implements on the clay or marl as in Burwell Fen, and the surprising number of implements, almost all of stone, in Burnt Fen. We may suppose that the Undley-Mildenhall promontory in Neolithic times extended nearly to Littleport, and that the Burnt Fen area was part of the East Anglian heathland, so rich in remains of this Age. The growth of peat in the shallow meres produced by subsidence was doubtless slow. Soham Mere and Whittlesea Mere may be regarded as the last surviving patches of open water in our area.

The distribution of the remaining finds in the region covered by our map may now be briefly analysed.

A few implements are met with in the fens west of the River Cam —at Whittlesea Mere, Manea and in the Isle of Ely—and finds in the Old West River at Aldreth may indicate an ancient ford near the present High Bridge.

In the Cam Valley it is noticeable that finds and sites rich in worked flint occur in parishes adjacent to the main river and its tributaries, or as at Oakington, Histon, Coton and Cottenham on patches of gravel or dry chalk upland which here in primitive times were probably enveloped or bordered by forest. The barrenness of the Great Ouse Valley is in striking contrast to that of the Cam, and suggests that *narrow* belts of open country offered comparatively little inducement to settlers.

The upper waters of the several streams which, running south and east, drain the densely forested uplands of Hertfordshire, Essex and Suffolk, provide the only possible routes in primitive times from the coastal districts and the lower Thames Valley through or into so forbidding an area: on their banks, moreover, well-drained gravel terraces replace the cold wet claylands. Into these natural gateways, then, pushed Neolithic man; and we find traces of his passage or settlement in almost every one.

THE NEOLITHIC AGE

A few finds, on the line which traffic proceeding along the chalk belt is forced to follow by the nature of the country and the position of the fords across the Essex Cam, the Bourn, the Kennett and the Lark, suggest that the "Icknield Way" may be as old as the Neolithic Age; consideration of the Long Barrow at Therfield [H] will provide us with further reasons for supposing that the route from the south-west along the chalk escarpment was in use at all events during the last phase of the Age. The traditional alignment is indicated on the map; the Way is discussed in detail in Chapter IV.

It is more necessary in this than in any later Age to warn the reader that the picture of settlement and of distribution of population presented by the Regional Map will be misleading, unless it be borne in mind that it is a composite picture, and cannot accurately reproduce any given phase of an Age the duration of which may possibly be counted in millennia. It may well be that in the closing phases of the Neolithic the preponderance of population in the East Anglian heath district was appreciably modified, and that it was then more in accord with that which is manifest in the Bronze Age; the map of this Age will suggest that the chalk escarpment bordering the fen and the River Cam maintained as large a population as did the heath.

Our knowledge of the actual sites where Neolithic man dwelt is scanty. Apart from the heath district and the region round Saffron Walden (Morris, 1922) only a few records deal with sites rich in flint flakes, scrapers and cores probably of the period. Detailed record of living-floors or middens such as would give indications of the mode of life, etc., of the inhabitants in the Stone Age, is conspicuously absent.

THE VALUE OF THE MAP RECORD

It is a widely held opinion that the preparation of a topographical map of Neolithic finds in this district is useless; that the whole of East Anglia was occupied in the period, and that implements are found everywhere. With this view I disagree; and it is indeed clear from the map that finds though widely distributed fall into well-defined areas and alignments, and are in fact almost entirely confined to those parts which under natural conditions may be assumed to have been more or less dry, well drained, and open, or which provided a line of route more or less easy, from one open district to another. The barrenness of the large triangle of forest west of the Cam, in particular, is striking evidence of the correctness of the contention here advanced, and of the importance to the archae-

THE NEOLITHIC AGE

ologist of a study of soils and subsoils. The scanty traces of occupation of the fen islands may be due partly to their wooded character, partly to their inaccessibility. The possibility that malaria may have hindered occupation both of fen and of forest cannot be excluded, but it could hardly have been a controlling factor.

In the great majority of cases we know nothing of the provenance of an implement beyond its derivation from a given parish; it may therefore be urged that in many cases where a parish contains both open and forest land the site mark has without justification been placed on the open country (in order to bolster up a case) and that the validity of the conclusion arrived at is thus seriously impaired.

The principle adopted, in this and subsequent period maps, where the exact provenance of an object is unknown, is to place the suitable symbol on the modern village, as the centre of the parish[1]. It is a definite, simple and obvious system, and precludes bias, conscious or unconscious. That the village is usually to be found on the dry well-drained site rather than the cold wet forest land is indeed true, and may be held to increase the probability of Neolithic man having made a similar choice; but the real answer to the criticism lies in the fact that of the many parishes situated entirely in forest country in our district hardly one has yielded undoubted Neolithic implements.

That Neolithic man hunted in the woodlands may be taken as certain; that outcasts took refuge there is highly probable; and that stone implements will from time to time, here and there, be found in such areas is to be anticipated; but it is clear from the rarity of such finds hitherto recorded, that settlements of this Age in the forest were very infrequent.

Polished axes and other implements have been found in the forest at Chrishall [E], and a polished axe at Sampford [E]. Rude implements (flakes and scrapers), possibly of Bronze Age or later date, are, as Dr Garrood informs me, here and there found in the forest area north of Huntingdon.

THE STONE AXE

It is not proposed to discuss in this chapter the character or distribution of the several types of implements found in the district. A brief note on the most characteristic weapon of the Age, the axe, is, however, desirable.

The axe, chipped, ground, or polished, is the commonest of all

[1] Save in the East Anglian heath area, in the present Age only, where a different method is adopted, for reasons already stated. Fen finds, moreover, are in this and subsequent Ages sited broadcast over the particular fen from which they come.

implements deriving from areas other than the heathlands of the north-east. It need not of course be concluded that the *variety* of weapons and tools (of which axes form only a small percentage) found on the heathlands is a phenomenon peculiar thereto; the probable explanation is that the collection of implements in these areas is carried out mainly by experts, and all artifacts are sought for; in other districts implements of high finish or striking form alone would be likely to be preserved by labourer or ploughman. It follows that the recorded finds in such districts inadequately represent the activities of Neolithic man therein; and were knowledge more widespread discoveries indicating closer settlement might confidently be looked for[1].

The range of axe-form found in the district is bewildering, and we have very slight data to go upon in indicating a chronological succession of types; but examples of practically every variety—from the (presumed) earliest to the latest—met with in Eastern England are to be found here.

The chronology of the stone axe in the Middle and Late Neolithic has been worked out in Scandinavia by Montelius and his school; and if Northern parallels could be accepted, a broad classification would be possible for this country. The axe of chipped flint with pointed butt, for example, met with in our eastern fens as well as on the East Anglian heathlands is a pre-dolmen type dated by them early in the IV millennium; its successor, the thin-butted axe, common in our region, belongs to the dolmen period (3400—2400 B.C.). Late forms of this axe showing squared sides are common; but the square section ultimately reached, by a development of this process, in Scandinavia, is represented in Cambridgeshire only by a few examples the provenance of which is not satisfactorily established.

The finely wrought and highly polished axes with sharp-pointed butt, of thin and flat or flattened-oval section, made of jadeite or other semi-precious stones, magnificent examples of which from Warkworth Street, Cambridge, Histon and Burwell Fen are in the Cambridge Museum, probably came from Brittany, where they are contemporary with the dolmens and "mark a definite phase of the Neolithic"; but their ultimate place of origin is obscure. The Histon specimen is figured on Plate V.

The present state of knowledge of this subject has been admirably reviewed by R. A. Smith (1918, esp. table on p. 499, and 1919 *a*, pp. 17–20).

---

[1] A recent survey by Morris (1922) gives the information we require for Saffron Walden and its neighbourhood, and confirms the opinion expressed in the text.

THE NEOLITHIC AGE

The determination of the origin of the "foreign" rocks of which numerous axes found locally are made might appear a promising line of enquiry, as giving ideas as to trade routes or racial movements in East Anglia during the Age; but though the range of material used is wide it appears that the glacial drift which covers the uplands is able to provide practically all [Fearnsides (1904, p. 40)]. That some implements made of mottled flint, of felstone or of greenstone may have been imported from Yorkshire or Lincolnshire is possible but unproven (Hughes, 1894 a, p. 88, and 1899, p. 299). The ease whereby ideas and forms, native to Yorkshire, might reach the culture pool formed by the fens—a chain of lakes and navigable rivers easily crossed in any direction by canoes—is evident on the small scale map of Eastern England (p. 13).

The discovery, however, in Burwell Fen of a grinding-slab of sandstone, associated with two axes of flint and fragments of greenstone (J. Evans, 1897, p. 263) of the right shape and size for manufacture into axes, places these speculations in their right perspective, showing as it does that axes of "foreign" rock were made in the district. It also suggests that flint axes were contemporary with these, and were, moreover, not the product of a different culture.

INTERMENTS. LONG BARROWS

It has been remarked that our knowledge of the dwelling-places of Neolithic man in our district is scanty. We are equally ignorant as to how or where he buried his dead.

The long barrow on Therfield Heath [H] already mentioned, of characteristic form though of small size—it measures 125 feet long by 65 feet broad at its base—lies significantly enough on the line of the Icknield Way, as do also two other long barrows at Dunstable [B] some few miles outside our area.

It was opened by E. B. Nunn in 1855, and his account of the excavation is preserved in an unpublished MS. in the Cambridge Museum.

A trench dug along the main axis (east and west) disclosed an inhumation interment, the bones having been disjointed before deposition, and, at the broad eastern end, a "bank of flint" which may have originally formed a cist or chamber. These were primary deposits on the original ground level. There were also two small pits about 2 feet in diameter sunk in the chalk rock, which contained ashes. The results are in many ways difficult to explain, but accord more closely with Neolithic burial custom in the south-western area than on the Yorkshire wolds.

No long barrow is known to exist in the thickly populated region of the north-east (the East Anglian heathland) and the type is said to be entirely absent from Norfolk. Many round barrows are found on the heathland as also along the entire chalk belt from Newmarket to Hitchin. In many of those which have been examined and of which records exist, pottery and cremation interments, referable to the Bronze Age culture, have been found. In others, however, no such definite evidence of date is available; and the possibility that certain of the inhumation burials in round barrows in our district are Neolithic can therefore not be excluded[1].

Long barrows, moreover (which are a local manifestation of the later Megalithic culture of Western Europe, the corresponding passage graves of Scandinavia being dated by Montelius 2400–2000 B.C.), are not in England characteristic of the Neolithic culture generally, but only of the closing phase of it. Though the barrows were designed for multiple interment, their comparatively small number, even in counties where they are most numerous, suggests that only for a short period could the type have been in use.

To return to the topographical problem: we have to account for a distribution of long barrows in our neighbourhood which indicates an extension of the culture associated with them north-eastward from Wiltshire and the Thames Valley along the line of the chalk escarpment into the Cambridgeshire borders, and no further. The small scale map (A, p. 13) serves to make this point clear. The most obvious explanation of the facts would seem to be that the population of the East Anglian heathlands and the dwellers on the borders of the eastern fens were able to hold their own against the invaders; or if the long barrows indicate commercial intercourse, that they preferred their own sepulchral customs, whatever these may have been.

[1] One of these is discussed in the next chapter (p. 32). Here one may note that a ground flint axe in the Bury Museum is labelled "From a Mildenhall barrow." This may have been associated with a Neolithic interment, such axes being very rarely found in Bronze Age burials.

From a barrow on Newmarket Heath (not included in the next chapter), opened and destroyed in the 80's of last century, several skeletons, and leaf-shaped arrowheads were obtained. One, of black flint, is in the possession of Dr Chas. Lucas of Burwell. I can find no confirmation of the statement of a second informant, that axes accompanied the skeletons. Neolithic date is, however, possible. The shape or size of the barrow is unknown.

From a "barrow at Triplow" the jadeite axe in the possession of Rev. E. Conybeare (the fourth found in our region) is said to have been derived.

THE NEOLITHIC AGE

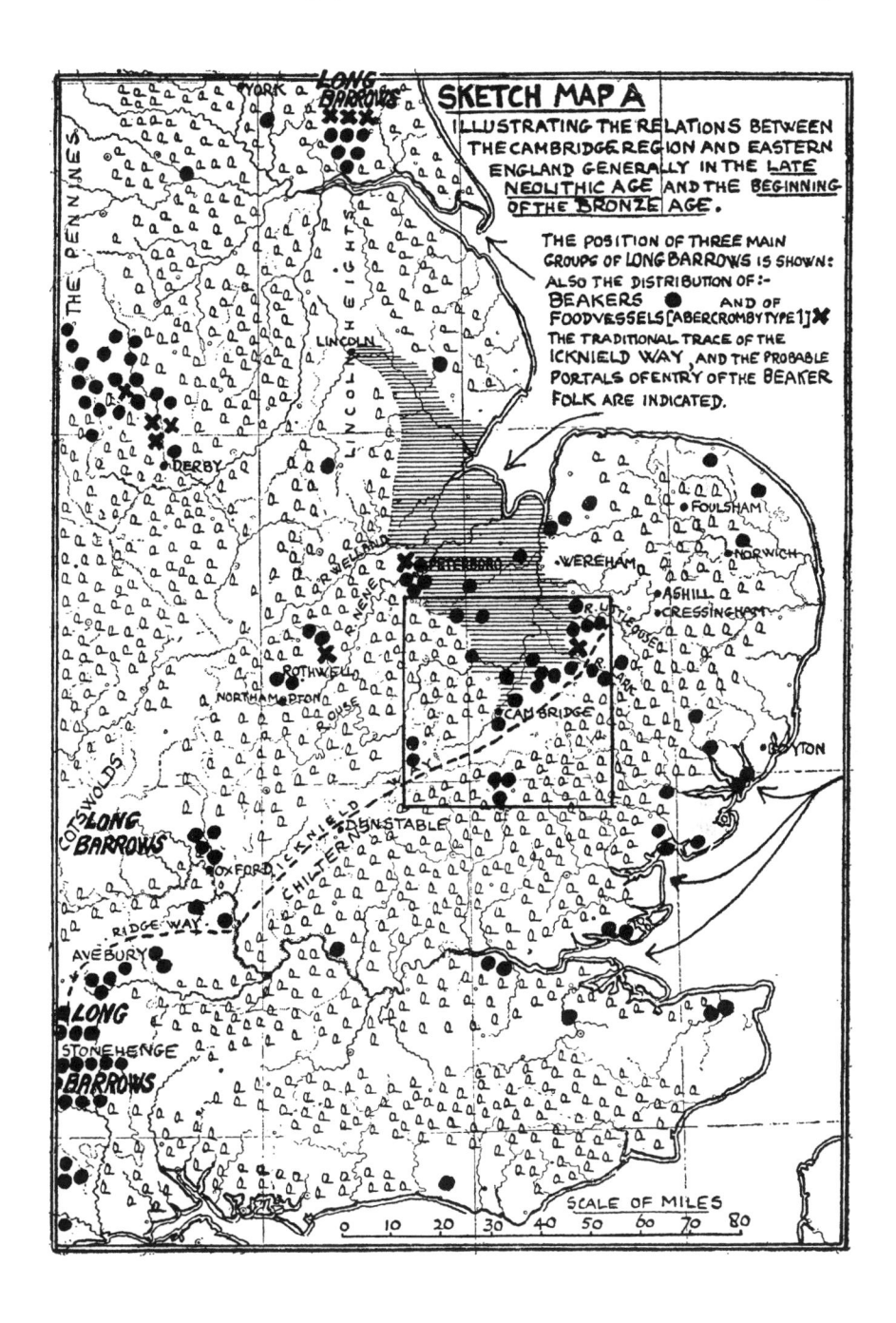

THE NEOLITHIC AGE

GENERAL CONSIDERATIONS

Little is known of the mode of life of the inhabitants of our region in Neolithic times. The character and distribution of their implements give us some clues; we can be sure that many tribes and groups were pastoral, others were hunters—witness the poleaxed urus in Burwell Fen (Babington, 1863 a); fishermen doubtless dropped many of the implements and weapons found in the fens, and the net-sinkers found here may in some cases be as old as the Stone Age. A primitive agriculture doubtless was practised on favourable sites near river or fen, but of this we have no evidence[1]. The skull of a wolf with a barbed and tanged arrowhead sticking therein, found at Barrington and now in Mr Conybeare's collection, is a vivid reminder of the dangers against which primitive man, whether of the Neolithic or Bronze Age, had to guard his flocks and herds.

We have, again, practically no direct evidence as to the racial type of Neolithic man in the southern fens. But since the slightly-built Iberian type is still recognizable in the existing population of Cambridgeshire and N.W. Suffolk, and since long skulls are met with in local inhumation interments of the Bronze Age, it is probable that the Iberian was the most important, if not the only, element in the population occupying our region in the Neolithic Age.

R. A. Smith (1919 a, pp. 23 ff), summarizing the evidence of commercial and other relations with the continent, emphasizes the prevalence of intercourse between Eastern Britain and Scandinavia in the later dolmen and passage-grave periods. Pottery found at Peterborough (see p. 15) has close Scandinavian parallels referred to both periods, while local evidence for connection in the cist-grave period which followed is afforded by the finds of flint dagger handles of Danish type already referred to.

This commerce, due primarily it is supposed to the demand for Baltic amber, seems to have dwindled after the Early Bronze Age.

Indications of trade with Western France, probably Brittany, in the dolmen period as afforded by the presence of axes of Breton type at Histon, Triplow, Cambridge and Burwell, have already been mentioned. Britain in this period was in the full stream of Western culture, and their occurrence is in no way surprising; the route by which these arrived in our district may have been the Icknield Way; they were all found close to its alignment.

The possibility that certain axes found in our region were derived

---

[1] Flint sickles do not occur in the district.

from the north has been noted; examination of representative collections from the Yorkshire wolds confirms the opinion that close cultural relations existed between this area and the southern fens during the later phases of the Age.

The survey of the remains of the Neolithic Age has been limited in scope; it is intended merely to serve as an introduction to our study of the Bronze Age. Information, essential to a correct understanding of the latter Age, as to the range of Neolithic man's activities in the Cambridge Region, has been obtained.

The duration of the Age is unknown; its closing phase, dating probably at the end of the III millennium, is marked by the appearance in the Cambridge Region of a new and characteristic type of pottery, the "beaker," and of a brachycephalic people who doubtless largely displaced the Iberian population. That the invaders brought metal with them is unlikely, that they knew of it is probable; and the developed forms of stone implements, to some extent influenced by metal, are doubtless their handiwork. No definite evidence, from refuse pits or stratified deposits, of the overlap of the two cultures, the transition from Stone to Metal, is available from our district; but immediately to the north-west thereof, on the edge of the western fens at Peterborough, such evidence has been obtained (Abbott, 1910; Leeds, 1922), and is, as will be seen, of importance in connection with the pre-history of the Cambridge Region. A series of shallow pits (hut sites) sunk in the gravel revealed in the lowest strata fragments of round-bottomed bowls, resembling the one in the British Museum from the Thames at Mortlake, and other Neolithic pottery. Flint flakes, scrapers, knives, and a few arrowheads were found in the pits, and numerous fragments of typical "beaker" pottery, which in one case were definitely in the upper layers of the deposit.

CHAPTER II

THE BRONZE AGE

INCLUDING THE TRANSITION PERIOD FROM STONE TO METAL

"Flint work is fool's work." KIPLING.

CHRONOLOGICAL AND OTHER PROBLEMS

THE chronology of the Bronze Age in Britain, as in Western and Northern Europe, presents problems of great difficulty, since the Age ended before the historical period began in the West. It is certain that a "community of ideas and forms" extended from the Eastern Mediterranean and more especially perhaps from the Aegean all over the continent of Europe during the earlier part of the Age, and that Mycenean (Minoan) chronology, thanks to the associations of its culture with Egypt, has been satisfactorily worked out; but the dates at which metal and successive types of weapons such as the dagger and the sword were produced in Western and Northern Europe are as yet only approximately known. The route, moreover, by which copper and the knowledge of metal-working arrived, is not yet agreed upon.

The presence, on the one hand, in graves of the transition period in Britain of dagger-blades of flint with thickened butts known to be of the passage-grave period in Scandinavia, and, on the other hand, the occurrence in Sweden of flanged axes of English and Swedish types, associated in the same hoard, would make it an easy matter to assign dates to the close of the Neolithic Age and the introduction of bronze weapons in this country if one could implicitly rely on Northern chronology, but the dating of the uniform scheme embracing all Europe, evolved by Montelius, is probably too early.

During the greater part of the Bronze Age the main culture routes in Western Europe were sea-routes, and the western seaboard of France shows a development parallel to that seen in this country. French chronology is therefore of importance. Déchelette's system (1910, p. 105) is based on that of Montelius; he suggests that the introduction of copper may date from 2500 B.C. and of bronze from 1900 B.C. and that the Bronze Age gave place to the Hallstatt (iron) culture in 900 B.C.

Montelius, in an important paper published in *Archaeologia* in 1908, extended his European system of Bronze Age chronology to these islands. Allowing a certain period for a copper age preceding the bronze—an age that is when metal was rare and when objects of copper or bronze poor in tin occur in association with stone implements, he assigned to the entire Age 1700 years—2500 B.C. to 800 B.C.

He subdivided this Age into five Periods based on pottery and implement forms to each of which he gave approximate dates. These dates are:

Period I.	Copper Age	2500–2000 B.C.
„ II.	First period of Bronze Age properly so-called ...	2000–1650 B.C.
„ III.	... ...	1650–1400 B.C.
„ IV.	... ...	1400–1150 B.C.
„ V.	... ...	1150– 800 B.C.

He therefore considers the Iron Age to have begun in Britain about 800 B.C.

Montelius' chronology has not been generally accepted by English archaeologists. It is regarded as assigning too high an antiquity for the introduction of metal, and as antedating by several centuries the arrival of the Iron Age. Though recent discoveries, which demonstrate the presence of certain elements of the Hallstatt culture in Southern Britain, have deprived contemporary criticisms of some of their point, the objections to Montelius' chronology raised by A. J. Evans (1908) and others still in the main hold good, and we may conclude that the first metal objects reached this country about 2000 B.C., and that the introduction of iron cannot be dated earlier than 600–500 B.C.

Before pursuing this aspect of the problem further, it is necessary that the value of the other elements of Montelius' system, which in this country have been little criticized, should be examined.

The system is a typological sequence cut up into five periods. In my original analysis I followed it closely, because it appeared to be the best hitherto attempted for the Bronze Age in Great Britain, and it is convenient for a worker like myself in a restricted field to arrange his material according to some recognized scheme. I found that while the typological sequence was satisfactory, the division into five periods was indefensible. Before proceeding to describe the modifications which I have adopted, it seems desirable to state the facts which led me to reject Montelius' five-period arrangement.

The provenance of no less than 298 bronze axes (flat and flanged axes, palstaves, and socketed axes) found in the Cambridge Region has been recorded, in addition to those which have occurred in hoards. Classifying these according to Montelius' system, I obtained the following figures:

| Period II. | 26 | Period IV. | 39 |
| „ III. | 114 | „ V. | 119 |

If Montelius' memoir (1908) be referred to it will be seen that he only allows certain "degenerated varieties" of palstave, and socketed axes with structural decoration in his Period IV.

Now it is certain that as the Bronze Age progressed the axe became more common—as the composition of the large hoards found in the district demonstrates. That so marked a fall in numbers occurs in Period IV must be due to errors in determining the types of axe proper thereto. Incorrect classification on my part of the local material might have been responsible for some misplaced examples; but the deficit transcended the limits of possible error in judgment.

Consideration of the hoards threw light on this difficulty. "Degenerated varieties" of palstaves dated by Montelius in Period IV occur occasionally in hoards otherwise of Period V character[1]. It was therefore concluded that the palstave was in full use throughout Period IV. It followed that too wide a range of development of the type is included by Montelius in his Period III. I am inclined to consider that palstaves with high stop ridge and "trident" (like Fig. 88 in Montelius' memoir—but not Fig. 87) in which the last traces of the flange are lost in a decorative pattern, and also those of similar form but with a slight median rib running down the blade, should be placed early in Period IV and degenerate varieties at the close of that period. The former are the types associated with the Grunty Fen armilla (Cambridge Museum), and are therefore contemporary with it. In the Downham Fen find (Plate VIII and p. 56) a palstave identical with one of them was associated with a sickle and rapier (both Period IV); the whole being probably not a hoard but the equipment of a well-to-do fenman.

Such a rearrangement as this would transfer some 34 examples of palstaves found locally from Period III to IV, producing the following alterations to the figures at the top of the page:

[1] Hoards: 1 Lakenheath (Camb. Mus.), 2 Meldreth (Evans, p. 462), 1 Arkesden (refer to p. 324), 1 Wilburton Fen (Camb. Mus.). The latter is almost wholly of Period V character.

A group of palstaves found at Eriswell were unfinished castings and their association with a socketed axe renders contemporaneity of manufacture almost certain. I am, however, not disposed to bring the Eriswell hoard forward as an argument for late use of the palstave. The fact that these poor thin blades are unfinished suggests that they may have been minted as currency from the close of the Middle Bronze Period onwards. See Déchelette (1910, p. 164).

THE BRONZE AGE

Axes, Period II.   26   Axes, Period IV.   71
„   III.   82   „   V.   119

In the case of the hoards, it would result in that from Grunty Fen being moved from Period III to IV; a few others now placed intermediately between Periods IV and V would fall wholly in V.

Now in the Cambridge Region almost all the Founders' and "Merchants'" hoards belong to the close of the Bronze Age; and when tabulated according to Montelius' classification practically all are found to be in Period V (or transitional between IV and V). The only important exception is the Meldreth hoard (Evans, J. 1881, p. 462, 44 objects), which is used by Montelius to illustrate Period IV. Examination of this hoard, however, shows that it might with equal justification be included in Period V; for the only objects of earlier type which it contains are a few palstaves and socketed axes with wing decoration.

The rearrangement which thus appears to be inevitable is more than a mere shifting forward of groups of objects on the border-line between two periods. It shows clearly that the appearance of Founders' hoards marks an abrupt change, and that Montelius' typological division between IV and V is arbitrary and obscures a clearly defined culture phase. There is, I think, no doubt that in the last period of the Bronze Age there should be included not only all our local founders' hoards but also all socketed axes and the leaf-shaped sword, the transitional forms of which are in this country rare or wholly absent.

One would be inclined to bring these changes in culture into relation with the first invasion of Celtic-speaking peoples, and to regard them as closing the period of seaborne culture, characterized by the rapier and the palstave, during which the British Isles were in the van of Western European civilization. Henceforward Britain occupies culturally the position which is historically familiar; a country on the edge of the known world, the last area to receive and absorb cultures moving transcontinentally from east to west (south-east to north-west). The central date of this invasion, which may have been a movement extending over a century or more in time, can hardly be earlier than 1000 B.C. The invaders may have been the Goidels, or Q-Celts; but no agreement has yet been reached as to the date of the first appearance of Celtic-speaking peoples in Britain. It is to be noted that the newcomers had apparently not been subjected to the influence of the Iron (Hallstatt) culture of Central Europe prior to their occupation of our region. They were in the last phase of the Western European Bronze Age. Exotic objects characteristic of the Hallstatt culture found locally probably drifted in in the way of trade or were brought in by later comers. The facts that our leaf-shaped swords are of Bronze Age types, and not that known to have been associated with the transitional bronze-iron culture of Hallstatt; and that winged axes occur not infrequently in hoards with socketed axes in our region and in Eastern England generally, tend to confirm this opinion and to justify the early date assigned to the invasion.

I cannot agree with Crawford (1922) in his argument that the invasion took place about 800–700 B.C. for the reasons given above. Peake (1922 b, p. 129) suggests that the movement which resulted in the settlement of leaf-sword folk in Eastern Britain commenced in Central Europe between 1200 and 1175 B.C. He regards the invasion postulated by Crawford as a later movement. Its importance in our region is clearly secondary.

SYSTEM OF CLASSIFICATION ADOPTED

It cannot be doubted that Montelius' division of the Bronze Age into five periods is unsound. I conclude, then, that the Age in the Cambridge Region presents two culture phases only; the one, commencing with the introduction of metal, about 2000 B.C., ended about 1000 B.C.; the other lasted some 500 years, being influenced by the Early Iron (Hallstatt) culture and eventually replaced either by it or by the later La Tène civilization about 500–400 B.C. (This date refers to the Cambridge Region; as we have seen, an earlier one may prove to be appropriate to Southern England.)

The first phase being a prolonged one and including profound evolutionary changes in form and type of weapons and implements may conveniently be subdivided; I retain the simple term "Transition" for the period when metal was rare, and stone weapons still in general use, and utilize the old terms "Early and Middle Bronze" for successive developments within this phase. The use of the familiar term Late Bronze Period for the second phase naturally follows.

Divisions and Chronology of the Bronze Age in the Cambridge Region		Characteristic metal forms
First Phase:	Approximate dates	
Transition Period.	2000 B.C.–1700 B.C.	Flat axes and daggers, very rare.
Early Bronze Period.	1700 B.C.–1400 B.C.	Flat and flanged axes, daggers.
Middle Bronze Period.	1400 B.C.–1000 B.C.	Palstaves, rapiers.
Second Phase:		
Late Bronze Period.	1000 B.C.–500–400 B.C.	Socketed axes, swords.

With respect to the dating: 2000 B.C. or thereabouts for the beginning of the Age and 500–400 B.C. for its close, command, as we have seen, a measure of assent. The date of the appearance of the rapier and the evolution of the palstave from the flanged axe which marks the Middle Period cannot, I think, be earlier than 1400 B.C. The close of the First Phase at 1000 B.C. has already been referred to.

This division into four periods corresponds to, and is influenced by, Déchelette's classification. Déchelette, however, while modifying Montelius' classification, has retained his chronology, and since the culture of Western Europe for the greater part of the Age was seaborne and the majority of the French deposits are on the western coasts, criticism of this element of Montelius' system as applied to Britain applies also in some measure to France. Déchelette himself (1910, p. 105) remarks that during the first half of his transition period (2500–1900 B.C.) the north of France was still in the Neolithic Age. He also notes (p. 109) in connection with his acceptance of so early a date as 900 B.C. for the close of the Bronze Age, that this does not apply to the western seaboard of France. The Iron culture came overland from Central Europe and iron weapons of the Hallstatt I period in France are almost entirely limited to the east and south of the country. Hence the Bronze Age persisted in the west for centuries, and was only effectively replaced in the Hallstatt II period. If the maps of the Bronze Age and the Hallstatt period accompanying Déchelette's *Manuel* (1910, Carte I; 1913, Carte II) be examined the distribution of finds will be seen to be in great measure complementary, not successive.

Incidentally, the French evidence provides one reason for the scanty traces of Hallstatt culture in Britain (see p. 85).

Our classification of the remains of the Bronze Age has been based on finds and hoards. It is not yet possible to include Bronze Age burials in such a system. We may be sure that interments associated with beakers save perhaps the very latest belong to the transition period and that all inhumation burials are of early date; but though Abercromby (1912, II, p. 109) has propounded a detailed chronological system largely based on the typology of Bronze Age pottery, his views have not commanded general acceptance, and are necessarily based on slender data. Interments attributed to the Age will therefore be treated separately and such correlations with our chronological system as are possible will be made in the course of analysis. Full treatment of this part of the subject is necessary, for the information is scattered in publications many of which are inaccessible, and in unpublished MSS., and has not hitherto been analysed.

In a survey of the Bronze Age one must begin with the beaker-folk and their pottery, and this leads to an examination of Bronze Age burials, prior to a consideration of finds and hoards.

THE BEAKER-FOLK AND THEIR POTTERY

The distinctive type of pottery to which the term "beaker" is applied is found in this country in certain well-defined areas; the beaker is as a sepulchral vessel associated with stone weapons and implements, with early types of bronze[1] daggers and other metal objects, with conical jet buttons with V perforations, etc., all the associated objects when of definite character being indicative of the transition period when metal was very scarce and stone weapons still in common use.

The distribution of beakers in the British Isles was worked out by Abercromby in 1904. The views on the type sequence of the pottery expressed at the time were subsequently (1912) in the light of further evidence revised and elaborated in his study of the Bronze Age pottery in Great Britain and Ireland.

Beakers are found along the whole east coast of Scotland, and in Yorkshire; in Derbyshire, Wiltshire and Dorset, the Upper Thames, and East Anglia; elsewhere they occur only sporadically. This distribution would appear to be the result of invasion—separate landings perhaps successive on the south and east coasts, the occupation of the Derbyshire area resulting from an advance up the Trent Valley; but Abercromby strongly upholds the view that a single landing took place somewhere on the south coast and that the distribution of beakers is a result of overland expansion. That some of the invaders landed in Kent is probable; but the presence on the coast of Holland and at the mouths of the Rhine of brachycephalic peoples (Ripley, 1900, p. 296) is an argument in favour of a more northerly point of embarkation than Abercromby seems to admit, and consequently supports the view that the more important landings took place on our east coast—in the Wash, and Humber-mouth, for example. The Sketch-map A (based on Abercromby) shows the topographical distribution of beakers in Eastern Britain.

The beaker type of pottery ranges from Spain to Germany, and from Hungary to Britain, forms closely resembling ours being found on the Middle Rhine. The craniological data collected by Abercromby

[1] In many cases probably copper. But few have been analysed.

render it probable that the tribe or tribes thus occupying our coastal areas belonged to a common brachycephalic stock, but their racial affinities are uncertain: from the characters of their skeletons they appear to be a mixture of Alpines with Nordics which may have originated in Eastern Central Europe. They were thus an inland people who had no knowledge of seafaring. Dr Haddon considers it possible that the invaders of this country made use of maritime folk on the Dutch and Belgian coasts.

This invasion is of special interest in that it is the first of which we have any definite and clear information, and because the beaker-folk are apparently the only round-headed people who have ever entered Britain *en masse*.

The beaker was not in this country exclusively used for sepulchral purposes; evidence is accumulating that it was the common domestic ware of the intrusive peoples. This is the more remarkable, in that the majority of beakers in refinement of decoration and craftsmanship, fineness of paste, thinness of body and excellence of firing are far superior to the later Bronze Age cinerary urns made, apparently, for the tomb. The quality, however, varies widely, as can readily be seen by a cursory examination of specimens in the Cambridge Museum; this has been thought to be due to progressive deterioration, but beakers of refined and of crude decoration have been found under conditions indicating contemporaneity, and the explanation is now discredited.

Distribution of Beakers in the Cambridge Region

The preceding remarks will have suggested that in the southern fens, as elsewhere in Britain, the Age of Metal was ushered in not by the peaceful operations of commerce, but by conquest. It is, however, very improbable that the beaker-folk brought metal with them; the earliest (copper) implements and ornaments probably reached Britain by a more southerly route, and by slow degrees seaborne trade brought a knowledge of metallurgy. No metal, but numerous scrapers and knives of flint, and one arrowhead, were found with the beaker fragments in the rubbish pits of the settlement at Peterborough already referred to (p. 15). This is to be expected; metal, if present, would have consisted only of rare and cherished articles in the possession of the chiefs.

Abercromby, in the valuable corpus already quoted, records twelve examples of the beaker class of pottery in the Cambridge Region. To these I am able to add fourteen, nine of which have not previously been published; fragments moreover from four additional sites are preserved.

An examination of the distribution of these beakers should give some indication of the route by which the invaders arrived here.

A list is given in Appendix I; the regional map (II) indicates their range.

Nine of the examples added to Abercromby's list strengthen the evidence which he provides for segregation in and around the fens; three of the remaining five, a cup found at Berden [E], and two at Chesterford [E][1] are situated on the natural traffic route formed by the inosculating valleys of the Essex Cam and the Stort, while the fourth, and fifth, found at Shefford [B] and (probably) Hitchin [H] show that the beaker-folk were settled around the headwaters of the Ivel, a tributary of the Great Ouse. Two more examples in Bury Museum, one of which is figured on Plate I, 4, almost certainly came from the valley of the Lark. It is a significant fact that the first colonists settled in greatest number in the area most favoured by Neolithic man.

The general distribution (see Sketch-map A, p. 13) suggests an invasion by way of the Wash, a view which receives strong support from the Peterborough discovery. The beakers found there were of early type and the site, a tongue of land bordering the western fens, is an obvious landing-place for seafarers advancing up the fen rivers.

The examples from Chesterford and Berden, on the other hand, when considered alone may be held to afford support to the theory of invasion *via* the lower Thames and the Lea Valley. We must await further evidence; but the latter examples may with equal justice be held to mark an extension of the invasion south-westward from the fens, rather than northward from the Thames. The Hitchin and Shefford beakers, found near the chalk escarpment and the "Icknield Way" route from the Thames Valley, are important. This portal of entry into the Cambridge district was a possible one, for the long barrow people came along it[2]; but in view of the absence of beakers on the line of the Way from the Thames to Hitchin, it is probable that the beaker-folk in the latter district made their way up the Cam Valley from the fens. (It is indeed more probable on general grounds that Wiltshire was colonized by invaders from the Wash than that the movement was in the opposite direction.)

[1] The provenance of one of these is not certain.
[2] The traditional route is indicated on the map. For discussion, see Chapter IV.

PLATE I

BEAKER POTTERY OF THE 'TRANSITION PERIOD' PRECEDING THE FULL BRONZE AGE
See pp. 25–7: also, No. 1, p. 28; No. 2, p. 45; No. 4, p. 24.

THE BRONZE AGE

Similar views as to the portals of entry of the beaker-folk are expressed by A. G. Wright, who takes a wider survey in his contribution to the review of the Berden finds. (See Maynard and Benton, 1920.)

It is to be noted that in Cambridgeshire no beakers occur, as do the later burials (see Map II), on the chalk escarpment, but in the river valleys, or on the edge of or in the fens. This distribution is probably to be accounted for in two ways: (*a*) we are dealing with domestic as well as sepulchral pottery; and (*b*) the newcomers were in the habit of burying their dead near their settlements which were by fen and river side.

Beakers are frequently found in gravel diggings: gravel implies well-drained soil suitable for settlement. One has been found on a chalk hill in N.W. Suffolk, in the parish of Barton Mills.

Typology of the Beakers found in the Cambridge Region

Basing his classification on form Abercromby, following Thurnam, divided beakers into three types, A, B, C. He elaborated this classification, distinguishing early and late phases of each type. In the tabular list (Appendix I) the type of each beaker is indicated; here it is sufficient to note that practically all Abercromby's forms are represented in the district, and to record a few examples illustrated in his *Bronze Age Pottery*. Those in italics are in the Cambridge Museum.

Type A. A "high-brimmed globose" cup, Phase I. *Eriswell* [S], Tuddenham [S].
　　　　　　　　　　　　　　　　　,, II. *Snailwell* (No. XXI).
　　　　　　　　　　　　　　　　　,, III. Barnwell (*Cambridge*).
Type B. An "ovoid cup with recurved rim" Near Methwold [N], Brandon [S] *Somersham* (No. XXIII).
Type C. A "low-brimmed" cup; a late and "debased variety" of A. *Snailwell* (No. XXII).

Of my illustrations, Plate I, 1, Wilburton and II, 2, Eriswell, represent Type A. Plate I, 3, Lakenheath, Type B, while Plate I, 4, Bury St Edmunds, is in form intermediate between B and C. Whether Abercromby's estimate of the duration of the beaker class of pottery (450 years) be correct or no, or his several phases a true indication of successive debasements, it is clear that in the Cambridge Region the range of types is similar to that in Southern Britain, and that the culture here lasted as long as anywhere in the country.

Plates I and II show the remarkable variety of decoration met with on the beaker class of pottery. The most characteristic ornament, employed on the most finely wrought beakers, is that produced by the toothed wheel or quadrant, the decoration being zonal (Plate I, Wilburton; Plate II, Eriswell). A similar effect is produced, possibly at a later stage in the history of the beaker, by scratching the surface with a pointed implement (Plate I, 2, March). Decoration consisting of a continuous coil or successive bands of ornament produced by the toothed wheel, or by a blunt implement (Plate I, 3, Lakenheath), is commonly met with. Often the fingernail is used to produce rows of deep incisions (Plate I, 4, Bury St Edmunds); a sharp-pointed implement is occasionally employed for the same purpose. Two or more of these methods may sometimes be used in decorating a given beaker. Beakers with coarse and with refined ornament are found in Abercromby's Types A and C; and it is difficult judging the pottery from this aspect to believe that Type C is really a late and debased variety of A.

In Bury Museum there is a fragment of a remarkable beaker from Great Barton near Bury, which is figured on Plate II, 3. Its vertical and horizontal decoration consists of raised ribs, and of depressions produced both by a sharp and a blunt implement. It is certainly late and probably unique. Its incised ornament is of Neolithic origin (cp. West Kennett). The bevelled rim is derived from beakers such as Plate II, 2, whereon are also apparent the early stages of the vertical ribs, and the horizontal ribs which limit these. The large beaker from Somersham in the Cambridge Museum shows well-marked vertical ribbing on the neck and may be contemporary with the Barton beaker; Abercromby considers it to be of late date.

The most important vessel of beaker type found in the district remains to be dealt with. The elaborate handled mug from Fordham (Plate II, 1) is of high importance topographically. Its only close parallel is a mug from Rothwell near Kettering [Northants.] figured by Abercromby; but one element of its decoration—a close band of thumbnail markings—is met with also on a Ramsey [Hunts.] beaker, at East Winch and Ingham [N], at Shefford [B] and at Peterborough. Here then on the western and eastern edges of the southern fenland and on the upper waters of rivers draining into the fens are evidences of a common and wellnigh exclusive style in form and ornament[1]. We may conceive of the fenland—a chain of lakes readily navigable in any direction—and its upland waterways as a culture pool, influ-

---

[1] Mr Wyman Abbott owns the Peterborough example. One from Norfolk is figured by Abercromby (Fig. 91), for the other see *Norf. Arch.* XVIII, p. xliv. Mortimer (1905, Fig. 217) figures a Yorkshire example and Abercromby one from Wiltshire (Fig. 4). The nail decoration thus occurs, so far as I have information, on seven beakers from the fenland basin, and on two from other districts.

PLATE II

BEAKER POTTERY OF THE 'TRANSITION PERIOD' PRECEDING THE FULL BRONZE AGE
See pp. 25–7: also, No. 1, pp. 45, 66; No. 2, p. 40; No. 3, pp. 39, 40, 45.

ences acting on any part of the periphery or developments produced within it being readily transmitted throughout its area. We shall frequently see reason to dwell on this aspect of our local archaeology.

Handled beakers of cruder type were also chiefly produced in Eastern Britain; of eight examples known to me, four come from Yorkshire, one each from Northants., Hunts. and Berks., and one from March in the fens —just outside the limits assigned to our region. The latter vessel, figured on Plate II, 2, was found with other pottery not preserved (Fisher, 1862). Handled "food vessels," probably contemporary, are similarly distributed, the most notable examples being derived from East Yorkshire, Northamptonshire and our region (Chesterford, Walden Museum). The range and quality of the pottery produced by the beaker-folk in the Cambridge region is very remarkable, as the Plates show. A recent addition to the local museum is a caliciform handled beaker from East Hunts.—probably Somersham. Its decoration—rows of deep cylindrical holes—is unique in this country. Similar ornament occurs on late Neolithic pottery from Uppland, Sweden[1].

Interments associated with Beakers

We cannot be certain that the beakers from our district of which no record of discovery exists are sepulchral, though the fact that most are perfect (indicating careful deposition) is in favour of association with a burial. However this may be, in the case of twelve only is there any definite evidence of sepulture[2].

In four cases, Wilburton (Plate I), Ramsey [Hunts.], Barnwell, and Berden [E], the interment was definitely by inhumation, in one, Brandon [S]—two beakers—probably so: moreover, the association of the Fordham mug (Plate II) with a skeleton may safely be accepted. This association is important in view of the extreme rarity of the type and the consequent difficulty of dating it.

The evidence in the case of the Worlington [S] beaker suggests cremation, as does also the existence of a deposit of carbon on the inside of the Somersham beaker (No. XXIII). But cremation is almost unknown during the beaker phase of culture; it is indeed doubtful if any fully authenticated case is on record. In three cases, Lakenheath (XVI and XVII) and Tuddenham [S], the beakers are known to have been found in barrows.

Barrow burial is in the Cambridge Region rare in this early period; evidence of burial in the fens and in gravel terraces by the fen borders without barrows is definite, and is peculiar to Kent and East Anglia.

---

[1] Stjerna (1910, p. 17). I owe this reference to Mr T. D. Kendrick.
[2] There is some evidence suggesting that the two Snailwell beakers were associated with an inhumed burial, but these are not included in the above total.

It may be suggested in connection with these and later Bronze Age burials that the barrows are destroyed on the fertile lowlands but suffered to remain on the hills. I do not believe it. Tumuli are met with on lowlying lands in Cambs., but they are always, when examined, found to be Roman (or Early Iron Age), and as destructive activity has been mainly confined to the last 1000 years, a Roman barrow is as likely to have suffered as one 2000 years older.

Objects associated with beaker burials. With the Brandon burial was a bowman's wrist-guard of stone, a not uncommon object in the graves of the earliest metal age; with the Wilburton skeleton and beaker was the horn of a urus; and, most important as confirming the ascription of the beaker in our district as elsewhere to the earliest metal period, the Berden skeleton (of a woman) had on the left arm a thin ribbon of metal, probably copper.

SUMMARY

This series of pottery vessels, then, is to be regarded as the product, during some 300–400 years, of an invading people probably of mixed Alpine-Nordic stock, who inhumed their dead, the culture being mainly Neolithic; at some time during this period, which may be dated from the close of the III millennium to about 1700 B.C., metal was introduced.

INTERMENTS NOT ASSOCIATED WITH BEAKERS

We may now consider the interments of the Bronze Age not associated with beakers. Their number is as remarkable as is the variety of sepulchral customs which they disclose. The majority are found in round barrows, the minority in "flat" graves. The barrow burials, being characteristic of the Age, may first be analysed.

I have found record, in one form or another, of the opening —frequently followed by the destruction—of no less than 78 barrows in our region; of these 20 are in S.W. Norfolk or N.W. Suffolk, 50 in Cambridgeshire and 8 in N. Hertfordshire and N.E. Essex.

In addition, the existence on the uplands of at least 84 other barrows is known, 45 being in the Norfolk-Suffolk corner of our area, 30 in Cambridgeshire, and 9 in Hertfordshire. The chief source of information concerning these latter is the 1836 one-inch O.S. map; the recent six-inch map and the Stowe MSS. (British Museum, 1025, fol. 15) provide some additional sites; while a few unrecorded examples have been at various times noticed by me. Many of these barrows, especially in the neighbourhood of Newmarket, have been destroyed in recent years.

THE BRONZE AGE

Of the majority of the 78 barrows of which some record exists, that record is inadequate; in many cases indeed it amounts to no more than that there exists in a museum an urn or urns from a tumulus in a given parish, or that a barrow contained "a skeleton," or "burnt human bones." In certain of these latter the ascription to the Bronze Age must be regarded as "probable" or "possible."

I am of opinion that on the Cambridgeshire uplands not more than half a dozen untouched examples remain for future investigation.

The number of barrows originally present on the chalk escarpment in the Cambridge Region must be counted in hundreds. Many of those of which record exists were, before examination, reduced by the plough to so insignificant an elevation as to be almost unrecognizable. In two cases this had occurred before 1860; and many must, before and since, have been completely obliterated in this manner. The 1836 Ordnance Surveyors one may be sure only marked considerable elevations. Many cinerary urns and other sepulchral vessels of local origin in the Cambridge and other museums, the provenance of which is only vaguely known, undoubtedly came from destroyed barrows.

It is due to the memory of a distinguished local archaeologist, R. C. Neville, afterwards 4th Lord Braybrooke, to record that the majority of the many barrows which he excavated in the middle of the nineteenth century are carefully described, and that from his printed papers, his unpublished MSS. and his collection in the Audley End Museum much of the material utilized in this chapter is derived.

Our archaeological evidence having been thus in large measure ignorantly destroyed, it seemed desirable to gather all the records of barrow burial, however slight, together; that much of the material was in unpublished MSS. and some not even written down was additional reason for careful and detailed treatment. Space, however, does not permit the presentation of more than a small portion of the information thus gained; but a referenced List of the Barrows attributed to the Bronze Age will be found in Appendix III.

The Map (II) shows the distribution of these[1], and of interments over which apparently no barrows were raised. With its aid we may first consider them topographically; then selected examples of barrow burial and of burial in "flat" graves, illustrating different sepulchral customs, will be examined in their probable chronological sequence; consideration of the typology of sepulchral pottery may provide additional evidence of relative date; and finally analysis of the objects associated with interments may give some indication of the material resources of the inhabitants of the Cambridge Region in the early Age of Bronze.

[1] Nine doubtful ones have been omitted from the Map.

THE BRONZE AGE

The Map also shows by means of *broken* circles the distribution of 77 of the 84 barrows, referred to on p. 28, unexamined, or destroyed without record of their contents having been preserved. It is thought that record in this form is justifiable and desirable, but such barrows will not again be referred to in the text.

Topographical Distribution of Round Barrows, etc.

Our Bronze Age barrows are all bowl-shaped. They are here, as elsewhere in similar districts in England, confined almost entirely to the uplands[1]; they are sited on the belt of open country along which the Icknield Way runs[2]. The small number of barrows so sited which can confidently be referred to later periods is remarkable; two or three (of course omitted from the Bronze Age Map) are of the Early Iron Age[3] and one is Saxon. No *primary* interment of Roman date in an upland barrow is known to me; tumuli of the period are not infrequent, as may be seen on the Roman Map, but they occur in the valley and forest lands and present an entirely different grouping.

Secondary interments of Early Iron, Roman and Anglo-Saxon date are met with in Bronze Age barrows; such are not referred to in the present chapter.

The Bronze Age barrows on the downs appear to be mainly segregated; the groups at Upper Hare Park[4], near the Fleam Dyke, and on Therfield Heath [H] may be cited. That this is partly due to the destruction of barrows formerly existing in the intervening areas is probable, but the main reason doubtless is that the groups are the sepulchres of local tribes and clans which dwelt on the edge of the fens or by the rivers. In support of this view it may be noted that the majority of the Fleam Dyke group (Nos. 2–10 and 20 in Appendix

---

[1] A few exceptions occur in the north-east of our district, and one "barrow" is in Mepal Fen; but this latter is probably a natural hillock.

[2] That the Way as a route along the chalk escarpment existed in this period is probable, and its traditional alignment is indicated on the map. That it determined the position of more than a very small minority of the barrows is unlikely.

[3] Certain of the Triplow group of 13 barrows (9 are omitted from the map) present unusual features. See List in Appendix (Nos. 68–70, p. 329). In view of the facts that the Chronicle Hills group, assigned to the first phase of the Early Iron Age, is only two miles away, and that an Iron Age pottery vessel from "a Triplow Barrow" is in the Audley End Museum, Iron Age date for the majority of this group is possible. The record of excavation is in all cases inadequate, and practically none of the finds are preserved (see pp. 79–80).

[4] In the neighbourhood of Newmarket Heath the rising ground on which Upper Hare Park is situated, and Allington Hill adjacent, are rich in prehistoric remains. This important site, between the Street and Icknield Ways, commanding wide views in every direction, has probably been utilized from the earliest period down to historic times.

III), all excavated by Neville, presented uniform and in some ways distinct characters.

No relation, it may here be said, can be established between the dykes and the barrows. Though groups occur near each they are not on the defended side alone, but indifferently disposed on either; and I am of opinion that the dykes were not in existence when the majority was raised[1].

Both inhumation and cremation interments are met with along the whole line of the uplands; and though local variations do occur the burials on the whole suggest that the culture of the district was fairly uniform, as might be expected from the ease of communication within its limits.

Burials which present no evidence of a barrow are all sited on low-lying ground by river or fen, or even within the fen, thus carrying on the tradition of the beaker-folk. Those near Cambridge and in the valley of the Essex Cam are known to be on gravel terraces. Of some, marked on the map as in this group, such as those at Lakenheath, nothing is known save the existence of a cinerary urn, and they *may* be barrow burials. The majority of burials on low-lying sites other than beaker burials of which anything is known are by cremation[2], and some are, as we shall see, of early date; others are late, but on only one site (Wenden, p. 37) have associated interments indicating a "flat cemetery" been recorded.

Details of representative Burials

Details of the several types of burial occurring in the district may now be given[3].

To the transition period (*circa* 2000 B.C.–1700 B.C.), doubtless, the following belong:

Barton Hill, Barton Mills [S]; No. 11 on List, Appendix, p. 325.

Four barrows stood on this commanding height; from one presumably came the beaker referred to on p. 25. A second was excavated in 1869.

In its centre on the natural surface was an unburnt contracted skeleton. Near it were found several pieces of "plain pottery," some flint flakes and three round scrapers.

Around this interment was a bank of clunch 7 feet thick and 2 feet

---

[1] Fleam Dyke is known to be later than the Mutlow Hill barrow which adjoins it (see pp. 130–1).

[2] At Soham (p. 37) a skeleton was found in addition to the cremation interment. Its chronological relation to the latter cannot be determined.

[3] References to authorities will be found in Appendix III.

3 inches high, the internal diameter being 38 feet[1]. On the top of, or just within, the clunch wall three interments were found, two by inhumation and one by cremation; the latter had not been burnt on the spot.

Within the clunch ring also, in a hollow, was a quantity of charcoal and burnt flints. The barrow had been lowered by cultivation and human bones had frequently been turned out by the plough when crossing it.

A round barrow (No. 48 on List, Appendix, p. 328) on Therfield Heath [H] may possibly be of even earlier date.

Opened in 1856 "by means of a central shaft" after the manner of the earlier excavators it was found to have been raised over nine human skeletons—men, women and children; these covered a space 2 feet by 12 feet, the bones lying in all directions. In a cutting made on the east side of the shaft a bone pin was subsequently found. The resemblance between this interment and certain of those of Neolithic date in Wiltshire is notable; but Mortimer (1905, p. xxxvi) met with dismembered bodies in round barrows in Yorkshire.

The Three Hills, Warren Hill, Mildenhall [S] (No. 28 on List, Appendix, p. 327). The three fine round barrows on this eminence, about 70 feet in diameter and 9 or 10 feet high, each being fossed, were destroyed in 1866. Adequate record of one interment, apparently the primary, in one of these barrows exists.

Overlying a grave sunk 2 feet in the gravel subsoil were eighteen fine antlers of the Red Deer disposed in a heap with the prongs projecting upward[2]. In the grave was a contracted female skeleton, the skull of which was "eminently brachycephalic." Behind the skull and nearly touching it was a perfect and finely wrought "food-vessel." It measured 5 inches high by 6¾ inches in width at the rim, had six pierced ears or lugs, and was decorated in three zones, two of herring-bone and one of zigzag, all being incised: in addition, the lip had "twisted thong" ornament (figured by H. Prigg, 1872).

Barrows not infrequently contain a primary inhumation interment attributable to the Transition Period, or possibly to the Early Bronze Period (*circa* 1700–1400 B.C.) with secondary cremation interments: No. 37 on List (Appendix, p. 327) provides a good example.

It was a round barrow situated a quarter of a mile north-west of Hare Park, Swaffham Bulbeck. In it was a large cinerary urn (in the Cambridge Museum) containing "the bones of children buried by cremation." Fragments of a second urn were found, and the excavators (Allix and Hughes) noted that all round the margin of the mound fires had been

---

[1] Mortimer (1905, p. xxii) noted that circles within barrows excavated by him were incomplete. There is nothing in the record to suggest that this was so at Barton Hill.

[2] Antlers of the Red Deer are similarly associated with an inhumation interment in a barrow at Hare Park (No. 44 on List, Appendix, p. 328).

lighted; burnt mussel-shells, moreover, were found, remains of the funeral feast (?).

The primary interment was by inhumation, bones, scattered by burrowing animals, being found in the centre of the mound below the urn.

Sometimes secondary inhumation interments are on record:

A barrow on Long Heath Field, Risby [S], No. 30 on List (Appendix, p. 327), opened by Greenwell in 1869, contained in a shallow grave a primary inhumation interment; the skeleton was contracted; four secondary inhumation interments of similar character were found at various levels in the barrow; and, in addition, one burnt interment, contained in an "urn of the usual British form," was found.

To the close of the Transition Period probably belongs a burial at Icklingham [S] (No. 22 on List, Appendix, p. 326)[1].

In a "stone kist," presumably in a barrow, was found a contracted skeleton; with it a flat tanged knife or dagger of bronze, 5 inches in length and $\frac{5}{8}$ inch wide (Plate V), and three hammerstones. The occurrence of such a cist is unique in the district.

Primary cremation interments in barrows are of course common. The date when inhumation ceased to be practised cannot be definitely stated; but it was probably during the Early Bronze Period. In this period burials by cremation associated with cinerary urns of the overhanging rim type may be held to occur first (pp. 39 and 45).

Wide variations in methods of sepulture in cremation burials in local barrows are noticeable. The ashes of the dead may be placed in an urn—upright or inverted—on the surface of the ground or in a hollow; sometimes a bronze pin is used to secure the cloth in which the bones are wrapped[2]. Frequently there is no urn, the ashes being collected in a heap and the barrow raised over them; similar deposits, usually superficial in barrows of earlier date, are met with and possibly represent the very latest phase of barrow burial in the Bronze Age. In each of the above cases the pyre may have been burnt on the spot or elsewhere.

Examples of these varied usages may be given. Barrow No. 34 on List (Appendix, p. 327) near Upper Hare Park may first be described.

It was an unusually large one, being 90 feet in diameter and 14 feet high. At its centre an inverted cinerary urn 5 inches high (in Cambridge Museum) was found surrounded by charcoal, burnt bones and earth,

---

[1] Barrows Nos. 5, 12, 15, 19, 35 on List (Appendix, pp. 325 f.) also contain inhumation interments of the Transition or Early Bronze Periods.
[2] Cf. *Iliad*, XXIV, 795 ff.

and containing charcoal and a fragment of bone. The body had apparently been burnt on the spot where the urn was placed. A partially burnt secondary deposit of human bones "apparently that of a young person" was found 10 feet to the eastward of the central interment. A mass of charcoal and burnt earth was found near the latter. Charcoal was everywhere mingled with the mass of earth composing the barrow.

Two barrows in Balsham parish, Nos. 2 and 3 on List (Appendix, p. 325), situated in Charterhouse Plantation east of the Newmarket-London Road, show variations on the above procedure.

No. 2 was 5–6 feet high, and 50 feet in diameter. It contained two basin-shaped cists about 3 feet in circumference and 20 inches deep scooped out of the solid chalk. In the centre of each a large cinerary urn was inverted over cremated remains; it appeared to the excavator as though fire had been kindled in the basin. In one case the burnt bones and ashes under the urn had been wrapped in coarse cloth—a fragment was preserved—and a small rude bronze pin, evidently used for fastening the shroud, was lying in the pile of ashes. The urns were very rotten and fell to pieces; one was very large, being 17 inches high. The excavator, Neville, remarked that he had "only to regret that the Britons had not been as careful in baking their pottery as their dead." Charcoal, due doubtless to the funeral pile, and a few burnt bones of oxen (from the funeral feast?) occurred at intervals all through the mound.

The neighbouring barrow (No. 3) was about the same size as the former.

A very large cinerary urn standing on its base was found in the centre; it was covered with an irregular pattern apparently made with the finger-nail; and was so rotten that it could not be removed. It contained the cremated remains of one individual. No cist had been hollowed out for it, nor were there any traces of a fire having been kindled around it. Eight black flint "arrowheads" [so-called, evidently flakes] "unused," were found very near it; they were so sharp as to require "great care in handling." A heap of six similar "arrowheads" was found near the edge of the mound, and three more elsewhere in the earth composing it[1]. A portion of a small bronze ornament must be regarded as a secondary deposit.

A tumulus within half a mile of the group at Five Barrow Field, in Melbourn parish, No. 26 on List (Appendix, p. 326), presents features not met with elsewhere in our district.

A hearth consisting of five or six flat slabs of sandstone was found bearing traces of fire on the upper surface, which was covered with a mass of human bones apparently burnt at the time of interment. There were no associated objects. There was in the mound a secondary deposit probably also of Bronze Age date; a small cist or nest had been scraped out of the original black mould of which the barrow was composed and filled with burnt human bones probably of one person only.

---

[1] Compare Mortimer (1905), p. xxv.

THE BRONZE AGE

The simplest form of primary cremation interment may be illustrated by a barrow at Bottisham, No. 14 on List (Appendix, p. 326).

This barrow, 40 feet in diameter and 3 feet in height (much reduced in elevation by the plough), was examined in 1852. In a cist at the centre of the mound, scooped out of the floor of the barrow, a quantity of burnt human bones reduced nearly to ashes was found. Five "flint implements" (probably flakes) and the skulls of a goat (?) and ox were the only other objects met with, the barrow having been turned over from end to end.

Two barrows yielding multiple cremation interments are of especial interest.

The Mutlow Hill Barrow (No. 20 on List, Appendix, p. 326), 67 feet in diameter and 10–12 feet in height, situated on the north side of the Fleam Dyke at or near the point where the "Icknield Way" crossed it, may first be described. It was excavated by Neville in 1852. Its contents were as follows:

(1) A small heap of burnt human bones with several chipped flints, part of a bronze pin, "six long beads of pottery each consisting of five smaller ones united" and a bone pin. (2) A large heap of burnt human bones. (3) Another heap of burnt bones. (4) An urn containing "burnt ashes, apparently of some plant." (5) An urn containing burnt human bones, enveloped in a cloth which fell to powder when touched. (6) An urn with a few bones, no trace of a cloth. (7) An urn, broken, but fragments indicated unusual size ("2 feet in diameter"), contents similar to (5). (8) and (9) Two urns, separately placed, no contents. (10) An urn containing burnt human bones. (11) A similar urn.

The barrow thus contained no less than eight (possibly ten) separate interments, all by cremation. From Neville's descriptions and illustrations, and from the examples preserved at Audley End Museum, five of the urns appear to have been of similar form, being overhanging-rim cinerary urns of latish type (see p. 40); the remaining three are small bowl-shaped vessels such as are met with in the Hare Park tumuli (Plate IV, 2, 5). One of the latter was empty; one (showing a decorated rim) had the plant ashes inside; but the third contained human bones, and is the second definitely recorded local example of this type of ceramic being employed as a cinerary urn.

The necklace of segmented beads found with one interment is the most interesting associated object in the whole series of our Bronze Age barrows. These beads are pottery copies of the vitreous paste beads of Mediterranean origin, in this country found almost exclusively south of the Thames, the earliest date for which appears to be XIV century B.C. (Abercromby, 1912, II, p. 66). One bead is preserved in the Audley End Museum. It is possibly of disintegrated faience; but I could see no trace of glaze.

It is difficult to determine from the published account which of the interments was primary. That all the urns of overhanging-rim type were morphologically similar suggests that the sepulchre was in use for no very long period. Two or three broad bands of dark earth, said to have run horizontally across the barrow, indicate no doubt successive additions to its bulk.

In the Neolithic Age the distinctive tomb was a chamber in which successive interments could conveniently be made; a similar result was in cases such as this obtained in a different manner in the succeeding Age of Metal.

Our second example is the Money Hill Barrow (No. 46 on List, Appendix, p. 328) on Therfield Heath [H] partially excavated by Beldam (1861) by means of a central shaft and subsequently destroyed[1].

It was 15 ft. high and 100 ft. in diameter. The primary interment, in a cist cut in the chalk 2 feet long by 18 inches in depth and width, was that of a child of about two years, whose bones, presumably cremated, were placed in an elaborately decorated cinerary urn. [See Plate IV, 6B; it is a characteristic example.] The barrow owed its height and size to its being raised after successive interments; the central shaft, by which the above-mentioned interment was reached, passed through successive layers of clay, charcoal and decomposed turf mixed with the bones of animals[2]; ashes and decayed turf, moreover, covered the cist at the base of the barrow. At a depth of 8 feet in the central shaft an "incense cup"(?) was found (Plate IV, 6A)[3]. When, shortly after this excavation, the mound was destroyed—the material being carted away—portions of "several vases" were found with "ornaments" as "elaborate" as those of the urn first mentioned, but "not so well baked." These are lost. In addition, thirteen small bars or ingots of metal 4 to 5 inches long were found together, "as in a nest," within about 2 feet of the bottom of the mound on the north-east side, and in a spot unspecified "a small copper tool" $3\frac{3}{4}$ inches long, rounded at the angles and the ends, which (preserved in the Beldam collection) is seen to be one of the bars, worked up into the form of a cold chisel. The bars on analysis were found to be almost pure copper (98.5 per cent.). Two of them are figured (Plate XVIII, 10); see also p. 63.

We may next examine the group of interments in graves without barrows, on gravel terraces near rivers, or in the fens. Of few of these has any detailed record been preserved.

---

[1] Beldam's account is in some respects obscure; but by a fortunate chance the collection of antiquities which he possessed has been recently placed in the Camb. Mus., and I was able to identify those from the barrow, which were amongst numerous unlabelled objects.

[2] Of pig, horse, roe deer and goat.

[3] This may have been—on the analogy of Hare Park interments—a cinerary urn. On the other hand, an incense cup of Yorkshire type was found apparently alone in a barrow (No. 24 on List) at Melbourn.

THE BRONZE AGE

A cinerary urn with well-defined foot and of unusually good workmanship, containing charcoal and fragments of bone, was dug up in Clipsel Field, Soham (see Plate III, 2 and p. 39). With it was a small pin (or awl?) of bronze and an unburnt skeleton. Urn, pin and skull are now in the Camb. Mus. Whether the pin was associated with the burnt interment as a fastening for the cloth in which the bones may have been wrapped (as at Mutlow Hill, p. 35), or with the skeleton, is unknown. There is no mention of a barrow and from the analogy of similar sites it is improbable that one existed. It appears likely that an inhumation interment was here followed by the cremated burial.

At Mepal two vessels, a cinerary urn with deep overhanging rim, about 7·5 inches high, full of burnt bones, and a tiny bowl decorated with an indented lattice pattern, were found together in 1859 in a "very low and broad tumulus" in the fen—probably a natural hillock. Both vessels are figured on Plate III, 3.

The definite association of urn and tiny vessel is of interest; the latter is doubtless of the "incense cup" class.

In connection with the possible ascription of certain Bronze Age burials in our district to a late date in the Bronze Age two interments at Wendens Ambo [E] at the head of the Essex Cam Valley are of interest.

In a field close to the railway viaduct showing no trace of tumuli on the surface, gravel-digging has yielded a short distance below ground at two different points cinerary urns with overhanging rims. One of these was associated with an unique fluted cylindrical implement or instrument of sandstone of unknown use. (Maynard, 1916, p. 13.)

An urn field such as this suggests late date; the urns were of advanced, but not of debased type.

This discovery may be associated with that made in 1856 in a gravel pit close to the Essex Cam in Saffron Walden [E] parish, where —there being no recorded trace of a barrow—a cinerary urn $7\frac{1}{2}$ inches in height, containing cremated human remains, was found in association with a pestle?—a roughly cylindrical instrument of granite 9 inches long. This and the urn are in the Audley End Museum[1].

If mention be made of two barrows in Balsham parish (Nos. 7 and 8 on List) which seemed to be almost entirely composed of greasy fatty ashes, as though many persons had been cremated at the same time, the range of type in Bronze Age burials met with in our district may be said to have been fully covered.

It remains to be seen whether we can obtain any information as to relative chronology, especially of the series of cremation interments, from a study of the typology of the associated pottery.

---

[1] Similar pestles from Hauxton and Barnwell are in the Camb. Mus.

SEPULCHRAL POTTERY OTHER THAN BEAKERS

Apart from the beakers, which have already been considered, the earliest type of pottery is the "Food-vessel," which is contemporary with the later phases of the beaker, and derived, as R. A. Smith has shown, from the Neolithic bowl.

(i) **Food-vessels.** One characteristic example (Abercromby, Type 1 *a*) was obtained from the Mildenhall barrow already referred to (p. 32). This, with two found in Northamptonshire, at Eyebury and Desborough (Leeds, 1915, pp. 119 and 124), represents the extreme southerly range of the type, and indicates contact with the north, probably with Yorkshire.

A few food-vessels are found in the south and west of Britain, but they are not characteristic. Abercromby (1912, I, ch. 7) records none of his types 1, 1 *a*, 1 *b*, south of Derbyshire and Staffordshire.

Several of the wide range of forms of food-vessel other than the above, figured by Abercromby, are found in the district. A fine handled mug from Chesterford, in Walden Museum, represents his Type 3; vessels from Brigg, Lincs., and Garrowby Wold, Yorks., may be compared with it[1].

A vessel—found during gravel digging on Midsummer Common, Cambridge, in 1860—figured on Plate IV, 1B, is of Abercromby's Type 5. It was associated with a small rude bowl, and may possibly have been used as a cinerary urn (see p. 41). A second vessel from the Midsummer Common gravel pits, though its associations are unknown, is certainly a food-vessel (Plate IV, 4); the diagonal depressions on the rim are characteristic, and the cuneiform incisions on the upper part are, I believe, a mark of early date in this district.

Similar incisions occur on urns with overhanging rims of the earliest type from Chatteris, and Fletton, near Peterborough; in Wisbech Museum and Mr J. W. Bodger's Collection, Peterborough, respectively. Compare Abercromby, 1912, I, Plate 32, fig. 63, and Plate 34, fig. 101, from Yorkshire and Derbyshire.

This community of ideas and forms with the north late in the Transition Period and in the Early Bronze Period is apparent throughout the Fenland Basin. Side by side on a shelf in the Cambridge Museum are two bowls almost identical, of Abercromby's Type 5, one from Rothwell [Northants.] on the western border, the other from Wereham [N] on the eastern (see Plate VI, and Sketch-map A). For their nearest relations we must look to Yorkshire (Abercromby, 1912, I, Plate 40, fig. 193).

[1] Abercromby (1912, I, Plate XLI, fig. 199); Mortimer (1905, fig. 353).

PLATE III

BRONZE AGE. CINERARY URNS

See pp. 39–41: also, No. 2, pp. 37, 44, and footnote, p. 31; No. 3, pp. 37, 42; No. 4, p. 328.

The Sketch-map A indicates the distribution of food-vessels of Abercromby's Type 1 in eastern England. It is analogous to that of handled mugs of beaker type (confined to Yorkshire and the Fenland Basin with an isolated example in Berkshire) which are doubtless contemporary; and viewed from our local standpoint suggests that during the earlier part of the II millennium B.C. our cultural connections were mainly with Yorkshire; and that whether tribal jealousy or geographical barriers to intercourse were the cause, the Thames Valley was the southern limit of the Northern influence.

(ii) Cinerary Urns: overhanging-rim types. The cinerary urns with overhanging rims found in the district present practically the whole range of form and decoration shown in Abercromby's Plates (1912, vol. II).

While it does not appear that it is safe to date all such urns on form alone, his typological sequence may be in broad outline accepted; and we may agree that the series begins with urns that are structurally tripartite and ends with those that are structurally bipartite.

Abercromby and others derive the cinerary urn from the food-vessel; but it has seemed to me possible that the later developments of the beaker may have had some share in its evolution. For example, the bevelled rim and vertical neck of the Soham urn (Plate III) are related to the similar elements of the Barton beaker (Plate II); the paste, of excellent quality, is in both cases similar in colour and texture[1]. The Soham urn should moreover be compared with the Northamptonshire beaker, No. 66 (Abercromby, 1912, I, Plate 9). Again, though many cinerary urns have a broad flat rim often decorated with thong markings undoubtedly of food-vessel ancestry, others have a rounded lip like a beaker. The paste of such is, moreover, of high quality, and all are typologically early.

That urns of the Soham type were derived directly from Neolithic pots with a cavetto moulding under a well-defined rim is by no means improbable; Abercromby hints at the possibility of this (1912, II, p. 9).

A recent (1922) paper by Leeds on Neolithic pottery found at Peterborough throws fresh light on these problems. He describes a large barrel-shaped Neolithic vase with a deep rounded rim which closely resembles a vase found by Mortimer in a Yorkshire barrow presumably of Early Bronze Age date[2]. These vessels show us whence the

---

[1] Cremation urns with moulded rims like the Soham urn are common in the Wiltshire barrows. It is significant that associated objects indicate an early date in the Bronze Age for such.

[2] A vase similar in shape, from Icklingham [S], is in the Brit. Mus.

hollow *internal* moulding at the lip of a large group of cinerary urns may have been derived; the Soham urn possesses this feature. Leeds also figures a beaker which possesses features derived from Neolithic ceramic. His work suggests that the bevelled rim of certain beakers of Abercromby's A type and of the Barton beaker (Plate II, 2 and 3) may be modifications of the caliciform cup due to the same influence.

We may perhaps conclude that the main line of evolution was Neolithic pot—food-vessel—cinerary urn, and that the former *may* have influenced the cinerary urn directly. The beaker, introduced at the close of the Neolithic Age, became modified by the native pottery; and the late types of beaker in turn influenced the development of the cinerary urn and the method employed in its manufacture. Such influence was to be expected; it would be surprising if the high skill as potters shown by the beaker-folk were to pass without leaving a trace.

It is noticeable that the local barrows provide few of the early forms under discussion. For such we must look chiefly to burials on low-lying sites, such as that from Soham[1]. This is at first sight unexpected, for one was prepared to find that burial on the uplands was the earlier phase, and that fen-side burial without barrows would be late; but since the beaker-folk preferred the lowland interment it is after all not surprising that during the first centuries after their disappearance (probably by racial absorption) the tradition should have been carried on.

Developed and late (bipartite) forms of the cinerary urn occur frequently in local barrows[2]. An example, from Money Hill, of a group with fairly well-defined shoulders is given on Plate IV. This urn is well baked and the decoration is carefully wrought. Bipartite urns from Mutlow Hill, Wilbraham, are well represented in the Audley End Museum, and characteristic examples from Mepal Fen and from a Therfield Heath barrow are figured on Plate III, 3 and 4. These are typologically the latest forms of the cinerary urn with over-hanging rim met with in our barrows[3]; but we are not yet in a position to say when their use was given up or when barrow building ceased in the Cambridge Region. We do not know, moreover, whether the secondary interments of burnt bones found in nests scooped out of

[1] Urns, the paste of which suggests beaker influence, are of forms held to be early by Abercromby; his type sequence thus receives confirmation.

[2] The four urns of over-hanging rim type, figured on Plates III and IV, give some idea of the range of forms which are found locally.

[3] It may be noted that many of these typologically late urns are of poor design, badly made and badly fired, and frequently so rotten as to fall to pieces when exposed.

PLATE IV

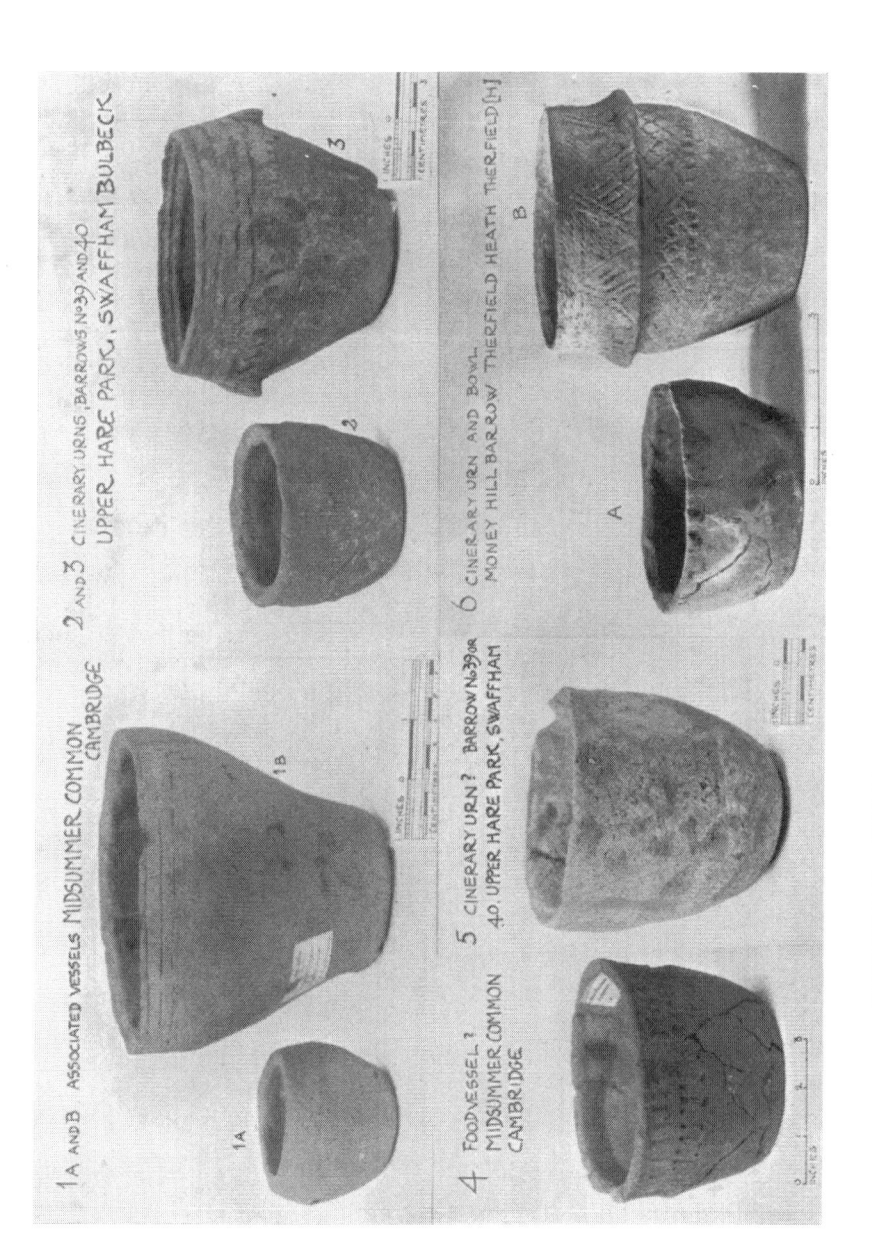

BRONZE AGE. CINERARY URNS AND OTHER SEPULCHRAL POTTERY

No. 1, p. 38; No. 2, pp. 35, 41; No. 3, p. 41; No. 4, p. 38; No. 5, pp. 35, 41; No. 6, pp. 36, 40.

the side of a barrow are contemporary with or altogether later than the deposits associated with overhanging-rim urns.

The difficulty of determining the lower limit of date of these urns is increased by the fact that very few cineraries of types related to the Deverel-Rimbury group of Wessex, associated by Abercromby (*op. cit.*) and Crawford (1922, p. 30) with an overseas invasion, have been found in our district. I can only record one or two bucket-shaped examples, and these fragmentary, from Lakenheath and Chesterton[1]. Such vessels occur in flat cemeteries at Ashford [Middx.], Colchester and Manningtree [E], and Troston Heath, Bury St Edmunds [S], and similar cemeteries may await discovery in the Cambridge Region.

(iii) **Cinerary urns and other vessels: anomalous forms.** Vessels of anomalous form are frequently met with in the district, usually in barrows; the outline of some, and the presence of lugs and ears on others suggest early date, and derivation from the food-vessel. It has already been noted (p. 35) that some of these are definitely cinerary. The majority are small and of rude manufacture; Plate IV, Nos, 2, 3, 5, are characteristic examples from the Hare Park barrows. A larger example (Plate III, 1) which contained burnt bones when discovered in 1876 during coprolite digging near Wadloes foot-path, Fen Ditton, resembles a food-vessel of Abercromby's Type 4.

These vessels then may represent the phase, dated in the Early Bronze Period, when inhumation was the rule, and cremation occasionally employed.

Some small vessels found in barrows may be of the "incense cup" class associated with cinerary urns. In the case of the small pot associated with the Mepal urn (Plate III) this may be held to be certain. The Melbourn "incense cup" (figured by Neville, 1848) is the only example of classic form found in the district.

The existence of examples of food-vessels and of other early forms of sepulchral pottery related to ours in the Nene Valley has been mentioned; it may be noted that a series of urns of overhanging-rim types from Fletton near Peterborough, which I have examined, as a group closely resembles ours. Thus the intimate connection with the Nene Valley manifest in the late beaker period may be held to have continued throughout the II millennium B.C.

Space will not permit consideration of the various styles and methods of decoration found on food-vessels, cinerary urns and

---

[1] In Camb. Mus. Vessels with curved ribs, probably related to this group, have been found locally on a settlement site assigned to the Late Bronze Period (see p. 47).

associated vessels; it must suffice to remark that that produced by a twisted thong is the commonest, but incised lines or depressions made by stick or bone are frequently met with; and that in range and character the patterns employed present few unusual features. The recurrence of a rouletted pattern on certain typologically late overhanging-rim urns (as Plate III, 3) is interesting.

ANALYSIS OF BRONZE AGE INTERMENTS

The general bearing of the interments we have considered on the pre-history of the Age may be left till later. Here an analysis may be given of the contents of all the round barrows in the district of which we have sufficient information for tabular presentation, and for inclusion in the period.

This analysis is set out in the attached table. It shows that in a total of 55 barrows about 38 inhumation interments were met with, and over 52 cremation interments with urns and 25 without.

Incidental mention has been made of associated objects; here all such finds are recorded; and the poverty of our district in the Transitional and Early Bronze Periods when the deposition of objects with the dead was customary, is apparent. From 55 barrows come four small bronze pins and a bead necklace (p. 35) only; there is no amber or gold. The result confirms Greenwell's and Mortimer's experiences in Yorkshire, and Abercromby's analysis of Bronze Age burials generally, as suggesting that during the early part of the Bronze Age metal was exceedingly scarce north of the Thames. The percentage of burials in which bronze occurred was 7·3, a percentage which would be increased to not more than 12·0 were we, analysing the whole series of burials of known provenance whether in barrows or no, to add the copper bracelet, the bronze pin and the tanged dagger tabulated separately. The inadequacy of the records makes the *exact* percentage of little value; it is not improbable that some bronze pins have been overlooked in barrow excavations. Thus, since Greenwell (*B.M.G.* 1920, p. 65) and Mortimer (1905, p. xxxiv), whose figures are of course dependable, found only 3·9 per cent. and 4 per cent. respectively of interments in Yorkshire contained bronze, and our percentage is at least 7·3, Abercromby's conclusion that at the beginning of the Age bronze becomes scarcer the further north one goes, is confirmed.

Flint flakes and chips are commonly met with in the material composing barrows, and sometimes rough scrapers. Such have not been recorded in the analysis save in one case where they were

THE BRONZE AGE

Analysis of Contents of Round Barrows of the Bronze Age in the Cambridge Region

Description of group area	Barrows examined	Inhumation interments	Objects associated with inhumation interments	Cremation interments with urns	Cremation interments without urns	Objects associated with cremation interments
Area north of River Kennet (List Nos. 1, 11, 23, 28, 30–32, 51–60)	17	12[1]	3 beakers (XVI, XVII, XXIV), food-vessel and 18 red deer antlers (28), pottery sherds and scrapers (11)	8 (2 known to have been inverted)	13	None recorded
Newmarket Heath–Hare Park area (List Nos. 12–17, 33–45)	19	11[2]	2 vessels (? beakers or food-vessels) with 3 arrowheads (15), 4 red deer antlers (44)	20 at least [possibly 25] (one known to have been inverted)	3	2 smooth balls of clunch 1 inch in diam. Associations doubtful (45)
Fleam Dyke group (List Nos. 2–10, 20)	10	5[2]	—	15 (4 known to have been inverted)	5	3 groups of black flint flakes (3), 3 bronze pins (2, 6, 20), bone pin and 6 segmented pottery beads (20)
Heydon-Triplow area (List Nos. 19, 24–26)	4	1	—	3	3	1 pierced incense cup (?), inverted, associations doubtful (24)
Therfield Heath area (List Nos. 46–50)	5	9 (in one barrow (48))	Bone pin; associations doubtful (48)	6 at least (1 known to have been inverted)	1	Bronze pin (49)
Totals	55	38		52 + x	25	—

[1] Beakers found in barrows in this area are presumed to have been associated with inhumation interments.
[2] In one case an unknown number is counted as 3.

Note. The occurrence of scattered flint flakes and of animal bones in barrows is not recorded in the list. Barrow burials for which the evidence is too indefinite for tabular presentation are omitted from consideration; as are all post-Bronze Age interments in Bronze Age barrows.

Objects, other than pottery, associated with interments of the Bronze Age not included in the preceding analysis[1].

Object	Associations		References
Horn core of urus	Beaker and skeleton	No barrow	Beaker No. XXV, Wilburton, pp. 25, 26
Stone wrist-guard	2 beakers	,,	Beakers Nos. IV–V, Brandon, p. 322
Copper bracelet	Beaker	,,	Beaker No. III, Berden, pp. 27, 28
Pierced stone axehead	"Urn"	? Barrow	Wilton Heath, p. 3
Bronze pin or awl	Cinerary urn	No barrow	Soham, p. 37
Flat bronze dagger	Provenance and associations doubtful	Barrow	Cambridge Museum
Flat copper dagger	Associations doubtful	Barrow	Litlington (?)
Granite cylindrical object (pestle)	Cinerary urn	No barrow	Walden, p. 37
Sandstone cylindrical object, fluted	Cinerary urn	No barrow	Wenden, p. 37
Tanged bronze dagger and 3 hammerstones	Skeleton	? Barrow	Icklingham, p. 33

disposed in groups. Very few other stone implements are recorded; a wrist-guard, a quartzite axehammer, three arrowheads and the two remarkable cylindrical instruments found with low-lying cremation interments (one of which was elaborately fluted) are practically all. Bone pins, doubtless used either to secure the shroud of the inhumed body or to fasten the cloth in which the cremated ashes were wrapped, have been met with in two cases. The discovery of red deer antlers with skeletons in graves in the chalk is interesting; fragments of deerhorn probably used as picks have also occasionally been found in local barrows. The associations of the two smooth balls of clunch found in one barrow are doubtful; they may possibly be of later date.

BRONZE AGE INTERMENTS: SUMMARY

The sepulchral pottery found in the district has been examined, the variety of type of interments has been illustrated, and the objects associated with local burials have been recorded. The rarity of such associated objects has made it difficult to determine the dates of the various pottery forms and of the sepulchral rites associated with them;

[1] Treated separately either because they were not found in barrows or because their provenance and associations were doubtful.

but before discussing the weapons and implements upon which the chronology of the Bronze Age has been mainly based, it is desirable to summarize the information gained, and to see where at the moment we stand.

The characteristic sepulchral pottery of the Transition Period (*circa* 2000 B.C.–1700 B.C.) is the beaker, which is invariably associated with skeleton interment. It is not known when the beaker died out; but it seems improbable that a duration of more than 300–400 years can safely be assigned to the type. To the end of the Transition Period, then, rare and developed forms of the beaker (as Plate II, 3) and the handled cups characteristic of the Fenland Basin (Plates I and II) probably belong; and certain inhumation interments in barrows without beakers (Burials No. 11 and 48, pp. 31–32), representing perhaps a recurrence of earlier sepulchral custom, may be approximately contemporary with these.

To the same period the food-vessel, regarded as a development from the Neolithic bowl, may be assigned; an example of a characteristic Yorkshire type occurs in a Mildenhall barrow (p. 32).

Many inhumation burials, the majority in barrows and without associated objects, have been recorded in our district; the Icklingham interment with bronze dagger and hammerstones (p. 33) being exceptional.

It is impossible to determine the duration of inhumation in the Cambridge Region, owing to the rarity of dateable associated objects. The literature of the subject reveals wide differences of opinion among English archaeologists as to the date of the establishment of cremation and the cessation of the earlier practice. I incline to the view that cremation in Britain which originated in Neolithic times, reappeared in the Bronze Age independent of the change of rite on the Continent.

Cremation is normally associated with the overhanging-rim type of cinerary urn which is seen to combine elements of Neolithic pottery, of the food-vessel, and of the beaker; the evolution of the type must have taken time and a date late in the Early Bronze Period (*circa* 1700–1400 B.C.) seems to be indicated for the establishment of cremation and the consequent extinction of inhumation; the two rites having, we may suppose, been employed concurrently for some considerable time. Anomalous forms of cinerary vessel such as those from certain Upper Hare Park barrows may date from this transitional period.

The earliest forms of the cinerary urn with overhanging rim, such as that from Soham (Plate III), may then provisionally be assigned to about 1500 B.C. That in paste and surface technique these early examples found locally resemble late beakers, and that they usually occur, like the beakers, on low-lying sites, are important facts confirmatory of a date earlier than would be admitted by some authorities.

The cinerary urn with overhanging rim undoubtedly had a long life, and Abercromby's views as to the evolutionary sequence from tripartite to bipartite forms are accepted. Many of the latter occur in our district, in barrows near Fleam Dyke and on Therfield Heath; they are for the most part very debased, shapeless and badly fired. The date of these late urns is very difficult to determine. That they did not in some parts of East Anglia persist until the close of the Bronze Age is rendered probable by the occurrence in flat cemeteries of cylindrical and bucket-shaped urns (as at Troston Heath and Colchester) differing both in form and decoration. These are related to the Deverel-Rimbury types found in Wessex. No such cemeteries are known in our region, and this is an argument in favour of the survival of the overhanging-rim types to the end of the Age; but similar vessels of which the associations are unrecorded from Lakenheath and Chesterford exist, and the evidence we need for a solution of the problem may in the future come to light.

The new type of pottery here referred to has been elsewhere correlated with an invasion of (Celtic-speaking?) peoples which seems to have taken place about 1000 B.C. If this were substantiated, the duration of the overhanging-rim type of cinerary urn in South Britain might be fixed at about 600 years. The beginning of the I millennium, then, may in the future be found to mark the cessation in our district of the practice of barrow burial on hill-tops; for I can find no record of urns of the novel types mentioned having been found in East Anglian barrows.

Abercromby remarks that the evidence of grave-goods shows that the tribes north of the Thames were in the earlier part of the Bronze Age at a lower level of culture than those south of the Thames; and this is clearly brought out by the analysis of local burials. The control of the island trade-routes exercised by the latter tribes, into whose territories all imported metal objects must in this early period first have come, sufficiently accounts for the facts.

The Fenland Basin, of which our region forms part, is seen, in the matter of pottery types, to present in the first half of the II millennium a uniform culture, which has close relations with Yorkshire. Cambridgeshire thus appears to have been at this time on the

THE BRONZE AGE

southern fringe of a north-eastern culture area distinct from that south of the Thames.

Towards the close of the Early Bronze Period a change in cultural relationships seems to have taken place, as we shall see, but pottery forms give us little help in estimating the character and extent of this change, and the custom of depositing grave-goods had become obsolete. The similarity between certain Wiltshire urns and the Soham urn referred to on p. 39*n.*, may be of importance in this connection.

SETTLEMENTS

The most important traces of Bronze Age settlements which have been recorded in our district are those discovered at Swaffham by Allix and Hughes in 1902 and those found recently at Grimes Graves, Weeting [N].

Swaffham. At a point immediately N.W. of Middle Hill Plantation at Swaffham a workman sinking trial pits for gravel came upon a deposit of black earth in a shallow trench 2 to 3 feet deep. The trench, which was completely explored, was found to be circular, 68 feet in diameter. It contained (chiefly in the black soil which occurred in patches) charcoal and pot-boilers; numerous flint scrapers, the majority with convex, some with hollow faces; hammerstones; numerous small spherical flint nodules (120 were counted); several hones, and one hammerhead partially perforated, the boring of which had been begun from either side. Jaws and teeth of ox, sheep and pig were recognized, as were teeth of the red deer, but no antlers were met with; animal bones in general were numerous, some being burnt and charred, others smashed to extract the marrow.

A portion of a child's skeleton was found in one part of the trench; and in another the skeleton probably of a woman; the latter was contracted, and the skull dolichocephalic. There was no definite indication of any grave-goods with either of these burials.

The pottery was important. It was all handmade. Small portions of a large vessel with rim of square section and with decoration of raised ribs were found, and another showed a band of nail markings round the shoulder. Numerous undecorated fragments were clearly contemporary, many rim fragments in section identical to that described above being found. The bases were all obtuse angled, the bottoms flat.

This pottery may be with fair certainty assigned to the close of the Bronze Age and possibly to the (Celtic-speaking?) invaders of whom we have spoken. Pots with raised ribs have not hitherto been recorded in East Anglia, but are common in Dorset (Abercromby, 1912, II, Plate 86). The recurrence of nail impressions as a decorative *motif* is significant.

Additional to this well-defined group of wares were two curious rim fragments smooth on the inside and very rough on the outside as though the vessel had been made by lining a hole in the ground with clay and then firing it. The broad rim was slightly concave as though it had been pressed over the lip of the hole (cp. *B.M.G.* 1920, Fig. 167).

One or two tiny fragments of pottery with rounded rims were clearly referable to the Early Iron Age, and possibly represent an overlap of cultures.

There was no metal, but one or two pieces of bone were stained green as with bronze.

The poverty of the settlement or family dwelling-place which these remains imply was its most marked characteristic; and it is difficult to reconcile this with the wealth of fine bronze weapons, which I suppose to have been contemporary, found in the neighbourhood[1]. That flint implements of simple form were in everyday use by the peasantry at the close of the Bronze Age is a fact of importance[2].

Weeting [N]. An occupation level of the Bronze Age was found just below the upper humus near the Tumulus Pit at Grimes Graves, in 1920. The remains consisted chiefly of a hearth on which a pair of bronze tweezers was found, and coarse pottery (Armstrong, 1921, p. 82).

A second living-floor on the eastern margin of floor 16 was found by A. E. Peake in 1916. Charcoal, pot-boilers, bones of the red and roe deer and of "domesticated animals" were noted; the occurrence of the dagger mentioned on p. 54 fixes the date as in the Early Bronze Period. Fragments of a Bronze Age pot were at the same time found near the graves, in Santon Field (A. E. Peake, 1917, pp. 429 ff.).

Eriswell [S]. To the Transition Period belongs, on the evidence of a fragment of beaker pottery with rouletted decoration, a living-floor at Foxhole Heath, Eriswell (W. G. Clarke, 1915).

Repell or Paille Ditches, Saffron Walden. Excavations in the Anglo-Saxon cemetery area within this earthwork in 1876 revealed, among objects of various dates, a portion apparently of a food-vessel of Abercromby's Type 1 ornamented with indented herring-bone patterns, and fragments of coarse pottery, undecorated, also probably

---

[1] The poverty of purely agricultural settlements of peasants in the district in the Roman period is, however, equally marked (see p. 231).

[2] An account of the discovery of the site was read to the C.A.S. by Mr C. P. Allix in 1902, but was never printed. All the finds have recently been presented to the Camb. Mus. by his son.

THE BRONZE AGE

of Bronze Age date; one piece had the impression of woven cloth (H. E. Smith, 1883, p. 319, and Plate VII, 1 and 8). The entrenchment is doubtless later than the Bronze Age. There is no evidence that the pottery was sepulchral; though the highly decorated piece was probably so.

FINDS AND HOARDS OF THE BRONZE AGE

The number of bronze implements, weapons and ornaments found in the district is very great, and consideration of them will be assisted by a preliminary analysis.

Chronological Analysis

In the table (p. 50) these objects are grouped in typological sequence, period by period. It will be seen that the total number of "Isolated Finds" is 537. This is less by a score or more than those known by me to have been found in the district, all finds of uncertain provenance (*e.g.* "Cambridge Fens") having been omitted in compiling the topographical index. The number of "Hoards" analysed is 35[1], containing, as the table shows, 512 objects; but this figure also requires correction. It occasionally happens that, of the total number of implements known to have been included in a given hoard, only a portion survive or have been described (*e.g.* the Arkesden hoard (p. 324) contained 50 or more, but the character of only 30 is known). The number of these unclassified objects is estimated at 48; the corrected total for the hoards is therefore 560. But even this large number is an underestimate. At least seven hoards from the district are inadequately described and partially preserved; the number of implements which they contained is therefore indeterminate. Furthermore, the wealth in bronze of our region is not fully realized if mention of founders' metal is omitted. Lumps of copper or bronze were found in twelve of the fifteen hoards attributed to founders, and no less than six depôts of such metal unassociated with implements are known. The weight of metal is not often specified; but in two cases[2] there was half a hundredweight or more.

The totals at the foot of the table show that the number of objects found increases rapidly and steadily as the Age advances. But the isolated finds of the Middle Period are as numerous as those of the Late Period, and the marked increase in numbers in the closing phase

---

[1] A referenced list of these is given in the Appendix, pp. 323–4.
[2] Rushden (Cumberlow Green), Bally (1877); Ashdon (Bartlow Hills), J. Clark (1873, p. 280).

CHRONOLOGICAL ANALYSIS OF FINDS AND HOARDS OF METAL OBJECTS OF THE BRONZE AGE, FROM THE CAMBRIDGE REGION

	Period	Objects	Nature of deposit			Totals
			Isolated finds	Associated objects and hoards other than founders'	Founders' hoards	
FIRST PHASE	Transition period about 2000 B.C.–1700 B.C.	Axes flat Daggers	4 0 [4]			4
FIRST PHASE	Early Bronze Period about 1700 B.C.–1400 B.C.	Axes flat Axes flanged Daggers Halberds Gold rings Other objects	19 20 8 [49] 1 1	25 [27] 2		76
FIRST PHASE	Middle Bronze Period about 1400 B.C.–1000 B.C.	Palstaves Daggers Rapiers Spears, looped Gold ornaments Other objects	133 15 28 [223] 35 12	5 1 [16] 1 9		239
SECOND PHASE	Late Bronze Period about 1000 B.C.–500-400 B.C.	Palstaves Axes, winged Axes, socketed Swords Spears, looped Spears, not looped Gouges, hammers, etc., socketed Knives, chisels, etc., tanged Razors Shields Scabbards and ferules Gold objects Moulds Miscellaneous	5 126 21 38 11 [221] 5 1 3 1 1 9	5 2 22 15 1[1] 126[2] 3 [216] 3 3 17 19	4 4 143 28 29 13 [253][3] 7 3 4 1 1 16	690
	Not placed	Miscellaneous	40 [40]			40

[1] Associated with a shield.
[2] Some spears, the type of which is unknown, are included in this total.
[3] The total number of objects known to have existed in founders' hoards is 301; many of these are destroyed, lost or unidentified. See List in Appendix, p. 324.

of the Age is due to its wealth in hoards which, as we have seen, is its distinctive feature.

I have arranged the hoards, both in the Table and in the Appendix, in two groups; in one those of the types classified by Evans as "Personal," and as "Merchants'"; in the other those probably or certainly "Founders'." In the former group, however, several, such as those of flanged axes from Grunty Fen (p. 63) and Mildenhall (p. 323), and the shields found together in Coveney Fen (p. 60), may be votive offerings; and in both groups some of the larger hoards may be those of chiefs, following the contemporary Homeric and later Teutonic custom. It may well be that the sudden appearance of numerous large hoards in the second phase of the Age is due to the immigrant leaf-sword people having a social organization hitherto imperfectly represented in Britain. We may suppose that each chieftain had his chest of arms, and that a weapon-smith was an essential member of his household. This surmise seems the more probable, since there was evidently no lack of bronze in the preceding period; the situation then was this, that accumulations of weapons were not customary, and but little actual manufacture was carried on in the district.

In addition to their finely wrought bronze weapons, the Cambridgeshire folk in the second half of the II millennium (the close of the Early and the whole of the Middle Bronze Periods) were wealthy in gold. Two gold rings were found with a hoard of flanged axes at Postlingford (p. 54); a gold torc (4 oz. 1 dwt.), a gold bracelet and ring-money with a rapier at Granta (*sic*) Fen, Stretham (p. 57) and the Grunty Fen armilla (p. 57) with three palstaves; nothing found locally which can be assigned to the last phase of the Age can compare with this armilla in beauty, or with any of these finds in value. All doubtless were made of Irish gold from the Wicklow Mountains; and their occurrence suggests that a trade connection existed between the southern fenlands and the west, which, initiated in the middle of the II millennium B.C., was broken some 500 years later by the invasion of the leaf-sword folk.

Similar finds have been made in Norfolk (Ashill and Foulsham) and East Suffolk (Boyton), and it may be that our region was then on one of the gold routes from Ireland to the Continent.

The objects associated with a remarkable inhumation burial of the Early Bronze Period, at Little Cressingham [N][1], included amber beads and articles of thin gold plate. The finds as a whole pointed to trade with Denmark on the one hand and Wiltshire on the other;

---

[1] Abercromby, 1912, II, p. 62, where further references will be found.

and the route through our district may have been the Icknield Way. On the other hand, the distribution of gold torcs of Grunty Fen (or "Yeovil") type in Wales and Britain as worked out by Crawford (1912 *a*) points to a trade-route from Ireland having crossed this country from the Mersey to the Wash. In any case, it is clear that the Little Cressingham burial is the earliest evidence we have of the changed conditions which brought wealth to East Anglia and, it may be, put an end to close cultural relations with Yorkshire.

The rarity of isolated finds of metal tools assignable to the Transition Period confirms the evidence yielded by interments. The numerous beakers found in the district (one associated with a copper ring) show that the Period was well represented; but metal was evidently very scarce.

The axe is the commonest weapon (or implement) in every period; the spear in both Middle and Late Bronze Periods comes next, the rapier, or the sword, taking third place. From the close of the Early Period onwards the number and quality of the weapons and implements discovered indicate that the civilization of the southern fens was as advanced as anywhere in Britain. In the closing phase of the Age the *variety* of tools and articles of use and ornament increases greatly.

Detailed analysis of the local hoards supplies evidence of the soundness of the typological sequence which Montelius elaborated, and of the completeness of the break in culture which divides the Middle from the Late Bronze Period. Of the 156 spear- or lance-heads found associated with Late Bronze objects only one is known to be of the looped type characteristic of the Middle Period (p. 60); one doubtful fragment of a rapier is recorded[1] in hoards which include at least 43 leaf-shaped swords, and there are, as we have seen[2], only five palstaves other than currency forms in hoards which contain 164 socketed axes.

Since many of these hoards contain large numbers of worn-out and broken weapons, the rarity of types attributed to the earlier culture suggests that the folk with the rapier-palstave-looped spear armature may have fled to the less desirable parts of the country at the approach of the invaders, as did the Romanized Britons 1400 years later.

In the pages which follow finds and hoards typical of each successive period are described. Examples of weapons and implements have, as far as possible, been chosen from the Cambridge Museum collection, or from those figured by Evans in his *Ancient Bronze Implements*, to limit the necessity for illustrations.

[1] In the Rushden hoard, p. 324.   [2] Footnote, p. 18.

PLATE V

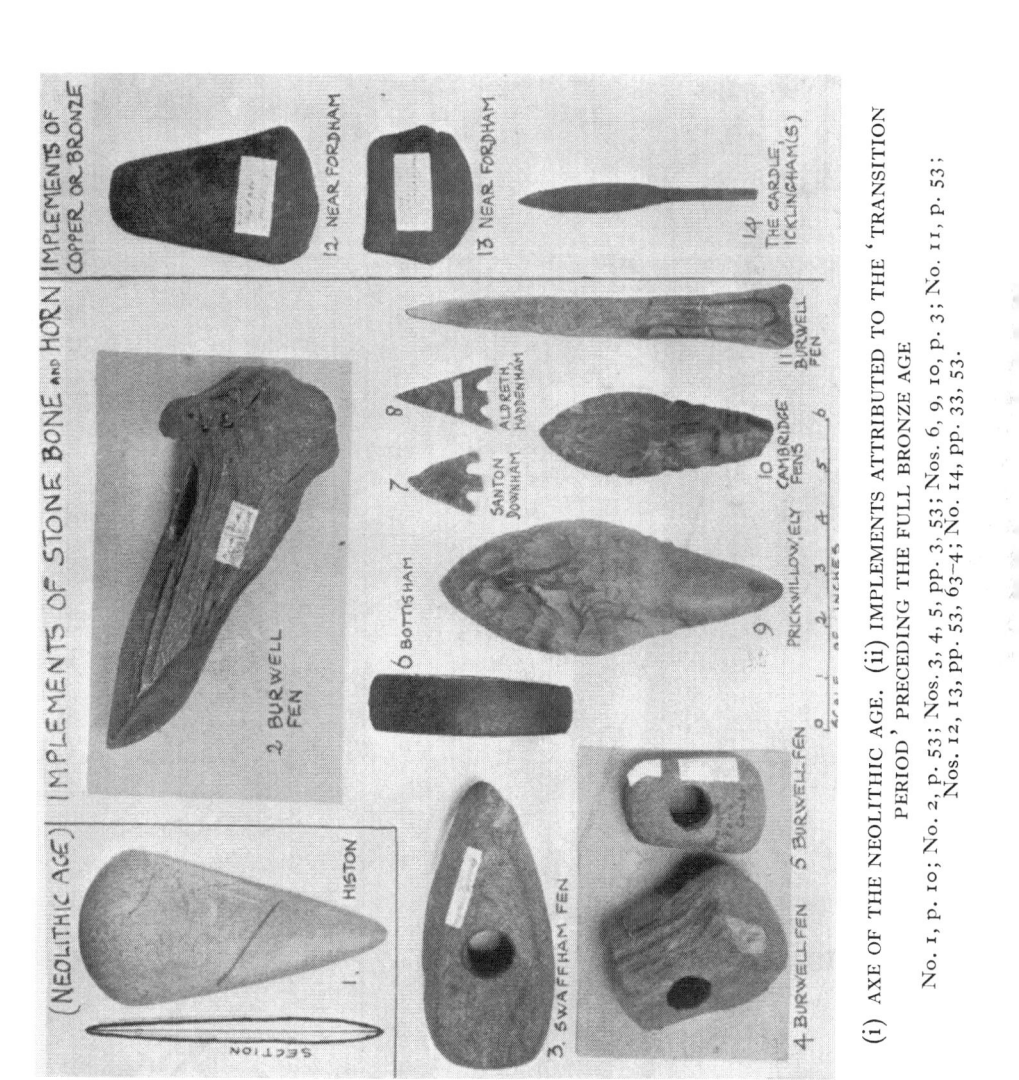

(i) AXE OF THE NEOLITHIC AGE. (ii) IMPLEMENTS ATTRIBUTED TO THE 'TRANSITION PERIOD' PRECEDING THE FULL BRONZE AGE

No. 1, p. 10; No. 2, p. 53; Nos. 3, 4, 5, pp. 3, 53; Nos. 6, 9, 10, p. 3; No. 11, p. 53; Nos. 12, 13, pp. 53, 63–4; No. 14, pp. 33, 53.

THE FIRST PHASE: ENDING CIRCA 1000 B.C.

I. *The Transition Period.* Circa 2000–1700 B.C.

Characteristic weapons. The stone axehammer, the flint dagger and the flat axe and dagger (or knife) of copper or poor bronze.

Weapons and implements of Stone, Bone and Horn. Perforated axes of stone and daggers of chipped flint have already been discussed (p. 3). Many of the implements of horn and bone found in the fens are thought to date in this Period, but it must be remembered that in the absence of associated finds, the attribution must be provisional. On Plate V are figured an axehead and macehead of deerhorn, the macehead of stone already referred to (p. 3), and a bone dagger from Burwell. Stone bracers are typical of the period; one was found at Sandy [B], another (in the British Museum), with a beaker, at Brandon [S].

Metal Axes. Two rudely wrought axes of copper or poor bronze without flanges or expanding blade from Fordham (in the Cambridge Museum) and one from Bottisham Lode (in Sir Wm. Ridgeway's collection) are manifestly of very early date, and can safely be assigned to the Transition Period. Two of these are figured on Plate V.

Daggers. The tanged knife or dagger from Icklingham [S] (on Plate V) has already been referred to; no other dagger found in the district of which the provenance is known can safely be assigned to the Transition Period.

Awls. It is probable that several of the small awls or pins of bronze found locally date from this Period.

II. *The Early Bronze Period.* Circa 1700–1400 B.C.

Characteristic weapons. The axe, flat and flanged, the halberd and the dagger. Bronze is scarce in the Cambridge Region until the close of the Period, when numerous flanged axes occur, and gold is introduced.

Flat Axes. The axes attributable to the first part of the Period are either flat or show the first traces of the flange—a thickening of the sides produced by hammering. The blades are expanded. On such axes there first appears the decoration characteristic of the flanged axe, cabled fluting on the sides and punched patterns on the faces. Plate VI, figs. 1, 2 and 3, from Bottisham Lode, Fordham, and Quy, may be referred to. The decoration on the faces of the latter weapon consists of parallel fluting and punched herring-bone.

Flanged Axes. These date from the latter part of the Period. A large number have been found locally, many of beautiful workmanship, with well-marked flanges (usually cast) and broad blades. The flange in some examples—Bottisham Lode (Cambridge Museum) and Burwell (Evans, Fig. 53)—is high, and such implements might be called winged axes.

The expansion of the cutting edge is a marked feature of the axe at this stage of its development, as may be seen in the examples from Stuntney, Ely and Burwell Fen on Plate VI. The two former are elaborately decorated, but the incised detail on No. 4 is so finely wrought as to be invisible in the photograph. No. 6 represents a stage in the evolution of the palstave, a well-marked curved stop-ridge being seen on the face of the axe. The finest series of axes found locally is that in the Postlingford (Clare) hoard; here, in 1844, nineteen flanged axes were found together with a gold armlet with a single small gold ring attached to it. Many were elaborately decorated, and had crescentic blades. This large hoard is especially worthy of note owing to the rarity of such in Britain at this early period (see p. 63).

Two smaller hoards of flanged axes from our district are listed in the Appendix (p. 323). Déchelette notes (1910, p. 171) that most of the hoards of similar axes in France come from the mouth of the Gironde. This observation is of importance to our enquiry; it is fairly certain that axes imported into the Cambridge Region came *via* the Icknield Way from S.W. Britain.

Daggers. Early blades, usually with notched hilt plate, sometimes with rivets *in situ*, have been found in the fens and in the Cam and Lark Valleys. One, in the Cambridge Museum, of unknown but probably local provenance, resembles a piece of sheet metal, having no central rib. Among other examples those from Soham Fen (Evans, pp. 244–5) and Lakenheath (Plate VI, 8) may be mentioned. One "found not far from Cambridge" is figured by Evans (fig. 304). A broad tanged blade from Saffron Walden (Plate VI, 7) is probably of this Period.

Two tanged daggers, from Swaffham and Burwell, also of this Period, are preserved; the former, beautifully wrought and of fine design, is figured on Plate VI, 11. For the latter, see Evans, p. 258. A third example has recently been found on a living-floor at Grimes Graves (A. E. Peake, 1917, fig. 87).

Halberd. One only has been found, in Manea Fen. This magnificent weapon, figured on Plate VI, is in splendid preservation. It has three large rivets still in position at the base and a small rib runs down

PLATE VI

A B

BRONZE AGE
Food vessels, p. 38; Implements, pp. 53–5.

the thickened centre of the blade. Its size (11¼ by 4 inches) and the dimensions of the rivets make it unlikely that it was a dagger.

Bead necklaces, partly composed of pierced plates, are widely diffused in Britain, and have been found with skeleton interments; two examples from our district are made of bone and jet respectively.

The bone necklace comes from Feltwell Fen; three plates decorated with rows of punctured dots and lozenge-shaped figures survive and are in the British Museum, where are also jet beads and plates of the second necklace, from Soham Fen.

The latter were associated with a skeleton—possibly a case of accidental death rather than of inhumation—and a socketed chisel-like axe of late type. It seems impossible that axe and beads should be contemporary; but A. J. Evans (1908, p. 127) is inclined to favour a late date for such necklaces, and judgment must be suspended. One plate of a third necklace of jet (from Burwell Fen), which was complete when found, is in the Cambridge Museum (*C.A.S. Rep.* XIV, 1854, p. 13).

Bodkin. A bodkin, pierced near the point, from Lakenheath, figured on Plate VI, is probably of this Period. The head is roughly hammered out to form three imperfect loops.

III. *The Middle Bronze Period.* Circa 1400–1000 B.C.

Characteristic weapons. The palstave (a development of the flanged axe), the looped spearhead and the rapier. The Cambridge Region is now in the full stream of Western European culture. Fine gold ornaments occur.

Palstaves. In the Middle Bronze Period the complete cycle of evolution from the flanged axe to the palstave is traceable and each stage can be seen in examples from the district in the Cambridge Museum collection. Special attention may be drawn to early examples with low stop-ridges from Reach (with its wings in three planes like many flanged axes), Quy, Hauxton, Wicken Fen, Croydon and Little Thetford. Two of these are figured on Plate VII, 1 and 2. In the development of the implement that portion of the flange which lies below the stop-ridge, becoming functionless, was curved inward to form the shield-shaped panel which, whether alone or combined with a vertical rib, is a characteristic feature of the palstaves of the Cambridge Region. Dozens of examples can be seen in the museum; Nos. 3, 4 and 5 on Plate VII, and Evans, figs. 59, 60, 61 and 65, may be examined.

Palstaves with central rib on the blade (Plate VII, 7), and those with "trident decoration" (Plate VII, 6) are also common types in our district; such were associated with the Grunty Fen armilla (p. 51). Forms presumably later show a very prominent stop-ridge (Plate VII, 8 and 9) and many lack the fine lines of the weapons just considered. A debased example from Teversham is figured on Plate IX, 6.

The typological sequence based on the development of the stop-ridge is shown on Plate VII, 1–9, and it may be noted that the crescentic blade—a legacy from the flanged axe—is characteristic of the early palstaves, the loop of the later forms.

Some narrow palstaves, such as those from Littleport (Burnt Fen) and Quy Fen in the British Museum, are probably chisels; sometimes the blades of such are set transversely. The chisel, unlike the gouge which is always of a late socketed type, is found in a variety of forms, and probably ranges over the greater part of the Bronze Age. Plate VII, 10, shows an example probably of the Middle Period, from Cambridge.

Daggers. Riveted dagger blades of developed type dating in the Middle Period are not infrequently met with. Examples from Wimblington (Wisbech Museum) and Soham Fen (Plate VII, 16) may be cited. The lengthening of the dagger produced the rapier, the characteristic weapon of the latter part of the II millennium; a few rapier-like dagger blades, such as that from Quaveney (Plate VII, 15), must therefore be assigned to the present Period.

Rapiers. A remarkable series of rapiers—of which perhaps the finest example is that from Feltwell [N], 25·8 inches long—have been found in the district, the majority in the fens. Evans figures specimens from Chatteris, Thetford [N] and Coveney (figs. 315, 316, 313): the latter is of the developed type with spade hilt. The Feltwell rapier, and a finely wrought reeded blade found in Isleham Fen, are figured on Plate VII. On Plate VIII is a plainer weapon from Downham Fen [N] with the rest of its owner's equipment. The bent tip of a rapier from Undley [S] in the Cambridge Museum illustrates the use of the weapon as a thrusting sword, and its weakness.

Spear- and Lance-heads. Looped spear- and lance-heads are numerous, and show wide variations in form and size. The loops, at first high up the socket, gradually approach the base of the blade, and finally become functionless vestiges—"protected loops." Plate VII, figs. 11, 12, 13, and Plate VIII, 1 A, show the chief types met with. See also Evans (figs. 394–396, 406 and 409).

Sickles. The attribution of socketed sickles to the Middle Bronze Period is justified by the occurrence of one with the rapier and palstave in Downham Fen (Plate VIII); the type, moreover, is rare on

PLATE VII

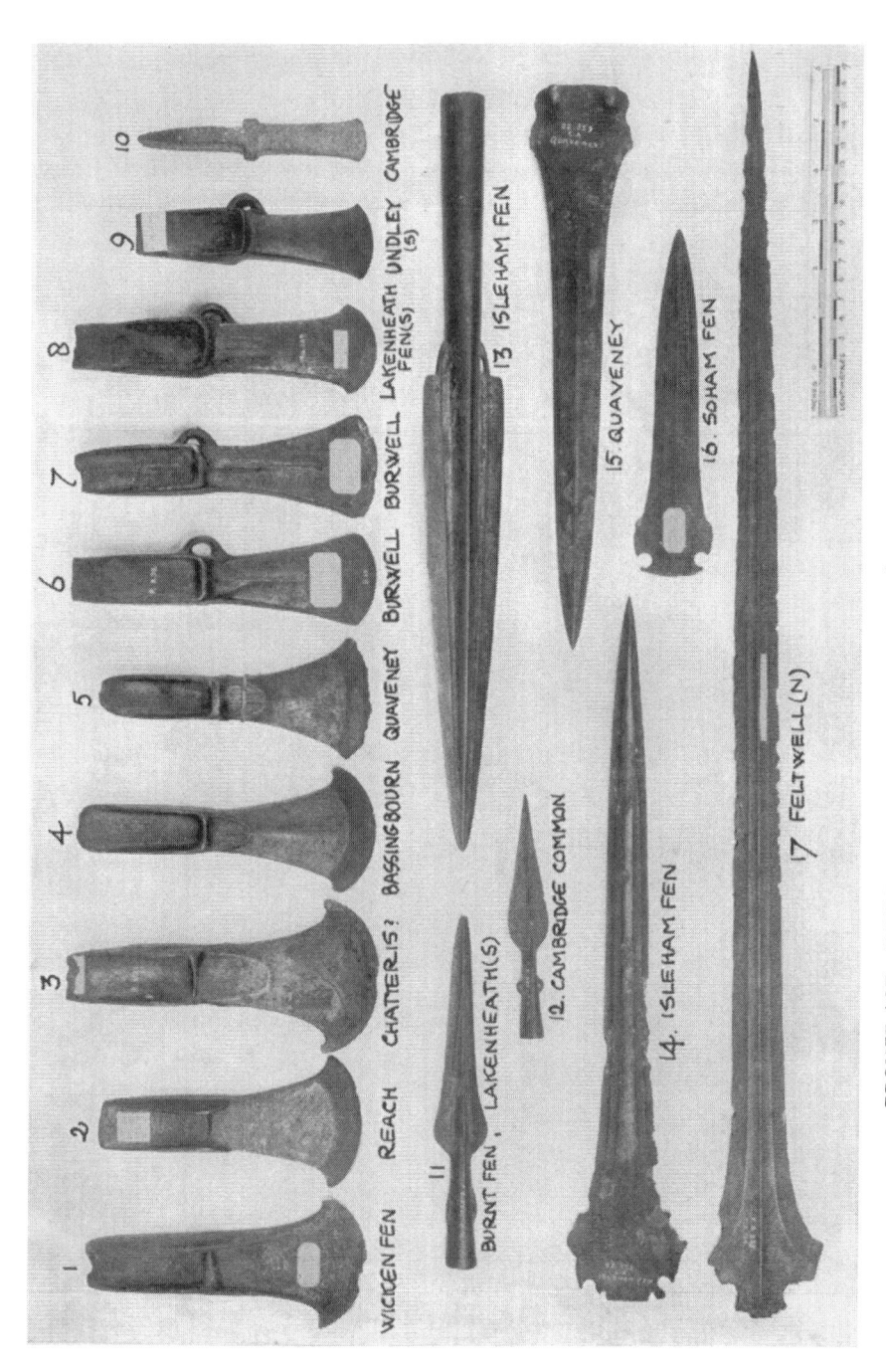

BRONZE AGE. IMPLEMENTS ATTRIBUTED TO THE 'MIDDLE BRONZE PERIOD'
See pp. 55–6.

THE BRONZE AGE

the Continent and is not an element of the leaf sword-socketed axe complex characteristic of the Late Bronze Period. A fine example, found in Stretham Fen in 1862, is in the Cambridge Museum.

Gold objects. The Grunty Fen armilla and the gold bracelet with six rings attached, found in 1850 with a broken rapier at Stretham (probably in Grunty Fen), have already been referred to (p. 51), and their importance estimated. The association of bronze objects with each is of great value for dating purposes.

Veasey (1853) says that a "wreathed torquis of pure gold" was found with the bracelet and rapier; this from the description was an ornament of Grunty Fen type, but I cannot find any subsequent record of it. The bracelet is figured in *B.M.G.* (1920, p. 54). The Grunty Fen armilla is figured by von Hügel (1908) and by Montelius (1908, p. 131).

Pins. A remarkable disc-headed pin, with expanded stem, from Lakenheath, in the Cambridge Museum, may be assigned to this Period[1].

The Second Phase. Ending 500–400 B.C.

The Late Bronze Period. Circa 1000—500–400 B.C.

Characteristic weapons. The socketed axe, the spearhead without loops and the leaf-shaped sword.

These weapons, and the abrupt appearance of numerous founders' hoards, mark a break in culture in our district, and are in this book correlated with an overseas invasion. The occurrence in hoards of exotic objects (winged chapes, razors, bronze buttons, tweezers, etc.) associated on the Continent with the early Hallstatt Iron culture is of importance[2].

Socketed Axes. Early types, with structural (wing) decoration, are not very common. Examples from Cambridge (Plate IX, 7), Foxton and Fordham, in the Cambridge Museum, may be referred to. Four were in the Meldreth hoard and one or more at Rushden [H] and Chrishall [E] (Appendix, p. 324). These were doubtless brought in by the invaders. Axes, the decoration on which is not structural (wings) but formed of ribs and dots (beads and pellets), are well represented. Examples from Horningsea (Plate IX, 10), Bassingbourn (very fine) and Fordham, in the Cambridge Museum, and those figured by Evans from Fen Ditton, Bottisham and Lakenheath (figs. 134, 135, 139), may be mentioned.

Axes decorated with three vertical ridges, either parallel (Plate IX, 9) or rayed, are commonly met with, and we have a few examples,

[1] Cf. a similar pin from near Lewes, Sussex (Dixon, 1849, p. 265).
[2] For an analysis of these exotic objects and their significance see Crawford (1922).

moreover, of the beautiful axes with triple ribs meeting at each angle. A fine example from Reach is in the possession of Dr Lucas of Burwell, and Sir Wm. Ridgeway has two such from Wicken in his collection (figured by him in *Man* (1919)).

Other designs are known; it will suffice to mention a St Andrew's Cross (a final phase of the wing pattern) on an axe from Chesterton (Plate IX, 8), and V-shaped incisions on one from Barrington (Cambridge Museum).

Plain axes present great variety of form, of which those with trumpet mouths, with bevelled sides, with indented sides, or of square section may be specially mentioned. The latter are important, since they are of a common Gaulish type. An example from Burwell is in Mr A. L. Armstrong's collection, and a small specimen from Royston Heath is figured on Plate IX, 15. Axes with indented sides are rare; the example figured (Plate X, 2) is in the Wilburton hoard.

Similar indented axes, from Frettenham [N] and Beverley [Yorks.], are in the Brit. Mus. The type is in this country confined to East Anglia and Yorkshire, so far as I can ascertain, and is probably derived from France.

Other plain forms are figured on Plates IX, 11 and 12, and X, 3; examples from Cambridge, Burwell and Cavenham [S], in the Cambridge Museum, may also be referred to.

A mould for casting socketed axes was found in New Street, Cambridge (Plate IX, 17); another was in the Arkesden hoard (Appendix, p. 324). These bronze moulds are characteristic of the Late Bronze Age.

Winged Axes. Six of these exotic weapons are known to have been found locally, in hoards at Rushden, Sawston and Arkesden (List Nos. 33, 19 and 21, Appendix, p. 323). A broken specimen from the Rushden hoard is in the Cambridge Museum. That they should occur in hoards and not as isolated finds suggests that they were never manufactured in our district; they were, it may be, elements of the stock of bronze brought into this country by the invaders, and the distribution in Britain may indicate the route followed by the latter.

Palstaves. The occasional occurrence of late forms in hoards of the Period has already been noted (see Plate X, 1), but of the continued use, as a weapon, of this type of axe in the Cambridge Region subsequent to the close of the Middle Bronze Period there is very little evidence. The triangular-bladed "currency" type of palstave (referred to as a survival on p. 18, footnote) and its prototype are figured on Plate IX, 5 and 6.

PLATE VIII

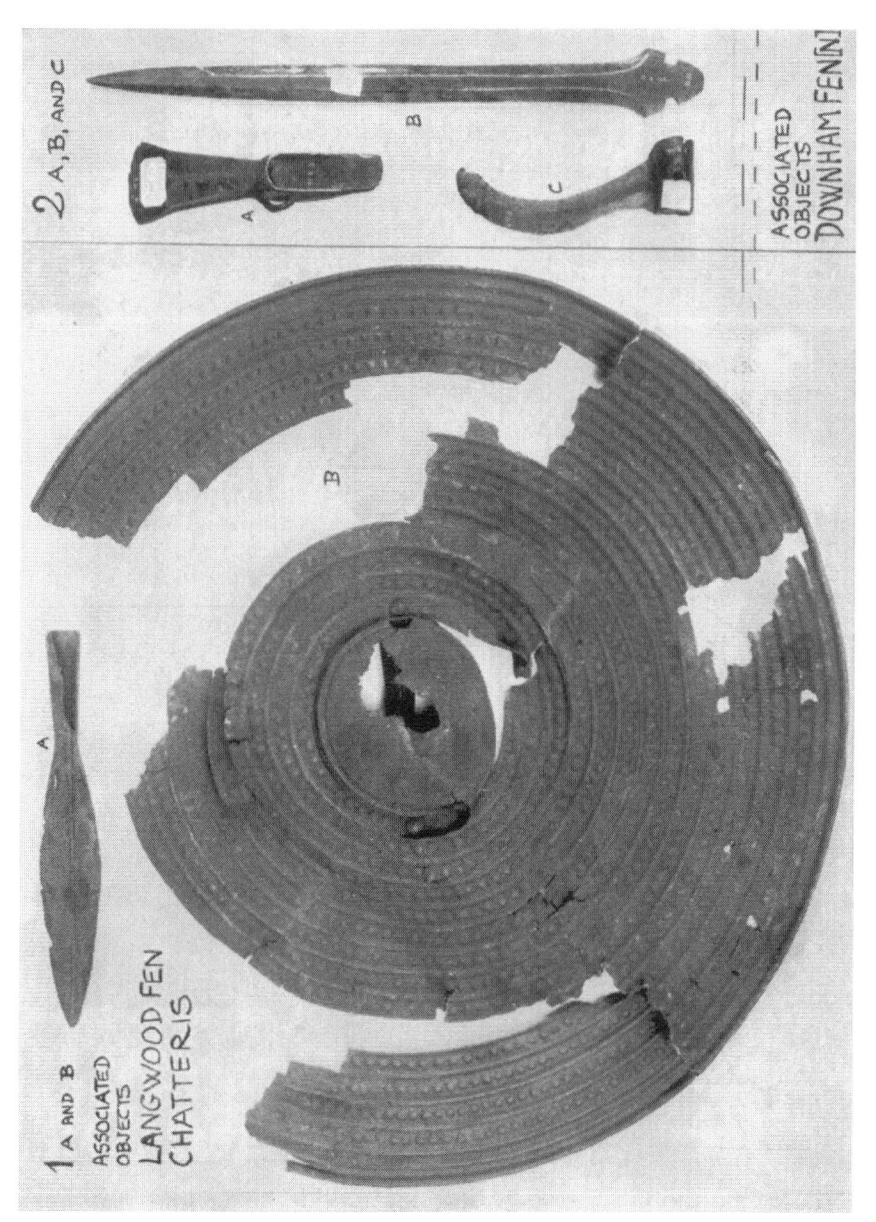

BRONZE AGE. TWO GROUPS OF ASSOCIATED OBJECTS
No. 1, pp. 56, 60, 65; No. 2, pp. 18, 56 (two references).

Swords. The transition from the rapier to the leaf-shaped sword in Eastern Britain is sudden. Such intermediate forms as occur are probably imported, and are in France contemporary with the rapier (Déchelette, 1910, p. 106) and the palstave. The most important local example, from the Ouse near Ely, is figured in *B.M.G.* (1920, p. 31).

The earliest leaf-shaped swords found locally have sloping shoulders, and lack the deep notches at the junction of blade and butt which are a feature of the later forms. A fine example of the early phase from Barrow (Evans, fig. 343) may be noted. A blade from Coveney (Plate IX, 2) is notched, but retains the sloping shoulders. The later notched swords usually show a broad slot in the hilt plate, and the shoulders are more accentuated. All the swords in the Wilburton hoard (Plate X, 15) are of this type; an isolated find from Aldreth (Plate IX, 1) may be mentioned as an additional example.

I have not found local examples of the latest bronze swords associated with the transition from Bronze to Iron at Hallstatt which have small punched rivet-holes in the hilt plates, shoulders concave in outline, and which lack the "fish-tail" pommel normal to the earlier swords.

Two unusual swords are figured on Plate IX. The leaf-shaped specimen with socketed hilt (No. 4) comes from the neighbourhood of Royston [H], the other, with flanged hilt and a blade almost, but not quite, parallel-sided, from Coveney. The latter is figured by Evans (fig. 348) as from Ely.

H. Peake (1922*b*, p. 87, and plate VI) classifies leaf-shaped swords according to the outline of the shoulder or butt, the sequence being from convex to concave. Figs. 1 and 2 on my Plate IX, and fig. 15 on Plate X, are varieties of his Type E.

One of the most interesting local hoards is that found at Chippenham; we possess exact details of the discovery which point to the existence of a small factory for leaf-shaped swords.

Work in a gravel pit in Chippenham parish, close to the line of the Street Way and Badlingham Ford, disclosed in 1884–5 a primitive foundry. In a shallow trench a deposit of blackened earth and charcoal contained pebbles bearing marks of fire and "several crude lumps of metal either copper or bronze" weighing in all nearly 5 lbs. Fragments of reddish-yellow friable pottery were found near by. Four yards away three portions of (one or more) leaf-shaped swords were found; ten yards away a perfect bronze sword was found and near it a quantity of burnt matter "like soot" which on being sifted contained no bones or metal. The sword was $2\frac{1}{2}$ feet below the surface and lay partly within a "stratum of picked flint stones"; it is of type E (Peake), 27¼ inches in total length.

This sword is figured by H. Prigg (1888 b). The association of perfect swords with selected stones and carbonized earth is paralleled by the discovery of two of these weapons at Barrow. These were 2–3 feet below the surface "surrounded by stones and much blackened earth" (*loc. cit.* p. 187). The Chrishall hoard was found in a hole full of burnt earth, as is recorded in a Neville MS. in Audley End Museum. In the same MS. it is stated that black earth was associated with the Furneaux Pelham hoard. The Arkesden hoard was found in a hole surrounded with stones, and the implements were associated with ashes. Black earth was noticed near the hole in which the Rushden hoard was deposited. The Chippenham and Barrow finds suggest that the craftsman hid his products near his forge, for safety. The stones might prevent earth from soiling the hilts; while the soot and calcined earth is to be accounted for by the probability that in the neighbourhood of his "foundry" soil entirely free from such might be difficult to find.

Bronze Chapes or scabbard ends. Several have been found in our district and four varieties are recorded. The most interesting is the winged chape from Mildenhall figured by Evans (fig. 375), of an early Hallstatt type. Sheath-like examples in the Wilburton hoard (Plate X, 14) are of a type rare on the Continent; while a bulbous form in the Reach Fen hoard (Evans, fig. 371) is contemporary with the leaf-shaped sword (H. Peake, type E) in France.

Shields. Three circular shields of bronze are among the chief treasures of the Cambridge Museum. A pair was found in Coveney Fen in 1846 and may have been deposited as a votive offering; one of these shows serpentine decoration of unusual character (Evans, fig. 430), the other concentric rings. Both are finely illustrated and described by Goodwin (1848). The third shield (injured by the ploughshare when discovered) was found with a spearhead with "protected loops" in Langwood Fen, Chatteris, an association which suggests the Middle Bronze Period. Its decoration, as the Plate (VIII) shows, is of the type most frequently met with in Britain—concentric rings alternating with circles of embossed knobs.

The association with a spear is of importance. No other shield has been found in this country with a dateable object, and it suggests that the type was contemporary with the rapier rather than the sword. Such a date, however, involves one in great difficulties; and the problem is too wide to be dealt with here. The spearhead is a late variety of its type, and it may possibly be a survival. See Ridgeway (1901, pp. 456 ff.), and a review of the subject by R. A. Smith (1919 b).

Spear- and Lance-heads. Such, without loops, of various

PLATE IX

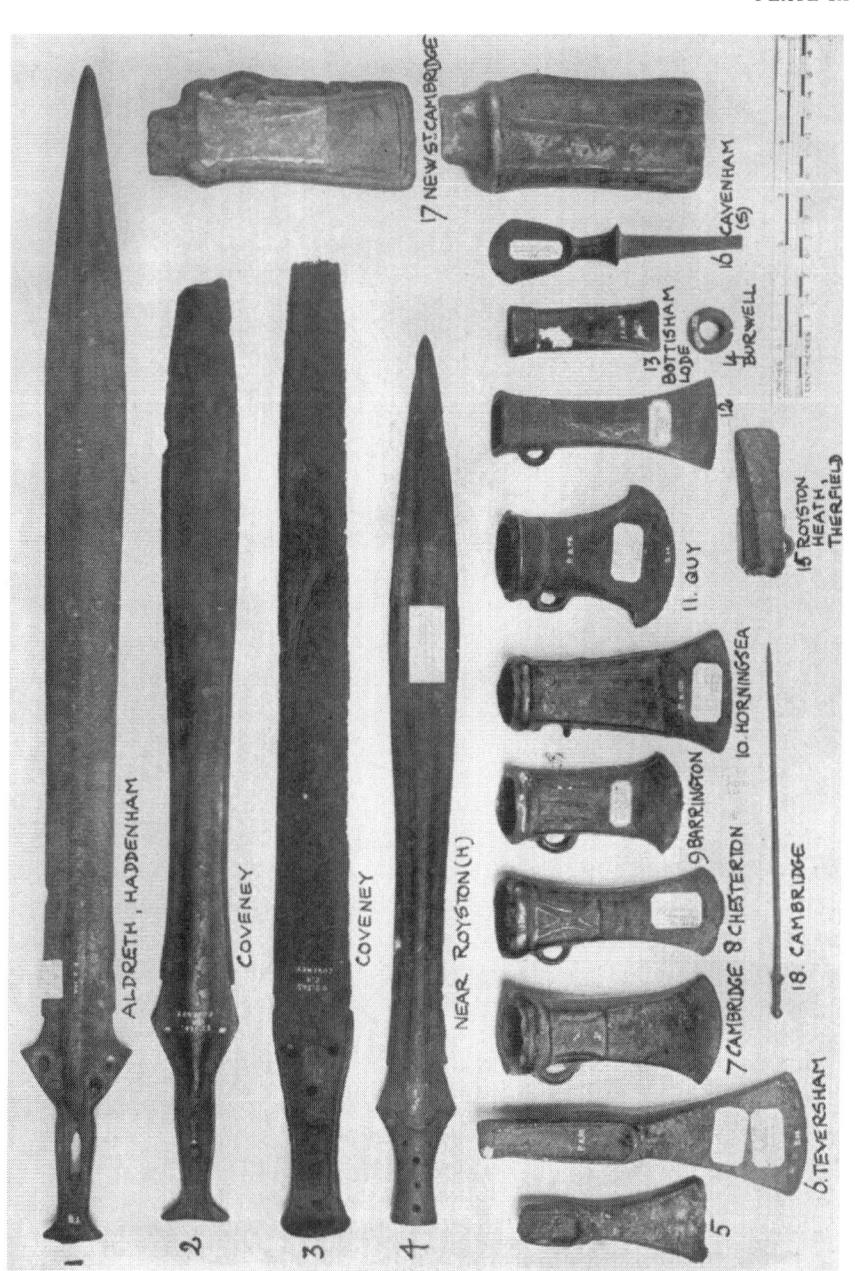

BRONZE AGE. IMPLEMENTS ATTRIBUTED TO THE 'LATE BRONZE PERIOD'
See pp. 57–9; also, No. 6, p. 56; Nos. 13, 14, 16, 18, p. 62.

types, are frequently found in the district. Some are very small, and were evidently used as javelin heads. The lightness and thinness of the metal indicates great skill in casting; the central hollow extends down the blade and is not confined to the socket, as in many of the spears and lances of the preceding period. Plate X shows a representative series from the Wilburton hoard; the handsome spearhead with lunate openings in the blade is specially noteworthy; another example, from Burwell Fen, is figured by Evans (fig. 420).

Spear ferules—some cylindrical, others with bossy terminals—are included in the Wilburton hoard (Plate X, 12, 13); many of these still contain fragments of the wooden shafts.

Other Bronze objects. Socketed hammers, knives, chisels and gouges are characteristic of the Period. Among the less common objects which are of importance in establishing a connection with France early in the I millennium B.C. are a tanged notched razor (Feltwell Fen hoard), bronze buttons (Reach Fen hoard), bugle-shaped objects (Reach Fen and Melbourn hoards and Malton, Orwell), tweezers (Feltwell Fen hoard and Grimes Graves, Weeting).

Crawford (1922) holds that these and other exotic objects were introduced by invaders who arrived about 800–700 B.C. This is probable; but the *main* invasion as far as Eastern England is concerned must be dated earlier. The Hallstatt bronze sword, as figured by Déchelette (1913, p. 722), to which Crawford refers (p. 27) does not occur in our local hoards, wherein the earlier (Bronze Age) type is common.

Hoards. The wealth in hoarded bronze of our district in the last phase of the Age has already been commented on. It is impossible here to do more than refer to one or two of the most interesting deposits. A full list will be found in the Appendix, p. 324.

The Reach Fen hoard contained a variety of objects (mostly broken): socketed axes, gouges, chisels, knives, swords and spears; a punch and hammer; buttons, rings, etc., and rough metal. This hoard admirably exemplifies the range of minor metal objects and tools in use at the close of the Bronze Age. Evans figures a number: figs. 371 (chape), 493–4 (looped tubes), 499 (buttons), 241, 250, 251, (knives), 256 (razor). The hoard was well described by H. Prigg (1880). A similar but smaller group of objects was found at Melbourn.

The Wilburton hoard, which has already been referred to, consisted of 163 objects, found in the fen in 1882 in a space 6 feet by 3 feet. The swords were all of one pattern, the 115 spears, though of varied types, were all without loops. Plate X indicates the more important objects here shown to be contemporary, and includes the only axes in the hoard; for a full account see J. Evans (1884).

Ornaments and objects of everyday use have been somewhat neglected in this survey; but it must suffice to remark that local examples of fishhooks, bodkins, pins and studs, bangles, rings (annular and penannular), and cauldrons (represented by ring handles), gouges and chisels are in the Cambridge Museum or British Museum collections. The majority of these date from the Second Phase of the Age, and a few examples are figured on Plate IX (Nos. 13, 14, 16 and 18).

A few isolated finds of imported fibulae of Hallstatt types, dating probably from VIII century B.C. onwards, occur in our district. Their relation to the Bronze culture is obscure; they never occur in hoards; and consideration of them and of pottery of Hallstatt character found locally is best deferred to the following chapter (see p. 72).

TOPOGRAPHICAL DISTRIBUTION OF FINDS AND HOARDS

The topographical distribution of finds and hoards is shown on the map (II), the details of which are filled in on the same principles as those adopted for the Neolithic Age.

All finds, the exact provenance of which is unknown, are placed on the site of the village or town whose name they bear. Fen finds are sited broadcast over the particular fen from which they come as in the Neolithic map. Each symbol represents one to three, or a multiple of three, finds.

Finds (weapons and implements) are seen to be mainly disposed along the eastern edge of the fens and in the valleys of the Lark and of the Cam. A fair number is recorded from the southern fen area generally, the majority of these, as might be expected, being on the east and south of the Isle of Ely adjacent to the mainland settlements. The Whittlesea Mere finds in the north-west are to be considered in relation to the abundant evidences of settlement on the fenland borders near Peterborough which cannot be dealt with in this book.

In the valley of the Great Ouse finds are rare, in that of the Cam south of Cambridge they are numerous; the contrast is clearly due to the fact that the Ouse Valley is bordered by cold claylands, the Cam Valleys by open chalk downlands.

The rarity of finds in the woodlands as a whole is striking; but several important hoards belonging to the Late Bronze Period show forest association. The parishes of Rushden (Cumberlow Green) and Furneaux Pelham [H], Chrishall, Clavering and Arkesden [E], between the Essex Cam and the headwaters of the River Ivel, a tributary of the Great Ouse, have each yielded a considerable mass of various implements and weapons, and scrap metal. This forest association is doubtless due in part to the need of the craftsmen for

PLATE X

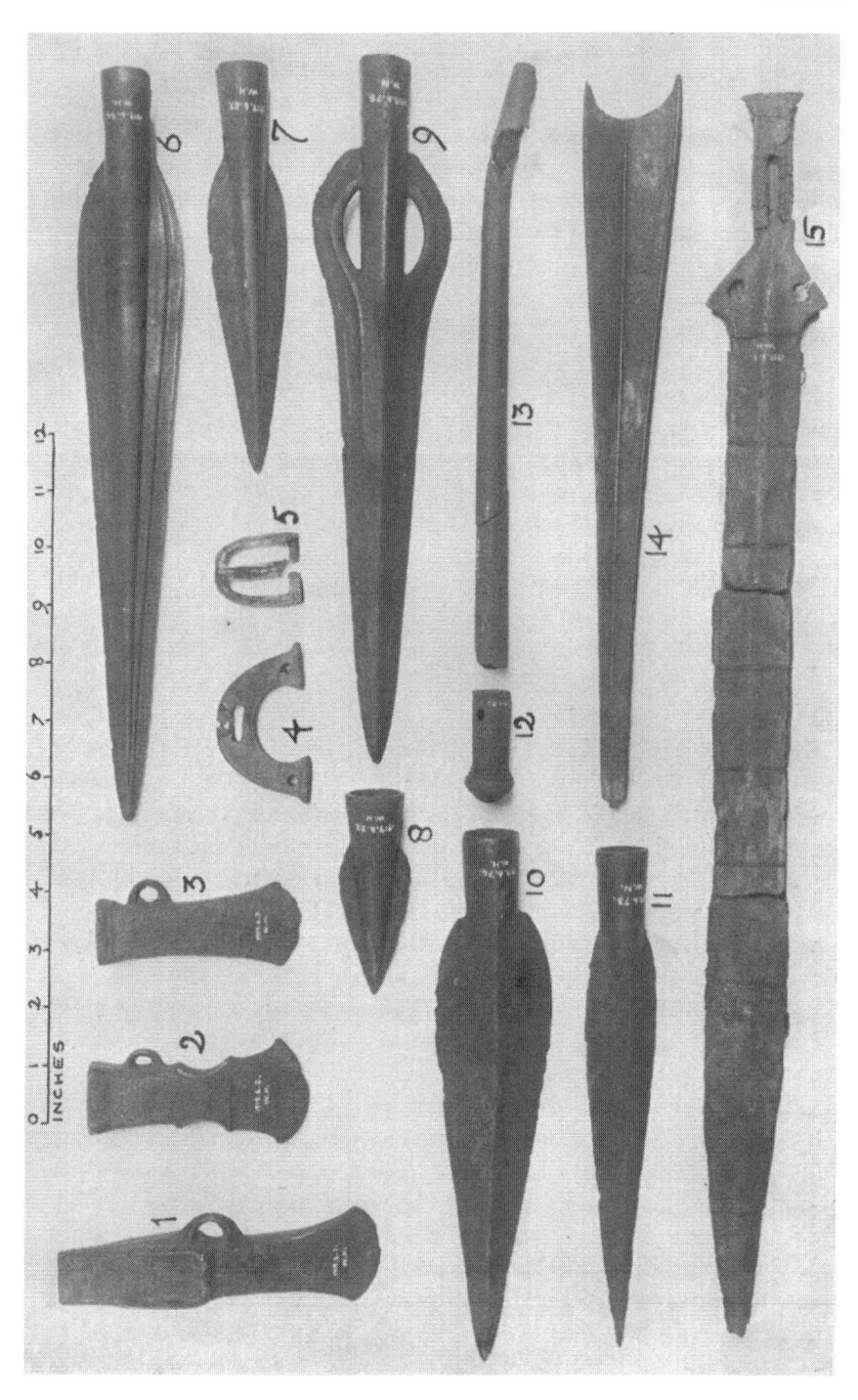

BRONZE AGE. PORTION OF HOARD OF THE 'LATE BRONZE PERIOD,' FROM WILBURTON FEN
See pp. 61 and 65: also, Nos. 1, 2, 3, p. 58; No. 14, p. 60; No. 15, p. 59.

charcoal[1]. The founder's hoard at Barrow [S] and the hoard at Pidley [Hunts.] may possibly be similarly accounted for.

The important (merchant's?) hoard of flanged axes associated with gold ornaments at Postlingford [S], and the occurrence of a gold torc at Boyton [S] (see Sketch-map A) suggest that the Stour Valley may, in the II millennium, have been a trade-route to the coast.

It is remarkable that Grunty Fen, S.W. of Ely, has yielded four hoards or groups of associated objects, but no isolated finds; and that all are of the Early or Middle Bronze Age. It is possible that in this secluded marsh, environed by forest, votive offerings were deposited; and that the custom died out when the leaf-sword folk occupied our district. The Chatteris and Coveney shields, also probably votive, were found in the fens not far away.

The remaining hoards are widely scattered throughout the district; as the map shows, the distribution accords with that of the finds, for hoards occur where finds are most numerous—along the eastern edge of the fens and up the Cam Valley. Occasional finds of rough metal (ingots and jets), implying the neighbourhood of a primitive foundry, as at Morden and Lakenheath, provide confirmatory evidence of this segregation which was indeed to be expected, if, as has been suggested, the smith was in the Late Bronze Age attached to the landed man's household.

That a number of copper bars (p. 36 and Plate XVIII) of a convenient size for barter and transport has been found on the line of the Icknield Way at Therfield [H] is indicative of the probable line of route by which first the finished article, and afterwards the raw material, reached our district.

The distribution of finds and hoards is complementary to that of barrows and interments, and to some extent explains the distribution of the latter. The tribes, clans, and families dwelt, doubtless, where their weapons are chiefly found, on the edge of the fens, by well-heads, by rivers; their dead were buried either near by, as at Cambridge, or on the downland adjacent. Finds in the neighbourhood of Abington on the Bourn River, and of Kentford on the Kennett, are scanty or lacking and should be looked for, in view of the aggregations of barrows adjacent to these villages.

The distribution of early bronze or copper axes (flat axes and those with slight flanges, hammered, not cast) is of interest. These occur in the Lark Valley near Mildenhall (two), and at Icklingham (two),

---

[1] Yorkshire provides an interesting parallel; Mr A. L. Armstrong tells me that in the Early Iron Age ore was taken to the woodlands for smelting.

and on the shore-line of the fens at Fordham (eight), Exning, Burwell (two), Bottisham (two), Reach and Quy. Elsewhere they are found in the Cam Valley "near Cambridge" (two), at Whittlesford and Duxford, and in the fens near Yaxley [Hunts.] and Littleport (see Crawford, 1912 b, pp. 307-9, Brit. Mus. and Camb. Mus. collections). It is thus seen that these early implements are most numerous where finds of the Bronze Age as a whole most frequently occur; and that the value of the conclusions derived from the preceding topographical analysis is not seriously impaired by the fact that the products of 1500 years have been dealt with as contemporary phenomena.

Comparison of the map of the Neolithic Age with that of the Bronze Age discloses parallels remarkably close and divergencies equally striking. In each case the population of the district was, it is clear, mainly confined to the borders of the eastern fens and the Cam Valley; the wealth of finds on the heaths and warrens of the north-east, so marked a feature of the former period, is not, however, repeated in the latter; and having regard to the greater scarcity of Bronze Age weapons, the map probably indicates a denser population in the Cam Valley in the latter period than in the former[1]. Finds in the fens and on the fen islands, too, are much more frequent in the Bronze Age and indicate, on the one hand, an extension from the eastern mainland, and, on the other, that movement to and fro across the "inland sea" which our examination of the pottery of the Fenland Basin led us to expect. A rapier found in a dug-out canoe below peat in the fen near Chatteris (J. Evans, 1881, p. 250) dates the latter, and indicates the methods of transit available. Inland waterways were, it is evident, an important factor in the diffusion of the Bronze culture.

For accounts of two other canoes, probably prehistoric, found in the fens see Marshall (1879) and Noble (1910). That recorded by the latter was found embedded in the gault underlying the peat in Warboys Fen [Hunts.]. It was of oak, monoxylous, 37 feet long, 3 feet 9 inches wide at the stern and 3 feet at the bow. The bottom was flat and 3 inches thick, the sides curved, $1\frac{3}{4}$ inches thick and 15 inches high. Transverse ledges were worked in the solid to give extra strength.

We may surmise that the greater ease with which monoxylous canoes could be made with metal tools, and the development of agriculture, were two of the causes which produced the changes we have been considering. The latter, surely, accounts for the proportional

[1] In Cambridge itself settlement appears to have been chiefly on the gravel terraces at Newnham and Barnwell, judging from finds the exact provenance of which is known. There was also a settlement at Chesterton.

increase in the number of finds and remains in the Cam Valley. Bronze sickles found locally (Stretham, and Downham [N]) are evidence that corn was grown in the Middle Bronze Period.

In several cases a detailed statement as to the exact position of objects found in the peaty fenland is available. The Chatteris spear and shield (p. 60), for example, were "lying on the clay under the peat"; the two Coveney shields and the Wilburton hoard (pp. 60, 61) were in a similar position. The Feltwell necklace (p. 55) was "in clay soil about 5 feet below the surface." A rapier found at Pond's Bridge, Whittlesea (Peterborough Museum), was "sticking in the clay," the upper part being in peat; the fact that the metal is corroded for some 6 inches from the point confirms the record. The canoes described on the previous page were similarly situated, as we have seen.

On the other hand, the Grunty Fen hoard (Middle Period) and the Reach Fen hoard (Late Period) seem to have been buried in peat.

The theory of subsidence in late Neolithic times adequately explains the facts. As a result of this subsidence much of the eastern fenland was in the Bronze Age and later times a shallow mere or meres, the extent of which was steadily being diminished by the growth of peat. It is also to be remembered that the courses of the fen rivers must frequently have changed; and the canoes mentioned above probably lay on the muddy banks of ancient water channels.

ETHNOLOGY

We know from sources external to our district something of the brachycephalic people who placed beakers in the graves with their dead. The race which here at a later date cremated its dead, placing the remains in urns or in a cloth fastened with a bronze pin, and who raised over the ashes barrows on the downs, may have been an intrusive dominant stratum of population overlying submerged races. There is little to support the view that this may have been the first wave of Celtic-speaking peoples—Goidels; more probably they represent mixed beaker-folk and Neolithic stocks either local or derived from another part of the country[1]. The four existing Bronze Age skulls from the Cambridge Region—which are dateable late in the Transition Period or early in the following Period—are, as the table

[1] Partial absorption of the beaker-folk by the aborigines in the district would adequately account for the elimination of the beaker; but the existence of examples of the food-vessel characteristic of the north in a few graves may point to a localized movement into the fens from Yorkshire.

shows, one brachycephalic, the others dolichocephalic; indicating the presence of the two racial types mentioned above.

List No. XII, p. 322

| Fordham[1] | With a handled mug | Late Transition Period | Skull dolichocephalic (index 72·3) |

List No. 28, p. 327

| Mildenhall | With a food-vessel in a barrow | Late Transition Period | Skull "eminently brachycephalic" |

List No. 36, p. 327

| Upper Hare Park[2] | In a barrow | Late Transition Period | Skull dolichocephalic (index 70·2) |

List No. 44, p. 328

| Upper Hare Park | In a barrow with four red deer antlers | Late Transition Period? | Skull dolichocephalic |

There are types of pottery found in valley burials in East Anglia quite distinct from the beaker, food-vessel, or the cinerary urn with overhanging rim, and which are, from analogies with other districts, known to be of late date—probably early in the I millennium B.C. These are thought to be associated with an invasion (of Celtic-speaking peoples, ? Goidels), with the arrival of the leaf-shaped sword and the socketed axe, and with the development of a bronze-founding industry in the Cambridge Region. This is rendered the more probable by the discovery in a midden trench near Cambridge of pottery with raised ribs—a type associated with the square-camp builders of Dorset, who were certainly of continental origin.

That the appearance of the cinerary urn with an overhanging rim is connected with any overseas invasion is rendered improbable by the fact that it is a type of pottery not, so far as is known, represented on the Continent; its evolution in this country has already been discussed. Abercromby (1912, II, pp. 110 ff.) indeed, being of opinion that the evolutionary sequence of sepulchral pottery of the Age in this country is unbroken, is led to affirm that no invasion—other than one localized (in his opinion) south of the Thames—subsequent to that of the beaker-folk took place till iron was introduced in the I millennium B.C.

[1,2] Measurements by Dr Duckworth, who remarks that in the flatness of its side walls the Fordham specimen reproduces the dolichocephalic type which Parsons (1921) claims as representative of the Long Barrow Race.

THE BRONZE AGE

But the evidence already analysed renders this view, based on a study of ceramic, improbable; and it is in conflict with the Irish evidence.

We must conclude that the ethnology of the Bronze Age in the Cambridge Region, as elsewhere in Britain, is very obscure. Our ignorance is largely due to the exclusive use of cremation in burials of the latter part of the Age.

A recent pronouncement from the philological side on the date of the first invasion of Celtic-speaking peoples does not, it should be noted, support the view taken in the text. M. J. Loth, writing in the *Revue Celtique* (1921) concludes that "les premiers établissements des Celtes en Gaule, comme leur première invasion dans l'île de Bretagne, remonteraient...au commencement du deuxième millénaire avant notre ère" (p. 288).

SUMMARY

Many aspects of the Age have been summarized in the course of the analysis; this final estimate may therefore be brief.

The phase of transition from stone to metal in the Cambridge Region is held to have lasted some 300–400 years, commencing with the invasion of the beaker-folk about 2000 B.C.; the full Bronze Age, commencing about 1700, closed some 1200 years later with the introduction of iron into the district about 500–400 B.C.

Montelius' typological classification of the remains of the Age has been in the main adopted, but his system of chronological subdivisions has been rejected, because it fails to elucidate important cultural changes.

The Bronze Age, then, has been divided into two Phases; the first a period of development, apparently unbroken, closing about 1000 B.C.; the second marked by the sudden appearance of a new culture. The first Phase includes the Transition Period when metal objects were very rare; the Early Bronze Period when flat and flanged axes and daggers were in use; and the Middle Bronze Period, the typical weapons then being the rapier, the palstave and the looped spearhead. Approximate dates have been assigned to each of these periods. The second Phase, which may conveniently be termed the Late Bronze Period, is characterized by the socketed axe, the leaf-shaped sword, and by founders' hoards.

In the Transition Period and the greater part of the Early Bronze Period—the first half of the II millennium B.C.—the Cambridge Region was poor in bronze and the cultural relations were mainly with the north—Yorkshire. A new orientation then becomes manifest; from

1500 to 1000 B.C. our district was comparatively wealthy in gold ornaments and has yielded numerous weapons of the finest craftsmanship; East Anglia generally was in the full stream of Western European culture. It is possible that a lucrative trade with the Continent in the gold of the Wicklow Mountains and in Baltic amber was centred here.

The connection with the west evidently ceased when the first Phase of the Age closed, practically no gold objects assignable to the second Phase having been found in the locality. The establishment of the culture of the Late Bronze Period by invasion from overseas may have altered the course of trade.

The local ethnography during the Bronze Age is obscure. We can be certain that the beaker-folk were invading brachycephals of mixed Nordic-Alpine stock, but of little else. It seems probable that the dwellers in the Cambridge Region during the Early and Middle Bronze Age were a fusion of the aboriginal inhabitants and the beaker-folk. The leaf-sword invaders may have been Nordic Celtic-speaking tribes. It is probable that these invaders, as well as the beaker-folk, crossed over to Eastern Britain from the Low Countries.

The distribution of the finds and remains of the Bronze Age in the Cambridge Region shows that settlement was mainly confined to the eastern borders of the fens and the valleys of the Cam and Lark; while the number of finds within the fens themselves points to the increasing use of inland waterways. Numerous round barrows— dating, it is probable, mainly in the II millennium—are disposed along the open hill country bordering the settlements. Poverty in associated objects and variety of funeral customs are outstanding features of these burials. The beaker-folk were buried for the most part *not* in barrows on the hills, but by fen and riverside, and even in the fens; and the distribution of beakers suggests that the invaders arrived by way of the Wash and the fen rivers.

As compared with the Neolithic Age, the diminution of finds on the East Anglian heathlands, and the evidences of settlement in the Upper Cam Valley, point to the growing importance of agriculture in the Bronze Age. The discoveries of sickles in the fens confirm this deduction. There is no evidence of any attempts to clear the forests, though the distribution of bronze-founders' hoards shows that many of the craftsmen dwelt in or on the edge of the woodland. As a recent writer (Maynard, 19—, p. 1) has well put it: "swampy valleys, forested hill-tops, and open grassy slopes scattered with thorn scrub, remained much as in Neolithic times, with probably more settled villages, wider clearings under corn, and a spreading system of trackways." It is difficult to point to any particular trackway, save the Icknield Way, which is certain to have been in use in the Bronze Age; the subject is discussed in Chapter IV.

The scarcity of recorded sites of Bronze Age settlement is remarkable. It is possible though improbable that some of the ring-works in the district may be of the Period, or their sites occupation areas; discussion of this point is deferred to a later chapter.

The use of the loom in the Bronze Age in our district is evidenced by the impression of cloth on a fragment of pottery from Walden, and by the discovery of woven material in cremation urns in barrows.

CHAPTER III

THE EARLY IRON AGE

"*Iron—Cold Iron—must be master of men all.*"   KIPLING.

INTRODUCTION

STUDY of the second Phase of the Bronze Age has suggested that the Hallstatt culture of the Continent influenced but did not replace the Bronze culture in the Cambridge Region; and examining the subject from a new angle in the present chapter we shall endeavour to determine whether there is any evidence for the use of Iron in our district prior to the second Phase of the Early Iron Age, which is marked by the appearance of the La Tène culture. It has already been noted that the "Iron" civilization did not effectively replace that of Bronze on the north-western seaboard of France until late in the Hallstatt period. The burial of Court Saint Étienne near Brussels, moreover, may be quoted in this connection as showing that Belgium was in a transitional phase in the VII–VI centuries B.C. An iron dagger of "anthropoid" type, an iron lance, horsebit and cutlass, evidently the equipment of a man of rank, were associated with a bronze socketed axe (Déchelette, 1913, p. 796).

The La Tène civilization, developed by the Celtic-speaking peoples in contact with Italian civilization, has been divided by continental archaeologists into three sub-periods, and the chronology is pretty well agreed upon. For example, the dating for France, which concerns us most closely, is:

	Montelius, 1901	Déchelette, 1914
La Tène I	400–250 B.C.	500–300 B.C.
,, II	250–150 B.C.	300–100 B.C.
,, III	150–1 B.C.	100–1 B.C.

It must be remembered that culture movements being now overland and not seaborne a given phase may be later in this country than in Western Europe, and it is unlikely that La Tène I is here dateable earlier than IV B.C.[1], or La Tène III than middle I B.C. Moreover, this Celtic culture survived to a later period here than on the Con-

---

[1] For brevity, Roman numerals will in future pages of this book frequently be used for the centuries: *i.e.* IV B.C. = Fourth century B.C.

THE EARLY IRON AGE

tinent, and a fourth sub-period, La Tène IV, has been added to cover the period 1–100 A.D.

Déchelette's system will be adhered to in this book whenever it is necessary to link up local finds with comparable discoveries on the Continent; but our finds of the earlier periods are insufficient to permit such detailed classification as is possible in France.

Several Greek writers use Pretan- for Britain, and this seems to go back to Pytheas (about 330 B.C.); if, as seems probable, Pytheas heard this name when actually in Britain it implies (as is well recognized) the presence of P-Celts or Brythons. Archaeological evidence points to a date not later than the middle of IV B.C. for the Brythonic invasion of Yorkshire; and it is probable that these invaders introduced iron into North Britain. In South Britain kindred tribes may have arrived earlier, or the Brythons may have been preceded by other iron-using immigrants in the Hallstatt period; a growing mass of material from sites such as Hengistbury, All Cannings Cross, and Eastbourne suggests that tribes in the Hallstatt phase of culture began to arrive in V, or even in VI B.C.

The series of uninscribed British coins originated in the southern parts of the country probably not earlier than the II century B.C.; and mention of these brings us to the next invasion, in dealing with which we are assisted by historical record. Caesar's reference to the Belgae—who probably spoke the same language as the Brythons, if the evidence of place and personal names can be trusted—suggests that they arrived in the same century.

From this time onwards burials, isolated finds, and evidences of settlement are met with not infrequently in S.E. Britain. La Tène art developed on remarkable and original lines, and during the early part of I A.D., when the art of Gaul was dominated by that of Rome, native work of astonishing excellence was produced in this country.

The Early Iron Age, properly so called, closes in S.E. Britain with the arrival of Claudius in A.D. 43; but the art associated with the La Tène civilization persisted for a considerable time side by side with provincial Roman art, which eventually—apart from certain survivals the history of which is obscure—replaced it.

We may now consider the evidence for and the characteristics of the Early Iron Age in the Cambridge Region. From classical sources we gather that the names and situations of the states which concern us are: (1) The Iceni (Cenimagni (?) of Caesar), occupying Norfolk and Suffolk; (2) the Trinovantes, whose chief stronghold was Camulodunum, occupying Essex and it may be portions of Hertfordshire; to the west of these, (3) the Catuvellauni, whose wide territories may have included Cambridgeshire and one of whose strongholds was Verulamium. Though the names of these political groups are known their ethnical affinities (were they Belgae or Brythons?) and boundaries are uncertain, and it may be hoped that the analysis of finds in our district, especially of coins and of interments, may give us some assistance on these points.

Oman (1913, p. 18) thinks that the Iceni were Brythons, the Trinovantes and Catuvellauni Belgae. But the parent tribe of the Catuvellauni dwelt on the Marne; they were a small and probably a subject tribe, and it is not at all certain that they were Belgians. Their distance from the sea suggests that the British representatives came over at an early date —the period of the Brythonic and not the Belgic invasions. That the Trinovantes were Belgae is probable; but it is not clear that Caesar's reference to the maritime states (*B.G.* v. 11-12) can be held to include them.

Very little evidence bearing on the development of the Iron culture prior to I B.C. or thereabouts is available from the eastern counties, but it is on general grounds unlikely that the settlement of the Parisii in Yorkshire in IV B.C. should be an isolated phenomenon. Two fibulae of Hallstatt II character and one of characteristic La Tène I type, occurring as isolated finds in our district, and one interment probably of La Tène II date have already been published, and I have gathered sufficient additional material from interments and from finds of pottery and bronzes to warrant the view that the Iron Age commenced here as early as, or possibly earlier than, in Yorkshire. It is not yet possible, however, to distinguish successive phases prior to La Tène III. The Age will therefore be dealt with in two phases, Early and Late; the one comprising La Tène I and II (probably with some admixture of the preceding Hallstatt culture); the other the remaining periods, La Tène III and IV, extending from some time in I B.C. till La Tène art was replaced by provincial-Roman in the second half of I A.D.

THE FIRST PHASE: CENTURIES V (OR IV) TO I B.C.

FIBULAE OF EARLY TYPES

Hallstatt Fibulae. Two fibulae of Hallstatt types have already been noted as occurring in the district; it will be convenient first to consider all such finds, providing as they do problems of great difficulty and interest. The following is a complete list, with the period to which they are assigned:

SKETCH MAP B
EARLY IRON AGE
SHOWING:
i. POLITICAL OR TRIBAL GROUPS
ii. PROBABLE S.W. BOUNDARY OF ICENIAN TERRITORY
iii. PROBABLE LINES OF COMMUNICATION INTO THE CAMBRIDGE PLAIN FROM THE SOUTH
iv SITES OUTSIDE THE CAMBRIDGE REGION MENTIONED IN THE TEXT
THE PENNINES
POCKLINGTON
ARRAS
PARISII
CORITANI
R. WELLAND
R. NENE
PETERBORO'
ICENI
IXWORTH
DEVIL'S DYKE
HUNSBURY
ROUSE
CATUVELLAUNI
CAMBRIDGE
COTSWOLDS
FOSSE WAY
ICKNIELD WAY
RING HILL
WALBURY
CAMULODUNUM
TRINOVANTES
WELWYN
VERULAMIUM
CHILTERNS
LONDON
CALLEVA ATREBATUM
ALL CANNINGS CROSS
ATREBATES
AYLESFORD
CANTII
BELGAE
VENTA BELGARUM
REGNI
EASTBOURNE
HENGISTBURY
SCALE OF MILES
0 10 20 30 40 50 60 70 80

Icklingham [S]	Two: leech-shaped, Italian type	Hallstatt II
Lakenheath [S]	One: broad bow with knobs and long foot, Italian type	Hallstatt II (late)
Chesterford [E]	One: swollen bow with three knobs on either side	Hallstatt II (late)?
Trumpington	One: La Certosa type	Hallstatt II (late)

One of the Icklingham fibulae is in the Bury Museum, the existence of the other was made known to me by Mr R. A. Smith, to whom it had been submitted for an opinion: it was very large and possibly later than the Bury example which has a short pin-catch.

The Lakenheath example is in the British Museum, and is figured in *B.M.G.* (1905, p. 99); the dating of the Chesterford specimen depends on a rather poor drawing by Neville (1847, plate 7, fig. 2), but I do not think that a later date than that given is possible. The Certosa brooch from Trumpington is figured on Plate XVIII, 2.

We have, then, five examples of pre-La Tène fibulae, four certainly of Italian type and evidently imported. Accepting Déchelette's chronology for France where similar types occur, we must date them from 700 to 500 B.C.

The evidence for the importation of Hallstatt fibulae into the fenland districts is, however, much stronger than this list of finds would suggest. Ridgeway and Smith, in a valuable paper published in 1906, collected all the examples then known of brooches of Hallstatt type presumed to have been found in this country; in particular, an important series in the Cambridge Museum, from Ixworth and its neighbourhood (north-east of Bury St Edmunds), was discussed and figured. The chief objects which concern us are six leech-, bow- and boat-shaped fibulae of both early and late Hallstatt date, a portion of bronze bowl-rim embossed with a design paralleled at Hallstatt itself, and a fragmentary spiral wire fibula of a type rare in Western Europe. In addition to these objects of Central and Southern European type, one fragment of a leaf-shaped fibula of Scandinavian type (such as are found in the later Bronze Age deposits of N. Germany) was included.

The association of none of these objects was known; they formed part of a large and varied collection of antiquities acquired by a watchmaker in Ixworth, and it was thought possible that they might have been introduced into this country in XIX A.D. Subsequent discoveries of similar bronzes elsewhere in England have however justified the authors in their opinion that they were contemporary importations.

The identification by the author of a fine early La Certosa fibula with semicircular bow among "Roman objects found on one site" at Ixworth provides additional confirmation. This is illustrated below.

This series does not exhaust the list of similar local finds.

In Bury Museum is a second leech-shaped brooch the provenance of which is unknown, but doubtless it also came from the Lark or Little Ouse Valleys; and in Peterborough Museum the writer noticed in the Artis Collection, obtained during excavations in and about the Roman site near Castor [Northants.], two fibulae of types not, so far as I know, elsewhere met with in Britain, but also of late Hallstatt date.

The drawings (Fig. 1) will give a better indication of the character of these latter brooches than detailed description. The horned springless type is of a handsome design and is certainly Italian. It does not stand alone; for a horned brooch of more common form, from the same neighbourhood, was figured by Artis (1828, Pl. XXXI, fig. 8. See also Ridgeway and Smith, 1906, p. 112).

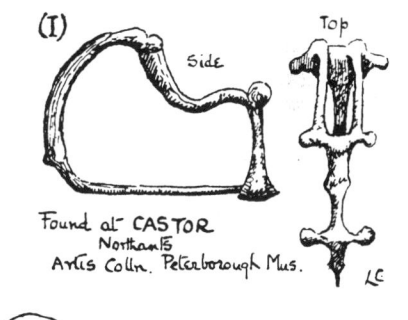

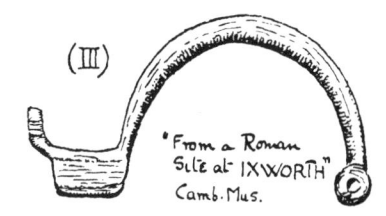

The second brooch is unusual, the bow being formed of a succession of coil springs, a feature met with in La Tène as well as in Hallstatt fibulae; but the flat hammered plate is an early feature and a date prior to La Tène I must be claimed for the fibula.

Early La Tène Fibulae. Three fibulae of La Tène I types[1] have been found in the district, and one of La Tène II. One of the former, from Barrington (Plate XVIII, 3), is a characteristic example similar to many found widely distributed in South Germany, and of a type attributed to V B.C. (Beltz, 1911, map); the others, from Barrington and Milden-

Fig. 1[2]. Scale ⅔.

---

[1] A rude bronze representation in the round of an animal form from Undley (Cambridge Museum) with reverted head, resembles in this latter respect a La Tène I fibula; but it has two studs and must have been fastened on to a metal plate.

[2] Fig. 1, i and ii are from drawings by Dr L. Cobbett.

hall [S], are degenerate forms. The La Tène II fibula was associated with an inhumation interment (p. 81).

The significance of these objects in connection with the problem of the introduction of the Iron culture may be deferred until the whole range of finds dateable prior to La Tène III have been surveyed.

Pins. Two early types have been found in the district.

1. A wire pin with the head bent in the form of a figure of eight. The type is met with in the late Hallstatt period in South Germany (Lindenschmit, 1911, Taf. 69, 1291). Our example, from Lakenheath (Cambridge Museum), has no spiral or other terminal above the figure of eight, and may be a late copy.

2. A ring-headed pin with shaft bent to hold it in place. A similar form, more ornate than our examples (from Bury St Edmunds, British Museum, and from Haslingfield, Cambridge Museum), was found in an interment of early La Tène date in Yorkshire. A specimen similar to ours from Crowland in the Lincolnshire fens is also in the British Museum.

A disc-headed pin from Haslingfield, in the British Museum, is probably to be included in the early group.

INTERMENTS

The evidence relating to the majority of the interments assignable to the first phase of the Early Iron Age in the district is as unsatisfactory as in the case of those of the Bronze Age, and the material available being more limited, the difficulties of interpretation are greater.

Déchelette (1913, p. 630) points out that the Hallstatt period in France was a barrow-building epoch and that the custom persisted in certain areas in the earlier phases of La Tène (1914, p. 1014); and in this country the early La Tène burials in Yorkshire are in barrows.

It seems justifiable, therefore, to include in our first phase all interments in tumuli in this district which appear to belong to the Early Iron Age; the more so as there is at present no evidence that the custom survived locally into La Tène III. The point is again discussed on p. 199.

Three isolated tumuli, and one group, are here considered.

1. A tumulus at Barrow Bottom [S] opened in 1813 contained hollow-bladed iron spearheads, fragments of which are in the Bury Museum; these, which presumably accompanied inhumation inter-

THE EARLY IRON AGE

ments, are of primitive—Bronze Age—types, and may be dated in the very beginning of the Iron Age in this country.

This tumulus is marked on the 6-inch O.S. Suffolk, XLIII N.E. From a neighbouring Bronze Age barrow at Risby Heath (No. 30) a rude plain vase of polished dark brown ware with well-defined foot (in the British Museum) was obtained by Greenwell in 1869. That it was a food-vessel, originally associated with an inhumed body, is probable, but no trace of such association was found. Mr R. A. Smith regards it as of La Tène I date, and drew my attention to its resemblance to contemporary Danish pots.

2. A large low elevation (? a tumulus) near Brandon [S], excavated in 1895, was found to contain numerous human skeletons of all ages and both sexes, as well as the skeletons of horses (p. 114 and Myers, 1896). The Early Iron Age seems a likely period, though there were no associated objects, other than pieces of iron.

Sixty-five inhumed skeletons of La Tène date were found in the tumulus of Lantilly, Côte-d'Or (Déchelette, 1914, p. 1044). In the Hallstatt period, moreover, the tumulus was frequently a cemetery (*op. cit.* 1913, p. 630).

3. In a barrow at Royston [H] six male skeletons (in 7-foot graves) each having an iron spear with wooden shaft $6\frac{1}{2}$ feet long were found in 1854; and three smaller graves within the barrow contained skeletons apparently of children. "Blades of knives and daggers, and one or two coins" were also found. Here, again, the Early Iron Age seems probable, but is by no means certain.

Record in Nunn's MS., Cambridge Museum. Roman coins are frequently found as superficial deposits in prehistoric barrows in this district. In this case the type of coin is unknown. Anglo-Saxon date is of course possible.

4. Greater certainty of pre-Roman date attaches to the group of tumuli destroyed in 1819 (*Gent. Mag.* 1819), of which the more prominent bore the name of Chronicle Hills; these were situated to the north of the Street Way and on the east side of a stream which divides the parishes of Whittlesford and Triplow. Being on low-lying ground, none is likely to be of the Bronze Age (see Sketch-map D, p. 144).

They were three in number, in line north and south. The middle one was 8 feet high and 27 yards in diameter; in it were four skeletons "lying upon their backs about 2 feet from the bottom." In the earth composing the barrow "broken pieces of terracotta with red and with black glazing which...seemed to be Roman, but this is uncertain" were found. There is a very inadequate account in the *Gentleman's Magazine* of the two other barrows; but Babington (1883, p. 63), who possibly had access to more detailed information (he gives an incorrect reference), says they also contained skeletons.

That the barrows were not Roman was the opinion of the original investigator—"rather Celtic than Roman" are his words; he points out that the tumuli ranged along an ancient wall of flints and pebbles, but that in clearing away the ruins not a single Roman coin was found. The pottery may have been the highly burnished black ware of which one example is known from the district (see Plate XVI, 5) and the polished red painted ware such as that from the Marne (La Tène I), of which one fragment was found in the War Ditches (p. 136).

It is, however, the two barrows about 100 yards to the north of the Chronicle Hills, levelled at the same time, which provide the most striking and incontestable examples of Early Iron Age inhumation burial in the Cambridge district.

In each of these, human skeletons were found in "soroi" (small vaults?) which consisted of "flints and pebbles[1] put together with fine gravel." These "soroi" were surrounded each by a circular wall $2\frac{1}{2}$ feet thick and about 3 feet high, and 22 feet in diameter; the mounds of earth which covered the whole rose in each case about 2 feet above the top of the "soros."

In the first "soros," 5 feet square and 8 feet deep, "brought to a point with pebbles," were found two skeletons, the uppermost of which appeared to be the larger; under the skull was the "blade of a poignard or knife" (metal not recorded), and the head of this skeleton rested on the body of the other. The "soros" had an oak bottom stained with oxide of copper owing to the decomposition of an "ancient bronze vessel." Large iron nails were also found "here."

In the other "soros," 4 feet square and 8 feet deep, was a human skeleton, and below it another "in a sitting posture with an erect spear the point of which was of iron." Nails were found here but no wood as in the other soros.

There are continental analogies to many features of these remarkable interments.

Déchelette (1914, p. 1033) mentions coffins of oak planks fastened with iron nails as occurring in burials in the Marne district and elsewhere in France in the La Tène I period, while similar coffins had gabled roofs in a cemetery at Vevey, Switzerland; it is probable that

---

[1] The wall adjacent to the Chronicle Hills is similarly described, and is probably contemporary.

THE EARLY IRON AGE

the iron nails found in each "soros" in the Cambridgeshire burials were from a decayed shell of wood.

Double and triple burials occur in the same period also in the Marne district. At Châlons, for example (*ibid.* p. 1036), two warriors lay side by side, the right leg of one crossed over the left leg of the other; the inequality of their rank was evidenced by differences in the objects deposited with each.

No information is given as to the sex of the skeletons in the first soros; but the uppermost skeleton, "larger than the lower," was probably a male, and it is not impossible that customs such as those met with in the Marne burials and described by Déchelette (1914, p. 1036) were carried on in this country.

The custom of encircling the central and primary burial with a ring of stones or low wall has been met with in this district in the Bronze Age (see p. 31); it commonly occurs in burials of the Hallstatt period in France[1].

The bronze vessel would have fixed the date of the interments, but it was not preserved; bowls and buckets (*ciste a cordoni*) are of course commonly met with in continental burials of Hallstatt date; the illustration in Déchelette (1913, p. 642) of the objects found in the tumulus of Monceau-Laurent, Côte-d'Or, may be referred to. Of this barrow, too, Déchelette remarks that it contained much broken pottery, widely disseminated, as was apparently the case with the middle barrow of the three "Chronicle Hills."

The soros or vault, roofed by inclining the walls inward, reminds one of the Etruscan tombs of V century date at Orvieto and other sites.

5. All the barrow burials hitherto discussed in this chapter have been by inhumation, and the association of this rite with the incoming Iron culture is, on the continental evidence, to be anticipated. But there is evidence which precludes us from drawing a clear-cut distinction in burial rites between the bronze and iron users. Mr A. L. Armstrong informs me that he has found fragments of Iron Age pottery associated with a primary cremation interment in a barrow in Weeting Park [N]. Moreover, there are three barrows on Triplow Heath (Nos. 68–70 in my supplementary list), situated not far from the Chronicle Hills, which present features of importance in this connection.

From one of these barrows (probably No. 70) was obtained a

---

[1] For a review of the evidence, see Déchelette, 1913, p. 635. Compare also the Armorican tumuli, p. 681.

typical Iron Age pot apparently associated with a cremated burial; another (No. 68) yielded a bone pin "made from the base of the rib of some small animal" and a piece of black pottery—both of which suggest Early Iron Age date. These were apparently associated with the primary deposit—a skeleton bearing marks of fire (as did also the soil) and "the jawbone of a horse." In another barrow (No. 69) was a cremation interment associated with the unburnt bones of a horse.

It is the presence of horses which suggests that these barrows may be entirely of the Early Iron Age, and hence examples of the transition from cremation to inhumation, the corpse of the dead warrior buried in No. 68 having, we may suppose, been passed through the fire as a ceremonial act.

Barrow No. 19 on my list (p. 326), in Chrishall parish on the border of Triplow Heath, contained a secondary interment probably of the Early Iron Age, but possibly Anglo-Saxon. With a cremated burial were associated the burnt bones of at least one horse, a small iron knife and fragments of bronze fibulae which also had been burnt.

Ridgeway (1905, p. 92) holds that the horse was probably introduced into Britain at the end of the Bronze or the beginning of the Iron Age; and in our barrow records I find very slight evidence of its presence, save in definitely secondary deposits and in these Triplow tumuli. Though some species of horse was utilized in this country as a food animal prior to the Iron Age, the known military and social importance of these animals among the Celtic-speaking peoples suggests that their ceremonial interment in this country may date from the Brythonic conquest. We can only record the facts, and await the production of further evidence.

No burials associated with brooches of Hallstatt types are known from the Cambridge Region; but it is a remarkable fact that the fibula of Italian type (late Hallstatt) figured by Artis and referred to on my p. 75 was discovered in clearing away a tumulus; moreover, at Pirton, near Hitchin [H], Dryden (1845, p. 21) records the discovery of an inhumation cemetery associated with pottery (of unknown types); some of the bodies were "sitting with urns between their knees"—a position similar to that of the skeleton in the "soros." The only associated object which is described is a brooch $5\frac{1}{2}$ inches long "of one piece of brass wire in which the spring is formed by four convolutions of the wire near the centre of it." Can this be anything but a serpentiform fibula of Italian type, or an allied form such as that figured by Hoernes (1905, Fig. XVI, 20)?

THE EARLY IRON AGE

In estimating the value of these records it must be remembered that so far as I am aware no fibula of Hallstatt type has been found in England under test conditions associated with an interment; and that many of them come from "Roman sites."

The burial of a warrior with his spear and two dogs in a grave at Soham may be of the earlier period (La Tène I or II) when the slaughter of dependents was a common custom (Déchelette, 1914, p. 1036). The spearhead (British Museum) has a sharp median rib and the junction of socket and blade is well defined; it is a characteristic La Tène form.

The next burial to be considered belongs to the close of our first phase (La Tène II), judging from the design of one of the associated fibulae, and is the only one of the early series which was carefully examined by a competent archaeologist. The interment in question was discovered by von Hügel at Newnham, Cambridge, in 1903, and the finds (see Plate XV, 5) are preserved in the Cambridge Museum. The elaborate fibula (Plate XVIII, 2 x) is closely related to a Marne type, and to several found in the chariot burials at Arras in Yorkshire, of early La Tène date (Greenwell, 1906, pp. 267-8 and 296; A. J. Evans, 1915). Plaques of shell are attached by central rivets to the bronze framework, and the portions of the brooch not thus ornamented are covered with incised decoration. Plaques of shell are seen also on the reverted terminals of a pair of penannular brooches. The bangle, finely patinated, is covered with scroll decoration in relief of developed La Tène character. The circular bronze object with projecting boss, found under the vertebral column of the skeleton, was almost certainly a harness mounting; the signs of wear at the attachment of the chains are visible in the plate. Dr Duckworth kindly examined the skull from this grave for me; he found it to be that of a middle-aged individual "almost certainly dolichocephalic." The skeleton was in a contracted position, as were the Arras burials.

A remarkable burial at Mildenhall is probably representative of the same culture phase. Bunbury (1834) records that "in 1812 some labourers while levelling skirt lands (by cutting down hillocks of sand and throwing them into the moorpits) discovered a human skeleton of large dimensions, stretched at its full length between the skeletons of two horses, arranged in parallel order. On one side of the warrior lay a long iron sword, on the other his celt; he had a torques of gold." Unfortunately none of the finds is preserved; the "torques" is known to have been melted down shortly after its discovery. The "celt" may have been of bronze (see p. 70).

FA

Weapons

The only isolated finds of weapons definitely assignable to the early phase of the Iron Age are two spearheads in the Cambridge Museum, from Grantchester and Orwell?, and the beautiful dagger of modified anthropoid type, from Hertford Warren near Bury St Edmunds, in the Walden Museum, dated by A. J. Evans (1915, p. 570) in II B.C.

Pottery

In sorting the collection of sherds from various local sites stored in the Cambridge Museum I found a few pot and beaker fragments, late Hallstatt in form and decoration, from Lakenheath in the northeast and from Hauxton Mill near Cambridge; finds which were confirmed by the discovery amongst the pottery obtained from the recent coprolite diggings at Grantchester of several sherds of similar character.

Though fragmentary, this pottery, all of which is handmade, is of the highest importance, suggesting as it does the occupation of the Cambridge district by invading elements at the close of the Hallstatt or the beginning of the La Tène period. Scale sections of the most characteristic forms will be found on Plate XI.

From few sites in this country has similar pottery been obtained. An important and fully illustrated series is the "A group" from Hengistbury [Hants.], a site which was explored by Bushe-Fox in 1911–12; the plates and figures in his *Report* (1915) will be taken as the standard of reference.

The Lakenheath pot (A 1) is a large one, 11·8 inches in diameter and about 10·6 inches in height; it is well made, of light-coloured (sandy) clay, and the decoration is carefully wrought. It is to be noted that another Lakenheath fragment of the Early Iron Age (Plate XVI, 3) is of similar paste, and both are clearly of local manufacture.

The Hauxton Mill bowl (A 5), about 8·4 inches in diameter at the rim, has, on the other hand, a black clay body, as have the majority of Early Iron Age handmade wares found in this district. The colour is partly due to the method of manufacture adopted, for a piece of a similar pot from All Cannings Cross, Wilts.[1], is indistinguishable from it, and such coarse wares are not likely to be imported.

These two fragments are undoubtedly products of the same culture as those of Class A, Plate xvi, figs. 10–13, at Hengistbury; while

---

[1] In Cambridge Museum. Type-series presented by Mrs M. E. Cunnington of Devizes.

PLATE XI

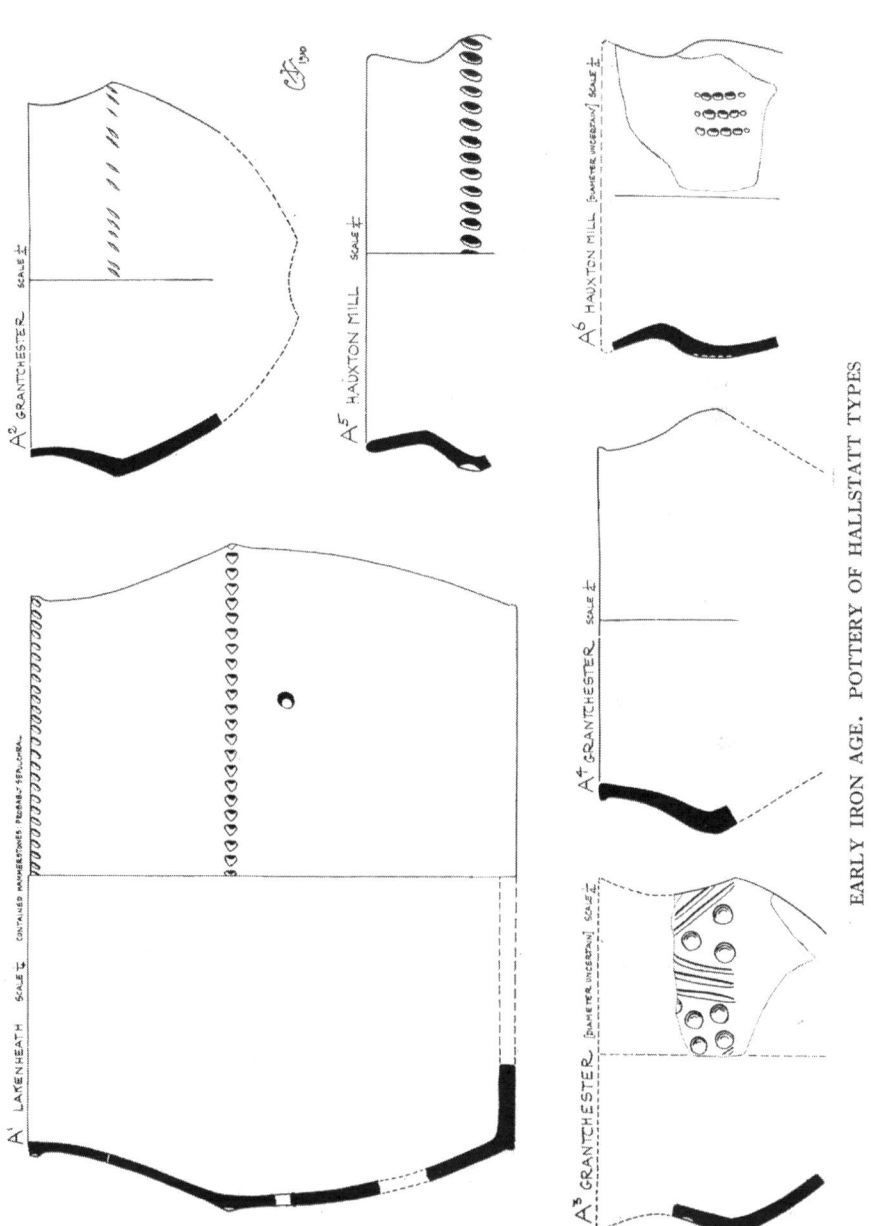

EARLY IRON AGE. POTTERY OF HALLSTATT TYPES
All one-quarter actual size. See pp. 82 and 83.

the two Grantchester beakers (A 2, A 3—and possibly also A 4) are, there can be little doubt, of the same type as figures 1 to 9 on Plate xvi, also of Class A. It is uncertain whether the omphalos base was present in our pots, for no bases were preserved. A 3 presented decoration resembling Hengistbury Class E (see Plate xi, Nos. 5 and 6), the earliest examples of which are considered by Bushe-Fox to be contemporary with his Class A pottery. All these Grantchester fragments are of blackish body, well baked, reddish-brown on exterior surface, which is fairly uniform in colour, smooth but not burnished.

The indented rim which is characteristic of certain of the Hengistbury Class A wares is represented by a fragment from Trumpington (A 7, Plate XIV), which has the black clay body mentioned above.

A well-burnished fragment from Hauxton (A 6), with an impressed decoration like the hobnails of a boot, showed the margins of the depressions rubbed down as though the surface of the pot had been ground smooth; this detail is noted on certain wheelmade pots from the Lark Valley (see p. 93) and must be a late feature. La Tène II would appear to be a possible date.

In addition to wares of this well-defined group, a fragment of burnished red pottery, of the type well represented in the national collection from La Tène I burials in the Marne district, of very rare occurrence in England, is present in a collection of sherds from the War Ditches, Cherryhinton (see p. 136).

Bushe-Fox remarks (p. 33) that parallels to every type of his Class A pottery may be found in the cemeteries of the Hallstatt period in S.W. France and the Pyrenees; but it is to be noted that the majority of the characteristic forms to which he draws attention have not yet been found in our district, and one would suspect that Cambridgeshire had closer connections with Northern France, Belgium and the Lower and Middle Rhine, than with any district further south.

Bushe-Fox (p. 33) dates his Class A group in the late Hallstatt period, V B.C. or earlier; Cunnington (1922) has found similar pottery associated with La Tène I fibulae and the culture cannot therefore safely be dated earlier than 500–400 B.C.

Much coarse pottery, some of it probably earlier than the wheelmade La Tène III–IV wares, has been found in our district; but until a stratified sequence is obtained by excavation it cannot be accurately dated, and will therefore be considered in the next section.

General Considerations

Having examined the material available for the study of the first phase of the Early Iron Age in the Cambridge Region, we may consider its bearing on the problem of the date and mode of introduction of iron into the southern fenlands.

The evidence for a date prior to the La Tène I period—an acceptable date for which in this country is the IV–III centuries B.C.—consists in the presence of imported bronzes and pottery of Hallstatt type, and possibly in the character of certain interments.

Leech-shaped, "Certosa," and spectacle fibulae and an early bronze bowl have, as we have seen, been found in N.W. Suffolk, horned fibulae near Peterborough, and one "Certosa" brooch in the neighbourhood of Cambridge. These objects range in date from about 800–400 B.C., and it is natural to suppose that they were obtained from traders by the Bronze Age folk, though the channel by which they arrived is obscure.

Leech-shaped Italian fibulae are found on the Middle Rhine and on the coast of Normandy. I have not yet obtained information of their occurrence in Belgium or the mouth of the Rhine. Ridgeway (1890, p. 94) regards it as improbable that any traders from the Mediterranean to Britain as early as 300 B.C. used a more northerly route than that *via* the Loire and Corbilo; and he does not think it likely that the most northerly route across Gaul of which Strabo speaks—that from the Rhine through the country of the Morini—was ever a direct medium between the Mediterranean and Britain. The Dover-Calais crossing, though used by invaders, was probably not then a trade-route; but it is not unlikely that in the Late Bronze Age and Early Iron Age a trans-Channel route from the Cotentin to the Dorset harbours was open. In any case the weight of evidence is in favour of the derivation of these fibulae from S. Britain and not direct from overseas.

We have already seen that the introduction of the leaf-shaped sword may have coincided with an invasion (of "Q.-Kelts" or Goidels?) and the connection between the Continent and Britain thus established may have resulted in these articles of luxury filtering through from the mainland, the majority coming ultimately from Northern Italy. But they could never have been numerous; and the survival of so many uninjured examples suggests that some at least were deposited in graves with inhumed bodies; that is to say, that their introduction coincides with a complete change of sepulchral custom and therefore probably with an invasion. In the case of one of the latest examples, a horned brooch found near Castor [Northants.], there is evidence that it came from a barrow (Artis, 1828, Pl. XXXI, 8); and what may have been a contemporary serpentiform brooch was associated at Pirton with an inhumation burial.

Finds of pottery of late Hallstatt type at several sites near Cambridge, and in abundance near Peterborough[1], suggest that the first waves of immigrants may have drifted in not later than V B.C., and such may have been possessed of late Hallstatt brooches. That they had not long been acquainted with iron might be deduced from the occurrence of spearheads—apparently slavish copies of bronze forms —in a tumulus at Barrow. Cunnington's excavations (p. 83) however show that Hallstatt pottery found in this country may not in any case be earlier than the La Tène I period on the Continent. Metal objects travel more quickly than domestic pottery, and invaders possessing, in the main essentials, Hallstatt culture might well have early La Tène fibulae.

We must therefore conclude that our evidence is insufficient to permit us to frame an hypothesis, much less to arrive at a decision, as to a pre-La Tène iron culture in Eastern England, and on the whole we must regard the problem presented by the local occurrence of fibulae of Hallstatt types as at present insoluble.

Hallstatt pottery has been found at several sites in Southern England; apart from the fenland finds under discussion I do not know that such has been found north of the Thames Valley.

There is a plain bowl with the omphalos base in Colchester Museum; but this is not necessarily earlier than La Tène II, for the decorated bowl referred to on p. 94 (footnote) shows the same feature.

It is of course not impossible that wares of Hallstatt type exist unrecognized in provincial museums, and it is at present of little use speculating on the causes of the apparently limited distribution in this country.

The Peterborough site, difficult of access by land except from the north, is on a gravel spur on the banks of the Nene, the first landing-place reached by men sailing up this river; and it seems likely that the iron culture reached the fens from overseas rather than overland from the Thames Valley. This is on other grounds not improbable; for Yorkshire was evidently colonized direct from the Continent.

The occurrence at Risby of a rude urn of a type met with in Denmark and of a leaf-shaped brooch (which apparently had a

---

[1] Mr Wyman Abbott was kind enough to show me his unpublished material from this district, which includes many early bowls with the omphalos base. Recognizing the southern fens as a culture pool, we are justified in using this evidence when dealing with the problems of the Cambridge Region.

swivel pin) at Ixworth, suggests that the invaders had Northern connections.

Whether the culture represented by our early pottery be called Hallstatt or no, it certainly proves that new elements were present in the Cambridge Region in La Tène I times. La Tène I fibulae; a fragment of Gaulish pottery from the Marne; inhumation interments in barrows such as those at the Chronicle Hills, or in flat graves as at Newnham and (?) Mildenhall confirm the presence of invaders prior to I B.C., and they reveal a connection with Northern France. The Newnham burial, moreover, being contracted, and associated with horse trappings and a fibula resembling several found at Arras [Yorks.], is important as indicating that the La Tène culture of the East Riding, associated with the Parisii, was present in our region.

As is now generally accepted, conquest and a new culture may be held to result only from successive and continuous movements of a people or peoples, reinforcing the spearhead of invasion and replacing losses by battle and racial absorption; and the jetsam of continental Iron cultures which chance has preserved to us may point to this—that elements drawn from the whole seaboard from Holland to France may have contributed to the establishment of the Brythonic Celts in England in general, and our countryside in particular; and that the process occupied a considerable period of time.

We cannot say whether the communities which in Eastern England coalesced when the conquest was complete are those with which history has made us familiar, but it seems highly probable that the Iceni and Catuvellauni are Brythonic rather than Belgic; the point may be better discussed when dealing with the later phase of the Age.

Mention should be made in this summary of two copper coins of the early Ptolemaic dynasty (both said to be of Ptolemy Soter 323–285 B.C.) found in the district; one in a Barnwell gravel pit (*penes* Mr T. D. A. Cockerell) and one at Barrington (*penes* Rev. J. W. E. Conybeare), both Early Iron Age sites. That they were contemporary importations cannot be affirmed; but the southward expansion of the Celtic peoples in IV B.C. and the development of Massilian trade with the north and west from about 300 B.C. onwards render it not improbable.

No attempt can be made, on the basis of the scanty finds we have discussed, to estimate the topographical range and distribution of settlements in our district in the first phase of the Iron Age. As in the first metal age, and as in the pagan Anglo-Saxon period a thousand years later, the valley of the Lark and the neighbourhood of Cambridge yield the earliest remains; the portal of entry—the Wash—being, as we may conclude, the same in each case. Of the actual sites we know very little, most of the material being chance finds and not the product of excavations competently supervised; discussion of these may thus conveniently be postponed till the end of the chapter, when all the Iron Age sites will be dealt with.

THE SECOND PHASE: LA TÈNE III AND IV.
I CENTURY B.C.—I CENTURY A.D.

The material available for the study of this phase will be dealt with in the following order: Firstly, coins; then pottery; shale vases; and interments. The evidence which finds and remains of these classes afford, as to the limits of Icenian territory and of the cremation culture associated with pottery of Aylesford type, will next be examined; and, finally, the weapons, bronzes, enamels, etc., of the period will briefly be considered.

COINS

Numerous coins of gold, silver, tin or copper, including a few hoards have been found in the Cambridge Region, the majority in the Ivel (upper Great Ouse) and Cam Valleys or adjacent to the rivers Lark and Little Ouse; their distribution corresponds, as might be expected, with that of the Early Iron Age finds as a whole.

The distribution of the several types met with, both of the inscribed and uninscribed series, is of importance, as it supplements the very inadequate historical evidence as to the names of British princes and their spheres of influence, and the boundaries of tribal areas.

The subject has been thoroughly worked out by J. Evans (1864 and 1890; see also 1902 *a*, p. 235, and 1902 *b*). The briefest possible statement, and the inclusion in the survey of a few coins discovered since he wrote or not included by him, is all that is necessary to enable us to apply the information to our particular problems.

Certain of the uninscribed coins with which we are concerned (found in the south of our Region) can safely be dated from II century B.C. to 30 B.C. or thereabouts, while the inscribed series dates from about 30 B.C. to the Claudian conquest, 43 A.D. Icenian uninscribed coins, however, are later, and contemporary with the inscribed series.

Inscribed coins of the Iceni not infrequently bear the legend Ecen or Ece. Those inscribed Ver and similar abbreviations were minted at Verulamium (certainly St Albans), the capital, we may hold, of the Catuvellauni, whence also came the majority of the coins of Tasciovanus (30 B.C.-5 A.D.). Coins of Cunobelinus, son of Tasciovanus, king of S.E. Britain about 5 B.C. to 40 A.D., who minted at Camulodunum (Colchester), are also frequently met with. Coins of Addedomaros, regarded by Evans as probably a prince of the Iceni contemporary with Tasciovanus, and of Antedrigus, a mysterious person who in I A.D. seems to have held power first among the Iceni and afterwards in the West, are also met with. These are the chief facts and names which concern us[1]. It follows that the relative distribution of Icenian coins, and of those minted by Tasciovanus at Verulamium or by Cunobelinus, will give us some indication as to which sphere of influence, the north-eastern or the southern, the Cambridge Region is to be assigned to, at all events during the period 30 B.C.-43 A.D. It is true that coins are portable property and isolated examples prove nothing, but the aggregate of finds is a reliable indication of the political orientation of a given district[2].

In the north-east of our region no less than three hoards have been found—or, if one at March (Akerman, 1839, p. 89) be included, four—38 of silver, uninscribed, at Stonea in the fens (Evans, 1890, p. 586), 90 uninscribed of gold at Freckenham [S] (Montagu, 1886), and 109 of silver at Santon Downham [S] (Evans, 1869). All the Stonea and Freckenham coins were Icenian. The March hoard—40 to 50 in number—also were all Icenian. So were those from Santon Downham, save two Roman, of Claudius, probably minted in 41 A.D. In the latter hoard were many coins inscribed Ecen or Ece, as well as 14 of Antedrigus. Isolated finds of Icenian coins are recorded from several other sites in this neighbourhood.

South of the Devil's Dyke Icenian coins are rare. Two of Addedomarus have been found in the Stour Valley, and one in the Cam Valley at Barrington. Barrington, Chesterford [E], and Bygrave [H] on the watershed between the Ivel Valley and the main valley of the Cam, have each yielded one uninscribed coin of Icenian type.

On the other hand, these are the areas wherein uninscribed coins of Evans' "central district[3]," dating from before 30 B.C., inscribed coins of Tasciovanus, coins bearing the Verulam mint mark, and coins of Cunobelinus, are commonly met with—not less than

[1] The problems presented by the coins inscribed Tascio-Ricon, and those with the legend Rufi or Ruli [a few of both types occur in the district] are omitted from consideration, and the reader is referred to Evans.
[2] This was clearly indicated by Evans, and I am merely expanding his analysis, and its results, in the greater detail which the survey of a limited area permits.
[3] See Evans (1864, p. 215).

THE EARLY IRON AGE

forty sites being recorded. Of the large number of coins found at Braughing [H] and in the Ivel Valley (the sites nearest to Verulamium) it may be specially noted that none is Icenian.

Only one hoard is recorded from the country to the south of the Devil's Dyke and of this, unfortunately, little is known. It was found in 1788 in Millfield, Place Farm, Haverhill [S], and consisted of about fifty coins; the known representative is of gold, uninscribed, of "central" type, and from Walford's account (1803 b, p. 72) it is probable that all were of similar type though of different values.

Topographical analysis of (a) uninscribed coins of "central" types, (b) coins of Tasciovanus and the Verulam mint, and (c) coins of Cunobelinus, showed me that each group is widely and evenly distributed within the area covered by the whole; they may, therefore, here be lumped together as representative of the civilization centred at Verulamium or Camulodunum.

Our material, then, may be analysed as follows: Of ten parishes[1] in the district north-east of the Devil's Dyke wherein coins have been found:

In 7 the finds are solely Icenian.
In 2 the finds are Icenian and of "central" types[2] mingled.
In 1 the finds are of "central" types.

Of 44 parishes in the remaining portion of the area covered by the investigation:

In 2 the finds are solely Icenian.
In 3 the finds are Icenian and central types mingled.
In 39 the finds are of the central types only.

The differentiation is more striking if the numbers of coins found are considered.

Of 253 coins from the north-east of our region:

249 (including 3 hoards) are Icenian.
4 are of central types.

Of 192 coins from the remaining portion of the district:

6 are Icenian.
186 are of central types[3].

---

[1] Excluding March as being outside our area.
[2] "Central" = Inscribed and uninscribed coins from the Eastern Midlands, probably all Catuvellaunian, and coins minted in Essex (Camulodunum). This term is open to criticism, but a short descriptive word is necessary to avoid repeated paraphrase.
[3] Including the Haverhill hoard. Almost all are from the Verulamium or Camulodunum mints, or are of types believed to be hence derived. One coin of the Regni (Sussex) comes from Barrington and two Gaulish coins from Braughing.

It seems certain:

(1) That the Icenian boundary was somewhere in the neighbourhood of the Devil's Dyke.

(2) That the southern fens were in Icenian territory[1].

(3) That there were obstacles to intercourse greater than those of political division—such as might be provided by the military barrier formed by the Devil's Dyke[2].

The boundary thus delimited is shown on Sketch-map B (p. 73).

POTTERY

The great majority of perfect vessels found in the district, and therefore practically the only earthenware of the period exhibited in museums, are cineraries, usually wheelmade, of the Aylesford (Belgic) class. These range in date probably from early in I B.C. to the Claudian conquest; some of the later forms indeed may be post-Claudian, and a distinctive feature of many such, convex roll mouldings on the neck and upper part of the shoulder, are commonly met with here on early Romano-British wares (p. 92).

As a class they form a characteristic and recognizable group, relying for their effect mainly on excellent proportions. Their decoration, apart from cordons and girth-grooves, is unimportant; when present it is confined to zigzags, lattice patterns and combed striations. In colour, black to brownish-red is common, a wide range of tones occurring on a given pot; grey and light red urns are also met with.

Five main local types may be distinguished: pedestalled urns; barrel- or butt-shaped cordoned urns; tazzas; globular urns with neck cordons; and wide-mouthed bowls and beakers. The plates in A. J. Evans' (1890) and R. A. Smith's (1912) memoirs on the Aylesford and Welwyn finds respectively indicate the range of form and decoration met with, and these will be referred to when necessary. Characteristic examples found near Cambridge are, moreover, figured in my plates.

Pedestalled Urns. These graceful vases, high shouldered, with everted rims, are represented in the Cambridge Museum by examples from Chesterton (Plate XII, 3) and Whittlesford. Urns of the same type from Chesterford [E], Walsworth (Hitchin) and Letchworth [H], and Arlesey [B] are also known.

In most of these the foot is flat or slightly dished, the ware blackish-

---

[1] Indeed, the fens as far north as the Wash were probably Icenian. See J. Evans (1890, map).

[2] The *direct* evidence for pre-Roman date of the Devil's Dyke is of a negative character. See Hughes (1913, p. 138), and p. 128 of this book.

PLATE XII

EARLY IRON AGE. POTTERY, MAINLY SEPULCHRAL AND OF AYLESFORD TYPES [EXCEPT NO. 6, OF THE ROMAN AGE]

Nos. 1–5, pp. 90, 91, 92; No. 6, p. 208.

grey or red, not polished, but slightly smoothed. The Letchworth example is one of the finest and earliest met with in the district; it was found with a bronze strap-link (?) of late La Tène character, the deposit apparently having been associated with a cremation interment (R. A. Smith, 1914, figured).

The Cambridge district, moreover, yields forms apparently late (second half of I A.D.?), but clearly of La Tène ancestry; an example from the Castle Yard, Cambridge, with rough incised zigzags on the neck, and another from a Roman pit at Chesterford (both in the Cambridge Museum) may be cited.

Barrel- or Butt-shaped Urns. These are common; many examples found in the district are known to have been used as cineraries, and probably the majority were. The type ranges from I B.C. (probably) to the Roman occupation; examples dating round about the Christian era from Hitchin and its neighbourhood are in the British Museum, others, possibly a little later, from Chesterford, are at Audley End Museum, whilst a series from the neighbourhood of Cambridge (Hauxton, Milton, Chesterton, Madingley Road) are in the Cambridge Museum. The Milton specimens are of good quality; the ware is thin and well baked, brick-red in colour; the rims are oblique, making an obtuse angle with the barrel, a feature frequently met with in early Romano-British or Romano-Belgic wares found locally.

A characteristic barrel urn is figured on Plate XIII, 1 B; it was associated at Hauxton with a handsome vase (Plate XIII, 1) which shows diagonal combings between girth-grooves, and with a fibula of Gaulish type[1] dating probably in the first half of I A.D. (see p. 106). Trumpington and Barnwell have yielded specimens similar to Hauxton 1, and I have recently found another on a living-floor at Foxton which was definitely pre-Roman. Late examples of both the Hauxton forms occurred at Silchester (May, 1916, Plate LXX), and a contemporary example of Hauxton 1 at Aylesford (A. J. Evans, 1890, Plate IX, 1).

Tazzas. These beautiful vessels, though not apparently represented at Aylesford, occurred at Welwyn, and are characteristic of the La Tène cremation culture. The ware in our local specimens is black to brownish-red on the surface, which shows a slight polish.

A fine early (probably I B.C.) example with hollow pedestal foot, from Haslingfield, is in the Cambridge Museum (Plate XII, 1),

---

[1] The *upper* fibula on Plate XIII is from Hauxton, the *lower* from Eriswell [S].

and two in the Audley End Museum are also of La Tène III date; these latter accompanied a burnt interment.

Tazza-like bowls are common; examples from Chesterton and Barrington are in the Cambridge Museum; the former contained burnt bones. A debased form from Ashwell [H], in the British Museum, was found with Roman remains and coins of I and II A.D.; the type, therefore, survived the Roman conquest.

A (? Romano-Belgic) form found locally is concave-sided, without cordons, has a bowl-shaped under-body and is of burnished black ware. An example from Chesterford, in the Audley End Museum, came from a Roman ashpit; others from the same site are in the Cambridge Museum (Plate XVI, 14).

Bowls, Globular Urns, and Beakers. Examples of these forms in the Cambridge Museum from Barton (? Haslingfield, see p. 258), Trinity Hall (Cambridge), Foxton, Ashwell [H] and Barrington—the two latter with holes pierced in their flat bases, a common La Tène feature—may be specially mentioned (see Plate XII, Nos. 4 and 5). A wide-mouthed pot from Great Chesterford, in the Cambridge Museum, has the characteristic Aylesford zigzag incised decoration on the shoulder; another, from Walsworth [Hitchin], had a conical cover with a knob terminal.

Urns with double cordons above the shoulder occurred at Aylesford (Evans, No. 6, Plate viii, and 7, Plate ix). A fine example from Odsey (Guilden Morden) is illustrated on my Plate XV; it has zigzag decoration incised with a smooth point in the characteristic La Tène manner, and may be dated round about the Christian era. A mass of iron rust adheres to the basal interior. Another example (handmade), from Stourbridge Common, Cambridge, also in the Museum, shows faint zigzags similarly incised extending from neck to base (Plate XII, 2); fragments of similar vessels from the War Ditches, Cherryhinton, and Grantchester, are also preserved.

Cognate forms, probably later in date, from Barnwell, Hauxton and Sutton, are to be seen in the Cambridge Museum.

Wide-mouthed bowl-shaped vessels, sometimes with broad cordons above the shoulder, are not uncommon in Romano-British cemeteries in the district; these may be derived from a La Tène type represented at Aylesford (A. J. Evans, 1890, Plate IX, 8).

Cinararies of hard paste with burnished girth-grooves, usually with a black wash on the upper part of the body, occur in the district. Examples from Litlington and Lakenheath, in the Cambridge Museum, and Icklingham (Bury Museum) may be cited. They

PLATE XIII

EARLY IRON AGE. POTTERY, MAINLY SEPULCHRAL AND OF AYLESFORD TYPES
No. 1, pp. 91, 106; Nos. 2 and 3, p. 93.

present some La Tène characteristics, but are almost certainly post-Claudian.

A curious vase, from Abbey Road, Barnwell, deserves brief mention. It is ovoid, of reddish paste covered with a black wash; two broad convex cordons decorated with rough incisions encircle the body, and the waist shows lattice pattern incised with a smooth point. A more refined and possibly later example of the class, showing metopic decoration, and probably related to No. 3, Plate ix, of the Aylesford series, was found near Royston; both are figured on Plate XIII, Nos. 2 and 3. Typologically the Barnwell urn is undoubtedly a development of the urn-with-cover of La Tène III date.

It will have been observed that many of these vases are in form and material transitional between La Tène and Roman; or rather that the wheelmade pottery usually described as Belgic lasted into the second half of I A.D. and profoundly influenced the wares made in Britain during the Roman occupation. A similar phenomenon is observable in the Belgic districts of Gaul.

La Tène influence is very marked in the case of the large olla from Castle Street figured on Plate XXIII, 1. Every element of its decoration —faint metopic and lattice patterns, neck cordons, and rows of incisions— occurs on pre-Roman wares.

The majority, if not all, of these vases were associated with interments; the significance of their distribution may therefore be considered when we deal with the contemporary burials.

In addition to wares of the Aylesford class, there is a wide range of pottery types, usually handmade, found in the district. These are not readily dateable, for the associations are for the most part unknown, and the examples fragmentary; but an analysis will suggest a possible sequence of types and indicate the importance of careful research on stratified Iron Age sites, such as the War Ditches.

The wheelmade vase, illustrated on Plate XV, from a grave at Mitchell's Hill, Icklingham, may first be mentioned. The decoration gives the clue to its relationships; it may be regarded as a late La Tène representative of wares such as those of Class E, Hengistbury (Bushe-Fox, Plate XX)[1], and not far removed in time or character from the fragmentary bowl, A 6, from Hauxton, dealt with on p. 83. The surface technique—clearly visible in the plate—is characteristic of a large group of Early Iron Age wares.

[1] This and subsequent references to Hengistbury finds relate to the *Report* already cited (p. 82).

Copies of this Icklingham vase in Romano-British ware are known: in decoration it resembles certain Anglian urns, and it has been regarded as post-Roman. It is relevant here to record, moreover, that it is extremely difficult to differentiate between the simple undecorated bowl-shaped vessels of the Early Iron and Anglo-Saxon periods respectively. One explanation may account for both these facts; the Anglo-Saxon wares of the V century A.D. may be held to present modifications of certain of the types in vogue in N. and N.W. Europe in the centuries immediately preceding the Christian era, the persistence of these types being due, it may be, to the freedom of the northern Teutonic tribes from foreign influence.

That the Icklingham vase is not an isolated instance in the Lark Valley is suggested by the presence of an ovoid pot in Bury Museum of the same school of decoration; its provenance is unfortunately not recorded, but it is certainly local, as Mr Barker, the curator, informs me.

There does not appear to be any pottery with flowing La Tène decoration in this district, or indeed in the Fenland Basin[1]. This is curious; for the style flourished at Hunsbury. Déchelette (1901), considers the culture thus represented to have been centred in Armorica; the ware is met with at Hengistbury and, of course, at Glastonbury. It may have reached Northants. (Hunsbury) by the ancient traffic-line afterwards followed by the Roman Foss Way (see Sketch-map B, p. 73).

Domestic Wares. Sectional diagrams of a representative series of the commoner, handmade, probably mainly domestic wares are given on Plates XIV and XVI. C 1 and C 2 (Plate XIV) are examples, the one probably from pit dwellings within Arbury Banks, Ashwell [H] (Beldam Collection), the other from Chesterford, of a coarse ware with roughly scored surface. These large vessels are doubtless cooking-pots; but there is a small beaker of the same type, from Coldham Common, in the British Museum, and a fragment from the La Tène site at Shoebury [E] is in the Colchester Museum. C 2 and C 3 show profiles resembling that of the Grantchester beaker, A 4; the history of the flat thickened rim present in these pieces is obscure. The fragment figured as No. 12 on Plate XVI, from Mutlow Hill, Wilbraham, gives us an upper limit of date for this feature, being associated with I A.D. Romano-British wares.

On the whole, it seems probable that C 1 and C 2 are cooking-pots of a date prior to the Christian era.

---

[1] A bowl with incised pattern of overlapping semicircles was, however, found in one of the Red Hills at Langenhoe on the Essex coast. F. W. Reader (1909, p. 191).

PLATE XIV

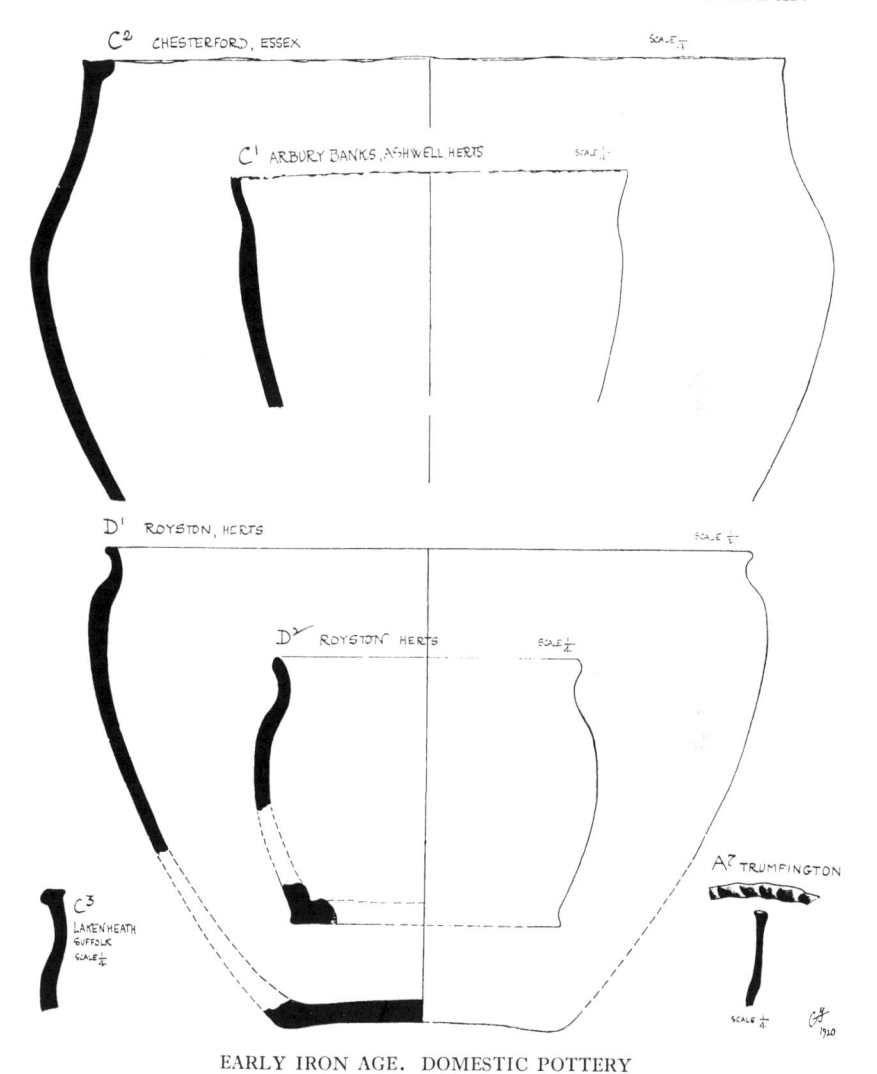

EARLY IRON AGE. DOMESTIC POTTERY
All one-quarter actual size.
C¹, pp. 94, 95, 109, 136; C², C³, pp. 94, 95; D¹, D², p. 95; A⁷, pp. 83, 95.

A pot from Freckenham [S], probably of similar character (being described as "of coarse black...clay ornamented apparently by the rough scratchings of a stick"), but with a well-defined neck and shoulder, more like No. 2, Plate XVI, from Newnham, is known to date from the beginning of the Christian era, for in it was a hoard of Icenian coins (see p. 88). It is figured and described by Montagu (1889).

Whatever their date may prove to be, these vessels doubtless preceded in domestic usage pots such as D 1 and D 2 (Plate XIV), which show the high shoulder, short neck and everted rim characteristic of certain Welwyn and Aylesford urns. They have bases either slightly dished (D 1) or flat and pinched out (D 2), the latter a characteristic local La Tène form[1]. D 1 has a profile of exceptional refinement. These two pots were reconstructed from a collection of sherds, obviously from a single site, in the neighbourhood of Royston; fragments of no less than five other similar pots were recognizable.

Beakers such as No. 1, Plate XVI, from Trumpington, with a flat base, present in their short necks and well-marked rounded shoulders a profile very characteristic of the period. Another nearly perfect example comes from Lakenheath. In paste (soft body, black or brown in colour), and surface quality (soapy or smooth), as well as in profile, these vessels are representative of a large group of local wares for which I B.C. seems a likely date. Lord's Bridge (Barton), Hauxton, Grantchester, Caesar's Camp (Sandy) and the War Ditches are sites additional to those already mentioned.

Types, presumably later, are distinguished by changes in rim-form. No. 10, Plate XVI (a roll-rim) and No. 11 (an oblique rim) may, from their resemblance to Romano-British forms, be provisionally dated in I A.D. No. 9, from Hauxton, with the same rim-form as No. 11, is an interesting pot. The upper surface of the rim has a cabled fluting; this at Hengistbury was a characteristic feature of certain late Hallstatt vessels, and is seen here also on the fragment A 7, from Trumpington (Plate XIV). Round the neck of the Hauxton pot runs a prominent applied cable moulding, and for it a late date in the La Tène period seems probable.

Another example of the persistence of decorative technique throughout the Early Iron Age may be noted. The depressions, produced by the fingernail, decorating the shoulders of the A class of pots (as in Plate x, No. 1, Hengistbury, of late Hallstatt type), show a projecting nick in the centre. A good example from Grimes Graves, Weeting, of uncertain date, is figured by R. A. Smith (1915 a, fig. 83).

[1] Mrs Cunnington has since shown me similar bases from the V–IV B.C. settlement site at All Cannings Cross, Wilts.

The writer found in the War Ditches a rudely made bowl of light red clay (Plate XVI, 6) similarly decorated, which has a La Tène pinched-out base; while the Mutlow Hill rim fragment (Plate XVI, 12), associated with Romano-British wares, shows the same ornamental detail.

Fragments of two shallow bowls of character unusual in the district come from the Early Iron Age site at Trumpington. One (Plate XVI, 5), with incurved rim, is highly polished; the other (Plate XVI, 8) has a carinated shoulder; in profile it resembles a Hengistbury type (No. 5, Plate xxvi, Hengistbury).

Round-bottomed shallow bowls with soapy surface, such as Plate XVI, 7, from Chesterford, closely resemble Anglo-Saxon "porringers."

The large pots with pierced lugs, commonly met with at Hengistbury, Hunsbury, Peterborough and other Early Iron Age sites, are represented in our district by one fragment from the War Ditches (not figured). In this connection examples of spoons or scoops with loop handles from Chesterford (Cambridge Museum), Sandy (Ransom collection) and Coldham Common (Ridgeway collection), deserve mention.

No. 4, Plate XVI, represents a class of wares met with in the northeast of our district—Reach and Brandon—characterized by a thin markedly everted rim; the exemplar is of sandy clay, evidently of local manufacture. The Reach beakers in Sir William Ridgeway's collection have rudely incised decoration not met with elsewhere in the district.

Fragments of pots and beakers of rough combed ware (Hauxton Mill), of a finer combed ware (War Ditches and Horningsea), of burnished vessels with lattice pattern—probably I A.D.—(Grantchester, War Ditches, and Trinity Hall) may be mentioned. Other forms and types occur in the collection in the Cambridge Museum; but consideration of these must await the discovery of less fragmentary remains. Sufficient has been said here to indicate the variety of these wares, assigned to the Early Iron Age, hitherto unrecognized and unrecorded in Cambridgeshire.

Shale Vases and Bowls

It will be convenient here to mention the two magnificent cordoned pedestalled vases of Kimmeridge shale from the Old Warden [B] cemetery, in the Cambridge and British Museums. One of these is figured on Plate XV, 3. Kimmeridge shale was frequently used for

PLATE XV

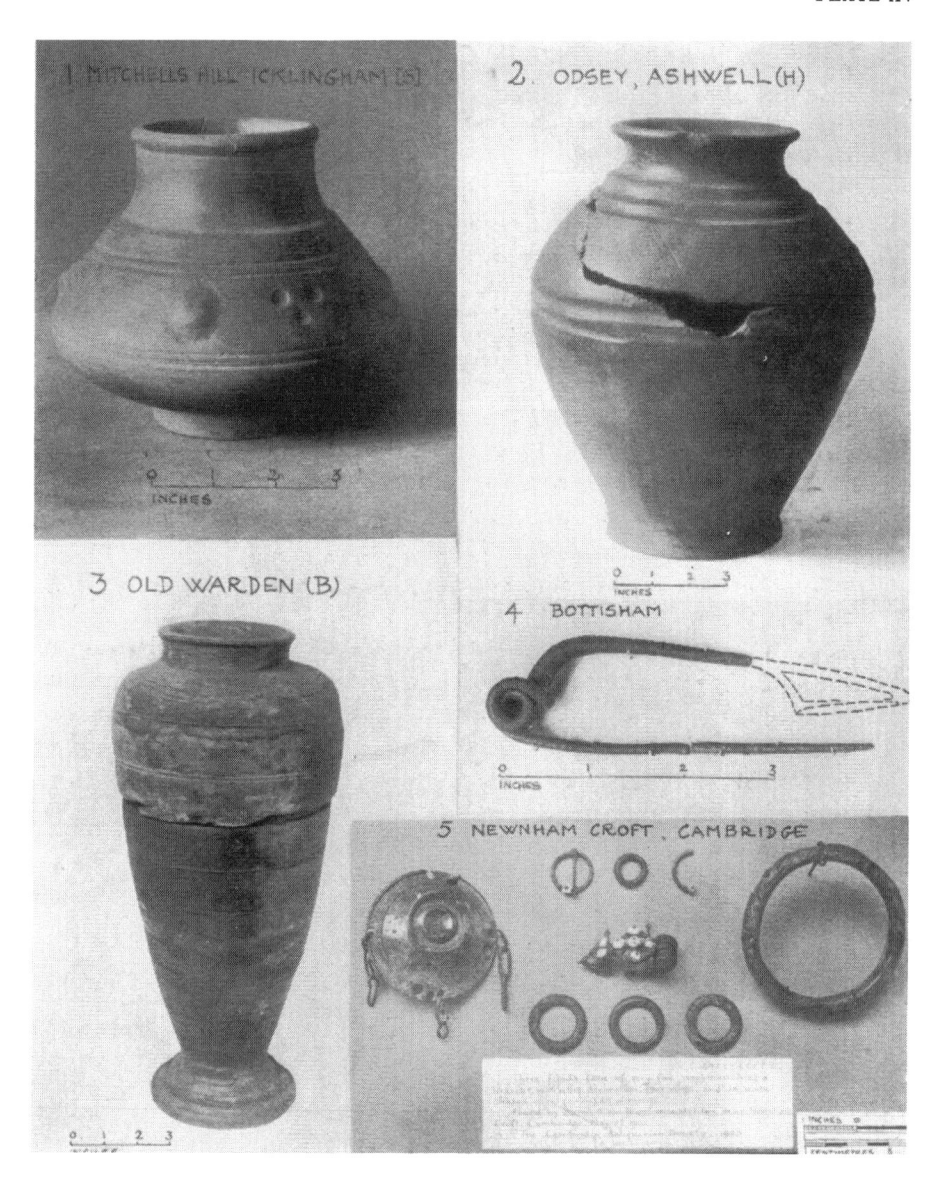

EARLY IRON AGE. POTTERY, SHALE VASE, AND BRONZES

No. 1, pp. 93, 94, 97; No. 2, p. 92; No. 3, pp. 96, 98; No. 4, p. 105; No. 5, pp. 81, 118.
Erratum. Odsey is in Guilden Morden parish.

ornaments such as bangles in the Early Iron and Roman Ages, but vessels of this material are rare in England, the majority having been found in East Anglia.

Fragments of a fine tazza of shale with pedestalled foot and concave sides, 11·5 inches in diameter at the rim, found at Barnwell, are in the Cambridge Museum, while two similar bowls were associated with the cremation interments at Chesterford referred to on p. 98. A fragment of a fourth tazza is in the Colchester Museum (No. 2397, 11).

It is probable that all these beautiful vessels owe their preservation to their use for sepulchral purposes; they are closely associated with the culture represented by pottery of Aylesford type. The two Chesterford tazzas would appear from associated objects to be of La Tène III date; and a similar date may be assigned to the Old Warden vases.

INTERMENTS

A. *By Inhumation*

Inhumation interments which can with fair certainty be ascribed to the second phase of the Age (La Tène III–IV) are two in number.

One, in a grave at Mitchell's Hill, Icklingham, was associated with the wheelmade vase already mentioned, equal in technique to the Aylesford urns but decorated in a fashion derived from an earlier style of art (p. 93). The site was probably a cemetery dating in I A.D. (Prigg, 1881, p. 154). Inhumation burials discovered near by, at West Stow Heath, are, I think, of the same date (*loc. cit.* p. 155).

At Lakenheath a skeleton was found, the dateable associated object being a fine "S-shaped" fibula, the design of which shows no trace of the formalization which the type afterwards suffered under Roman influence (G. Clinch, 1911, p. 271; R. A. Smith, 1909 a).

If these burials are correctly dated, it follows that inhumation was practised in the north-eastern part of the Cambridge Region at a time when the Kentish folk, presumably Belgic, were cremating their dead and forming family-group deposits at Aylesford; at a time, indeed, when at sites only a few miles away, Hitchin, Chesterford, Old Warden, the new customs associated with the new types of wheel-made pottery already described, were in use.

B. *By Cremation*

Cremation interment in our district in the Early Iron Age, apart from the obscure survivals referred to on p. 79, is associated with vessels of pottery and shale of the Aylesford class, and thus indicates here, as in the south-east of England, an intrusive culture. Both isolated burials and flat cemeteries are met with. The more important deposits may now be considered.

In Brambleshot Field, Great Chesterford, on a hill-slope to the east of the Roman town, two important interments dateable in I B.C. were discovered in 1856 by Neville (1857 b, and Neville MS.). The chief objects found are now in the Audley End Museum. The deposits consisted of two pairs of silver fibulae of admirable workmanship and design, each pair connected by a silver chain; an urn containing burnt bones; two elegant earthenware vases; the two tazzas of shale already mentioned, and the hafts of two iron knives. One vase and a fibula are figured in *B.M.G.* (1905, pp. 101 and 141).

At Great Chesterford also other interments possibly from an adjacent site associated with earthenware tazzas with feet are recorded. The evidence for cremation burial is that in one of these vases, now at Audley End Museum, a fragment of a bronze fibula which had been burnt was found.

Of the several barrel-shaped cordoned beakers found by Neville in his Chesterford excavations one at least is known to have contained burnt human bones; and the whole series may be assigned to a flat cremation cemetery or cemeteries of Aylesford type dating in La Tène III and IV.

Near by, at Wendens Ambo [E], urns of Aylesford type containing burnt bones (now in Walden Museum) have been found in a gravel pit in a field overlooking the Essex Cam Valley, close to the railway viaduct. This urn-field is the more interesting as it provides an example of continuous use of a given site for sepulchral purposes through a prolonged period, the Bronze Age urns previously described having come from the same spot. These later finds suggest the possibility of *late* Bronze Age date for the earlier urns; if this be not the case we must suppose that a cemetery disused for many years was re-used by accident by a later people; that the cemetery was in continuous use seems more probable.

The cremation burials north of Quint's Hill at Old Warden [B] were associated with "two hoops of iron" (evidently the remains of a situla); two "earthen urns of large size with long handles"—almost certainly amphorae of Italo-Greek type; and the two fine cordoned vases of Kimmeridge shale already mentioned, which were inverted and contained only "ashes and earth."

See Dryden (1845, p. 20). Inskip (1851, p. 169) confirms the conclusion

PLATE XVI

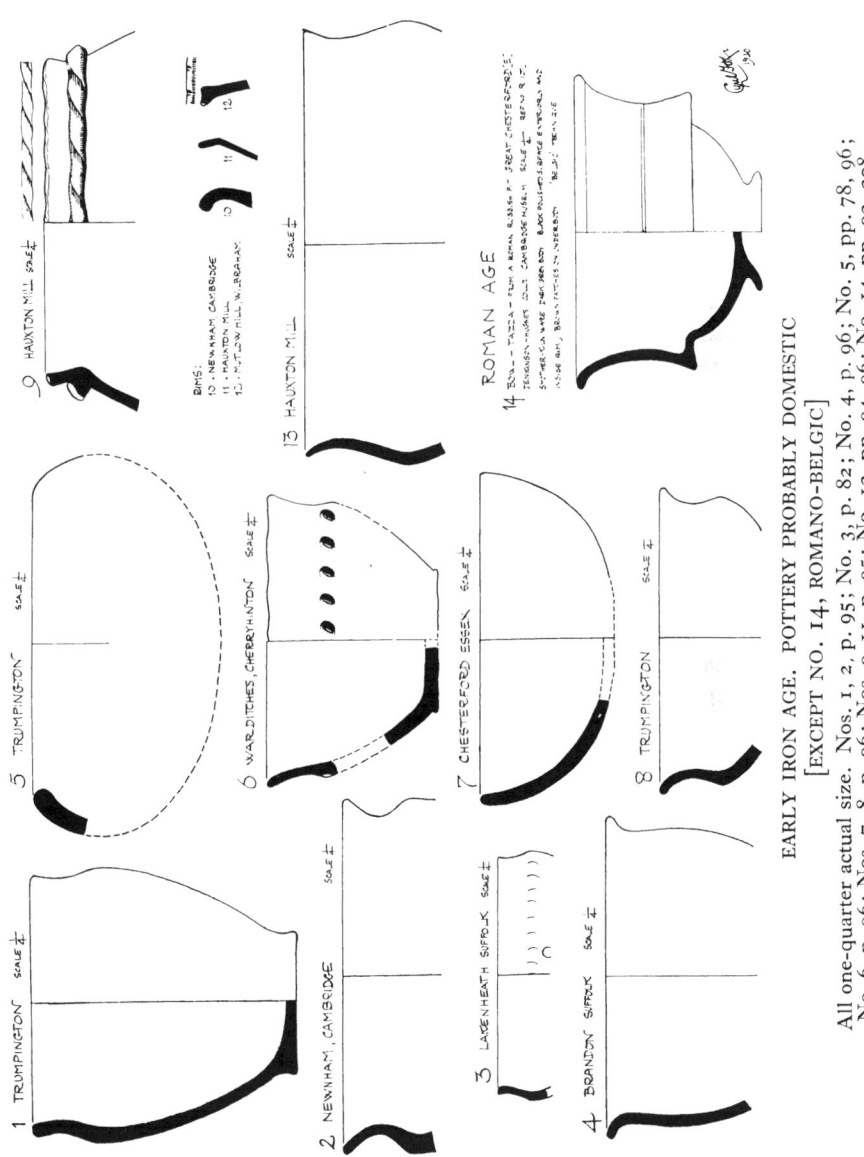

EARLY IRON AGE. POTTERY PROBABLY DOMESTIC
[EXCEPT NO. 14, ROMANO-BELGIC]

All one-quarter actual size. Nos. 1, 2, p. 95; No. 3, p. 82; No. 4, p. 96; No. 5, pp. 78, 96; No. 6, p. 96; Nos. 7, 8, p. 96; Nos. 9–11, p. 95; No. 12, pp. 94, 96; No. 14, pp. 92, 208.

THE EARLY IRON AGE

as to the character of the "earthen urns." There is a La Tène III mirror in Bedford Library from another site in the same parish (p. 108); this was probably associated with an interment (R. A. Smith, 1909 d, p. 333).

More closely related, perhaps, in sepulchral custom to the Aylesford interments were the Walsworth (Hitchin [H]) burials; here a line of group interments was found with urns of pedestal, barrel and other forms (Ransom, 1890, figured). Since similar pottery has been found in the neighbouring parishes of Shillington (Ransom collection), Letchworth (see p. 91), Arlesey (British Museum) and Stotfold (British Museum) it is probable that the new culture had taken firm hold in the valley of the Ivel.

Urns of Aylesford types have from time to time been found in gravel pits at Chesterton; one is *known* to have contained burnt bones. The fine tazza of shale and other vases in the Cambridge Museum from the opposite side of the river at Barnwell were, there can be little doubt, also associated with burials; and we have here two cemeteries of late La Tène folk who dwelt in the neighbourhood of the present town.

It is unnecessary to describe all the cemeteries of this type, but a burial at Elveden deserves special mention, coming as it does from a district (N.W. Suffolk) otherwise barren of cremation interments. The deposit consisted of a two-handled bronze-plated wooden tankard adorned with repoussé medallions together with three globular earthenware urns with striated decoration. That the interment was of late date is highly probable; the middle of the I century A.D. may be suggested. See H. Prigg (1889), A. J. Evans (1890, p. 351, and fig. 10), *B.M.G.* (1905, fig. 99), G. E. Fox (1911, p. 304).

Two of the most remarkable burials of the La Tène III period found in this country, those at Welwyn [H], were associated with a wide range of objects including La Tène fire-dogs or andirons and amphorae of Italo-Greek type (R. A. Smith, 1912).

Firedogs and amphorae accompanied cremation interments of character similar to those at Welwyn, but of Roman (mid I century) date, found near Stanfordbury Farm, Southill [B] in 1832 and 1834.

The finds were imperfectly recorded, and there are many obscurities in the account written by Dryden in 1845; the illustrations, moreover, are in certain respects inaccurate. But Inskip, the discoverer, did not publish the finds (accounts in his name appear in 1845 and 1851; they appear to be derived from Dryden's memoir), and full credit is due to Dryden who, some thirteen years after the discovery, collected and published all the information that was then available. A recent analysis of this find and others of similar character by R. A. Smith (1912, pp. 9 ff.) may be consulted;

7—2

half a dozen British sites where amphorae of Italo-Greek type have been found are recorded in his paper. To this list four local sites may be added (see p. 101). The most important objects from Stanfordbury are in the Cambridge Museum.

The most remarkable objects in the pit first discovered, which was floored with Roman tiles, but which otherwise resembled a large grave, were what Dryden called an "extraordinary kitchen range," consisting of a tripod of iron with dependent hooks—the latter identical with several found in Bigbury Camp, Kent (Dawkins, 1902)—the rings of a cauldron, a pair of firedogs and four spits. There were also six amphorae of Italo-Greek type and a bone flute. Numerous vessels of terra sigillata and other ware, a bronze oinochoè, bowl and skillet were the chief distinctively Roman objects in this interment. Plate XXVI, 1, shows two Roman bronzes; Plate XX three of the sigillata vessels. Plate XVII shows the chief iron objects, and one amphora. (This latter may be contrasted with a typical specimen of the Roman Age on Plate XXIII, 3, which contained a cremation interment and was found at Haslingfield.) The pointed ends to the tripod suggest that the whole outfit was designed for use in the open.

The place where the associated objects were found is described as a vault; but it apparently was not roofed, but a mere pit, floored, and filled with earth subsequent to the interment. It may perhaps be a developed example of the grave pit of Aylesford type such as that figured by A. J. Evans (1890, p. 318) which contained the La Tène III pail.

The vault at Mount Bures [E], the contents of which are figured by C. R. Smith (1852), was probably of similar character.

The second pit, somewhat later in date, contained two amphorae, two iron bars of unknown use[1] and the bronze mounts and plating of an oaken box showing La Tène decoration (Plate XVIII). A shale armlet, "melon" beads, two silver buckles, two La Tène IV fibulae, four glass vessels and a few sigillata dishes were the chief additional objects found.

The civilization revealed by these burials, La Tène overlaid by Italian influences, is met with in Artois, where, at St Nicolas-lès-Arras, there were discovered similar pits containing cremation interments associated with bronze ewers, amphorae, numerous pottery vessels and iron frames of Welwyn type (R. A. Smith, 1912, p. 12).

A firedog of the same type as those at Stanfordbury, but with the ox-head terminals of finer design and, therefore, probably earlier in date, was found early in the XIX century at Lord's Bridge in

---

[1] But see R. A. Smith (1912, p. 10).

PLATE XVII

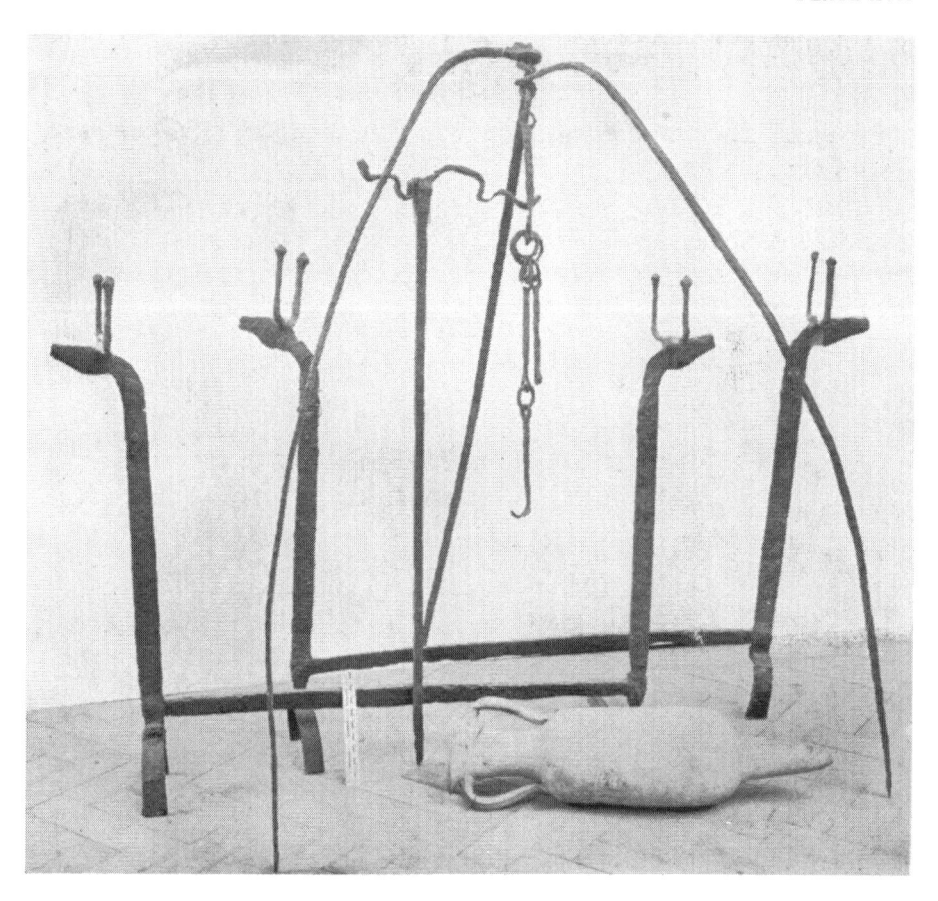

EARLY IRON AGE. OBJECTS ASSOCIATED WITH A BURIAL BY CREMATION; STANFORDBURY, SOUTHILL [B]

See pp. 99–100.

NOTES. The scale on the plate is 7 inches in length. The amphora is one of six, the 'spit' one of four. The latter is imperfect, and it is probable that the hook on the left side of the head, affixed by a restorer, belongs to the other end of the bar (see Dryden, 1845, pl. 3). The 'pothook' also is imperfect; there were originally two terminal hooks, one for each ring of the pot.

Barton parish, and is now in the Cambridge Museum (Walker, 1908 b, Plate xviii)[1].

Nothing of the circumstances of the discovery is known, save that a chain with six collars for conducting prisoners, also in the museum, was found at the same time. Similar chains of Early Iron Age date were found in Bigbury Camp, Kent (Dawkins, 1902). The site was of some importance. A Roman road crosses the ford of the Bourn near by, and there is a tumulus of Roman date immediately adjacent (p. 194). Moreover, evidence of occupation in La Tène times has recently come to light (p. 102).

Whether the Lord's Bridge firedog was associated with an interment cannot be known, but it is improbable that it would have survived uninjured for so prolonged a period unless it had been carefully buried.

The significance and distribution of interments of the Stanfordbury class, associated with firedogs, amphorae, and sacrificial utensils of Italian origin is discussed by R. A. Smith in the paper already several times quoted. He notes the persistence of elements of the ritual thus exemplified in burials of Roman date at Bartlow and elsewhere which will be considered in Chapter V.

It seems probable that much wine and oil was imported from the Mediterranean in the century preceding the Claudian invasion; four other sites in our district, at Lindsell and Thaxted [E] (Walden Museum), Dam Hill, Trumpington, and Jesus Lane, Cambridge (Cambridge Museum), have yielded amphorae of Italo-Greek type, in one case (Lindsell) known to have accompanied a burnt interment.

Arretine Ware. Amphorae of Greek type are not the only evidence of trade with the Mediterranean in the century preceding the Roman occupation met with in the district. Barrington and Foxton have each yielded vases of Arretine fabric of the Augustan Age. The fine crater from the latter parish, by Xanthvs, in the Cambridge Museum, was found in an amphora, together with platters of Belgic ware from N. Gaul (p. 201 and Plates XXII, 3, 3 A, and XX, 4, 5. See also Babington (1852), Walters (1908 b), Haverfield (1917), Oswald and Pryce (1920, p. 5)). That these were associated with a cremation interment is rendered the more probable by the discovery in 1818 of an undoubted burial of this character at Lord's Bridge, Barton; a rude stone slab covered the mouth of an amphora within

---

[1] Since these firedogs are of the greatest rarity in Western Europe it is remarkable that four sites in East Anglia should have yielded examples. See R. A. Smith (1912, pp. 6, 7, 8).

which was a "black terra-cotta vase of elegant form half filled with human bones, also two other smaller vessels of red terra-cotta with handles" (E. D. Clarke, 1821, p. 61).

Wheelmade Iron Age pottery, indications of settlement, and an inhumation interment have recently been found by Mrs H. M. Chadwick at Lord's Bridge probably within 100 yards of the site of this burial.

Topographical Range of the Aylesford Cremation Culture

We may now deal with the problems presented by the topographical distribution of pottery of Aylesford type, of which the pedestal urn is the most striking form, and of the rite of cremation.

The Aylesford class of wares is in our district commonest in the corn-growing belt, drained by tributaries of the Great Ouse, extending from Hitchin [H] to Sandy [B], and in the upper Cam Valley, being found at eighteen sites in these regions. Typical forms have not up to the present been found in the north-east of our district or in the southern fens (the class being represented only by late and possibly post-Claudian forms as at Elveden and Lakenheath [S] and Sutton in the Isle). The most northerly sites at present recorded are Milton and Barnwell. At Peterborough, as Mr Wyman Abbott informed me, they do not occur, though remarkable quantities of the coarser late handmade wares (as well as of the earlier La Tène forms) are here met with.

This distribution thus accords with that of the coins minted at Verulamium and Camulodunum; the Aylesford class of pottery was not, it would appear, in the La Tène III and early IV periods in use in that area which we have seen reason to regard as Icenian territory.

Cremation burials associated with "Aylesford" pottery are common in the Ivel (upper Great Ouse) Valley, and in the Cam Valley as far north as Chesterton, but (again with one reservation, Elveden) the rite was apparently not in use in the La Tène III and early IV periods in the Icenian territory adjacent.

It is possible that cremation was not so universal in the Cam Valley as was the pottery normally associated with it in the latter part of the Early Iron Age; Belgic bowls associated with skeletons at the War Ditches, Cherryhinton, suggest that inhumation here survived the Roman Conquest (see p. 190). A reoccupation of this hill fort by Icenian folk in the middle of I A.D. provides an alternative explanation.

There is no evidence that in the west of our district the Aylesford culture extended further north than Old Warden and Sandy in the

Great Ouse Valley. A settlement site at Alconbury [Hunts.] has yielded late La Tène pottery[1] but no cordoned vessels.

Any conclusions drawn from the facts already detailed must be regarded as provisional, the material available for generalization being so limited; but they strongly suggest that the wave of Belgic conquest, or to use a more guarded form of expression, the influence of the new culture held to be associated therewith, spent itself on the edge of the southern fens.

That this culture is found to be dominant in areas which are certainly Catuvellaunian (N.W. Herts. and S.E. Beds.) suggests but does not prove this tribe to be Belgian.

Close correlations such as those existing between the burials at Arras (France) and Stanfordbury and Welwyn, referred to on pp. 99 ff., and the fact that a La Tène III bowl-shaped vase from Sandy, of rare type, is duplicated in a cremation burial near Soissons, at first sight suggest Belgic conquest in our district and not the infiltration of a novel culture. (See R. A. Smith, 1905, p. 349.) The explanation may however be found in the existence of a political union which facilitated trade. Diviciacus, king of the Suessiones about B.C. 70, held sovereignty in Britain (Caesar, *B.G.* II, 4).

The evidence hitherto examined throws no light on the Trinovantian boundaries; but the upper Stour Valley which has yielded a few pots of Aylesford type at Long Melford, Sudbury and Great Waldingfield[2], as well as many British coins, may be in our district the northern boundary of this presumably Belgic kingdom, in which the Aylesford culture was well established.

Numerous cremation cemeteries are known in Essex. Much fine pottery of the class is in the Colchester Museum. Very little has been found to the north of the lower Stour Valley either in Suffolk or in Norfolk. The boundaries of the Icenian kingdom were thus probably similar to those of East Anglia in 600 A.D. (see pp. 289-90).

This culture may then have reached our district not only from the south-west (Verulamium) along the chalk belt, but also from Camulodunum, *via* the Colne and Stour Valleys. Another possible line of infiltration is that from the Thames *via* the Lea-Stort-Cam Valley route; the existence of a La Tène III cemetery at Hallingbury near Bishop's Stortford, at no great distance from the settlements at Chesterford and Wenden, renders this not improbable; the route may have been in Trinovantian territory, but we have no means of settling the point (see p. 140).

[1] In the possession of Dr Garrood.
[2] Examples in Bury Museum and Sudbury Institute.

Reference to the Sketch-map (B) of Eastern England will make these arguments clear; briefly put, it would seem probable that Cambridge marks the northern limit of Catuvellaunian and Trinovantian influence, and of the extension in the Fenland Basin of the intrusive cremation culture up to, say, the first quarter of I A.D.

HOARD

The important hoard of scrap bronze from Santon Downham [S], now in the Cambridge Museum, was found in 1897, together with a few iron tools in a large bronze cauldron, by a labourer. The cauldron appears to have been a water-clock; a similar one has been found at Baschurch in Shropshire. The more important products of the La Tène culture were two openwork bronze plates for harness[1] with red champlevé enamel (one is reproduced on the cover), and a horse's bit (with these the Polden Hill finds may be compared), ferules of cast bronze, a bronze linchpin and six bronze nave-bands—the whole probably being chariot furniture. Amongst the objects of a different character were a thin bronze band embossed with a repeating scroll pattern and other fittings probably of a wooden casket; a bronze plate with "duck-shaped" rivet-heads and engraved rosettes characteristic of the latest phase of La Tène art in this district, graven discs of bronze, fragments of coloured glass, a piece of leather and a steelyard and weight. Ten of the eleven brooches in the hoard are of I century forms met with on Roman as well as La Tène sites (see Plate XVIII, and pp. 106-7).

The distinctively Roman objects include a fine bronze jug with trefoil spout and the bronze handle of a patella with an animal's-head terminal (see p. 213). R. A. Smith, in his analysis of the finds (1909 e), dates the deposit about the middle of I A.D., a few years after the arrival of Claudius. The more important objects are illustrated in Smith's paper.

BUCKETS, BRONZE VESSELS, FIBULAE, WEAPONS, ETC.

Wooden Buckets, etc. with bronze mounts; water-clocks and other bronze vessels. Buckets made of wooden staves with bronze mounts are not infrequently met with in the La Tène period[2]; the technique, indeed, may be held to have survived the Roman conquest and influenced the Anglo-Saxon metal-workers.

---

[1] Decayed leather was adherent to the back of one of these.
[2] See A. J. Evans (1890, p. 360) for a discussion of the origins of the type in Italy and the Eastern Mediterranean.

Fragments of bronze, probably from two buckets or tankards, were included in the Santon Downham hoard, and a complete bronze-mounted two-handled tankard was associated with the Elveden interment (see p. 99).

Staves and the bronze mounts of a wooden bucket from Great Chesterford are in the Cambridge Museum. The bronze plates show embossed decoration of provincial-Roman character, but the handles have applied boar's-head terminals with enamelled buttons—typical La Tène design. The phase of development shown by this situla is probably to be dated in the middle third of I A.D.; it is also represented in the museum by a small bronze bowl (fragmentary) acquired at the same time and from the same site—possibly, therefore, found in association with the situla.

That the bronze mountings of a wooden box, with embossed La Tène scroll work, should have been found in the second of the two Stanfordbury vaults (see p. 100, and Plate XVIII) emphasizes the lateness in date of work of this type.

Several thin bronze vessels, some of which are probably water-clocks (having a minute perforation in the basal centre), have been found in the district. They are of two types. (*a*) A shouldered cauldron-shaped vessel like the Santon Downham example—one from Ickling-ham [S] is in the British Museum and two, probably from the fens near Ely, are in the Cambridge Museum. (*b*) A shallow bowl with an omphalos base and with turned-in rim; examples from Sandy [B] and Lakenheath Fen [S] are in the British Museum, and there are specimens in the Cambridge Museum, one from the fens near Mildenhall. The latter may be the earlier type, since the Santon Downham example is undoubtedly of I A.D.

The resemblance in form of these vessels to some of the earlier types of pottery found in the district is noticeable. For illustrations and a discussion of the problems connected with them see R. A. Smith (1915 *b*).

Fibulae. The finest examples of the characteristic La Tène III fibula, which has a bilateral spring (the chord of which is frequently hooked round the base of the bow) and in which the foot forms an open or fretted plate, are those of silver from the cremation burial at Chesterford (p. 98), one of which is figured in *B.M.G.* 1905, p. 101. Others of bronze from this site are in Audley End Museum, and a small finely-wrought example from Lakenheath is in the Cambridge Museum, where also are typical though damaged specimens from Bottisham Fen (Plate XV, 4) and Stanfordbury.

Simpler and smaller forms of the same type with solid or pierced plate—La Tène IV in date—are commonly met with, and examples from all parts of our district then inhabited are in the local museum. Many are undoubtedly post-Claudian: the knobbed foot may perhaps serve to differentiate the late forms from the earlier.

The "S" fibula from Lakenheath, associated with an interment, has already been referred to (p. 97). Numerous examples of the Backworth type of fibula[1], and of harp-shaped fibulae with or without pierced catch-plate occur in the district; but the majority of these are probably not earlier than the second half of I A.D. and will be referred to in Chapter V. A harp-shaped fibula from the Santon Downham hoard (50 A.D.) is figured on Plate XVIII, 5.

The type of brooch in which "the bow takes the form of a ribbed band passing through the centre of a circular or lozenge-shaped plate and widens out into a fan-shaped ornament over the catch"—like a bird's tail—occurs in the district. It is of Gaulish origin (developed from a La Tène III form) and was, on the Continent, common in the first half of I A.D. Several were included in the Santon Downham hoard, and one occurred with a burial at Hauxton. Typologically early (La Tène) forms, as well as forms in which the design is simplified, occurred in association at Santon Downham, and all must therefore be considered together. Two of the former are figured by R. A. Smith (1909 *e*, p. 159) and a third (with an annular plate moving freely on the bow) is shown on Plate XIII A (Hauxton). The simpler form is well represented by Fig. 8, Plate XVIII, from Santon Downham.

All these brooches can be dated about the middle of I A.D. or earlier. Such are said not to be common in Britain; but the type was acclimatized, and related forms are found on Roman sites.

For a La Tène III continental example see Déchelette, 1914, Plate XII, fig. 13. Notes on the history of this class of fibulae will be found in Bushe-Fox (1913, pp. 23-24), from whom my description is quoted, and R. A. Smith (1909 *e*, p. 159).

A bronze plate fibula with iron pin, "embossed with the figure of a somewhat grotesque quadruped"—work of the school of the Aylesford and Marlborough buckets—was included in the Santon Downham hoard (Plate XVIII, 9).

The fibula types in the Santon Downham hoard not yet referred to are two in number and are figured on Plate XVIII, Nos. 6 and 7. They are provincial-Roman rather than La Tène in character (that the change of type occurs so early is doubtless due to the Romaniza-

---

[1] No early example of the form with trumpet-shaped head of which this is a derivative is known to occur in the district.

PLATE XVIII

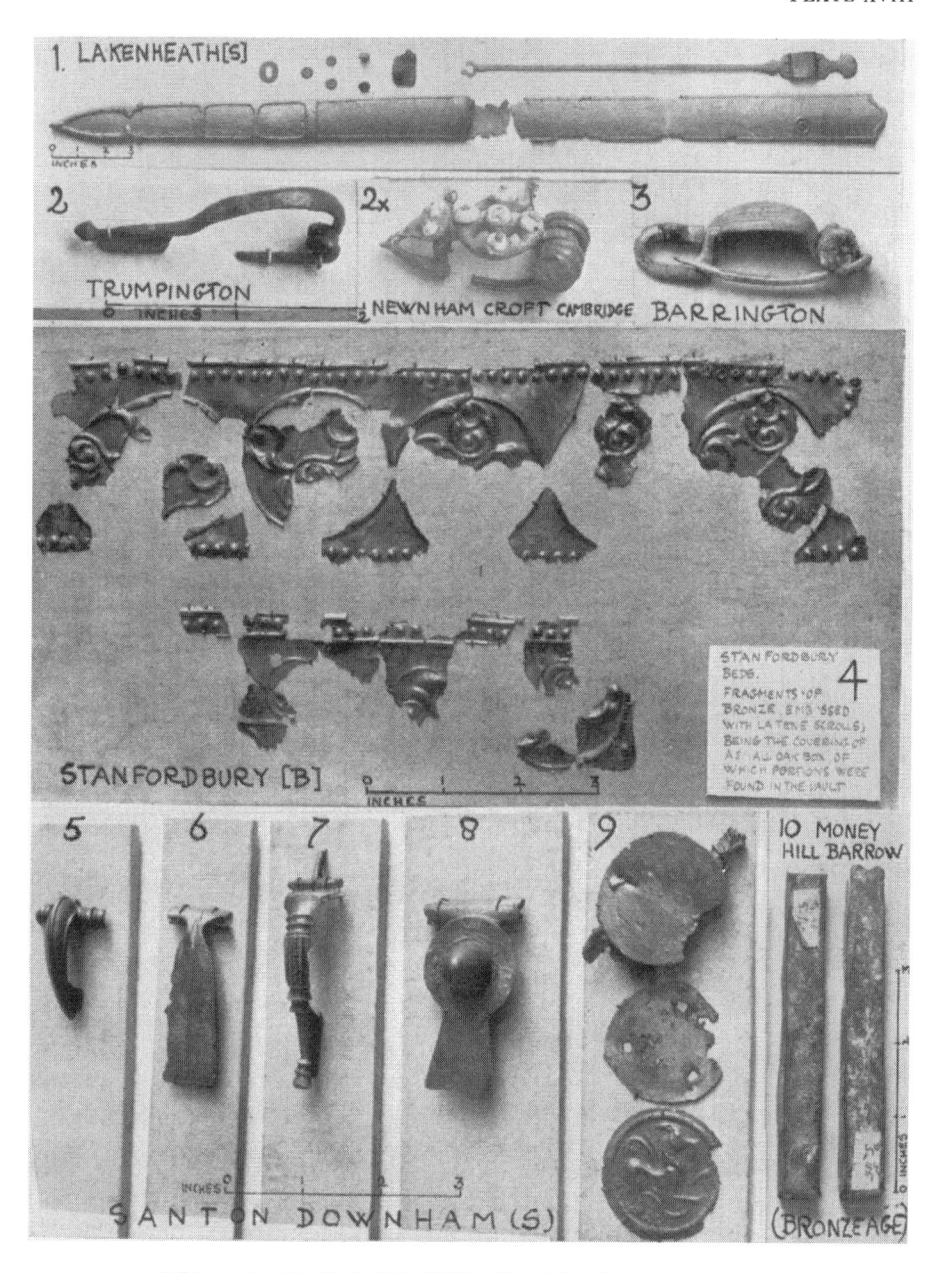

NOS. 1–9. BRONZE AND IRON OBJECTS. EARLY IRON AGE
NO. 10. COPPER BARS. BRONZE AGE

No. 1, p. 107; No. 2, p. 74; No. 2×, p. 81; No. 3, p. 75; No. 4, pp. 100, 105;
Nos. 5–9, pp. 104, 106, 107; No. 10, pp. 36, 63.

THE EARLY IRON AGE

tion of Gaul); but the whole series merits record here as indicating the range of forms met with in about 50 A.D.

One has a broad wedge-shaped nearly flat bow, heavily tinned, with a delicate incised wavy median line, the spring having a cylindrical cover; the other has a hinged pin, a foot-plate pierced with a round hole and a high bow with deep and sharply cut transverse and longitudinal mouldings. These are not mentioned by R. A. Smith in his otherwise exhaustive analysis of the hoard. The wavy line decoration in the fibula No. 6 is a native device, being met with on a La Tène torc at Newstead (Curle, 1911, Plate XC, and pp. 335–6). Fibulae resembling No. 7 were found at Hod Hill, Dorset (*B.M.G.* 1922, p. 52).

An important fibula type with hinged pin, dating in the La Tène III and IV sub-periods, is that which has been termed Aucissa from the fact that many are thus inscribed. Some specimens found in Britain may be of Gaulish origin, but plain forms such as those from Barrington and Cambridge, in the Cambridge Museum, were doubtless made in this country and may be post-Claudian (see Bushe-Fox, 1913, p. 24, and *B.M.G.* 1922, p. 53).

Examples of the fibulae with flat slightly wedge-shaped bow and unpierced catch-plate, having the chord of the spring hooked round the bow, occur in the north-east of our district—at Eriswell and Lakenheath. They are late La Tène IV in character.

Pins. Characteristic forms of the later La Tène periods from several sites in the district are in the Cambridge Museum. The most interesting is an "ibex-headed" pin from Newnham, similar to one from Sandy [B] associated with a La Tène III vase (p. 103).

Weapons. The finest example from the district of a La Tène III weapon is the bronze sword-sheath (still containing the rusted remains of the sword) from Lakenheath (Plate XVIII), which is in the Cambridge Museum. Another such was found at Icklingham (Clinch, 1911, p. 276).

A dagger chape from Cambridge showing basket pattern decoration (probably La Tène IV) is also in the local museum. The strap-work of a shield in the Walden Museum, knives from the Foxton settlement site (Cambridge Museum) and a few iron spearheads of La Tène types with whole sockets practically complete the list.

Horse trappings. It might have been expected that the importance of the chariot in the La Tène period would have resulted in numerous finds of horse trappings and chariot fittings in the Cambridge Region, but the fragment of a horse-bit from Cambridge

(Cambridge Museum), and a cap or boss, probably from a chariot axle, found in Burwell Fen (British Museum) are practically the only examples of this class of bronzes dateable in the La Tène III and IV sub-periods, except the Santon Downham harness plates, bit and other objects already referred to.

It may here be noted that pony shoes of iron with frilled outer margin, of the type which may possibly prove to be of Celtic origin, have been found in the peaty bed of the Slade at Walden (Walden Museum) and at Bury St Edmunds (Bury Museum).

Domestic Appliances. Weaving-combs of bone of La Tène type, from Malton, Haslingfield, Wandlebury Camp and Hauxton, are in the Cambridge Museum, and a pottery spindle-whorl from the living-floor at Foxton is in the collection. Triangular pottery loom-weights from Abington Pigotts (p. 110) and other sites are certainly British, but the earthenware rings in the Cambridge Museum, derived from several parishes in the district, are all probably of Anglo-Saxon date. Shears of iron, used by the weaver, have been recorded in cremation interments at Hitchin and Hauxton.

The characteristic Roman querns or handmills of imported Niedermendig lava are common on Roman sites in the Cambridge district, as are the native beehive querns of Hertfordshire pudding-stone; but in addition to these a number of rude mills, consisting of a large stone with flat or concave surface and a smaller muller with a corresponding ground face, have been found locally. Two pairs (possibly of the Early Bronze Age) come from Mildenhall and Bottisham, and consist of large slabs of flint (with the upper surface ground flat) and mullers of the same material (see *C.A.S. Report*, 1861, p. 8). From the Early Iron Age site at Hauxton Mill a number of slabs and mullers of sandstone (derived from the "drift") were obtained during the excavations for coprolites in 1889 (Hughes, 1891 *b*, Plate IV). In the Sedgwick Museum local examples of all the types mentioned above are exhibited.

Enamels. A few characteristic La Tène enamelled objects have been found in the district; the majority have been referred to in the previous paragraphs. The open-work bronze plates from the Downham hoard and the mirror from Old Warden (figured by R. A. Smith, 1909 *d*, p. 333) are especially noticeable. The horse-bits from Cambridge and Santon Downham had enamelled roundels. Lockets, seal-boxes and fibulae of Roman type, enamelled in a variety of colours[1],

---

[1] In the La Tène period red appears to have been the only colour used.

show the craft persisting throughout the following period, while the enamelled mounts of a situla from Mildenhall point to a revival in Anglo-Saxon times which will be discussed in a later chapter.

EARTHWORKS, SETTLEMENTS AND COMMUNICATIONS OF THE EARLY IRON AGE

Dykes

There is slight but definite negative evidence for the pre-Roman origin of the Devil's Dyke and, as has been noted already, the indirect evidence for its use as a barrier late in the La Tène period is very strong. It is fully described in the succeeding chapter, as are other dykes which are possibly pre-Roman.

Settlements

Our knowledge of the sites occupied by the Early Iron Age peoples is scanty, but greater than that of either of the preceding periods.

Of fortified settlements the War Ditches, Cherryhinton, claims precedence as the only one of which we have detailed knowledge. Pottery from the lower layers of silt in the fosse, preserved in the Cambridge Museum, indicates occupation probably from La Tène I onwards. No remains of the Bronze Age were found in the excavations carried out in 1904 and subsequent years, and the earthwork may be regarded as of Iron Age origin.

For references and a description see p. 136. The skeletons found in the fosse are discussed on p. 114.

Caesar's Camp (Sandy [B]), Wandlebury (Stapleford), and Arbury Banks (Ashwell [H]) were all occupied if not constructed during this period.

Undecorated smooth soapy handmade pottery, dated in I B.C by Mr R. A. Smith, was dug up within the enceinte of Caesar's Camp in 1905 and is now in the Cambridge Museum; Wandlebury has yielded bone weaving-combs and British coins; a portion of a cooking-pot in the local museum, obtained from Arbury Banks (see p. 135 and Plate XIV), suggests that the pit dwellings and hearths within this entrenchment may be those of a I B.C. settlement.

All these earthworks are discussed in Chapter IV. What is almost certainly a fortified Iron Age village site was disclosed during coprolite diggings at Barrington in 1889. Within an area of unknown size, probably completely enclosed by a rectangular fosse (14 feet wide and 8 feet deep in the sector examined), was a collection of roughly circular pits, distributed in no recognizable system, some of which were as much as 13 feet in diameter and 8 feet deep, "but in general they were smaller and shallower." "Rude pottery," doubtless of types with which we are now familiar[1], as well as better class wares definitely Romano-British, was found in these pits together with greasy earth and bones split to extract the marrow. It is unfortunate that no examination of the infilling of the fosse was made. See Foster (1883, pp. 7-10).

Pigott (1888) records the discovery of hut circles, a gold coin of Cunobeline, pottery of Aylesford type and other remains at Abington Pigotts.

In 1922 I examined cooking-trenches and a refuse-pit at Foxton dating in the first half of I A.D. Numerous sherds of soft paste wares both hand- and wheel-made were found; these showed close correspondence with some of the War Ditches' pottery, but nothing resembling the Hallstatt pots described on p. 82 was found. Sufficient fragments of a Belgic vase of fine red ware and a bowl of late La Tène type were available for reconstruction. A spinning-whorl and knives of iron were found, and numerous bones of domestic animals—horse (pony), pig, ox, etc.

Fragments of burnt animal bones were associated with the handmade pottery already referred to (p. 96) as having been found on the edge of the fen at Reach. At Grimes Graves, Weeting [N], living-floors have been recorded, possibly of the first phase of the Iron Age; the La Tène potsherds found by Fox and Palmer (1923) adjacent to Mutlow Hill, Wilbraham, mark on the other hand a settlement of the Roman Age, being associated with Romano-British wares.

In Milton parish, on the site of the Sewage Farm, finds indicative of a Romano-British settlement were discovered some years ago (Hughes, 1903 c). The presence here of cordoned urns of Aylesford type suggests that it was occupied prior to the Claudian conquest.

Though no deposits of pre-Roman date are recorded from the site of Roman Chesterford, the existence of a La Tène III cremation cemetery in the immediate neighbourhood of the Roman town is established. Native pottery and coins from "Chesterford" in museums and private collections are additional evidence of pre-Roman settlement.

Certain objects obtained by Walker (1908 c) from ancient living-floors at Barton Moats, led him to conclude that a "Late Celtic

---

[1] In the Camb. Mus. (Conybeare Coll.) are two handmade La Tène pots probably from this site.

THE EARLY IRON AGE

people" had occupied the spot in I A.D.; but there was little to differentiate this settlement from a poor Romano-British one.

The cooking places of a living-floor on Barnham Common, Thetford [N], found by W. G. Clarke (1915, p. 41), yielded much fragmentary pottery dated in I B.C., which I have seen; it was handmade and not of Aylesford type.

At Alconbury [Hunts.] within the angle formed by the junction of the Alconbury and Ellington brooks, gravel digging recently revealed a shallow pit containing charcoal, bones of animals and fragmentary pottery, now in the possession of Dr Garrood. The latter was both wheel- and hand-made, but Aylesford types were not present. The roll-rim of one piece indicated late date, but the paste, finish and character of the sherds were purely Celtic and we have here indications of La Tène IV settlement.

The traces of settlement here recorded are scanty, but they all seem to emphasize the poverty of the inhabitants of the Cambridge Region in the Early Iron Age. The primitive life which these refuse-pits indicate was however not inconsistent with material wealth and even luxury; fragments of a red ware vase of the finest workmanship were found in the midden at Foxton, and the owners of the tazzas of shale and silver fibulae found at Chesterford, and of the grave-furniture found at Stanfordbury, probably lived in wooden houses of some pretensions.

The most interesting settlement sites of La Tène date in our district, other than those within earthworks, are at Hauxton Mill, Grantchester and Trumpington. Of none of these, unfortunately, is any detailed record preserved; and our estimate of their importance is due to the character and variety of the pottery (almost certainly domestic) derived from them, which has already been fully described.

The Hauxton site is adjacent and to the north of the important ford over the Essex Cam by Hauxton Mill, which was in use in the Bronze Age and earlier; the material was obtained during coprolite digging in 1889 and subsequent years (Hughes, 1891 *b*). A section of a filled-in trench, containing fragments of Early Iron Age pottery, is now (1920) visible in the chalk pit cut in the face of the spur which here abuts on the stream.

The Settlements of Trumpington and Grantchester

From a gravel pit on the east side of the main road opposite Trumpington cemetery, the series of wares, probably of I B.C. and earlier, already described, was obtained in 1907 and deposited in the Cambridge Museum; but their importance was at the time not suspected. Close by, in Anstey Hall grounds, Roman remains have been found; and the church and hall are probably on the site of an early settlement. A late cordoned urn and other remains, also in the museum, are derived from Dam Hill at the N. end of the parish.

Of the associations of the Grantchester pottery, some of which as we have seen may be as early as 500 B.C., very little is known, for it was for the most part obtained from workmen during the extensive excavations for coprolites carried out by Government during the war, on a site west and south of the village. That any was preserved is due to the energy of Mr and Mrs Porter of Cambridge (Porter, 1921).

These two early inhabited sites lie on either side of what was doubtless an ancient ford across the Cam. This ford was, as we shall see, utilized by the Romans for their road from Red Cross to Barton and beyond, and a rectangular earthwork by the schoolhouse in Grantchester village (p. 175) may have guarded this important crossing. No early pottery comparable with the Grantchester-Trumpington series has been found at any point in the borough, and it is probable that Cambridge as a crossing-place of the Cam and the most important site on the river is of Roman creation.

The distribution of Early Iron Age remains in Cambridge of which the exact provenance is known is similar to that of the Bronze Age, the gravel terraces of Barnwell and Newnham yielding the most important evidences of settlement. No pottery to which pre-Roman date can safely be assigned has been recorded or preserved from Castle Hill, and only two vessels from its neighbourhood—one a barrel-urn probably of La Tène III date found in Madingley Road. It seems probable that the Castle site, apparently an ideal one, was then of little importance. The breadth of the marshy valley at this point, and the absence of a convenient ford, may be the reasons for the neglect.

If the map of the district be examined it will be seen that the Chesterford-Cambridge road, which passes through Trumpington, has to cross an awkward belt of marsh and a stream (Vicar's Brook). This is quite unnecessary, for the road could have skirted the chalk spur of Clarke's Hill and reached Cambridge without any such difficulty. No trace of a Roman road from Chesterford to Trumpington has ever been found; and the reason is probably that in this sector, and in its continuation the Essex Cam-Stort-Lea Valley route to the Thames (as in the Stour and Colne Valley routes to Colchester)[1], good chariot roads of La Tène date existed and were utilized by the Romans, who confined their energies mainly to the construction of straight roads where no decent routes existed before their time.

If, then, the modern highway to Cambridge preserves pre-Roman

[1] The probable course of these trackways is shown on Map V.

alignments the facts elucidated supply a reason for its course through Trumpington; its objective was the lowest convenient ford of the Cam and the settlements which flanked that ford; the extension to Cambridge, which in Roman days seems to have been along a line drawn from Trumpington Hall to the buildings of the Leys School (parallel to and west of the modern road)[1], probably followed the line of an ancient trackway linking up the settlements on the right bank of the river.

The sites we have considered whereon living-floors, or objects of domestic character implying settlement, have been found, are fourteen in number. That this represents an absurdly small proportion of the total number existing in the district in the Early Iron Age may be taken for granted. Some archaeologists, with whom the writer is inclined to agree, would affirm that one reason why remains of the Age are so scanty is that the great majority of the valley settlements were on the site of existing villages; hence evidence of pre-Roman occupation is to a great extent either destroyed or inaccessible. Yorke (1911), in discussing the history of the parish of Fowlmere, attacked this interesting problem of the continuity of village life in Cambridgeshire, and concluded that Fowlmere was a Celtic settlement laid off in the Tyddyn and Randir of a British Trev, the plan of which had survived with but little alteration to the present day.

COMMUNICATIONS

Brief references to certain of the routes by which our district may have been reached from the upper Thames Valley and from Norfolk (Icknield and Street Ways); from the lower Thames (Stort and Essex Cam Valleys); from the Essex coast (Stour and Colne Valleys) have already been made. These will be discussed in Chapter IV.

Turning to local communications, the conclusions outlined above with regard to the antiquity and original objective of the Chesterford-Cambridge road are of special interest. Further discoveries of a like nature to those at Grantchester and Trumpington will in the future, we may be certain, permit the attribution of a number of existing routes to the same early period; it may indeed be that, Roman roads apart, the foundations of our modern road system (governed then as now by the requirements of an agricultural population) were laid in the centuries immediately preceding the Roman occupation, if not

---

[1] Judging by finds in the Latham and Chaucer roads, and on Dam Hill (see pp. 205, 227, and Map G, p. 246).

in the later Bronze Age. So scanty is our knowledge of the period that it is impossible to press the point; but in addition to through routes such as the Street and Icknield Ways which are certainly wholly or partially prehistoric, there are a number of lesser routes presenting features which suggest an origin in the Early Iron or preceding Ages. These also will be dealt with in the next chapter.

RACIAL TYPE OR TYPES IN THE EARLY IRON AGE

The scanty material available for the determination of the racial type or types present in our district in the Early Iron Age is as follows:

1. Icenian area. Numerous skeletons in a large low tumulus (?) at Brandon: date uncertain, but Early Iron Age seems probable.

2. Trinovantian or Catuvellaunian area.

(*a*) Numerous skeletons in fosse of War Ditches below Romano-British occupation level.

(*b*) Inhumation burial of La Tène II date, Newnham.

1. The Brandon interments, 63 in number, were reported on by C. S. Myers (1896). He found "no trace of the elements of a Round Barrow race" and only one skull presented "in any degree the characters of Saxon crania." The Long Barrow type was represented, and other dolichocephalic skulls suggested a "Germanic infiltration," while the intermediate skulls indicated "ethnic admixtures." Some were identified as of the continental type known as "Batavian."

2. (*a*) A summary of the evidence with regard to the War Ditches' skeletons, the situation of which indicated a date in I A.D. and massacre rather than burial, is given by Hughes (1904, p. 478). Duckworth reported on these (in 1895). His opinion[1] may be quoted. "By the process of exclusion, as they are not of the long barrow or round barrow races, nor of the broad-faced coffin-shaped type of the Saxons of Southern England, they must be either Belgic or Anglian, and hitherto there are no definite criteria upon which we can depend for distinguishing these."

(*b*) The calvarium of the middle-aged individual buried with such a wealth of ornaments at Newnham, probably about 250 B.C., was, in Dr Duckworth's opinion, almost certainly dolichocephalic (p. 81).

Dolichocephaly was thus characteristic of practically all the skulls of our period examined, and it was a marked characteristic of

---

[1] The archaeological horizon on which the skeletons were found was, when this summary was written, thought to be post-Roman; the conclusions drawn by Duckworth are all the more important.

the Belgae. As Myers remarks (1896, p. 124): "the provinces formerly occupied by the Belgae are now inhabited, as M. Collignon has shown, by the longest headed people of France. Therefore if any migration of Belgic Gauls took place at or before the Roman invasion it was a wash not of brachycephalic but of dolichocephalic people that the British shores received."

Admitting a doubt as to the date of the Brandon interments it would seem clear that the neighbourhood of Cambridge at least was Belgic; that is, that either the Catuvellauni or the Trinovantes, whichever of these tribes future research shall prove to have occupied our district, were Belgae. But further considerations suggest that the evidence does not justify this conclusion.

The skull form of the early La Tène barrow builders of the East Riding was definitely dolichocephalic (summary of evidence in *B.M.G.*, 1905, p. 82): these invaders were doubtless Brythons, in any case they certainly antedated the Belgic conquests. We cannot assume that this dolichocephaly was the result of admixture with long-headed aborigines in Yorkshire, for the pre-Belgic burial at Newnham presents similar characters; and it may be that the Brythonic Celts who invaded Britain in general and East Anglia in particular were a tall, fair, long-headed folk[1] who had not suffered that admixture with conquered races which subsequently altered the type of those who occupied Gaul. Thus we cannot differentiate anthropologically between Belgian and Brython[2].

Neither can we with any confidence draw a cultural distinction; it has already been observed that the boundaries of Belgic settlement and of the cremation culture are not coterminous; the connection between the race and the culture is not necessarily intimate.

TOPOGRAPHICAL DISTRIBUTION OF FINDS AND REMAINS OF THE EARLY IRON AGE

We have already obtained useful results from an analysis of the local distribution of certain classes of Iron Age objects such as coins and pottery, and of settlements such as those at Grantchester and Trumpington; we may now consider what deductions are to be drawn from the map (No. III) in which the distribution of the remains of

---

[1] Characters indicated by the descriptions which classical writers have given of the Gaul. See Ridgeway (1901, pp. 370–3). It must be remembered, moreover, that in Yorkshire, and in the fenlands, elements drawn from Northern Europe may have been mingled with Brythonic Celts. The Brandon interments and certain local finds suggest that this may have been the case in the Cambridge Region.

[2] Confirmed by Dr W. H. L. Duckworth (letter to the author Nov. 11, 1921).

the Age as a whole from the introduction of Iron, possibly in V B.C. down to I A.D., are presented.

The remains of the Age, apart from coins of which some hundreds are recorded, are surprisingly scanty. The valley of the Ivel, from the source of its tributary the Hiz at Hitchin, to Sandy, and that of the Cam south of Cambridge provide the greatest number of finds and sepulchral deposits. Evidences of settlement are found in the valleys of Little Ouse and Lark and at Lakenheath in the north-east, and in the upper valley of the Stour in the east; and numerous coins indicate a pre-Roman settlement at Braughing.

Only isolated finds occur elsewhere, but some of these are suggestive. Finds of imported wine-jars at Thaxted and Lindsell, for example, near the watershed of streams draining into the Blackwater estuary suggest that the ships of the Veneti and other Gallic traders were seen in the Essex creeks.

Compared with the preceding Age we notice:

(1) That the southern fens and their eastern borders from Quy to Fordham, so rich in remains of the Bronze Age, are in the Iron Age almost entirely barren; and (2) that Iron Age burials are absent from the chalk belt from Kentford to Hitchin, except for a few on Triplow Heath; like the beaker-folk the La Tène Celts buried their dead near their settlements. The next point (3) is that the population of the Ivel Valley has increased in the latter Age; while (4) in both Ages alike the forests are bare of settlement.

Having regard to the lesser number of finds in the present than in the earlier Age, the population of the Cam Valley, as well as that of the Ivel Valley, must be held to have increased in proportion to the entire population of the district; and the changes shown by the map suggest that the shifting of population from north-east to south-west, from the hunting and pasture grounds to the alluvial lands, manifest when the map of the Bronze Age was compared with that of the Neolithic Age, has been accentuated in the Early Iron Age. The valley of the Ivel has been a famous wheat-growing district; and the explanation of the distribution of population in our period may be found in the importance which agriculture attained in the Early Iron Age, an importance for which we have historical evidence (see Strabo, IV, 5, § 2; Caesar, *B.G.* V, 12 and 20).

But this explanation is incomplete; it does not account for the rarity of finds in the Quy-Fordham area or in the fen islands.

Dealing with the fens first, it is clearly inconceivable that these fertile islands were depopulated and then left waste during the whole

THE EARLY IRON AGE

of the La Tène period, four centuries or more. Could malaria have hindered the invaders from settling in the fens? It was very prevalent up to the middle of XIX A.D.

Again, we must consider the suggestion that there was an overlap of cultures; that in the fens men lived on in the Bronze stage of culture, while the Iron Age was in full swing on the uplands. This is not impossible, for the scantiness of the finds and the fact that the majority are assignable to the years round about the Christian era suggest that the new culture did not take a firm hold of the district until late; its dominant period was short.

On the other hand, it may be regarded as important evidence against the theory of an overlap that local examples of objects of typical Bronze Age form with La Tène decoration do not occur; nor in any of the Late Bronze Age finds in our region which have been preserved is there any admixture of Iron Age implements or weapons. Changes in fashion in decorative arts are readily transmitted, and if the Bronze culture persisted side by side with La Tène in this district some traces of it would probably be noticed.

The iron spearheads with hollow blades referred to on p. 76 are transitional forms; but since they were associated with inhumation interments they probably belonged to invading elements, and thus represent not a local but a continental overlap of the Bronze and Iron cultures.

The absence of coins of the "central district" and of pottery of Aylesford type, in Icenian territory north of the Devil's Dyke, has suggested that trade along the Icknield Way N.E. of Cambridge in the years round about the Christian era was almost non-existent, that, in fact, at this point there was a military frontier, and that the narrow belt of open country spanned by the Devil's Dyke was then a march between hostile confederations. We learn from Caesar how frequent tribal wars were. Such warfare may have made the area between the Lark Valley and Cambridge a belt wellnigh bare of culture, the population of which was the prey of both parties; and the absence of finds on the borders of the fens is thus explicable.

SUMMARY

That this is the first attempt to estimate the duration and character of the Early Iron Age civilization in Cambridgeshire may excuse my somewhat lengthy descriptions and analyses; that the conclusions arrived at are of a guarded and provisional character is due to the scantiness of the evidence and to the absence of detailed information as to the earlier phases of the Age in Britain generally.

THE EARLY IRON AGE

The chief points brought out in the course of the investigation are here briefly summarized.

In the Hallstatt period (800–500 B.C.) brooches and other objects mostly of North Italian make were brought or imported into the fenlands. It is not improbable that certain of these early brooches were associated with inhumation burials, but it cannot yet be definitely asserted that the Iron Age commenced in the southern fens prior to the La Tène culture phase, and the true significance of these discoveries is not yet known.

Pottery of Hallstatt type, inhumation burials in barrows, early La Tène fibulae, etc., clearly show that at the beginning of the La Tène phase on the Continent (500–400 B.C.) an iron-using people or peoples who inhumed their dead entered the Cambridge Region. Similar pottery found at Peterborough and the presence of Iron Age barrows at Crowland—sites difficult of access save by water—suggest that the invaders came from overseas direct; to the Wash and up the fen rivers. The existence in our region of Early Iron Age cremation burials in barrows is established, but their significance cannot at present be assessed. A rich inhumation burial at Newnham and a burial at Mildenhall provide interesting and hitherto isolated parallels to the chariot burials of Yorkshire and the Marne.

The La Tène III period (which in Eastern Britain commenced some time in I B.C.) is marked by the appearance in the southern parts of our district of pottery of Aylesford type, and of the rite of cremation. No barrows are used; burials are occasionally isolated, but are usually massed in flat cemeteries. This culture is usually described as Belgic. Its distribution (the counties of Kent, Essex, Middlesex, Hertford, Buckingham, (southern) Bedford, and (southern) Cambridge) is not, however, coterminous with that of tribes known to be of Belgic stock, and the problem of the origin, range and mode of introduction of this cremation culture into S.E. Britain demands further research[1]. It undoubtedly reached Cambridgeshire from the south, and failed to establish itself in the southern fens and N.W. Suffolk. Coin finds suggest that this was territory of the Iceni; and this tribe may have built the Devil's Dyke to prevent both military and peaceful penetration. The Iceni were almost certainly Brythons; of the two neighbouring tribes on the south and west, the Trinovantes, in spite of Caesar, may perhaps be considered Belgic, but whether

---

[1] Many of the characteristic pottery forms occur at Silchester (Calleva Atrebatum) and two at Rushmore, Dorset (Pitt-Rivers, 1887, Plate xxxv), and future discoveries may extend in this direction the limits of cremation burial.

the Catuvellauni were Brythons or Belgae cannot be considered settled, nor can the mutual boundaries of these latter tribes in our district be determined. Ethnological data give us little assistance; all Early Iron Age crania in Eastern Britain seem to be dolichocephalic.

Professor Chadwick tells me that he thinks that the various Celtic invasions were merely successive movements of the same people—probably all coming from Belgium, Holland, and N.W. Germany. Differences therefore are not to be expected, except in so far as the various invasions coincided with different waves of cultural influence from the south.

Our conclusion that the Fenland Basin is an area upon which geographical conditions impose unity of cultural character at any given period, valid for the Bronze Age and apparently for the earlier phase of the Iron Age, seems to be incorrect for the later La Tène periods. This is doubtless because we see a new culture, approaching the region from the south, destroyed before the factors we have mentioned have had time to overcome the temporary check imposed by a political barrier; the Roman conquest fixed for us the evidences of what must have been an unstable equilibrium.

The Roman domination, in another aspect, becomes of the highest importance when we attempt to deal with the later phases of the Early Iron Age. Evidences of the overlap of the higher and lower civilizations meet us on every side and increase the difficulty of determining the value, as illustrations of pre-Roman civilization, of finds of La Tène character of which the associations are unknown. La Tène fibulae and pottery come from Roman ashpits at Chesterford; fire-dogs with barbaric ox-head terminals, and bronzes embossed with Celtic scrolls are associated with sigillata vessels at Stanfordbury, while in the hotch-potch of bronzes from the Santon Downham cauldron we see, in the words of Mr R. A. Smith, "British art in the act of being overwhelmed at least temporarily by the more formal and commonplace traditions of the Empire." The saving clause is justified; La Tène art did not pass without profoundly and permanently influencing provincial Roman craftsmanship in pottery, bronze and enamel work.

The distribution of population, densest in the fertile valleys of the Cam and Ivel, supports the view that these districts were predominantly agricultural[1]; being, in the La Tène III and IV periods, on the fringe of the highly civilized south-eastern portion of Britain which Caesar differentiates from the barbaric interior. Finds of

[1] It is possible that some of the well-marked cultivation terraces in Cambridgeshire may date from this period. See Plate XXXVII. Early Iron Age fields in Sussex are, however, square.

La Tène metal work and enamels, of finely-wrought vases and bowls of shale, of Arretine wares and wine-jars from Italy, as well as the numerous coins of various denominations confirm this estimate of the standard of civilization here attained.

Of the barrenness of the southern fens in the Early Iron Age no satisfactory explanation can be given.

While some, if not all, of our early (Hallstatt) bronzes may have reached the fenlands by the southern trade-route from the Mediterranean area *via* Corbilo on the Loire, later importations into our district from Italy (and Belgic Gaul) almost certainly came by the more northerly routes across the Straits, of which Strabo speaks; it is, indeed, not improbable that the wine-jars found at Thaxted formed part of a cargo unloaded in an Essex estuary from a Gallic merchantman. Such imports were doubtless paid for directly or indirectly by the export of cattle and corn produced locally[1].

Evidence exists of the occupation in the Early Iron Age of several of our hill-forts: at least one is held to have been constructed during the period; possibly all were, but of this we have no proof. Great Chesterford and Sandy, Roman towns, overlie or are close to La Tène settlements; and it is likely that many of our village sites, and highways such as that from the Thames to the Cam Valley past the hill forts of Starbury and Wallbury, originated in this period. Settlements at Grantchester and Trumpington are thought to have flanked the lowest convenient ford across the Cam, Cambridge being, as in the Bronze Age, represented mainly by settlements on the gravel terraces of Barnwell, Newnham and Chesterton.

Domestic pottery probably extending in date over the whole of the Age has been obtained from various sites in the district; but in the almost complete absence of associated objects determination of type-sequence is not yet possible.

[1] See Strabo, IV, 5, §§ 2 and 3.

CHAPTER IV

EARTHWORKS AND TRACKWAYS, POSSIBLY OR CERTAINLY PREHISTORIC

"Let us go into the defenced cities." JEREMIAH.

INTRODUCTION

HAVING examined the finds, hoards, interments, and other remains which are definitely assignable to one or other of the three Prehistoric Ages under investigation, it seems desirable, before proceeding to a consideration of remains of the Historic Period, to discuss the ring-works, dykes and trackways which are possibly or certainly pre- or proto-historic.

If multiplication of maps is to be avoided, these must be entered on one or other of the Period Maps. Now while we can be fairly certain that our hill-forts, whether excavated or no, are of pre-Roman origin, the date of the lowland ring-works must be regarded as doubtful.

The Fleam Dyke, the only one of the dykes which has been excavated, is, as we shall see, Roman or post-Roman. Therefore, though in my opinion indirect evidence favours pre-Roman origin for the Devil's Dyke, it is clearly inadvisable to insert this, or any of the unexcavated dykes, on a pre-Roman Period Map.

Again, of only two trackways, the Icknield Way and the Street Way, can pre-Roman origin be with reasonable certainty affirmed.

Briefly put, the date of the majority of our local earthworks and trackways is uncertain, and it would clearly be misleading to mark such on any Period Map earlier than the Anglo-Saxon. The earthworks (except the hill-forts) and tracks (except the Icknield and Street Ways) discussed in this chapter therefore are marked on this Map. The exceptions are marked on the Iron Age Map; for if pre-Roman they must then have been in existence. Moreover, such evidence as we have suggests that this is the Age in which the hill-forts were constructed.

Since so little is known, description and discussion in the following pages will be as brief as possible, being intended mainly as an indication of the directions in which research is desirable.

122   EARTHWORKS AND TRACKWAYS

The following is a list of the earthworks and routes which will be dealt with:

I. *Earthworks (all marked on Map V)*

(*a*) Defensive Dykes.

> Black Ditches, Cavenham [S].
> Devil's Dyke [C].
> Fleam Dyke [C][1].
> Brent Ditch, Pampisford [C].
> Bran or Heydon Ditch [C].

Also discussed:

> Worstead Street [C].
> Foss Ditch, Weeting [N].
> Royston or Mile Ditches [H] and [C].

and other works.

(*b*) Hilltop fortresses:

> Wandlebury, Stapleford [C].
> Ring Hill (Starbury), Littlebury [E].
> Caesar's Camp, Sandy [B].
> Arbury Banks, Ashwell [H].
> War Ditches, Cherryhinton [C].
> Grim's Ditch, Saffron Walden [E].

(*c*) Forts and camps on less lofty ground:

> Arbury, near Histon [C].
> Belsar's Hill, Willingham [C].
> Round Moats, Fowlmere [C].

Also discussed:

> Repell or Paille Ditches, Saffron Walden [E].

II. *Trackways (Marked on Map V)*

Icknield Way: crossing the Cambridge region diagonally from south-west to north-east.
Street Way: parallel to Icknield Way.
Mare Way: known only in short sectors in the neighbourhood of Haslingfield and Hauxton.

A few other ancient routes, the prehistoric origin of which is for varying reasons probable, will also be discussed.

---

[1] More conveniently discussed here than in a later chapter, though undoubtedly Roman or post-Roman.

POSSIBLY OR CERTAINLY PREHISTORIC

THE CAMBRIDGESHIRE DYKES

So much has been written about the defensive dykes which extend from fen to forest across the belt of open chalk downland which crosses Cambridgeshire diagonally from south-west to north-east, that it will be sufficient if their main features are indicated, a few notes dealing with points which have hitherto received little attention added, and the results of recent excavations discussed.

The dykes are five in number; six if the Royston or Mile Ditches be included.

The five differ markedly in dimensions and in length, but they possess important features in common.

(i) The defensive work in all cases (save possibly the Black Ditches) rests on the one flank on ground originally forest (boulder-clay overlying chalk), on the other on the fen, or marsh. That is, they were all constructed when the fens were impassable, the river valleys morasses, the clayey heights forest-clad.

(ii) The ditch is on the south-western side; that is, the defences were erected to prevent access to Norfolk from the south-west. The Brent or Pampisford Ditch alone is doubtful; only faint traces of a bank exist, here on one side there on the other.

No sequence of strength can be established indicating unity of construction, but rather the reverse; the outermost defence, Heydon Ditch, is the third strongest, Brent Ditch, the next, is the weakest; the Black Ditches, the fifth and final line of defence, is but a feeble work; the strongest are the Fleam and Devil's Dykes. Two, it may be added, are exactly aligned for considerable distances; the others are more or less sinuous. These variations suggest that, taken as a whole, their construction covers a considerable period of time, and that different races may have had a share in the work.

The salient characteristics of each dyke may now be dealt with. For topographical details the 1-inch Ordnance Survey map, as well as my Map V, should be consulted[1].

Black Ditches. Two sectors survive, lying the one to the north (1100 yards in length) the other to the south (1¼ miles in length) of the Icknield Way, covering the ford at Lackford where the ancient way crossed the River Lark.

The total length of the original work, assuming its flanks respectively to have rested on the River Lark and on forest country, was about 4½ miles.

---

[1] Black Ditches, Sheet 189; Devil's Dyke, Sheet 188; Fleam Dyke, Brent Ditch and Heydon Ditch, Sheet 205.

The northern sector, constructed in sandy soil with no advantage of position, shows a bank much spread and wasted, but still formidable, and a broad shallow fosse; the southern (though less well marked, the fosse having been filled in) is much more imposing, being aligned along the crest of the slope[1] at the bottom of which the little Cavenham Brook flows. Here the bank is about 27 feet wide and from 4 to 6 feet above ground level.

Beyond the ridge the southern sector of the dyke is traceable across Risby Poor's Heath, and is lost in the arable land south-east of the common. This sector is thus well marked for 1200 yards and traceable for a further 1000 yards.

A hedge line marked on the 1836 Ordnance Survey carries the line of the dyke nearly to Barrow Bottom; there is little doubt that it originally extended to a point south of the turnpike road where the clay capping over the chalk indicates natural forest.

It is difficult to understand why the northern sector was needed. It might have been supposed that the marshes of the Cavenham Brook were sufficient protection (see 1-inch O.S. Sheet 189); or, in any case, that the brook might have been utilized as part of the defences, instead of constructing the bank in front of the brook[2]. A similar problem will confront us in connection with the Fleam Dyke.

In any case it will be clear that though comparatively weak, this earthwork is not unworthy of the system of which it forms part. The name "Black" Ditches is apposite, the northern sector being of dark sand covered with old heather stumps and ling.

Devil's Dyke. This is the longest and finest, differing from the other dykes also in that no effort was made to select the shortest distance between forest and fen; its fenside termination, Reach hamlet, lies on a promontory. It is $7\frac{1}{2}$ miles long: had an adjacent alignment (Dullingham to Swaffham Bulbeck) been selected it would have effected a saving of over two miles.

The dyke is aligned with remarkable exactness, no less than $5\frac{1}{2}$ miles being in the same straight line; but each end is slightly deflected. This is undoubtedly due to the fact that from a point on the edge of the forest adjacent to Stetchworth House the $5\frac{1}{2}$ miles' stretch was visible, and could thus be accurately plotted out; the terminations, on the other hand, were aligned by "rule of thumb" methods. The builders did not know, as did the Romans, how to stake out a straight line between points mutually invisible. (See 1-inch O.S. map, Sheet 188.)

[1] It is seldom that the builders of the dykes took any advantage of position; this sector is especially interesting on that account.

[2] But see pp. 132, 134 and 146.

The differences in the estimated proportions of the dyke as recorded by various observers are very remarkable (Babington, 1883, p. 98) and an accurate survey is much needed. At a point where vallum and fosse are undamaged, namely on the knoll 300 yards south-east of the Swaffham-Burwell road cutting, the ditch was estimated by me to be 15 feet deep, the distance from the top of the bank to the bottom of the ditch being 62 feet; and the "over-all" breadth of bank and fosse was 37 yards.

The dyke maintains its immense proportions to the end, on both flanks[1]. On the hills it stops abruptly at the edge of a little wood by Camois Hall, Wood Ditton, and does not tail off into a mere boundary bank as does the Fleam Dyke. But the flank was adequately protected, for the dyke extends well into the ancient forest belt.

There are several gaps, of which that which permits the passage of the main Newmarket road (approximating to the line of the ancient Icknield Way) may be original. It should be noted that the dyke presents here no indication of the recurved valla and flanking defences so commonly met with in the entrances to the larger hill-forts.

There may also have been an original passage way at Running Gap, where Street Way crosses the dyke. But I should not be surprised if the dyke is shown by excavation at some future date to be continuous from forest to fen.

Fleam Dyke. There are two sectors: that extending from a spur of the forest ridge north-west of Balsham to Fulbourn Fen, over 3 miles long, and that running from the northern end of the fen to the bank of the Cam at Fen Ditton, $1\frac{1}{2}$ miles long.

(i) *The Balsham sector.* This is a magnificent work, rivalling the Devil's Dyke in its proportions. Its over-all breadth near Fulbourn Fen is 28 yards, depth of ditch 11 feet, vallum 55 feet on the slope.

The point of passage of the Icknield Way will be discussed later. The Dungate Farm gap is modern: at the Fulbourn Fen end, though the dyke does not continue down to the fen, the ditch does so, and the bank is undoubtedly destroyed. There is thus no proof that a gap originally existed permitting the passage of the Street Way. The dyke is aligned on "Shardelow's Well"—a spring rising actually in the fosse, and making it for the last 100 yards a wet ditch.

There is no adequate topographical evidence for the continuation of the dyke from Shardelow's Well to the "W" of Great Wilbraham (as suggested in the 1-inch O.S. Sheets 188 and 205)[2].

---

[1] A small sector at the northern (fen) end has been destroyed.
[2] The excavations carried out in 1921-22 are discussed on p. 129.

(ii) *The Fen Ditton sector.* This has been for the most part destroyed. The present east-and-west road through Fen Ditton roughly preserves its alignment; in the village the road represents the ditch[1]; further to the east on the outskirts of the village both bank and ditch are faintly visible to the north of the road; beyond the railway and a narrow boggy valley the road follows the crest of the bank, which is very well marked near the Newmarket road junction. Further trace is lost; but the dyke descended into Teversham Fen, the alignment being undoubtedly preserved by a deflection of the Cambridge-Newmarket road at this point.

The almost complete destruction of the dyke prevents a comparison with its southern sector; but it may be doubted if it were ever so magnificent a defensive work.

The use of this part of the Fleam Dyke is not clear; behind it is Quy Water, which must have been a formidable obstacle; and if artificial defences were needed, an entrenchment on the right bank between Quy Bridge and Mill would, one might suppose, have been sufficient. The tactical situation is identical with that presented at the northern sector of the Black Ditches (see pp. 124 and 134).

Brent or Pampisford Ditch. This ditch is remarkably short, the distance between forest and marsh being only $1\frac{1}{2}$ miles. It originally extended from a boulder-clay covered spur S.S.W. of Great Abington (Abington Park) to a spring head at Dickman's Grove, Pampisford, which feeds a small tributary of the Cam; but about 450 yards of the lower portion has been destroyed. Though it is difficult to realize the natural physical conditions of the district, there can be no doubt that formidable obstacles, river, marsh and forest, to an advance from the south-west existed for many miles to north and south of this narrow gap. (See Sketch-map D.)

The alignment of the ditch is sinuous; no definite bank exists; sometimes a slight ridge is apparent on one side, sometimes on the other[2].

That it is a boundary ditch is unlikely. Such structures usually have a bank ditched on either side: the Brent Ditch is deeper and wider than is likely to have been constructed for the latter purpose. The "covered ways" of the South Downs (shown in one case (Curwen, 1918, p. 62) to be pre-Roman) present very similar features, and must not be neglected in a survey of the possible uses of this curious work.

---

[1] Sir William Ridgeway drew my attention to the fact that all the better-class farmhouses in the village are on the north of the road—on the site of the high dry bank—and the poorer cottages on the south side.

[2] See footnote, p. 130.

Bran or Heydon Ditch. This dyke extends for $3\frac{1}{4}$ miles from the spur (natural forest) on which the village of Heydon stands, to the "Black Peak" in Fowlmere parish where strong chalk springs still rise—springs which fed the mere (now drained) which gave its name to the parish.

The bank was levelled and the fosse filled in, in part at some unknown date, in part when the parishes bordering it were enclosed in 1845.

Parish boundaries, however, mark its line, which is approximately straight throughout its course, and absolutely straight for over $1\frac{1}{2}$ miles. Moreover, definite traces of it still exist and in places, after ploughing, the line of the destroyed vallum is very apparent as a raised belt of white chalk contrasted with the brown of the natural surface soil adjacent. Beldam (1868, p. 36) records that in his day a small undestroyed portion of the vallum was probably 7 feet in vertical elevation above ground level, and that the breadth of the work was at least 80 feet—which is equal to that of the Fleam Dyke at several points. It is clear that the Heydon Ditch was a formidable defence. The alignment is indicated on Sketch-map D.

Royston or Mile Ditches. These ditches are situated $1\frac{1}{2}$ miles to the west of Royston, and originally extended, according to Beldam (1868, p. 37), from a tumulus on Pen Hills, Therfield Heath, to Bassingbourn Springs, a distance of 2 miles. They are now visible only for a few hundred yards on the heath, from the Icknield Way southward; there are three ditches with banks to correspond, roughly parallel save at their upper end, where they diverge. The most westerly, which is the best preserved example, appears to be banked on both sides. Of slight elevation, the banks do not suggest defences of the type we are now familiar with; but they are certainly ancient, for they are partially destroyed where they cross the belt of trackways, 100 yards wide, which here marks the trace of the Way.

Beldam also states that Drays Ditches, N. of Luton [B], extended across the Way from a tumulus on Warden Hill towards Ravensburgh Castle and were similar in character. These I have not examined. A similar series of parallel banks extends from Grimes Graves, Weeting [N], southward, one forming the boundary between Weeting and Santon parishes. Nothing is known of these works save what can be seen; but they are probably prehistoric. (See W. G. Clarke, 1920, p. 206.)

ARCHAEOLOGICAL EVIDENCE BEARING ON THE DATE OF THE DYKES

Though weapons of stone and bronze are recorded as having been found "at" or "near" one or other of the dykes, there is no reason for supposing that any such were found either in vallum or fosse. Iron weapons of types occurring in Anglo-Saxon graves of the pagan period, on the other hand, have been found, in one case certainly in the other probably, in the valla of the Devil's and Fleam Dykes. These are discussed on pp. 292-3.

Numerous barrows adjoin each of the dykes, but after studying the distribution of each group I cannot but think that the relationships are accidental. The dykes one and all seem to have been driven through barrow areas, rather than the barrows disposed along a military barrier. If there be an exception it is the Black Ditches; three tumuli, one on Cavenham Heath, the others on Risby Poor's Heath, adjoin the dyke on the defended side. (See also p. 31.)

Beldam (1868, p. 38) found traces of prehistoric settlement at the lower end of the Mile Ditches near Bassingbourn Springs. He showed by excavation, moreover, that the fosses of these ditches (each about 5 feet deep) were not continuous across the main road (Icknield Way), a causeway of solid chalk 16-18 feet wide being left. The present metalled road thus marks the crossing point of the ancient Way, which is older than the Ditches. There is little doubt that these works are prehistoric, but their purpose cannot be guessed at. Their southern termination, it may be noted, is over a mile away from the forest plateau, and the ditches could not therefore have been intended as barriers across the open chalk belt.

Important evidence of a similar character in connection with the Heydon Ditch is recorded by Beldam (1868, p. 36). Near Heydon Grange, where the Icknield Way crosses the dyke, he found solid and undisturbed chalk on the line of the fosse at a depth of about $2\frac{1}{2}$ feet. Thus the road is older than the dyke.

On the other hand, there is evidence that the Brent Ditch, Pampisford, was "filled up for the Icknield Way to pass over it"; but this is probably the Roman not the prehistoric way. See Babington (1883, p. 101) and pp. 145-6 and 166 of this book.

Hughes was present when the Devil's Dyke was cut through by the Mildenhall Railway in 1883-4. He made (1913, pp. 137-9) the important observation that though much evidence of Roman occupation was visible in the neighbourhood of the dyke, no Roman remains occurred under it, though a few Roman objects lay below the turf covering the bank itself. This is evidence of pre-Roman date, and though it is but slight, the later pre-history of the Early Iron Age seems to confirm it (see p. 117).

The section thus made showed that a slight bank and fosse, facing *north*, lay under the great vallum and was earlier than it. This may have been a tribal boundary.

That the dyke was *used* in the Pagan Anglo-Saxon period is fairly certain; but the evidence on which this conclusion is based does not fix the date of construction of the earthwork.

Excavations in 1921–22: Worstead Street and Fleam Dyke

Such, up to 1921, was all the direct archaeological evidence[1] available for the student; and it seemed to the writer desirable to attempt by excavation the solution of the problem of at least one of the dykes.

A preliminary investigation was carried out (in March, 1921) to determine whether or no the ramp which carried the Roman road, known as Worstead or Wool Street, across the chalk downs was the partially levelled vallum of a pre-Roman dyke. Hughes (1904, p. 458) suggested that this was the case, and his view was adopted by Allcroft (1908, p. 507).

In order to settle the point it was only necessary to cut a trench down to the chalk rock on either side of the ramp at a point where the latter was well marked; the presence or absence of a filled-in fosse could thus be readily demonstrated.

The trench was cut at a convenient point on the Gog-Magog Hills; and it was definitely shown that there never had been a ditch on either side; moreover, the construction of the ramp—a floor of puddled chalk, then turf, then a layer of chalk rubble upon which was a capping of gravel—showed that it was an example of Roman civil engineering (C. Fox, 1923). A diagram of this excavation is given on Plate XIX, A.

This being settled, work was begun on the Fleam Dyke by Dr W. M. Palmer and myself[2]. This dyke was chosen because its site (the most conveniently defensible one on the chalk belt) and sinuous trace suggested an antiquity second to none in the series of which it formed part.

The investigation was confined to that portion of the Fleam Dyke which lies between the disused railway cutting and Dungate Farm a distance of 2500 yards. The dyke here presents uniform characters,

---

[1] For a note on the historical evidence, see p. 160.
[2] See Fox and Palmer (1923). This is the first report; the final report will be published in a subsequent volume of *Proceedings, C.A.S.*

the ditch being about 10–11 feet deep and the scarp measuring 40–50 feet on the slope[1].

A section across the vallum at the railway cutting showed an original core—a bank some 7 feet high—increased to the present dimensions mainly by two additions. A second section, some 75 yards to the south-east of the railway cutting, showed evidence of these later additions, but no definite "core."

Sections across the fosse at several points many hundred yards apart revealed a main trench with a flat floor some 4 to 6 feet below the silt, and showed the counterscarp to have been steeper than the scarp[2]. A secondary trench or shelf on the scarp, sometimes flat, sometimes V- or U-shaped, was a constant feature and may represent, with the "core" of the vallum mentioned above, the first phase of the defensive work. Since, however, the second section through the vallum revealed no definite "core," the ramp corresponding to the original ditch may never have been completed as a military work. The history of the construction of the dyke must thus remain for the present obscure; it may, however, be noted that the striking uniformity in the profile of the fosse revealed by the fosse sections suggests that if the existing dyke be the result of successive reconstructions, these were on each occasion carried out along the whole length of the sector under investigation.

The crossing point of the Icknield Way, which a Saxon charter (Birch, 1893, 1305) refers to as a "highway" and which was therefore probably an unmetalled track and not a Roman road, was undoubtedly in the neighbourhood of the Bronze Age barrow on Mutlow Hill (p. 35). Excavation showed that the fosse of the dyke was continuous up to the metalling of the present London-Newmarket Road on either side, and its presence was demonstrated at several points between the road and Mutlow Hill. Rubble filling was also demonstrated on the line of the fosse at other existing gaps between the main road and Dungate Farm, Balsham. As a result of these investigations, we are convinced that the dyke formed a continuous barrier from forest to fen, and was designed to prevent, rather than to control, ingress to the territory which lies behind it.

A lower limit of date for the construction of the work was ob-

---

[1] Except where local causes have produced deep silting, as at Dungate.

[2] This observation may enable the disputed point as to which side of the ditch the bank of the Brent or Pampisford Ditch lay to be determined by a short day's digging. A tentative examination at one point showed me that the silting of the ditch was derived mainly from the south side; but the results obtained were not followed up.

PLATE XIX

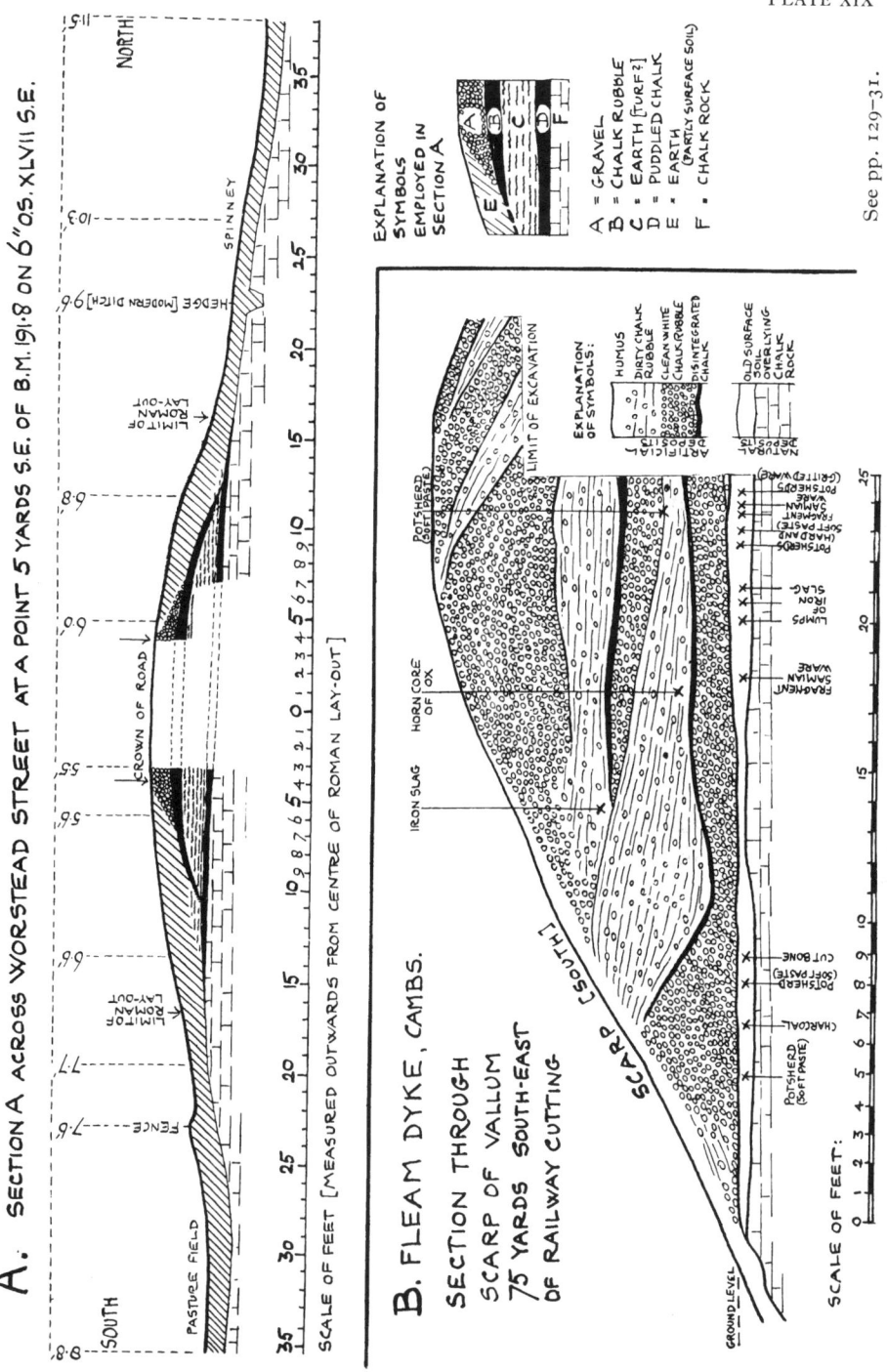

See pp. 129–31.

tained in the course of the excavations. At a point 75 yards southeast of the railway cutting, sections through the scarp and reverse slope of the ramp revealed, in the old surface soil thereunder, iron slag, sherds of soft paste native ware, of hard Roman grey ware, of "gritted ware," and of terra sigillata. All the finds were paralleled in a deposit dateable within the Roman period, excavated at the same time near Mutlow Hill; and it is clear that the dyke had at the point in question been aligned across the rubbish-strewn fringes of a Romano-British settlement. Section through the partially levelled scarp of the vallum near Mutlow Hill also revealed Roman remains in the subsoil. Moreover, it may be noted that no single fragment of deerhorn, and nothing which is necessarily earlier than the Roman period was found in the course of the excavations, either in the fosse sections or in the vallum. See Plate XIX, B.

Very little was found in the fosse sections. This suggests that the earthwork may, subsequent to its final reconstruction, have been very little used, and in brief time entirely and permanently deserted.

The evidence yielded by the excavations, in our opinion, warrants the conclusion that the Balsham sector of the Fleam Dyke is of a date posterior to I century A.D.

The only one of the dykes which has been excavated thus provides us with a new set of problems. Consideration of the results, which point to an Anglian origin for the Fleam Dyke will be found in Chapter VI, p. 292.

General Considerations bearing on the date of the Dykes not yet Excavated

Indirect evidence pointing to the existence of the Devil's Dyke in I A.D. has already been quoted; consideration of its scale and character justifies the view that it must date from a time when the energies of a large part of the population of Norfolk and N.W. Suffolk were controlled from a single centre.

The second phase of the Early Iron Age is obviously a very probable period for its erection, an age when inter-tribal wars (probably carried on by chariot warfare) were endemic, as the chapters in Caesar's Commentaries dealing with the invasion of Britain indicate[1]. As a defence against chariots the great dyke must have had

---

[1] *B.G.* Bk. v, 11: "Hitherto there had been continuous wars between this chief [Cassivellaunus] and the other states." See also Bk. v, 20, and Tacitus Agricola, xii. Cassivellaunus had under his command at least 4000 charioteers (Bk. v, 19).

peculiar advantages, as is well recognized. Moreover, Ridgeway (1892) has given reasons for supposing that Ostorius in his campaign against the Iceni in A.D. 48 "met at least one dyke," and since it could not have been the Fleam, it was in all probability the Devil's Dyke.

That a Celtic tribe was quite capable, in spite of Caesar's statement as to the laziness of the Gauls, of constructing so mighty a work as the Devil's Dyke is evidenced by Caesar's account of the fortifications of Avaricum (*B.G.* VII, 22–24), and by the feat of the Nervii, who built an entrenchment 3 miles in circumference the vallum of which was 9 feet high and the trench 15 feet wide, in less than three hours (*sic*) using only their swords and cloaks (V, 42).

Of none of the remaining dykes is adequate information available; it may be urged that even if the Devil's Dyke be pre-Roman, the probabilities are that it is the only one; that the Heydon Ditch, Brent Ditch and the Black Ditches, like the bulk of the Fleam, are works of the historic period.

I admit the possibility; but suggest that there are considerations not yet dealt with which hint at a prehistoric origin for the Fen Ditton sector of the Fleam Dyke, and a part at least of the Black Ditches.

It is not unlikely, moreover, as will be seen when the distribution of the hill fortresses is considered, that the Heydon Ditch was an outer defence of the Devil's Dyke system, and of Early Iron Age date.

The probability of pre-Roman date for the former works depends on the significance to be attached to certain dykes in W. Norfolk and N.W. Suffolk. This district is singularly bare of the ordinary type of defensive earthworks. No ring fortress indeed of any importance exists in the area and there are but few minor ones. The principle adopted by the inhabitants was to provide defence for a maximum amount of ground with a minimum of labour; to construct, in short, dykes across the necks of peninsulas.

In the neighbourhood of the great dykes there are no less than three examples of what are, geographically, promontory forts, though on a large scale.

Two (the Foss Ditch and the Devil's Dyke) extending respectively from the Little Ouse river to the Wissey, and from the Wissey to the Nar, protect areas bounded on three sides by fen and marsh; the third (also called the Devil's Ditch) encloses a tongue of land between the rivers Thet and Little Ouse.

These works, though not now perfect or traceable for their entire length, undoubtedly rested on marsh or river at either end; their lengths are $4\frac{1}{2}$, 5 and 2 miles respectively. In strength and character two of these resemble the Black Ditches, and they have their fosses on the east; the remaining dyke (the Thet-Ouse defences) I have not examined.

The sketch-map gives the essential topographical features of these earthworks.

Nothing in our knowledge of the Roman Age, or of the Anglo-

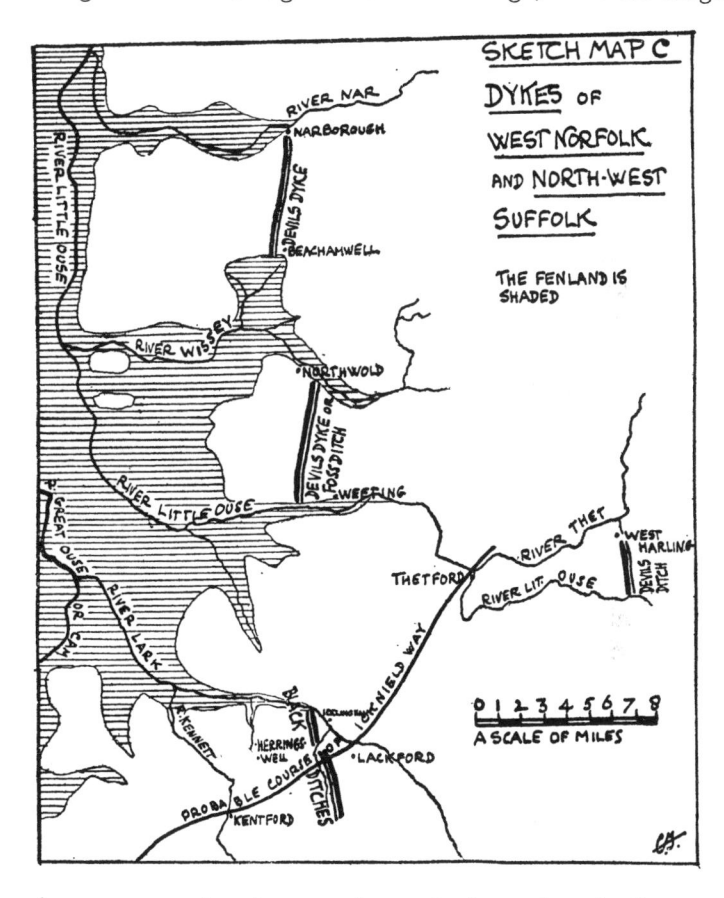

Saxon Age, suggests that these works can be later than the I century A.D.; though no conclusion can be arrived at without excavation[1], it seems likely that they were built by the prehistoric inhabitants of the district. In any case it is true that the Cambridgeshire dykes prevent access to a territory wherein lived, at some period, peoples who

---

[1] A section has since been cut across the fosse of the Wissey-Nar Dyke by my friend the Rev. J. F. Williams, of Beachamwell. It was V-shaped. Nothing was found that gave any clue to the date of the work.

in their tribal or clan defences were not fortress builders, but who utilized the principle of the protected flank in constructing their earthworks.

It appears to me probable that the Fen Ditton sector of the Fleam Dyke was originally a local defensive work, on the same lines as those which we have been discussing, enclosing the tongue of land on which Horningsea stands, subsequently incorporated—at all events in popular nomenclature—in the larger system. The northern sector of the Black Ditches may perhaps be similarly accounted for.

Summing up our scanty information, we see that one of the dykes, the Fleam, is Roman or post-Roman, while there is a possibility of pre-Roman date for the others. The question may be asked, why, if the dykes belong to different periods, are they all constructed as a defence against the south-west by the Norfolk peoples? Surely at some time in the long military history of the district the Norfolk peoples must have been aggressors and defence required by the inhabitants of the area now included in Hertfordshire and Bedfordshire. It is difficult to account for the fact, but it may be remarked that, other things being equal, the inhabitants of a small and agriculturally poor area like Norfolk are at any period from the Late Bronze Age onward likely to need defences more than the inhabitants of central and southern Britain, who must have been more wealthy in man-power and in metal for weapons.

HILL-TOP FORTRESSES[1]

Very little is known concerning the examples in our district.

Caesar's Camp, in the parish of Sandy [B], is a true contour fort, occupying a steep-sided narrow spur 200 feet above O.D. overlooking the Ivel Valley (see Goddard, 1904, p. 271). It is much damaged and its original extent is uncertain; the area of the existing portion—probably the lesser part—is 7 acres. It was occupied in the Early Iron Age; characteristic domestic pottery of this period from within the rampart is in the Cambridge Museum (see p. 109).

Wandlebury, in Stapleford parish, a plateau fort, circular, 1000 feet in diameter, occupies the crest of the Gog-Magog Hills about 240 feet above O.D. British coins and weaving-combs have been found within the area, and Stukeley records querns, fibulae, beads, etc. (ed. Lukis, 1883, p. 36). It is in a commanding position; anyone coming from the west and crossing the Cam by the fords at Hauxton or Grantchester would be forced to pass close to the fortress

[1] Marked on Maps III and V.

on his way eastward, Fulbourn Fen on the north side and the Bourn River on the south preventing a wide detour. Under primitive conditions the Gog-Magog ridge is a "key position."

This fortress has been described by a succession of antiquaries as being, in the words of Camden, "girt with a threefold rampire"; this was its character in the days before the hill-top was planted and a house built within the enceinte[1], but, unfortunately, it is not true to-day. The earthwork now consists of a double bank and single fosse, the fosse 6 to 9 feet deep, the ramparts 2 to 5 feet above ground level. The outer rampart is in places higher than the inner; this is probably due to the inner bank having been to some extent levelled. The distance on the slope from bottom of fosse to top of either vallum varies from 20 to 30 feet; the over-all width 70 to 80 feet.

Slight traces of the destroyed defences, which consisted of the main vallum and its ditch, are apparent inside the existing works.

The nature of the original entrance defences cannot now be determined, but it is probable that the two existing entrances on the north and south sides respectively are the points at which access to the fortress was originally obtained.

Ring Hill or Starbury[2], in Littlebury parish near Audley End [E], is an oval single-ramparted contour fort occupying a narrow chalk spur 300 feet above O.D. overlooking the Essex Cam Valley. Its dimensions are 840 by 1250 feet and it encloses an area of about $16\frac{1}{2}$ acres. It has recently been surveyed and described (*R.C.H.M. Essex*, 1916, pp. 191 and 193; see also Gould, 1903, p. 280). The whole area has been afforested, and the vallum partially levelled. The ditch is "generally about 50 feet wide," and the defences must have been formidable. The original entrances cannot be identified. There is no record of finds within the area other than those of Roman coins and a "silver cup."

Arbury Banks, on a low chalk hill near Ashwell [H], about 290 feet above O.D., is an oval entrenchment measuring 930 by 770 feet, and is about 12 acres in area; with a single vallum, much wasted. The Street Way passed close to it; but the Icknield Way, $1\frac{1}{2}$ miles to the south-east, was not visible, being hidden by Claybush Hill.

Aylott (1911, p. 270) notes that between the camp and the valley a ledge commands a view of Ravensburgh Castle to the south-west, and of Caesar's Camp, Sandy, to the north-west.

---

[1] In 1694. Wandlebury formerly had "two other ditches which were levelled for lord Godolphin's gardens and plantations" (Lysons, 1808, p. 73).

[2] For the evidence for the name Starbury, see Braybrooke, 1836, p. 136.

The defences were formerly double on the north-east and south-west sides. Traces of two entrances and of pit dwellings within the area formerly existed. Beldam (1859b, p. 285) provides a detailed record (with plan) of excavation carried out here before the enclosure of Ashwell parish. The fosse was found to have been 15 feet deep and 20 feet wide, V-shaped with a steep counterscarp. See also Montgomerie (1908, p. 105) and *R.C.H.M. Herts.* (1911, p. 38).

In the pits mentioned above were cooking-hearths: coarse pottery ("in which are numerous pebbles"), with scratched decoration, and bones of animals were found, also a bone piercer and a bone pin described as rude. In the Beldam collection (Cambridge Museum) there is nothing from the camp save half a cooking-pot of Early Iron Age date (figured on Plate XIV); this at least proves occupation of the site in the period immediately preceding the Roman conquest.

War Ditches. This circular single-ramparted fortress, 500 feet in diameter, the vallum of which is completely levelled, is situated on the Reservoir Hill, Cherryhinton, 150 feet above O.D.

It was discovered in 1893 in quarrying for chalk, and was partially excavated by Hughes and others (see Hughes, 1904). In the lower levels of the filled-in fosse, which was 15 feet deep, bones of domestic animals, dressed flints and pottery were found; and also skeletons of the Early Iron Age discussed on p. 114. Above these were deposits of the early Roman period, described on p. 177. The pottery from the lower levels is described by Hughes as "of a coarse quality and of no great variety" (*loc. cit.* p. 480). Examination of the material obtained during this excavation and stored in the Cambridge Museum revealed no pottery of Bronze Age character, but many fragments of Early Iron Age wares; and we may thus safely date the earthwork in the latter Age; a fragment of Gaulish ware of La Tène I character which has been preserved suggests construction in III or IV B.C.

Grim's Ditch, Saffron Walden [E]. An irregular enclosure, some 550 yards in greatest diameter, defended by a single rampart and ditch of no great strength, situated on a clay-covered spur flanking the chalk valley at the head of which Little Walden is situated. The boundaries of Grimsditch Wood are approximately those of the earthwork, which is not marked on the O.S. maps (see *R.C.H.M. Essex*, 1916, p. 260). In form it more closely resembles the polygonal Iron Age fortresses of Southern Britain (Karslake, 1920 and 1921) than any others in our district, and its position is such as the Britons of Caesar's time favoured. The Early Iron Age is thus a probable date for its construction; but no remains of this, or of any Age, have been found within it.

POSSIBLY OR CERTAINLY PREHISTORIC

FORTS AND CAMPS ON LESS LOFTY GROUND[1]

Tentative excavations have been made on the sites of two of the five low-lying ring-works in our district which may be prehistoric. Of the others nothing is known save what can be seen.

Arbury is situated on level ground, on gravel subsoil, near the village of Histon, 40 feet above O.D.

The existing remains consist of a very much wasted semicircular vallum with traces of a filled-in external fosse. The work was probably circular and, judging from the existing segment, 300 yards in diameter.

Several sections were cut through the bank and fosse by Hughes (1906 *b*); the fosse was found to be shallow, and must have been for the greater part of the year a wet moat. No objects were found that gave the slightest clue to the age of the work, but it was demonstrated that it could never have been of any great strength.

Belsar's Hill, Willingham. A circular ring-work 880 feet and 750 feet respectively in long and short diameter, with single vallum and ditch, lying on the edge of the fen 18 feet above O.D. The vallum is much wasted; the area is now pasture, but has been under plough. The driftway which leads to Aldreth Causeway and which is in a direct line therewith now bisects the camp. This driftway was from Norman times onwards for 600 years the chief land route into Ely from the south. Though it now goes *over* and not *through* the vallum it is not necessarily later than the earthwork; reference to the 1836 O.S. map shows that the track then skirted the camp on the east side. An original entrance lies to the west; faint traces of an eastern entrance are also to be seen. The ditch where it and the vallum are most perfect is marshy; and it must when the camp was in use have been a wet moat. Under natural conditions the site must have been very inaccessible.

The Round Moats, Fowlmere. This small oval ring-work, 300 feet in greatest diameter, and a little over an acre in area, is situated on the floor of a marshy valley, adjacent to the church of Fowlmere (Sketch-map D, p. 144). It is, for its size, very strongly defended, the bank being now 7 to 12 feet above natural level, and the wet moat 20 feet wide, and as originally excavated, 11 feet deep (below ground level). The waters of the adjacent brook were led into the moat by a channel now silted up. There are two entrances, both possibly original. Tentative excavations made by Yorke (1908) failed to yield any objects which would give a clue to the date of the work.

Orwell. The earthwork at Orwell, destroyed during coprolite

[1] These are marked on Map V.

digging in the XIX century, was apparently a work of the same class as the Round Moats. It is not marked on my map.

Paille or Repell Ditches, Saffron Walden [E]. This remarkable work challenges attention for its size, situation and regularity of form.

The existing remains (the south-western angle, 530 feet of the southern side and a similar length of the western) lie outside the west end of the town on the south slope of the Walden Valley and close to the "Slade," one of the chalk streams which flow through Walden (now piped). Its situation is doubtless due to the existence here of an important ford on one of the routes from the Cam Valley to the Thames Valley. (See p. 153.)

Indications at various points to the east of these remains point to the earthwork having been an elongated rectangle over 20 acres in area (1780 feet from E. to W. and 520 feet from N. to S.) enclosing a considerable part of the modern town, and bisected by the High Street, the line of which probably marks the original north and south entrances.

On the west side the rampart is "about 9 feet above the bottom of the ditch which is 30 feet wide from crest to crest."

Though rectangular, the proportions of the fortress are not Roman; its situation, however, is such as that people might select, and it may be the work of Early Iron Age Celts copying Roman methods. A few fragments of coarse badly-baked pottery, a portion of a decorated food-vessel and fragments of clay bearing the impress of wattle, found under Anglo-Saxon burials in the western part of the work, suggest a Bronze Age settlement, but it is very doubtful if the fortification can be assigned to so early a date. (See *R.C.H.M. Essex*, 1916, p. 259. H. E. Smith (1883) and Gould (1904) should also be consulted.)

GENERAL CONSIDERATIONS BEARING ON THE DATE OF THE FORTRESSES

THE HILL-TOP FORTRESSES

It is generally held that hill-top fortresses, especially those on open chalk downs or moorland, suitable environment for a pastoral people, are, special circumstances excepted, older than those earthworks which, hidden in marshes or forests, represent strongholds of a period when a settled agriculture has to a large extent cleared the valleys and effected a complete alteration of distribution of population. In point of size and strength the fortresses of the former class are here as elsewhere superior to the latter.

POSSIBLY OR CERTAINLY PREHISTORIC

We have, however, no evidence which permits us to assign an earlier date than the Early Iron Age to any of our hill camps, which are of two well-known types, "contour" and "plateau." For one of the latter, War Ditches, a date within this period may be regarded as certain; while scanty remains found within the enceinte of three others, Wandlebury and Arbury Banks (plateau), Caesar's Camp (contour), are in each case of the same Age. Of Ring Hill (contour) nothing is known; in form and situation it resembles Caesar's Camp.

Topographical Distribution. Ring Hill lies on a spur overlooking the Essex Cam Valley, on the line of what must have been an important route from the fenlands to the Thames Valley. The existence of the fine fortress of Wallbury, near Bishop's Stortford [H], 13 miles to the south on the same route is significant.

See Sketch-map B. Wallbury is a large irregularly oval work 31 acres in area, occupying the flat crest of a steep-ended spur by the River Stort. No excavations have been made in it and there are no records of any finds; but the discovery of a pedestal-urn cremation cemetery at Little Hallingbury, half a mile from the camp, proves that the district was occupied in the Early Iron Age. See Laver (1905) and *R.C.H.M.* Essex (1921, p. 93).

That the relation of these fortresses to this, the most convenient route for traders from the lower Thames and Kent, was of design and not accidental may be safely affirmed.

Wandlebury and the War Ditches bear no ascertainable relation either to the dykes or the Icknield Way, from which they are some miles distant. Study of the district suggests, as far as Wandlebury is concerned, that the most suitable and central site in this downland area was chosen purely on local and tactical grounds; on the other hand, it may be that this great ring-work is to be considered as the last of the line of fortresses controlling the Thames-Stort-Cam Valley route[1].

Since writing the above I have received an interesting letter from Mr G. Maynard, lately the curator of the Saffron Walden Museum. He says that from Ring Hill the Gog-Magog Hills can be clearly seen—and "Wandlebury before the site was planted with trees," also "Little Trees Hill and probably the Wandlebury camp site are visible from far up the Cam Valley beyond Audley End. It always struck me that Wandlebury would in early days serve as a great signalling centre for a very wide area. Signals from it could be observed far up both the Walden and Linton valleys and from the high ground by Ashdon and many other points. Any enemy movement along the escarpment could thus be easily communicated to the population of the sheltered valleys opening on to the open chalk country." Oct. 10, 1919.

[1] The relation between the forts and the dykes can be studied on Map V.

Similar observations with regard to Arbury Banks are noted on p. 135. I doubt, however, whether these facts will bear the interpretation placed on them. Hill-top sites were probably selected because of the facilities they afford for defence; a wide range of view from such sites is inevitable.

Speculation as to the relation between the inhabitants of these hill-forts and the dyke-building peoples of Suffolk and Norfolk is wellnigh valueless. Finds and remains dating from the century immediately preceding the Claudian conquest have given some indications as to the probable boundaries of the Iceni at that period; but of the history of the conquest of Goidel by Brython, or of the civil wars which may have marked the earlier phase of the Iron Age we are absolutely ignorant.

There are three observations which may, however, safely be made.

(i) One is that it is probable that these fortresses were used by the Celtic peoples in their struggle against the Romans, and that the Stort-Essex Cam Valley route was then important. The position of the Roman station of Chesterford between Ring Hill and Wandlebury, and at a point which blocks the northern outlet of the Stort Valley population, is suggestive.

(ii) Another concerns the Heydon Ditch.

The population of the Stort and Essex Cam Valleys must have been, when Wallbury and Ring Hill were built, sufficiently numerous to have been a potential source of danger to the inhabitants of S.W. Norfolk. Now the Cambridgeshire dykes are entirely confined to the belt of open country along which the Icknield Way runs, and it is clear that when Heydon Ditch, the most westerly of the series, was constructed no danger was apprehended from the left flank (the Essex Cam Valley district). Otherwise we should, I suggest, find barrier earthworks across this valley in the neighbourhood—say—of Chesterford. It follows that whatever people built Heydon Ditch must have controlled the Stort Valley-Cam Valley route. A confederation of East Anglian peoples such as this suggests was clearly possible in the Early Iron Age; and indeed such a war as that between Cassivellaunus and the Trinovantes to which Caesar refers (*B.G.* v, 20) might provide the military and political situation which on this view the facts require.

(iii) My last observation refers to Caesar's Camp, Sandy. The increase of population in the Ivel Valley which, as finds suggest, took place in the Early Iron Age renders it extremely probable that this fortress was then constructed as a camp of refuge for the more southerly of the settlements in this district.

POSSIBLY OR CERTAINLY PREHISTORIC

THE LOWLAND RING-WORKS

Arbury, Belsar's Hill and Round Moats, topographically, are distinguished by their natural inaccessibility, low-lying situation and wet moats.

Excavation has given no clue to the age of Arbury or the Round Moats; Belsar's Hill has not been excavated.

Belsar's Hill commands an ancient causeway (and ford?) giving access to the Isle of Ely, which the Bronze Age finds near Aldreth High Bridge suggest may have been in use at an early period. Arbury lies close to the mediaeval route from Cambridge to Aldreth; and the whole length of this Way, from the fords across the Cam to Ely Island, may be prehistoric[1]. Round Moats lies in a marshy valley at Fowlmere close to the line of the Street Way, but has not necessarily any connection therewith.

There is nothing in the character of Arbury or Belsar's Hill to suggest post-Roman construction. Concerning the Round Moats I am less confident. Circular or regularly oval moated sites with high valla of mediaeval date are uncommon, but the small size of the Round Moats certainly favours a late rather than an early period. It is unfortunate that no dateable objects were found during Yorke's excavations.

PITS OR SUBTERRANEAN CHAMBERS

Several pits and chambers excavated or sunk in the chalk have been recorded in the Royston district. Whether their original use was as habitations or refuges, or whether they were flint mines is unknown; the majority were probably pre-Roman. Beldam (1868) remarks that "in this neighbourhood tradition speaks of several caves or caverns having been broken up within the present century." The best known example is the Royston cave situated at the point where Icknield Way crosses Ermine Street; but this may be of Roman or later date.

PREHISTORIC TRACKWAYS

The general characteristics of roads and routes used by peoples in varying stages of culture may be differentiated.

1. Ridgeways. These follow the crest-line of the hills. On the chalk downland of South England they appear to be the earliest type of trackway; probably earlier even than any of the hill-forts. Their characteristic is that of a bundle of tracks converging and creating

---

[1] See Map V and p. 155. For the distribution of finds in the area traversed by the route, see the maps of the Neolithic and Bronze Ages.

deep holloways when descent from the high land (in order to cross a river) is necessary.

2. Hillside Ways. These follow the contours of the hills, running on a level alignment just above the spring line. They have been held to mark the period when the hill population began to leave the uplands and to form settlements by the springheads on the edge of the uncleared jungle; but my investigations show that in the Cambridge Region settlements on such sites are of very high antiquity, and such ways may here be as old as the ridgeways.

3. Valley routes, usually late; but may be early, as when a trackway has to cross a watershed; in such case the easiest route is usually found by following a valley up to the saddle or col, crossing the hills at this point and following an adjacent valley down.

4. Engineered and metalled roads, carefully aligned; necessarily the product of a high civilization; well represented by Roman roads.

We are concerned here with trackways of the first three types only. The subject as far as Cambridgeshire is concerned has been dealt with by Babington (1883) and partially by Codrington (1918); and the Icknield Way has been the subject of numerous monographs[1]. The 1836 1-inch Ordnance Survey map, moreover, is of the greatest value, for the survey was made prior to the enclosure of many parishes in the district.

A brief account of the chief routes which are likely to be pre-Roman is all that is possible here. The subject is a very difficult one; the whole countryside is a network of communications, both new and old, and enclosure in XVIII–XIX A.D. caused the destruction of many old ways and diverted others from their ancient alignments. In these circumstances chief reliance must be placed on careful study of a given route in relation to primitive geography; on the existence in its immediate neighbourhood of prehistoric earthworks such as camps and barrows; on the occurrence of portable antiquities along its course; and on the extent to which it forms parish boundaries, in order to determine whether or no an ancient trackway is likely to be prehistoric. Few will be found to yield much evidence of this character.

The alignments of our ancient roads or tracks are determined by the position of the river crossings. The belt of marsh must at the chosen spot be narrower than elsewhere and the river fordable. Examples of such points

---

[1] See Beldam (1868) and W. G. Clarke (1918), the latter especially for sector Lackford-Thetford. Beloe (1896, p. 93) and Bullock-Hall (1901) may be consulted, but their papers are of little value for my purpose. For the Herts. sector, U. A. Smith (1913) is most useful.

are: on the Little Ouse at Thetford, the Lark at Lackford, the Kennett at Badlingham and Kentford, and the Essex Cam at Hauxton, Whittlesford Bridge and Ickleton.

Topographical details are recorded where difference of opinion exists as to the exact trace of an ancient way. Such details are worked out on the O.S. maps, 1-inch scale (see Sheets 174, 187, 188, 189, 204 and 205). The routes are plotted on my Map V.

ICKNIELD WAY[1]

The crest-line of the chalk belt which crosses Cambridgeshire diagonally, and along which the Icknield Way runs, is clay-capped, and under primitive conditions forest: the Way, therefore, is not a true ridgeway but follows the line of the open downs below the summits. Its importance for East Anglian pre-history has been frequently noted in this book directly or by implication, and need not be further emphasized.

The Alignment. The course of the Way is pretty clear and is well known from the Berkshire downs and the Thames to the borders of our district. From Dunstable to Newmarket it takes for the most part a midway course between forest-clad hills and watered valleys. In discussing its trace it must be remembered that in places several parallel routes may have been followed at different seasons of the year, and that alternative routes may occur where obstacles have to be crossed. Each route was a broad band of tracks: at certain points where the Icknield Way passes round a spur of the downs the whole hillside viewed against the sky is seen to be serrated, like the teeth of a saw, for a distance of two or three hundred yards, each indentation representing a separate track[2]. These broad routes were in historic times gradually reduced by enclosure. Moreover, in prehistoric times the alternative routes must have coalesced into one narrow track if dykes barred the way.

It will be convenient to commence our brief survey at the point where the Way crosses the ford of the Hiz at Ickleford, 1½ miles north of Hitchin. From thence to Baldock its trace is known, being marked by parish boundaries, though the Way is partially disused and ploughed up. Passing Willbury Hill it crossed Norton Common, skirting the claylands of Letchworth; and, following a course approximately that of the railway, passed through the northern part of Baldock town.

[1] Codrington, 1918, pp. 191-3, 197-9; Babington, 1883, pp. 55-6, and refs. on my p. 142.
[2] Thus no indication of the line followed by the Way can be other than approximate.

EARTHWORKS AND TRACKWAYS

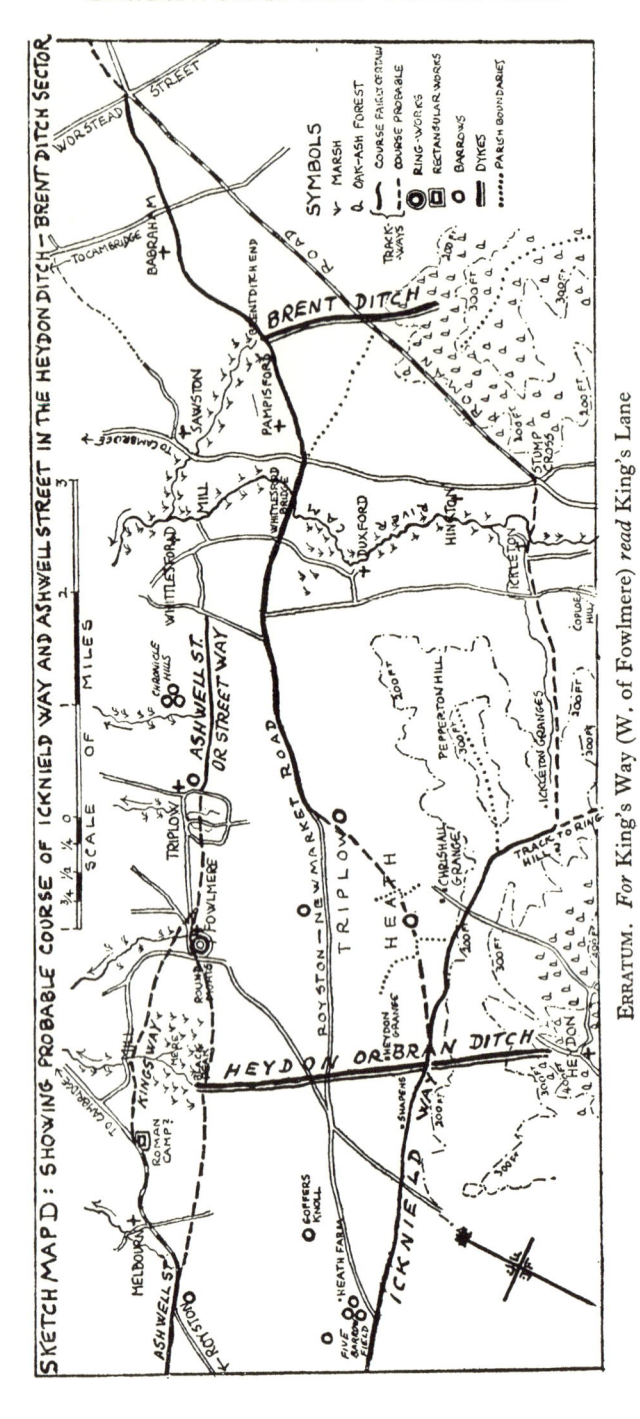

SKETCH MAP D: SHOWING PROBABLE COURSE OF ICKNIELD WAY AND ASHWELL STREET IN THE HEYDON DITCH—BRENT DITCH SECTOR

ERRATUM. *For* King's Way (W. of Fowlmere) *read* King's Lane

POSSIBLY OR CERTAINLY PREHISTORIC

From thence to Royston it forms the modern turnpike road and is marked by parish or county boundaries throughout its length[1].

From Royston to Heydon Ditch the course of the Way is known: it passes Noon's Folly Farm and Shapens, crossing the Ditch 600 yards S.S.E. of Heydon Grange. Here the excavations previously mentioned showed that the fosse was not continuous, that the road was older than the dyke, and that the line indicated above is the original alignment.

The Way, in my opinion, here divides: one route, a track in part a county boundary passes south of Chrishall Grange, crosses the saddle of Pepperton Hill and follows the valley by Ickleton Granges (a track branching southward at this point possibly led to Ring Hill and the Essex Cam Valley settlements) to Ickleton, where an ancient ford over the Cam, and a track, carry the line on to Stump Cross.

The other route, crossing Triplow Heath, makes, I think, straight for the tumulus 500 yards N.W. of Chrishall Grange, then following a parish boundary and passing a second tumulus it joins the present Royston-Whittlesford road south of Triplow. From this point the Way is a parish boundary to the crossing of the Essex Cam at Whittlesford Bridge and beyond. The alternative routes are shown on Sketch-map D[2].

From the cross-roads east of the bridge to Newmarket the trace is not accurately known. Mediaeval itineraries show that the route was then *via* Babraham; the evident antiquity of the holloway north-east of Babraham village, and the probability that this branch of the Way skirted and did not cross the high ground at Brent Ditch, are important factors influencing my solution of the problem, as indicated on the Sketch-map.

A charter of X A.D. (p. 130) records that "the highway" crossed the Fleam Dyke at the western end of the Wratting parish boundary, while the parish boundary west of Steeplechase Course on Newmarket Heath almost certainly fixes for us its point of passage of the Devil's Dyke. These indications enable the alignment marked on Map III to be laid down.

The alignment of the parallel track which we left at Stump Cross in Ickleton parish cannot be determined. It has been Romanized

---

[1] Beldam (1868, p. 24) records that in documents of XII and XIII A.D. from Royston Priory the road is called Hickneld or Ykenilde Street.

[2] The 1836 O.S. map is of great value here; it fixes the route from Ickleton Granges to Ickleton, and indicates the alternative track across Triplow Heath. It also shows the branch track (Walden Way, now partly destroyed) passing through Strethall parish as indicated on my Map III.

in this sector (Stump Cross to Worstead Lodge), being utilized as a route to the north from Chesterford (see p. 166). It may have crossed the Bourn by the ford at Bourn Bridge, rejoining the main track at Worstead Lodge. If so it crossed Brent Ditch at or near the point where the Ditch is said to have been filled in to permit the passage of the Roman road.

From the Devil's Dyke, through the town of Newmarket to Kentford, the course of the Way is marked by parish and county boundaries, and is approximately that of the Newmarket-Bury road. In Newmarket it was, as a mediaeval document records, known as the Ykenildeweie in XIII A.D. (Babington, 1883, p. 55).

From Slade Bottom, a mile beyond the crossing of the Kennett at Kentford (where there is a mediaeval pack-horse bridge) to the crossing of the Lark at Lackford (the name of a Hundred, testifying to the importance of the ford in Saxon times) the Way resumes its primitive character, that of a sinuous track. It crosses the Black Ditches near Cavenham.

That the trackway across Cavenham Heath (west of the Cavenham Brook) to Farthing Bridge, Icklingham, and the Pilgrim's Path beyond, is an ancient alternative route to Thetford, is possible: the northern sector of the Black Ditches may in that case have been designed to cover the crossing of the Lark at Icklingham. This alignment is marked on Map V.

From Lackford to the boundary of the Liberty of Thetford an existing track (which, though nowhere called Icknield, is certainly a continuation of the Way) forms parish and hundred boundaries, running by a sinuous yet direct course past Shelterhouse Corner, Barrows Corner, and Marmansgrave Wood. Here parish boundaries fail us; but W. G. Clarke in his valuable paper on the Way (1918, p. 544) indicates its probable objective, the ancient fords across the Little Ouse and the Thet. This track passes by the Castle Hill earthworks, and its course incidentally supplies a reason for the position of the Norman castle.

Some trace the Way beyond Thetford[1]; but the alignments are doubtful; and a glance at the Sketch map (B), p. 73, indicates the reason. The Way has served its purpose; directly the forest and fen are past travellers may go east or north at will; Norfolk forms the northern reservoir which feeds or is fed by the Way.

For the same reason the Way as a definite route is lost near Avebury in Wiltshire; the southern reservoir has been reached.

[1] To the Peddars Way on Bridgham Heath. For this and other routes see W. G. Clarke, 1918, pp. 545-6.

Evidence of Antiquity. The Icknield Way is known historically as far back as Anglo-Saxon times; here and there in its course through our Region, as elsewhere, round barrows mark its trace[1]; the extension of the long barrow culture into Eastern Britain, marked by examples at Dunstable and Therfield, strictly follows the course of the Way; four dykes are crossed centrally by the Way and are clearly secondary to it; and for the greater part of its course in our district the traditional route forms parish or county boundaries.

As we have seen, weapons of various dates have been found on the line of the Way; but in a countryside so fully occupied from earliest times the evidential value of the majority of the finds cannot be rated very highly.

See W. G. Clarke (1918, p. 546) for antiquities found near the fords at Thetford. He mentions also that "more than a dozen dagger handles of Danish type" have been found on the Suffolk course of the Icknield Way nearly all in North Stow: none has occurred elsewhere in the neighbourhood.

The absence of villages on its line, frequently a distinguishing characteristic of *Roman* roads, is due, in this prehistoric instance, to the fact that the Way keeps well above the spring line, traversing a waterless area unsuitable for permanent habitation.

Ashwell Street: Street Way

The roads that go by these names undoubtedly form one system parallel to the Icknield Way from Ashwell [H] to the River Lark.

Evidently Roman or Romanized in one sector, it presents the characters of a pre-Roman way in others. In general, its type is that of a "Hillside Way," for it keeps on the foot-hills of the chalk just above the spring line, the position of which is determined by the outcrop of Melbourn Rock at the base of the Middle, or of Totternhoe Stone at the base of the Lower Chalk. The alignment of the Way at Ashwell, Litlington, Kneesworth, Melbourn, Triplow, Wilbraham, Exning and Snailwell illustrates its character and explains its function. It duplicated the Icknield Way for travellers who desired to be near wood and water, and it may indeed have been the "summer road" of, and therefore as old as, the Way itself. It is not probable that the dyke-builders would leave two gateways to guard where one sufficed, and certain peculiarities and breaks in its course may be, as we shall see, due to artificial deflections.

---

[1] Apart from the groups which seem to have no connection with it, we may note the landmarks of Mutlow Hill (p. 35) and Bury Hill, Moulton [S]; and also several tumuli on the line of the Way between Kentford and Cavenham.

Trace. South-west of Ashwell the alignment is very uncertain, but parish and county boundaries and old roads existing in 1836, now destroyed, suggest that the route was Willbury Hill - Radwell Mill-Newnham-Ashwell, which skirts the clay lands, as a glance at Map III will show. From Ashwell to Ermine Street it is, as its name "Ashwell Street" indicates, a straight road of Roman character; but this road keeping as it does on the margin of the water-bearing stratum must preserve the ancient alignment. From Ermine Street to Melbourn its sinuous course is marked by parish boundaries, and suggests pre-Roman origin.

From Melbourn to Triplow the route is doubtful. The majority of writers believe it to have gone south of Black Peak to Fowlmere, along a track marked on the 1836 O.S. map (Sheet LI); a view which I shared until I had the advantage of consulting the Rev. A. C. Yorke of Fowlmere, whose knowledge of the district is unrivalled. Mr Yorke considers that the Way skirted the mere on the *north* side; this route also is shown on the 1836 survey. The alternatives are indicated on Sketch-map D. The fact that in local tradition the track considered by the Rector of Fowlmere to be the ancient way is known as Ashwell Street in one part (King's Lane in another) goes far to confirm his hypothesis. There was no doubt an ancient ford by Fowlmere Mill[1].

The two views may be reconciled on the assumption that the Way originally passed to the south of Black Peak—a route consistent with its character; but that after Heydon Ditch was constructed the route usually adopted was that by Fowlmere Mill.

From Triplow to Whittlesford a green lane flanked by several tumuli of the Early Iron Age may with reasonable certainty be held to fix the line of the ancient way: but its course for a further six miles is very doubtful. It may originally have swung southward to Whittlesford Bridge and become merged in the Icknield Way (see Sketch-map D).

Assuming that it retained its individuality, two possible alignments are[2]:

I. Whittlesford Mill: footpath to Sawston; lane passing by Sawston Church; then field track running north-north-east continued by footpath to Cott Farm on Cambridge-Linton road: thence to Fulbourn Lodge, the line suggested being approximately that of the post-enclosure track, passing the great tumulus Copley Hill. From the spur on which the Lodge is situated the Way is presumed to make for Shardelow's Well at the Fulbourn

[1] In many cases in Cambridgeshire, mills are on the site of ancient fords: and the reason is, no doubt, that there is naturally a slight head of water just above a natural ford which a little embanking renders serviceable water power.

[2] The 1-inch O.S. Sheet 205 should here be consulted.

POSSIBLY OR CERTAINLY PREHISTORIC

end of the Fleam Dyke (its trace being obliterated by enclosures) beyond which an existing green lane takes up the alignment.

II. The second possible trace is parallel to, and west of, No. I. To Sawston Church as before; proceeding thence N.N.E. towards Wormwood Hill (a tumulus adjacent to the 5-mile stone on the Cambridge-Linton road), by a route marked by the track to North Farm, and by a parish boundary; Worstead Street is then reached by a sinuous trackway undoubtedly ancient, skirting Gog-Magog Hills park. From this point the Way is presumed to have made straight for Shardelow's Well.

Dry gravelly subsoil renders the crossing of the Bourn Valley at either of these points, marked to-day by footpaths, easy; but I am not satisfied that the marshy valley of the Cam could conveniently have been passed at Whittlesford Mill. It is, however, clear that the chief feature of a "summer way" is that it utilizes down-stream fords and crosses marshes impossible in winter.

I have not felt justified in indicating either of these hypothetical routes on Maps III or V.

Near Shardelow's Well, Great Wilbraham, we are once more on firm ground. An existing green lane, henceforward known as the Street Way, runs parallel to, and at a distance of 1–1½ miles from, Icknield Way for 7 miles to Exning [S], making for the spring-head known as St Mindred's Well. Though breaks occur its course is clear thence past Snailwell, through Chippenham Park; crossing the Kennett at Badlingham Hall[1], an ancient manor, it makes by a well-defined ancient way for the River Lark at Worlington [S]. I have been unable to trace it further; for a conjectural alignment see Babington (1883, p. 65).

I have treated the Way in this analysis as a *through* route; but in prehistoric and Roman times it may have been mainly of *local* importance, linking up hamlets and villages grouped round the never-failing chalk springs.

Evidence of Antiquity. The Street Way consistently presents throughout its course from Ashwell to Worlington the characteristics of a "summer" or "hillside" way; that portion of the Way west of the Essex Cam which is not Roman, marked as it is by barrows such as that which gives its name to Triplow, and by the Chronicle Hills group, links up with the Romanized portion in a manner which suggests that it is older, not younger, than the Roman road. For the sector east of the Cam: though an Anglo-Saxon cemetery adjoins the Way near Wilbraham, and barrows lie beside it at Hare Park, the evidence for high antiquity lies more, I think, in its choice of route

---

[1] Very close to, if not actually on, its line between Chippenham and Badlingham the bronze-founder's hoard described on p. 59 was found.

than in any definite associations. Sections of the Way are in this part of its course exactly aligned, and the name "Street Way" may correctly record its type, that of a pre-Roman Way in places straightened and metalled by the Romans. Enclosure has in many places destroyed evidence of its precise alignment; but that its general character is as described will be apparent to anyone who will follow the route here indicated.

Mare Way

In one of the two existing sectors the Mare Way is a true ridgeway. It begins near Coomb Grove Farm on Ermine Street, 1¼ miles south of the Old North Road railway station, and keeping to the crest of the ridge follows the spur which ends abruptly as Chapel Hill,

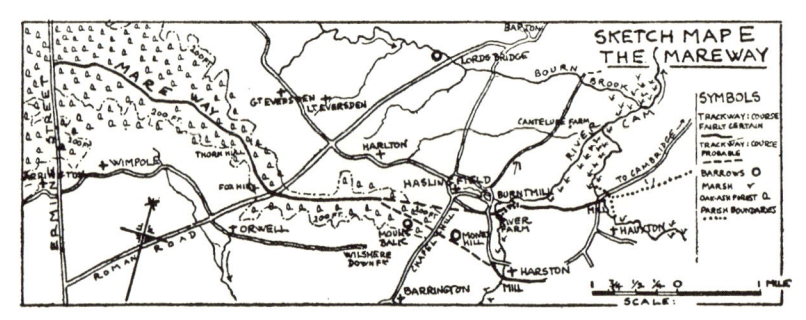

Haslingfield. As an existing track it ceases at Thorn Hill[1], but its original alignment is probably marked by parish boundaries which follow the ridge up to within 700 yards of the site of the chapel of "Our Lady of White Hill" on the Barrington-Haslingfield road, a place of pilgrimage in the Middle Ages. The second existing sector commences at valley level, namely at the crossing of the River Cam (Ashwell branch) between Burnt Mill Bridges and River Farm, from which point a field track leads to its next objective, the ford of the Cam (Chesterford branch) at Hauxton Mill.

From the Mill a parish boundary continues in the same alignment to Red Cross on the Cambridge-Linton road, and suggests the prehistoric settlements on the Gog-Magog Hills as the objective (see Map V).

See Walker (1910, p. 172). An excellent summary, which, however, neglects careful consideration of the crucial sector, Chapel Hill-Cam Valley. The track to Hauxton ford, for example, could not have passed anywhere near Money Hill which is in a re-entrant facing south-east.

[1] In the 1836 edition of the O.S. map the Way continues a few hundred yards further, joining the Ermine Street at Fox Hill.

The Sketch-map (E) indicates the probable trace in the gap between the two known sectors. It is usually assumed that the (Ashwell) Cam was crossed at Burnt Mill Bridges (close to the R of BURNT on the Sketch-map). This involves bad going across two tributary brooks on the left bank, and neglects the highly significant detached portion of Hauxton parish on the right bank[1]. Clearly the significance of this patch of isolated territory is that the Anglo-Saxon lords of Hauxton Manor who held the bridgehead at Hauxton Mill (see map) controlled the Haslingfield ford as well[2]. There is a patch of gravel in the river bed near River Farm and this is probably the original crossing: the construction of the Mill with its convenient bridge and the deep channel known as the New Cut deflected the course of the Way. The New Cut in particular obscures the ancient topography.

Study of the ground in the neighbourhood of Money Hill, a tumulus on the slope of the Chapel Hill spur, suggests the possibility of a branch of the Way having led to Harston Ford (by Harston Mill); a continuous hedge-line running past the tumulus and pointing direct to the ancient "Fordway" (as an old inhabitant of Harston described the forgotten track to me) is also suggestive. The fordway is marked on the 1836 O.S. map.

That the road apparently originates from Ermine Street is no doubt due to the fact that its continuation westwards was not used in the Middle Ages; its objective may have been Caesar's Camp, Sandy, and the adjacent ford across the Ivel; if so, a route *via* Gamlingay may be looked for.

Evidence of Antiquity. In the ridge sector, parish boundaries and two barrows (Mount Balk, now destroyed, and Money Hill) on the tip of the plateau afford the only evidence of the antiquity of the Mare Way, apart from its primitive character as a true ridgeway.

In the valley sector the archaeological evidence is confined to the neighbourhood of Hauxton Mill. Here it is prolific; remains of all ages from the Neolithic onwards have frequently been found, and not only at the Ford; a fine bronze sword, for example, was found in 1908 on the line of the parish boundary a quarter of a mile north-east of the river-crossing (Walker, 1910, p. 173).

The Mare Way, as Walker notes in the paper several times quoted, is, with very slight exceptions, a parish boundary for over 10 miles —from Ermine Street to Red Cross.

[1] Walker (1910, p. 173) is in error here.
[2] Domesday Book states that Havocheston Manor (Hauxton) lies, and always lay, in the demesne of the Church of Ely.

The apparent importance of the valley sector of the route in Anglo-Saxon times suggests pre-Saxon origin; we have already noted that Lackford, the point where the Icknield Way crosses the Lark, gives its name to a Hundred; and the men of the Hundred of Chilford assembled close to the point where the trackway discussed on p. 153, and held to be prehistoric, is considered to have crossed the Bourn River.

While convinced that the upland sector of the Mare Way is a prehistoric track and that its course is as here described I do not wish to exaggerate the cogency of the evidence. In the first place, even assuming that Mount Balk is of the Bronze Age, it may have no relation whatever to the track, being placed as was commonly done in that Age in a conspicuous position on the end of a spur. Moreover, the existence of parish boundaries along the whole length of the ridge is only confirmatory evidence. Parish boundaries follow the crest-line of the spur (Pepperton Hill) north of Ickleton Granges; they follow the crest of the watershed between the Bourn River and the Essex Cam from Abington Park to Woodstone, east of Saffron Walden, six miles as the crow flies. No one has suggested the existence of an ancient way along either of these ridges; the explanation is much more simple. As the villages in the valleys extended their arable up the hill-slopes, questions as to rights and boundaries inevitably arose when contact was established on the hill-top, and the boundary was naturally fixed on the crest-line. The term Mare Way (Maerweg), moreover, as Grundy (1917, p. 104) has shown, indicates an occupation road on the edge of the ploughland; when it occurs in charters it suggests that the arable had extended up to the limits of the parish. Our Mare Way may have been such a road; they are common in our district. The tracks, for example, bearing the name "Mere Way," between Hemingford Grey and Hemingford Abbots [Hunts.], between Wyton and Houghton [Hunts.], and between Willingham and Long Stanton are probably not of pre-Saxon antiquity.

Many other roads and tracks in Cambridgeshire are probably prehistoric, certainly in the Iron Age at least there must have been a network of them, as we know was the case in Essex and Hertfordshire (Caesar, *B.G.* v, 19). But in none is the archaeological evidence sufficiently strong to justify *detailed* consideration. They cannot, however, be wholly neglected in our survey: some half-dozen routes of varying type have therefore been selected and are indicated on the Anglo-Saxon Map (V), and their salient characteristics and features of interest will be briefly described[1].

A. **Stansted Mountfitchet [E] to Trumpington.** (A portion of the Stort-Essex Cam Valley route from the Thames to the Fenland Basin.)

[1] Babington (1883) discusses others, possibly pre-Roman, such as the Moat Way and the Bullock Way.

POSSIBLY OR CERTAINLY PREHISTORIC

The importance of this route has frequently been referred to, particularly in connection with the Wallbury and Ring Hill fortresses and with finds of the Early Iron Age at Trumpington and Grantchester. The probable alignment, which provides good going on well-drained gravel terraces, is as indicated on Map V; the Way may have crossed the Cam at Chesterford, but in ancient (as in modern) times this valley road from Wendens Ambo [E] northward was doubtless duplicated, running on either side of the river[1]. The marshland by Audley End House necessitated a detour through Walden for the traffic on the right bank; the importance of the ford across the "Slade" at this point may account for the position of the Paille Ditches.

The absence of traces of a Roman road on the alignment we are discussing is perhaps evidence that in the Early Iron Age a road suitable for wheeled vehicles already existed; for the route is geographically so important that it must have been in use in Roman times.

This point will be amplified in Chapter V when dealing with Roman roads; a similar argument suggests the probability that good roads from Colchester (Camulodunum) and the Essex coast up the Stour and Colne Valleys existed before the Claudian conquest. If so, the modern highways up these valleys may closely follow the ancient alignments. The Stour Valley road is marked on Map V.

B. Trackway: Linton-Balsham-Stetchworth. (Probably part of a route to the north-east from the Essex Cam Valley settlements at Chesterford and Walden, duplicating the Icknield Way.)

This track is certainly not of Anglo-Saxon origin. Its relation to the villages which are distributed along the margin of the forest belt is clearly accidental. Its distinctive character is well brought out on the Map (V); it skirts the forest closely, but while avoiding the clay lands as much as possible it does not hesitate to cross the tongues of woodland which here and there mark an outlier of the drift. Disused chalk pits are to be seen beside it.

From Stetchworth a possible continuation is marked by footpaths, tracks or modern roads (best shown on the 1836 O.S. map) through Cheveley, Ashley, Gazeley and Higham, joining the Icknield Way at Cavenham [S]. This route is more closely related to the villages than is the Linton-Stetchworth Way; and it may be of later date.

From Linton southward the course of the Way is doubtful; but here again routes consistent with its character are available; those, namely, across narrow belts of forest to Chesterford and Walden.

[1] Compare the parallel roads in the Valley of the Bourn River.

We may provisionally then regard the Way as a short cut from the Essex Cam Valley settlements to the heathlands of N.W. Suffolk.

C. Ridgeway: Eltisley to Madingley Hill. (Probably part of a route from the Great Ouse Valley to the Cam Valley.)

The modern road is a parish boundary for nearly the entire distance of 9 miles. This fact, its character as a true ridgeway (it strictly follows the watershed), and the discovery of a gold coin of Cunobelinus on its line at Childerley Gate, which is forest land apparently unoccupied in pre-Roman days, suggest that it may have been one of the British woodland roads to which Caesar draws attention[1].

Eltisley is geographically a nodal point at which many modern roads meet; and several prehistoric ways ascending from the lowlands of the Great Ouse Valley by lateral ridges may in like manner have coalesced here.

One well-defined ridge is that which extends from Great Gransden to Sandy [B] terminating in the steep-ended spur on which Caesar's Camp is situated[2]. Broken segments of what is undoubtedly an ancient track follow the crest of this dry and well-drained greensand ridge through Everton [B] to Tetworth [Hunts.]; if, as is not improbable, its objective was Eltisley, our ridgeway may have served as one of the connecting links between the Ouse and Cam Valley settlements.

It may be urged that the suggested route is too circuitous to have been in general use. But anyone who has traversed forest country in which the subsoil is clay will understand the impossibility of a primitive people using in winter any track across this belt of upland save the one which keeps to the crest-line. Bogs and quags would force the traveller back to the ridge should he attempt to deviate. That there was a shorter route—perhaps a summer road—from Gamlingay to the valley of the Bourn Brook and thence to Grantchester and Trumpington is, however, highly probable.

I can offer no suggestions as to its course from the forest to the fords of the Cam; but Babington (1883, p. 49) records a possible route *via* Hardwick to Grantchester known as Deadman's Way, and the 1836 O.S. marks a track from Childerley Gate to Hardwick. Or the Way may have passed by Coton, and crossed the Cam in the neighbourhood of Cambridge.

D. Hillside Ways. (i) Croydon-Arrington-Wimpole Hall-Orwell-Wilsmere Down Farm-Haslingfield (or Harston?).

(ii) The Eversdens-Harlton-Haslingfield.

---

[1] The points raised on p. 152 in connection with the Mare Way, however, apply with almost equal force to this road.

[2] The ½-inch O.S. Sheet 24, layered, is of great service here.

The former, on the south side of the Fox Hill-Chapel Hill spur, is a true hillside way; it is sinuous, and old chalk pits mark its course, which runs just above the spring line wherever possible. A ringwork (now destroyed) existed at Orwell and finds of pre-Roman date at several points on its alignment are recorded.

Finds in 1879 in the channel of a small streamlet just below the 100-foot contour, 700 yards south-south-west of the Money Hill tumulus, suggest that Haslingfield was its objective. (Information from Mr A. F. Griffith, 21.10.21.)

The latter road on the north slope of the same spur, is of similar character.

The whole system, part of which is shown on sketch-map E, may be closely connected with the valley sector of the Mare Way.

E. Aldreth Causeway. The mediaeval route to Ely from Cambridge (*via* Histon-Lamb's Cross-Rampton-Aldreth) may, as has been suggested (p. 137), preserve some elements of a prehistoric track. Whether this be so or no finds of Neolithic and Bronze Age date near Aldreth High Bridge suggest that a ford existed here in pre-Roman times and the situation of the camp of Belsar's Hill which controls the southern approaches thereto is certainly significant.

F. Two Trackways crossing a Watershed. (i) Walkern-Clothall-Baldock [H]; and

(ii) Walkern-Cumberlow Green-Slip End, Odsey, near Ashwell [H].

From the upper valley of the River Beane two sinuous tracks running north cross the watershed—here a narrow belt of clay (forest) land—into the Ivel Valley, being traceable as far as the Icknield Way. Parish boundaries follow almost the entire length of both; on the line of the latter the Cumberlow hoard of bronze was found (p. 324) and its objective, Slip End, is close to a well-known Early Iron Age and Roman settlement site.

The southward extension is uncertain; but that it originated at Verulamium, passing through Welwyn and Woolmer Green [H], is highly probable.

The Walkern-Clothall-Baldock road has every appearance of antiquity; and seems to have been used in part by the Romans (see p. 170).

G. The Droveway. Many tracks across the warrens of the north-east of our district present ancient characters (parish boundaries, tumuli, etc.). The Droveway, a track north of and for several miles parallel to the Little Ouse river, analysed by Clarke and Hewitt (1914) is the most interesting. Pilgrim's Walk, Weeting,

Pilgrim's Path, Icklingham, and a track across Lakenheath Warren may also be cited as examples. All these are marked on Map V. But the whole area is so seamed with tracks new and old that accurate determination of a prehistoric route is wellnigh impossible.

SUMMARY: EARTHWORKS AND TRACKWAYS

Dykes. Of the five dykes which span the chalk belt from forest to fen, preventing access to East Anglia from the Midlands, only one, the Fleam, has been excavated. The main sector of this Dyke, which is the second in point of size, has been shown to have been constructed after the Claudian conquest, and, therefore, probably in the Anglo-Saxon Age. For the date of the others we are mainly dependent on probabilities. The existence of areas protected by dykes in S.W. Norfolk, and the absence in this area of ring forts, suggest that works such as the Black Ditches, and the Fen Ditton sector of the Fleam Dyke, may be tribal defences, the work of pre-Roman people or peoples who employed similar methods in the district indicated above. On the other hand, it is held that the Devil's Dyke, by reason of its size, and the Heydon Ditch, on account of its advanced position on the chalk belt, may have been national rather than tribal works, dating from a time when the energies of a large portion of the inhabitants of East Anglia were controlled from a single centre. This period may have been the Anglo-Saxon; but a body of indirect evidence suggests that the Devil's Dyke at least is a work of the Early Iron Age, the builders being the Iceni.

Ring-Works. It is significant that in none of our hill-forts, whether they be contour forts (such as Caesar's Camp) or plateau ring-works (such as Wandlebury), have any objects been found earlier than the Iron Age; moreover, War Ditches, the only hill-fort which has been adequately examined, is certainly of this period. We can at present know nothing of the part which these fortresses played in the tribal or racial wars of the Age, or of their relations to the defensive system of the dykes; but we can get hints from their topography; the existence of Ring Hill (and of Wallbury to the south thereof) must, for example, be largely due to the importance of the Stort-Cam Valley trade-route from the Kentish ports and the lower Thames. The increase in the population and wealth of the Ivel Valley, again, which is a marked feature of the Early Iron Age in our district, sufficiently accounts for the appearance of Caesar's Camp, which occupies an ideal site for a hill-fort.

Though so little is known of our hill-forts and dykes one probability emerges from the preceding analysis; namely, that organized warfare, of which such works are the visible outcome, was unknown in Eastern Britain until the Iron Age.

Concerning the smaller ring-works, low-lying, inaccessible, wet moated, little can be said; Arbury and Belsar's Hill are probably prehistoric, but the possibility of a mediaeval origin for the small work at Fowlmere cannot be excluded.

Trackways. The alignment of the Icknield Way, a route probably in use from Neolithic times, and the most important factor in the prehistory of the Cambridge Region, has been discussed at length. The Way is thought not to exist beyond Thetford because Norfolk is its objective, and the canalization of traffic, which its existence implies, necessarily ceased when East Anglia was reached.

The characters of the Street Way, a "hillside Way" running just above the spring line, have been shown to be constant, and it is regarded as a "summer road," alternative to the Icknield Way, and not improbably of equal antiquity.

There is evidence in the shape of implements of all periods, from the Neolithic Age onwards, that a track which crosses the Essex Cam at Hauxton Mill is of high antiquity; it is thought to be connected with the ridgeway known as the Mare Way which followed the crest of the forest-clad spur south of the Eversdens to Ermine Street (and beyond?). Another road which follows a watershed for many miles and is, like the Mare Way, continuously a parish boundary, is that from Madingley Hill, west of Cambridge, to Eltisley; that both these forest ways may date only from Anglo-Saxon times is considered possible though improbable.

That the Romans used trackways of the Early Iron Age folk is a view put forward to account for the absence of roads recognizably of Roman origin in the more fertile areas of our district known to have been inhabited by Celtic tribes. Modern highways such as that along the Stort and Cam Valleys, past Ring Hill and Wallbury, and that following the course of the Stour from Long Melford to Haverhill are thought to preserve pre-Roman alignments. Pre-Roman origin, again, is regarded as probable for a curious track following the borders of the ancient forest from Linton to Stetchworth, for the tracks crossing the north Hertfordshire watershed from Walkern to the Ivel Valley, and for the hillside ways on either side of the Fox Hill-Chapel Hill spur, on the crest of which runs the Mare Way. Many ancient ways exist in Breckland; of these the Drove Way is the best attested.

That numerous other routes existing, wholly or in part, to-day have a claim to discussion equal to many of those mentioned is admitted, but proof of antiquity is lacking; and it has been thought better to confine discussion to a few examples varying as widely as possible in character.

The paucity of evidence bearing on prehistoric traffic routes emphasizes the importance of obtaining the exact provenance of objects of all periods deposited in the future in our museums. That a bronze sword, or a stone axehammer, is known to have been found in a particular parish is a useful piece of information; it might clearly be many times more useful if the particular field, hedgebank or ditch of origin, and the conditions of deposit, were recorded.

For very few of the thousands of objects indexed and utilized in the preparation of this treatise, are such necessary data available.

CHAPTER V

THE ROMAN AGE

"*Today the Roman and his trouble*
"*Are ashes under Uricon.*"   HOUSMAN.

INTRODUCTION

THE situation of the writer, passing from the Early Iron to the Roman Age, may be likened to that of a traveller who, traversing a countryside inadequately surveyed and utilizing in his journey such boggy paths and rutted droveways as appear to lead in the direction he wishes to go, suddenly reaches a broad metalled highway with its guideposts and milestones.

Prehistoric trackways have, in fact, been left behind; and before us stretches the exact alignment of the Roman Road.

The analogy must not be pressed so far as to imply that our difficulties are over; even Roman roads only survive in broken segments, and we may yet lose direction before reaching our goal.

This trope may also serve to remind us that a clear understanding of the Roman road system is a primary necessity for the study of the remains of the Age in our district. "Transportation is civilization" as the Romans well knew; and though not necessarily the lines on which settlement developed, the roads were the channels by which the Roman culture penetrated the country.

The analysis of the Roman period in its topographical aspect, then, will begin with the roads and the camp sites or towns thereon and with the canals of Roman origin; then further evidences of civilization afforded by remains of rural dwellings of Roman type, and by Roman burials will be noted; finds of terra sigillata, fine bronzes, etc., will be discussed, but scattered finds, which do not *in themselves* indicate more than the partial Romanization of the native inhabitants, are too numerous to be treated independently; all such finds are, however, indicated on the Map (IV)[1]. An estimate of the duration and character of the Roman occupation completes the survey.

---

[1] For the border counties of Norfolk, Suffolk, Hertford and Bedford, excellent topographical indices in the *V.C.H.*, prepared by Page, G. E. Fox, Haverfield and their assistants, have been made use of; and I have been able to limit my work in this connection mainly to the collection of the Cambridge material.

Summaries will be given at successive stages of the analysis.

A brief note of the chief events which may be held to have most closely affected the Cambridge Region during the Roman Age is perhaps a necessary preliminary.

That Aulus Plautius in his campaign in 43 A.D. reached Cambridgeshire, the southern half of which was in Trinovantian or Catuvellaunian territory, is fairly certain; for the Iceni, impressed by the defeat of the latter tribe, submitted to his master Claudius. Details, preserved by Tacitus, connected with the rebellion of the Iceni and its suppression by Ostorius in 48 A.D. suggested to Ridgeway (1892) that the Fleam and Devil's Dykes were utilized as a means of defence by the tribesmen; though it is not improbable that the latter was thus employed, recent research has shown that the former work was not then in existence.

There is ample evidence, as will be seen, that Roman civilization and Roman manners were being rapidly absorbed by the dwellers in the southern part of our district during the next decade; an orderly development which was checked by the revolt of the Iceni in 60 A.D., suppressed by Suetonius in the same year.

To the period covered by the campaigns of Aulus Plautius, Ostorius and Suetonius such slight evidences of Roman military earthwork as exist in the district may provisionally be ascribed (see p. 182).

From this time onwards we have no knowledge of aught to disturb the process of peaceful development in our region until the close of the II century, when (in the reign of Commodus, 180–192) disaster in the north and mutinies in the army must have to some extent disturbed even the civilian area.

The III century and part of the IV century were, as Haverfield remarks (1915, p. 77), a period of progressive prosperity for Roman Britain as well as parts of Gaul. The close of the III century was, it is true, marked by pirate raids; these dangers and the disturbances connected with the death of Allectus (296 A.D.) must have affected Southern Britain, for hoards of coins dating up to this time are not infrequently found.

Such troubles were, however, temporary; and the peaceful years of the IV century were probably in our district uninterrupted until the disaster of 367 A.D. when the then Count of the Saxon Shore and the *Dux Britanniae* were defeated and slain, and Picts, Scots and oversea raiders came flooding into the Midlands. The situation was soon afterwards restored; but the security of life and property was probably

THE ROMAN AGE

permanently lessened. East Anglia must have suffered from recurrent raids until temporary relief was obtained by the reorganization of imperial defence, carried out in the closing years of the century, as indicated in the Notitia Dignitatum (see Oman, 1913, p. 168).

The severing of direct connection with Rome following on the invasion of Gaul by the Suevi, Vandals and other Teutonic tribes in 406[7] is a fact of importance in British archaeology, for the importation of articles of luxury and of coinage probably ceased.

Constantine, the usurper, took the best of the British troops with him to Gaul in 410, and Zosimus records the defection of the provincials which followed his departure (Oman, 1913, p. 174)[1]. Only legend and a few isolated items of information permit us to gain an idea of the progress of the destruction of Roman civilization in Eastern Britain during the next half century[2]; but the closing years of the V century certainly found the Anglo-Saxon invaders in full possession of the Cambridge Region.

ROMAN ROADS

The Cambridge Region lies athwart the Ermine Street, one of the most important highways in Britain, which linked up London and the Continent with Lincoln and the North.

From that portion of Ermine Street which lies within our district two roads branch off in a north-easterly direction; the one from Braughing, the other from near Royston. The former (*via* Chesterford) seems to be making for the Peddars Way near Thetford; the latter (*via* Cambridge and Ely) was evidently designed to provide communication with N.W. Norfolk.

There are two important east-to-west roads, both probably originating at Colchester; the one (Stane Street) passing through Dunmow and by Bishop's Stortford may be held not to concern us, since only the last half-mile, south of Braughing, is within our area; the other crosses Cambridgeshire from south-east to north-west and joins the Ermine Street at Godmanchester.

These highways, in part linked up with pre-Roman ways such as the Icknield Way, form the main framework of communications, and will first be dealt with; minor and vicinal ways will then be discussed.

---

[1] See however Bury (1922), who points out that the final overthrow of Roman power probably did not take place until some thirty years later.

[2] *E.g.* Saint Germanus in 429 A.D. was able to visit, unmolested by Pict or Scot or Saxon, the shrine of St Alban, wherever that may then have been.

THE ROMAN AGE

Reference should be made by the reader to the Sketch-map F showing the road system of Eastern Britain in its relation to the Cambridge Region, the inclusion of which justifies the brevity of the above analysis.

All roads that may fairly claim Roman origin are indicated on the regional map (Map IV) by continuous red lines where the trace is reasonably certain, and by broken lines where it is highly probable. The system as here depicted is manifestly incomplete. It might easily be made more complete; but it is best to follow Codrington's wise rule: "to refrain from conjecture as much as possible and to follow the roads only so far as there is evidence available for tracing them."

Apart from missing segments of known roads, it is clear that the network of communications is not as close as might be expected. This is probably due to the readiness with which vicinal ways went out of use and were destroyed in the Dark Ages; to the use by the Romans of British tracks unmodified or slightly improved for byways; and to the elimination of so large a number of ancient ways, Roman as well as prehistoric, in the enclosures of the XIX century.

The main lines of Roman communications in the neighbourhood of Cambridge are, however, fairly clear to this day. In many cases excavation has proved that roads believed to be Roman are actually of that date, in others we are dependent on probabilities—a succession of rights-of-way or parish boundaries in the required alignment, unmistakable signs of Roman engineering methods in the setting out of a road, may be mentioned as examples.

The consideration of Roman roads in this book would in any case necessarily be far briefer than the subject deserves; but since it has been so adequately treated by others[1] I have reduced it to little more than a catalogue, only discussing routes when my opinion differs from the authorities quoted, to whom the reader is referred for details[2]. No discussion of the itineraries is attempted[3].

---

[1] General survey: Codrington, 1918. For Cambs.: Babington, 1883; Walker, 1910. For Herts.: U. A. Smith, 1913. For Essex: Christy, 1920.

[2] Codrington, for example, records as Roman on his map the road Cambridge-Coton-Ermine Street (Caxton Gibbet). For this road (the Portway) I do not consider the evidence adequate (see p. 171).

[3] For a recent analysis of the evidence so far as it relates to our district, see paper by Yorke (1905).

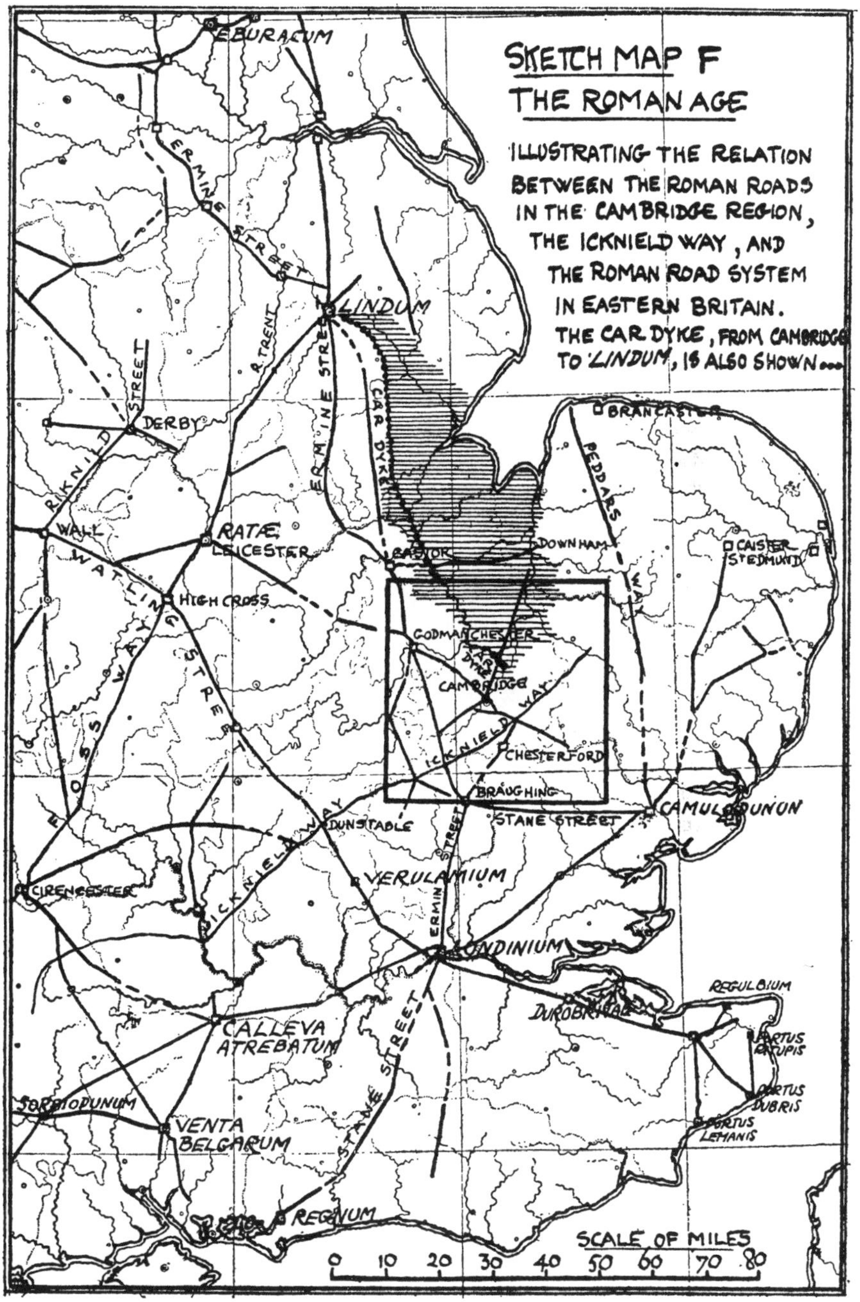
SKETCH MAP F
THE ROMAN AGE
ILLUSTRATING THE RELATION BETWEEN THE ROMAN ROADS IN THE CAMBRIDGE REGION, THE ICKNIELD WAY, AND THE ROMAN ROAD SYSTEM IN EASTERN BRITAIN.
THE CAR DYKE, FROM CAMBRIDGE TO LINDUM, IS ALSO SHOWN...
EBURACUM
ERMINE STREET
LINDUM
TRENT
CAR DYKE
STREET
DERBY
ICKNIELD
WALL
RATAE
LEICESTER
WATLING STREET
HIGH CROSS
FOSS WAY
BRANCASTER
PEDDARS WAY
DOWNHAM
CAISTER
STEDMUND
CASTOR
GODMANCHESTER
CAMBRIDGE
ICKNIELD WAY
CHESTERFORD
BRAUGHING
STANE STREET
CAMULODUNUM
DUNSTABLE
VERULAMIUM
CIRENCESTER
LONDINIUM
REGULBIUM
DUROBRIVAE
CALLEVA
ATREBATUM
PORTUS RITUPIS
PORTUS DUBRIS
PORTUS LEMANIS
SORBIODUNUM
VENTA
BELGARUM
REGNUM
SCALE OF MILES
0 10 20 30 40 50 60 70 80

THE ROMAN AGE

The following summary will facilitate reference:

	PAGE
I. ERMINE STREET	164
II. Roads leading from ERMINE STREET into N.W. SUFFOLK or NORFOLK:	
(A) From ARRINGTON BRIDGE to CAMBRIDGE, ELY and DENVER [N]	165
(Note on HILL LANE, OLD WARDEN [B]) . . .	165
(B) From BRAUGHING [H] to CHESTERFORD [E] and WORSTEAD LODGE	166
(Note on ASHWELL STREET)	167
III. East-to-West road, HAVERHILL [S]-RED CROSS-CAMBRIDGE-GODMANCHESTER [HUNTS.]	168
(Possibly preceded in the western section by the RED CROSS-GRANTCHESTER-BOURN BROOK VALLEY road) . . .	169
IV. Roads, apparently of lesser importance, west of ERMINE STREET:	
(a) BRAUGHING [H]-BALDOCK [H]	170
(b) BALDOCK-BIGGLESWADE [B]-SANDY [B]	170
(c) SANDY-GODMANCHESTER [HUNTS.]	170
(d) BALDOCK-GRAVELEY [H]-? SAINT ALBANS [H] . .	171
(e) ALCONBURY HILL [HUNTS.]-TITCHMARSH [NORTHANTS.] .	171
V. Notes on roads showing alignments possibly Roman, north-east of HUNTINGDON	171
VI. Notes on roads possibly Roman in the neighbourhood of CAMBRIDGE	171
VII. North-and-South road probably Roman, near RADWINTER [E]	172

I. ERMINE STREET[1]

The sector included in our district, Braughing [H]-Godmanchester [Hunts.]-Stilton [Hunts.], is unmistakably Roman and offers few topographical difficulties.

Chief evidences of Roman origin:

1. Parish boundaries mark nearly half (21 miles) of the entire length under investigation (45 miles).

2. Distinctive Roman method of setting out. Great stretches are laid out on the same alignment, changes in direction coinciding with hill-crests. Note particularly the angles on the hill south of Royston, at King's Bush S.E. of Godmanchester, and at Green End, Great Stukeley, N.W. of Huntingdon.

The Ouse was forded or bridged at Huntingdon below the Alconbury

[1] Codrington (1918), pp. 117-19; Babington (1883), pp. 52-4; Walker (1910), p. 163, footnote 3 a and d.

Brook junction (almost certainly between the railway and the road bridges) to avoid two river crossings. Compare the crossing of the Arun at Pulborough, Sussex, by the Stane Street (Belloc, 1913, p. 89).

3. Ancient usage in this sector of the name Ermine Street.

4. Sections at Godmanchester, and at Lattenbury Hill 3 miles to the S.E. thereof, showed typical Roman construction, and Stukeley records the road as being in 1722 perfect and in some parts paved with stone, near Stilton.

II. (A) ROAD BRANCHING FROM ERMINE STREET AT ARRINGTON BRIDGE: PROCEEDING THROUGH CAMBRIDGE TO ELY AND DENVER [N][1]; KNOWN, IN THE SECTOR NORTH-EAST OF CAMBRIDGE, AS MEREWAY OR AKEMAN STREET

The adequately authenticated portion of this road extends from its junction with the Ermine Street through Cambridge to the edge of the fen at Chittering, but its alignment from Fox Hill (Little Eversden) to Cambridge is known only from historical record and as a result of excavation. It has been traced northward through Ely to Denver; its course beyond is quite uncertain (but see Beloe (1891) and Walker (1910, p. 156)). To the south-west beyond Ermine Street it is said by Walker to have passed through Tadlow and Biggleswade [B], but the evidence on which apparently he relies, Baker's Map of Cambridgeshire, 1821, is valueless.

Beyond Biggleswade for 3 miles a lane (Hill Lane) and parish boundary, exactly aligned, run westward to Old Warden [B]. Walker links our road up with this track. It is doubtless Roman; but its origin and objective are alike unknown.

If a westward continuation of our road be sought, it may be noted that existing lanes and roads suggest the possibility that, crossing the Cam, it passed through Shingay and Guilden Morden to join the Biggleswade-Baldock road by Caldecote [H].

Chief evidences of Roman origin:

Sections made at Barton and Chittering, the one to the S.W. the other to the N.E. of Cambridge, showed unmistakable Roman construction, and the presence of the road has been demonstrated at Ely (*Standard*, Nov. 21, 1902).

Near Goose Hall, Landbeach, the raised agger is distinctly visible west of the present road; it is likewise clearly visible in the arable fields north-west of Manor Farm, Chesterton; and is said by Bennet to have been seen

---

[1] Codrington (1918), pp. 195 and 196. Walker (1910), pp. 154-61, is of primary importance. He gives a full description, with record of sections cut by him. His view as to the alignment through Stretham, by Bedwell Hay Farm to Ely is supported by topographical evidence, and may be accepted as in the main correct; the visible traces are, however, very slight. Babington (1883, pp. 14-21 and 24-6) quotes Bishop Bennet and others; but the alignment from near Denny Abbey to Ely which he favours is certainly incorrect.

in 1808 at Cold Harbour Farm, Southery [N], where Roman remains have been found.

The engineering skill shown in the trace of the road whereby, while preserving the accuracy of alignment, every advantage is taken of high ground, and the fens crossed at their narrowest points (see map) is a distinctive mark of Roman work.

It may be noted too how the junction with Ermine Street is carried out so as to avoid two bridges over the Cam; and on a clear day one may see how the alignment on Castle Hill, Cambridge, was taken from Fox Hill north of Orwell. The road coincides with a straight line joining these two points.

II. (B) From Braughing [H] to Chesterford [E] and Worstead Lodge

Study of this interesting route, linking up London and the Ermine Street with Norfolk, explains why no trace of a Roman road from Chesterford southward along the inosculating Essex Cam-Stort Valleys can be found: such a road was not needed for through traffic, and pre-Roman roads probably were sufficient for local needs (pp. 152–3).

The trace from Braughing to Chesterford is represented only by short sectors, but these are sufficient to make the alignment tolerably certain. These sectors are indicated on the map, and, as will be seen, the alignment is direct from the high ridge by Strethall to Braughing. There are in all $4\frac{1}{4}$ miles of existing road spaced out at about equal intervals, the total distance being 14 miles[1].

From the Roman town of Chesterford five miles of straight road bring us to Worstead Lodge, the junction with the Roman road from Haverhill [S] to Cambridge, and with what is undoubtedly an old trace of the Icknield Way (p. 145). Beyond this point I do not think that a Roman road can be made out. Codrington (pp. 116 *b* and 192 (8)) traces it to Newmarket and beyond, but the evidence for regarding the existing main London-Newmarket road as preserving its alignment is of little value. In connection with the excavation of the Fleam Dyke the writer examined the documentary evidence for the point of passage of the Icknield Way. The "Highway" in a charter of 974 (Birch, 1893, No. 1305) was said to be at the western apex of West Wratting parish, at which point it was joined by a "straet"—apparently the existing road to Lark Hall. The ancient road was thus not on the present alignment, and was, moreover, described as a "Way" not a "Street."

---

[1] Codrington, 1918, p. 116 (*b*). Haverfield, in *R.C.H.M. Essex* (1916, p. xxv), confirms this alignment. See also Christy, 1920, pp. 221–2.

THE ROMAN AGE

This record illustrates the risk of assuming that roads which form parish boundaries, as does the main London-Newmarket road immediately south of the Dyke, are necessarily of high antiquity. Worts Causeway from Trumpington Drift to Red Cross is also a parish boundary, but this is of XVIII century date; its predecessor the Roman road was situated some distance to the west. In both cases the alteration of the boundary is probably recent, coinciding with the enclosure of the adjacent parishes.

There is thus no evidence that the Icknield Way was Romanized where it crossed the Fleam Dyke. The conclusions to which this argument leads are of wide application and general importance; they are already familiar to the reader (Chapter III, pp. 112-3), but need brief re-statement from a new aspect.

One of the most remarkable features of Roman roads in this country is their partial survival. A road manifest as a raised ridge for a considerable distance, aligned it may be on a known Roman site, will suddenly cease; and no further trace of it will be apparent on the closest scrutiny of the intervening area.

It is not improbable that in this remote province, the Romanization of which was incomplete, the Roman road system was to some extent a patchwork. The pre-Roman civilization had developed, at least in the Belgic districts, an extensive system of routes suitable for wheeled vehicles; and that the conquerors should have utilized these, linking them up where necessary by straight stretches of road built in the Roman manner, is to be expected.

Such a pre-Roman road was the Icknield Way; such a link, it may be, was the Roman road from Chesterford to Worstead Lodge. Examination of the map (Map IV) justifies this solution of the problem, and until definite evidence of Roman construction between Worstead Lodge and Thetford be discovered we may hold that communication between Southern Cambridgeshire and N.W. Suffolk throughout the Roman Age was by a pre-Roman track in places straightened and possibly hardened, but not reconstructed.

The "Summer road" of the Icknield Way, Ashwell Street-Street Way (see p. 147), is another example, it is held, of a pre-Roman road partially Romanized. The "Ashwell Street" sector in the south-west[1], and the Badlingham-Worlington [S] sector in the north-east, present some Roman characteristics.

---

[1] One side of the enclosing wall of the Roman cemetery at Litlington was found to be parallel to the Ashwell Street, to which it was adjacent (p. 188).

III. Road from Colchester (?) through Haverhill [S] to Cambridge and Godmanchester [and ? Leicester]

The course of this road from Haverhill to Godmanchester, where it joins Ermine Street, is well known. There is little doubt but that it originated at Colchester (CAMVLODVNVM), though the exact trace thence to within a few miles of the borders of Cambridgeshire is conjectural. Christy (1920, p. 223) considers that its line through Birdbrook [E] and Sturmer [E] parishes can be fixed with fair certainty, and there seems no reason to doubt that Walford's account (1803 *b*, p. 68, and map) of its trace in Ridgewell [E] parish in 1801 is correct. The Ridgewell trace is marked on my map. Its alignment for 7 miles from the neighbourhood of Chilford Hall to the Gog-Magog Hills (where it is known as Worstead Street) has been supposed that of a pre-Roman dyke, but recent excavation has shown the ramp to be entirely of Roman construction, and has failed to reveal any trace of a filled-in ditch. (See p. 129 and Plate XIX.)

Further evidences of Roman origin are[1]:

(1) Sections made near Horseheath, in the Perse School grounds on Hills Road, Cambridge, and in Godmanchester disclosed typical Roman construction and Roman remains.

(2) Two Roman milestones apparently dating from 305-353 A.D., in the Fitzwilliam Museum, were found by the road nearly 3 miles north-west of Cambridge in 1812.

(3) The road is a parish boundary for the greater part of its length, 19 out of 31 miles.

(4) Roman cemeteries have been found adjacent to the road near Gravel Hill Farm and Girton, one and two miles respectively from Cambridge, and a Roman barrow, Emmanuel Knoll, Godmanchester, until recently stood beside it (see p. 195).

(5) Names indicative of Roman origin occur on its course: Streetly End and Silver Street near Horseheath, Fen Stanton near Godmanchester.

(6) Stukeley (1740) records that "here and there a piece of the raised part of the road" (near Godmanchester) was still left (ed. Lukis, 1883, p. 219).

For details of the causeway, ford and bridge (?) across the Cam Valley at Cambridge, see Babington (1883, pp. 7-9 and 26-27) and Gray (1910).

The failure to trace this Roman road from Colchester to Ridgewell and the doubt as to its trace in the neighbourhood of Haverhill may be due to its never having been built in these sectors; the Roman engineers may as we have seen (p. 153) have utilized a pre-Roman way up the valley of the Colne, reconstructing it in places as the names

[1] See Walker, pp. 161-8; Babington, pp. 26-42; Codrington, pp. 193-6.

THE ROMAN AGE

Pool Street and Swan Street suggest. They then, let us suppose, built straight roads in the Roman manner past Ridgewell village across the narrow belt of forest which separates the head of the Colne Valley from the basin of the Stour, and from the head of the Stour Valley near Haverhill to the Cam Valley, across the watershed; in these thinly populated areas the pre-Roman communications may have been inadequate or devious.

The marked change of direction which this road manifests at spot level 222 on the Gog-Magog Hills has attracted much attention. This may, as Codrington (1918, p. 194) points out, have had "no other object than to keep the road on the higher ground between Cherryhinton and Trumpington Fen, but it is suggestive of a road across the Cam to Grantchester[1] in the first place, before the station on the north of Cambridge was established."

This latter hypothesis is here based entirely on the Roman evidence; its probability is greatly increased by the evidence detailed in Chapter III, that in pre-Roman times the lowest crossing of the Cam was not at Cambridge, but between two Iron Age settlements at Grantchester and Trumpington. Let us examine the evidence for this supposedly earlier road, which has been traced from the junction at Red Cross to Toft and beyond.

The sector Red Cross-Grantchester is now almost entirely destroyed; evidence of its existence, and Roman origin, is to be found in Babington (1883, pp. 43-47) and Walker (1910, p. 168). A Roman cinerary urn, it may be noted, was found on the right bank of the river not far from the ford (*C.A.S. Rep.* 39, 1879, p. xvii). From the earthwork at Grantchester, which is probably Roman, the alignment is preserved by a short sector of the modern road to Coton, then by an ancient track known as Deadman's Way; at the junction of Deadman's Way with Akeman Street was a tumulus almost certainly of Roman origin (p. 196). Before enclosure the road existed from Barton through Comberton to Toft immediately south of their respective churches; thus explaining the situation of these at an unusual distance from their villages. The trace is clearly shown on the 1836 O.S. map, and there is a tumulus (since destroyed) marked on its alignment near Comberton. The road possibly joined the Ermine

---

[1] Was the Grantchester-Trumpington-Red Cross-spot level 222 road part of a pre-Roman (and partially Romanized) route to the Stour Valley *via* Weston Colville and Thurlow [S]? There is a Roman settlement probably of Claudian date at Thurlow, and the ridged way forming the north boundary of West Wratting parish, described as a "Straet" in the Saxon charter of 974 already referred to, is on the required alignment (see Maps IV and V).

THE ROMAN AGE

Street near Caxton, passing through Bourn: but this is conjectural. Walker regards it as a pre-Roman way, re-made in Roman times as far as Toft or Caldecote. I have not been able to trace it beyond Toft; but if the hypothesis which is presented above be correct, it formed, doubtless, a link in the chain of communications from CAMVLODVNVM to the Ermine Street, largely native in origin, used by the Romans in the years immediately following the Claudian conquest.

Pursuing the same line of argument, one may suppose that the development of the Castle Hill area as the chief Roman centre in the district, resulting in the construction of the Red Cross-Cambridge and the Cambridge-Godmanchester roads, quickly reduced the more southerly route to the Ermine Street to insignificance.

The Alconbury [Hunts.]-Titchmarsh [Northants.] road, mentioned on p. 171 may be directly connected with our road, the whole forming a through route from the Essex seaboard to Leicester and the Midlands.

In dealing with the roads which, as far as our knowledge goes, are of local rather than general importance, those lying west of Ermine Street may first be considered.

IV. A ROMAN ROAD (OR SERIES OF ROADS) ON THE WESTERN BORDERS OF OUR DISTRICT RUNNING FROM THE NEIGHBOURHOOD OF BRAUGHING [H] TO BALDOCK [H] AND GODMANCHESTER [HUNTS.] *via* BIGGLESWADE AND SANDY [B][1]

(*a*) The Braughing-Baldock route is represented by some four miles of road of Roman character traversing the forest-clad uplands west of the former village, and by a mile of straight road near Baldock. The trace for 3 miles between these two sections is uncertain; the pre-Roman track referred to on p. 155 may have been utilized.

(*b*) The Baldock-Biggleswade road is directly aligned on Chesterfield, Sandy, where numerous finds indicate the neighbourhood of a Roman settlement of some importance; but the trace of this road north of Biggleswade is partially effaced for the last two miles (Watkin, 1882, p. 258)[2].

(*c*) From Sandy northward the road is laid out in the Roman manner for $5\frac{1}{2}$ miles (Watkin, *loc. cit.*): beyond this point there runs a sinuous track probably pre-Roman, partially straightened and

[1] Babington, pp. 91–94. Codrington, p. 116 (*c*). U. A. Smith (1913, p. 124).
[2] The east-and-west road, Hill Lane, which joined or crossed this road at Biggleswade has already been mentioned. For a discussion of the roads which may have existed on the left bank of the Ouse in this region, see Watkin (1882).

improved by the Romans[1]. It is certainly of Roman construction at the point where it enters the Roman town of Godmanchester, as Walker (1910, p. 163, footnote 3 e) has shown. The most remarkable fact connected with this route as a whole is that the two roads, the direct and the sinuous, overlap; one may surmise that the pre-Roman way was in course of replacement by a road more directly aligned which was never completed.

(d) A branch road from Baldock, which runs southward for $4\frac{1}{2}$ miles and is continued in the same alignment for another $1\frac{1}{2}$ miles in the neighbourhood of Stevenage [H] by parish boundaries, may be of importance.

This road points directly towards St Albans [H] $11\frac{1}{2}$ miles distant; but further traces are lacking. Whether there was a direct route to VERVLAMIVM or no[2] it is probable that this piece of road formed the terminal sector of the main line of communications between that city and the Cam Valley (see Sketch-map F, p. 163).

One short sector of road west of Ermine Street alone remains to be dealt with.

(e) North-east of Huntingdon at Alconbury Hill, indications of a branch road to Titchmarsh [Northants.] in alignment with a known road to Leicester are apparent.

East of Ermine Street but few roads remain for consideration.

V. ROADS IN THE AREA NORTH-EAST OF HUNTINGDON

Exact alignments, associated over long stretches with parish boundaries, suggest that roads such as the Sawtry Way from Houghton to King's Ripton [Hunts.], the road from Hartford Hill to Old Hurst [Hunts.], and the southern portion of the St Ives [Hunts.]-Chatteris road, are of Roman origin; but I am not aware that any definite evidence of Roman construction exists to support this ascription.

VI. MINOR ROADS IN THE CAMBRIDGE AREA

(a) An ancient trackway known as the Portway seems to have linked the Cam Valley with the Ermine Street, via Hardwick. It may have been Roman but more probably is an earlier Way. Enclosures in the XIX century have obliterated nearly every trace of it: but lanes and footpaths near Hardwick bear the name to this day. No evidence of Roman construction has been found on its traditional alignment here.

---

[1] This track, if pre-Roman, may have led to the crossings of the Ouse at Hartford [Hunts.], for which there is evidence of use in prehistoric times.

[2] U. A. Smith (1913, p. 129) hints at the probability of this.

The 1836 O.S. map (Sheet LI) gives but little assistance in determining its original course west of Hardwick. On this map, however, a track is indicated branching from the Arrington Bridge-Cambridge road at a point adjacent to Deadman's Hill, Barton (see Map IV), and making for Hardwick. This track, now obliterated, was known as the Hardwick Way, and Babington[1] brings forward evidence suggestive of Roman origin. It may have been connected with the Portway.

(*b*) That an ancient road from the Ermine Street at Royston passed through Melbourn and Harston to Trumpington is probable. The existing main road, which passes the Roman camp at Melbourn, was there known as the Portway. It was doubtless a pre-Roman way (for the ancient settlements were numerous in this fertile valley) and may have been used by the Romans; but no trace of Roman road construction has been found on the alignment indicated.

(*c*) The northern termination of such a road in pre-Roman times would doubtless have been the Iron Age settlements at Trumpington; but it is probable that a Roman road ran from Trumpington to Cambridge, the trace being along the ridge of high ground to River Farm, across Vicar's Brook, thence along the margin of Coe Fen to Milne Street and the Great Bridge (Walker, 1911 *d*). Evidence in the shape of much Roman pottery and other remains found from time to time on this alignment between the Vicar's Brook and Trumpington Hall increases the probability of the existence of such a road, which would be necessary in order to link up the upper Cam Valley settlements with Cambridge.

Road near Radwinter [E]

The writer has long been of opinion that lanes and parish boundaries in the neighbourhood of Radwinter suggest that a Roman road passing through Thaxted [E] to join Worstead Street west of Haverhill [S] should be looked for; and the probable course of this road has recently been studied by Christy (1920, p. 213). I cannot agree, however, that its trace *southward* from Bowcroft Wood[2] in Thaxted parish through Thaxted town and Monk Street towards Dunmow [E] can be regarded as proven; and if its course *northward* from Radwinter to Ashdon [E] and beyond be as he suggests, it is

---

[1] Pp. 49, 50; see also Walker, p. 169.
[2] The possibility of a change of alignment at the wood must be considered; for over a mile hedgerows and tracks run due south-west to Mill Hill Farm which, situated on a ridge, may be the site of a mound of Roman origin. (See 6-inch O. S. Essex, Sheet XIV, N.E.)

in this part not a Roman road, in the strict sense, at all. This may give us a hint as to its true character; it may be another of the roads, most difficult of all to elucidate, which are partially Romanized pre-Roman trackways.

ROMAN TOWNS, EARTHWORKS, ETC., AND CANALS

Before summarizing the results of the preceding survey, it will be convenient to examine Roman remains intimately connected with the road system; fortified towns, camps, and open towns[1]. The following is a list of the chief sites dealt with:

Site	Character	
i. Chesterford [E]	Fortified town	page 173
ii. Cambridge "The Borough"	,, ,,	,, 174
iii. Grantchester	Rectangular earthwork	,, 175
iv. Melbourn	,, ,,	,, 175
v. Cambridge railway station	Earthwork	,, 176
vi. Braughing [H]	Probably a small town	,, 176
vii. Sandy [B]	Probably an open town	,, 176
viii. Godmanchester [Hunts.]	,, ,, ,,	,, 176

The War Ditches, Cherryhinton, an important Romano-British settlement, is also considered; and the Car Dyke (a Roman canal), and Reach Lode, are discussed in relation to the problem of fen reclamation and the use of water transport in Roman times.

(i) Great Chesterford. This well-known town site in the Essex Cam Valley, situated on the north-west of the modern village, has been described and discussed by many generations of archaeologists. At least one Roman road (Braughing-Great Chesterford-Worstead Lodge) passed through it. Stukeley records that its walls were existing in part in his time; now no trace of them can be seen[2]. The admirable and readily accessible summary by Haverfield[3] of the evidence relating to the Roman settlement, and the references given below render detailed description here unnecessary. It suffices to note that the walled town occupied a rectangular area of 35 acres or

---

[1] None of the town sites in our district has been satisfactorily identified save perhaps Godmanchester (Dvrolipons). See Yorke's paper (1905) on the "East Anglian Itineraries," in which he summarizes the views of earlier writers.

[2] July 12, 1719. "I had the pleasure to walk round an old Roman city there, upon the walls, which are still visible above ground; the London road goes 50 yards upon them, and the Crown Inn stands upon their foundation....I saw the wall to the foundation; they pulling it up with much labour to mend the highways...for which I heartily anathematized them" (ed. Lukis, 1883, p. 148). This destruction was still going on in 1769; see note in *Arch. Journ.* XII, 123.

[3] In *R.C.H.M. Essex* (1916, p. xxiii); see also Hughes (1907 *a*) and references in Lyell (1912, p. 23).

more[1]; that it was apparently occupied by a peaceful and settled population of Romanized Britons during the whole period of Roman domination (see p. 227); and that there had been a La Tène settlement either on or immediately adjacent to the Roman town (p. 110).

Neville, to whose excavations our knowledge of the site is chiefly due, laid bare in 1847 a small rectangular temple with a mosaic floor, of Celtic type, situated on rising ground a mile to the east of the settlement, with which it may be held to be connected. Such buildings are not common in this country. Neville (1848, p. 89); see also Haverfield (*loc. cit.* p. xxii, and 1915, p. 36).

The Audley End Museum contains a large collection of objects found at Chesterford by Neville, the majority from pits within the walled area, or to the north thereof, or in the rectory garden adjacent to the churchyard. The terra sigillata and Castor ware, the bronzes, glassware and iron objects, are especially noticeable. Attention may also be drawn to the sculptured stone from Chesterford, figured and described in *B.M.G.* (1922, p. 21).

Strategically Chesterford controlled the northern exits of the Stort-Essex Cam Valley area and the traffic along the Icknield Way. The more the topography of the district is studied the clearer the military importance of the site becomes, and the greater the likelihood therefore of its having been a military station in the middle of I A.D. But we have no evidence bearing on the date of the defences.

(ii) **Castle Hill, Cambridge.** In the Borough of Cambridge is a four-sided enclosure of some 28 acres, the limits of which can fairly accurately be determined and which is almost certainly a Roman fortified town. Two important Roman roads, as we have seen, crossed here, and the numerous finds recorded within the area (especially on the site of the Norman Castle in 1802-9) and in the neighbourhood indicate prolonged occupation and an extensive settlement. Coin finds range from Nero to Honorius. Babington records the alignments of the vallum and ditch; excavation at Blackamore Piece in 1802 showed the latter to be 10-12 feet deep and 39 feet broad. Babington estimated the rectangle formed by the vallum to measure about 1320 feet in length and 930 in breadth: the area was thus less than Chesterford. Bowtell records the destruction of what was apparently a portion of the Roman wall and gate near Castle Street in 1804.

Hope, writing in 1905, considered the earthwork to be Roman, and likened the settlement which it protected to a small town like

---

[1] Roman remains occur also outside the area of the station.

Caerwent. An excellent plan of it will be found in his paper quoted below; I have utilized this in preparing the map on p. 246.

Walker carried out excavations in 1910 in the grounds of Magdalene College on the line of the probable Roman boundary. He discovered a bank at least 11 feet in height along the margin of the watercourse (a branch of the Cam) which passed through the grounds of the college. From the coins and associated objects found, the date of the work was placed at between 320 and 420 A.D. The excavator points out that other Roman towns are known to have been fortified at as late a date as this; and concludes that the existence of a Roman station is demonstrated[1]. No Roman house foundations have however been discovered.

(iii) **Grantchester.** A small rectangular earthwork adjoining the village school, a portion of two sides of which remains, is on the line of the road (p. 169) from Red Cross to Barton and Toft. It is sited on the crest of the steep bank below which the River Cam flows, and a well-marked holloway can be traced on the slope.

The north-east angle is very distinct and what is probably the greater part of the northern vallum and fosse is tolerably well preserved, being 100 yards in length. The eastern defences can be traced for a distance of 54 yards. The road to the ford appears to follow the line of the ditch. Roman coins have frequently been found in the schoolhouse garden, which is partly within the entrenchment[2].

(iv) **Melbourn.** Close to the ninth milestone on the east side of the Cambridge-Melbourn road (the ancient way known in this part at least up to the middle of the XIX century as the Portway), and immediately adjoining the road, are traces of a rectangular earthwork (see Sketch-map D, p. 144).

All that can now be seen is one corner of the work; a portion of the fosse and much wasted vallum lies at right angles to the road in a small orchard, while the roadside hedge at this point is on the top of the bank.

Beldam (1868, p. 31) records that in his time "it formed a quadrangle of about 200 yards surrounded by a vallum with a second vallum towards the east." Babington (1883, p. 62) notes that various antiquities of Roman date have been found near the camp and in Melbourn.

---

[1] See Babington (1883, p. 3), Hughes (1894 b), Gray (1896), Hope (1907), Walker (1911 c), Bowtell (MS. II, 89) and Stukeley (ed. Lukis, 1883, p. 36); also pp. 182, 205 and 221 of this book.

[2] For a detailed description and plan of the camp and its approaches, see Babington (1883, pp. 44-46). Walker found 3rd brass coins of Gallienus and Tetricus on the site (1910, p. 169).

On the east side of the work, between it and the fen there was a Roman cemetery, which was probably in use in I A.D. and certainly in II A.D.[1] The position of the earthwork, on the line of the Street Way (see p. 148) and abutting on the Portway (which presumably linked up the Cam Valley settlements) is significant, and suggestive of construction at the time of the first advance into the district, but there is no direct evidence to support such an hypothesis, and no proof even that the work is Roman.

(v) G.E. Railway Station, Cambridge. Scanty remains of the earthwork of what may have been a Roman camp lying just to the east of the Roman road, Red Cross-Cambridge, close to the Hills Road railway bridge, and apparently bisected by the wall of the cattle market, were, until recently, visible (Walker, 1910, p. 167). The greater part of the work was destroyed in building the goods station. Fragmentary pottery from the site is in the Cambridge Museum.

(vi) Braughing [H]. The Roman station here, if there be one, has not yet been determined with certainty. But numerous finds of Roman date in the neighbourhood of the junction of five Roman roads suggest that one existed, and its site is probably close to the ford below the junction of the rivers Rib and Quin. Earthworks in Larksfield, between the rivers, may however be those of the settlement[2]. Numerous finds of British coins suggest, as we have seen, that it was of pre-Roman origin.

(vii) Sandy [B]. Discoveries of grave-furniture, etc., made from time to time during the XVI to XIX centuries suggest that a Roman settlement of some importance existed in or near the area known as Chesterfield, which lies between the two spurs on which Caesar's Camp (pre-Roman, p. 134) and Galley Hill Camp are sited. The latter is rectangular, and may be Roman (see Map V, and Goddard, 1904, p. 273). Coins and other objects found at Chesterfield and its neighbourhood indicate occupation from I to early V A.D.; a fine south Gaulish bowl, Form 30, in the British Museum, dates from the middle of I A.D. But it should be noted that no foundations of Roman buildings have been recorded, and the actual site of the settlement which these remains imply is yet to seek[3].

(viii) Godmanchester. Walker (1910, p. 163) records that he

---

[1] Walters (1908 a, Index, Melbourn). There are urns of coarse ware in the British Museum from this site, probably of I century date.
[2] For a summary of the evidence see M. V. Taylor (1914, p. 150, and map, p. 141).
[3] For full account see Page and Keate (1908, p. 9); Babington (1883, p. 92), Watkin (1882, p. 271) and Stukeley (ed. Lukis, 1883, p. 150) may also be consulted. For the oculist's stamp found near Sandy see *B.M.G.* (1922, p. 33).

has seen sections of the three Roman roads that meet in Godmanchester; and in another paper (1909) dealing with the site describes numerous Roman remains found in the neighbourhood of the meeting-place of these roads. He defines the Roman town (which does not appear to have been fortified) as bounded on the west by Post Street, Causeway, Silver Street; on the south by London Street, on the east by Ermine Street and on the north by East Street.

In a small cemetery here—probably the private one of a villa—he found a third brass of Aurelianus (270–275 A.D.) in an urn with ashes; and coins dug up near by ranged in date from 76 to 337–361 A.D. Very little information is available from earlier writers. R. Fox (1831, p. 30) records a remarkable number of coins. His list includes Julius Caesar, Augustus, Tiberius, Claudius and Nero onwards. The occupation of the site doubtless, therefore, dates from I A.D. No remains of buildings have, however, yet been unearthed.

There was a settlement also probably dating from I A.D. on the Huntingdon side of the river. In digging a deep trench for a sewer in St Mary's Street, close to the line of the Ermine Street through the town, much Roman pottery—terra sigillata, Castor ware, mortaria, amphora fragments and coarse sherds, now in the possession of Dr Garrood of Alconbury—was found. Pottery with horizontal striae on the shoulder, pottery burnished in the La Tène manner and fragments of late La Tène ware suggest an early date for the occupation.

(ix) War Ditches, Cherryhinton. The early history of this ring-work, so far as it has been revealed by excavation, has already been discussed (p. 136). It is probable that the first phase of occupation was closed by a massacre; the skeletons lying in the fosse, if I understand Hughes' report correctly (1904, p. 464), were covered by silt representing a period during which the earthwork was presumably uninhabited.

Deposits in the fosse above these layers indicated occupation of the earthwork by a people who left behind no fibulae or ornaments of the usual Roman type[1], and practically no terra sigillata; moreover, no coins were found during the excavations and only an occasional oyster-shell. These people used in addition to coarse pottery (some of Horningsea manufacture), a fine thin biscuit ware with patterns applied in slip (p. 208); this is almost certainly of the late I and early II century.

These remains were in places near what was the surface of the

---

[1] The only bronze object found was a fibula of rare type figured in Hughes' paper (1904, p. 468), and now in the Cambridge Museum.

fosse floor before the levelling of the vallum in recent years completely obliterated the work. They therefore represent the final occupation. Inhumation burials, associated with pottery of different types, almost certainly of the second half of I A.D., were situated on the west side of the enclosure, and Roman pottery (including II century terra sigillata and Castor ware, now in the Cambridge Museum) has been found at various spots on the hill-top.

Though many points, such as the exact provenance of the sigillata mentioned above, are by no means clear, it seems probable that in the middle of I A.D. the inhabitants of the War Ditches—a long-headed race (whether descended from the first Celtic-speaking invaders, or representing the Belgic conquest cannot be determined)—were slaughtered. Before the end of the century the earthwork was re-occupied by a folk who had little direct contact with Roman settlers or traders, but who used Romano-Belgic and Horningsea wares, and practised inhumation. This occupation cannot have been prolonged, for the pottery types in the upper layer of the fosse were limited in number; but scattered finds of II century terra sigillata show that the hill-top was not entirely deserted when the Romanization of the district was complete.

Hughes (1904, p. 481) commenting on the rarity of Roman objects in the upper layers of the fosse, concluded that the last occupation was later than the "distinctively Roman period." But the study of coarse pottery has made great advances since he wrote, and I am confident that the character of the wares found at the War Ditches justifies the conclusions outlined above. It may be noted that an early date is as consistent with Hughes' observations as a late one.

There are several earthworks in the district other than those already discussed, which may possibly be of the Roman Age. Four are mentioned below; the list might easily be extended with but little advantage to the reader.

King's Hedges, Chesterton. Traces of a rectangular earthwork, one side of which borders the Mereway in Chesterton parish, are manifest in the pasture fields by the farmstead known as King's Hedges. Roman coins have been found in it (Babington (1883, p. 14)).

Other Earthworks. Granham Manor Camp, Shelford, and the Paille Ditches, Walden, both rectangular works, may *possibly* be Romano-British. The latter has been described in Chapter IV; the former is most likely to be mediaeval.

A rectangular entrenchment, destroyed over a century ago, at Watsoe Bridge, Steeple Bumpstead [E], which may well, from its situation (close to a ford, at the junction of the Colne Valley and Stour Valley roads to Colchester), have been Roman, is described by Walford (1803 b, p. 70). As the Map (IV) shows, there is much evidence of Roman occupation in the neighbourhood. The record of its position will enable its filled-in fosse to be examined, and its date determined, on some future occasion.

Civil Engineering Works

(A) Car Dyke. A wet ditch five miles in length, the material from which has been thrown out on either side, extends from a feeder of the River Ouse (Old West River) in Setchel Fen north of Cottenham to the River Cam near Waterbeach.

A ditch of similar character bearing the same name is traceable on the west of the fens near Peterborough and from the River Glen to the River Witham in Lincolnshire.

See Wheeler (1897 and 1906). He notes that its total length is 55 miles and its width from 50 to 60 feet. The present writer was struck by the similarity in profile and dimensions between the section north of Peterborough and that at Waterbeach.

Some regard our Cambridgeshire Car Dyke as a work connected with the drainage of the fens—a channel for the upland waters at a time when the Cam joined the Ouse at Earith and the Ely channel was silted up (see Cunningham, 1909, and Bull, 1904), others (see Babington, 1883, pp. 105 ff.) consider it to be, at least in its southern sector with which we are concerned, a canal forming a short cut from the Cam westward to the waters of the Great Ouse[1]. I am inclined to think that both explanations may be correct, and that the work was a canal and drainage channel combined. The link between the local Car Dyke and the Peterborough-Lincoln Dyke is provided by the old West Water from Earith to Benwick, then it may be by Knut's Delph (a channel and causeway very possibly Roman), or by the ancient waterway of the River Nene, to Peterborough.

See Miller and Skertchly (1878, map), Babington (1883, map), Skertchly (1877, pp. 13 f.) and Cunningham (1909, p. 82). Tacitus, *Ann.* XI, 20, mentions a similar work carried out in 47 A.D. by Corbulo "to keep his soldiers from idleness." This canal between the Rhine and the Meuse was 23 miles long.

The Dyke may best be examined near Waterbeach on the east side of the Waterbeach-Landbeach road. Here it consists of a broad and deep artificial cut, banked on either side, bearing "not the least

---

[1] Assuming it to be a canal, it would save, on the journey from, let us say, Earith to Cambridge, 9 miles.

resemblance to a natural watercourse," as Babington rightly says. It is here called "The Old Tillage, or Twilade, a dialect word meaning 'to load, unload, and return for a second'" (Babington, p. 109).

Though its sinuous trace does not suggest Roman work, the fact that large quantities of Roman pottery were found actually in the bed of the Dyke at Cottenham is conclusive evidence that it was in existence during the Roman period; and if the whole system from the Cam to the Witham be examined its scale and character are demonstrably such as no pre-Roman people would have designed and carried out.

Other evidences of antiquity might be brought forward. Much Roman pottery has been found at various points on the line of the Dyke between Akeman Street and Cottenham Fen. The Dyke is, moreover, a parish boundary for a considerable part of its length—from Waterbeach to the Akeman Street (itself a parish boundary from the point of junction onwards). This may be regarded as evidence that both dyke and road were ancient landmarks in the Christian Anglo-Saxon period.

Stukeley's suggestion that these canals were used for barge traffic, conveying corn, it may be, from Cambridgeshire and the upper Ouse Valley to Lincoln and the North does not seem improbable. On the return journeys Northamptonshire stone and pottery from the Castor kilns were doubtless transported into our region.

Castor ware is common enough on local Roman sites; in the foundations of the Roman houses at Comberton and Ickleton Ketton stone was used. Barnack Rag is also known to have been used in Roman building in Cambridgeshire.

The regional map (IV) shows the line of the Dyke as far as the local sector is concerned and indicates its value as a short cut; the Sketch-map (F) shows its trace from Peterborough to Lincoln. A short distance only separates the navigable Witham at Lincoln from the navigable Trent, whence the water route is clear to York; this short distance may have been canalized in Roman times; a dyke, certainly ancient, known as the Foss Dyke, links up the two river systems.

The discovery in the bed of the Foss Dyke of a statuette of Mars renders Roman construction highly probable (*B.M.G.* 1922, p. 89).

(B) **Reach Lode.** Another (minor) work, possibly of similar date, is Reach Lode, which runs from the end of the Devil's Dyke at Reach to the River Cam near Upware. Roman remains have been found along the whole length of the ancient causeway which runs parallel to the Lode. Hughes considered that this road was constructed by the

Romans to connect their settlements at Reach and Upware; and the Lode may have been designed by them, to provide adequate water transport facilities for the Burwell-Quy area.

Was there a clunch-quarrying industry at Reach in Roman times? The quarries, now disused, cover an immense area, and are clearly of high antiquity. Clunch, flint, and brick are the materials commonly employed in the foundations of Roman buildings in this district.

Discussion of these ditches raises the whole problem of Roman engineering and navigation works in the fens, which can best be dealt with when the range of finds of the Roman period has been analysed (see p. 222).

Summary of Analysis of Roman Roads and other Engineering Works, Fortified Towns, etc.

Nothing further need be said here of the Car Dyke and its problems. This apart, the points of major importance that have been elucidated in the preceding analysis may briefly be reviewed.

We have, in the first place, seen that in order to understand the Roman road system in our district some knowledge of the probable alignments of pre-Roman tracks is necessary, since such were undoubtedly utilized by the Romans. The Braughing-Chesterford road, for example, joining the Icknield Way at Worstead Lodge, provides a convenient route from the Ermine Street to N.W. Suffolk and Norfolk; Ashwell Street is a portion of an older Way straightened and hardened; the Haverhill-Gog Magog Hills road may be regarded as a Roman link connecting roads mainly of native origin in the Stour and Cam Valleys.

Reasons have been given for the view that the objective of the last mentioned road was originally Grantchester, and not Cambridge. That this interpretation of the topographical facts, though it solves several difficulties, creates others, is apparent; for the upland way is not aligned on Grantchester[1]. It may be that the Grantchester-Trumpington-Red Cross-Gog Magog Hills road was pre-Roman and originally extended to Wratting, and to Thurlow in the upper Stour Valley, and that the Roman short-cut from Haverhill (a later work) joined this at the most convenient spot, the spur of the Gog Magog Hills. No definite conclusion on these points is at present possible. In any case, the Colchester (?)-Haverhill-Cam Valley road, whether

[1] Nor for that matter on the Roman site at Cambridge, but half a mile to the south thereof. The three other roads meeting at Cambridge are exactly aligned on Castle Hill.

it originally crossed the Cam at Grantchester or Cambridge, was linked up with the Ermine Street, and was probably part of a main line of communications to Leicester and the Midlands.

The roads which can definitely be said to be entirely Roman in design and construction are, first, the Ermine Street, which, it cannot be doubted, was primarily a military Way; and, secondly, the roads which—to take for a moment a fresh point of view—we may regard as radiating from Cambridge. The Cambridge-Godmanchester, Cambridge-Ely, Cambridge-Arrington Bridge[1] and Cambridge-Red Cross[2] roads are throughout their courses of this character; this fact adds weight to the evidence which suggests that Cambridge as a town, and probably as the administrative centre of the district, was a Roman creation, and communications worthy of it were part of the Roman design.

It follows that the roads radiating from Cambridge are later than others. We have no direct evidence bearing on the point: and, in any case, it would be a difficult matter to prove, for dateable finds (see p. 205) render it probable that the Roman town is of I century foundation.

A glance at the small scale map (F) emphasizes the probability of the Cambridge-Ely-Denver road having been constructed in order to provide more direct access to the Brancaster fortress and the Norfolk coast generally, from the south and midlands, than was afforded by the Icknield Way-Peddars Way route. The remarkable skill shown in the construction of this road—it utilizes to the best advantage all the patches of dry ground in its passage across the fens, while preserving a direct alignment—indicates preliminary surveying of the most careful and exact character. That both it, and the fen road which crossed the drowned lands from east to west (from Peterborough to Denver) in a manner equally skilful, are military works (it may be of late III or IV A.D., connected with coast defence), is highly probable.

Other sources of evidence will enable us, in the course of the present chapter, to confirm and extend certain of the above conclusions and deductions.

Rectangular earthworks which may *provisionally* be regarded as Roman are not common in the district. This is to be expected; the legionaries defeated the natives in a few sanguinary engagements, and there was no further need of purely military works. Confining

---

[1] A pre-Roman settlement adjoined the Bourn Brook ford at Lord's Bridge utilized by this road; but other considerations suggest that the relation is accidental.

[2] Accepting for the moment the view that the road to the east out of Cambridge was linked up with an earlier route at Red Cross.

THE ROMAN AGE

our attention to the two which are best attested we see that Melbourn Camp is sited at the junction probably of two pre-Roman highways (the Portway and the Street Way) and Grantchester at an important ford of the Cam; both districts being as we have seen centres of Early Iron Age civilization and doubtless thickly populated.

The strategical importance of Chesterford has been emphasized, and the town may have been fortified in the *early* days of the Roman occupation—but the walls are destroyed and with them the evidence of their date. Cambridge may have been an open town until IV A.D.; the earthen bank which defines its limits on the riverside, at any rate, is not of earlier construction.

ROMAN HOUSES IN RURAL DISTRICTS

The quality and extent of the Roman civilization in the rural districts may be tested by an examination of the character and distribution of houses of Roman type.

It will be convenient to deal with these on a county basis. The remains of such houses found in Southern Cambridgeshire have not previously been treated comparatively, and may therefore be dealt with here in greater detail than those situated in adjacent counties[1].

Cambridgeshire

Though we have definite evidence, in the recorded presence of foundations, of the existence of buildings of Roman type all up the Cam Valley from Landwade to Litlington, none save the Ickleton farmstead examined by Neville (1849 *b*) has been completely excavated and planned; much information that might have been available bearing on the history of the Roman occupation is therefore lacking. Of one house indeed, and that probably the finest, discovered at Litlington in 1829, the records of excavation are lost and we only know of its existence[2].

We are, however, able to show within the county borders examples of corridor, basilican, and courtyard types of building.

Ickleton. Farmhouse, and barn (?). The house in Church Field at Ickleton on the west bank of the Cam, of corridor type, was of moderate size, 97 by 66 feet, and formed a compact block. The chief rooms and portico faced east. In plan and siting it closely resembled

---

[1] Lyell's Bibliographical List (1912, p. 5) has been of great service. His references to Arbury and Burwell, however, refer to foundations at Shepreth and Landwade respectively.

[2] The account was communicated in 1841 to the C. A. S. by the Rev. W. Clack, the excavator, but was never published. See Babington (1883, p. 60).

a house at Brading, Isle of Wight, but had a more extensive series of secondary rooms. It was built subsequent to 117 A.D., a coin of Hadrian being found under the foundations[1]. An adjacent building (56 by 24 feet) was connected with the main block by a single wall running diagonally from the south-west angle.

Thirty or forty yards to the south-east of this house a building of basilican type (82 by 41 feet) was uncovered; it was possibly a barn or granary[2]. Its walls were of flint and clunch with tile quoins, and each of the pier bases was topped by a small block of Ketton stone. A few coins, mainly of the early IV century, were found in the excavations. Neville's plan (1849 b, p. 365) shows the character of the building, which was probably of wood, for no trace of the superstructure (except stone roofing slabs) was met with during the excavations.

Swaffham Prior. Corridor-courtyard type. A house found in 1893 in Swaffham Prior parish on the south side of the Devil's Dyke was only partially uncovered, but it was sufficiently explored for its type to be determined (Atkinson, 1894).

It was a medium-sized country residence intermediate between the courtyard and the corridor types, symmetrically planned, with an apsidal projection in the front of each wing. The main block was at least 130 feet in length; the wings on either side of the open courtyard which faced south-east, projected 42 feet. Its walls, like those of the Ickleton house, were of flint with brick quoins, and portions of two tesselated pavements and of a hypocaust were laid bare. No attempt was made to date the pottery and other finds. The site is marked on the 6-inch O.S. Cambs. XLI. N.E.

Litlington. Courtyard type (?). The villa at Litlington mentioned on the previous page, situated near the Manor Farm, south of the church, is said to have contained "30 rooms and a bath" (Babington, 1883, p. 60; Lyell, 1912, p. 5). It was clearly a house of some pretensions and had at least one mosaic pavement; if the plan shown on the map accompanying the report by Kempe (1836) of the Litlington cemetery (see p. 188) be approximately accurate it was of the developed courtyard type with rooms on all four sides; the external dimensions of the rectangle being not less than 500 by 300 feet! The village was of some importance, or the villa with its dependent dwellings very extensive; for the existence of Roman house

---

[1] See Neville (1849 b), Ward (1911 a, pp. 163 ff.), Lyell (1912, p. 5). Ward gives a plan of the Brading house (Fig. 48 B).

[2] For details and a discussion of buildings of basilican type see Ward (1911 a, p. 175).

THE ROMAN AGE

sites in the immediate neighbourhood has since been reported on three separate occasions (in 1850, Nunn's MS.; in 1881, Babington (1883, p. 62) and Lewis (1881, p. 340); in 1913 (*Proc. C.A.S.* XVIII. p. 4)).

Bartlow. A small dwelling in Church Field, about 100 yards north-east of the Bartlow Hills, was excavated by Neville in 1852; "the block (43 by 48 feet) contained in the northern half two heated rooms and their furnaces; the southern half was rougher and less habitable." Coins found in a rubbish pit indicated a long occupation ending about 350 A.D. See Neville (1853, p. 17) and Haverfield (1916, p. xxiv).

Of few other buildings in Southern Cambridgeshire have records of value been preserved.

Comberton. A house at Fox's Bridge, Comberton, close to the Bourn Brook was partially explored in 1842 (Babington, 1883, p. 22; Lyell, 1912, p. 5). The walls consisted of masses of Ketton stone, chalk marl and flints. Hypocaust piers were disclosed, but the plan of the house was not made out. Painted plaster, glass and iron fragments and "much pale yellow pottery ornamented with red lines" (probably IV century) were met with; and the few coins found ranged from Vespasian (69–79 A.D.) to Gratian (367–383 A.D.).

Landwade. The fine mosaic pavement showing a guilloche border and geometrical patterns, in the Cambridge Museum, is practically the sole existing record of a house at Landwade, on the eastern borders of the fens, discovered in 1904 (Hughes, 1906 (*a*)); it is the only pavement found in the county which has been preserved.

Evidence for a house of some importance situated north-north-east of Carter's Well, Grantchester, was revealed during coprolite digging in 1917–8 (Porter, 1921). At Stapleford a hypocaust was ploughed into in 1852 (Neville, 1854 *c*, p. 213); and at Shepreth traces of three cottages or out-buildings were exposed in 1885 (Hughes, 1886).

In addition to the known sites of villas in Cambridgeshire there are several places where the character of the finds renders the existence of a house of Roman type in the immediate neighbourhood certain. Jenkinson (1882) found Roman tiles and freestone on the site of the Anglian cemetery at Girton, and in a rubbish pit the fragments of sculpture referred to on pp. 187–8. At Eye Hall, Horningsea, finds pointing to the former existence of a house of some pretensions are recorded (Walker, 1913, p. 69); the potteries are in the adjacent field, and the works manager may have lived here. Considerable portions of a frieze of clunch with egg-and-dart mouldings built into the foundations of the Lower Mill at Barrington (adjacent to numerous Roman ashpits, from one of which the fine Arretine bowl, referred to on p. 101, was said to have come) suggest a building of some importance (p. 236 and Conybeare, 1884). The O.S. maps record a "villa" at Harlton, close to the Wheatsheaf Inn; but I have not found any other record of Roman finds here.

NORTH-WEST ESSEX

The majority of Roman houses discovered in North-West Essex[1] were excavated by Neville in the middle of the XIX century. A summary by Haverfield of the evidence which these, and a house at Ridgewell excavated in 1794, afford, with plans and references, will be found in *R.C.H.M. Essex* (1916).

Here notes of three will suffice. The Ridgewell house was a fairly extensive building round a courtyard (120 by 200 feet); it had one elaborate mosaic, and several tesselated floors; and "coins show that it was occupied during most of the Roman period down to its end." Two small houses at the head of the Bourn Valley at Ashdon (17 by 52 feet) and at Hadstock (60 by 85 feet) contained, like the house over the Cambridge border at Bartlow just described, little beyond apartments for heating and bathing. Haverfield remarks that such houses may originally have included rooms built in wood or clay, besides the stone-built rooms which have alone survived. The Hadstock house yielded evidence of date; pottery of late II century and coins of 250-370 A.D. For buildings at Chesterford see pp. 173-4.

NORTH HERTFORDSHIRE AND EAST BEDFORDSHIRE

Though the evidence from cemeteries points to the complete Romanization of the inhabitants of the Ivel Valley, very few houses of Roman type have come to light. Detailed record, indeed, is preserved of only one, at Purwell Mill, Great Wymondley [H], but finds of Roman débris make the existence of a second near Great Wymondley church probable, and the foundations of a small (30 by 20 feet) rectangular building of uncertain use at Shefford [B] were found in 1826. For a detailed account of the Purwell Mill house see Ransom (1886, p. 43); six rooms were examined, three of which had pillared hypocausts, and one a tesselated pavement with a "gridiron pattern"; these represented probably a portion only of a large build-

---

[1] There are six in all of which four are planned; those at Ridgewell, Ashdon, Hadstock and Wendens Ambo. Practically nothing is known of the dwellings at Stansted and Thaxted. The sites of two additional buildings near Bartlow have been pointed out to me.

THE ROMAN AGE 187

ing of unknown type. Coin finds in the débris ranged from Gallienus (253–268) to Valentinian II (375–392); and in the field in which the building stood from Severus (193–211) to Gratian (367–383). These suggest that the house was not built till the end of II A.D. Many traces of structural alteration provided confirmatory evidence of prolonged occupation.

WESTERN SUFFOLK

The only dwelling-house which has been excavated in Western Suffolk is in the valley of the Lark at Icklingham, though there is indirect evidence (e.g. at Great Thurlow and Kedington) for the existence of several in the upper valley of the Stour. The Icklingham house was explored in 1877. It was of simple type; the main block, consisting of two heated rooms, measured externally 30 by 21 feet; smaller unheated rooms formed projecting wings on either side of the main entrance; the recessed portico thus formed faced south-east. The coins found were of the late III century[1].

BUILDINGS OTHER THAN HOUSES

Two buildings of unusual character, at Mutlow Hill, Wilbraham, and at Heydon, deserve mention. Both were constructed of clunch blocks; the one was circular, 35 feet in diameter with walls 3 feet thick; the other, rectangular, measuring internally 10 feet by 8 feet (see Neville (1852 *b*, p. 229), and Clarke, J. (1849)).

Coins, pottery and fibulae found near and in the former indicate occupation of the site all through the Roman period[2]; in the latter a coin of Constantius II was found. The position of each ensures a wide view over the surrounding country; but they differ greatly in character and the evidence is insufficient to permit the use or purpose of either to be determined.

SUMMARY

As a whole these rural dwellings give the impression of comfort rather than wealth; they are farmhouses (dwellings of natives who had adopted Roman fashions) rather than the residences of large landowners. Several are very small; none, save that at Litlington, is large; and fine mosaic floors are uncommon. Finds indicating the former existence of important structures, such as stone columns or sculptured friezes are rare; the frieze of clunch at Barrington and a portion of a Doric column at Carter's Well, Grantchester, are the only examples recorded. The rudely sculptured lion's head and

[1] For plan and record see H. Prigg (1878), also G. E. Fox (1911, p. 309).
[2] Vespasian (69–79) to Valentinian (364–375); I century "gritted ware"; wire fibulae (I century) and a crossbow fibula (late III century?).

human torso found in a Roman rubbish pit at Girton College suggest the former presence of a house in the neighbourhood.

Clunch—derived it may be from the great quarries at Reach—flint and tile, are the chief building materials, but Ketton stone from Northamptonshire has been met with at Comberton and Ickleton.

Coin finds in the Ridgewell house suggested construction in I A.D.; the Ickleton house was built subsequent to 117 A.D.; while the Wymondley dwelling was probably erected about the close of the same century, and that at Hadstock somewhat later. These two houses and that at Comberton and Bartlow seem to have been deserted in the second half of IV A.D. The significance of this will be discussed later (p. 232).

The dwelling-houses we have examined occur usually in the fertile river valleys, as at Icklingham, Ickleton, Grantchester; sometimes near springheads as at Wymondley and Litlington. A few are on the edge of the forest, as at Hadstock and Ashdon; and one is in the woodlands at Thaxted. I have failed to find record of any on the fen islands. A southern or eastern aspect was usually chosen; but the four small houses near Bartlow are on the north slope of the valley of the Bourn River. This suggests that the domain of the builders of the Hills may have been on the south slope of the valley.

INTERMENTS

(A) IN FLAT CEMETERIES

Cremation appears to have been wellnigh universal in Roman Britain up to the beginning of IV A.D., when the influence of Christianity secured its abolition in favour of inhumation.

The latest dated cremation interment in our district is one at Godmanchester; in the cinerary was a coin of Aurelianus (270–275 A.D.).

Both pure cremation cemeteries (as at Wymondley [H]) and those containing only inhumed bodies (as at Chesterford [E]) occur in our district; on many sites both rites are met with. Kempe's description of the cemetery at Litlington, explored by Webb in 1821, may be quoted as indicating the general character of these cemeteries and their contents; my selection is influenced by the fact that most of the cineraries and associated vessels are in the Cambridge Museum.

The cemetery was situated in a field known from time immemorial as Heaven's Walls; the foundations of one side of the Roman enclosing wall (which measured 38 by 27 yards and was of flint and brick) were found to be immediately contiguous to the Ashwell Street.

THE ROMAN AGE

The persistence of tradition or the unrecorded discovery of foundations accounts for many curious names locally attached to Roman sites; both probably operate in this case. "Church Field" or "Sunken Church Field" are the sites of Roman houses at Ickleton, Bartlow and Hadstock. These names probably date from pre-Conquest times when churches only were built of stone, and it was assumed that such foundations were ecclesiastic in character.

The cineraries had been placed "in rows parallel with the road" surrounded as usual by other vessels, the groups being about 3 feet apart.

"A roof-tile sometimes covered the whole deposit; sometimes a sort of square 'septum' of roof-tiles environed it, or it had been surrounded with a little wall of flints, or had been placed in a wooden box, the large nails and brasswork fastenings of which alone remained perfect."

In very few instances was the urn (an olla or beaker) unaccompanied by a vase or bottle (frequently of cream-coloured ware) and a patera[1].

"At the S.E. and S.W. angles of the inclosure, were two heaps of wood ashes, as much as would have loaded five carts; these were undoubtedly the remains of the funeral piles. On the spots where these ashes lay no sepulchral deposits were found, so that they remained in all probability on the very places where the piles had been raised."

The shovel and pincers used for collecting the bones and ashes were in one instance found with an interment.

The regularity of disposition of these cremation burials has been noted, and it implies visible memorials probably of wood. Where this regularity was interrupted, it was

"occasioned by the interment of numerous human bodies; and in the graves where they lay were found many fragments of sepulchral urns which had thus been displaced....Only in one instance were the remains of a human skeleton found *under* a sepulchral urn[2]."

The occurrence of a coin in the mouth of one of these skeletons is sufficiently uncommon in this country to be worthy of record.

This cemetery, though doubtless mainly for the poorer classes, was not lacking in objects of beauty and value, such as the incense-burner (Plate XXI, 3, 3A) and a fine glass ewer (Plate XXV, 4).

The burials of the wealthier Romanized Britons were similar, but the quality of the earthenware was finer and bronze vessels frequently occur. The most remarkable cemetery of Roman date in the district is that near Stanfordbury Farm, Southill [B]. The two most important interments are described in Chapter III (p. 99), and the chief

---

[1] A small bowl or dish usually of terra sigillata: forms Drag. 35-36 (with curved rim decorated with ivy leaves), 33, 27 or 18/31 are the most common.

[2] This account is taken from Kempe, 1836, pp. 368-72.

Roman bronzes are figured in this chapter (on Plate XXVI). We undoubtedly have here powerful native influence persisting into the Roman period; the date of one of the deposits may have been in the reign of Titus (79-81) or thereabouts. A coin, thought to be of this emperor, was found in one of the vaults; the date is not impossible, though later than might have been expected.

Though cremation was undoubtedly normal in our district during the early Roman period evidence is not lacking which points to the sporadic occurrence of inhumation in the second half of the I century and possibly in the early II century.

The inhumation cemetery at War Ditches, Cherryhinton, wherein two skeletons were associated with pottery almost certainly of the I century; and a burial at Toppesfield [E] associated with a bronze trefoil-lipped jug and patella (see pp. 192 and 213) may be cited. These, I think, are to be considered in connection with the history of cremation and inhumation in the Early Iron Age. We saw that the incoming cremation culture had not succeeded, at the date of the Roman Conquest, in entirely replacing inhumation; and these post-Claudian burials may be regarded as the latest manifestations of the traditional burial rite of the Brythonic Celts.

The War Ditches burials are especially interesting. Walker (1908 a) describes interments situated outside the fosse on the west side; he figures a handsome pot which was associated with one burial, the profile of which is strongly suggestive of I century date. Hughes had previously (1904, p. 477) described an inhumation burial in a similar situation in a grave 3 feet deep associated with bowls of smother-kiln ware with polished surfaces; the best preserved specimen being a typical I century Belgic product (see p. 208, and Plate XXII)[1].

The burials at Limlow Hill, Litlington (*Gent. Mag.* 1833) are probably of the same class. On the breast of one skeleton were numerous pieces of broken pottery, and coins of Claudius, Vespasian and Faustina.

The inhumation burials of the IV century yield, as might be expected, very scanty grave-furniture. Braybrooke (1860), for example, examined seventy graves in a cemetery lying on the north side of the Roman town at Great Chesterford. "Some fragments of Roman pottery, third brass coins, bone pins, etc.," were the only associated objects found during the excavations. The late indented beaker, figured on Plate XXVI, 3, from Birdbrook [E] accompanied an inhumation interment.

[1] See May (1916), Plate LXXI (Type 164), and p. 171.

THE ROMAN AGE

(B) IN BARROWS

There are a number of mound burials proved by excavation to be of Roman date in the Cambridge Region, which merit detailed consideration; no less than five separate barrows or groups of barrows, in addition to the Bartlow Hills series, exist within a few miles of Cambridge. Their positions are such as the Bronze Age peoples did not utilize in this district; a fact which justifies consideration, in this section, of barrows similarly sited which are either (i) destroyed, (ii) destroyed and inadequately recorded, (iii) unexplored. The regional map (IV) indicates the topographical distribution, and differentiates between those of known, and those of presumed, Roman origin.

The barrows known to be of Roman origin may first be dealt with.

(i) **Barrows in Ashdon Parish—The Bartlow Hills.** These form two parallel rows running nearly north and south. The western row consisted probably of five small barrows of which two remain; the eastern of four steep-sided mounds the largest 40 feet high and 145 feet in diameter.

Two of the destroyed barrows in the western alignment are said to have contained inhumation interments in stone coffins; but there is no contemporary record of these discoveries.

See Gage (1834, pp. 3-4) quoting Camden. Compare Gale's account: Roger Gale to Dr Stukeley, July 14, 1719, "Two of them were formerly opened and some chests of stone with bones in them taken up" (ed. Lukis, 1883, p. 153).

The remaining three barrows on this alignment were examined by Gage in 1832. Of these and the larger barrows subsequently opened by him an adequate record is preserved[1]—fortunately, since the fine grave-furniture which they contained was destroyed by fire at Easton Lodge, Dunmow [E], in 1847.

In each of two of the barrows first investigated (in 1832) an oak chest was found together with burnt bones, glass vessels and an iron lamp; one contained also a fine trefoil-lipped bronze jug and a patella; the other two beakers evidently of Upchurch (Belgic) ware and platters and cups of terra sigillata, one of which bearing the mark OFIC VIRILI is probably of Flavian date.

In the third was a brick tomb. In it a glass urn half full of charred human bones was found on which a second brass of Hadrian (117–

---

[1] In *Archaeologia*, XXV, XXVI, XXVIII and XXIX.

138 A.D.) and a gold signet ring were lying[1]. The intaglio figured two blades of corn[2]. Fragments of basket-work, and of a wooden metal-bound bucket and coffer, a glass cup and a small glass vase were also found.

Of the four larger barrows excavated in 1835-40 one, the largest (Gage, 1836), contained in an oak chest a large glass urn full of burnt bones, three glass vessels containing liquids, a folding chair of iron and bronze with leather seat, strigils, pottery and many fine bronzes —a globular situla enamelled in red, green and blue embodying a phyllomorphic design[3], a magnificent bronze lamp, a patella with ram's-head handle and ewer, etc. Leaning against the chest was a globular amphora containing ashes and fragments of bone.

Another (Gage, 1840) contained the usual bronze jug and patella, an iron lamp, glass and pottery vessels. The third was found to have been previously rifled. This is probably the barrow opened in 1815, the objects from which, an "iron lamp, a bronze patera and a small sickle-shaped knife" are in the Walden Museum (Goddard, 1899).

The fourth and last of this group, opened in 1840 (Gage, 1842), contained objects similar to the one last described, and several earthenware vessels evidently of Upchurch (Belgic) ware.

Gage remarked on the similarity of the earthenware and terra sigillata vessels in this series of interments; the Upchurch ware is probably late I century; and there is little doubt that an approximate upper limit of date for the whole is that of the coin of Hadrian found in one of the smaller barrows. An important feature is the constant presence of the sacrificial utensils, the ewer—usually trefoil-lipped with mask-decorated handle—and the handled pan or skillet[4]. These, to take examples solely from our district, were seen in the Stanfordbury vault (Plate XXVI), were associated in the Santon Downham hoard and were met with in the inhumation interment at Toppesfield[5] in Essex. R. A. Smith (1912, p. 28), discussing the Welwyn burials (where bronzes of similar use but of an earlier type were met with),

[1] An urn found at Sandy contained with the burnt bones a signet ring (bearing the device of an eagle) and a coin (Watkin, 1882, p. 272). Coins are not infrequently found in urns (see p. 188).

[2] This may be significant. An ear of corn occurs on the reverse of a coin of Cunobelin struck at Camulodunum. But the device is of classical origin; and it may be mere coincidence that an intaglio—probably imported—worn by a man of rank in Eastern Britain should present it.

[3] The remains of this vessel, salved from the Easton Lodge fire, are in the British Museum.

[4] In one of the Bartlow deposits the ewer was placed on its side in the patella (Gage, 1836, plate xxxiii).

[5] Walford (1803 a). A variation on the same theme occurred at Shefford; the ewer was of glass, the patella a vessel of unusual form with constricted waist; see p. 213 and Plate XXV.

THE ROMAN AGE

remarks that these later deposits seem "to reflect the same feelings with regard to the dead, and the same ceremonial observances under Roman rule as in the days of independence."

Comparison with the Stanfordbury interment (p. 99) is interesting also as showing the changes which half a century, it may be, has produced. The barbaric fire-dogs and spits do not occur at Bartlow, nor do pottery vessels in immoderate number and for the most part broken; but the other features are constant.

Two rich interments at Girton (preserved in Girton College and the Cambridge Museum), which can safely be dated in the Antonine period, perhaps two or three decades later than the Bartlow burials, afford another interesting comparison. The deposits were contained in wooden boxes which had perished. In each a glass jug formed the cinerary; iron lamps resembled one found in a Bartlow burial; there were glass dishes and flasks, platters and a cup of terra sigillata, and a glazed pottery vessel (p. 209); but no bronze ewer or patella (Jenkinson, 1881). Another large group of objects, including a lamp, associated with a cremation interment and approximately contemporary with the Girton burial, found at Chesterford (Braybrooke, 1860, p. 118), may also be referred to in this connection.

In many respects the careful record of the Bartlow burials throws welcome light on the sepulchral rites of the period and invests the dry details with human interest. The floor of one of the chests had been strewn with branches of box; two of the lamps had charred wicks showing that they had been lighted before being placed in the tomb: and several of the vessels contained food, or liquids.

Wine is recorded also by Ransom (1886, p. 41) in flasks associated with cremation burials at Wymondley [H].

The Bartlow barrows are probably the family graves of Romano-British nobles, and the poverty and comparative unimportance of the adjacent dwelling-house (p. 185) is all the more remarkable. This may, however, have been an outlying portion only of an extensive building, for "ancient foundations" were discovered when the railway cutting was made close by in 1864. It is unfortunate that no detailed record of the discovery of the inhumation interments is available; these may represent the usage of mound-burial continued by the family into the IV century. Such was probably the case at Rougham east of Bury St Edmunds, where a row of four barrows, doubtless representing a series of family tombs as at Bartlow, is situated close to the foundations of a Roman house. These were explored in 1843-44; three contained cremation interments, while in the fourth was an inhumation burial in a brick chamber (see C. Babington, 1874, and G. E. Fox, 1911, p. 315).

(ii) **Barrow at Lord's Bridge, Barton.** The barrow, Hey Hill, at Lord's Bridge, 100 yards from the ford where the Roman road to Cambridge crossed Bourn Brook, excavated by Walker (1908 b), measured 48 by 24 feet and was 8½ feet in height.

In a large stone coffin, probably of Barnack Rag, without a cover the disjointed skeleton of a young woman was found. Two or three fragments of Roman pottery were found at ground level just outside the coffin and a broken Roman urn was placed round the sides of the wider end of the coffin. Many Roman remains have been found in the immediate neighbourhood.

Fragments of pottery were placed round the head of an inhumed body in a grave at War Ditches, Cherryhinton (see p. 190 and Walker, 1908 a).

(iii) **Barrows at Bourn.** The barrows at Bourn, also excavated by Walker (1911 b), were three in number, all close together, and known as Arms Hills. They were ditched, and it is of great interest to have determined their date and origin; for several mounds with surrounding fosse occur in our district and but little is known about them.

Other examples are: a mound at Trumpington close to the line of the vicinal way from Red Cross to Grantchester (and therefore probably Roman), and Limlow Hill, Litlington. The latter was situated on a prominent knoll adjacent to the Roman houses and cemetery at Litlington, and was 18 feet high and 42 feet in diameter. It was surrounded by a ditch the bank of which was apparently *outside*. When destroyed in 1888 the mound was seen *not* to be composed of material from the fosse. Hughes, who reported on it (1891 a), states that a rectangular pit 4 feet by 2 feet, filled with large flints, was said to have been found at the bottom of the mound. There is no indication of date save that a fragment of red deer antler (? a pick) was found close by; and the outer bank—present at Mutlow Hill—suggests prehistoric origin. (In a Bronze Age barrow (No. 47 on list) on Therfield Heath was a cist lined with large flints.) Coins of the early Caesars with inhumation burials, at or by the mound, are recorded: but details are lacking, and these are therefore not adequate evidence of date. See Kempe (1836, p. 374) and Hughes (1891 a).

These mounds must be distinguished from moated mounds on marshy sites which are probably mediaeval, such as that at Knapwell, 7 miles west-north-west of Cambridge.

The Bourn barrows varied from 60 to 82 feet in diameter and from 5 to 8 feet in height, while their respective fosses were from 15 to 22 feet in width.

Barrow No. 1 contained a patch of black earth apparently in the centre and on ground level, with a variety of bronze objects and pottery and fragments of burnt human bones; also a coin of Marcus Aurelius (161-180 A.D.). The bronzes were submitted to the British Museum and reported on as being "Late Keltic or Roman." Under these remains and below ground level Roman remains, probably occupational, were found.

Barrow No. 2 was remarkable: one barrow was found to be superimposed on another, both being fossed. In the centre of the inner mound remains similar to No. 1 were found; and in the inner fosse remains of "Roman or Late Keltic" occupation.

The outer barrow was post-Roman, of unknown date.

There is no record of Barrow No. III in the paper. Mr Walker, in response to my enquiry, writes (Nov. 21, 1921): "No, I did not open the third tumulus. It was exactly like the other two and fragments of Roman pottery turned out in the small hole I made in it."

The finds indicate cremation burials of II A.D. by Romanized Britons. Roman remains have been found at Bourn Hall near by.

(iv) Barrow at Emmanuel Knoll, Godmanchester. This barrow was on the top of a hill on the south side of the Roman road from Godmanchester to Cambridge, one mile from the former town. It was noticed in 1740 by Stukeley, who says that urns, etc., had been dug up there (ed. Lukis, 1883, p. 219).

The barrow was destroyed in 1914 being then 32 feet in diameter and 5-6 feet in height; a careful record of its character and contents was made by Ladds (1915). There was no trench round it. Almost in the centre at about 18 inches below the original surface was a patch of black earth and ashes some 18 inches square, in the middle of which was a Roman urn containing calcined bones and clay. Round the edge of the black earth were iron nails with decayed wood, evidently the remnants of the box in which the urn had been enclosed.

The urn was of "black Castor ware, slightly burnished," $9\frac{3}{4}$ inches high, plain save for four parallel grooves on neck and shoulder.

(v) Barrow at Hildersham. On a low-lying site in the valley of the Bourn River, 150 yards from the west end of Hildersham Church, a barrow very regular in form—originally a perfect cone[1]— 190 feet in circumference, was examined by Neville in 1852, and his record is preserved in the Audley End Museum. The barrow was found to have been rifled by previous excavators at some unknown date. Its construction was peculiar. A basin-shaped hollow was first exca-

[1] Compare the Bartlow tumuli.

vated in the somewhat peaty soil[1] and lined with puddled clay; on this floor, doubtless, the interment was laid. Fragments of Roman pottery which smeared the finger when touched were found during the removal of the mound and had doubtless been associated with a cremated burial. Additional evidence of Roman origin was found in the fact that in the undisturbed clay puddling there were fragments of Roman pottery and tiles.

(v *a*) **Barrow at Langley [E].** Ample evidence for a primary cremation interment of Roman date in a large barrow at Langley is recorded by Neville (1858, p. 194).

Barrows thought to be of Roman origin

(vi) **Deadman's Hill, Barton.** (Destroyed.) The tumulus at the junction of the Red Cross-Toft road (here called Deadman's Way) and the Roman road running south-west from Cambridge, in Barton parish, was examined by Walker in 1909. It was almost entirely levelled, and the printed account of the excavation (*C.A.S. Proc.* XIV. p. 53) suggests that its date is indeterminate. But in a letter to me (Nov. 21, 1921) Mr Walker remarks: "I found nothing but Roman nails, fragments of iron and Roman sherds, etc., but quite enough to satisfy me that it was a Roman tumulus originally a little smaller than the one at Lord's Bridge." I do not think, therefore, that there need be hesitation in assigning the barrow to the Roman Age; its situation supplies strong confirmation of Mr Walker's conclusions.

(vii) **How House, Impington.** (Destroyed.) A barrow adjacent to the Roman road (Cambridge-Godmanchester) was destroyed in making the present road. It contained "several Roman coins" (Lysons, 1808, p. 44). From its situation it may well have been Roman; but the discovery of the coins is very poor evidence of date.

(viii) **Linton Heath, Linton.** (Destroyed.) The large barrow at Linton Heath, which was shown to be an Anglo-Saxon cemetery (see p. 260), was undoubtedly of earlier origin. The Anglo-Saxon interments were all by inhumation, but one deposit of burnt human bones with a "Roman vase" was found by Neville (1854 *b*) who explored the site, and it may be regarded as the original interment over which the barrow was raised.

Of four other barrows in the immediate neighbourhood opened by the same investigator in 1853 little evidence of date was obtained. They are mentioned in his paper, but no details are given; in a MS.

---

[1] Compare the similar basin-shaped hollow above which the Roman or post-Roman tumulus at Broxbournebury [H] was raised. J. Evans (1902 *c*).

THE ROMAN AGE 197

note, however, in the Audley End Museum it is recorded of one that such finds as were dateable were either "Roman or Saxon." It is thus possible that in this area, adjacent to the Bartlow Hills and to at least three Roman houses, barrows commonly marked the resting place of well-to-do persons in Roman times.

(ix) **Six Hills, Stevenage [H]**. These, like the Bartlow and Rougham tumuli, are in line running north and south; they are situated by the side of the Stevenage-Welwyn road one mile to the south of the town. J. Evans (1892) marks this road as Roman. "Wood and iron" were found in one, excavated in 1741 (Evans, *loc. cit.* p. 260).

(x) **Clifton [B]**. A bowl-shaped urn, containing cremated bones, in the Cambridge Museum is labelled "from a barrow at Clifton." The situation is one where a Roman barrow might be expected; the Roman cremation interment is therefore probably primary.

It has already been noted that secondary interments of Roman date are known to occur in Bronze Age barrows on the chalk uplands[1]; but I have found no record of a primary Roman burial in a barrow in such a situation. The barrows of proved Roman date are, as we have seen, differently disposed. They occur in the valleys, by streams, as at Bartlow, Lord's Bridge and Hildersham; those on the uplands (Emmanuel Knoll (Godmanchester), and Bourn) adjoin Roman roads or are in forest districts not occupied by earlier peoples. The topographical distinction is striking, as comparison between Map II and the Roman map (IV) will show.

A number of unexplored mounds, the great majority of which are probably sepulchral, may thus, on topographical grounds alone, be provisionally assigned to the Roman Age; that some of these may, however, on the analogy of the Chronicle Hills group, be of the Early Iron Age, is possible, and the point must not be lost sight of. The probability of Roman date becomes almost a certainty in some cases when mounds (as at Tetworth [Hunts.] or Biggleswade [B]) are situated by the side of roads definitely of Roman origin.

Such mounds are listed below; the majority are inserted with a special symbol on the map. It is hoped that opportunity may shortly be afforded of testing by excavation in selected cases the value of the preceding argument.

[1] Examples: Burwell, No. 17 on List, Appendix, p. 326; Swaffham Bulbeck, No. 44. Balsham, Nos. 3, 4, 6, 8 ought possibly to be included. In the museum at Audley End, moreover, is a Roman cinerary urn from a barrow on Triplow Heath, obtained by Neville in 1848. This barrow is No. 16 in his MS. list in the museum, and from his account the urn which was found near the edge of the mound was clearly a secondary deposit.

Mounds, unexplored, the position of which suggests Roman origin

The mound at Comberton on the line of the supposed Roman road, Barton-Comberton-Toft, marked on the 1836 O.S. map, is now destroyed, and the opportunity of determining its date is past. The mound at Swavesey on the line of the old road from Swavesey to Fen Drayton is about ¼ mile north-east of the windmill. The Rev. F. G. Walker, its discoverer, in a letter to me says that he found "a fragment of Niedermendig lava and bits of Roman pottery on the surface." To Mr Walker I also owe my knowledge of the mound at Fen Drayton. This mound, known as Low Hill, is situated on the south side of the railway in Fen Drayton parish; it is circular, 80 feet in diameter and 4 feet high. Ladds, in the paper referred to on p. 195, mentions a second mound near Emmanuel Knoll, Godmanchester, which is presumably a barrow and doubtless of Roman origin.

The mounds at Wilburton (Isle of Ely) are in two pairs; one pair in a grass field south of the church, the other pair in an old orchard lower down the slope of the hill and nearer to the fen. They may be prehistoric; but I am not aware that any barrows of the Bronze Age have been found on the high lands in the fens.

Mounds at Sturmer [E] near the head of the Stour Valley where many Roman remains have been found, and at Shudy Camps, between Haverhill and Bartlow, are from their situation probably of Roman date.

Mounds, now destroyed, at Furzenhall Farm north of Biggleswade [B] beside the Biggleswade-Sandy (Roman) road, at Crane Hill in Tetworth [Hunts.] parish beside the Sandy-Godmanchester road and at Great Stukeley [Hunts.] beside the Ermine Street, are here recorded for a similar reason.

In the *R.C.H.M. Essex* (1916) mounds at Newport (Shortgrove House) and Quendon Park (½ mile north of church) are recorded, and in the *R.C.H.M. Herts.* (1911) mounds at Anstey (Hale's Farm, moated), Brent Pelham (moated, west of Cole Green) and Little Hormead (Bummers Hill). Some of these may be Roman.

Barrow Burial in the Roman Age; General Considerations

The frequent occurrence in our district of primary interments of Roman date in barrows is worthy of remark. It is especially to be noted that mound burial is not associated with any particular rite; the contents of the Bartlow Hills, though exceptional in quality, are in character similar to those occasionally met with in flat graves. The use of a wooden chest to contain the sepulchral objects is frequently recorded, and the brick tomb within one of the "Hills" is paralleled in a flat grave at Fulbourn[1]. Interments as simple as those commonly

---

[1] At Fulbourn a "square brick grave" was found—there is no record of any barrow surmounting this interment and the use of the word grave renders it improbable—in which were "some glass and pottery vessels"—evidently a burnt interment of Roman date. Roman remains were found close by the tomb (Babington, 1883, p. 31, and Neville, 1854 c, p. 212).

THE ROMAN AGE

met with in cemeteries occurred in the barrows at Bourn and Emmanuel Knoll; while Roman interments in stone coffins as at Lord's Bridge, Barton, and probably at Bartlow are known to have occurred in flat graves near Gravel Hill, Cambridge (Babington, 1883, p. 36), and in a brick tomb at Litlington (Kempe, 1836, p. 374). Incidentally, this variety of sepulchral usage indicates prolonged duration of the custom of mound burial in the Roman Age; and we observe that the only constant feature of these sepulchres is the mound itself.

It is not easy to supply a theory which will satisfactorily account for the reappearance of barrow burial in East Anglia. It is possible that during the Late Bronze Period the construction of barrows in our district went out of fashion. If so, it was reintroduced, as we have seen, in the Early Iron Age, to be (apparently) again discontinued; and in the years round about the Christian era cremated burials were massed in cemeteries. It may be that the apparent gap in the later years of the Early Iron Age is due to the imperfection of the archaeological record, and that the erection of barrows persisted as a tradition in certain families or certain districts in the La Tène sub-periods III and IV, and was thus carried on into Roman times. The fact that the Bartlow tumuli lie in exact lines north and south conforms to ancient custom, the Chronicle Hills at Triplow having been in the Early Iron Age so aligned.

One of the Bartlow barrows is described as being built of horizontal strata of black mould and white chalk. A similar structural feature was recorded by Neville (1848, p. 18) in a Bronze Age tumulus on Five Barrow Field near Royston, and also by Hughes in respect to Limlow Hill, Litlington (p. 194).

The high conical profile of the Bartlow Hills and the Hildersham barrow, on the other hand, does not occur in our prehistoric tumuli.

Haverfield (1916, p. xxiv), in discussing the Bartlow Hills, pointed out that mound burial in Roman times occurs on the Continent (in Belgium) as well as in South-eastern England. He mentions examples in the counties of Essex, Suffolk, Kent, Hertford and Buckingham, but none in Cambridgeshire save Limlow Hill, Litlington, which is certainly dubious. Mr O. G. S. Crawford tells me (1920) that he has recently met with a group in Gloucestershire, so the distribution is less limited than has been supposed.

The chief significance of barrow burial in the Roman period is this: that it represents a survival, mainly in the most effectively Romanized areas of Britain, of a La Tène custom; this survival being prolonged far beyond that of the distinctive La Tène art in these regions. It is desirable that the phenomenon should be further studied by means of the careful exploration of tumuli, hitherto unopened. We do not know the date at which the custom became extinct. The absence of grave-furniture in one Rougham barrow suggests a Christian burial, probably of IV A.D.

POTTERY, BRONZES, ETC., ASSOCIATED WITH INTERMENTS, OR CHANCE FINDS

The mass of portable objects of the Roman period from our district preserved in museums and private collections is so great that a detailed analysis is not practicable; moreover, our knowledge of the Age, derived from other sources, permits a broader treatment in this treatise than has been possible in dealing with the prehistoric Ages.

In view of the chronological importance of pottery in general and of terra sigillata in particular, however, a brief note on this subject appears desirable: objects of glass or metal of outstanding interest found in the district are also discussed[1].

(I) POTTERY

The variety of pottery derived from the numerous cemeteries, country houses and village sites in our district is very great. Of a fair proportion of the large collection in the Cambridge Museum information is fortunately available regarding exact provenance, but records of stratification from excavated sites are almost completely lacking, and we have very few groups of associated vessels. Chronological analysis must, therefore, be based mainly on analogies with dated pottery from areas external to our own; no excavations have here been carried out comparable to those at Wroxeter, for example. Chesterford provided us with a magnificent opportunity; but its partial examination was carried out by Neville before the possibilities of archaeology as an exact science had been appreciated. The value of the work done in Cambridgeshire by Hughes and Walker at War Ditches and Horningsea must not, however, be underestimated; these men provide us with a valuable basis on which to build, by research in the future, an independent chronological survey of the local pottery of the period.

The lack of detailed record of the excavation of Roman sites is peculiarly unfortunate in the case of imported wares such as "terra sigillata" and "terra nigra." In the Stanfordbury pits, for example, was "a great quantity of red, grey and black pottery"—probably

---

[1] The coin hoards are dealt with later (see p. 231).

PLATE XX

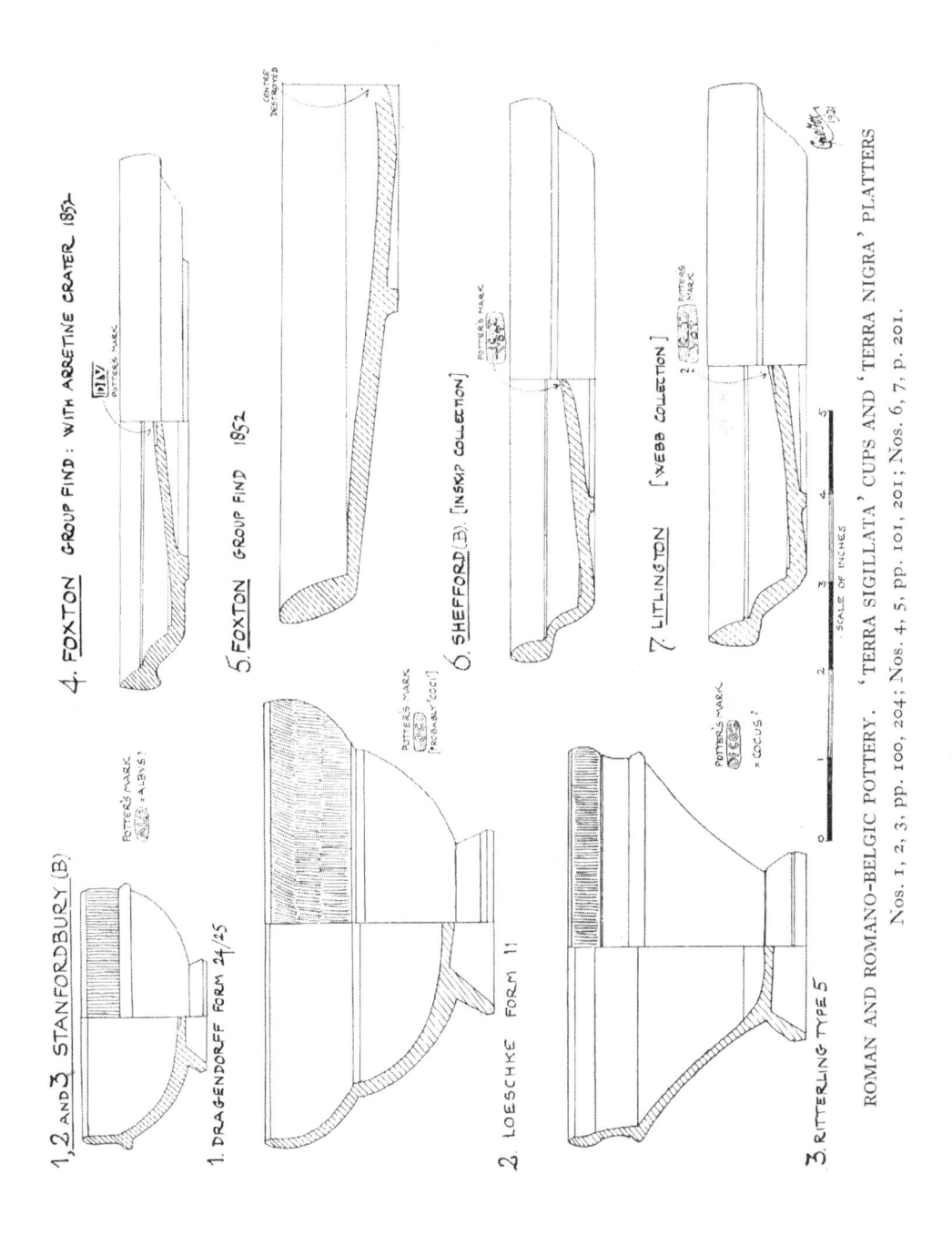

ROMAN AND ROMANO-BELGIC POTTERY. 'TERRA SIGILLATA' CUPS AND 'TERRA NIGRA' PLATTERS

Nos. 1, 2, 3, pp. 100, 204; Nos. 4, 5, pp. 101, 201; Nos. 6, 7, p. 201.

Belgic platters as well as sigillata cups; the value of the proofs of contemporaneity and of date which the careful preservation of this collection would have afforded cannot be overestimated.

Terra Nigra

The importation of Continental wares began, as we have seen, before the Claudian Conquest; and in addition to Arretine vases[1], finely designed Belgic copies of Italian platters, in grey ware coated with graphite and known as "terra nigra," are met with. These are dated in the first half of I A.D.

Such a platter, in the Cambridge Museum, was included in a large collection of pottery from the Roman cemetery at Litlington already referred to; another, in the Inskip collection, was obtained from a burial at Shefford.

The little that can justifiably be inferred as to the associations of these two plates renders it probable that they were imported in the years immediately following rather than those preceding the Claudian Conquest, and both may thus conveniently be considered in this chapter. The ware is not common in Britain; Colchester and Silchester have yielded the chief examples.

The diagrams (Plate XX) showing form and section of the local specimens render detailed description unnecessary; they show concentric rings of tooled lines on the basal interior; the black wash which covered the surfaces has almost entirely disappeared.

For comparison with these, sections of two of the platters associated with the Foxton chalice (see p. 101) are figured on the same plate, and one is reproduced on Plate XXII, 3A.

The Shefford and Litlington examples, so far as I can ascertain, have not previously been described. The Foxton platters are described by Babington (1852), and are mentioned by Haverfield (1917, p. 58).

It will be seen that the Shefford and Litlington examples are almost identical and come from the same workshop; the stamps, in two lines, Arretine fashion, are only partially decipherable; such letters as can be made out are indicated in the drawing. A third Foxton platter, similar to the smaller one figured which shows a partially effaced mark, is stamped $\frac{\text{TORNO}}{\text{VOCAR}}$; this specimen also is in the Cambridge Museum. The centre of the large dish, which is of coarser fabric, is lost, but it is said to have had no mark.

---

[1] See p. 101. A fragment of Arretine ware in the Cambridge Museum, marked L.R. PIS ("*in planta pedis*"), from the "Bartlow Hills," has not previously been mentioned. Unfortunately, nothing is known of its history; it may be post-Claudian. See Oswald and Pryce (1920, pp. 5 and 6). Two cups, possibly of Italian fabric, are discussed on p. 204.

The Belgic platters from Silchester are figured by May (1916, Plate LXXIV). None is identical in profile with our examples. Platters from the Mount Bures [E] burial are figured by C. R. Smith (1852, p. 35).

Terra Sigillata

Notes, in many cases limited to a record of the potter's mark, of some dozens of vessels from our district are to be found in archaeological publications, and a few (chiefly from the Melbourn cemetery) are exactly recorded by Walters (1908 a). These might easily be listed, but it appears to be of more use here to analyse the hundred or more examples, complete or fragmentary, preserved in the Cambridge Museum. They cover a wide range both in form and date; they are derived from all parts of the district and are thus representative. Moreover, apart from references to the Shefford and Litlington specimens[1], the material is almost entirely unpublished[2].

The table on the next page gives the provenance and type of each specimen in the collection. The rarity of late types shows that there was very little terra sigillata imported subsequent to the Antonine period. No examples of incised sigillata, or of the later developments of barbotine decoration, are present, and III century rouletted ware is seldom met with. The table also shows that early forms such as Drag. 15/17 are confined to a few sites—Chaucer Road (Cambridge), Great Thurlow, Shefford and Stanfordbury, Ely; it also shows in the range and character of forms met with the difference between a typical I century and a typical II century deposit, such as those from Great Thurlow and Chesterford respectively. The only form common to these two groups is Drag. 27 which "had a long life extending from the early South Gaulish period down to the middle of the second century" (Oswald and Pryce, 1920, p. 186).

An analysis of the marked sigillata shows that of 56 specimens, the makers of which can be identified with reasonable certainty, 20 come from the South Gaulish potteries, 21 from Central Gaul, and 6 from East Gaul; the remaining 9 being the work of potters of uncertain locality. The names of individual potters and the forms on which their marks occur are recorded in the following account of the chief sites whence the collection was derived.

Shefford and Stanfordbury. Over 30 cups, bowls and platters (Inskip and Webb collections) are derived either from the Roman

[1] For Shefford and Stanfordbury: Dryden (1845), Inskip (1845); summary by Page and Keate (1908, p. 11). For Litlington: Kempe (1836, p. 372, footnote).
[2] My analysis is based on Déchelette (1904), Oswald and Pryce (1920), May (1916), Walters (1908 a), Curle (1911) etc.

THE ROMAN AGE

CAMBRIDGE MUSEUM

Analysis of over One Hundred Specimens of Gaulish Terra Sigillata, Complete and Fragmentary

Parish and site	County	Decorated sigillata			Plain sigillata																				
		Drag. 29	Drag. 30	Drag. 37	Drag. 24/25	Drag. 15/17	Drag. 18	Drag. 18/31	Drag. 31	Drag. 27	Drag. 22	Drag. 33	Drag. 35	Drag. 36	Drag. 46	Curle 15	Walters 79	Drag. 45	Drag. 38	Ludowici To'	Drag. 30	Drag. 44	Curle 11	Drag. 42	Ludowici Tg'
Ashwell	H.	.	.	.	.	.	.	.	.	.	.	.	.	.	.	.	.	.	.	.	.	.	.	.	.
Bartlow	C.	.	.	1	.	.	.	.	.	.	1	.	1	.	1	.	.	.	1	.	1	.	1	1	1
Cambridge, the Borough[1] Chaucer Road	C.	1	1	3	.	2	.	.	.	.	.	.	1	.	1	.	.	.	1	.	.	.	.	.	.
Cherryhinton	C.	.	.	.	.	.	.	.	1	.	.	4	1	1	1	.	.	.	.	.	.	.	.	.	.
Chesterford (rubbish pits)	E.	.	.	3	.	.	.	2	1	1	1	1	1	1	.	.	.	.	2	.	.	.	.	.	.
Chesterton	C.	.	.	.	.	.	.	.	.	.	.	6	.	.	.	.	.	.	2	.	.	.	.	.	.
Ely	C.	.	.	.	.	.	.	.	.	1	.	.	.	.	.	1	.	.	.	.	.	.	.	.	.
Great Thurlow	S.	.	.	.	.	.	.	.	.	.	.	.	.	.	.	.	.	.	.	.	.	.	.	.	.
Haslingfield	C.	.	.	1	.	1	1	.	.	1	.	1	1	1	.	.	.	.	.	.	.	.	.	.	.
Horningsea (Biggin Abbey)	C.	.	.	2	.	.	.	.	.	.	.	5	4	3	2	1	1	.	1	.	.	.	.	.	.
Lakenheath	S.	.	.	.	.	.	.	.	.	.	.	.	.	.	.	.	1	1	.	.	.	.	.	.	.
Litlington (cem. and R. house)	C.	.	.	2	.	4	4	3	2	4	.	1	.	1	.	.	.	.	1	.	.	1	.	1	.
Milton (village site)	C.	.	.	1	.	.	.	.	.	.	.	1	6	.	2	.	.	.	.	.	.	.	.	.	.
Saffron Walden	E.	.	.	.	.	.	.	.	.	1	.	1	.	.	.	.	.	.	.	.	.	.	.	.	.
Shefford and Stanfordbury	B.	.	.	.	.	.	.	.	.	.	.	1	.	.	.	.	.	.	.	.	.	.	.	.	.
Wilburton	C.	.	.	1	.	.	.	.	.	.	.	.	.	1	.	.	.	.	.	.	.	.	.	.	.
Wimblington (Stonea)	C.	.	.	.	.	.	.	.	.	.	.	.	.	.	.	.	.	.	.	.	.	.	.	.	.
Wixoe	S.	.	.	.	.	.	.	.	.	.	.	.	.	.	.	.	.	.	.	.	.	.	.	.	.
Totals		2	3	14	1	9	7	14	9	10	1	22	14	7	4	1	3	1	6	1	1	1	1	2	1

[1] Barge Yard, Barnwell, Northampton Street, St Sepulchre's and Thoday Street.

NOTE. The cups, Ritterling 5, and Loeschcke 11, figured on Plate XX, are excluded from this list, their Gaulish origin being unproven.

cemetery at Shefford explored by Inskip in 1826 or from the pits at Stanfordbury containing La Tène and Roman objects.

Though some of these vessels are labelled Stanfordbury and the rest Shefford the differentiation is not to be depended upon; and we cannot therefore, as might easily have been possible, accurately determine the date of the former burials.

Dryden (1845, p. 14) remarks: "The Samian ware cups and bowls found at Stanford were not at the time distinguished from those at Shefford."

It is, however, highly probable that three fine and delicately moulded cups—Drag. 24/25, Loeschcke 11 and Ritterling 5—with rouletted decoration, closely resembling Arretine fabrics but probably South Gaulish ware of Tiberian or Claudian date are *correctly labelled* as being from Stanfordbury. These are sufficiently uncommon to merit reproduction (see Plate XX). The marks are indistinct but the La Graufesenque potters Albvs and Cocvs may perhaps be identified.

The assignation of two of these (Loeschcke 11 and Ritt. 5) to South Gaulish potters requires justification. The former is identical with an Arretine cup from Silchester (May, 1916, Plate V, 12) bearing the stamp SILVA and May notes that a specimen marked XANTI is in Mainz Museum (*op. cit.* p. 13). The chalice, Ritt. 5, again, is of Arretine character. No less than six fragmentary examples from Silchester are figured by May (Plate IV) and examples with rouletted mouldings, like ours, have not been recorded from South Gaul. The stamp, however, so closely resembles that on a platter by Cocvs OF COCI in the Cambridge Museum that it appears almost certain that this potter made both. Now Cocvs is, according to Walters (1908 a, p. 51), a potter of La Graufesenque. Moreover, OF (Officina) rarely occurs on Arretine fabrics. If this piece, then, be considered South Gaulish there is little justification for assigning Arretine origin to the cup, Loeschcke 11, which in paste and technique so closely resembles it, and which is probably also by Cocvs.

The scale sections and reproductions of the stamps, enable the reader to form an independent judgment as to date and provenance.

The South Gaulish potters Bilicatvs (?), Logirnvs and Silvanvs, of Claudian to Flavian date, are represented by finely moulded platters of Drag. form 15/17. The marks on two platters, Drag. 18, have not been deciphered; they are probably of Claudian date. Several examples of the cup, Drag. 27, with constricted curvilinear wall occur; two bear the name of Maccivs. Lezoux ware is represented by a dish, Drag. 31, of Rebvrrvs; another dish, Drag. 18/31, is of East Gaulish fabric, Reginvs being the potter. Numerous examples of Drag. 35, a cup with rim decorated *en barbotine*, the majority probably of Flavian date, may also be mentioned. From this col-

PLATE XXI

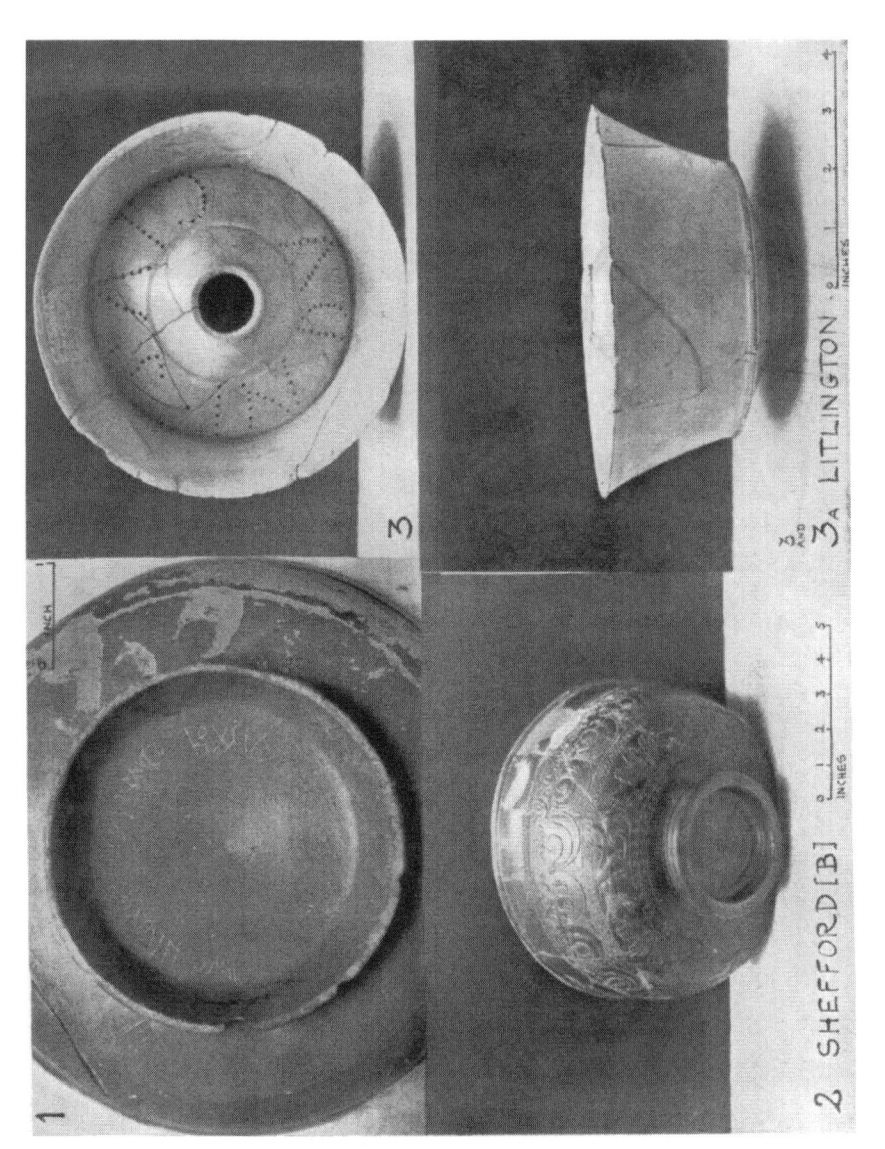

ROMAN AGE. POTTERY

No. 1, p. 207; No. 2, p. 205; Nos. 3 and 3 A, pp. 189, 208–9.

THE ROMAN AGE

lection, again, comes a magnificent early example of Drag. 37. The photograph (Plate XXI, 2) renders description unnecessary; the character of the decoration suggests South Gaulish fabric and Flavian date.

Other potters represented here are Maccarvs (Drag. 18), Cracisa (Drag. 18/31) and Calvinvs (Drag. 33). See also Watkin (1882, p. 277).

As a whole, the series attests the early date of the settlement in the Ivel Valley.

Ashwell [H]. Two platters (Drag. 18 and 15/17) from this parish bear the stamps of Germanvs and Mascvlvs, and date probably from the early Flavian period.

Great Thurlow [S]. Examination of the sigillata fragments obtained from a rubbish pit at Great Thurlow, on the Upper Stour, gives similar results. The deposit consisted of wares of South Gaulish fabric with dull matt surface and of high quality, probably mainly of Claudian-Neronian date. Finely decorated bowls (Drag. 29 and 30) and a variety of plain forms were met with. The two marked specimens (Drag. 18) were by Albvs and Cotto.

Cambridge. Early occupation of the low gravel ridge between the River Cam and the Cambridge-Trumpington road is attested by the recent discovery at Upwater Lodge, Chaucer Road, of a pair of fine platters (Drag. 15/17) by Ardacvs and Lic[invs?], La Graufesenque potters of the Claudian-Neronian period.

And by the discovery in 1711, in an extensive cemetery of which these deposits evidently formed part, of paterae bearing the name of the latter potter, Licinvs, and of a contemporary, Damonvs; also of an amphora of Italo-Greek type (Babington, 1883, p. 48, and Stukeley, ed. Lukis, 1883, p. 37). The site is marked on Map G, p. 246.

Scanty finds of sigillata within the Borough to which dates can be assigned suggest occupation from the Flavian period onward. A fragment bearing the stamp of Calvvs was found among much rubbish from the Castle Hill settlement in the Lady Margaret Road area (Macalister, 1896, p. 30), and a dish (Drag. 42) with rosette stamp comes from Barnwell. A large quantity of sherds from excavations carried out in 1862 in Barge Yard yielded examples of forms Drag. 29, 30, 35, 37, etc., but no potters' marks were preserved. Much of the ware was of Flavian date, and from La Graufesenque, judging from the character of the paste and glaze.

Litlington. La Graufesenque potters are represented at the

Litlington cemetery and house site[1] by a platter (Drag. 18) by Damonvs and possibly by a bowl (Drag. 27) with constricted curvilinear wall which bears the same stamp as M. 832 in Walters' catalogue (1908 *a*). The majority of the wares were, however, of later date. The work of Central Gaulish potters (such as Primvlvs, dating from the Flavian period, Elvillvs, Albvcianvs, Divicatvs and Borillvs, of the II century) occurs on shallow bowls, Drag. 18/31 or 31, or conical cups (Drag. 33). The stamps of Tittivs, Cracissa, Calava, Satinvs (represented also at Chesterford) and Pecvliaris, an East Gaulish potter of the Hadrian-Antonine period, are also met with. Of the unmarked wares, cups (Drag. 35) of Flavian type and the later forms (Drag. 36) of the same vessel occur here as elsewhere in the district; and the fragment of a mortarium (Drag. 45) of a Rheinzabern type dating in the second half of II A.D. deserves mention.

We see, therefore, that occupation of this area from pre-Flavian times to the Antonine period is probable; other evidence, as we have seen, extends the use of the cemetery to a much later date.

Walden [E]. A quantity of fragments from an unknown site at Saffron Walden date probably from the beginning to the end of II A.D. The potters Sabinvs and Criciro (probably of Banassac) are represented; a Rheinzabern bowl (Drag. 37) by Comitialis represents the modified form of metope decoration used in East Gaul in the Antonine period. An example of Ludowici form Tó may be noted[2].

Chesterford [E]. The Chesterford collection was obtained by Messrs Jenkinson, Hughes and von Hügel in 1879 and subsequent years from rubbish pits within the settled area. A fine bowl in free style (Drag. 37) and a fragment of another in the style of Cinnamvs are probably Lezoux wares. A campanulate cup with cornice rim and handles (Drag. 46) and a cup (Drag. 27) with a partially obliterated mark (? Macrianvs of Lezoux) are worth mentioning. A bowl (Drag. 38) and dish (Drag. 31) show the marks of the East Gaulish potters Constas and Sextvs; other dishes (Drag. 31) are by Criciro and, probably, Celticvs.

The range in form and date of terra sigillata from Chesterford is of course very much wider than the small museum collection indicates. South Gaulish potters of the I century (e.g. Silvanvs and Maccivs) are represented in the Audley End Museum.

---

[1] The majority of the vessels come from the cemetery; a few from the Clack collection (Beldam collection) may have been from the villa. Some potters' marks listed by Kempe (1836, p. 372) are not to be found in our collection.

[2] As Oswald and Pryce, 1920, Plate LXIX, 4.

PLATE XXII

ROMANO-BELGIC POTTERY; ROMAN AND ROMANO-BRITISH POTTERY
AND FIBULAE

No. 1, pp. 190, 208; No. 2, p. 212; No. 3, p. 101; No. 3 A, pp. 101, 201;
Nos. 4, 5, 6, p. 215.

THE ROMAN AGE

Ely. An interesting range of fragmentary vessels from a site in Ely town has recently been acquired (Cole Ambrose collection). Primvlvs, Rebvrrvs and Atilianvs, Lezoux potters of I and II A.D., are represented by Drag. 33 cups; and the mark of one early South Gaulish potter, Scottivs, is met with on a platter, Drag. 15/17. Sherds from an unknown site near the town yield stamps of Marcellinvs (Drag. 18/31?), Macrinvs, Asiaticvs (Drag. 33?) and others, all probably II century.

The remaining marked wares may be briefly dealt with. The I century potter Pavllvs of La Graufesenque is represented by a bowl (Drag. 27) from Wixoe [S]. Wares of the II century Lezoux potters Namilianvs, Maccalvs, Illiomarvs, Albvcianvs (all Drag. 33), Belliniccvs (?) and Albvcivs (Walters 79), Paternvs (Drag. 37) are derived from Cherryhinton, Chesterton, Wilburton, Milton or Bartlow. A cup by Cvcalvs (Drag. 33, Wilburton) and a fragment from Undley [S] bearing the stamp of Sennivs complete the list.

On the basal exterior of a platter probably from Henlow [B] of I century date, Drag. 18, there is a graffito in cursive script, which is reproduced on Plate XXI, 1. I am much indebted to Mr A. B. Cook for the translation and notes printed below. Such graffiti are rare in Britain[1]; the example under consideration resembles those found at Pompeii and other Italian sites. It appears to be a message sent by a Roman centurion to a comrade, and thus has not necessarily any bearing on the question as to whether or no the Romano-British population spoke Latin.

Esico Litullus c(enturio) Commit(t)o Hoxaico (?).

"I, Litullus, centurion, (send this) to Esicus. I entrust it to Hoxaicus (?)."

Æsica was a British town near Netherby in Cumberland (*Notitia dignit. occident.* 38).

Esica for Æsica occurs in Anonym. Rav. p. 432 Pind.

Litulla occurs as the name of a woman, probably a barbarian, in *Corp. inscr. Lat.* III, no. 4906, Litulla Touti f.

Commit(t)o. The dropping of second *t* is not unusual in vulgar Latin.

Hoxaico (?). Name not elsewhere recorded. But the initial *H* is very possibly a vulgarism. If so, cp. the name *Oxtaius* borne by a Gaul in H. Dessau, *Inscriptiones Latinae selectae*, III. 2, no. 9307: Aug. sac. | deo Apollin[i] | Moritasgo, | Catianus | Oxtai.

---

[1] The evidence for Bedfordshire provenance may therefore be stated. Inskip (1845) describes a Samian dish with graffiti inscribed on the bottom, which was dug up in "Penlowe Park, Herts." Taylor (1914, p. 159) suggests Henlow for "Penlowe." The whole of the Inskip collection obtained, from Shefford [B] and its neighbourhood, is in the Cambridge Museum.

Haverfield (1915, p. 33) figures and discusses a fragment of an urn found on the Ickleton house site by Neville which bears a graffito which he restores as "*ex ha*]*c amici bibun*[*t*," "from this jar friends drink."

Other imported wares

1. Examples of the so-called Upchurch (Romano-Belgic) pottery dating probably in the second half of the I century occur in this district. Bowls of polished grey and black ware (examples from War Ditches (Plate XXII, 1) and Barge Yard, Cambridge, may be cited) decorated with incised concentric semicircles and parallel lines are met with, and an interesting series of beakers and ollae, some with raised dots in rhomboidal patterns (evidently of types common at Upchurch), was found in the Bartlow Hills. The plain tazzas or bowls with concave sides and pedestal feet found at Chesterford (see sectional drawing, Plate XVI, 14) also were probably imported; as, doubtless, were the globular beaker (Plate XII, 6) with black polished surface from Stourbridge Common, which has a slightly everted rim resembling a La Tène III form, and the fine olla with silver-grey polished surface decorated in two zones with delicate combed zigzags from Chesterford (Plate XXIII, 2). Others in the Cambridge Museum and elsewhere were, it is probable, made in Britain by native potters.

A remarkable range of beakers made of a fine biscuit ware, white, pink or yellow in colour, decorated *en barbotine* with patterns of circles or dots in white or coloured slip, was found by Hughes in the upper layer of the infilling of the fosse of the War Ditches, Cherryhinton (see p. 177). I have not been able to ascertain the origin of this ware; it is possibly Romano-Belgic, and certainly of late I or early II century date. Portions of flagons with mouthpieces of I century forms and of coarse wares showing La Tène influence occurred in the same layer, and Belgic bowls from the same site referred to above may well be contemporary. Plate XXIV, 2, shows characteristic examples.

2. An incense-burner of exceptional interest from the Litlington cemetery is shown on Plate XXI. It is of fine creamy-white biscuit, unglazed; the underbase is coned inwards and the perforated domed cover with a central aperture rises to the level of the rim of the vessel. Parallel examples in Britain are recorded from Silchester and the Wall; and similar Continental forms are ascribed to the period Domitian-Hadrian (May, 1916, p. 119, and Plate L, 71). Our example is unique in that the perforations form the letters of the name Indv[l]civs. It is probably of Rhenish origin.

PLATE XXIII

1. CASTLE STREET, CAMBRIDGE
2. CHESTERFORD [E]
3. HASLINGFIELD
4. ISLEHAM FEN

ROMAN AGE. POTTERY
No. 1, pp. 93, 212; No. 2, p. 208; No. 3, pp. 100, 256; No. 4, p. 209.

THE ROMAN AGE

This vessel is mentioned in Kempe's account of the Litlington cemetery (1836, p. 372), and is there figured (plate XLV), but on a very small scale. The name is recorded as Indulcius, without comment; the "l" is not now traceable, but it must be accepted that before restoration some portion of the letter was apparent.

3. The green-glazed earthenware bowl with flat auriculate handles (resembling Drag. 39), which was found with a sigillata vessel at Saffron Walden, is probably an early II century product of the St Remy en Rollat workshops[1] in Central Gaul: the same factory may have produced the globular vase with raised striae from Girton in the Cambridge Museum, dated by the associated terra sigillata, in the Antonine period (p. 193).

Vessels painted in white slip

In the Lewis collection at Corpus Christi College is a Rhenish beaker, probably of III century date, bearing the inscription *Vtere Felix* in white slip, which was found in a Roman cemetery at Guilden Morden in 1879 (Lewis, 1881).

Some other beakers found in the district with scroll decoration in white slip are, doubtless, also of Continental origin; but the style was in vogue at Castor, and the majority of our examples certainly came thence. A series in the Cambridge Museum from Trumpington, Bourn, Haslingfield, Litlington and Madingley Road, Cambridge, may be referred to.

Similar decoration is seen on flagons and amphorae in the Cambridge Museum. An example from Isleham Fen (Plate XXIII) may be late III A.D., while a flagon of debased form and crude ornament from the neighbourhood of Royston (Plate XXV, 2) clearly belongs to the close of the Roman Age in Britain.

Wares of British manufacture

(*a*) **"Castor" wares.** As might be expected from the convenience of water transport, colour-coated beakers and cups which can safely be ascribed to the Nene potteries are found everywhere in our district. The indented beakers vary widely in form and cover the whole period of the Roman occupation (No. 4, Plate XXVI, being a very late type); and beakers of "hunt cup" form, dating from about 135–200 A.D. (May, 1916, p. 108), with scroll decoration, animals, gladiators, etc., *en barbotine*, commonly occur. Two are figured on Plate XXV, 1, 3. Of the former group, examples in the Cambridge

---

[1] Figured and described by A. G. Wright; see Maynard, 1916, p. 16.

Museum from Madingley Road, Haslingfield and Chesterford, with overlapping scale pattern or bold scrolls applied to the ridges between the indentations, deserve special mention.

See also examples of "hunt cups" and beakers from Horningsea, Chesterford and Shefford (Cambridge Museum), Wymondley (Ransom collection) and Chesterford (Audley End Museum).

(b) **New Forest Wares.** These evidently could not compete with the Castor products in their own neighbourhood, and I have met with only one beaker of local provenance with the purple glaze characteristic of the New Forest kilns. This is in the Ransom collection, and was found at Wymondley [H].

(c) **Wares produced in the Cambridge Region.** Pottery kilns have been discovered at Horningsea and West Stow [S] and wasters from kilns (not yet located) at a third site, Jesus Lane, Cambridge.

(i) **Horningsea.** The potters' field at Horningsea, producing vessels which have been recognized as occurring in many parts of South Cambridgeshire, is close to Eye Hall. The remains—wasters from the kilns, etc.—were described by Hughes in 1901 (see Hughes, 1903 a), but the actual kilns were not found until 1911, when excavations were carried out in the neighbourhood by F. G. Walker.

Walker notes that Horningsea ware occurs on Roman sites at Littleport and on the banks of the Old Croft River to the north thereof, at Castle Hill, Cambridge, at the War Ditches and at Godmanchester. The present writer has seen examples from several other sites in Cambridge, from the Roman house at Swaffham, from Ely and from Wilbraham, and there is one vessel undoubtedly from these kilns in the Ransom collection at Hitchin, found in that neighbourhood.

Walker's investigations, which were published in 1913, showed that an important manufactory of varied types of coarse ware was in existence in the I century. The small area which he excavated yielded forms ranging down to the III century, and it is therefore possible that the potteries were active throughout the Roman occupation. No ware recognizably Anglo-Saxon, or mediaeval, was found. Almost all the product of the kilns was light or dark grey in colour, and was of hard paste. Beakers and ollae decorated with combed and other patterns on neck and shoulders, and large grain jars with broad flanged rims and bold grooved decoration on the lower part of the body, were common. One of the latter, figured on Plate XXIV, measures 2 feet high and 21 inches in diameter at the bulge; and this was not exceptional. Saucers and shallow bowls with straight sides and flat

PLATE XXIV

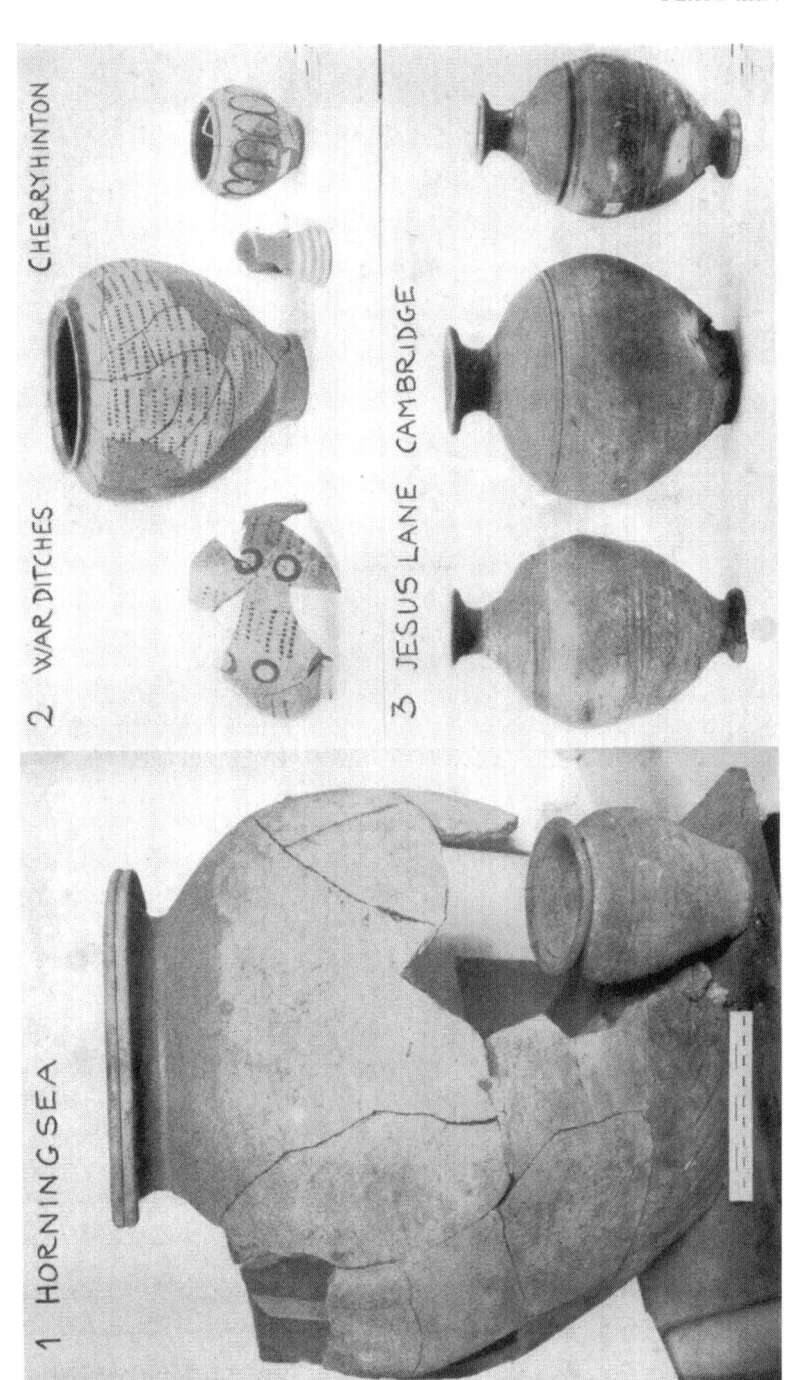

ROMAN AGE. POTTERY
No. 1, p. 210; No. 2, p. 208; No. 3, p. 21

bases and small pots from two to three inches in height were also manufactured. The occurrence as wasters of some indented beakers with the metallic glaze associated with the Castor potteries suggests that such were made at Horningsea, but no examples decorated *en barbotine* were found. Walker suggests that pottery was made on the site in the La Tène period, but no pottery indubitably of pre-Roman date was found. A series of fragments from the kilns or their immediate neighbourhood shows La Tène technique—burnished surfaces and girth grooves, lattice patterns, broad raised bands, with incised decoration, etc.; but none is, I think, necessarily earlier than middle I A.D. A platter in the Cambridge Museum is of special interest. It is clearly a copy of a Belgic imitation of an Arretine plate, having moulded sides and a foot-ring.

All the chief types found are figured in Hughes' and Walker's papers; and the existence of a representative series in the Cambridge Museum renders further description here unnecessary.

(ii) **West Stow [S].** The only other potters' field in the district, that on West Stow Heath, was discovered in 1879. Nothing is known of its products save that "fragments of fawn-coloured, bottle-shaped vases with handles were found in the ashes close to the kilns." Walker (1913, p. 34) gives a convenient summary of the original record. A vessel from "Kiln No. 1" is in Bury Museum.

(iii) **Jesus Lane, Cambridge.** Globular narrow-necked flasks and bottles of hard light grey ware ornamented with girth grooves and neck cordons were found in 1901 in Jesus Lane, Cambridge, on the east side of the King's Ditch, and reported on by Hughes (1903 b). They are of hard Roman ware, in form showing native influence, and are probably of late I century date. The majority have some defect, as Plate XXIV, 3, shows; this suggests that kilns existed somewhere in the immediate neighbourhood. Specimens of the Jesus Lane ware are found in the district, as Hughes remarks, in Roman rubbish pits or cemeteries, as at Haslingfield, where good class pottery occurs; but it is nowhere common. (Cf. May, 1916, Type 147, p. 165.)

(iv) Other kilns of Roman date found in the district are listed below. All are probably tile or lime kilns.

Ashdon. See Neville (1853, p. 21).

Great Chesterford. Found within the area of the Roman town in 1879 (Hughes, 1903 a, p. 178).

Kilns with a filling of Roman remains, apparently lime kilns (since slaked lime was found near by), were found near Fulbourn half a mile on the Cambridge side of the railway station in 1875. They had perhaps been used as rubbish pits subsequent to disuse as kilns (Hughes, 1903 a, p. 177).

(*d*) **British Gritted Ware.** To the class thus characterized by May (1916, p. 178) belongs a group of ollae and beakers without handles, with stout flattened rims rolled well outwards, made on the wheel. The majority have the surface roughened with minute parallel horizontal striae, and all show in the clay much pounded flint, the surfaces of the vessels being thus everywhere speckled with white. The colour varies from drab through red to smoky black.

Such vessels occur frequently in local cemeteries; the example figured (Plate XXII, 2) comes from Litlington. In form and material they closely resemble certain pre-Roman wares and are undoubtedly of native and probably of local (East Anglian) manufacture.

Fragments of one such vessel, inaccurately reconstructed, as I am disposed to think, is figured by Walker (1913, fig. 46, and p. 56), but the evidence that it was made in a Horningsea kiln is very indefinite.

A La Tène pot of the same form from "Near Hitchin" is in the Ransom collection.

The author has found numerous fragments at Mutlow Hill, Fleam Dyke, in deposits considered to date from the I century onwards, and an example in Peterborough Museum is said to have been deposited as cinerary, in a cist covered by a tile (also in the museum) bearing the stamp of the IX Legion ("LEG. IX HISP")[1]; a date not later than 60 A.D., when the Legion was destroyed, is here indicated. The chronology of the type is of some local importance, for several fragments of one such pot were found under the vallum of the Fleam Dyke (see p. 131).

Survival of La Tène forms. Much has been said in Chapter III about the overlap of La Tène and Roman pottery forms; our "gritted ware" and the undecorated wide-mouthed ollae and bowls (in form closely resembling certain Aylesford types) which are usually assigned to the late I century[2] show native influence and are probably of East Anglian origin. The remarkable olla from Castle Street, Cambridge (Plate XXIII), dating probably in II A.D., shows La Tène feeling strongly marked. It is decorated with raised neck cordons, lattice and metopic patterns made with a smooth point, and rows of incisions. This olla may have been made locally; it has features resembling the Jesus Lane (Cambridge) flasks, and also certain pots made at Horningsea. Other vessels showing La Tène

---

[1] At Hilly Wood, Northants., on west side of "King Street," a Roman road. Information from Mr J. W. Bodger, honorary curator.

[2] This is probably correct, but definite evidence is lacking. See examples in Cambridge Museum from Hauxton, Chesterford [E], Madingley Road (Cambridge), Litlington, Exning [S], etc.

technique, found in and around the Horningsea kilns, were probably made by native potters at the commencement of the Roman occupation (see p. 211). The influence exerted by native craftsmen in Britain (as in Gaul) on the form and decoration of earthenware throughout the Roman period was very marked and is especially shown in the colour-coated wares manufactured at Castor.

Space does not permit discussion of the development of the potter's art during the Roman occupation, and several important classes of ware have not even been mentioned. I have endeavoured in the selection of examples for illustration to cover as wide a chronological range as possible and to show the decadence which overtook the potter's art in the closing phase of that occupation. Beakers Nos. 4 and 5 on Plate XXVI, and the flagon figured on Plate XXV, 2, late IV century wares, tell their own story.

Owing to the disuse of pagan burial customs, perfect vessels belonging to the later centuries of the Roman occupation are rare, and can for the most part be at present only approximately dated.

(II) Vessels and Objects of Metal and Glass

A. *Of Bronze*

Bronze vessels of exceptional quality or interest found in the district are, like the pottery, mainly derived from interments; and reference has already been made to those found in the Bartlow Hills, at Toppesfield and Stanfordbury. The majority of the trefoil-lipped ewers and patellae with reeded handles which occurred in these deposits are undoubtedly of I century date. Such were associated in the Santon Downham hoard (middle I A.D.), and R. A. Smith (1909 *e*, p. 161) notes that the trefoil-lipped jug occurs at Pompeii, destroyed in 79 A.D. In this connection a dated bowl with constricted waist (probably an incense pan?), found at Shefford and now in the Cambridge Museum, is of special interest. It has two handles, one looped, of cast bronze bearing a mask and lion's claw, almost identical with that on the Santon Downham oinochoè; the other, horizontal, cylindrical, with zöomorphic terminal like that of a patella. It thus, in itself, combines features of both vessels. The label, evidently contemporary with its discovery (1836), records that it was found with a coin of Vespasian (69–79 A.D.) and with a fine blue pillar-moulded glass jug, also in the museum (Plate XXVI, 2).

The bronze bowl is much restored; but such fragments as exist, and the shape of the loop handle, make the restoration highly probable.

Dryden (1845) figured the vessel as a shallow patella. That its loop handle should be that normally used for jugs suggests that such fittings were made in a central foundry or foundries, and sold to local bronze workers.

The associations of a bronze bowl found at Braughing, with naturalistic decoration in champlevé enamel, are unknown; but it resembles the situla from Bartlow, which is well illustrated by Gage (1836, Plate 35)[1]. The latter is one of the finest known examples of La Tène enamel work carried out under classical influence in the Roman period.

These apart, enamel decoration of the Roman period is in our district confined to small objects such as fibulae, lockets, and seal-boxes. La Tène ornament is seen on one of the latter in the Cambridge Museum.

Special mention should here be made of the magnificent bronze bowl or skillet—with "vine scrolls on the handle filled with niello," a winged genius and dolphins. This bears the name of the maker BODVOGENVS; it was found in the fens at Prickwillow, Ely, and is now in the British Museum. The Stanfordbury ewer was accompanied by a vessel similar in form but less elaborate (see Plate XXVI).

See *B.M.G.* (1922, p. 85) and Ward (1911 b, pp. 186–188). The latter discusses the range and uses of the type. The Stanfordbury skillet resembles one from Herringfleet, Suffolk, figured by G. E. Fox (1911, p. 308).

Of interest as a dateable object is the bronze strainer from Chesterford, figured by Neville (1848, p. 95); the most recent coin of a large hoard deposited in it was one of Commodus (180–192); the type has, however, a long history, as it occurs at Pompeii.

A number of statuettes and votive figurines of bronze of great interest have been found in the district. Several of Hercules are in the Cambridge Museum, the majority probably from near Ely. A figure of Mercury was found on Castle Hill, Cambridge (Bowtell MS. II, 191); one of Jupiter, now in the British Museum, at Earith [Hunts.]; one of a River God at Chesterford (Braybrooke, 1860, p. 125, figured). The Barkway hoard (p. 216) included a bronze figure of Mars. A bronze plaque with head of Mercury in high relief from Sandy [B] is figured by Page and Keate (1908, p. 10).

Babington records (1883, p. 84) the discovery in a field at Willingham Fen, in 1857, of a number of bronzes which are evidently votive and other objects from a shrine. These bronzes, now in the Cambridge Museum, were, as Baron von Hügel tells me,

---

[1] The range of the type is given by Taylor (1914, p. 151); it is confined to Britain, Scandinavia and N. France.

PLATE XXV

ROMAN AGE. POTTERY AND GLASS VESSELS: PEWTER DISH
Nos. 1, 3, p. 209; No. 2, pp. 209, 213; No. 4, pp. 189, 217; No. 5, p. 216; No. 6, p. 217.

THE ROMAN AGE

in a wooden box, and therefore represent a carefully hidden deposit. The most remarkable object is a bronze club surmounted by the bust of an Emperor, and showing figures and symbols in high relief on the central zone. The statuettes include two mounted soldiers—Roman cavalry; and there is a diminutive (votive) horsebit of bronze. Professor Rostovtzeff, who has examined the hoard, suggests that it comes from a sanctuary connected with the cult of the Emperor—possibly Commodus—and of a Celtic God equated with Jupiter; a sanctuary visited by Roman soldiers.

To the same period (II A.D.) and the same shrine may possibly belong a remarkable helmeted bust, illustrated and described by Babington (1883, p. 82), which was also found on the southern margin of the fens, at Cottenham, four miles from the Willingham hoard. It is in the Fitzwilliam Museum, Cambridge.

Arms and armour of the Roman period rarely occur; in the first rank of such objects, however, is a bronze helmet lined with iron and with cheek-pieces, front and neck guards, found in the fen peat at Witcham Gravel and now in the British Museum (figured, *B.M.G.* 1922, Plate IV). The mouth of a bronze trumpet found at Chesterford, also in the National Collection, was probably for army use (*B.M.G.* 1922, p. 82).

Fibulae. The range of types found in the district is such as all students of the period are familiar with; a few examples, characteristic, or of special interest, may be mentioned.

The fibulae occurring in the Santon Downham hoard have already been considered in connection with the Early Iron Age; they are of importance to our present study, showing as they do the stage of development in the middle of I A.D. of the chief forms met with in the Roman Age. Other fibulae of the period figured in the plates are:

(i) A characteristic early example of the Backworth type with trumpet base, floriated expansion on bow, wire spring and ring, probably of early II century date, from Mildenhall (Plate XXII, 5). (ii) A double disc fibula from "near" Cambridge (Plate XXII, 6)—introduced here as an example of the bizarre forms, which defy typological classification—characteristic of the Age; and (iii) a magnificent knobbed cruciform fibula of IV century date (and Continental origin?) from Barrington. The latter is of gilt bronze, the ridge of the bow and the foot being inlaid with silver; along either side of the foot the cusping is unusually well developed. The workmanship is admirable, the general effect barbaric. It illustrates the influence of oriental fashions on the art of the period (Plate XXII, 4).

From Stonepit Hill, Icklingham, is derived a similar fibula heavier and larger but no less ornate; it is in the Bury Museum. Another is in the Peterborough Museum. These three fenland examples are perhaps finer than any in the National Collection.

B. *Of silver and pewter*

Of chief importance is the hoard of votive objects found in 1743 in Rokey Wood, near the village of Barkway [H] and the Ermine Street, on the crest of the southern escarpment of the Cam Valley. There were seven variously-shaped plates of silver, four with figures of Mars helmeted and two bearing a figure of Vulcan with his attributes, in addition to the bronze figure of Mars already referred to.

One of these plates bore a dedicatory inscription to Mars Toutates, another to Mars Alator, while a third, fragmentary, refers to Vulcan.

The find possibly represents the plate of a neighbouring shrine where Romanized Britons worshipped their ancient gods, stolen during the V century and hidden in the wood.

See Taylor (1914, p. 149) for a full account of these finds and a discussion of the Celtic deities commemorated; Haverfield (1915, p. 69) emphasizes the rarity of references to the god Teutates. The hoard is in the British Museum.

Finds of silver are rarely met with; but pewter vessels (cups and platters) have been found, singly or in hoards, in several places; at Lakenheath and Icklingham, and in the fens at Sutton, Isleham, Stretham Mere, and West Row, Mildenhall. The Icklingham find consisted of a large table service which had been carefully hidden; it was discovered in 1840 and some forty pieces are now in the British Museum. Characteristic platters from Sutton and Mildenhall, and a table service—platters and cups—from Isleham, are in the Cambridge Museum. Pewter flagons from the fens are also in the museum. On Plate XXV one of the platters from Sutton, with an embossed border, is reproduced. Most of this pewter is of the IV century.

C. *Of Glass*

One of the treasures of the Cambridge Museum, the blue glass jug from Shefford (Plate XXVI) has already been mentioned; the Bartlow barrows, the Stanfordbury pits, Chesterford, Hauxton and the Litlington cemetery have yielded a characteristic range of bowls, jugs, ewers, and beakers; it may, indeed, be said that the whole range of forms illustrated by Ward (1911 *b*, p. 181) has been found in the

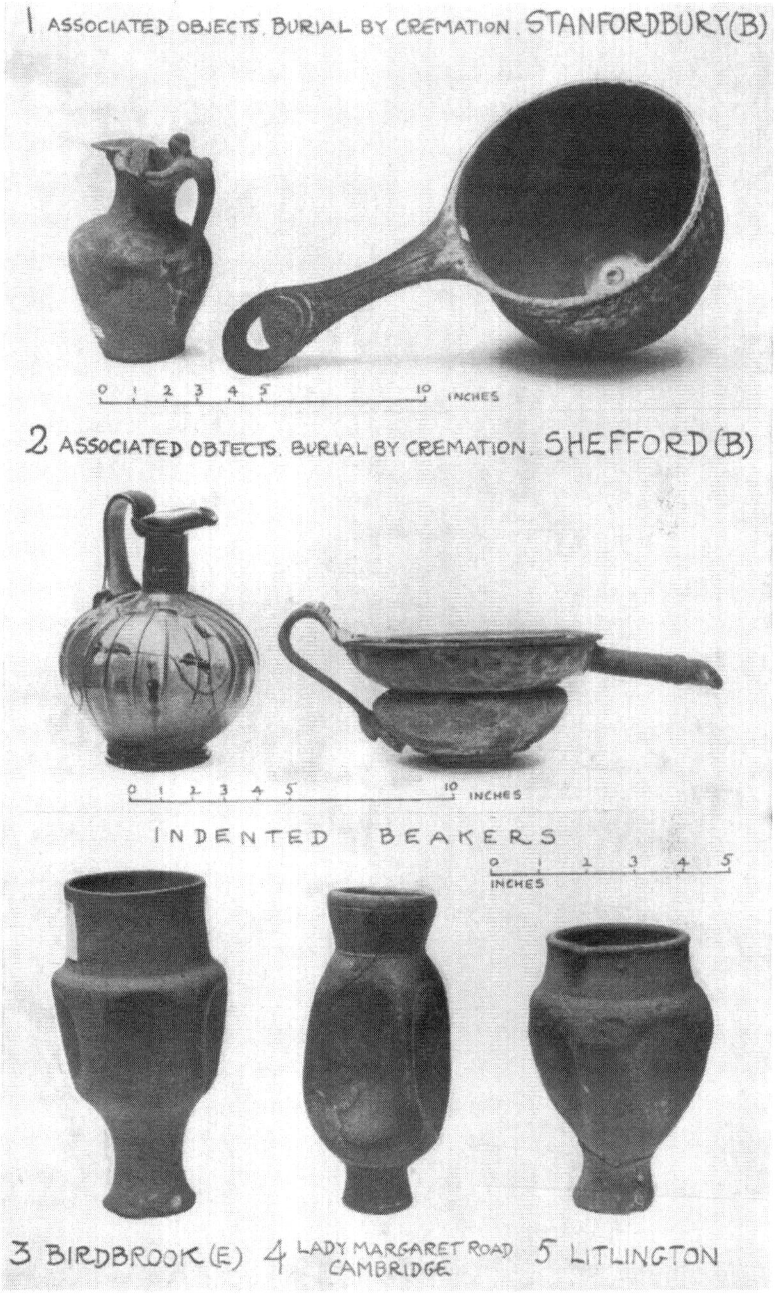

PLATE XXVI

1 ASSOCIATED OBJECTS. BURIAL BY CREMATION. STANFORDBURY (B)

2 ASSOCIATED OBJECTS. BURIAL BY CREMATION. SHEFFORD (B)

INDENTED BEAKERS

3 BIRDBROOK (E) 4 LADY MARGARET ROAD CAMBRIDGE 5 LITLINGTON

ROMAN AGE. BRONZE, GLASS AND POTTERY VESSELS
No. 1, pp. 100, 189–90, 192, 214; No. 2, pp. 213, 216; No. 3, p. 190;
No. 4, pp. 209, 213; No. 5, p. 213.

district. On Plate XXV is figured a square bottle of green glass, with reeded handle, from Wicken Fen: it is of the type frequently employed as a cremation urn. The Litlington decanter is also reproduced. Much fine glassware of the period is in the Audley End Museum.

D. *Of Iron*

Illustrative of the fine craftsmanship of the period is the hoard of ninety-six iron objects found carefully covered over in a rubbish pit in the grounds of Chesterford Rectory in 1854 and now in the Audley End Museum. It apparently consisted of a smith's tools and stock-in-trade (finely illustrated by Neville, 1856).

The writer was much struck by the close resemblance to mediaeval ironwork shown in this and other local finds of Roman date in the refinements of decorative detail; but reflection suggested that smithying was the one craft likely to survive, unimpaired, the breakdown of a high civilization; and that the noble ironwork manufactured in Cambridgeshire forges as late as the XVIII century may well have represented a tradition unbroken since the Early Iron Age.

TOPOGRAPHICAL ANALYSIS OF THE REMAINS OF THE ROMAN AGE

Before discussing topographically the evidence afforded by Roman remains in our district it must again be emphasized that the greater number of portable objects of which records of provenance are preserved come from cemeteries.

Practically all the unbroken glass and pottery vessels and many of the bronzes in our museums were, there is little doubt, associated with burials. Our record is, however, inadequate, and in many cases there is no information connecting a given group of such finds with interment. The practice adopted is to place on the Roman Map the symbols **I** or **III** only when there is definite evidence of burial.

It is clearly desirable that on the map important finds or extensive groups of objects (such as the Icklingham hoard of pewter, the Witcham helmet or the votive bronzes from Willingham) should be differentiated from minor finds (such as coarse potsherds in no great quantity). For the former the "hoard symbol" ♣ is employed, for the latter the "find symbol" ●.

The practice hitherto adopted of placing on the map one symbol for finds up to three in number, and one for each multiple of three thereafter —quite satisfactory for the earlier periods—is found to be unsuitable for the Roman Age. Each "find symbol," therefore, as far as the available evidence permits, marks a "site find."

The differentiation between important and unimportant finds described above is, however, impossible on a small-scale map in closely settled areas such as Cambridge; here the "find symbol" alone is used.

As in maps of the earlier periods when the exact provenance of the find is unknown the symbol is placed on the modern village site; and separate finds in a given fen are widely spaced in that fen (see p. 9).

It is not proposed to discuss in detail the sites and parishes in which remains of the Roman period have been found; lists of names and of objects so lengthy as these would add nothing to the reader's comprehension of the extent and character of the civilization portrayed. The regional map (IV) indicates the range, and as far as possible the nature, of the finds; and the outstanding material evidences of the Roman civilization which survive in our district have already been referred to in this chapter under their respective headings.

It is proper to add, however, that the map cannot fully indicate the remarkable universality of civilized occupation in the more fertile areas of our region[1]. This is impressed upon the mind of every local archaeologist who has intensively surveyed a limited field.

Hughes (1909, p. 147) has rendered striking testimony in this connection.

"All along the valley," he says, "from Chesterford to Cambridge and up the hills on either side traces of Roman sojourn have been turned up; not merely a few potsherds which may have been left by the wayfarer, but rubbish pits which have been slowly filled with household ware and kitchen refuse....So if we follow the river to the north by Barnwell, Chesterton and Fen Ditton to Biggin Abbey or Horningsea; or out to the north-east by Reach or to the north-west by Madingley and Girton, the record is the same."

In the borough of Cambridge the evidences of widespread settlement are especially striking. The whole of the Castle Hill area and the warm southern slopes abutting on the Madingley Road have yielded quantities of household rubbish. To the south and west the cemeteries of the settlement fringed the Roman roads. On the east side of the river the site of the mediaeval town was occupied, as was the Barnwell area; to the south of this district finds occur on the gravel terraces which border the right bank of the river as far as the borough boundary and beyond. The well-drained gravel terraces at Newnham too were occupied.

[1] Of many local finds the provenance is only approximately known.

THE ROMAN AGE

The Cam Valley at Cambridge and its neighbourhood is probably not exceptional save in the extent to which the archaeological record has been studied. Such evidence as is available suggests, for example, that a similarly dense and Romanized population dwelt in the Ivel Valley from Hitchin to Sandy.

Absence of Evidence of Settlement along the Highways

The first point which is evident on studying the Roman Map is that, while towns and settlements not infrequently occur at road junctions, the occupied areas as a whole bear little direct relation to the main Roman roads. One might go further and suggest—too hastily—that the native population seem to have avoided the neighbourhood of the great highways. The Ermine Street throughout its length, and the Cambridge-Godmanchester road may be cited as examples of this tendency.

This topographical feature is generally held to be exclusively characteristic of the Anglo-Saxon settlement; the "tons" and "hams" of our forefathers were surrounded by their common fields and the great roads were used mainly to define territorial limits; but since it is here found to be equally marked in the Roman period, the accepted explanation is clearly inadequate.

It appears probable that the La Tène communities which received and absorbed the Roman civilization, like the Anglian settlements which followed them, represented a culture based on agriculture; the distribution of the Celtic hamlets was, therefore, the result of influences similar to those which determined the sites of the later villages. The Romans came, and drove their great roads from nodal point to nodal point across wide stretches of country largely uninhabited and uncultivated; these were the roads designed for through communication, and suitable sites for settlement did not frequently coincide with their alignment. The analysis of the Roman road system in our Region has provided us with the corollary to this; namely, that the occupied areas had, when the Romans came, a network of reasonably good roads and these, hardened and straightened in places, became vicinal ways, and occasionally, it would appear, main roads; in either case essential elements of the Roman system. But since the roads did not present the characteristic features of Roman engineering (the chief of which is exact alignment) they are not now readily recognizable; hence they cannot for the most part appear on our map; and the Roman road system appears curiously enough to ignore the most fertile and populous areas, and to be most highly developed in the forest lands, which in truth was certainly not the case.

It follows that when a road, recognized as Roman, is driven *through* (not *to*) populous areas it will probably be found to be a pre-Roman road utilized by the Romans. Ashwell Street and the Trumpington-Barton-Toft road are the most notable examples in our district. The former is, as we have seen, a piece of pre-Roman trackway straightened and hardened; the latter, crossing the Cam by the pre-Roman ford, suggests by its sinuous course that its origins also are to be sought for in prehistoric times.

If our explanation be correct, it follows that the Roman Conquest produced no profound disturbance and, indeed, changed very little the topographical distribution of the British settlements. The deduction can be tested further by a comparison of the Roman Map (IV) with the Early Iron Age Map (III).

Scanty as are the finds of the earlier period, the relative distribution of the population is seen in both cases to be similar, for the fertile valleys of the Cam and Ivel yield the most numerous evidences of settlement. The greater topographical range of the Roman finds is quite consistent with this essential similarity; for the historical evidence suggests that the policy of the conquerors was such as to permit the free development untrammelled by war of the social and economic tendencies which had been in operation before their arrival. There is, of course, topographically speaking, more in the Roman occupation than this. The road system while it linked up old centres—Sandy, Braughing, Chesterford—created at its junctions new ones—Castle Hill, Cambridge, Godmanchester; the engineering works carried out in the fens and the development of river traffic opened up new areas for profitable tillage; and there are indications, as we shall see, that clearances were effected in the forests.

(a) The New Towns

These points may with advantage be treated more fully. What first of all were the causes which gave in Roman days the pre-eminence to Cambridge, a pre-eminence which with brief eclipse it has ever since held? It is not necessary here to go over the ground discussed in the chapter on the Early Iron Age; it suffices to say that, while evidence of settlement on the gravel terraces bordering the river is apparent in that Age as in the preceding Bronze and Neolithic Ages, there is no evidence that Cambridge as a central settlement—a meeting-place of trackways—the most important crossing-place of the Cam, existed before the Romans came.

The only pre-Roman objects from within the area of the walled town, preserved or recorded, are, so far as I can ascertain, three "British coins," mentioned by Babington (1883, p. 6).

The causes of the predominance of Cambridge must have been important; they must have continued to operate in spite of the relapse into barbarism at the close of the Roman Age, or the eclipse of the town in the VII century attested by Bede would have been permanent and not temporary, and the University, if it had developed at all in our county, might have been sited at Trumpington or Grantchester.

The question can, I think, be answered; it was the Roman road system which secured for Cambridge her permanent importance.

It is a commonplace that, next to the mouth, the most important site on any river is the crossing-place nearest the upper limit of the tidal flow. When the Romans made a causeway across the marsh from the gravel spur at St Sepulchre's to the edge of the river opposite Castle Hill spur, and, as we may hold, bridged the river there, they created what was, other factors being constant, a more convenient crossing-place than was the Grantchester ford. But this was not necessarily the case; the permanence of Cambridge depended on a stream of traffic from the north-west to the north-east[1]; that is, on good communications from Northamptonshire and beyond (from Leicester and Lincoln) eastward. This the Ermine Street, with its extensions, and the Godmanchester-Cambridge road provided. Both were, in our Region, driven through forest country which, we have seen, was for the most part uninhabited and uninhabitable in prehistoric times. In such times all traffic from Northamptonshire (the Nene Valley) in this direction was doubtless by river; there is certainly no evidence of any land-ways. Once these Roman roads were built their obvious advantages (see Sketch-map F) secured their permanence within our Region. They survived, as we see, the breakdown of the Roman civilization; since they survived they must have been continuously used; since they were continuously in use Cambridge, as a "deserted little city[2]," must necessarily have been a temporary phenomenon.

That this explanation is correct further considerations attest. The

---

[1] Though there is at present no evidence to prove it, the value of the Grantchester-Trumpington crossing probably depended on the existence of a track from the Ouse Valley at Sandy to the Bourn Brook Valley.

[2] Bede, *Ecc. Hist.* Bk. IV, xix.

route which the Romans thus created crossed the Ouse at Godmanchester; here again there is no evidence of the existence of a pre-Roman town; here grew up the second of the only two important settlements which, so far as our evidence goes, the Romans created in the district[1]. One explanation suffices for both; for Huntingdon-Godmanchester[2] and for the twin Cambridge towns.

(b) Traffic and Settlement in the Fens

The Roman Map shows that finds are widespread in the fens —not on the fen islands merely, but in the marshlands. These occurred in previous Ages, but they then consisted mainly of weapons presumably lost in the swamps or meres. In the Roman Age cinerary urns and a wide range of objects indicating settlement occur in the peat, frequently in areas which must under natural conditions have been waterlogged for a considerable period of the year.

These finds suggest that the Roman engineers drained the fens, and there is a certain amount of evidence which supports this conclusion. It is well known that the problem of fen drainage is threefold; the floodwater from the uplands has to be controlled, the rain falling on the fenlands has to be disposed of, the tidal sea has to be shut out.

In the first place, the Car Dyke, which has been shown to be Roman, probably served a twofold purpose; that of a catchwater drain for the upland floodwater as well as a canal for traffic. Far to the north and outside our area, the sea-bank which prevents Wringland from being flooded at high tide may possibly be as old as the Roman period. It is, at all events, certain that the Roman fen road from Peterborough to Denver [N] could only have been maintained as a serviceable route by confining the tidal flow and floodwater to the river channels; for the thick deposits of silt and peat which now cover it show that under natural conditions (which prevailed in this region for a long time after the Roman Age) the district was frequently flooded and always waterlogged (see Beloe, 1891, p. 121). Hence it is probable that the rivers were embanked and canalized.

The fenland being above, and not below, mean sea level, dykes and drains discharging into the river by means of sluices would dispose of much of the rain falling on the area, and such additional

---

[1] A settlement of Roman origin probably existed at the junction of the Stour and Colne Valley roads from Colchester to Cambridge (see p. 179).

[2] There was a Roman settlement of some sort at Huntingdon. See p. 177.

works may have been undertaken, though we have no direct evidence of it. In any case, we may conclude that during the Roman period much of the fenland was "cultivable and habitable."

There is in the fens adjacent to the Car Dyke on Bullocks Haste Common, in Cottenham parish, an elaborate system of shallow ditches, frequently parallel, or enclosing geometrical figures, which are possibly irrigation works of Roman date (Evelyn-White, 1904). Similar systems occur near Smithey Fen Farm, Cottenham, and in fields to the north of Denny Abbey; but the latter is on ground which is well above fen level. No evidence of date was obtained by a partial excavation of the Bullocks Common system carried out by the Rev. F. G. Walker.

Certain finds of Roman date in the fens are known to have been lying on the clay below the peat (*e.g.* Babington, 1883, p. 19). It is, therefore, probable that the wide meres which we have seen reason to suppose were in existence in the Bronze Age had not in the Roman Age been entirely overgrown with peat. Many such sites again may be ancient water channels; for there is abundant evidence that the courses of the rivers have been continually changing by the operations of nature and of man throughout the historic period. "Rude draining tiles, Samian and other pottery," were found in the bed of an ancient river in Isleham Fen (*Standard*, 19 Aug. 1907).

Discussion of the probable extent of fen drainage and reclamation carried out by the Romans leads to a consideration of the extent to which the waterways were used for transport and as a means of communication. Quantities of broken pottery—sigillata and Castor wares as well as coarse sherds—have been found on the margins of the Car Dyke and in its bed, at Cottenham; along the banks of the Old Croft River north of Littleport; and along the line of Reach Lode. Near Stanground, Peterborough, on the banks of the Nene, the timber foundations of a hithe and a roadway formed of broken Roman sherds represent, doubtless, one of the places where the products of the Nene Valley potteries were shipped[1].

Similar finds at Stuntney (Ely) where an ancient river course (Rolls Lode) borders the bluff on which the village stands, at Clayhithe, and at Upware, indicate the sites of Roman quays, places of call for the barges that plied up and down the river. At Upware, adjacent to these Roman remains, traces of a mediaeval quay show how convenient the place has always been for water transport. It is probable that as much use was made of the rivers in the Roman Age, as in mediaeval and modern times down to the XVIII century.

[1] Information from Mr J. W. Bodger, of Peterborough.

(c) WERE THE FOREST AREAS CLEARED AND INHABITED?

We have concluded in our analysis of each preceding period that there was no evidence of clearance and settlement in the forest areas. So numerous and widespread are the finds of Roman date in our district that one was prepared to see, on the map, marked and definite evidence of such clearance. Such evidence exists, but it is scanty. Symbols indicating civilized occupation—important finds, house foundations, extensive cemeteries—occur in the river valleys (such as the Quin, the Stort, the Essex Cam, Bourn Brook and Bourn River, and the Stour) which pierce the forest areas, and here and there on the forest borders as at Red Hill, Sandon and Kelshall [H], Little Walden and Ashdon [E], but are rare elsewhere in these regions.

Symbols [●] indicating small and unimportant finds, usually of coarse pottery, and those indicating coin hoards [&] are widely, though sparsely, scattered over the cold claylands, but these do not necessarily imply civilized settlement. In the large collection of Roman objects from all parts of the district, preserved in the Cambridge Museum, nothing but coarse potsherds and an occasional fibula is derived from any parish entirely situated in a forest district.

What the evidence does show, is this: that in the Roman Age, for the first time in history, there was sparse but widespread occupation of the claylands, probably by partially Romanized peasants, and that a good deal of destruction of the woodland took place. It is evident that there must be present, before woodland is turned into arable, (i) a certain measure of civilization (so that sharp tools are readily obtainable), and (ii) political security. Agricultural activity in forest areas requires much labour for which there is no immediate return, and ordered and stable government is thus essential. The civilization was present in the Early Iron Age, the security, here on the marches between the Catuvellauni and the Iceni, in all probability lacking; not until the Roman Age, then, were both requirements satisfied. The direct stimulus resulting in the extension of the arable at the expense of the forest was, as my friend Mr H. Peake suggests, the increase of population naturally following on prolonged peace. Professor Myres reminds me that the special features of the southern civilization, such as the central heating system in houses built after the Roman fashion, and the manufacture on an extensive scale of tiles and pottery must have resulted in a large fuel consumption, and seasonal occupation and destruction of forest areas by the woodcutters; moreover, the development of pig-breeding which doubtless took place in Britain as in Gaul may have materially aided in this destruction.

Such considerations amply account for the evidence of limited occupation which the archaeological record yields; but it must be emphasized that there is nothing to suggest a wholesale and general destruction which should have transformed the forest uplands of the Cambridge Region as a whole into prosperous corn-growing districts such as for the most part they are to-day.

I am aware that in expressing these views I am, in respect to the south-eastern part of the Cambridge Region, at variance with our highest authority on Roman Britain. Haverfield (1916, p. xxiii) pointed to the existence of Roman houses at Stansted, Ashdon, Bartlow, Thaxted, Wenden and Ridgewell and the Roman town at Chesterford as evidence that N.W. Essex was a "well populated corn-growing district." I cannot think that he had examined a topographical map with the claylands (forest) defined. The situation of Chesterford and of the majority of these houses, on chalk slopes or gravel terraces bordering rivers or streams, is such that their presence cannot afford proof that the hundred square miles and more of dense woodland in this area had been cleared. There remain only the houses at Ridgewell and Thaxted, a tile kiln at Ashdon and minor finds to sustain the argument.

The former is situated on the narrow belt of forest across which all traffic from the Colne Valley to the Cambridge plain must pass, and this belt would doubtless have been cleared at a very early date in the Roman period. The Thaxted hypocaust is important evidence in support of Haverfield's views, but situated as it is close to the gravel terraces of the River Chelmer, it is a small foundation on which to build so weighty a superstructure.

Neville's evidence (1858, p. 193) is important: "The greater part of this county" (Essex) "seems to have been originally covered with forest which accounts for the numerous horns and bones of the red and fallow deer, with tusks of the wild boar, found invariably on all sites of Roman occupation."

That N.W. Essex was, as we shall see, to a great extent forest in Anglo-Saxon times has no bearing on the problem. If the district had been cleared in the Roman Age, natural reafforestation may have taken place in the V, VI, and VII centuries.

DURATION OF THE ROMAN AGE IN OUR REGION

Evidence, individually slight, but cumulatively important, indicative of effective occupation of certain sites in our district in pre-

Flavian times (43–69 A.D.) is available, and coin finds in many parts prolong that occupation into the V century.

The information provided by the latter type of evidence necessarily ceases in 406 A.D. when the supply of imperial coinage was cut off by the barbarian invasion of Gaul.

Area South of the Fens

It will have been noted from incidental remarks in the preceding pages that there were probably two lines of infiltration into Southern Cambridgeshire in the I century: from CAMVLODVNVM up the Colne and Stour Valleys, and from the lower Thames *via* Ermine Street or its native predecessors. We may first examine the chronological evidence provided by finds on the line of the former route, almost certainly the one first used.

The rubbish pits at Great Thurlow [S] near the head of one of the main sources of the Stour (see p. 205) have provided ample evidence of peaceful settlement from the middle of the I century onwards; it was probably a contemporary extension of the Claudian occupation of north-eastern Essex. Coin finds at the Ridgewell [E] villa site (see p. 186) ranged from Nero (54–68) to Arcadius (395–408), and a coin of Nero has been found at Wixoe [S] (Walford, 1803 *b*, p. 71); on the other hand, a hoard of gold and silver coins found in a pot under a Roman tile at Sturmer [E] (*ibid.* p. 71) belongs entirely to the last phase of the occupation, the majority being those of Honorius and Arcadius. On the forest ridge at Horseheath, a pot found in 1832 contained silver coins representative of nearly all the emperors from Nero to Marcus Aurelius (Babington, 1883, p. 35).

On the other side of the watershed in the basin of the Bourn River the evidence for occupation in the V century is similar, but for early occupation is very slight. Neville (1854 *c*, p. 213) remarks that "coins of the whole series" are found in the neighbourhood of Bartlow, the greatest number being "of the very lowest Empire, Theodosius (378–395), Honorius (395–423) and Arcadius in particular." Recent finds, my friend Mr C. G. Brocklebank informs me, confirm this conclusion. The earthenware in the Bartlow Hills burials appears to have been mainly of late I century types, and from the same area comes a fragment of Arretine sigillata from the workshop of L. R. Pisanvs who was active in the middle of the century (see p. 201 *n*).

Certain sites on the traffic lines from the lower Thames to the Cam Valley, and finds in the Ivel and Cam Valleys, yield testimony similar to that from the Stour Valley. A single site at Braughing yielded "thousands of Roman coins," from Augustus (31 B.C.–14 A.D.) to Constantine (306–337), and continuity of occupation was indicated by the presence of numerous British coins. Other sites in the parish confirm this chronological range, late IV century coins being absent (Taylor, 1914, p. 150). Much pottery of transitional character, I century terra sigillata, and Romano-Belgic ware, together with a wide range of coin finds, from Roman rubbish pits and elsewhere at Chesterford point to Roman occupation of this site from pre-Flavian times down to the V century.

Hughes (1907 a, p. 142) records pre-Flavian coins of Tiberius, Caligula, Claudius and Vitellius; his long list closes with those of Theodosius and Arcadius (395–408). Neville (1854 c, p. 214) remarks that "a perfect series of coins might have been formed, if all those removed [from Chesterford] by antiquaries at different periods were now available."

Coins "of the early Emperors," moreover, have been found at Whittlesford and Hinxton, a few miles to the south of Chesterford (Babington, 1883, p. 63). A gold coin of Claudius found at Ring Hill is mentioned by Stukeley (ed. Lukis, 1883, p. 150). Platters of Belgic terra nigra and pre-Flavian terra sigillata (see pp. 201–6) from the Litlington and Shefford cemeteries, and pre-Flavian coins from Litlington, Shefford and Sandy are indicative of early settlement. The latter site has yielded pre-Flavian pottery, the coin finds range from I to early V A.D., and there is evidence for continuous occupation throughout the Roman period (Page and Keate, 1908, pp. 2 and 9). Coins at the Shefford cemetery range from Tiberius (14–37) to Maximian (286–305) (*ibid.* p. 13), while the last emperor represented at Litlington is the usurper Magnentius (350–353). Evidence of similar character points to the last civilized owners of the Roman houses at Wymondley having left in the last quarter of the IV century (Ransom, 1886, pp. 42 and 45).

So much for the upper Cam Valley and the area west of Ermine Street; the Cambridge district may now be considered, and here also we have evidence of early (and prolonged) occupation.

Fine South Gaulish terra sigillata obtained on several occasions from a cemetery on the gravel spur by Vicar's Brook and River Farm (see p. 205) attests peaceful occupation of the area north of Trumpington in the Claudian-Neronian period. Coin finds on a site (Latham Road) immediately contiguous indicate occupation as late as the reign of Gratian (367–383) (Walker, 1911 d).

In the town itself the Castle Hill area yields evidence of prolonged occupation. Here a few pre-Flavian coins (of Germanicus, Claudius and Nero) have been recorded; and the long list closes with third brass coins of Theodosius, Gratian, Arcadius and Honorius (Babington, 1883, p. 6). Romano-British pottery which certainly dates from the I century, has been obtained from this area, but it is important to notice that no terra sigillata of pre-Flavian date is preserved or recorded. On the right bank of the river (where the La Tène Celts lived) Flavian terra sigillata and a coin of Claudius have been found, and evidence suggesting continuity of occupation is provided by rubbish pits at Trinity Hall, which yielded early Roman wares mixed with La Tène sherds. Similar material (now in the Cambridge Museum) was found under the Union Society's buildings at the tip of the gravel spur from which the causeway to Castle Hill originated; and, as we have seen, pottery kilns must have been established at or near Jesus Lane at an early date. It is fairly certain, then, that the town on Castle Hill is of I century foundation; and the Romanization of the La Tène folk on the east side of the river may date from pre-Flavian times. The Horningsea potteries four miles to the north of Cambridge were producing characteristic Roman wares in the I century, and this is important evidence of effective occupation.

Barrington, on the River Cam a few miles to the south-west of Cambridge, has yielded a remarkably complete series of Roman coins now in the possession of the Rev. E. Conybeare; Roman *denarii* of the Republican period, many pre-Flavian coins, and an *aureus* of Valentinian III (425–455) may be specially mentioned; the latter must surely have been brought in by an Anglian settler.

The settlement at Godmanchester has yielded numerous pre-Flavian coins—those of Julius Caesar, Augustus, Tiberius, Claudius and Nero are recorded by R. Fox (1831, p. 30); and Walker (1909, p. 287) found coins ranging from Gallienus to Constantius II (337–361) in a cemetery on the site. Pottery of early types, probably late I century, has been found in Huntingdon.

This evidence is of some importance; for we have seen reason to hold the view that the foundation of the town or settlement resulted from the creation of the road junction. The Cambridge-Godmanchester road, and that portion of Ermine Street which bisects Huntingdonshire may therefore be of I century construction. It is unfortunate that there is so little direct evidence of value bearing on the date of the Roman roads in our district. The interments at Emmanuel Knoll (date uncertain but pot appears to be an early form) and at Girton (II century) were undoubtedly placed beside the Godmanchester-

Cambridge road and are therefore posterior to it (see pp. 195, 193); evidence of burials beside other main roads should be sought for.

Such is the evidence of early and prolonged occupation of the southern part of our region.

The Southern Fens and North-West Suffolk

There is but little evidence of effective occupation of the southern fenlands, or of the valleys of the Lark and Little Ouse (our north-eastern area) in I A.D., and practically nothing indicative of settlement prior to the Flavian period. Coin finds here, as elsewhere, show that occupation continued into IV and early V A.D.

Mr W. G. Clarke has found a denarius of Vespasian at Santon [N]. In the Lark Valley at Icklingham [S] scattered coin finds range from Marcus Aurelius (161–180) to Honorius (395–407)[1], while a hoard of silver coins (400 in number of which 349 were examined) covered the period 305–6 to 395–407 (G. E. Fox, 1911, p. 309). A hoard found at Undley [S] is known to have contained coins of Maximian (286–305) and Valens (364–378) (*C.A.S. Rep.* 43, 1883, p. lxxvii), and a large hoard found in a pot on Wangford Heath (in Bury Museum) seems to have been deposited in the III century. I have seen coarse pottery and fibulae of I century types from this district but no early South Gaulish terra sigillata.

Turning to the fens and the fen islands; it may first be noted that a find at Ely provides, so far as I can ascertain, the only evidence for pre-Flavian occupation. This is slender enough, being the base of a terra sigillata vessel by Scottivs, a potter of La Graufesenque. A few scattered coins found at Ely range from Vespasian to Gratian (Babington, 1883, p. 16), and coins of Vespasian, Hadrian and Constantine were found with a deposit of bronzes in Burnt Fen in 1852 (*ibid.* p. 19). A coin of Vespasian is recorded from Manea, and one from Stonea (Wimblington). Apart from these I find scanty record of I century coins from the southern fen area; and such sigillata as I have seen (other than the fragment by Scottivs and a Flavian cup by Primvlvs) is of the II century[2]. Coarse pottery of I century character however, comes from one or two sites near Ely. Coin hoards are fairly numerous in the district, though for the most part inadequately recorded; the following may be noted. Doddington (Vespasian to Antoninus Pius, Lukis, 1883, p. 20); Willingham Fen (Gallienus to

---

[1] Coins of the later years of Honorius do not occur either here or elsewhere in the district for reasons already given.

[2] From Wilburton, Lakenheath Fen, Ely, and Stonea (Wimblington).

Diocletian, Jenkinson, 1884); Stonea, Wimblington (2000 of about the time of Gallienus, Babington, 1883, p. 72); Chatteris (of the early IV century—Constantine family, *ibid.* p. 90); Somersham (60, of the "later Emperors," *ibid.* p. 91). One of the latest coins found in the southern fens is an *aureus* of Theodosius (378–395), which had been placed in an indented beaker of Castor ware at Stonea (Fisher, 1862, p. 365).

Summarizing the evidence, we may first note that finds particularly of early terra sigillata, coarse pottery and coins suggest that the whole of our district as far north as Cambridge and Godmanchester was effectively occupied in the I century, and that from certain sites in the Stour, Ivel, Cam and Essex Cam Valleys definite evidence of settlement in pre-Flavian times exists. Occupation of the southern half of our district may possibly date from the first campaign in 43 A.D. (for it was, as we have seen, within the Catuvellaunian and Trinovantian boundaries); if not so early, then certainly as a result of the campaign of Ostorius in 47 A.D. On the other hand, the evidence for I century Roman occupation of the southern fens and their borders, or of the East Anglian heathland north-east of the Devil's Dyke, is scanty, and for pre-Flavian occupation practically nonexistent. It is unwise to base conclusions on negative evidence when the archaeological record is so inadequate; but it must be significant that this is precisely the area which we saw reason (in Chapter III) to include in the Icenian kingdom, and the Roman evidence, such as it is, confirms the boundaries there laid down. For though the Iceni submitted to Claudius, the process of Romanization might be expected to have been slower in an area where the native organization persisted, than in one where it had been destroyed and replaced by that of Rome.

The phrase "effective occupation" has in this section been used to imply the free inpouring of Roman products, and conditions permitting civilized life in the Roman manner by Roman officials and soldiers. The Romanization of the native population, which in the case of wealthy nobles and landowners had begun long before the Claudian Conquest, was for the mass of the population a slow process, and the country houses and farms built in Roman fashion which are, as we have seen, widely scattered throughout our district belong for the most part, we may hold, to the II and III centuries[1]. In the less favoured regions it is not probable that the Roman occupation changed the mode of life of the inhabitants to any great extent. Coarse

[1] For example, the house at Ickleton was not built till after 117 A.D. and coin finds suggest that the Wymondley villa dates from the end of the II century.

pottery of Roman type and Roman fibulae are superficialities. What little we know of Romano-British agricultural settlements—even in the lowlands at sites such as Barrington (pp. 109-10), Hauxton (*C.A.S. Rep.* 47, 1887, p. cvii) and Barton (p. 303)—suggests that they were essentially primitive communities of Early Iron Age peasants with but a slight veneer of Roman civilization.

The War Ditches is the most interesting settlement dating in the early years of the Roman occupation of which we have record; it shows how slow the process of Romanization might be under certain circumstances. At a date later than that represented by the purely Roman deposits in the Cam Valley at Trumpington and elsewhere, it was possible for the native inhabitants of this windy hill-top overlooking Cambridge to be almost entirely lacking in the characteristic appurtenances of the new civilization, and to retain the old (Brythonic?) custom of inhumation. What they did possess, moreover, is important, for it shows that they obtained without difficulty wares of distant and possibly Rhenish origin.

Within and without the area of War Ditches shallow trenches were found, cut in the chalk, which contained bones of domestic animals and fragments of pottery of Roman type. We may recall the midden trench of the late Bronze Age at Swaffham Prior; and may agree with Hughes (1904, p. 478) who remarks that such ditches are "found round the several dwellings in all the rude agricultural settlements of the district, from the Bronze Age to that of the Romanized Britons...who frequently seem to have followed their ancient habits of life long after they had adopted all the domestic appliances of the Romans."

EVIDENCE ILLUSTRATING THE VICISSITUDES OF THE ROMAN OCCUPATION

It may be worth while to see whether the material we have gathered provides any evidence illustrating the vicissitudes of the Roman occupation.

There are certain recognized hoard periods in the Roman Age; an early one is the reign of Commodus (180-192) when disasters in the north and mutinies in the army weakened authority throughout the province. The prevailing sense of insecurity was doubtless the direct cause of the deposit at Chesterford of 200 coins (Braybrooke, 1860, p. 121), the date limits of which were Caligula (37-41) and Commodus; of 500 silver coins at Ashwell End (Taylor, 1914, p. 148)—Nero (54-68) to Marcus Aurelius (161-180); of the silver coins at Horseheath (Babington, 1883, p. 35)—Nero to Marcus Aurelius; and of the deposit of votive bronzes in Willingham Fen.

The Willingham coin hoard fully described by Jenkinson (1884) ranged from Gallienus to Diocletian, and evidence was brought forward to suggest that it was deposited in 285 or 286 A.D. In this decade we have the first historical record of the piratical descents of the Franks and Saxons to whose attacks East Anglia was particularly liable; and it is reasonable to connect this hidden treasure with their activities. The house at Icklingham in the Lark Valley (p. 187) was deserted about the same time and was then or subsequently partially demolished.

Evidence of the effect of the growing insecurity of the second half of the IV century is afforded by the desertion of country houses. It is to be expected that the breakdown of civilization would first affect well-to-do people dwelling in isolation, and that the occupation of places like Chesterford and Cambridge would be more prolonged; and this is in fact the case. No doubt the landed gentry, their wives and families, flocked into the towns for safety.

The sequence of coins found at Purwell Mill, Great Wymondley, suggests continuous occupation from 193 to 375 A.D. or thereabouts; of the adjacent settlement at Great Wymondley from Vespasian (69–79) to Julian (361–363). The Purwell Mill villa (p. 186) had been altered from time to time, and Ransom, the excavator, noted the gradual decadence of the material used at each rebuilding. A similar observation was made by Neville in connection with the Bartlow house (p. 185). Building like all other arts reflected the slow decline of civilization. The occupation of the latter dwelling, and of that at Hadstock close by, terminated about 350–370 A.D.

The evidence yielded by these country houses is therefore entirely and remarkably consistent, and accords with historical record. In 367 A.D. "the whole defence of Britain was shattered owing to two simultaneous disasters...and the barbarians came flooding into the Midlands" (Oman, 1913, p. 161). That the cemeteries at Shefford and Litlington (p. 188) appear to have been disused at the same period is confirmatory evidence of the profound effect of these reverses.

The evidence of coins suggests a later date for the effective occupation of the Ridgewell villa (p. 186) than others; but its position on the important line of route to CAMVLODVNVM suggests that even if deserted it may have in the last years of the Roman occupation have provided a shelter for coin-dropping travellers.

We have no information as to when either Chesterford or Cambridge were first fortified; the latter may have been an open town till the IV century; the earthen bank some 11 feet high which apparently formed the riverside defences is, at any rate, not of earlier origin

THE ROMAN AGE

(p. 175), and its construction may well date from the time when the country houses came to be deserted.

The significance of the numerous coin hoards hidden in the early years of the V century is too obvious for comment. The date of deposit cannot be fixed within the same narrow limits as can that of earlier hoards, for the supply of imperial coinage ceased after 406, and during many years, no doubt, Roman money was from time to time hidden by the provincials, until the destruction of the Roman civilization in Eastern England by the Anglo-Saxon raiders was complete.

NOTE ON THE ETHNOLOGY OF THE ROMAN AGE

The difficulties which beset us in attempting to determine the racial type to which inhumed skeletons of the Iron Age found in the district belong, are present equally in the Roman Age. Inhumation burials of dolichocephalic people are on record at the War Ditches, and at Hauxton, and crania of similar type from other local Romano-British sites are in the Anatomical Museum. It is evidently normal for the period in our district, as might be expected; our inhumation cemeteries contain almost exclusively native elements; and since the absorption of the beaker-folk such appear to have been in our Region almost entirely of long-headed types.

Three skeletons from War Ditches are set up in the Anatomical Museum, Cambridge. The Hauxton burials have not previously been referred to here; the cemetery was a poorly furnished one of dolichocephalic people apparently of Roman date. It is recorded in *C.A.S. Rep.* 47 (1887), p. cvii; the skeletal remains are in the Anatomical Museum and the Leys School Museum, Cambridge.

The burials were partly cremation and partly inhumation; they were revealed by coprolite digging in 1879 and subsequent years on the east side of the main road to Hauxton Mill, on the right bank of the mill stream. The pottery, some of which is in the Leys School Museum, was mostly of a common greyish wheelmade ware similar to much produced at Horningsea.

SUMMARY

The wide range covered by the finds and remains of the period has made it necessary to take stock of the results obtained from time to time in the course of the analysis. This general summary may therefore be brief, and the reader is referred to pp. 181–183, 187–188, and 198–200 for a more detailed survey of the conclusions to which study of certain aspects of the Age has led us.

Though the finds and remains of the Age are much more numerous than in any preceding period, the topographical distribution presents close analogies with that of the Early Iron Age.

The densest population in both periods dwelt in the fertile Upper

Ouse and the Cam Valleys; and the Roman Age may be said to represent the expansion and development, during 400 years, of pre-Roman communities whose interests were agricultural.

This expansion is well marked in the fens, where Roman engineering works such as the Car Dyke and (?) Reach Lode, and finds in the fen peat and alongside rivers and canals indicate drainage, settlement and extensive use of the waterways. In the forest areas, too, clearances had begun, mainly on the borders of the open country; but it is improbable that any general transformation of the woodland into arable took place during the Age.

Southern Cambridgeshire lies athwart the main Roman road to the north (Ermine Street) and two roads branching therefrom north-eastward—through Chesterford and Cambridge respectively—were clearly designed to facilitate communication with north-west Suffolk and Norfolk.

The rare occurrence of evidences of *settlement* on the alignment of these (and on other main traffic routes such as the Cambridge-Godmanchester road), and the imperfection of the Roman road system as it exists to-day in the Cambridge Region, are thought to be correlated facts; the explanation being that in the more fertile and populous areas pre-Roman roads hardened (and in parts straightened) were used by the Romans[1], who drove their great military roads, exactly aligned, across districts largely uninhabited. The former are now for the most part unrecognizable, the latter survive; hence the difficulties which beset a student of the Roman transport system in East Anglia. Attention is drawn to the fact that the absence of villages on the great highways is not an exclusive feature of the Anglo-Saxon settlement.

But little evidence of value bearing on the date of the roads has been obtained; evidence of early settlement at Cambridge and Godmanchester is thought to imply I century date for two at least of the roads which unite at these junctions. General considerations suggest a late date for the Cambridge-Ely-Denver road to Norfolk.

Cambridge (Castle Hill) and Godmanchester are thought to be the only purely Roman sites of importance in the district. That these proved permanent is held to be due to the creation of the roads referred to, along which for nearly two thousand years traffic from the Midlands to East Anglia has proceeded, necessarily utilizing the river crossings which these towns control.

Occupation of the southern half of our district (as far north as the fens) is shown to be of early date (pre-Flavian and possibly Claudian). Occupation of the southern fens and N.W. Suffolk

[1] Partly, no doubt, to avoid unnecessary disturbance of taxpaying communities.

(north-east of the Devil's Dyke) is apparently later, no pre-Flavian coins, so far as I have ascertained, having been recorded from these regions, and early terra sigillata being exceedingly rare. The line of demarcation thus drawn coincides with the boundary of Icenian territory in pre-Roman times as deduced from evidence detailed in Chapter III; that this should be so was by me unexpected, but *a priori* not improbable, for though the Iceni submitted to Claudius, they retained for some time their native organization. In this respect, then, consistent results have been attained by detailed analysis of two successive periods, and it is therefore probable that future research will confirm the limits of Icenian territory in our district in the I century A.D., as defined on Sketch-map B.

The cemeteries and isolated flat graves of the period present few unusual features; but the prevalence of barrow burial is of great interest. The distribution of these barrows—in river valleys and by Roman highways—is shown to be distinct from that of the Bronze Age barrows—sited mainly on the chalk uplands; this generalization permits the provisional ascription on topographical grounds to the Roman Age of a number of unopened mounds. It is noted that both cremation and inhumation occur in our Roman barrows, and that the only feature common to all such burials is the presence of the barrow.

The character and standard of the Roman civilization in the district would appear to have been little if at all below that normal in Southern Britain; apart from interments in the Bartlow Hills and certain discoveries at Stanfordbury and Litlington there are it is true no evidences of great wealth or luxury, but comfort and prosperity appear to have been fairly general in the more populous areas. Terra sigillata was freely imported from the middle I century onwards and is widely distributed, and fine glassware, bronze vessels, and table services of pewter are commonly met with.

The points that impress one most in surveying the remains of the period here, as elsewhere, are the evidence of orderly and civilized life continuing apparently unbroken for a considerable period of time, and the uniformity of the culture. House sites never show any sign of defensive fortification, and in mode of construction and decoration they follow one tradition: the ashpits in the neighbourhood of dwellings and towns are filled with the slow accumulations of centuries. As Hughes (1899, p. 305) says, "Villas with outhouses and signs of occupation everywhere show that it was as safe for farmers and traders in and around the fens in Roman times as it is now, and far more safe than it was for 1000 years after the legionaries were withdrawn from Britain."

THE ROMAN AGE

Study of the Roman Age in Southern Cambridgeshire suggests many analogies with the period immediately preceding the industrial revolution in the XVIII century. We have in each era wealthy landlords—the Bartlow Hills and the Litlington villa are evidence of such in the Roman period—well-to-do farmers, craftsmen and traders, and a poor peasantry. As wide differences in the circumstances and character of the burials of rich and poor existed in the Roman Age as in the XVIII century. In each period, we may safely say, agricultural development had made the Cam Valley a corn-growing district, and an adequate system of metalled roads had been developed; in this latter respect the intervening centuries cannot offer any analogy. The parallel is drawn closer by the vigour of the classical renaissance which culminated in XVIII. Conybeare, discussing the carved frieze from Barrington Mill referred to on pp. 185-6, was compelled to say that it was work either of the Roman Age or of the XVIII century; and only extrinsic considerations permitted a verdict in favour of the earlier craftsman.

The peace and prosperity typical of the Age was of course not entirely unbroken. Coin hoards reflect the weakening of authority due to civil discord and external pressure on occasions in the II and III centuries; and the steady decline in the arts of the potter and the builder in the later years of the Roman dominion is manifest in our district as elsewhere.

But for definite archaeological evidence of the break-up of civilization in our district one has to wait until the latter half of the IV century, when the desertion of country houses illustrates the growing insecurity of life and property. At this time probably, and because of this insecurity, the earthen vallum which defended Cambridge on the river side was constructed.

There is little recorded evidence as to the fate of Roman dwellings, of the towns and their occupants, in the V century. In some cases it appears that country houses crumbled down into ruin and were not destroyed by violence; this appears to have been the case also at Chesterford; there is, at all events, nothing to indicate that the town was burnt.

At the Roman house near Purwell Mill (Wymondley), which, from the evidence obtained by excavation, had had apparently a long history as a civilized habitation, there was abundant evidence of subsequent occupation by semi-barbarous people who cooked their food in the middle of the floors of the principal rooms and left the evidences of the feast, bones broken to extract the marrow, around their fires (Ransom, 1886, p. 45). This gives some indication of the character, but unfortunately not of the chronology, of the Anglo-Saxon Conquest.

CHAPTER VI

THE ANGLO-SAXON AGE

" 'Tis opportune to...Contemplate our Forefathers."
SIR THOMAS BROWNE.

INTRODUCTION

WHEN we lost sight of Roman Britain at the beginning of the V century it was a wealthy and civilized country with a uniform culture; the civilization had, it is true, been impaired by raids and invasions, but was still coherent. When, in 597, contact with the South was re-established we find the greater part of the country occupied by a number of semi-barbaric Teutonic kingdoms. The sequence of events in the intervening period can only approximately be determined. A variety of sources, however, permits the date of the first permanent settlement of the invaders, that in Kent, to be fixed not long before the middle of V.

The remains of the Anglo-Saxon Age in our district fall naturally into two periods, the Pagan, mid-V to mid-VII centuries, the Christian, mid-VII to 1066, the latter with an interlude of heathenism resulting from the Danish invasion of 866 A.D.

The archaeological material available for the study of the former period is confined to grave-goods; within this limitation, it is ample.

That available for the study of the latter period is, owing to the absence of grave-furniture in Christian burial, very scanty, apart from churches and church monuments. I had originally intended to include such architectural and monumental remains; but, on reconsideration, have omitted them, as somewhat outside the scope of this treatise[1]. The section dealing with the Christian period, then, is confined to a description of such finds as are on record, and a consideration of the evidence for the Anglo-Saxon origin of homestead moats and other earthworks. The chapter closes with an examination of the distribution of Anglo-Saxon settlements at the end of the Age, as recorded in Domesday Book; as an exact picture of distribution of population at the close of our survey, this is of value for comparison with the necessarily incomplete record of the preceding Ages.

---

[1] For the monumental remains see C. Fox (1922).

A. THE PAGAN PERIOD, MID-V CENTURY TO MID-VII CENTURY

The remains of the Pagan Anglo-Saxon period in the Cambridge Region have been more adequately treated in recent years than those of any earlier age. The distribution of the cemeteries and the character of the grave-furniture have been examined and discussed by Brown (1915), Leeds (1913) and others; and a detailed survey of the numerous and important remains in N.W. Suffolk has been made by R. A. Smith (1911). Monographs on special problems, such as that of the saucer brooch by Leeds (1912), are also available.

Something, however, remains to be done. The finds from several of the Cambridgeshire cemeteries have as yet received little attention; other sites and objects have not been published, and there are many obscurities and errors in records of provenance of local finds which require to be cleared up. Treatment of the material, moreover, from our local point of view may throw fresh light on the problems of the period.

It is proposed, then, to centre the enquiry on the remains found in Southern Cambridgeshire, and the border counties on the south and west, using the Suffolk material analysed by Smith for comparative purposes.

In dealing with the problems of the invasion and settlement in our district we shall have occasion, using archaeological evidence, to test the conclusions arrived at, mainly on historical grounds, by Chadwick in *The Origin of the English Nation* (1907). He holds that the "invaders of Britain belonged not to three but to two distinct nationalities which we may call Jutish and Anglo-Saxon" (p. 88). The former came from the Danish peninsula north of Slesvig, the latter from Slesvig and the coastal districts between the Elbe and Weser[1]. The Jutes "occupied Kent and Southern Hampshire," the Anglo-Saxons "the rest of the conquered territory....The Anglo-Saxons may not originally have been a homogeneous people...but there is no evidence that any national difference survived at the time when they invaded Britain" (pp. 88–89). The kingdoms are held to originate not from the migration of separate tribes, but from the settlement in geographical areas of bodies of warriors attached to certain families or individual princes, the organization of the conquest being military and not tribal (p. 182). Such archaeological differences as exist between "Anglian" and "Saxon" districts must therefore

[1] There is little doubt that as in earlier invasions elements from the whole seaboard from Denmark to Northern France took part.

on this theory have arisen since the invasion: and it will follow that the extent of such differences between two given districts should be correlated with their mutual inaccessibility or comparative accessibility. The theory will be tested on this basis, so far as the material permits.

The kingdoms which closely concern us are those of the Middle Angles, the East Angles and the East Saxons. With regard to the former kingdom, Chadwick concludes that at the beginning of the Christian period (mid-VII century) it included a considerable part of Cambridgeshire as well as Huntingdonshire and hence that in all probability it bordered upon East Anglia[1]. This is generally accepted: but the views of scholars differ as to the position of the boundary, and attention will be given to this problem in its archaeological aspect. The boundary between Middle Anglia and Essex is uncertain, as is the limit of the westward extension of Essex. W. J. Corbett (1913) places the "Hendrica" of the Tribal Hidage in Hertfordshire, regarding it as a province of Essex[2]; the kingdom of Essex proper being thus confined approximately within the limits of the present county. The boundary between East Anglia and Essex at this period also is unknown (Chadwick, 1907, p. 11).

To the west and north the extent of Middle Anglia, and therefore the position of the Mercian and West Saxon boundaries are uncertain; but these do not directly concern us.

The southern fenlands were, according to Bede, part of the East Anglian territory in VII; but other evidence points to this area, apparently in the occupation of the "Southern Gyrwe," being part of Middle Anglia (Chadwick, 1907, p. 8). For these discrepancies the political history of the Middle Angles and the East Angles offers ample explanation. The kingdom of East Anglia came into prominence under Redwald before the death of Ethelbert of Kent in 616 A.D., and Redwald held the Imperium over all the kingdoms south of the Humber for many years. The Middle Anglians, on the other hand, were absorbed by Mercia a generation later, for Penda gave the throne to his son Peada in 653 A.D. This absorption proved permanent, and suggests that the "Middil Angli" (whatever their original status) had been militarily impotent for some time. The transference of the fenlands from Middle to East Anglia, therefore, during Redwald's hegemony seems not improbable.

[1] (1907, pp. 8 ff.) Supported, on purely archaeological grounds, by Leeds (1913, pp. 37 and 39).
[2] See his map, and p. 553. Essex was probably in the pagan period largely uninhabited; cemetery sites are very scanty.

Correlation of local finds with those in Slesvig and Hanover will give us an idea of the date of the first settlements in the Cambridge Region, but we can hardly expect to obtain from an archaeological survey much information as to the date of the establishment of the kingdoms. We may on general grounds agree with the view that the invasion of Eastern England was practically contemporary with that of Kent, and that a period of destructive raids which resulted in the abandonment of the Roman towns in our district[1] preceded the period of settlement; and it is also probable that the crystallization of the settlers into political entities followed the defeat of Mons Badonicus, c. 500 (or 517) A.D. Chadwick (1907, p. 183) notes that the East Anglian kingdom is said, on fairly good authority, to have been founded by the great-grandfather of Redwald, which indicates a date in the first half of VI.

One other point needs preliminary notice as bearing on the problems presented by our archaeological material.

The Saxons, prior to their conquest of Britain, had been a maritime people, as Roman history records; but by the time of Bede they had apparently lost the habit of seafaring. The close parallelism in development which exists between the cruciform fibulae of Scandinavia, Norway particularly, and those of the eastern districts of England, together with the occurrence here of examples apparently of Scandinavian origin, suggests that during V and early VI at least direct communication was maintained with the north, probably to some extent by English keels. Frankish jewellery such as the radiating brooches of V, again, may have been brought by English traders from the Rhine ports, if there be any truth in Procopius' story (*Goth.* IV. 20) of the English fleet which attacked the land of the Warni. Chadwick (1907, p. 19) suggests, on historical grounds, that direct communication between England and the North ceased before the middle of VI. The commerce of the North Sea certainly in early VII and probably from mid-VI onwards was in the hands of the Frisians, who, in Charlemagne's time, held the Continental coastline northward to the mouth of the Weser if not beyond.

The close of the pagan period in our district is marked by the establishment of an East Anglian bishopric at Dunwich (631 A.D.) and, further west, by the conversion of Peada son of Penda in 653 A.D.

For the chronology of the grave-furniture I follow Brown, R. A. Smith and other English archaeologists, their dating being largely

---

[1] We have seen (Chapter V) that there is no evidence of the burning of Chesterford or of any Roman house in the district.

THE ANGLO-SAXON AGE

based on the typological studies of Salin (1904) and Schetelig (1906) whose works are frequently referred to. The results attained by the typological method—which is, in most cases, the only one available—can, however, be regarded as only approximate.

CEMETERIES AND ISOLATED FINDS
I. IN SOUTHERN CAMBRIDGESHIRE

Though the Cambridgeshire cemeteries are numerous, and the material available for analysis adequate, it was soon evident to me that in many cases the reputed provenance of even large groups of objects was open to grave doubt, that in others the record of the discoveries was inadequate, while in one case the site of a large cemetery was only vaguely known. The majority of the cemeteries were discovered during the extensive coprolite diggings carried out in all parts of the district in the '60's, '70's, and '80's of last century; workmen went about with their pockets full of grave-furniture and much came into the hands of collectors through the intermediary of dealers in antiquities in Cambridge. I feel sure that villages where workmen happened to reside sometimes came to be the recorded provenance of objects found in adjacent parishes. From a ring of villages and hamlets, Orwell, Malton, Barton, Harlton, round the great cemeteries of Edix Hill, Barrington, and Haslingfield, objects indicative of an Anglo-Saxon cemetery are derived: in no case, as will be seen, has the site of the reputed cemetery ever been recorded. Similarly, reputed finds from Fordham and Quy probably came from the adjacent known cemeteries of Exning and Soham, and Wilbraham.

An effort is here made to unravel this tangle; I have been content to err on the side of caution and have omitted, from Map V, record of all doubtful sites.

In discussing the objects derived from the several cemeteries I shall be as brief as possible, concentrating attention on those of special importance to the present research, since the field has, in general, been dealt with by other workers.

The cemeteries in or near Cambridge will first be examined—Cambridge, Girton, Trumpington, Grantchester; then the Chapel Hill group—Barrington A and B, Haslingfield. The cemeteries at Foxton, Hauxton and Sawston, and at Linton on the Bourn River will next be dealt with, followed by those on the eastern margin of the fens, and in the fens, at Wilbraham, Burwell, Soham and Chatteris. Record of interments on the chalk escarpment will complete the list.

THE ANGLO-SAXON AGE

Cemeteries at or near Cambridge

Cambridge. One large cemetery, that in St John's College cricket field, and one small one (possibly an outlying portion of the former) only are on record from the ancient borough; but there are a number of finds recorded only in museum accession lists, and search in the stored collections of pottery in the Cambridge Museum has disclosed material from other cemetery sites.

Certain grave-furniture in the Cambridge and other museums —such as the Ashmolean at Oxford (Evans collection)—is entered as from "Cambridge," or "near Cambridge." Some of this material may have come from the St John's cemetery; but it has already been observed that dealers in antiquities in Cambridge acquired grave-goods brought in by workmen from the neighbouring villages, and the provenance of objects thus labelled can only be regarded as "Cambridge district." For a national survey this is perhaps sufficiently exact; but for a detailed analysis of a limited area the value of these objects is slight. Such are therefore ignored, unless they show features of special interest, or are of a date and character which render the determination of exact provenance possible.

Belt-plates and a fibula in the Ashmolean for example, thus labelled, have been identified as from Haslingfield and St John's respectively.

(i) *St John's*. An important cemetery, mainly on the site of the racquets courts[1] in St John's College cricket field, adjacent to the Roman Akeman Street and to the knoll on which the Roman town was situated, was excavated in 1888. It was a mixed inhumation and cremation cemetery, the two rites being apparently concurrent. Though many hundred skeletons and urns were destroyed before investigation, no less than 100 cinerary urns and other vessels and 30 skeletons, together with a representative range of associated objects were secured for the Cambridge Museum. Unfortunately, no detailed record of the cemetery was published[2]. Examination of the unsorted pottery from the site in the Cambridge Museum reveals much fragmentary coarse Roman ware, and several Roman brooches and many Roman coins pierced for suspension are in the collection. Of the relation between Roman and Saxon here little is known; but the condition of the earlier material suggests that Roman rubbish strewed the field selected as a burial-ground by the newcomers. One Roman harp-shaped brooch is known to have been found with two annular (Anglo-Saxon) brooches on a woman's skeleton (cf. Girton, p. 247),

---

[1] As I am informed by Mr F. J. H. Jenkinson, University Librarian, who was one of the excavators.   [2] Note of discovery in *C.A.S. Rep.* 48, 1888, p. cxl.

PLATE XXVII

ANGLO-SAXON AGE. GRAVE-FURNITURE OF THE PAGAN PERIOD
The scale is in inches.
No. 1, pp. 243, 248, 270; No. 2, pp. 248, 271 (two refs.), 280 (footnote); No. 3, pp. 243, 269, 276; No. 4, pp. 257, 268; No. 5, p. 244.
NOTE. One 'ward' of the girdlehanger in No. 2 is broken off, and the side knobs of the cruciform fibulae, Nos. 3 and 4, are lost.

and all Roman brooches found on the site were probably buried in Anglo-Saxon graves.

The unusual length of time during which the cemetery was in use is attested by the objects discovered which seem to range in date from about mid-V to early VII.

The earliest objects, two cruciform fibulae, the long snouts of which resemble examples met with in Mecklenburg and Hanover (see p. 268), cannot have been buried much later than 450 A.D., and tend to show that the Roman town or its immediate neighbourhood was occupied by the first settlers to reach the district. One of these is drawn on Plate XXXIII. The cruciform fibulae figured on Plate XXVII, 3, may be a few decades later, and were doubtless brought in from the Baltic (see p. 269)[1]. One of the latest objects, a rectangular buckle chape of bronze gilt, inlaid with glass or garnets, which are for the most part missing, is figured on Plate XXXIV, 9; another, a bronze buckle with triangular chape inlaid with silver is figured by Leeds (1912, p. 191, fig. 19).

The more characteristic finds from the cemetery included cruciform (see p. 248, under "Girton," and Plate XXVII, 1), square-headed, "small long," and annular fibulae; and wrist-clasps. The latter were common, occurring in cinerary urns as well as on inhumed bodies. There were no bronze girdle-hangers, but iron keys, as Plate XXXVI, 5, occurred. Saucer brooches were absent also, but two applied brooches probably of mid-VI, and two of VII date with naturalistic decoration, were met with. (The latter are figured by Leeds, 1912, p. 191.) A fine set of five bronze-gilt belt-plates with zöomorphic decoration, in the Cambridge Museum, dating in VI, deserve special mention. The range of form and decoration of the cinerary urns from the site is unusually wide. There were no swords.

(ii) *Grange Road*. The St John's cemetery was 150 yards from the Roman road which gave access to Cambridge from the south-west. On the opposite side of this road, at "Saxmeadham," less than 200 yards from the cemetery, one inhumation and one or more cremation burials (together with interments of Roman date) were recorded by Walker (1912); and near these remains an umbo, an axe, spears, and an urn had previously been unearthed.

(iii) *Madingley Road*. At some point beside the Madingley Road, which is here distant about 200 yards from the preceding deposits, cinerary urns, in the Cambridge Museum, "and other remains" not preserved, were found in 1900 and 1909.

[1] All these have lost their lateral knobs.

It is clear, from an examination of the large-scale map (G, p. 246), that these three burial sites are essentially one cemetery area; the existence of the Roman road which gave convenient access thereto in some measure accounts for their distribution.

(iv) *River Cam*. A remarkable and perhaps unique discovery is that of a large number of fragments of decorated vessels of cinerary urn type, dredged up (in 1910) from the bed of the River Cam by Strange's boathouse near the north-east corner of the Roman town, and now in the Cambridge Museum. With them was much fragmentary coarse Roman ware, and one Anglo-Saxon spearhead was found in the river on another occasion either there or close by.

The river now runs close to the foot of the bluff on which the town stood; and the most probable explanation of the find is that one of the cemeteries of the Anglo-Saxon settlement was situated on low-lying ground containing Roman rubbish; that subsequently the river changed its course in the marshy valley or was artificially deflected, with the result that part of the cemetery area became its bed.

That this cemetery was partly or wholly cremation is rendered probable by the character of the pottery. Large and finely decorated vessels of cremation-urn type are exceedingly rare in inhumation burials.

(v) *Chesterton*, (vi) *Gravel Hill*. Finds (now in the Cambridge Museum) on the west side of the river in the neighbourhood of the town at Swan's gravel pit, Chesterton, and at Gravel Hill Farm (1903) are of little intrinsic interest, but are evidence of one or more interments at these points.

(vii) *Newnham Croft*. A third site, Newnham Croft, is of greater importance. In the garden of Croft Lodge two interments were found in 1910: wrist-clasps and a cruciform fibula with one; three fine cruciform fibulae with another. The former group-find is drawn on Plate XXXIV; and one of the latter is figured on Plate XXVII.

The date of each is probably not earlier than mid-VI. An equal-armed fibula from the site, dating in V, is also in the Cambridge Museum; it is very similar to a Norwegian form figured by Salin (1904, figs. 174 and 176). Two typical large cinerary urns from "Newnham," in the British Museum, and spearheads, labelled "Barton Road 1893" (Cambridge Museum), are doubtless from the same cemetery.

(viii) *Coldham*, (ix) *Mill Road*, (x) *Newmarket Road and Barnwell*. Turning to the right bank of the river, scattered finds or isolated

THE ANGLO-SAXON AGE

interments from Coldham Common (British Museum, 1870), Barnwell (Ashmolean Museum), Mill Road (Cambridge Museum, 1847) and Newmarket Road (Cambridge Museum, 1904) attest Anglo-Saxon occupation of the gravel terrace bordering the river on which every race of which we have remains has in turn settled.

(xi) *Jesus Lane*, (xii) *Sidney Street*, (xiii) *Rose Crescent*, (xiv) *Trinity Hall*. It is not to be expected that the partial and casual excavation which is from time to time carried out in a town should reveal an extensive cemetery; but the discoveries which have been made in Jesus Lane (1895, pair of "small long" fibulae), Sidney Street (189–, decorated and plain pottery), Rose Crescent (1901, spearheads, knives, three shield bosses, portion of buckle[1] and fragment of decorated pottery), Trinity Hall (1880, decorated pottery) point decisively to the existence of an important cemetery (or perhaps, as at St John's, an area reserved for sepulchral purposes) and suggest, moreover, that cremation as well as inhumation was practised. All these finds are in the Cambridge Museum. The sites in question form a belt across the neck of the gravel spur, the long axis of which is defined by the Roman road from Red Cross (see Map G).

The significance of these Cambridge finds may best be appreciated if reference be made to the valuable paper by Gray (1908), on *The Dual Origin of the Town of Cambridge*. Such of his conclusions as are relevant to our enquiry are:

(1) That Cambridge was originally two settlements; the northern town mainly within the Roman walls, and the southern town, which I judge from his evidence to have been centred round St Benet's Church. (To these we may add Old Newnham, by Newnham Mill.)

(2) Even in post-Conquest times (1278 A.D.) when the northern town had extended to the south side of the river and dwelling-houses bordered each side of the Roman road leading to the bridge, there was a wedge of uninhabited land between the two settlements (which waste land is now represented by the parishes of All Saints, St Rhadegund, Trinity and St Andrew).

Gray made no use of archaeological evidence; but his conclusions afford so complete an explanation of the position of the cemeteries and burials that we may accept them as true; and may further accept his view that each of the settlements as defined by him originated in the pagan period: and that Bede's "waste city" (695 A.D.) was only temporarily deserted, probably as the result of civil war between Mercia and East Anglia.

[1] This is figured on Plate XXX. It is thought to be part of the tongue of a Frankish buckle of VII date (cf. Ipswich, R. A. Smith, 1911, p. 332, Plate II, 5).

We may assume also, on the evidence already detailed, that a settlement existed in the pagan period somewhere in the neighbourhood of Barnwell.

The archaeological evidence permitting this conclusion is as follows:

(1) Of the cemeteries and burials of the pagan period in the borough, the provenance of which is exactly known, none is situated on a settlement area as defined by Gray.

(2) Cemeteries exist which can confidently be assigned to each of his townships.

The cemeteries of the northern township are (*a*) the St John's cricket field area and (*b*) that now forming part of the bed of the Cam opposite Strange's boathouse. The cemetery of the southern town was probably mainly at Rose Crescent; but interments are widely distributed along the borders of the settled area. The cemetery of the Newnham settlement is evidently that at Newnham Croft.

That the northern township was in pagan times situated on the knoll within the circuit of the Roman walls, is suggested by the position of the burial places. Chesterford, the only other fortified town in our district, was not occupied; the occupation of Cambridge was due no doubt to the military importance of the site in the pagan period which forced the Anglo-Saxon settlers to utilize the Roman defences.

These points are illustrated on Map G.

Girton. An important cemetery in the grounds of Girton College, close to the main entrance and adjacent to the Roman Cambridge-Godmanchester road, was explored by F. J. H. Jenkinson (1881, 1882). The fullest record of this excavation is contained in a MS. in Girton College Library, and the objects found are preserved either there or in the Cambridge Museum. Further investigation in 1886 (*C.A.S. Rep.* 46, 1886, p. lxxiv) in an adjacent field revealed several more inhumation and urn burials, and the bare fact that urns had been found in 1871 is also on record. The finds from the 1886 excavation are all in the Cambridge Museum.

The cemetery had many features of interest. It was a large one, containing cremated and inhumed burials in fairly even proportions; during the 1881 digging at least 130 urns and over 80 skeletons were disinterred[1]. Cremation and inhumation must have persisted side by side for a considerable period; in several cases undisturbed cremation interments were found overlying inhumed bodies.

An important Roman building probably existed near the site and

---

[1] The notes which follow are largely taken from Mr F. J. H. Jenkinson's MS. at Girton College.

Map G. Cambridge. Illustrating the relation between the Roman Town and Roads and the Pagan Anglo-Saxon Cemeteries, Etc.

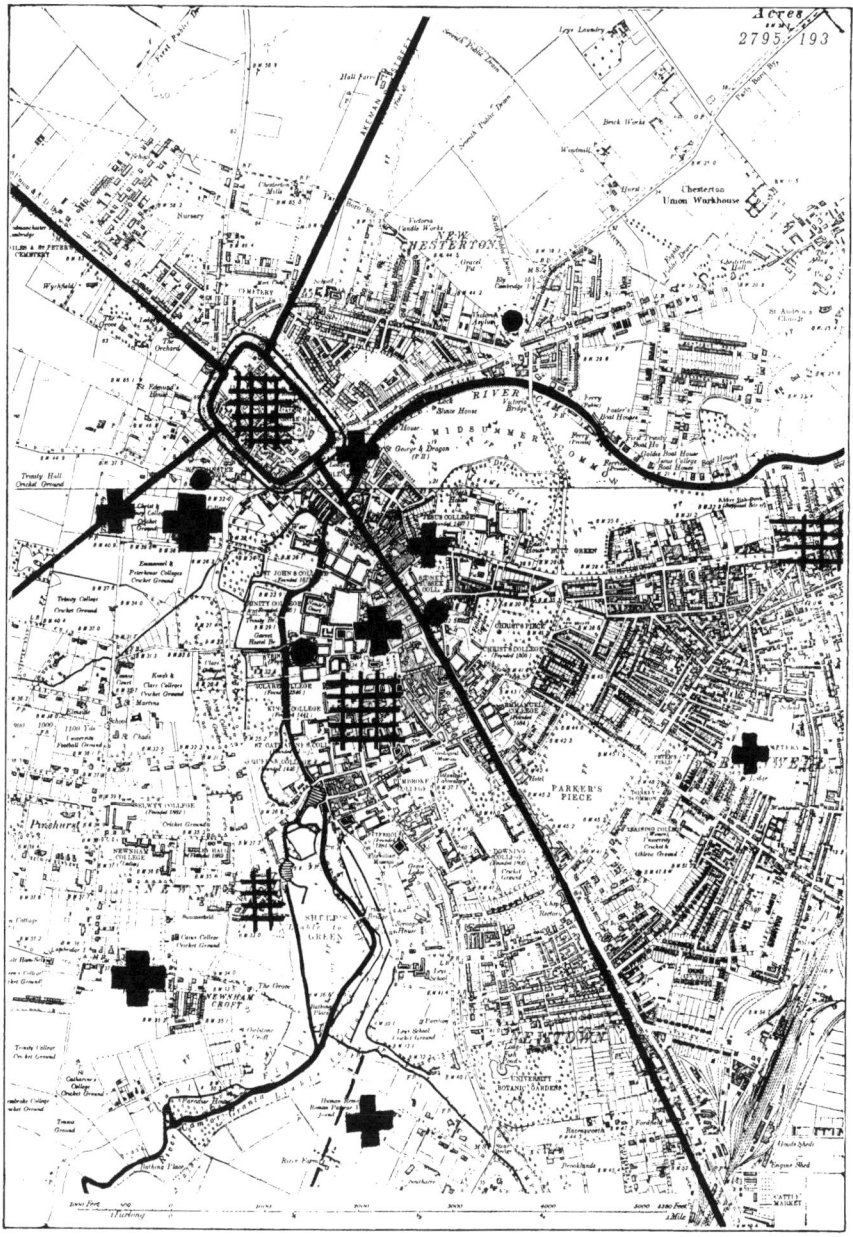

Printed by the Cambridge University Press

The probable sites of settlements of the pagan period are indicated by cross-hatching.
✚ Cemetery or isolated burial; size indicates relative importance.   ● Four finds not certainly sepulchral.

Based upon the Ordnance Survey Map, with the sanction of the Controller of H.M. Stationery Office.

Roman burials both inhumation and cremation were found close to Saxon[1]; a Roman bow fibula with enamel inlays, moreover, was found on the shoulder of a skeleton (grave No. 2), on the other shoulder of which lay a "common Saxon fibula" (see Plate XXX, 3). Roman worked stone, tiles, masses of mortar, as well as rough fragments of oolite were in some cases used to cover the bodies or to protect the urns (cf. Brown, 1915, p. 151).

Some of the urns are elaborately decorated: two of the finest (at Girton College) are figured (Plate XXXI). On No. 2, which contained beads as well as burnt bones, the decoration is unusual, on the other it is of normal character. Plain pipkins ("accessory vessels") were common, being placed close to the head of the skeleton; in one case a "decorated urn" was in this position.

The range of finds was typical of the district; cruciform fibulae and wrist-clasps were common. Two bronze-mounted buckets were met with and also a bronze basin (as Brown, 1915, Pl. cxvii, 3); these are in the Cambridge Museum. Weapons were rare save the knife; a few spearheads and a small double-horned axe (found at the right shoulder of a skeleton) are recorded. A bone comb-case in the Girton Library is an exceptional find; and the occurrence of bangles of Kimmeridge shale is notable. Cremated burials rarely yield objects of interest; but at Girton, as at Wilbraham (p. 280), important objects occurred occasionally in urns.

In one fragments of a glass vessel "very thin with raised striae $\frac{1}{4}$ inch apart" were found: in another "fused pieces of tawny glass"; both were probably drinking-vessels, and are notable in view of the rarity of such in our district. Remnants of bronze from two cinerary urns, showing zöomorphic decoration, preserved in the College, are probably parts of cruciform fibulae of advanced type: on Plate XXXV (No. 2) are figured two out of three fragments derived from a third urn (Jenkinson MS. p. 19). For a discussion of the significance of these finds in relation to the history of cremation in England see p. 279.

Apart from the glass and bronzes the range of recognizable objects, partially burnt, found in cremation urns here may be mentioned as typical. The list includes tweezers, beads, knives, iron shears (as Plate XXXVI, 4), bone needles, girdle-hangers. Bone combs of which many examples were found were, it is noted, unburnt.

At the waist of one skeleton (Grave No. 10) was a buckle of gilt bronze with rectangular plate, having a silver centre; opposite to this lay its complement; and in a different position a plate of identical

[1] As at Grange Road, Cambridge, Haslingfield, and Dam Hill, Trumpington.

type and a strap-end (Plate XXXV; one plate is reversed to show method of attachment to belt). The position of the third plate on the body is not recorded; it was probably fixed at the back of the belt. Complete sets of belt fittings such as this are rare in other parts of England[1]. The whole must have been imposing and most decorative, and the workmanship is excellent. A knife and iron tweezers were the only additional objects found in the grave.

A similar buckle is in the British Museum and studs in the same technique are in the Bury Museum; both from Icklingham. The four-leaf or star design is characteristic of the best period of Anglian art in our district; it is seen on the cruciform fibula from St John's on Plate XXVII, 1, admirable alike for its proportions, restrained ornament (confined to the double star on the plate and the triquetra at the foot) and workmanship. This fibula and the buckles may be dated in VI, probably in the middle of the century.

Plate XXVII shows also a rich deposit from Girton, probably a little later in date than the above, selected as an illustration of the characteristic grave-furniture of the district (see *C.A.S. Rep.* 46, 1886, p. lxxiv). The cruciform fibula is evidently by the same craftsman as the St John's example and merits equal praise. [It is to be noted that the ornament (zöomorphic) is here applied to the knob and the wings, the panel on the head-plate and the foot being left plain. In every detail these two brooches repay careful study as works of art.] The associated objects are two plate fibulae, a girdle-hanger (with moulded terminal), and wrist-clasps; pin, tweezers, and amber necklace: the latter is not figured.

A third fibula (from the same workshop?) with a niello inlay round the collar of the foot, in the Ashmolean, labelled "Cambridge 1888," is without doubt from St John's. The date is that of the exploration of the cemetery.

That *inhumation* burial in the Girton cemetery commenced not later than 500 A.D. is indicated by the presence of "small long" brooches of a type met with in Slesvig, associated with blown-glass beads (Plate XXX, No. 5)[2], and by the occurrence of fine early cruciform fibulae as in the associated find illustrated on Plate XXXIV, 1 and 1 A. Early date for cremation burial is attested by the presence of an urn with a piece of thick granular greenish glass in the bottom[3]. The

---

[1] See Brown (1915, p. 357). A plain set from Barrington A is in the Ashmolean. Finely wrought sets of belt-plates from Haslingfield (classical decoration), Barrington A and St John's (zöomorphic) are also preserved.

[2] The beads are figured by Brown (1915, Plate cvi, 6) and dated in late V (p. xv). Such have, however, a wide chronological range in our district. See p. 257.

[3] "There was nothing remarkable in the position or contents of this urn which had lost all the upper portion" (Jenkinson, 1882).

glass is figured on Plate XXXII, 4 B. A similar vessel has been found at Haslingfield (see p. 256), a third and fourth are recorded from Kempston and Stamford, cemeteries with affinities to the Cambridge group. Several have been found in Hanover (Leeds, 1913, p. 92); and that all the English examples are in the eastern district is well recognized to be significant.

Trumpington. Though no detailed record of the objects from Dam Hill, near Vicar's Brook, Trumpington (in the Deck collection, Cambridge Museum, obtained prior to 1854), exists, there is no reason to doubt that they came from an inhumation cemetery (see *C.A.S. Rep.* 14, 1854, pp. 12 and 14). The remains consist of a spearhead, clasps and long brooches. One of the latter is very early and of Hanoverian type (as No. 2 on Plate XXXIII, probably mid-V). A second, small and finely wrought, with attached side-knobs, is figured on Plate XXIX, 5. A third (Plate XXXIII, 6), the derivation of which from Trumpington is not fully attested, is a fine example of developed character with detached side-knobs, dating about 500; attached to the nose of the horse-head foot by a hinge with an iron pin is a thin bronze plate. This was sewn on to the dress (two holes indicate this) and prevented the loss or disarrangement of the fibula when fixed in position in the usual manner, foot uppermost.

The loop at the nose occurs in other brooches from Eastern England (one, from Tuddenham, is in the Cambridge Museum), and these probably had originally a similar plate; but none has survived. The extension of the foot beyond the horse's nose, so marked a feature of cruciform brooches of the "Londesborough type," may have originated in an addition of this character; if so, it is one of many examples of the atrophy of a structural member. A V century fibula from Norway, with traces of a loop at the foot, figured by Schetelig (1906, fig. 31), is almost identical in the elaborate mouldings of bow and foot, but the head-plate in our example is later and characteristically English.

Grantchester. A few knives and spears in the Cambridge Museum were obtained, as I am informed by Mr A. F. Griffith, some forty years ago from a small gravel pit on the south side of the road to Coton, close to the three-way junction in the village. A small decorated vessel from Grantchester of the type frequently associated with inhumation interments (as on Plate XXXII, No. 6), in the Cambridge Museum, also doubtless came from this site; and we may conclude that further excavation would disclose the cemetery of the settlement.

Cemeteries of the Chapel Hill Group

There are three known cemeteries in the Chapel Hill district; two in Barrington parish, and one at Haslingfield. The existence of the two former in the same parish has resulted in wellnigh hopeless confusion; and the preparation of a monograph on the group as a whole is a piece of work which would amply repay the labour spent on it. Here an attempt is made to set out the facts relating to them so far as they are known.

Partial record, good as far as it goes, of the exploration of the Barrington cemeteries exists; of Haslingfield there is no record.

The first Barrington cemetery to be examined (which I will call Barrington "A") was opened in 1860 by Wilkinson, who recorded the results of his excavations in *Collectanea Antiqua*, vol. VI, and by C. C. Babington, whose paper will be found in *Communications, C.A.S.* vol. II. Other burials on the site were revealed by coprolite digging in subsequent years. The cemetery was situated in a field called Edix Hill Hole near the western boundary of Barrington parish[1]; it was thus nearer to the village of Orwell, and to a large farm in Orwell parish known as Malton Farm, than to Barrington itself.

The second Barrington cemetery (Barrington "B") was examined by Foster in 1880, having been discovered, according to his account, in the same year, in the course of coprolite digging. It was situated at the west end of the village, in "Hooper's Field," and the site is marked on the 6-inch O.S. Sheet LIII, N.E. Foster recorded the results of his excavations in vol. V of *Communications, C.A.S.*, in 1883.

I can find no record or local knowledge of any cemetery in these parishes other than the two above mentioned[2]. Since "Barrington A" is closer to Orwell and Malton than to Barrington, it is not surprising that numerous objects which have found their way into private and public collections should be thus labelled. Many objects, moreover, dug up in "Barrington A" cemetery and correctly labelled "Barrington" are ascribed to the better known of the two cemeteries.

In this connection I may cite the evidence of an old coprolite digger of Barrington, aged 80, whose working life covers the period from 1860 onwards. This man, William Coote, described to me (in May, 1921) the exact position of the Edix Hill cemetery: he had never heard of anything being found at Malton, or at any sites in the neighbourhood other than the two above mentioned. Precisely similar testimony was elicited in April 1922 from another coprolite digger, Philip Jude of Barrington.

[1] Close to the road and immediately to the north of the footpath joining spot-levels 67 and 69 on the 1-inch O.S. map.
[2] But A.-S. weapons have been found at a ford of the River Cam at Barrington.

THE ANGLO-SAXON AGE

Fortunately it is possible to differentiate between objects from these two cemeteries. Barrington A was excavated in 1860 and subsequent years. Barrington B was not discovered till 1880[1]. Hence all objects dated before 1880 are to be regarded as coming from Barrington A (Edix Hill); again, all objects in museums labelled Orwell and Malton ought, I think, to be definitely ascribed to the same cemetery. The whole of the Barrington, Orwell and Malton objects in the Ashmolean, and the Barrington and Malton objects in the British Museum, obtained before 1880, then, are regarded as being from Edix Hill (Barrington A).

Mr E. T. Leeds, of the Ashmolean Museum, informs me that the Orwell and Malton objects in the Evans collection are dated from 1867 to 1872; the Barrington objects 1870, 1875 and 1876. The objects from "Malton and Barrington" in the British Museum were purchased in 1876.

To avoid confusion, such objects are in this book described as Barrington A (Malton) or (Orwell) or (Barrington).

Barrington A (Edix Hill) was apparently entirely an inhumation cemetery. No pottery was found in any of the 26 (or ? 30) graves opened by Wilkinson (nor apparently in the ten or more recorded by Babington), but broken fragments apparently of Anglo-Saxon vessels occurred on the site[2], and a bronze-mounted situla was placed by the head of one skeleton (Grave VI). A number of the objects then found have passed into the Cambridge Museum as the Trinity College Loan Collection; the few objects recorded by Babington (beads, "small long" fibulae and weapons) are also in the museum. The six plates in *Collectanea Antiqua* show the range of Wilkinson's finds; clasps, cruciform fibulae, large square-headed and "small long" fibulae, a plate fibula with the swastika cut therein and saucer fibulae may be mentioned. A pair of the latter with geometric (scroll) decoration was found in Grave XI, one on the right hip, the other on the left shoulder. A gilt square-headed fibula lay on the right shoulder; a ribbed silver bracelet on the left wrist. These are illustrated on my Plate XXX. The saucer fibulae cannot be traced, and one is reproduced from an illustration in the original record. The grave also contained beads, a clasp, a knife, an earring. The association is of interest as suggesting a date not earlier than mid-VI

---

[1] Definite statement by Foster in the paper alluded to above. Confirmed by Mr A. F. Griffith who examined the cemetery with Foster and who lived, as he informs me, in the immediate neighbourhood from 1873 onwards.

[2] A few plain and decorated vessels are known from this cemetery (in the Camb. Mus., and Brit. Mus.—"Malton and Barrington 1876"). The Cambridge pots are such as are known to occur with inhumed burials.

for these geometric saucer brooches and for the ribbed silver bracelet, another example of which, from Sandy (?), is in the Cambridge Museum. Both Babington and Wilkinson remark on the exceptional size of the skeletons in this cemetery; many were "about six, and some nearly seven feet high." The objects discovered during these excavations were probably all of VI century date; but certain items of grave-furniture in the Cambridge Museum from the site, such as the disc, formerly enamelled, from a bronze bowl (Plate XXXIV, 5, and p. 283), may turn out to be later. This object must be the result of later and unrecorded excavation, as doubtless are the numerous objects from Barrington A ("Barrington," "Malton" and "Orwell") in the Ashmolean (Evans collection). Among the latter is the cruciform fibula dating about 500 (resembling my Plate XXVII, 3) figured by Leeds (1912, p. 180) and considered by him to be an importation from Denmark, and the remarkable and unique fibula with Romanizing ornament also illustrated by Leeds.

Many objects in the Conybeare and other collections, Cambridge Museum, are from Barrington A. A curved knife or bill, with bronze mount and rivets, which is figured on Plate XXXVI, 12, a fork and a billhook are probably also from Barrington A. Such tools rarely occur in English cemeteries.

A large number of "small long" fibulae of Maltese cross or trefoil-head types—the majority of which probably date in VI—clasps, girdle-hangers, two geometric saucer and several applied fibulae are also in the Ashmolean. Three applied fibulae in the Cambridge Museum, one from Barrington A (the others dated 1880, and undoubtedly from Barrington B), are perhaps the earliest found in the district; the plates are decorated in the simplest fashion with punched patterns. Of special interest is a group of silver objects in the Ashmolean—finger rings, a bracelet, a pair of finely wrought square-headed fibulae dating in mid-VI, and an annular fibula set with projecting studs of gold and garnets. If mention be made of a radiating fibula in the British Museum ("Malton") the more important objects from the Barrington A cemetery have been passed in review and we can date it in late V and VI. The folk who buried their dead here appear to have been especially prosperous in early and middle VI. The absence of imported objects of late VI or VII date may be connected with the rise of East Anglia which probably involved the subjection of the dwellers in the Barrington district (see p. 295).

Barrington B. Much of the grave-furniture obtained from this cemetery, a portion only of which is recorded in Foster's paper

ANGLO-SAXON AGE. GRAVE-FURNITURE OF THE PAGAN PERIOD
The scales are in inches.
No. 1, pp. 255, 269, 270, 280 (footnote, two refs.); No. 2, p. 269;
No. 3, pp. 260, 269 (two refs.), 283; No. 4, p. 269 (two refs.);
No. 5, pp. 249, 269; No. 6, p. 257.

(1883), is in the Cambridge Museum (Foster and Conybeare collections and Trinity College Loan Collection)[1].

Though only six months elapsed between the discovery and Foster's exploration of the cemetery, he is careful to note that the "larger part" had been opened by the coprolite diggers before his arrival. Many objects found haphazard during this period are now in the local collection, but others may have been widely distributed; all objects of Barrington provenance bearing the date 1880 should, I consider, be regarded as from Barrington B.

The cemetery was almost entirely inhumation. That cremation occurred we know from Foster's record[2], which, though somewhat indefinite, is supported by the presence of a large decorated "cinerary urn" in the Cambridge Museum.

The contents of 114 graves recorded by Foster may be briefly indicated, as giving a picture of the relative frequency of various classes of objects. Thirty-one of these contained no deposit. The interments were usually but not consistently east and west, with the feet towards the east[3]. Of 55 fibulae (from 29 graves) there were 8 "applied," 2 annular, 14 plate, 1 large cruciform, 2 small squareheaded, the majority of the remainder being "small long" fibulae of various forms. There were 12 pairs of clasps; situlae with bronze and iron mounts, girdle-hangers, bracelets, buckles, bangles, pins, and one set of horse trappings, were also found. Of weapons there were 2 swords, 8 shield bosses of the ordinary types, 15 spears, and many knives.

Certain of the latter are figured on Plate XXXVI. One shield boss is unusual, in that it has a button of bronze, incised with a zöomorphic pattern (Foster, 1883, p. 14, and my Plate XXXVI, 10).

The urns figured by Foster are of the type frequently found in Southern Cambridgeshire associated with inhumation interments; they are small, bowl-shaped, usually with a markedly carinated shoulder, and thus suggest Frankish influence. I figure one of the Barrington examples (from Grave 66, Foster) on Plate XXXII, 6. These were at Barrington always found, like the situlae, close to the head.

[1] See also notes by Conybeare (1904, p. 437) and in *C.A.S. Rep.* 41, 1881, p. xii; the evidence contained in the latter has been carefully weighed.
[2] *Loc. cit.* p. 9: "In this cemetery cremation seems to have been quite the exception, very few cinerary urns having been found."
[3] This suggests Romano-British influence. But the position is by no means the commonest in the district. At Wilbraham the majority of skeletons lay with feet towards the north.

It will be convenient to base our review of Barrington B on the entire collection from the cemetery in the Cambridge Museum; but it must be remembered that with few exceptions nothing is known of the associations of any objects save those from the graves excavated by Foster.

The saucer and applied brooches are perhaps of chief interest. Practically all the specimens found in our district have been tabulated and discussed by Leeds (1912); he records four saucer and no less than twenty-five applied brooches from "Barrington" (some of which are undoubtedly from Barrington A). The following brief note is based on his researches, but is confined to specimens known to be from Barrington B.

The design most frequently met with locally in the applied brooches is that of "a central cross, each arm containing a rude face, the intervening spaces occupied by legs. An outer border is filled with a zöomorphic pattern[1]." Leeds (1912, pp. 179–180) agrees with R. A. Smith in assigning the type to early VI; but the associated wrist-clasps figured on my Plate XXX, 4, suggest the second half of the century for at least two Barrington examples. Brown (1915, Vol. III, p. xxxvii), indeed, dates these wrist-clasps in VII; and they certainly are of advanced type. Other applied fibulae of similar design from Barrington B have a central boss of blue glass.

Two pairs of applied fibulae with zöomorphic decoration in the Cambridge Museum show a central stud set on a tall waisted stem; this type, as Leeds shows, is very rare outside Middle Anglia. Barrington B has yielded the only example of an applied brooch with geometric decoration (that of a six-point star) found in Eastern England (Leeds, 1912, p. 200). Its associations, unfortunately, give little assistance in fixing a date for the type.

The few saucer brooches need little comment here; the rough cruciform division of the design in one may be derived from Kentish brooches set with four garnets, and therefore may date in late VI.

See Leeds, 1912, p. 192. Brown (1915, Plate CXLVI, 5, and p. xxiv) dates the prototype in early and middle VI, Leeds in late VI.

Clasps. The finest examples of clasps of developed types with triangular extensions found in the district are derived from this

---

[1] Leeds records four examples from Barrington B (Camb. Mus.), three from Barrington A ("Malton"), one each from Haslingfield and Hauxton, two from Linton and eight from Kempston [B]. To these may be added two of uncertain, but certainly local, origin in the Camb. Mus.; and two probably from Ashwell, in the Ransom collection.

PLATE XXX

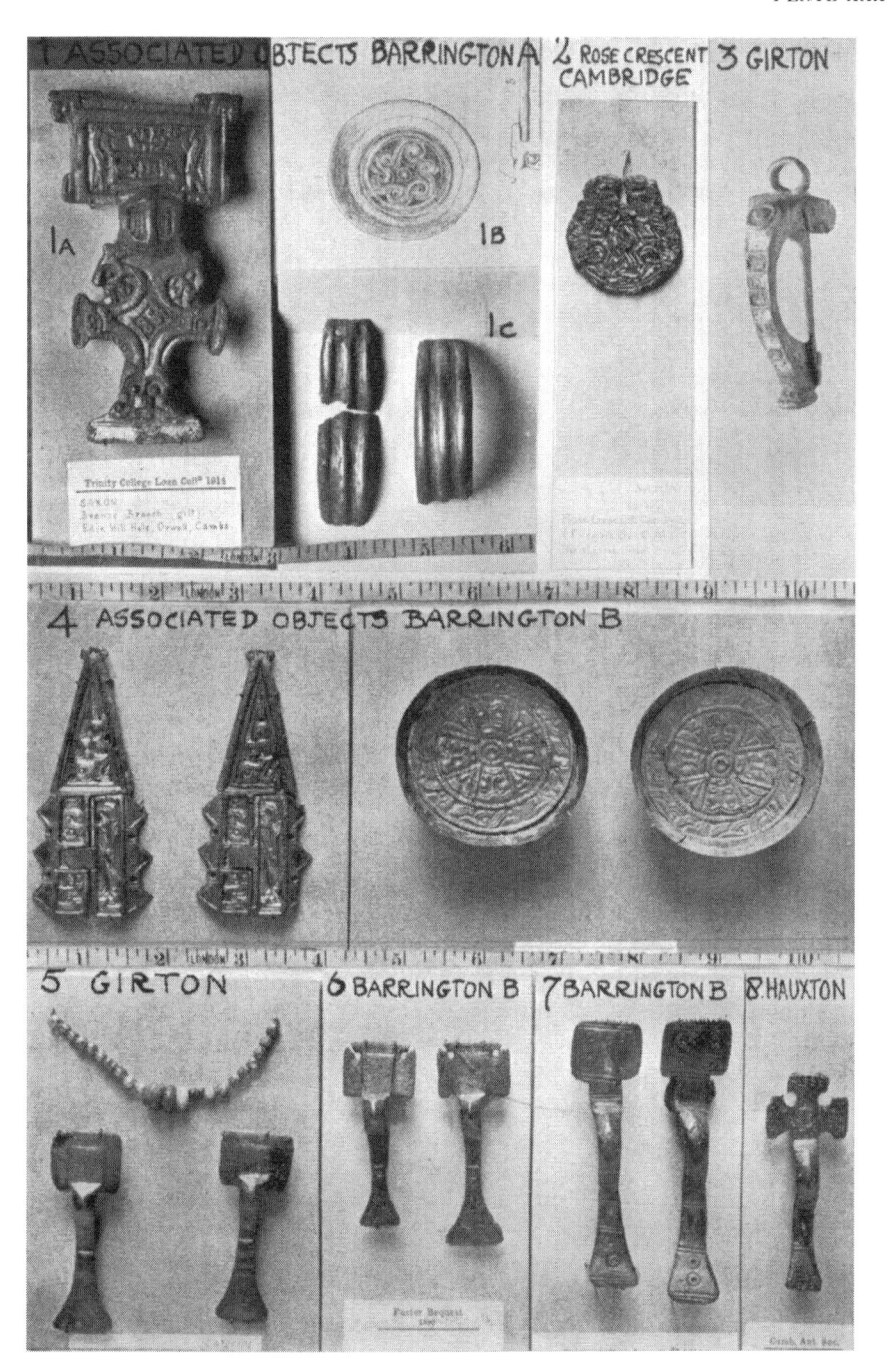

ANGLO-SAXON AGE. GRAVE-FURNITURE OF THE PAGAN PERIOD
The scales are in inches.
No. 1, pp. 251–2; No. 2, p. 245 (footnote); No. 3, pp. 247, 281; No. 4, pp. 254–5, 272; No. 5, pp. 248, 269; No. 6, pp. 255, 269, 270; No. 7, p. 269; No. 8, pp. 259 (footnote), 269, 270.

cemetery. There are two patterns and associated objects are recorded in each case. The earlier, dated in late VI by the presence of a florid square-headed fibula, shows a volute pattern, the triangular extension being separate; the later (typologically if not chronologically) shows the extension cast in one piece with half the clasp. The latter are figured on my Plate XXX; the former are in the Cambridge Museum and are figured by Brown (1915, p. 365, and Plate 79, 1).

An interesting group of associated objects is that figured on Plate XXIX, derived from Grave 82 (Foster). The developed character of the large cruciform fibula, and of the zöomorphic design on the wrist-clasps indicates a date in the second half of VI, which is interesting in view of the simplicity of the associated "small long" brooches and the shape of their head-plates. These latter lay on each shoulder; over that on the right shoulder was the larger fibula. The looped handle of bronze (part of a Roman key, the iron stem and wards having perished) lay on the finely moulded bronze ring at the left hip, "with knife and other fragments of iron surrounded by remains of cloth."

It is probable from its situation that the latter group of objects formed part of a "sporran." In Grave 75 (Foster), together with the brooches and wrist-clasps figured on Plate XXX, 4, were found, "between the legs and partly beneath the hips...four rings inside one another," the outer one (5⅛ inches in diameter) of ivory, the second and third of iron and the fourth of bronze: "under all lay a knife." Here we have similar association and position.

A remarkable pierced "girdle-hanger" from Grave 72, Linton Heath (figured by Brown, Plate xcii, 2), no doubt belonged to a similar sporran, since it lay on the legs of a skeleton—presumably a male, for a situla was found by the head (Neville, 1854 b, Fig. 13 and p. 108).

Among the early objects from Barrington B are a fine cruciform fibula with detached knobs, small square-headed fibulae (as Plate XXX, 6) and a buckle of Kentish type with shoe-shaped studs (Grave 101 (Foster) and Cambridge Museum). It is not possible, unfortunately, to give a date to the remarkable iron fibula with bronze wire pin sketched on Plate XXXIII, 4, the "cruciform bronze" fibula with which it was associated (Grave 47, Foster) not being identifiable; but a later date than V is unlikely.

Haslingfield. A cemetery was disclosed in this parish near spot level 71 on the Cantelupe Farm-Haslingfield trackway, in 1874-5, during coprolite digging. Occasional Roman and Saxon finds on the site had, however, been previously (1865) recorded.

In *Proc. Soc. Antiq.* 2 S. III. pp. 36, 77, a Roman cremation interment on this site, contained in the amphora figured on Plate XXIII, is described; near it was an inhumation interment, and a sword and two spears were found. Much Roman pottery from Haslingfield, in the Cambridge Museum, doubtless comes from the same area.

Practically our only knowledge of the Anglo-Saxon cemetery is derived from finds which at various times were acquired from workmen by collectors or museums; that the site is some distance from the village accounts for many finds being labelled "near Haslingfield."

Mr A. F. Griffith is my authority for the exact site and for the date; he lived in Haslingfield in 1873–1881. But it may have been opened as early as 1872, for objects in the Ashmolean Museum bear that date. I place on record here the statement made by Mr Griffith that he had heard "a second cemetery" spoken of as being in the parish. I have not been able to obtain confirmation of this; coprolite diggings may have trenched on the site at two different points.

Sufficient material has been preserved (Cambridge Museum, British Museum and Ashmolean Museum) to enable a good idea of the character of the cemetery to be obtained; its range of finds was similar to that of Barrington B, but it contained objects of early date and exceptional interest. I had considered it to be entirely inhumation, the only pottery known to me until recently being such as occurs with inhumed bodies in the district; but I have lately seen three vessels of cinerary urn type from the site in the Ashmolean Museum, and the occasional occurrence of cremation must be considered as highly probable. An example of the former type of pot (Plate XXXII, 4 A) contains a piece of glass in its base, and was probably made by one of the first settlers.

It is interesting to notice that of the two finds of this type in the district presumably of mid-V date and contemporary, one (Girton) was a cremation urn, the other (Haslingfield) in all probability associated with an inhumation interment, as was the Kempston bowl. See R. A. Smith (1904, p. 183).

Other interesting and early objects are the equal-armed silver brooch with Romanizing ornament, figured on the Frontispiece (see Brown, 1915, p. 561), and the bronze-gilt belt-plate with classical metopic and egg-and-tongue ornament and garnet centre (Plate XXXIV, 10). The latter is one of a set of three, of which two (labelled "near Cambridge" and dated 1876) are in the Ashmolean Museum. To the V century also, probably, belong several plate brooches in the Cambridge Museum.

Of the few groups of associated objects which have been preserved one deserves mention here. Two "small long" brooches of a type intermediate between the Girton and Barrington examples figured on Plate XXX, 5 and 6, were found with a string of beads, the central pendant of which was a tiger cowrie shell (*Concha Veneris*); the nearest habitat of this is the Red Sea. Two of the beads were small and of blown glass. This necklace is figured by Brown (Plate cvii, 1). Blown-glass beads have a wide chronological range in our district; in a group find from Icklingham, in the Ashmolean, such are associated with a late cruciform fibula.

A pair of "S" fibulae from Haslingfield, in the Ashmolean, showing early zoömorphs is figured by De Baye (1903, Plate 4). A third "S" fibula from the cemetery is also in the museum. It has silver discs (an Anglian fashion) at each terminal, replacing the garnets which decorate Frankish examples otherwise identical. This suggests that local copies of imported objects were made.

Two cruciform fibulae, figured on Plates XXIX, 6, and XXVII, 4, are of some importance. The slender type (6) is more like a Frisian than a local form; but it shows a vertical incision above the horsehead which is an English feature, according to Schetelig. The other shows to what a late date fibulae with knife edges to the head-plate and with side-knobs forming terminals to the spring, survived in the district. This fibula must be nearer 550 than 500 A.D. It also shows on the panel of the head-plate mock spirals—stamped circles attached by a diagonal line—which are, I think, not met with outside East Anglia as an element in Anglo-Saxon decoration. They occur in Scandinavia and may be survivals of the familiar Bronze Age *motif*. The design is, however, also met with on bone objects of the Roman Age in this country (cf. Pitt-Rivers, 1887, Plate XLV).

This brief review shows that the cemetery may be regarded as belonging to one of the early settlements; it contains also late objects, including a very debased square-headed fibula which is probably of VII date.

Harlton. An interesting group of objects, evidently from an inhumation cemetery of the usual Cambridgeshire character, including a very large (6·7 by 3·3 inches) gilt square-headed fibula, two saucer fibulae[1], a fine pair of clasps, beads, weapons and pottery was presented to Trinity College in 1879 by the late Professor McKenny

---

[1] This pair of saucer fibulae with zoömorphic decoration, in the Camb. Mus., 40 mm. in diameter, now labelled "Harlton," is included in the Barrington series by Leeds in the tabular list already referred to.

Hughes as from Harlton (a village on the north side of the Chapel Hill ridge adjoining Haslingfield). These objects are now at the Cambridge Museum. Investigation has failed to yield any other record of a cemetery in this parish. Again, Mr A. F. Griffith, whose connection with Haslingfield and Barrington has previously been mentioned, informed me (in 1921) that he had never heard of a cemetery at Harlton, and suggested that the objects may have been brought from Barrington (a mile and a half away over the hill) by a coprolite digger of his acquaintance then (1879) resident in Harlton.

The fact, however, that the most striking ornament in the group of objects under review—the square-headed fibula—was by Hughes himself figured as from Haslingfield in his *Cambridgeshire* (1909) renders it almost certain that the whole came from the cemetery in this parish already referred to. The ring fibula from Harlton (acquired 1872), in the Ashmolean Museum, is, doubtless, of similar origin; Mr Leeds tells me that no details as to provenance are known.

The fibula referred to above, being the best example found near Cambridge of a characteristic "Anglian" type, is figured on the Frontispiece with two others from Tuddenham and Lakenheath respectively, to show the variety of zöomorphic ornament on this class of brooch in the district. The Lakenheath specimen with silver plaques on the disc terminals of the foot (characteristic of the Anglian region) is mainly geometric in design, but the wings at the base of the bow show zöomorphs. It closely resembles, and is doubtless derived from, V century Scandinavian forms (several examples are figured by Schetelig): but is probably not earlier than 500 A.D.

The decoration of the "Harlton" and Tuddenham specimens is entirely zöomorphic; in the latter fairly coherent, in the former, to some extent, incoherent. It is not probable, however, that there is much difference in date between them. The notched head-plate which each shows is an early feature, and bow and foot resemble the Lakenheath fibula; in the Tuddenham specimen proliferation of ornament in places obscures but cannot hide the essential identity in design. Both probably date in the middle of VI. The "Harlton" specimen is almost identical with one from Fairford, figured by Leeds (1913, p. 64).

On the Frontispiece is shown, for comparison, the earlier provincial-Roman ornament represented by the equal-armed fibula from Haslingfield, of the V century, and the interlacing, coherent zöomorphic decoration (Salin style II) of VII, represented by the Allington Hill plaque.

Barton. An escutcheon probably of a bronze bowl, from Barton, is referred to in a paper by R. A. Smith (1909 *b*, p. 82). It is in the Evans collection, as is a spindle-whorl of Anglo-Saxon character; both were obtained in 1874. No other objects of the pagan period, so far as I can ascertain, come from this parish, which adjoins Haslingfield, and, since a large number of objects were being obtained from the latter cemetery in that year, the recorded provenance of the finds must be considered open to grave doubt.

The Sawston, Linton, Wilbraham and other cemeteries

Cemeteries in the Cam Valley at Hauxton, Foxton, Sawston and Linton may first be considered.

Hauxton. The wealth of antiquities of all periods, found during coprolite digging in 1879 and subsequent years on the right bank of the Cam by Hauxton Mill and the ancient ford, has frequently been referred to. A few Anglo-Saxon objects—undoubtedly grave-furniture accompanying inhumed burials—from the site are in the Cambridge and Ashmolean Museums. These include plate and "small long" (Maltese cross) fibulae[1] and an applied fibula; a large knobbed vessel of pottery in the Cambridge Museum suggests that cremation was also practised. One interment recorded by Hughes (1891 b, p. 26) is of especial interest. In a "pit" (? grave) at a depth of about two feet was a skeleton accompanied by a two-horned axehead of a type occurring in Hanover and France as well as this country, an iron key, knives, and a hilt-plate for knife or seax (?) 3 inches long, slightly curved, with a central slit (see Plate XXXVI, 3 and 11). No record, other than this, of the associations of any Anglo-Saxon objects from the site is preserved.

Foxton. Excavation of a La Tène settlement site about half a mile north-west of Foxton Church in 1922 revealed two Anglian inhumation burials; two others had previously been discovered by gravel-diggers, and the site is doubtless the cemetery of the Foxton folk. A small bronze buckle found at the waist of one of the skeletons is probably unique; a bronze fish, in high relief, certainly a pike, was attached by rivets to the chape (C. Fox, 1923 a).

Sawston. An interesting interment at Huckeridge Hill, Sawston, by the side of the Cambridge-London road, is on record (E. D. Clarke, 1816).

The skeleton was three feet below the surface. With it were: two vessels of bronze, the larger 15 inches across having a flat rim ornamented with a row of bosses all round; a vessel of black coarse earthenware; an iron sword and shield boss and an S-shaped bronze fibula.

---
[1] The latter of VI century type. See my Plate XXX, No. 8.

The bowl is of a type widely distributed in Western Europe, dating in V and VI; examples from Sussex and Kent are figured by Brown (Plate cxvi) and one from Norway by Du Chaillu (1889, 1, p. 269). Such are usually held to be of Rhineland origin; but Conway (1918, p. 83) suggests they may be derived from the East (Egypt).

The previous discovery of iron spearheads on the site is evidence of the existence of an inhumation cemetery.

Linton. An important cemetery on Linton Heath, adjacent to the village of Bartlow, was discovered and excavated by Neville (1854 *b*). A large tumulus on the heath was found to be filled with Anglian graves; the primary interment by cremation being probably Roman (see p. 196). The remains were reported on in detail, and the majority of the finds are preserved in the Audley End Museum.

The cemetery was entirely inhumation; 104 skeletons were exhumed and there were traces of many more graves which had been disturbed by agricultural operations. The general character of the finds was such as we are now familiar with, but several large gilt square-headed fibulae (in Graves Nos. 21, 32 and 39) bore red or yellow plaques of enamel or paste. These are features not met with on similar fibulae from Cambridgeshire cemeteries west of the Cam, but they occur in the River Lark district in N.W. Suffolk (see Plate XXIX, 3).

There were no bronze girdle-hangers in the cemetery; but the distribution of these is curiously irregular. Only two are known from Girton. There were three pairs of applied or saucer fibulae, and eight or nine pairs of clasps. In several cases small decorated pottery vessels were, as at Barrington A, placed near the heads of skeletons.

An interesting find at Linton was that of a funnel-shaped vase of thin greenish glass $5\frac{3}{4}$ inches in height, which lay by the head of a skeleton (Grave No. 73), together with a large sea-shell (*cypraea*); the date of such vases, according to Brown (Pl. cxxviii, 2), is late VI. The cemetery may have originated in late V; there are, for example, cruciform fibulae with detached side-knobs and one radiating fibula in the Audley End Museum. No markedly late objects are recorded.

The cemeteries adjoining the fens (Wilbraham, Burwell, Soham), or on fen islands (Chatteris), may next be dealt with.

Little Wilbraham. This well-known cemetery adjoins the Street Way (see p. 149) in Little Wilbraham parish. Some of the graves are now exposed in a chalk pit on the site. It was excavated by Neville in 1851: a complete illustrated record of his discoveries is

PLATE XXXI

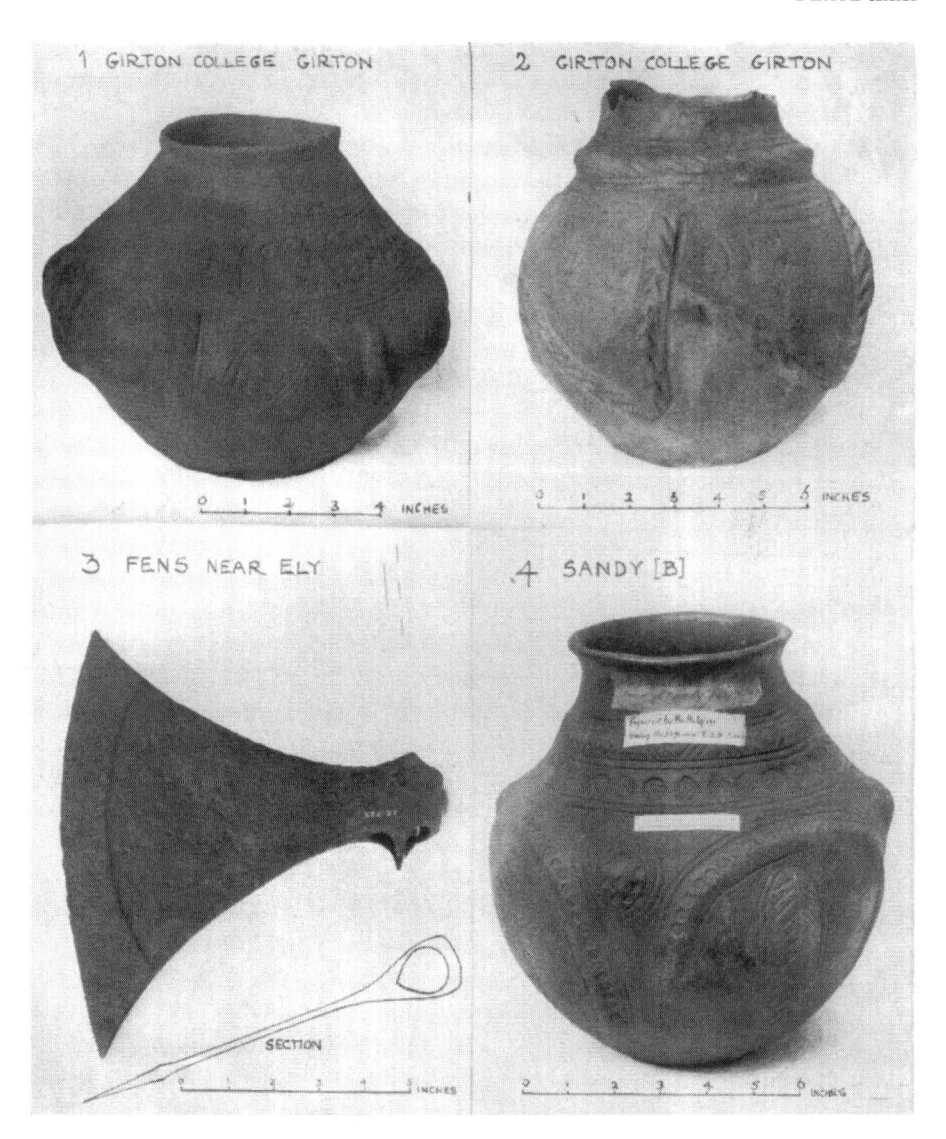

ANGLO-SAXON AGE. CINERARY URNS OF THE PAGAN PERIOD: WEAPON OF
THE CHRISTIAN PERIOD
Nos. 1, 2, pp. 247, 273; No. 3, p. 299; No. 4, pp. 267, 273.

contained in *Saxon Obsequies*[1], and the majority of the objects found are in the Audley End Museum. One hundred and eighty-eight graves and 121 cremation interments are here recorded; in addition, other interments are known, for a number of objects from the cemetery not mentioned by Neville are in the Cambridge, Ashmolean and British Museums.

The general character of the grave-furniture was similar to that met with in other large cemeteries in our Region, the number and variety of the cruciform fibulae being a marked feature. Many skeletons, as at Barrington B, were unaccompanied by any deposit. Beads were very numerous and widely distributed among the graves, the large parti-coloured rectangular and cylindrical beads of vitreous paste, characteristic of the Anglian region, being especially noticeable (Plates 18–21). Girdle-hangers were met with; two situlae (Plate 17) and two bronze vessels (Plate 16) may also be mentioned. Of weapons, knives were universal; numerous umbos and spears were recorded and there were four swords. An iron adze and a francisca or axe deserve mention.

The skeletons were laid at full length in graves from 3 to 4 feet deep; the orientation, as in other local cemeteries, varied widely. Cremation burials occurred with the inhumation interments in such a manner as to convince the excavator that the two rites were contemporary.

This cemetery may be used to illustrate the normal position of the grave-furniture in the local Anglo-Saxon burials. A pair of fibulae was found on the breast; if a third occurred it was deposited near the lower ribs and was always the largest. The clasps were close either to wrists or knees; the beads about or under the collar-bones, the girdle-hangers near the centre of the person; in fact, as Neville observed, "all the appendages occupied their natural, and proper places." The situlae and bronze vessels were placed near the heads of male skeletons equipped with shield and spear (and in some cases a sword also). Shield and spear and knife were always found together in the warrior's grave, and where a sword occurred it was additional. The swords were always by the right thigh, spearheads above the shoulder, but occasionally reversed, at the feet; the shield bosses varying along the whole body, the knives near the hip. One horse, with iron bit and remains of head-stall, was found buried with its rider. Urns with cremated bones contained the usual range of objects which had passed through the fire.

[1] Published in 1852. References in the notes which follow are to the plates in this publication.

These urns exhibited great variety in form, size and decoration (see Plates 24–33); plain jug- and bowl-shaped vessels being found here as elsewhere (see p. 273).

To sum up: the cemetery was mixed cremation and inhumation and was of "Anglian" type; cruciform and square-headed brooches, many late and florid, were a marked feature of the finds. The objects, as a whole, suggest an average date in VI; but several simple cruciform fibulae of early type, with detached side-knobs[1], in the Audley End Museum, a pair of radiating fibulae (probably imported, see Plate 8), and an equal-armed fibula (Plate 2) indicate that the cemetery originated earlier, possibly in middle V. A few applied, but no saucer brooches were found. A late cruciform brooch, at Audley End, has two circular depressions apparently for enamel, and two large gilt square-headed fibulae have small plaques of blue or red enamel. We see here, as at Linton, connections with the River Lark cemeteries.

A circular plate fibula set with keystone panels of shell and garnet is an importation from Kent, and dates in VI.

Burwell. There is brief record, in the *Reports, C.A.S.*, for 1884 (p. cxxvii) and 1887 (p. civ), of a cemetery on the site of the Victoria lime-pits, close to the village. The burials were apparently entirely inhumation, and numerous skeletons were unearthed during these years.

Two finds only, so far as can be ascertained, have been preserved; these are sufficiently remarkable to make one regret that so little is known of the cemetery or its contents.

On a skeleton, probably of a woman, were found a tooth of beaver set in bronze, one amethyst (probably an earring) and some glass beads, a silver wire ring, and the objects sketched on Plate XXXIV, 8. The perforated spoon and ear picks are almost certainly of Kentish fabric and early VII date, and the disc pendant of embossed silver on a bronze base may be of the same provenance, though such are not uncommon in East Anglia. Amethysts are a Mediterranean importation and are rare outside Kent. This being so, it is remarkable that the only other object preserved from the cemetery should be a gold disc fibula inlaid with garnet and shell, of Kentish or Frankish fabric and dating probably in early VI. It was found in 1884 and is in the Cambridge Museum. Other grave-goods mentioned in the record are knives, fragments of iron, and a small iron (*sic*) fibula.

---

[1] The head-knob of one has a tang as in the St John's fibulae, Plate XXVII. It is figured by Schetelig (1906, p. 98) as a V type.

C. R. Smith (1856, Plate XII, 1) figures ear picks similar to the Burwell examples from Kingston, Kent, and many embossed discs, one (of gold) being associated with the Kingston fibula (*ibid*. Plate I, 2, and esp. Plate IV, 22 and 24). Brown (1915, p. 406), discussing the function of perforated spoons which commonly occur in Kentish graves, remarks that the one indication of value is, "that in the museum at Wiesbaden a perforated spoon is joined in the same bunch with a pair of tweezers and a 'cure oreille' which seems to show that it was used in some way for toilet purposes." Our Burwell specimen provides a diminutive example of similar usage.

From Burwell Fen is derived a buckle bow (in Cambridge Museum) figured by Brown (Plate cliv, 2) and dated by him in V.

Soham. The cemetery in this parish is entirely an inhumation one, so far as is known. It is situated in the modern cemetery to the S.E. of the town and finds are recorded for the years 1856–65–67. There is a small collection from the site in the British Museum, acquired in 1873; this includes six fibulae of common types, two being "horned"; girdle-hangers, beads and spearheads (see 6-inch O.S. map XXXV, N.E.; and *Soc. Antiq. Proc.* 2 S, v. p. 496).

Chatteris. In 1757 the grave of an Anglo-Saxon fighting man was found on a "piece of elevated gravelly ground towards Somersham Ferry" in this parish. A sword, spear, umbo, and "claw" glass goblet were in the grave; and as the record (Stukeley, 1766, and Lukis, 1883, p. 49) states that "there were more bodies interred in the same spot" we may infer the existence of a cemetery.

Tumblers of the character found in this grave are widely distributed in Western Europe (and England), and are probably of Rhenish origin; but no other example from our district is recorded. It serves to date the burial as in the late VI or early VII century.

Manea and Mepal. Amber and glass beads found in 1838 with a skeleton in Manea Fen (Babington, 1883, p. 72) may represent accidental death rather than interment[1]; but a large plain jug-shaped pot typically Anglo-Saxon, found in 1859 with Bronze Age urns in a "tumulus" in Mepal Fen (now in the Cambridge Museum), probably represents a "secondary" cremation interment of our period.

Fleam Dyke. Iron weapons of the pagan period found at the Dyke in 1861 indicate burial by or in the earthwork. See p. 293.

Devil's Dyke. Similar objects were found in the vallum of the Devil's Dyke in 1822 (p. 292).

Bottisham. A plain pottery vessel in the Cambridge Museum, found in 1887 at Anglesey Abbey, may represent an interment of the pagan period.

[1] I cannot accept the recorded association of a bronze spear with the beads.

Burial in a Barrow on the Chalk Escarpment

Bottisham. At Allington Hill, Bottisham, close by the Bronze Age burials at Upper Hare Park, a primary inhumation interment of our period in a grave sunk about 5 feet in the chalk (surmounted by a mound some two feet high when excavated) was revealed in 1876. Hughes reported the discovery to the C.A.S.; and the contemporary note (*Report* 36, May 15, 1876) records that one of the well-known pair of jewels—bronze-gilt plaques decorated with bosses of shell (?) and garnet and bands of zoömorphic ornament—lay on the skeleton (see Frontispiece). The other (figured by Leeds, 1912, p. 177) is in the Ashmolean Museum; it was obtained from "Alton" (evidently Allington) Hill in 1860, and Hughes' excavation must be held to have been a re-examination of the barrow. He noted that only portions of the skeleton were present. These jewels were probably breast ornaments, of VII date and of Kentish fabric; they are practically the only examples of Salin's style II found in the district.

This completes the record of cemeteries and burials in Southern Cambridgeshire; reputed finds of minor importance at Quy (Ashmolean) and Fordham (Ashmolean and Cambridge Museums) are thought to have been derived respectively from Wilbraham, and from Soham or Exning.

II. BORDER COUNTIES

(a) Cemeteries in South-West Norfolk and West Suffolk

Thetford. There is practically nothing of the pagan period to record in the Little Ouse Valley; R. A. Smith (1901, p. 335) mentions finds indicative of a cemetery at Thetford, but of this cemetery practically nothing is known.

Cemeteries in N.W. Suffolk. In the Lark Valley and its neighbourhood, on the other hand, there are numerous cemeteries, and the available material is analysed and discussed by R. A. Smith in his admirable article in vol. 1 of the *V.C.H.* of Suffolk. I do not go in detail over the ground thus covered by him; but the cemeteries of N.W. Suffolk are recorded on the topographical map, and the material is used in this chapter for comparative purposes. A collection of objects from these cemeteries is in the Cambridge Museum. Axes from Newmarket and Tuddenham, spearheads and a bronze ferule from Exning, moreover, are figured on Plate XXXVI, which illustrates the range of iron tools and weapons of the period.

The following notes may be of use if read in conjunction with R. A. Smith's article.

THE ANGLO-SAXON AGE

A dozen or more cremation urns were found at Lackford in 1914, probably on the same site as that found in 1874. One (in the Bury Museum) shows an interlacing pattern which is unique in the district (Barker, 1917).

A sword of the period from Herringswell is in the British Museum.

A fragment of "Anglian" pottery, in the British Museum, obtained by Greenwell (1869 b, p. 40) from a barrow on Risby Heath probably represents a secondary interment of our period.

Evidence additional to that adduced by Smith (1911, p. 344) shows that there was a cemetery at Holywell Row (see Bunbury, 1834, p. 611). An isolated burial in a field west of Mildenhall town, with fibulae of late VI, was found in 1906.

The site of the Tuddenham cemetery is a gravel pit close to the Cavenham road, ½ mile from Tuddenham Church, as I am informed by Mr Chas. Brown. The burials at Barrow referred to by Smith (p. 343) are I think of the Early Iron, not Saxon, Age.

Great Thurlow. The importance in earlier days of the Upper Stour Valley as a settlement area renders the absence of Anglo-Saxon cemeteries here the more surprising. A find at Great Thurlow is thus of some interest. This find (in the Cambridge Museum), consisting of a corroded iron buckle, a knife, and bronze tweezers, was unearthed in 1891, apparently on the site of the Roman settlement described in the previous chapter.

(b) Cemeteries in North-West Essex

Wenden. Spearheads, pottery and an umbo of iron from Wenden, recorded by Neville (1848, pp. 9 and 49), indicate a cemetery. The form of the umbo suggests Kentish origin, as does the narrow neck of a vessel from the site preserved in the Audley End Museum. The site is called Mutlow, which points to the former existence of a barrow. The burials are early rather than late in our period.

Chesterford. One decorated vessel of cinerary urn type is in the Cambridge Museum, together with plain pipkins characteristic of the period; one of these latter was associated with charcoal, a bone spindle-whorl and a fragment of bronze. A plain bowl of Anglo-Saxon type 4 inches high, in the Audley End Museum, is said to have been found "to the west of Borough Field," and this may have been the site of the cemetery of the settlement. A late VI century cruciform fibula in the Liverpool Museum, from "Chesterford," is figured by Brown (Plate xlv, 7, and p. 270).

Saffron Walden. I cannot persuade myself that the cemetery within the Paille Ditches at Saffron Walden is of the pagan Anglo-Saxon period. One grave containing a large range of objects was definitely of late X or XI (see p. 299). Another burial yielded fifteen bracelets of Romano-British types.

Many other objects from the site are described, of the Bronze, Roman and Anglo-Saxon Ages. The majority are of Romano-British character; to the Anglo-Saxon pagan period may belong a buckle with forked shank, a cylindrical box of iron and a bell. Parallels to these three objects, as H. E. Smith (1883, pp. 327 ff.) noted, occur in Kentish graves; the two former are unique in our district. They may be chance finds; their association with burials is not definitely recorded; and they are the only evidence justifying the inclusion in the pagan period of a cemetery, from which 150 skeletons were carefully examined.

Anglo-Saxon knives were found in the cemetery; but since one was with the late X interment they are no evidence for pagan burial. Neither are the crystal beads mentioned by Brown (1915, p. 601), also found with this interment. Were it not for the late burial referred to I should be tempted to suggest that the cemetery was that of Christian Romano-Britons who continued to occupy the site for some time after the conquest of the district as a whole was completed (see p. 282).

(c) Burials in North Hertfordshire

Therfield Heath. A secondary inhumation interment in one of the "Five Hills" barrows on Therfield Heath was discovered in 1858; and the buckle found on the skeleton, in the Cambridge Museum, is, according to Brown (p. 107, and Plate v, 12), of V century date.

King's Walden. Until recently no burial of the pagan period in North Hertfordshire, other than the above, was known: but in 1913 R. A. Smith published an account of the objects associated with an inhumation interment at King's Walden, four miles south of Hitchin. A trefoil-headed fibula indicates relations with the counties of Cambridge, Bedford and Northampton, and the district may be included in Middle Anglia. A broken urn found at the same time suggested a disturbed cremation interment.

Ashwell. Fibulae have been found on a site near the station. Beads and a fibula from Ashwell are in the Ransom collection.

J. Evans (1892, p. 257) mentions as Anglo-Saxon an "interment with ornamental bronze tag" at Hitchin. This doubtless refers to a burial on Willbury Hill, Norton; the belt tab found on "the middle of" the skeleton is in the Cambridge Museum, and is illustrated on Plate XXXIII. It is classical in design (showing oriental influence) and probably of late provincial-Roman workmanship. The cast and chased technique is that which the Teutonic peoples adopted; a similar tab from Ixworth is in the Ashmolean Museum.

PLATE XXXII

ANGLO-SAXON AGE. SEPULCHRAL POTTERY, AND SHIELD BOSSES, OF THE PAGAN PERIOD

Nos. 1, 3, pp. 273-4; No. 2, pp. 267, 274; No. 4 A, pp. 256, 276; No. 4 B, pp. 249, 276; No. 5, pp. 273, 281; No. 6, pp. 253, 273 (two refs.); No. 7, p. 293.

(d) East Bedfordshire and East Huntingdonshire; Cemeteries in the Great Ouse Valley

Shefford, Henlow, Langford, Astwick. These are comparatively unimportant. Two saucer brooches in the Cambridge Museum, from Shefford, indicate an inhumation interment. A small plain pot from "a field near Henlow" (British Museum) also suggests a burial. Of the associations of an axehead (francisca) from Langford in the Ransom collection, nothing is known. An inhumation cemetery at Astwick is fully attested (Ransom, 1886, p. 40); a sword, a shield boss, spearheads and a knife, which were found with skeletons, are now in the British Museum.

Sandy. That a cemetery existed in the parish is certain; it was apparently close to the foot of the spur on which Caesar's Camp is sited. R. A. Smith (1904, p. 184) has summarized the scanty information on the subject. Sepulchral vessels, some large, of cinerary urn type[1], others small, bowl-shaped with carinated shoulder[2], suggest cremation as well as inhumation burials. A magnificent urn in the Cambridge Museum (figured on Plate XXXI, 4, and previously by Battely, 1745, Tab. X, 2) is said to have been found with skeletons and the remains of wooden coffins. No grave-furniture, save a silver armlet in the Cambridge Museum, doubtfully attributed to Sandy, is recorded or preserved.

Eynesbury and St Neots. Similar obscurity shrouds two cemeteries six miles further down the valley, at Eynesbury and St Neots. The evidence is contained in a brief note by Gorham (1820, p. 12): "Fragments of...pottery are frequently turned up on Eynesbury Conygeer." "Urns of inferior workmanship have also been found on the same spot," Gorham continues, and he figures one of these latter found in 1816, the only survivor. This urn is in the Cambridge Museum, see Plate XXXII, 2. It is of smooth handmade well-baked red ware, decorated with punctured dots, and lines drawn with a blunt point. The lip is broken away. In decoration it is unlike any pottery hitherto known of our period, but in form it resembles certain Kentish wheelmade accessory vessels. Mr R. A. Smith thinks it "can hardly be anything but Anglian, about 500 A.D."

Gorham's narrative may now be resumed:

"Several urns, of nearly the same form and dimensions, but devoid of pattern, were found a few years since in St Neots...on the East side of

---

[1] In Camb. Mus., Brit. Mus. and Bedford Library.
[2] In Brit. Mus. Resembles many associated with inhumation burials in Cambridgeshire. See my Plate XXXII (6).

Huntingdon Street...The mouth of each urn was covered by a tile: it was not noticed whether bones or ashes were enclosed; but skeletons were dug up in the immediate neighbourhood."

It only remains to add that I have found no record of any grave-furniture of our period from St Neots or the neighbourhood.

NOTES ON CERTAIN GRAVE-GOODS SPECIALLY CHARACTERISTIC OF THE CAMBRIDGE REGION

Before examining the problems presented by the topographical distribution of the cemeteries, it is convenient to consider certain well-defined groups of objects specially characteristic of our Region. Those selected are cruciform, "small long," annular, and plate fibulae; girdle-hangers and clasps: and I add a brief note on the local pottery.

Saucer and applied brooches, equally important, have been discussed on pp. 254 and 251-2, and are again referred to in connection with the differentiation between Middle Anglia and the West Saxon area and between Middle and East Anglia (pp. 287 and 292).

Cruciform Fibulae. The lines of development of the cruciform fibula are perhaps better known than that of any other single form commonly met with in the cemeteries; here a few notes on local types, bearing on origins and evolution, will suffice[1].

Perhaps the most primitive form found in the district is from Mildenhall (Plate XXXIII, 1), which shows the beginnings of the horse-head terminal and in certain details resembles a Slesvig type (Brown, 1915, Plate xl, 2; compare also Schetelig, 1906, fig. 137). The long narrow horse-head met with in Hanoverian brooches is seen in two examples from the St John's cemetery (Plate XXXIII, 2): with these compare Salin (1904, figs. 434-5), from Hanover and Mecklenburg; and Mestorf (1885, fig. 589) from Borgstedt, Slesvig; a similar (broken) specimen comes from Dam Hill, Trumpington. These are undoubtedly among the earliest cruciform brooches found in Britain and attest the early date of the settlement in our district.

Of the next phase, that of the cruciform brooch proper, the district yields numerous examples. The Lakenheath specimen (Plate XXXIII, 3) is characteristic of a large group dating towards the close of V. It has lost its side-knobs.

The transition from the type with detached side-knobs to those in which the side-knobs are cast in one piece with the plate is in our district by no means well defined. Brown (1915, p. 261) suggests that the former date up to about 500 A.D.; but Plate XXVII shows an example from Haslingfield (No. 4) of *developed* type with detached

[1] See also p. 249, paras. 2, 3, and 257, para. 3.

PLATE XXXIII

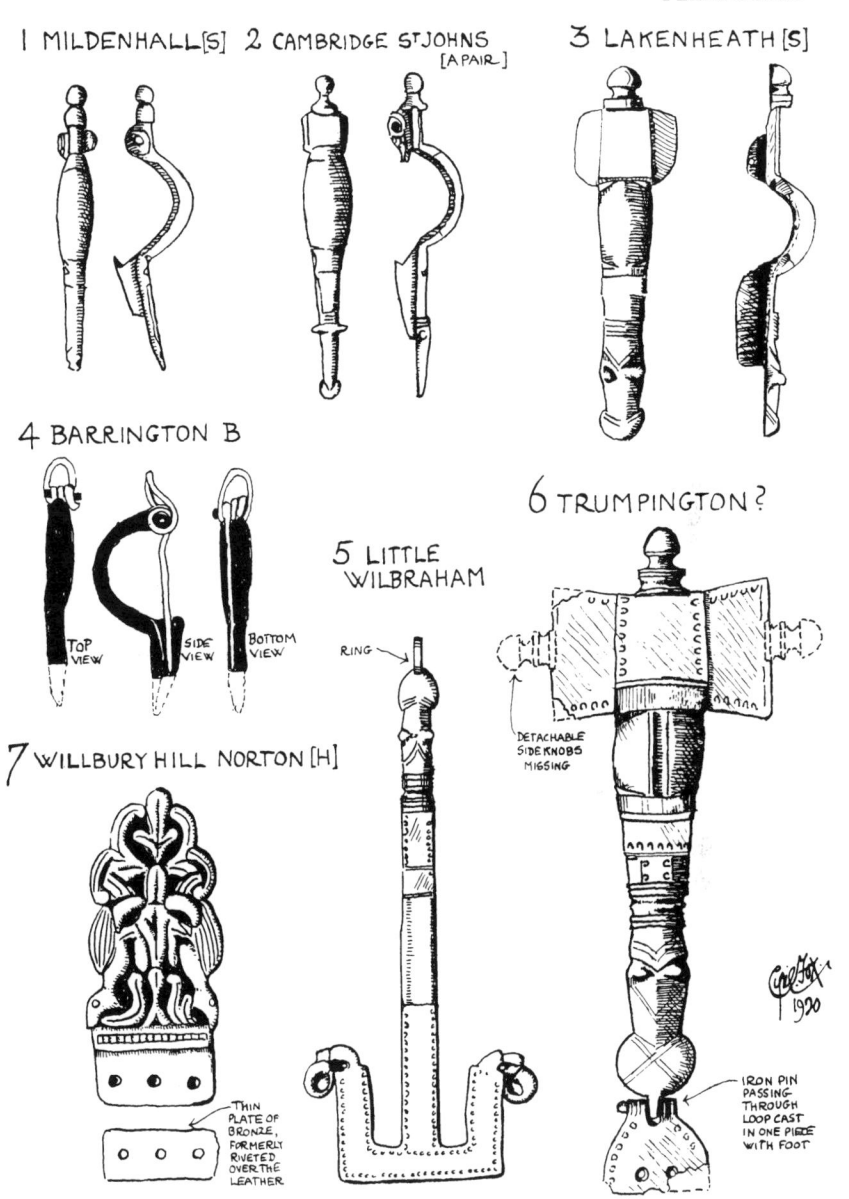

ANGLO-SAXON AGE. GRAVE-FURNITURE OF THE PAGAN PERIOD
[EXCEPT NO. 7, LATE PROVINCIAL-ROMAN]

All two-thirds actual size.

No. 1, pp. 268, 276; No. 2, pp. 243, 268, 276; No. 3, pp. 268, 276; No. 4, pp. 255, 281; No. 5, p. 271; No. 6, p. 249; No. 7, pp. 266, 272.

NOTE. The cruciform fibulae, Nos. 2, 3, have lost their side knobs.

side-knobs which cannot be earlier, one would suppose, than mid-VI. An early example with side-knobs cast on to the plate, from Trumpington, is figured on Plate XXIX, 5.

The weakness manifest in the former type was tentatively solved in one example in the Cambridge Museum, from Lakenheath, by affixing a half-knob to an extension of the plate.

It is important to notice, moreover, that the practice of casting the knobs in one piece with the plate could have been universal for a short period only; in several elaborate cruciform fibulae from N.W. Suffolk, dating in late VI or VII, the earlier method is reverted to, but the decorative adjuncts are *riveted* on the plate and are not as in early times an extension of the spring-bar (Plate XXIX, 3, 4).

The knobs of our cruciform fibulae are usually round or halfround; but polygonal knobs occur as on the early example from Girton (Plate XXXIV, 1). This is a feature of the Hanoverian brooch already referred to (Salin, 1904, fig. 434); it occurs also on Danish and Norwegian examples.

The early English cruciform brooches usually have the *terminal* knob cast in one piece with the head-plate; but an interesting pair of fibulae from the St John's cemetery, figured on Plate XXVII, 3, shows this knob as a separate feature (as in Salin, fig. 436, from Sweden, and Schetelig, figs. 30 and 31, from Slesvig and Norway). The former have in many details—such as the absence of facetting, and the rounded contours—un-English features; a similar bow-form is seen in Salin, No. 454, also from Sweden; and our brooch most probably belonged to late comers (between 470–500 A.D.) or is a trade importation. Leeds (1912, p. 180) figures a related example from Barrington A (Malton): fibulae with detached head-knobs from Wilbraham (Audley End Museum) and Tuddenham (Cambridge Museum) are also known.

The majority of the later cruciform fibulae of the Lark Valley and its neighbourhood (N.W. Suffolk) exhibit characters quite distinct from those found in the Cam Valley. The decoration is less restrained and the general appearance richer; it is indeed usually possible to differentiate at sight fibulae from these two areas. Compare Plate XXIX, No. 1, from Barrington B, with Nos. 2, 3 and 4 from Exning and Lakenheath. The variation is doubtless due to the existence of a political boundary, operating in restraint of trade (see p. 292).

"Small long" fibulae. This term, applied by Brown to a wellknown group of fibulae, examples of which are figured on Plate XXX (Nos. 5 to 8) and Plate XXXIV, 3 and 4, is very convenient, and has been adopted.

Salin (p. 74) noted that types commonly occurring in Slesvig are met with in our district, and a date in V may perhaps be assigned to Fig. 6 on Plate XXX. Square-headed brooches similar to those on the same plate from Girton (Fig. 5), moreover, were found with an early cruciform fibula with tanged head-knob at Wilbraham (Neville, 1852, Grave 143). The associations of the trefoil-headed types (Plate XXXIV, 3 and 4) show that they flourished throughout the greater part of VI in our district; a specially late example being that found in Grave 81, Wilbraham, with a debased cruciform fibula. The brooches with a "hammer" or Maltese-cross head, such as that figured on Plate XXX, No. 8, held by Salin to be typologically the earliest, also had a long life in our district; those on Plate XXIX, 1, for example, must date from the second half of VI.

A distinctive local form is that which has curved horns projecting from the upper angles of the head-plate. It is met with in Cam Valley and in Lark Valley cemeteries alike. Examples associated with clasps with "volute" decoration ("Barrington B," Camb.Mus.) may be dated in the second half of VI.

Annular fibulae. Those which consist of a flat ring of bronze, the upper surface of which shows simple geometric decoration, are exceedingly common in the district. A dozen examples from Lakenheath are in the Cambridge Museum; and four characteristic specimens are figured by Neville (1852, Plate 3), from Wilbraham.

The type has been held to date in V, and a pair in the St John's cemetery was associated with a harp-shaped Roman fibula; but it certainly survived well into VI, another pair in the same cemetery having been found with a cruciform fibula of developed type (Plate XXVII, No. 1); moreover, a pair in the Ashmolean Museum, from Grave No. 1, Mitchell's Hill, Icklingham, was associated with a cruciform fibula which on typological grounds might be assigned to late VI or early VII.

Plate Fibulae. A characteristic local form has the centre cut *à jour* to form a swastika. Wilbraham yielded two (Cambridge Museum and Audley End Museum); there is one in the Cambridge Museum from Barrington A, and one in the Ashmolean from Haslingfield. Evidence of date is provided by one only of these, from Wilbraham, associated in Grave 116 with a cruciform fibula of "Londesborough" type, presumably dating in the middle of VI (Neville, 1852, Plates 3 and 8). Others from the counties of Rutland, Huntingdon and Lincoln, are known. The design may have been introduced by invaders from Slesvig (see Mestorf, 1885, Plate xlii, fig. 499).

Two plate fibulae which show a cross as the central device, also cut à jour, were associated at Wilbraham (Neville, 1852, Grave 3) with a square-headed fibula showing very debased zöomorphic decoration which may be dated in VII; the occurrence of the symbol is significant, but it is, of course, improbable that the interment was other than pagan. Similar plate fibulae, from Haslingfield, are in the Ashmolean Museum.

Plate fibulae simply decorated with punched circles or geometrical patterns are very common. These are not necessarily of early date, as may be seen by the associated objects figured on Plate XXVII, No. 2.

No one, as yet, has worked out in detail the chronological range, or sequence of forms, of the key-shaped girdle-hanger and the clasp in Eastern England. Since these originated on English soil, such an analysis should prove of interest. It cannot be done in a limited area such as ours or in the space available in this treatise; but the following notes are relevant to the enquiry.

Girdle-hangers. The simplest forms are a close copy in bronze of the housewife's keys of iron (a Roman type), the possession of which they doubtless symbolized. An example from Barrington B (Cambridge Museum) may be cited. Such girdle-hangers are plain, or show punched decoration of the simplest character.

Stylization rapidly set in; a purely decorative form, such as that from Grave 158, Wilbraham, figured by Neville (1852, Plate 14), was associated with objects indicating a date in the first half of VI.

Occasionally the craftsman adopted motives derived from the cruciform fibula, as in the pleasing example from Wilbraham, found with beads and a Roman coin, and sketched on my Plate XXXIII. The simple zöomorphic terminals suggest that this is somewhat earlier than the group of objects including a girdle-hanger figured on Plate XXVII, 2, from Girton. The latter shows a moulded shaft of classical character and is one of three examples of such design met with in the district; the mouldings, being hand-wrought, not turned, are very irregular.

A similar pair of girdle-hangers from Grave 2, Mitchell's Hill, Icklingham, is in the Ashmolean. A pin with a similar moulded shaft from Barrington A is in the same museum.

Clasps. A wide variety of types is met with in the local cemeteries, and practically every technical process employed by "Anglian" craftsmen is utilized in their manufacture and decoration. Though clasps range widely in Eastern England, Brown (1915, p. 364) is no doubt correct in suggesting that they were chiefly made in the district of which Cambridgeshire is the centre.

The earliest type found locally which can be dated is that figured on Plate XXXIV, 1 A, from Girton. The association with the cruciform fibula with detached side-knobs (also figured) suggests it to be not later than 500[1]. The satisfying proportions of this clasp suggest classical influence, as does the character of the design; but, as we have seen (p. 248), the local Anglo-Saxon craftsman of, let us say, 500–550 A.D. is shown by many examples to have had a fine sense of form and to have exercised that restraint in the use of decoration which we usually describe as classical.

The type was popular in the district and numerous examples, from Barrington A and B, Wilbraham, Girton, Icklingham (Mitchell's Hill) and other cemeteries, dating probably in the first half of VI, are in the Cambridge and other Museums. The brooches figured on Plate XXXIV, 3 and 4, were associated with such clasps. That degradation should set in was inevitable; the associated find from Newnham Croft, Plate XXXIV, shows an example, probably dating from the second half of VI, illustrating this tendency.

Clasps made not of cast bronze chased, as in the group under consideration, but of sheet bronze, are also common. Some are plain, some show punched or embossed decoration. The example from "Cambridge" (Plate XXXIV, 7), with flowing phyllomorphic pattern and a border probably of provincial-Roman origin (seen on the Willbury Hill belt tab, Plate XXXIII) is in two parts, the upper plate being riveted on to a supporting plate, and may be early; unfortunately, nothing is known of its history. Others appear to cover the whole of the VI century; a characteristic series from Wilbraham is figured by Neville (1852, Plate 12).

The development of the clasp culminated in the splendid ornaments from Barrington B which have already been referred to (p. 254). Those showing a volute pattern and with separate triangular extensions have a wide range in our district, occurring, for example, at Barrington A and B, Lakenheath and West Stow (and at Rothwell, Northants.). The design in which the triangular plate is attached is met with at Haslingfield, Icklingham and Barrington B; the latter, figured on my Plate XXX, may be dated early in VII (see Brown, Plate lxxix, and p. 365).

[1] A plain bronze ring 4·4 inches in diameter accompanied the objects figured (Grave No. 7, Jenkinson MS.).

PLATE XXXIV

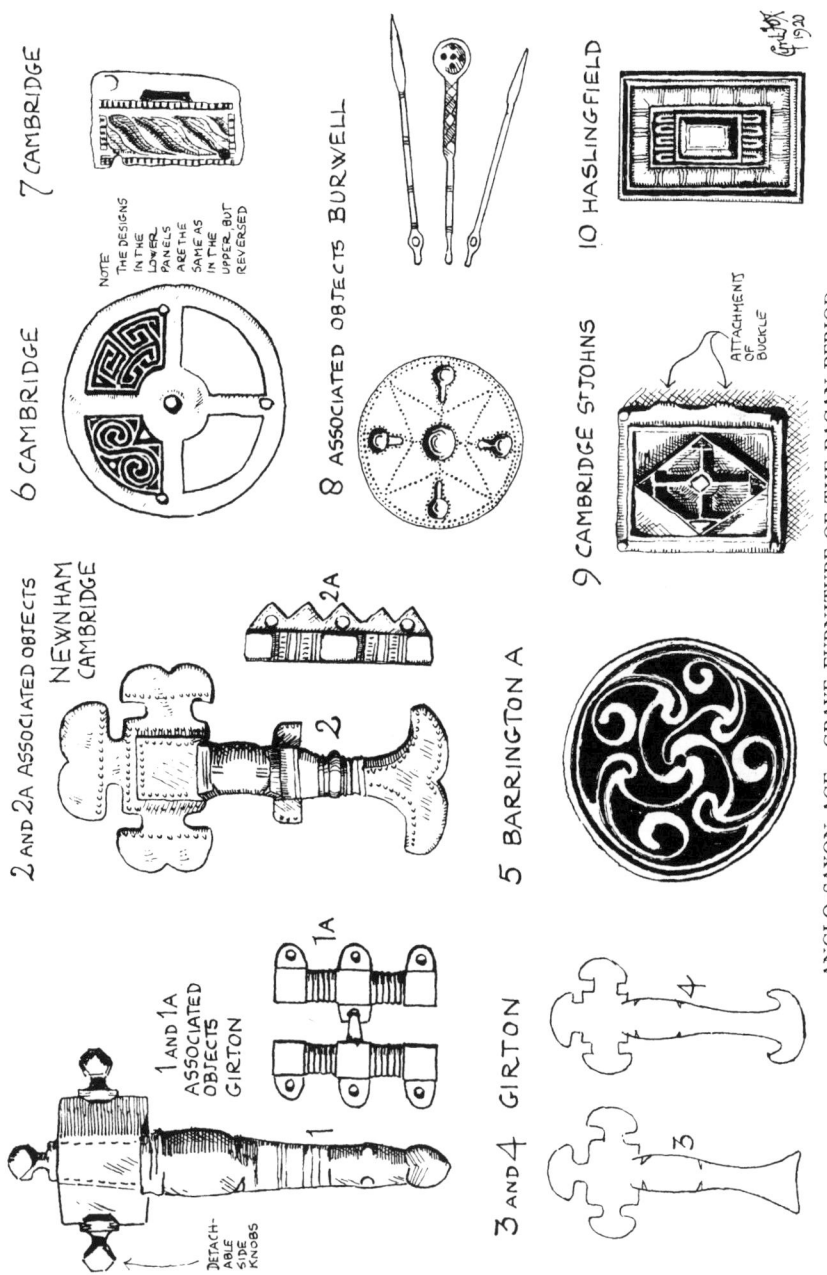

ANGLO-SAXON AGE. GRAVE-FURNITURE OF THE PAGAN PERIOD
[EXCEPT NO. 6, A BRONZE ORNAMENT OF THE CHRISTIAN PERIOD]

All two-thirds actual size [except Nos. 3 and 4, not to scale].

No. 1, pp. 248, 269, 272; No. 2, pp. 244, 272; Nos. 3 and 4, pp. 269, 270, 272; No. 5, pp. 252, 283; No. 6, p. 297; No. 7, pp. 272, 280 (footnote); No. 8, p. 262; No. 9, p. 243; No. 10, pp. 256, 280.

Pottery. The wide range of pottery forms found in the Cambridge region is that characteristic of East and Middle Anglian cemeteries. Such has been frequently described, and its Continental relationships are established.

The large and elaborately decorated vessels such as those figured on Plate XXXI, from Girton and Sandy, are, it would seem, almost invariably associated with burnt interments.

In addition to the ribbed and knobbed urns, and urns with stamped patterns, plain bowl- or jug-shaped vessels are not uncommonly used as cineraries. These may be domestic ware applied to sepulchral purposes.

Pots decorated in a similar manner undoubtedly occur with skeleton interments; but these are nearly always small bowls or beakers (see Plate XXXII, 6, from Barrington B), frequently with a carinated shoulder, and are readily distinguishable from the cremation urns. The position of these vessels—and the plain pots which serve a like purpose—conforms to ancient usage, such being placed by the head.

These small pots bear some resemblance to vessels found in Frankish graves. See Brown (1915, Plate cxxix), and compare my Plate XXXII, 5 and 6.

Small, plain, usually coarsely made cups or bowls with round bottoms, averaging about 3 inches in height, have been met with on many of our local sites—Linton, Wilbraham, Barrington A and B, St John's (Cambridge), Lakenheath, Mildenhall and Tuddenham [S]. These, like the small decorated vessels, appear usually to have accompanied unburnt interments. They are not confined to our district, but are perhaps commoner here than elsewhere. Examples from Northants. are figured by R. A. Smith (1909 c) who also notes their occurrence in Leicestershire and Rutland. One small porringer (2·5 inches high) was, at Girton, found with a baby's skeleton, and this may be the normal use. See, in this connection, H. Prigg (1888 a, pp. 60, 61 and 70).

Accessory vessels were in our district found by the heads of skeletons in Graves 56, 80, 93, Linton Heath; Graves 73 and 66, Barrington B. The situlae with bronze and iron mounts and the bronze vessels such as those figured by Neville (1852, Plate 16), probably served a like purpose—whatever that may have been—in the grave of the warrior.

The majority of the local urns have a slightly rounded or flat base but others have a moulded foot. These latter, Brown remarks (1915, p. 500), are more commonly met with in Continental cemeteries than in this country, and their occurrence in our district may be another mark of early settlement. Such urns are of special interest, for several which have "cordons" above the shoulder are very similar to La Tène urns of I A.D.; and it seems not improbable that these may represent a definite survival of La Tène motives among peoples only indirectly in contact with Roman culture (see my Plate XXXII, Nos. 1 and 3, and p. 94).

Vessels which do not conform to the normal range of types are rare. The Eynesbury vase (p. 267, and Plate XXXII) is an outstanding example, as is the wheelmade vessel from Lakenheath, figured on the same plate, which is of Frankish type and doubtless imported[1]. It was bought in 1897 together with a quantity of grave-goods of typical Anglian character from a cemetery near Lakenheath, the site of which has never been made known. Enquiry at the time of purchase elicited the information that three brooches, described as "plain cruciform, small plain square-headed and square-headed with ornamental base," were associated with it; these are also in the collection, but, unfortunately, cannot now be identified. The evidence, such as it is, suggests that the vessel was associated with an inhumation burial of normal character.

TOPOGRAPHICAL DISTRIBUTION OF THE CEMETERIES AND FINDS

All save two of the cemeteries are situated in river valleys[2], or on the edge of or in the fens. They are most numerous in the Lark Valley (N.W. Suffolk) and its immediate neighbourhood, and in the Cam Valley from Cambridge to Barrington; in these two areas, indeed, the villages must have been as numerous as they are to-day.

In Chapter II it was shown (p. 24) that the local distribution of the characteristic pottery suggested that the beaker-folk, at the close of the III millennium B.C., entered our district from overseas *via* the Wash and the fen rivers. The general distribution of the Anglo-Saxon settlements in the pagan period points (as has been fully recognized) to a similar conclusion; a conclusion which is in this case buttressed by evidence of similar character from all parts of Eastern England, and by the known position of the Continental homes of the invaders, which rendered this channel of entry into Southern Cambridgeshire the natural one. If the distribution of beakers (30 in number) and of Anglo-Saxon burial sites (about 50 in all) be compared—on Maps II and V—the correspondence will be seen to be singularly close, the only marked difference being the greater mass of Anglo-Saxon settlement on the River Cam near Cambridge. This correlation between phenomena over two thousand years apart in

---

[1] See R. A. Smith (1911, p. 344). Similar vases from Kent and Essex are on record [De Baye (1893, Plate XVI, fig. 6) and R. A. Smith (1903, p. 323)].

[2] Girton, on a knoll 1¾ miles from the River Cam, and King's Walden, 4 miles S. of Hitchin, are the exceptions.

THE ANGLO-SAXON AGE

time, attests the dominance of the influence exerted by the geography and superficial geology of a given district on primitive man's activities. This is a trite fact, but it is perhaps seldom that its truth is so signally demonstrated. For it is to be remembered that the Anglo-Saxon settlers did not enter as did the beaker-folk a countryside wellnigh virgin; Southern Cambridgeshire had been for five hundred years largely an agricultural district, and the *apparent* range of choice of sites for habitation must have been immeasurably wider.

The limitation of burial sites of our period to the most fertile parts of the district suggests further speculations of some interest. Since not less than fifty such sites are known, and the distribution is thus strictly limited, it may be inferred that the expansion of Anglo-Saxon settlement resulting in occupation practically of the entire district before 1066 (see Map V, and p. 307) is almost entirely a development of the Christian period, mid-VII to mid-XI. If this be conceded, then the numerous "-hams," the "-inghams" and the "-ings" in our forest districts, the which are usually held to be a mark of early settlement, may not be earlier than the second half of VII. The problem of the origin of such villages is, however, a complex one; it concerns the English settlement as a whole, and cannot profitably be discussed in a survey dealing with a limited area.

The limitation of Anglo-Saxon settlement in a district necessarily one of the first to be overrun, and settled, as we shall see, at an early date—certainly in V—confirms the general opinion as to the small numbers of the invaders. The most favourable areas offered, it is evident, an ample field for the agricultural activities of the original settlers and their descendants, during a period of two hundred years.

In the previous chapter it was pointed out that the establishment of a bridge (or paved ford) and causeway at Cambridge, with roads leading thereto from four directions, ensured the permanence of the Castle site as the most important in the countryside. The truth of this is fully demonstrated by the number and importance of the Cambridge cemeteries. Traces of the beaker-folk are found on the outskirts of Cambridge at Barnwell and at Chesterton; but the evidences of Anglo-Saxon occupation in the pagan period are chiefly in the immediate neighbourhood of the Roman town and bridge. Thus early, then, in the subsequent history of this district did the influence of the Roman genius make itself felt.

THE DATE AND MODE OF THE ANGLO-SAXON SETTLEMENT

The early date of the settlement in our district has been incidentally referred to, and most of the evidence detailed in the description of the cemeteries; it may here be summarized.

There is ample evidence, in the presence of early cruciform fibulae (such as those figured on Plate XXXIII, 1 and 3, from Mildenhall and Lakenheath), in the abundance of flat annular fibulae and of small long fibulae of early types, that N.W. Suffolk was occupied in V. Cruciform fibulae such as those from Trumpington (p. 249) and St John's (Plates XXXIII, 2, and XXVII, 3); pots with glass in their bases from Girton and Haslingfield (Plate XXXII, 4), and equal-armed fibulae—two with Romanizing ornament—from Wilbraham, Newnham and Haslingfield (Frontispiece, 1); early small long fibulae from the Barrington cemeteries and many other objects show that settlement in the Cam Valley at and near Cambridge was equally early. That settlement before the end of V extended up the Bourn River Valley to Linton is highly probable; but of the date of the settlements at Chesterford and Wenden on the banks of the Essex Cam we have no evidence. The recorded finds in the upper (Ivel) valley of the Great Ouse are not markedly early, but are too scanty to permit any conclusion to be drawn as to the date of settlement in this area. The urn found lower down the river at Eynesbury has been dated by Mr R. A. Smith at about 500 A.D. (p. 267). The only burial on a fen island of which detailed record survives, at Chatteris, is of the late VI century.

That the Lark and Cam Valleys were occupied contemporaneously and probably nearer 450 than 500 A.D., is in accord with the evidence; contemporaneity is a natural result of the use by the invaders of the fen rivers as highways (see Map H, p. 285).

I have had occasion to make use of Gray's valuable paper on "The Dual Origin of the Town of Cambridge" (1908). Working backwards from known facts he concludes that late in the VI or early in the VII century the Mercians and East Anglians faced each other at Cambridge, the one on the left the other on the right bank of the river. So far his arguments are convincing (though for Mercians we perhaps might more accurately read Middle Angles); but when in the following words he leads me into the still earlier period in which we are groping I must part company with him:

"South-eastern Cambridgeshire and the fen country about Ely were occupied at a later date" [than the settlements of the East Anglians in Norfolk and Suffolk, perhaps completed before 500 A.D.]. "When the East

Anglian colonists had advanced as far as Cambridge they found their progress barred by Mercians who had entered the district from the region of Huntingdonshire and Northamptonshire. The settlement of the southern parts of the county by the two peoples was completed before the end of the 6th century" (p. 23). No support is rendered to this argument by archaeological evidence. The river system is the key by which the history of settlement can be unlocked. The valley of the Cam was settled as early as the valley of the Lark, *i.e.* in V; and that colonization in Cambridgeshire came across country from west and east meeting on the line of the river at some date in VI is, I venture to think, directly opposed to the archaeological evidence. The facts on which Gray's induction is based are, I hold, the result of political developments subsequent to the settlement (see p. 295).

It is well recognized that early cruciform and small long brooches, and cremation urns from Anglian districts such as ours have close counterparts in Slesvig cemeteries such as Borgstedt, and that connection with the district between the Weser and the Elbe is also manifest, mainly in respect to pottery forms. Certain exceptional objects found in Southern Cambridgeshire—equal-armed fibulae, and "window-urns"—have their only Continental parallels in the latter area (Leeds, 1913, p. 91). It is probable that the great majority of our early settlers came from these regions; and that the radiating fibulae and other early objects of Frankish and Rhineland provenance are evidences of trade rather than of Frisian settlement in Cambridgeshire.

It is generally held that the Anglo-Saxon conquest was marked, as was the Danish invasion of 866, by two phases: plundering raids (in which the invaders must have left their ships and taken to the roads) followed, after an interval, by colonization. The inhumation interment in a barrow on Therfield Heath, accompanied by a V-century buckle, and the Willbury Hill burial (p. 266) may be relics of the earlier phase. Both are strictly on the line of the Icknield Way.

CREMATION AND INHUMATION

The cemeteries of the district are predominantly inhumation, but cremation was practised on several sites and there is evidence that both rites date from the settlement in V[1]. On the one hand, the "window-urn" found at Girton was a cremation urn; and the close resemblance afforded by many other East Anglian examples to Con-

---

[1] It may here be noted that there is no indication in the cemeteries of our district of small tumuli marking the sites of the graves; one *primary* inhumation burial in a hill barrow (Allington Hill) is known, and the Warren Hill (Mildenhall), and Linton Heath cemeteries partially or entirely occupy the burial mounds of earlier peoples.

tinental cremation urns establishes close chronological relationship. On the other hand, the numerous cruciform and other fibulae of V date found in the district certainly came from inhumed burials. In those cemeteries where cremation was practised it appears to have been carried on for a long period side by side with inhumation. No fully explored cemetery in the district is exclusively a cremation cemetery. The significance of the contemporaneous occurrence in our district (as elsewhere) of the two rites may be better appreciated by consideration of the distribution of the cemeteries wherein cremation occurs.

There are five such cemeteries. These are, in Cambridgeshire, at Cambridge itself [the St John's cemetery (30 skeletons, 100 urns), its annexe on the Grange Road, and probably the River Cam site, Newnham, and Rose Crescent], at Girton (80 skeletons, 130 urns) and at Little Wilbraham (188 skeletons, 121 urns). In north-west Suffolk—the Lark Valley—West Stow Heath and Lackford have yielded "several" or "many" cremation burials.

There are also sites, such as Barrington B, where the sporadic occurrence of cremation is proven; sites imperfectly recorded, which have each yielded from one to three vessels of cremation-urn type—Chesterford [E], Haslingfield, Hauxton, Sandy [B], Tuddenham [S], Culford [S], King's Walden [H][1]. These may for the moment be omitted from consideration.

The well-attested cremation cemeteries are marked ("C") on the map. Both in the Lark Valley and in the Cam Valley they are seen to form well-defined groups indicative of contiguous settlement; in the former the cemeteries are within two miles of each other, in the latter nine miles separate those furthest apart. In the neighbourhood of each group are cemeteries wherein none but inhumation burials are recorded.

These facts seem to me to suggest when considered in relation to the proved early date of inhumation burial, and to the evidence of the two rites being practised for prolonged periods in the same cemetery, that in the group of invaders—under one military leadership, as one may suppose—who settled in the Lark Valley, or the Cam Valley, some practised one rite, some the other[2]; that those who practised cremation tended to segregate, and to settle down on adjacent holdings;

[1] Reference to the Eynesbury and St Neots cemeteries is omitted on account of the inadequacy of the evidence as to their date and character.

[2] In Denmark, and the Danish islands, both rites are known to have been in use in the V century; and there is evidence in our grave-furniture that elements from further north than Slesvig settled in our district.

PLATE XXXV

1 GIRTON

2 GIRTON

3 WESTLEY WATERLESS

4 WEST STOW [S]

ANGLO-SAXON AGE. GRAVE-FURNITURE OF THE PAGAN PERIOD [EXCEPT NO. 3, A LEADEN VESSEL OF THE CHRISTIAN PERIOD]
The scale applicable to the Girton finds is in inches.
No. 1, pp. 247–8; No. 2, pp. 247, 279; No. 3, p. 300; No. 4, p. 281.

that the bond of tradition and a natural conservatism tended to perpetuate the older burial rite in the group area thus formed, but that among the settlers in a given district the lack of any powerful religious motive and the general tendency of the age towards inhumation, prevented its becoming exclusive. The sporadic occurrence of cremation in other cemeteries in the district mentioned on the previous page would naturally result from intermarriage.

It has been remarked that the two rites were carried on side by side in the same cemetery for a prolonged period. When did cremation cease in the district?

It is on historical grounds improbable that cremation survived into the VII century in *Eastern* England. For example, there is no mention of cremation in any ecclesiastical document promulgated in England; its practice is not forbidden. The inference is that it had gone out of use when Augustine landed in 597. And, again, in the poem of Beowulf, which many believe to be in the main of pre-Christian origin, all references to heathen gods have been eliminated. Detailed accounts of cremation, on the other hand, have been allowed to stand; and it may fairly be assumed that such references were not an offence in the ears of converts and their priests; the rite had been forgotten[1].

Leeds (1913, p. 74), however, brings forward archaeological evidence for cremation in VII. Of the two instances of so late a use of the rite cited by him, one is at Girton; consideration of the point is thus relevant to our enquiry, but it will be confined to the local evidence.

From Mr Jenkinson's MS. account of the Girton excavations, p. 19, the following notes are taken:

"Ap. 7. From a shattered urn the workmen produced some remarkable pieces of ornamental bronze."

"1. Half of a brooch, a paste in the centre, a ring on the back on which the pin probably hinged."

2. Half a rectangular plaque of similar ornament and technique.

These objects, part respectively of a saucer and a square-headed fibula, are figured on Plate XXXV, 2. A third piece of bronze (possibly part of another saucer brooch which had suffered much from the action of the fire) was included in the deposit.

Both fibulae show zöomorphic ornament (Salin, Style I) of degenerate character; the square-headed fibula, in addition, has a panel of geometric incised decoration. I cannot agree that these —they must be considered together—are *necessarily* later than the

---

[1] These arguments I owe to Professor Chadwick.

second half of VI. That cremation was practised then in the district there is further evidence. Fragments probably of elaborate cruciform fibulae which have passed through the fire, also from Girton, are preserved in the College Library, and two examples from Little Wilbraham are recorded and figured by Neville, 1852, Plate 11.

INFLUENCE OF THE ROMAN CIVILIZATION ON THE ANGLO-SAXON SETTLERS

It would *a priori* seem hardly possible that the arts and crafts of a primitive people coming suddenly into possession of the material apparatus of a high civilization should fail to be influenced thereby. That provincial-Roman art had on the Continent an important influence on Teutonic art (which was partly La Tène in origin) is well known; and it might have been expected that the art and craftsmanship of our semi-barbarous immigrants, cut off by the sea from the traditions of their homeland, would by contact with Romano-British civilization have been further modified if not entirely changed.

The determination of the extent to which such influences operated is extremely difficult. It is a problem which affects the whole country, and it cannot adequately be dealt with on the basis of a limited district. The prevailing view is that the culture of the invaders was not markedly modified by the Roman civilization in Britain, such elements of that civilization as the grave-furniture reveals being mainly acquired prior to the invasion, or derived subsequently from France.

Detailed examination of objects of the pagan period which were probably made in the Cambridge Region reveals, it must be admitted, but little evidence[1] of the influence of Roman art and technique other than that which has properly been assigned to Continental sources; the most markedly classical objects met with, the belt ornaments from Haslingfield (Plate XXXIV, 10), can hardly be of local manufacture[2].

The geometric patterns and scrolls seen on certain saucer and applied fibulae in our district are perhaps the most important evidence of Romano-British influence, as Leeds (1912, p. 174) has recognized; he gives reasons for supposing that these designs originated in the West Saxon area; none, it is probable, developed in the Cambridge Region. Penannular fibulae, undoubtedly of Roman (or La Tène) origin, are not common in our district.

---

[1] The girdle-hanger on Plate XXVII, the bronze ring on Plate XXIX, 1, and possibly the clasp on Plate XXXIV, 7, may be regarded as showing such influence. The handle on Plate XXIX, 1, is probably a Roman survival. See example from Canterbury, figured on p. 358 of vol. XXI, *Proc. Soc. Antiq.*

[2] These are Teutonic (Gothic) in form; but the decoration is purely classical.

Two fibulae of some interest, both undoubtedly V century, and closely related to provincial-Roman originals are figured as exceptional. The one of bronze, from the West Stow cemetery (Plate XXXV, 4) shows, in the high bow, the transverse mouldings at the base thereof, and the ring for chain attachment at the head, provincial-Roman features. This ring is cast in the same plane as the bow doubtless for technical reasons (the Roman fashion is seen in the fibula on Plate XXX, from Girton). The other fibula, of iron with a bronze pin and with a ring formed by the loop of the wire spring, was found in Grave 47 (Foster) at Barrington B. The construction is very primitive, as the diagrams show (Plate XXXIII, 4).

Though the invaders were settled in V at Cambridge, probably in the Roman town itself, the only well-marked trace of their predecessors in the grave-furniture at St John's is the presence of loot; Roman fibulae and coins. Girton, where a Roman building of some importance must have stood, presents similar evidence.

The evidence afforded by the pottery is most striking. There is no indication of the use of the wheel, or of Roman technique in manufacture, in any one of the hundreds of vessels from local cemeteries —save one: and that is doubtless a Frankish importation (Plate XXXII, 5).

Hughes was, however, inclined to consider that though for sepulchral purposes the Anglo-Saxons adhered to traditional methods in the manufacture of their pottery, they used ware of Roman character for domestic purposes. He thought it probable that much of the common "Romano-British" ware found locally unassociated with finer Roman wares might belong to the Anglo-Saxon period. He suggested, to take a concrete example, that the manufacture of pottery at Horningsea was not discontinued, but that the wares produced there became modified eventually into the familiar mediaeval pottery of our laystalls and ditches. He based this theory on his frequent discoveries in excavations in the town of Cambridge of "Roman" pottery in intimate stratigraphical association with "early mediaeval" pottery. Such ware, in such association, he called "Romano-English"; and the corollary is that when the pottery débris of Anglo-Saxon settlements is from time to time discovered it is not recognized as such but is described as Roman.

The importance of Hughes' theory—which must be studied in his papers (esp. 1893, 1902 and 1907 *b*)—is obvious. He regarded it as a "line of enquiry along which there is most hope of finding the true explanation of the supposed scarcity of domestic pottery of

Saxon age." The theory can only be tested afresh, as opportunity arises, by excavation, and I can neither confirm nor disprove it by direct observation; but all the indirect evidence known to me which bears on the problem tends to discredit Hughes' solution, attractive and reasonable as it undoubtedly is.

It would thus appear that the influence of the Romano-British civilization on the arts and crafts of the invaders in the Cambridge Region was almost negligible. But there is no doubt that a case could be made out for the opposite view, though its presentation is hampered by imperfect knowledge of the range in form and decoration of articles of use and ornament at the close of the Roman period in this country.

It is a mark of the barbarian that he applies objects of civilized use to ornamental purposes; the Scandinavian bracteate is a case in point. The Anglian girdle-hanger may be the Roman key similarly employed and consequently modified. The characteristic plate and annular fibulae, moreover, may be derived from Romano-British models.

The question as to whether elements of the Romano-British population survived in the district is important in this connection, and we have some evidence suggesting an answer in the affirmative. (i) The basic elements of many of our Cambridgeshire place-names —*Trump*-ington and *Mad*-ingley may be cited—can hardly, Professor Chadwick tells me, be Teutonic in origin.

(ii) H. E. Smith describes "debased Roman-British wares"—Roman in form but coarse and friable—found in 1876 on the site of the Walden cemetery (see p. 266). Such may have been produced by elements of the conquered people in the less accessible areas of Eastern England subsequent to the conquest. The loss of the potter's wheel, among other civilized arts and crafts, is not necessarily incompatible with survival, in poverty and on sufferance, of erstwhile civilized groups.

(iii) That Celtic-speaking elements survived in the population of the fens into early VIII is to be inferred from a passage in Felix's *Life of St Guthlac*; the saint in Crowland was disturbed by demons in the likeness of Britons whose "strident speech" he had learnt when in exile.

See Gray (1911, pp. 45 ff.) for an analysis of this and other evidence of like character.

(iv) Again, in the rules of the Thanes Guild at Cambridge (X century) the amount of compensation to be paid by each guild-brother for the slaughter of a "twelfhyndeman," a "ceorl," and a

"Welshman" respectively is laid down; this implies the presence of Celtic-speaking elements in the neighbourhood.

See Thorpe (1865, p. 612). But too much stress must not be laid on this; the phraseology may have been taken over direct from Wessex.

It is, then, significant that the use of enamel on cruciform and square-headed fibulae is in this country practically confined to the eastern borders of the fens—Lakenheath and the Lark Valley, Wilbraham, and Linton. It is reasonable to regard the art of enamelling here as a Romano-British survival.

An enamelled fibula, from Lakenheath, is figured on Plate XXIX, 3. The examples from Wilbraham are in Graves Nos. 28 and 40; at Linton in Graves Nos. 21, 32 and 39.

There is evidence of the superimposition of Anglo-Saxon settlements on Roman sites in the Cambridge Region. Apart from Cambridge itself, Roman houses at Litlington, Bartlow, Wymondley [H] and Stansted [E] are sited in or immediately adjacent to the Anglo-Saxon village nucleus. But this is not necessarily to be regarded as evidence of continuity; it may be merely a result of the operation of economic laws (see p. 307). Not every Romano-British site in the lowlands was, however, re-occupied: in what are now the open fields between Chesterton and Milton, for example, abundant traces of a pre-Saxon settlement have been demonstrated.

Evidence of the use by the pagan Anglo-Saxons of the burial sites of their predecessors is available. Roman burials (and a disturbed Bronze Age burial) were discovered in the cemetery at Girton, and Roman burials in the Haslingfield cemetery. The Anglian burial at Shefford was immediately adjacent to a Roman cemetery. This continuity has been noticed in many parts of the country.

RECURRENCE OF LA TÈNE ART

What is more unexpected than a Romano-British reflex is the recurrence of La Tène art. In the Cambridge Museum is a disc of bronze, formerly enamelled, found in the Barrington A cemetery[1]. The C-scrolls, which form its decoration, reproduce the work of the earlier age as represented in our district by the Santon Downham plaques, *circa* 50 A.D. These scrolls are, however, not set out truly, as may be seen in the drawing on Plate XXXIV; the enamel, moreover, has completely perished, and was therefore of an inferior quality. The disc probably decorated the base of a bronze bowl, the type of

---

[1] A second disc, from Barrington A (Edix Hill), is in Sir A. Evans' collection. It is possibly from the same bowl; but I have not examined it.

which is now well known, as a result of the researches of J. R. Allen (1898) and R. A. Smith (1909 b). Typologically our disc would appear to be one of the earliest examples met with; it shows no trace of the close spirals which occur on examples such as that from Chesterton-on-Fossway, or in MSS. of late VII, such as the Book of Durrow. A late VI date is not improbable; early VI date not impossible.

The well-known escutcheons and mounts of a bronze bowl found at Mildenhall bear a much less close resemblance in design to La Tène originals, showing debased palmette and other classical elements; the date cannot at present be determined, but the early VII century is probable. These are in the Cambridge Museum, and have been figured and described by R. A. Smith (1909 b, p. 75).

The escutcheons of some bronze bowls are heart-shaped. Of this form is an example from Lakenheath with phyllomorphic decoration which Brown (1915, Plate ix, 4, p. 107, and p. xviii) considers early (V century), comparing with it the decoration of a bronze fragment from Hanover illustrated by Salin (fig. 408). The similarity is certainly striking. Our example has no hook and ring attachment, as have the disc-shaped escutcheons, but is hinged; and it may have belonged to a different type of vessel, as may escutcheons with decorations of birds with spread wings from Wangford and Barton (? Haslingfield).

The Wangford escutcheon shows pellets filling up the vacant spaces of the design, and closely resembles in this respect a sceat coin found at or near Cambridge dating from about 650. The vessel to which the Wangford hinge belonged may thus be of the Christian period. Compare Brown (1915, Plate ix, No. 1) with J. Evans (1894, Plate II, No. 3).

That such vessels, when they show La Tène ornament, were manufactured in the British Isles is certain; but Conway (1918, p. 83) reminds us that the hanging bowl is of eastern and ecclesiastical origin, and some of the later examples, found in Kent, and showing the Christian symbol, may have been imported.

There is no reason to suppose that the recurrence of La Tène design is in any way connected with the possible survival of Romano-Britons in our district; so unbroken a tradition could only have survived through four centuries of Romanization in some part of the British Isles where Roman civilization did not penetrate.

SAXONS AND ANGLES

The theory formulated by Chadwick that there is no national or racial difference between Saxons and Angles in England, with its implications, has been stated on p. 238. We may now consider to

THE ANGLO-SAXON AGE 285

what extent it is supported by the archaeological evidence. The cultural characteristics which differentiate the Middle Angles from the West Saxons and East Saxons require attention, as do the relations between Middle and East Angles.

That the line of demarcation between Middle Anglia and its neighbours on the west and south is approximately that of the watershed of the Cam-Ouse-Nene basin is recognized. Within the basin thus

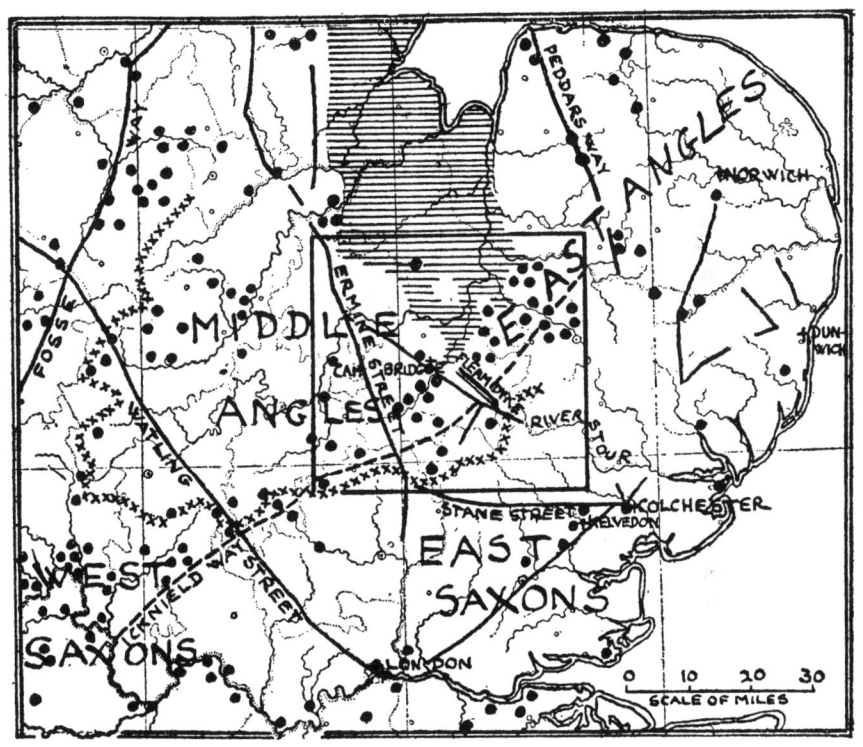

SKETCH MAP H. *The Anglo-Saxon Age.* Showing (1) Distribution of cemeteries [•] in East and Middle Anglia and their borders. Based on Brown (1915). (2) The Watershed of the Cam-Ouse-Nene-Welland basin thus: × × × × × × ×. (3) The Icknield Way and the Fleam Dyke. (4) Surviving sections of the more important Roman Roads.

defined (see Map H, above) the culture as a whole is uniform. Large square-headed, cruciform, saucer, applied, annular and small long fibulae, wrist-clasps and girdle-hangers are normal, and cremation is not uncommon.

(A) WEST SAXONS AND MIDDLE ANGLES

The traditional view of the significance of such cultural differences as exist between Middle Anglian and West Saxon districts has recently been restated by Brown (1915, p. 626), who may be quoted as giving a convenient summary of the position. While surrendering "the two old-established criteria, cremation and the saucer brooch" and admitting that "in patterns of funereal pottery, in florid square-headed brooches, in arms, in vessels and numerous other objects substantial differences are not to be discerned," he holds that "the cruciform brooches, the wrist clasps, and the girdlehangers, abundant on one side of the line" (separating West Saxon from Middle Anglian) "but so sparingly represented, if represented at all, on the other do furnish us with very distinct differentiae between the two regions and races."

That they differentiate between the two regions, is admitted. That they are evidence of racial divergence, cannot, I think, be established.

We may consider the cruciform brooch first of all. It is well known that in the cemeteries of the Saxon areas where V century settlement is apparent, early forms of the cruciform brooch occur, though rarely. On the Upper Thames, for example, they are found in the cemeteries of East Shefford and Reading (Brown, 1915, pp. 650 and 644). Fig. 6 on Plate xli, from the former cemetery, in Brown's corpus may be cited as being as typical an "Anglian" brooch of early VI as could be found in the Cambridge Region. These are usually regarded as "borrowed" culture elements; but the possibility that "West Saxon" and "Angle" alike had at the time of the settlement the cruciform brooch cannot be excluded. Maintenance of contact with Scandinavia may account for its popularity, and development, in the Anglian area.

There remain the wrist-clasp and the girdle-hanger. Now these objects so far from providing support for the theory of racial differences between Angle and Saxon are directly opposed thereto; since both are developments on English soil. They, in fact, tend to establish the truth of the theory under review, which regards such differences as exist between Angle and Saxon as being due to the isolation, partial or complete, of group settlements within defined geographical boundaries.

It has already been noted that there is one group of objects common to the West Saxon area and to Middle Anglia, rare or absent elsewhere; this is the saucer brooch and its variant, the applied brooch.

This is a striking fact; and it must be examined in relation to the dictum that the convergence or divergence in cultural characters of adjacent group areas, is, other factors being equal, determined by the extent to which facilities for intercommunication exist or are lacking.

The distribution of the saucer and applied brooches in these regions has been worked out by Leeds (1912), and since all the facts are accessible it is only necessary to note that such brooches commonly occur on the Upper Thames and the Warwickshire Avon on the one side of the divide; and on the other side are numerous on the upper waters of the Cam, the Ouse, and the Nene. Elsewhere they occur sporadically. In the Middle Anglian area, then, they are most numerous in the cemeteries closest to the West Saxon area.

We must first enquire whether any facilities for intercommunication exist between the two districts to account for this distribution. The Icknield Way affords a direct route from the Upper Cam to the Upper Thames Valley, and its existence may explain the close similarities between the earlier saucer and applied fibulae in these valleys. The use of this natural highway by the V century raiders is more than probable; and it may incidentally be noted that this would explain the exceptionally early character of certain finds in the Upper Thames Valley—at Dorchester, for example.

The invasion of Loðbròk's sons in IX offers a close parallel; the Danish army rode from East Anglia to Reading in the spring of 871, evidently by the Icknield Way. *A.S.C.* Laud MS. (E), Earle and Plummer (1892), p. 71.

It may, however, be urged that saucer and applied brooches are common to Middle Anglian and West Saxon areas further north, areas which could not be affected by the existence of the Icknield Way route. The districts in question are the Upper Avon (West Saxon) and the Upper Nene (Anglian). The divide between these two rivers approximately delimits on Leeds' map the respective "tribal" areas.

This divide is composed of Jurassic rocks, and along it, in this sector, the Foss Way runs. It was probably fairly open country; hence the watershed between these two rivers might be easily crossed, and intercommunication readily established.

The strongest argument against the theory we are testing is the absence of an "Anglian reflex" on the line of the Icknield Way in the Upper Thames Valley. No *late* cruciform brooches, girdle-hangers or clasps have, so far as I can ascertain, been found in this region;

and in the absence of a satisfactory explanation for this, the theory cannot be considered established. Such a reflex is, however, well marked in the Upper Avon Valley, where Anglian forms occur with some frequency (Brown, 1915, pp. 667 f.).

If the 571 A.D. entry in the Chronicle (MSS. Ā and E, Earle and Plummer (1892, pp. 18–19)) relating to "Bedcanford" or "Biedcanford" can be accepted as referring to Bedford, we have an explanation, consistent with Chadwick's theory, of the absence of VI century Anglian forms in the Thames Valley, and for the development of the applied fibula on independent lines in Southern Cambridgeshire. We may suppose that the Icknield Way route, open in V, was closed in VI owing to the presence of Britons at Bedford. But the existence of an Anglo-Saxon cemetery close to Bedford (Kempston) indicating peaceful settlement here during VI renders it very unlikely that this identification is correct. There is no early evidence to support it. Oman (1913, p. 230) considers that the entry relates not to Britons but to Teutons hostile to the West Saxons. In any case the context suggests that Bedcanford is a crossing-place on the Thames, not the Ouse.

Leeds has attacked the problem (1913, p. 81). He considers it possible that a Saxon tribe originally in possession of parts of Middle Anglia had been dispossessed by a subsequent invasion of a tribe or tribes of Angles; and he suggests that the cemeteries furthest to the west (in the Anglian area), where the Saxon brooch occurs most frequently, may be those of parts of the tribe retreating before the new immigrants. All this is very hypothetical, and the solution of the problem of the distribution of saucer and applied brooches which it presents cannot be regarded as final.

(B) Middle Angles and East Saxons

The relations between the Middle Anglian region of Cambridgeshire and the East Saxon district may now be examined. Here we have no natural channels of communication of importance, and wide expanses of forest-bearing clay lands, which we have seen reason to suppose would rapidly recover their natural impassability, divide the few known cemetery sites on the coast of Essex from our Cam Valley cemeteries. We have, however, means of communication which may in some measure have taken the place of natural routes; to wit, a number of Roman roads. So far as I am aware, no study of the breaks in continuity of Roman roads in relation to the boundaries of Anglo-Saxon kingdoms has been made: but if there be any truth in the theory under consideration in this chapter, the isolation of the settlement areas which crystallized into kingdoms should be thus traceable; and the continuity of Roman roads across such boundaries, if it is anywhere demonstrable, must be of historical importance.

That the break-down of the Roman system of communications took place mainly in the V and VI centuries will not be doubted. It may be regarded as certain that throughout the historical Anglo-Saxon period there was, on the whole, an increasing demand for interstate communications; and but little loss of such facilities (apart from the foundering of causeways and decay of bridges, remedied by a detour to the nearest ford) can be held to have taken place in this period.

Let us therefore examine the Roman roads in Essex; and see what measure of communication they afford with East as well as with Middle Anglia. On Sketch-map H (p. 285) the sectors of roads in Essex *which still exist without material breaks in continuity* are indicated.

(i) It is seen that the Roman coast road is practically continuous from near London to Colchester, where it divides; the continuity of both the northern extensions is broken, at the Stour Valley (Codrington, 1918, p. 177).

(ii) The east-and-west road, Stane Street, is practically complete from near Colchester (Marks Tey) to Braughing, where it links up with Ermine Street.

For 32 miles the Stane Street is practically continuously in use; the loss of the last 1½ miles from Horse Cross to Ermine Street is due doubtless to the deflection of traffic at an early date to adjacent villages on the line of that street. Codrington (1918, p. 115 a) doubts whether the sector Bishop's Stortford-Horse Cross is Roman; personal knowledge of it convinces me that it must be accepted as such.

(iii) Though the course of Ermine Street from London to Braughing is known, its track through Middlesex and Southern Hertfordshire is for long stretches disused, as the ½-inch O.S. map (Sheet 29, St Albans) clearly shows.

(iv) The Roman road from Colchester to the Ermine Street *via* Cambridge cannot now be traced with certainty between Colchester and Haverhill; but since it may have been but a sinuous pre-Roman trackway hardened by the Romans and hence now not recognizable (pp. 168-9) we can draw no conclusions from its apparent absence.

The significance of the relevant facts may now be considered. The continuity of the Essex coast road was preserved, we may conjecture, because it linked up a chain of settlements; while the loss of the roads north of Colchester points to the antiquity of the line of the Stour as a division between East Anglia and Essex[1].

The absence of East Saxon settlements in Southern Hertfordshire may account for the partial loss of the lower segment of Ermine Street. It was not, we may suppose, in use in the centuries immediately following the invasion.

Stane Street presents a different phenomenon. It crosses a wide belt (34 miles) of forest country, bare of Anglo-Saxon settlement in the pagan period (and thus had it been disused at any time, its trace must surely have been quickly lost); linked with the Ermine Street, it forms an unbroken channel of communication far beyond the limits of Essex.

Such a survival expands our conception of the importance of Roman roads in the pagan period. This survival is due, I hold, to a force greater than those making for isolation as between group-areas (kingdoms); namely, the necessity for communication with the outside world (in this case the sea-coast, Kent, France and the south generally) felt by settlers in an inland area such as Middle Anglia. If the Sketch-map be examined it will be seen that a practically unbroken sector of the Ermine Street extends from the River Nene to Braughing. Its survival may very probably be due to the political homogeneity of the Middle Angles; I suggest that it was their line of communication to an East Coast port.

Similarly, Watling Street was the vital link which connected Mercia with the outside world; the capital, Tamworth, was situated on it. It is not suggested that the necessity for such communication was in early days formulated; certainly it was not maintained by political action but as a result of continuous use by traders and travellers.

It is recognized that the few known Essex cemeteries, as a whole, present characters widely different from those of the Cam Valley group. This is readily explicable on the hypothesis we are considering; the wide belt of forest upland enforced isolation from Anglian kingdoms on the one hand, the coastal situation of the Essex settlements encouraged close relations with Kent and the Continent on the other.

The failure of the Ipswich finds to conform fully to East Anglian type is similarly explicable, as R. A. Smith recognizes (1911, p. 333). The cemetery was one of a people on the fringe of the Thames estuary group-area, who were influenced from the south as well as from the north and west.

---

[1] This may have been the Icenian boundary in early I A.D. See p. 103.

We cannot say that the finds indicate a culture materially different from that found in Essex until more Essex cemeteries are revealed and explored.

But if my explanation of the survival of the cross-country Roman road from the Essex coast to Middle Anglia be correct there should be definite evidence of the contact between southern Cambridgeshire and the settlements of Essex in one place, namely, in the neighbourhood of Colchester. Evidence of such relationship does here exist. From a large and imperfectly explored cemetery on the boundary of Feering and Kelvedon parishes, close to the coastal termination of the great road and 30 miles from the nearest Cam Valley settlement, a few objects obtained in 1882 are preserved[1]. These include two applied fibulae—the only examples found on the east coast between the Thames and the Wash[2].

The natural boundary between Middle Anglia and the kingdom which developed in the Essex area is the southern watershed of the Cam and its tributaries. The political boundary of the kingdom of Essex on the north-west in early VII is unknown; it may have included Chesterford as does the modern county. But the pagan settlement here was geographically part of Middle Anglia, and that it also was so culturally is probable, for the only important object preserved from its cemetery is a cruciform brooch of Cam Valley type (Brown, 1915, p. 788). I conclude, therefore, that the watershed of the Cam was probably the political boundary of Middle Anglia in the south-east of our Region. That it was so in the south I am less certain. The boundary probably was not defined until the Christian period, for in earlier times southern Hertfordshire was apparently almost entirely unoccupied. The distribution in northern Hertfordshire of the term "Bury" used to signify the manor (see p. 303), which is of common occurence in the upper Cam and Ivel Valleys, suggests that the former area was colonized from Middle Anglia; if so, the southern boundary of this kingdom extended beyond the limits of our Region[3].

(C) THE BOUNDARY BETWEEN MIDDLE AND EAST ANGLIA

Broadly speaking, the pagan Anglo-Saxon culture in the Fenland Basin as a whole is uniform; and it will be recalled that in discussing

---

[1] Colchester Mus.; note in *Essex Naturalist* (1888), II, 124. See also R. A. Smith (1903, p. 326).

[2] The occurrence of the place-name Feeringbury, 1 mile N.W. of Feering, may also be due to contact with Middle Anglia. See the following paragraph, and pp. 303–4.

[3] At a later period—subsequent to the absorption in Mercia of Middle Anglia—Hertfordshire was in all probability attached to Essex (see p. 239).

a similar phenomenon in the Bronze Age (p. 26) it was pointed out that the geography of the area was such that a tendency to unity of cultural characters might in all periods be expected.

But though the grave-goods of East Anglia (as represented in our district by the cemeteries of the River Lark) are closely similar to those of Middle Anglia (as represented by the cemeteries of the Cambridge and Chapel Hill groups) there are well-marked minor differences. The most important objects which are common in the one area, partially or entirely absent from the other, are the saucer and applied brooches. The numerous cemeteries of N.W. Suffolk have yielded only one pair of the latter; while no less than 18 of the former, and 48 of the latter, occur in Southern Cambridgeshire. The limits on the east of these West Saxon and Middle Anglian types is thus the belt of country between Cambridge and the Lark Valley.

In this same region, it will be remembered, we found that a cultural break existed in the later phase of the Early Iron Age, and we concluded that a political boundary (reinforced by a military barrier, the Devil's Dyke?) checked the tendency to unity of which we have spoken.

That the facts just mentioned are due to the maintenance by the East Anglians of a political and military barrier seems highly probable. We have evidence suggesting that the Devil's Dyke was thus utilized by them, and it is likely that they constructed the Fleam Dyke.

Devil's Dyke. The axe figured on Plate XXXVI, 7, is of a type frequently met with in inhumation burials of the pagan period. It was found (as a note in *C.A.S. Rep.* 36, p. 21, records) with another axe of the same form, a "lancehead, spur, and stirrup, all of iron," in 1822, by a "workman levelling the Devil's Dyke on Newmarket Heath." The spur and stirrup I cannot find in the Museum; the "lancehead" has a split socket and a long slender blade. It is probable that relics of more than one period were intermingled; there is no evidence as to the nature of the deposit.

Fleam Dyke. The investigations detailed on p. 130 showed that the main sector of the Dyke between the forest plateau near Balsham and Wilbraham Fen was of Roman or post-Roman origin.

Nothing that we know of the history of the Roman occupation of Eastern Britain renders it likely that defence was needed against attack from the south-west. The development of the Anglo-Saxon kingdoms, on the other hand—East Anglia, Middle Anglia, and later Mercia—and the numerous wars of which we have record, afford ample ground for the belief that the East Anglians of the pagan period,

PLATE XXXVI

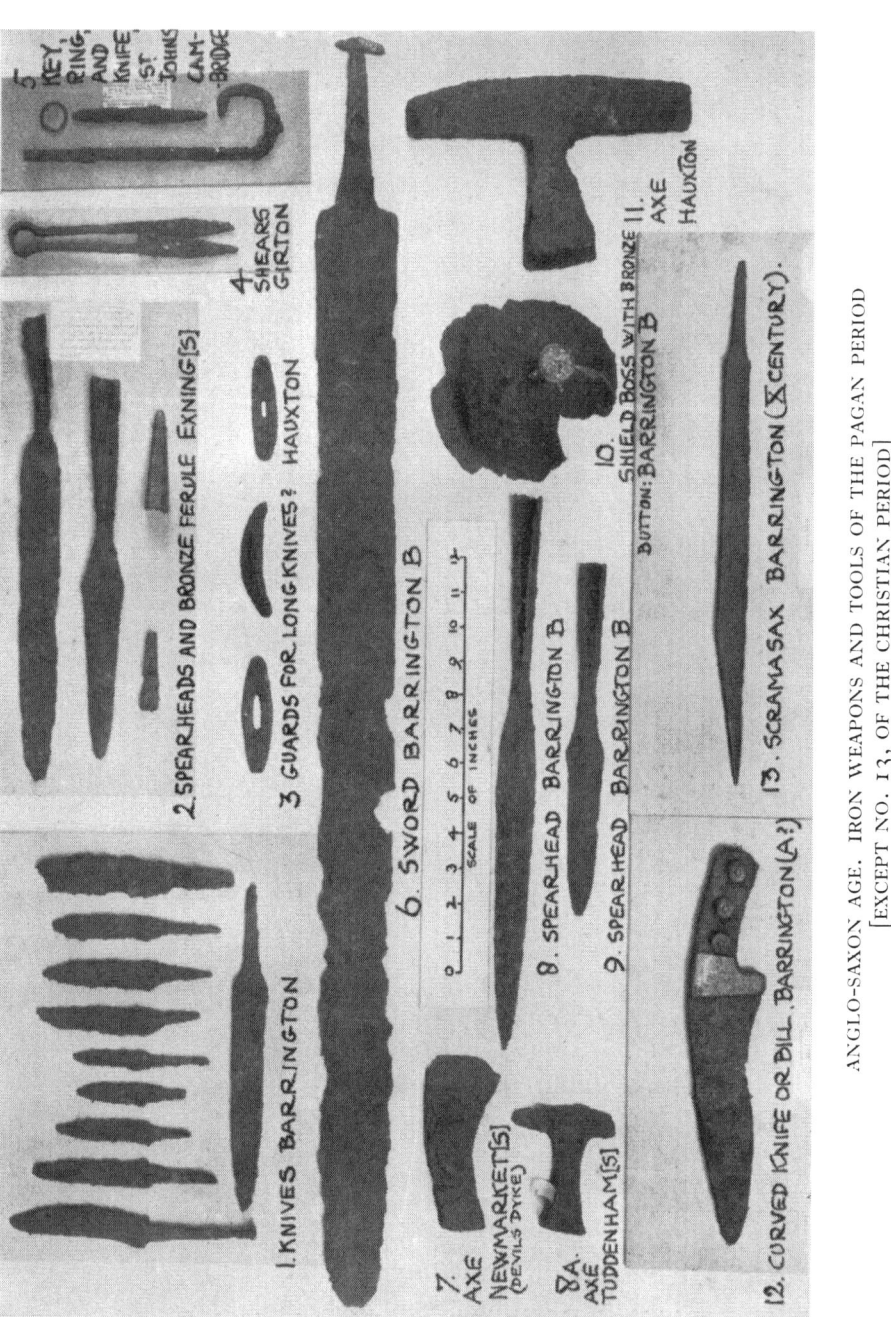

ANGLO-SAXON AGE. IRON WEAPONS AND TOOLS OF THE PAGAN PERIOD
[EXCEPT NO. 13, OF THE CHRISTIAN PERIOD]

Nos. 1, 6, 8, 9, 10, p. 253; No. 2, p. 264; Nos. 3, 11, p. 259; No. 4, p. 247; No. 5, p. 243; No. 7, pp. 264, 292; No. 8 A, p. 264; No. 12, p. 252; No. 13, p. 301.

like their predecessors the Iceni, would find a defensive dyke barring access to their territory of the utmost value.

That one, the Devil's Dyke, already existed, and was at some time in the pagan period in use, may provisionally be accepted, and it at first sight seems improbable that the East Anglians would trouble to construct a second. But we have seen that the Teutonic population of Eastern England must have been small for a considerable period after the conquest; and the fact that the situation of the Fleam Dyke permits the vulnerable frontier of East Anglia to be defended by less than half the number of men required for the Devil's Dyke affords an adequate reason for building a barrier at this point (see Map V).

That no such earthworks in this country are known to have been constructed by the Anglo-Saxons in the pagan period is true[1], but we learn from Tacitus that the Germani in I A.D. constructed boundary dykes, probably similar in character to our dykes. In dealing with the campaign of Arminius, 16–17 A.D., he describes the gathering of the Cherusci "in a spot closed in by a river and by forests, within which was a narrow swampy plain. The woods too were surrounded by a bottomless morass, only on one side of it the Angrivarii had raised a broad earthwork as a boundary between themselves and the Cherusci[2]." Offa's dyke, moreover, though not an original work of the Mercian king, was most likely extended and completed by him[3].

Interesting evidence (similar to, but more definite than, that already recorded in connection with the Devil's Dyke) which suggests that the Fleam Dyke was in use as a military barrier during the pagan period has recently come to light. Balsham men, employed on the work of excavation, referred several times to skeletons having been found in the ramp within living memory between Balsham and Mutlow Hill, and I find in the Cambridge Museum two umbos (Plate XXXII) of types characteristic of the pagan period in our district, labelled "found at (or by) the Fleam Dyke between Balsham and Mutlow Hill, 1861." One of these has the boss and rivet-heads silvered, a feature of common occurrence in local cemeteries. At the same time was found a spearhead (also in the museum). That any settlement-cemetery existed on the open chalk downs between these two points is improbable, and the evidence, vague and inadequate as it is, points to the burial of men fallen in battle at the earthwork.

[1] The Wansdyke in Wiltshire was at one point shown by Pitt-Rivers to be post-Roman, but was probably Romano-British, as was Bokerly Dyke.
[2] Tacitus, *Ann.* II, 19, trans. Church and Brodribb.
[3] The authority for this is late and poor. Vitae Duorum Offarum (St Albans, XII century).

It is not suggested that the Fleam Dyke was the permanent political boundary between East and Middle Anglia. What seems probable is that in time of danger to the East Anglian state, defence, in the late pagan and early Christian periods, may have been concentrated on the most easily defensible spot on the vulnerable frontier, namely, the narrow belt of open country spanned by the Dyke. This hypothesis amply accounts for the successive reconstructions, revealed in one section of the vallum.

Survey of the features in the grave-furniture which differentiate Middle from East Anglia may now be resumed. It has been noted (p. 283) that the use of enamel on cruciform and square-headed fibulae is met with in the cemeteries of N.W Suffolk; enamelled fibulae are found also at Wilbraham and Linton, but none is known from the cemeteries of the Chapel Hill group, west of the Cam. Objects of that distinctive character which is commonly called Jutish, and which are probably of Kentish fabric, dating in late VI and early VII, have a similar range in our district. A few examples occur in the Lark Valley and several at Tostock and Ixworth near Bury St Edmunds; we have recorded such also at Burwell (p. 262), at Allington Hill, Bottisham (p. 264), at Little Wilbraham (p. 262) and at Cambridge, St John's (p. 243). The distribution of imported glass vessels, probably of late VI date (Linton, Chatteris and (?) Girton), is somewhat similar, and may be a correlated phenomenon.

Special attention may be directed to the bronze pyramidal stud set with shell and garnets from Tuddenham in the Cambridge Museum. Similar studs from "near Canterbury" are in the Ashmolean Museum, where are also certain Tostock and Ixworth finds of Kentish origin.

An earlier date than the close of VI is possible for the circular brooch, with keystone garnets, from Wilbraham, referred to above.

It is interesting to observe that while the Lark Valley and Chapel Hill cemeteries are typical of their respective kingdoms, the intermediate cemeteries such as St John's, Cambridge, and Little Wilbraham show features belonging to both groups.

The limitation of the late imported ("Kentish") objects to the north-east half of our district—their furthest extension therein to the west being, apparently, the cemetery of the Castle Hill settlement, Cambridge—is evidence which is, so far as it goes, of importance. No such limitation is observable in the case of objects imported from the south in the early period of the settlement.

There was evidently a trade connection between Southern Cambridgeshire and Kent (France also) during the century following the conquest. Radiating fibulae, for example, occurred at Barrington A as well as at

Linton and Wilbraham; both the Barrington cemeteries have yielded large silvered buckles and square-headed fibulae of types commonly occurring in Kent, and the Haslingfield belt-plates are almost certainly of southern origin. Finds of Kentish character at Saffron Walden and Wenden [E] are referred to on pp. 265-6. The route of entry was doubtless Stane Street; possibly also the Stour Valley road.

It was pointed out on p. 239 that the rise of East Anglia to her position as the dominant military power in South England under the leadership of King Redwald at the beginning of VII was sufficient to account for the transfer of the southern fens from Middle to East Anglia. The archaeological evidence, then, suggests that the Cambridge bridgehead was held by Redwald, within whose dominions many inlaid jewels of Jutish character have been found[1]; and that in his day the boundary of East Anglia to the south of Cambridge was the line of the Essex Cam. This boundary, moreover, includes the district wherein enamelled fibulae are met with. Gray (1910, p. 137) arrives at similar conclusions from an analysis of historical data.

It should be added that, as Gray (1908, p. 29) pointed out, the distribution of place-names ending in "ham" points to the permanence of some such political boundary. "Ham," "stead," and "field" seem, in our district at least, to mark off settlement by East Saxon and East Anglian elements from that of Middle Anglians.

Such differential place nomenclature is probably only another manifestation of divergence due to isolation. If so, it provides additional evidence for the late date of certain "ham" names in our district (see p. 275).

Note on the Anglian Culture Area

That the Anglian culture area extends so widely as to include not only Middle and East Anglia but also Lincolnshire and Yorkshire is no doubt due in part to the stimulus of intercourse with Northern Europe. Parallelism, as Schetelig points out (1906, pp. 99ff.), in the development of the cruciform brooch in Scandinavia and in Eastern England existed in the latter half of V. In this period contact with Denmark is most manifest, while in early VI changes in cruciform and square-headed brooches in our district and in Eastern England generally find their closest parallels in Norway. After 550 we may suppose that the Frisian stepped in and that direct intercourse between the North and England was at an end.

---

[1] See R. A. Smith (1911). The portal of entry into East Anglia was probably Dunwich, the selection of which as the bishop's seat by Felix is indicative of its importance at the close of the pagan period. Redwald's close relations with Kent are attested by Bede, *H. E.* Lib. II. xv.

SUMMARY

The distribution of the cemeteries and finds of the pagan period in Cambridge points to the existence of at least three settlements within the limits of the modern town, one being on or by the Roman town on Castle Hill.

The apparent multiplication of cemeteries in the neighbourhood of Chapel Hill, Cambridgeshire, has been shown to be due, in all probability, to errors of provenance in the records of museum and private collections; three only are attested, Barrington A and B and Haslingfield.

Settlement in the district is limited to the river valleys[1] and fen islands and shows close similarity to that of the Early Bronze Age as defined by beaker burials, both being the result, it is held, of invasion *via* the Wash, and of the control exercised by environment on peoples of primitive culture.

There is ample evidence that the more important areas of our district, the Lark Valley and the Cam Valley near Cambridge, were settled before the end of the V century; the date of settlement in the Ivel and Great Ouse Valley cannot yet be determined. The character of the early grave-furniture suggests that the majority of the settlers came from Slesvig and Hanover.

The culture of our Region is that known as "Anglian"; but in the presence of applied and saucer brooches relations with the West Saxon culture of the Upper Thames Valley are apparent.

The hypothesis that divergencies of cultural characters between Angles and Saxons are the result of the isolation of districts which developed into kingdoms has been tested; while not affording a complete explanation of all the facts, it throws light on many difficult topographical problems.

Slight differences in cultural characters between Middle and East Anglian areas in our district are considered to be due to the establishment of a political and a military frontier; the military frontier is thought to have been, at some time within the period, the line of the Fleam Dyke, which was probably constructed by the East Anglians.

Evidence indicative of the advance of the political boundary of East Anglia to the line of the Essex Cam at the close of the pagan period has been brought forward.

The influence of Roman arts and crafts on the Anglo-Saxons in our district subsequent to the invasion appears to have been slight. There is some evidence pointing to the survival of Romano-British

[1] Save at King's Walden [H] and at Girton.

elements in the fens and their borders. The discovery of remnants of two or three bronze bowls showing La Tène ornament is important; their place of manufacture is unknown, but is certainly not in our neighbourhood.

The distribution of cremation and inhumation in the Cambridge Region shows that those invaders who employed the former rite had a tendency to segregate. Inhumation burial is contemporary with the settlement.

The importance in this period of Roman roads and of pre-Roman trackways has been emphasized; the breaks in continuity of the former have in one case been shown to be coincident with a probable boundary between kingdoms; and causal relationship is indicated. The possibility that the Stane Street from Marks Tey, near Colchester, to Braughing was used as a traffic route from the sea-coast to Middle Anglia in the pagan period has been investigated.

B. *THE CHRISTIAN PERIOD*

We may next consider what remains we possess referable to the Anglo-Saxon Christian period, from the middle of VII to 1066 A.D. (with a break of about 100 years following the Danish invasion of 866 A.D.).

Remains known to be of this period in the Cambridge Region are almost entirely monumental—churches and sculptured grave-slabs and crosses; and such are excluded from consideration in this book (see p. 237).

So scanty are the other remains, and so little light do they throw on the history of the period, that a mere inventory of the chief finds arranged chronologically will suffice.

(I) MIDDLE VII CENTURY TO THE DANISH INVASION, 866 A.D.

(i) A relic of early Christianity in East Anglia is the gold cross with garnet and glass inlays, probably of Kentish workmanship, framing a gold coin of Heraclius (610–641 A.D.), found at Wilton [N] on the Little Ouse. It is in the British Museum.

(ii) Four bronze strap-ends in the Cambridge Museum, one found at Cambridge, the others at Hauxton Mill, show how wide was the range of ornamental *motifs* available for the IX century craftsman. The former shows scrolls in niello and silver; the latter show geometrical, interlaced, and animal forms.

(iii) The bronze-gilt disc (Plate XXXIV, 6), dug up somewhere in Cambridge during the laying of a sewer in 1905, is of unusual interest. Its decoration—close spirals like those in the Book of Durrow and step-patterns—suggests a date in VIII. The rivet-holes (centre and base) and the two lateral holes show that it formed one of a trio of disc-headed pins like those found in the Witham at Lincoln, finely illustrated by Allen (1904) and now in the British Museum[1]. The ornament of the Lincoln pins is mainly zöomorphic as on the similar example from Ixworth [S], figured and discussed by R. A. Smith (1911, p. 337); but the bronze plaques which link the pins one to another show spirals resembling those on our disc. Allen dated the Lincoln example in early IX. A quadrant of another disc showing interlacing patterns, but otherwise similar to the Cambridge example, comes from Hauxton Mill. It also is in the local museum.

(iv) A leaden weight with bronze-gilt decorated disc, found at Mildenhall, is by R. A. Smith (1911, p. 345) dated in VIII or IX.

(v) A bronze-gilt boss of Irish work of VIII (in the British Museum) is said to have been dug up at the east end of Steeple Bumpstead Church (R. A. Smith, 1915 c).

(vi) *Coins.* A hoard of nine sceattas, found in or near Cambridge, is described by J. Evans (1894), the date suggested by him being mid-VIII, but I understand from Mr Bruce Dickins that the first half of VII would now be considered a more probable date; one is in the Fitzwilliam Museum, Cambridge. The Rev. E. Conybeare has a sceat found at Barrington. Inscribed coins are rare; some of Mercian origin are of special interest; two of Coenwulf (796–821), found at Haslingfield and Mildenhall[2]; and one of Offa (757–96) found at Barrington; another of Offa and one of his widow Cynethryth from "near Hitchin" (R. A. Smith, 1902, p. 260). A styca of Burhred (852–874) and one of Eanred (810–840) are recorded from Hauxton Mill (*C.A.S. Rep.* 48, p. cxxxvi); the latter is the only Northumbrian coin of the pre-Danish period of which I have record.

(II) PERIOD 866–950 A.D.

There are a few objects that are referable to the interlude of heathendom resulting from the Danish invasion and settlement in the Cambridge Region. Remains of the phase are rare in East Anglia generally.

1. Conybeare (1904, p. 438) records that a bronze bracteate stamped with "quasi-arabic characters" has been found at or near Barrington; and coins of Alfred found in the parish are also in his collection.

---

[1] Our disc has a diameter of 1·85 in.; the Lincoln pins are 1·92, 1·75 and 1·65 in.
[2] *Quart. Journ. S. I.* (June, 1869, p. 45) and *C.A.S.* (*Rep.* 36, 1876, p. 25).

2. A tri-lobed fibula with conventional foliage ornament, found on Lakenheath Warren, is dated by R. A. Smith (1911, p. 352) in the Viking period; a similar date is suggested for a gold ring from Thetford, in the Norwich Museum (Cat. No. 486), which shows "the characteristic pattern made by a triangular punch enclosing pellets."

3. In the Ashmolean Museum there is a square bronze plate from West Stow Heath, the face of which shows an animal device characteristic of the Viking period. It was probably a brooch.

4. On the skeleton of a woman in the cemetery at Paille Ditches, Walden, referred to on p. 265, was found a necklet on which were two bronze discs showing Carlovingian decorative *motifs* which are found in England and the North. To these Viking ornaments form "the closest parallels." See H. E. Smith (1883) and Brown (1915, Plate xvi, 2). This burial is considered by R. A. Smith (1903, p. 331) to date not later than 1000 A.D.: it is probably that of a nominal convert to Christianity.

5. At Santon on the Little Ouse the grave of a Scandinavian warrior of the early X century was discovered in 1867. See Greenwell (1874) and R. A. Smith (1907). There was no tumulus: the skeleton was in a grave 2 feet below the surface and the associated objects were an iron sword of Danish type and two characteristic oval bronze-gilt "tortoise" brooches (all in the British Museum). These are rarely met with in England. A buckle from Lakenheath in the Cambridge Museum exhibits similar pierced ornament.

6. An axe-blade of iron, of the Viking period or later, is in the Ambrose collection, Cambridge Museum; its patination shows it to have been derived from the fen peat. This beautiful weapon of war is illustrated on Plate XXXI. It is very light; but the strength necessary for its purpose is obtained by increasing the thickness of the blade near the edge, as the section shows.

(III) Period 950–1066 A.D.

(*a*) The settlement which existed on the north side of the River Cam at Hauxton Mill from the Early Iron Age onwards would appear to have been occupied more or less continuously throughout the Anglo-Saxon Age; and the inadequacy of our knowledge of the site is a grievous loss to local archaeology.

Wessex coins of Ethelred I and Alfred the Great are recorded (Kimmins, 1887), as well as the coins and other objects already mentioned; and amongst the pottery (La Tène, Roman and pagan Anglo-Saxon)—preserved in the Cambridge Museum—are some fragments of coarse hard-baked ware with pinched rim in the mediaeval manner. I submitted these fragments to Mr R. A. Smith who considers them to be pre-Norman.

(*b*) *Leaden Vessels.* A note on a leaden vessel measuring 18 inches in diameter, elaborately decorated with vandyked panels of interlaced work, found prior to 1879 deep in clay in a field behind the post office and school at Westley Waterless, was communicated to the C.A.S. in 1879 (Hughes, 1879). It contained a bill, spearhead with split socket, plough share, punch, hasps and other fragments which perhaps formed "the stock-in-trade of a small worker in iron." The illustration (Plate XXXV) shows that the interlaced work (cast in a mould) is of the debased type met with on the local gravecovers to which the date 975–1066 is assigned (C. Fox, 1922). The circular panels present four triquetrae, forming a cruciform pattern. A second vessel in the Cambridge Museum, similar in shape and character, and probably of local origin, has ornament of Romanesque (Norman) type, and it may be that both are nearly contemporary.

It is, however, to be noted that a triquetra resembling those on the Westley Waterless vessel occurs on a VII century sceat found at or near Cambridge (J. Evans, 1894, Plate II, No. 3).

The care taken in the ornamentation of these vessels suggests that they performed a function of some dignity and importance. Professor Chadwick suggests that the ale-mugs at the beer-drinkings may have been refilled from such a vessel which would thus be kept permanently in the thegn's hall.

(*c*) Camden (quoting from Hickes) records the discovery in 1694 at Sutton of "three silver plates," on one an inscription in Anglo-Saxon and in Runes, together with coins, a plate of lead, and "divers large rings of gold." This inscription is figured in the *Britannia*[1]; Mr Bruce Dickins translates as follows: "Aedwen owns me. May she own me. Lord, Lord, protect him who me to her shall bring, unless she give me of her own free will" ✠. The Runes are, in Professor Chadwick's opinion, "apparently an attempt to write Scandinavian runes by someone who did not understand them," and the plate is of XI century date, judging from certain Anglo-Saxon spellings in the inscription.

(*d*) A leaden tablet inscribed with a portion of one of Aelfric's homilies—probably the front cover of an MS. volume of the Homilies—was found on the site of Bury Abbey (see R. A. Smith, 1911, p. 353).

---

[1] Eng. trans. ed. Gibson, 2nd edn. vol. I, p. 493.

(e) A small flanged bronze plate, with three rivet-holes, from Mildenhall, in the Ashmolean Museum, shows incised decoration of late X century style, as does a bronze fragment from Cambridge in the Cambridge Museum.

Weapons of the Christian Period

To the period 950–1066 probably belongs a fine scramasax from Barrington (Plate XXXVI, 13) with damascened blade. Damascening is not known to occur in weapons from the pagan cemeteries[1], and a similar weapon in the British Museum was associated with coins of Ethelred II, as I am informed by Mr R. A. Smith. Iron swordblades from Lakenheath Fen and Waterbeach, in the British Museum, cannot be exactly dated. The former has a reeded bone pommel; the character of both suggests a date definitely later than the pagan period. A long blade like a sword with the tang hammered out to form a rough socket, found "near Cambridge," and probably a weaving batten, may be of IX or X century date.

EARTHWORKS

Only one branch of topographical archaeology remains to be surveyed in order to complete our brief consideration of the Christian Anglo-Saxon period, and, in a barren archaeological period, it is the most unsatisfactory branch of all.

The fact is that while there are many earthworks in the district which *may* be of Anglo-Saxon date, there are few, if any, which can be with certainty assigned to this period. Gannock's Castle, Tempsford [B], has been ascribed to the Danes, and Edward the Elder is known to have constructed a fortress at Huntingdon, while many moated and banked enclosures and homestead moats may possibly be pre-Norman, as may also be a dyke at Childerley.

Motte-and-bailey castles, and rectangular fortress-like manorial sites, such as that at Rampton, are not considered in this book, as they are regarded as of post-Conquest origin. One structure of the latter type, that at Clavering [E], must, however, be mentioned, since it had been thought to be the "Robert's Castle" mentioned in the A.-S. Chronicle (Laud MS. E), under date 1052: "gewendon sume west to Pentecostes castele. sume norð to Rodbertes castele."

Armitage's analysis (1912) of the castles known to have been constructed by the Normans during XI, 84 in number, shows that all are motte-and-bailey or keep-and-bailey constructions. It is extremely improbable, therefore, that a rectangular moated work such as Clavering Castle would have been constructed by a Norman favourite of Edward the Confessor.

---

[1] The art is mentioned in *Beowulf*, where it is probably reminiscent of Roman times; the blades in the Nydam Moss find are damascened. Weapons thus decorated first appear in England in the Viking period.

302   THE ANGLO-SAXON AGE

Tempsford. At Tempsford the Danes are known to have constructed an earthwork in 916 (921) A.D. An extensive fortification is clearly implied in the Anglo-Saxon Chronicle record[1], and it is called "burh" later on in the same year.

Situated about 200 yards from the former bank of the river in this parish is Gannocks Castle, a small ramparted moated rectangular work measuring 120 by 84 feet within the ramparts; the banks are 11 to 12 feet above the bottom of the moat, and the moat is 20 feet across. At one angle is a small circular mound about 20 feet across the top, probably the base of a stockaded tower[2].

Allowing two men to the yard of rampart, one to fight and one in reserve, the "hold" would provide a defence for 270 men. It certainly would not have accommodated the large army from Huntingdon and from East Anglia mentioned in the Chronicle.

Goddard considers the fort to be part only of the Danish defences, and speaks of "fields to the south and east [of the work] scored with traces of other lines...too faint to decipher." The work, however, is complete in itself and shows no traces in moat or vallum of any connection with larger constructions; moreover, it is *a priori* unlikely that citadels of this type would be built by the Danes.

It is difficult to assign a date to Gannock's Castle; but the XI–XII centuries may, on several grounds, be considered a more probable period for its construction than the X century.

Cambridge. It is possible that the "army which owed obedience to Cambridge[3]" improved or reconstructed the Roman defences on Castle Hill. But no evidence can be brought forward in support of this suggestion save that the town is described as a burgus in Domesday Book and was, therefore, presumably fortified in 1066 A.D.

Burhs of Edward the Elder. One certainly existed in our district (originally a Danish work repaired and rebuilt by Edward), that at Huntingdon[4]; but it was later on destroyed or merged in the existing (Norman) castle.

Moated and Banked enclosures. The ramparts in works of this class are usually slight. Certain indirect evidence is available pointing to an Anglo-Saxon origin for some small enclosures of this type in Bedfordshire.

---

[1] "Þy ilcan siþe for se here of Huntandune 7 of East Englum 7 worhton þæt geweorc æt Tæmeseforda 7 hit budon 7 bytledon." Parker MS. A; Earle and Plummer (1892, p. 101).
[2] Described by Goddard (1904, p. 281).
[3] *A.-S. C.* (Ā) *Ann.* 921. Earle and Plummer (1892, p. 103).
[4] *A.-S. C.* (Ā) *Ann.* 921. Earle and Plummer (1892, p. 103).

At Wyboston, Keysoe and Harrowden, where Domesday Book records the former presence of 12, 12 and 14 sokemen respectively, a series of slightly banked and moated enclosures occurs. Goddard (1904, p. 308) suggests that since the number of moats closely corresponds to the number of sokemen, and since similar groups do not occur in other parishes, these are probably the sites of pre-Domesday yeomen's farmsteads.

I have not been able to establish any relation in Cambridgeshire between moated sites of this (or any other) class, and the number and distribution of sokemen in the Domesday record.

One such moated site in Cambridgeshire, at Barton, has been excavated by Walker (1908 c), and was considered by him to be of late Anglo-Saxon date. This was the ancient manorial site of Barton; and was proved to have been occupied since Roman (or possibly late La Tène) times. Walker concluded that the "earthworks which appeared above ground" (the enclosure showed a low bank within the moat) were probably to be dated at from 800 to 1000 A.D. The evidence does not, however, appear to me to be conclusive as to the date at which the site was moated; and, indeed, the signs of Anglo-Saxon occupation are of the slightest.

Until further evidence of the date of works of this type is available it appears to be safer to exclude them from a survey which closes at the Norman Conquest.

Homestead Moats. We may now consider whether a large and important group of minor earthworks, very numerous in Cambridgeshire, is to be assigned to the Anglo-Saxon Age. These level-surfaced, small, water-moated enclosures are usually described as "Homestead moats"; the feature which distinguishes them from the works discussed above is the absence of any bank, mound or rampart.

I do not know of any archaeological evidence which will enable us to date these enclosures with certainty. If we turn to such historical records of the Anglo-Saxon Age as are likely to help us, we find frequent mention of "burhs."

Maitland (1897, pp. 183 ff.) explains the *early* uses of the word; in the Laws it means the residence, fortified or protected in some way, of an individual landowner—a thegn or "gesithcund man." "Burhs" of this type are undoubtedly represented, as far as the site is concerned, by the manorial halls of Anglo-Saxon villages as they existed after the Conquest, and as they exist to-day. Such sites and such dwellings in Bedfordshire, North Hertfordshire and here and there in adjacent counties are, as Maitland noted, to this day called "burys"; it is thus evident that in these districts the word has precisely the same significance as it had in the VII century.

Thus in our own district we have:

>Chrishallbury by Chrishall [E].
>Millowbury by Millow [B].
>Heydonbury by Heydon.
>Elmdonbury by Elmdon [E].
>Arlesey Bury by Arlesey [B].
>Melbournbury by Melbourn.
>The Burystead by Sutton.
>The Bury, Foxton.
>The Bury, Stapleford.
>The Bury, Great Shelford.
>The Bury, Ashwell [H].

Map J (p. 310) shows the village of Elmdon, with Elmdonbury adjacent.

Of the manorial character of these we have precise and definite information. For example, the manor in Melbourn called the Bury Manor was given by King Edgar to Ely. "The principal manor [in Foxton] called the Bury...belonged to the nuns of Chatteris." "The principal manor [in Stapleford] called the Bury was part of the ancient possessions of .. Ely." "The Bury Manor [Great Shelford] was given to the monastery of Ely by the parents of Leofsin" (Lysons, 1808, pp. 234, 195, 256, 249).

In the region covered by the present survey, "burys" are frequently moated; but the proportion of moated manors with this distinctive appellation is much the same as those not so described. "Homestead Moats" are, indeed, the normal protection provided for "manorial" sites[1]. Are we justified in regarding these moats as of Anglo-Saxon origin?

Some may be of pre-Conquest date[2], but the writer knows of no evidence which will enable us definitely to assert that "homestead" moats are the normal defence of a "burh" or even that moats of Anglo-Saxon origin are anything but exceptional. Many sites that are not manorial are moated; and the use of the moat without raised banks for defence was common down to the end of the Middle Ages.

It is quite possible that a rude stockade, as at Bamborough[3], was normally the sole defence of the Saxon thegn's dwelling; it may even

---

[1] Fleta, II, ch. 71, shows that in the time of Edward I a moat was the normal attribute of the manor house.

[2] Roman villas are never moated. It is entirely a post-Roman development.

[3] A.-S. C. 547 A.D.: "Ida...getimbrade Bebbanburh; sy wæs ærost mid hegge betined, þær æfter mid wealle." Laud MS. (E). Earle and Plummer (1892, p. 17).

THE ANGLO-SAXON AGE

be the case that there was often no specifically defensive construction at all, the steading being built four-square with all the constituent buildings facing inwards, ingress to the courtyard being provided by a gate.

Farmsteadings still exist scattered about the countryside arranged on this plan. The farmhouse occupies one side of the rectangle, the farm buildings the other three sides; all windows save mere slits open inwards on the yard where the stock is folded; entrance is gained by means of the yard gate. The arrangement is commonly seen in Western France.

In view of this uncertainty, it is not proposed to include in this survey any of the homestead moats in our district.

Childerley Dyke. Childerley is an upland parish 6 miles west-north-west of Cambridge. Its western boundary (see 6-inch O.S. XXXIX, N.W. and S.W.) for a distance of 730 yards is formed by a dyke of some strength, facing west; where well-marked, the crest of the vallum is about 6 feet above the floor of the ditch and the overall width is about 17 yards. An entrance, apparently original, is centrally situated. There is no evidence that the defences extended either to the north or the south beyond their present limits (see Map V). Ending "in the air," as the earthwork does, it seems useless for defence; but dense woodlands may have encompassed the settlement when the work was built and the only access thereto from the west may have been spanned by it. A cottage 700 yards to the west of the dyke, situated beside a hedge-line which leads to the gap in the defences and no doubt marks an ancient road, is called, significantly enough, Battle Gate. No tradition attaches to the site; the only recorded find, that of a chain-shot, does not seem relevant. No ancient through-road, so far as I can ascertain, traverses the parish, and it is in a wooded district where no trace of early occupation has been recorded. On the whole, I am inclined to suggest that it may have been designed for the defence of the Anglo-Saxon settlement of Childerley; it would thus be an earthwork of a type not known to occur elsewhere in the Cambridge Region.

Tradition would surely survive had the earthwork been constructed in the XVII century as the discovery of the chain-shot suggests. Charles I slept at Childerley Hall in 1647 for two nights (June 6–8) on his way from Holmby House to Newmarket when in charge of Cornet Joyce and his troopers.

Non-Military Earthwork. Numerous traces of the open-field system of cultivation which survived in Cambridgeshire into the XIX century are to be seen on our hillsides.

Plate XXXVII, 4, shows a series of lynchets at Chishall Down, Chishall; three acre strips and one half-acre strip are here visible. On the same plate are the tremendous series of terraced banks at Coploe Hill, Ickleton. These appear too large to be due to natural agencies—denudation and accretion—even when aided by man, who followed the practice of turning the sod downhill (Seebohm, 1896, p. 5); but a hillside road well known to me, across an arable countryside near Elmdon [E], shows a bank of similar scale; and here no conscious effort to make a level terrace can be predicated.

That terrace cultivation is in some districts older than the Anglo-Saxon period is probable; the cultivation of our chalk downland doubtless commenced in the Bronze Age; and such a system as that at Coploe Hill seems to require an antiquity greater than an Anglo-Saxon origin can give.

The most interesting unenclosed parish in the district is that of Clothall [H]. Though many of the balks dividing the acre strips are ploughed out, one is able to obtain from certain positions—such as that from which the photo on Plate XXXVII, 3, is taken—a good idea of the appearance of the open fields surrounding an Anglo-Saxon settlement. The hillside in the background in this photograph is terraced from top to bottom, as may be seen in Plate XXXVII, 2, taken at close quarters. This is perhaps the most remarkable series of lynchets in East Anglia (Seebohm, 1896, p. 5).

TOPOGRAPHICAL DISTRIBUTION OF SETTLEMENTS IN THE CAMBRIDGE REGION AT THE CLOSE OF THE ANGLO-SAXON AGE, AS RECORDED IN DOMESDAY BOOK

In preceding chapters of this book the distribution of finds and other remains of successive culture phases has been investigated, and the position and range of settlements in our district deduced.

Not until the close of the Anglo-Saxon Age are we able to provide ourselves with a topographical picture of settlement in the Cambridge Region based not on the result of chance finds, but on historical record; and consideration of Domesday Book from this aspect will be of value for comparative purposes.

The sites of the Domesday vills which are marked on the Anglo-Saxon Map[1] fall, broadly speaking, into two groups. Firstly, there are those sites which by reason of well-drained and fertile soil, shelter,

---

[1] Based on maps by J. H. Round, C. Johnson, B. A. Lees, and F. W. Ragg in the *V.C.H.* of *Essex, Suffolk, Norfolk, Hertford* and *Bedford*: on Evelyn-White's edition of the Cambridgeshire Domesday, and, for Huntingdonshire on information kindly supplied to me by Mr W. J. Corbett, of King's College, Cambridge.

PLATE XXXVII

ANGLO-SAXON AGE. BALKS AND LYNCHETS: SURVIVING TRACES OF THE OPEN FIELD SYSTEM OF CULTIVATION

See pp. 305–6.

proximity of water, and convenience of communication, are most suited to be dwelling-places of agriculturists in all culture periods, and, secondly, those which represent the extension of man's activities into the less favoured (forest) regions in the neighbourhood of Cambridge.

The majority of the sites in the first group undoubtedly have been the dwelling-places of man from the earliest times onward, as the period maps demonstrate.

In this group are included villages on certain islands in the fen, and on the eastern and southern borders of the fenland; and those adjoining the fertile alluvium of the valleys of the Cam and Ivel.

In the second group are sites whereon few evidences of occupation other than Roman and late Anglo-Saxon are to be found; it includes nearly all the villages situated in the forest country (claylands) in the south-east and north-west of our district, bearing in mind that these areas are intersected by river valleys wherein *limited* settlement has been possible from the earliest times.

So long as the countryside is inhabited, whatever changes may take place as a result of invasion, civil war, or famine following on bad seasons, the settlements of the former group will, as a whole, continue to be occupied. The effective occupation by a people mainly agricultural of districts covered by the second group is correlated with and dependent on a certain standard of civilization.

The Early Iron Age in its later phases followed by the Roman Age is such a period of expansion; the first two centuries at least which followed the Anglo-Saxon conquest one of contraction; and comparison between the Roman Map and the distribution of pagan cemeteries on the Anglo-Saxon Map clearly shows the decline from civilization to barbarism. The four hundred years of the Christian Anglo-Saxon period, broken though it was by war and by the weakening from time to time of ordered government, was on the whole one of progress; and the range and character of the settlement in our Region attained at its close were such that the topography of Domesday Book is in essentials that of the present day.

A more detailed examination with the aid of the Map (V) of the siting of the Domesday vills may prove useful.

(i) Areas of primary settlement.

The vills (eighteen in all) in the fens are confined to islands which are geologically distinguishable from the marsh lands[1].

[1] Those portions of the fen islands which possess a heavy clay soil, were probably not occupied prior to the Roman Age.

Settlement in the East Anglian heathland (the area north-east of the River Kennett) is confined to the Lark and Little Ouse Valleys and the fen margins, where there are in all thirty-one vills (in the 64 square miles of upland between these rivers there is one village only, Elveden). It is probable that the range of settlement has in this area not changed materially since the Bronze Age, for lack of water and an infertile soil strictly limit cultivation. It is noticeable that cemeteries of the pagan Anglo-Saxon period in the Lark Valley are wellnigh as numerous as the Domesday vills.

Settlements by fen and riverside, bordering the open chalk downland from the River Kennett to Hitchin, are very numerous. The upper limit of settlement is determined by the outcrop of water-bearing strata[1]; along a line approximately that of the Street Way are numerous vills, each of which adjoins a springhead. Settlements also are numerous on the banks of the streams which cross the chalk belt (the Bourn River and the Essex Cam, and the head-waters of the Ivel (Great Ouse)); on the southern margins of the fens, as at Over and Somersham and Cottenham, where well-drained gravel deposits cover wide areas; on either side of the Chapel Hill spur close to Haslingfield, west of the Cam; and in the heathy district by Sandy and Gamlingay. In these districts there are in all some ninety-six vills.

(ii) Areas mainly of Secondary Settlement.

At first sight the vills in the woodland areas seem to be evenly distributed, but analysis yields some evidence as to the nature of the process which transformed a countryside almost entirely forest into one largely arable.

The great forest triangle in the south-east, geologically boulder-clay overlying chalk, the western edge of which borders the open chalk downlands, may first be considered.

If the distribution of the vills, 178 in number, be closely examined, it will be seen that comparatively few (30 only) lie *deep* in the forest. The majority are in the river valleys or on the forest margins adjacent to the open country. In the latter situation there are, for example, no less than eleven between the Kennett and the Bourn River. That these are sited on cold clayland, dry well-drained chalk soil being immediately adjacent, emphasizes the chief factor which governs settlement; *water*. Dry well-drained soil is of secondary importance, though both are essential for primitive communities.

---

[1] The Melbourn rock at the base of the Middle, and Totternhoe Stone at the base of the Lower Chalk.

THE ANGLO-SAXON AGE 309

Both, therefore, are present in the areas of *primary* settlement; and it is the absence, partial or complete, of the second factor which marks the areas of secondary settlement.

Another important difference is that in districts of secondary settlement, the open ground is so limited that agricultural communities cannot flourish unless they have reached the stage of civilization when the clearing of the woodland becomes possible and profitable.

It is apparent that in the district under consideration the clearing of the woodland was initiated mainly by the dwellers in the river valleys or the forest borders; only when the area of the intervening forest was too great to be conveniently utilized from such points, either for wood-cutting, for arable or pannage for swine, did independent settlements (Domesday vills) spring up in the heart of the woodland. Such an area is shown in part on the map to the east of Newmarket (square C 6).

In the country to the west of Cambridge, also, most of the forest villages are situated at the edge of the boulder-clay-covered area; but since in many parts of this district the boulder-clay overlies other forest-bearing clays the geological factors governing settlement are not clearly indicated on the map. The selection of village sites is certainly due in some cases to the existence of springs issuing at the junction of strata; in others to the fact that boulder-clay covers the plateaux and hill-tops, and forest settlements where possible are sited on hill slopes. In many cases both causes, doubtless, governed settlement. Be the cause what it may, close to such junctions of strata lie strings of villages; bordering the Cam Valley west of Ermine Street those of Croydon, Tadlow, Eyworth, Dunton, Millow and Edworth may be noted, and in the triangle west of Cambridge formed by Roman roads (see Maps IV and V) we find twelve villages near the edge of the boulder-clay, and only two, Hardwick and Childerley, deep within it. Taking the area west of the River Cam as a whole I find that of fifty-three villages situated on ground naturally forest only fifteen are deep within a boulder-clay-covered area. We may suppose that in this part of our Region the earliest settlements were in open country on the edge of the forest; that when clearances commenced villages grew up on the slopes of the hills—the margins of the boulder-clay; where (as in the district to the east of Cambridge already analyzed) the extent of the plateau or hill country was too great for it to be utilized by dwellers on its margins, settlements sprang up within it.

It must not be supposed that the clearance of the forests, initiated from foci situated for the most part on their margins, was an ordered process of expansion of the arable at the expense of the woodland. We are not to conceive of the adding of field to field, but rather of the development here and there of clearings—"assarts of the waste"— which in process of time (in the later Middle Ages) coalesced by the destruction of intervening woodland. Besides the comparatively few settlements deep in the forest recognized in the Domesday record there were a number of hamlets in the woods which were not "geldable units" but sub-tenancies of large manors, the existence of which we can only ascertain indirectly. Domesday Book, in fact, represents in our Region the penultimate phase of settlement when inhabited sites, some of which afterwards attained manorial rank, were hamlets, groups of swineherds' cottages, it may be, attached to the manor from which their occupants hailed. Mr Corbett of King's College has been good enough to permit me to make use of his unpublished researches on the Huntingdonshire Domesday to illustrate this point. From vills which are known to have had forest settlements arrows are drawn on the map the points of which indicate the position of these. The process whereby the forest land to the north of the Great Ouse Valley, for example, may have been cleared and settled from original foci at Hartford and Slepe (St Ives) on the banks of the river can readily be envisaged[1].

The modern O.S. map of Dullingham parish, again, provides us with an admirable example of the process (see Map J). The hamlets of Dullingham Ley and Widgham Green are held to have originated as forest clearings, Dullingham being the primary settlement. In the least accessible portion of the parish much woodland still remains.

It is to be noted that the presence at the close of the Anglo-Saxon Age of large numbers of vills in forest areas in the Cambridge Region was compatible with the existence of large tracts of forest.

J. H. Round (1903, p. 377) brings forward interesting evidence proving the existence of large areas of woodland in N.W. Essex at the date of the Conquest, and showing how rapidly it diminished as a result of the energy of the new landowners. At Clavering the woodland had in 1066 sufficed for 800 swine; in 1086 it had only enough for 600. At Walden the diminution was from 1050 to 830 in the same period; at Wimbish 500 to 400; at Thaxted 1000 to 800. "Judging from such evidence as we have," he remarks, "we must assume that this loss of woodland represents that extension of the cultivated area that was always in progress."

Village structure in open and in forest areas contrasted

That such processes as we have been considering might result in a type of settlement profoundly differing from that which developed

[1] For the conclusions drawn from the facts I am responsible. D.B., as Mr Corbett reminds me, offers no evidence as to the age of these hamlets relative to the vills in which they are included.

Map J. Portions of parishes in Cambridgeshire and North Essex
(1) Ashdon, Castle Camps and Kirtling. Diffuse village structure in forest land. (2) Dullingham. Primary and secondary settlement in forest land. (3) Triplow. Typical nucleated village in open country. (4) Elmdon with Elmdonbury (p. 304).

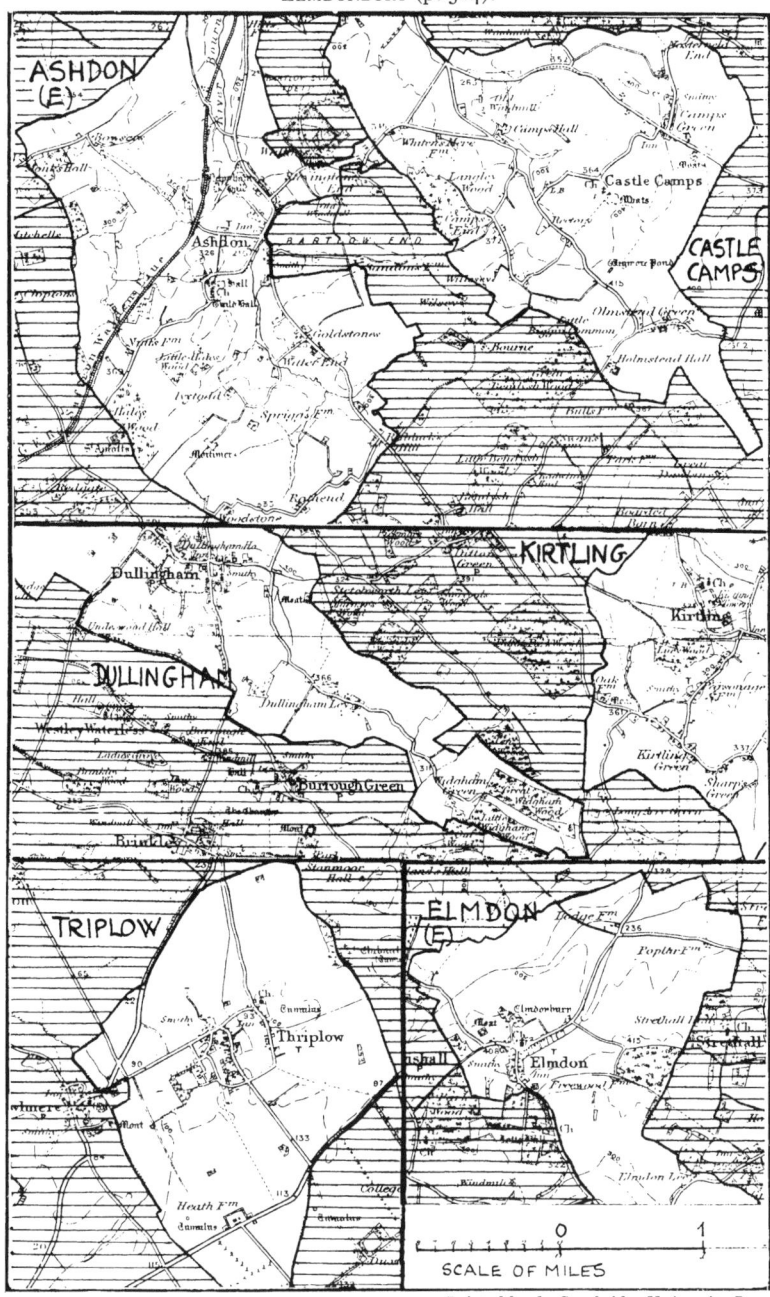

Printed by the Cambridge University Press

Based upon the Ordnance Survey Map, with the sanction of the Controller of H.M. Stationery Office.

in the open areas of primary settlement which we have examined, is to be expected.

The nucleated village containing a cluster of houses in the midst of its fields is the normal type in Cambridgeshire, well illustrated by the O.S. map of Triplow reproduced on Map J. Here no pre-enclosure farmsteads exist save in the clearly defined village area.

In the woodland district in the south of our Region, however, a more diffuse structure was prevalent. The map of the parishes of Castle Camps and Ashdon [E] illustrates this tendency.

Ashdon has a central nucleus round church and hall with open fields to the north; the process by which the forest in the southern part of the parish was transformed into arable is illustrated by the tangle of roads and lanes linking up farmsteads and hamlets; these doubtless originated in the paths leading from clearing to clearing in dense woodland. The adjacent parish, Castle Camps, is an area of diffuse settlement almost without a nucleus. Kirtling, another Domesday vill, is an even better example of the type. Though only a small parish it consists of five hamlets evenly distributed throughout its area. A portion is shown on Map J.

It would therefore appear that such a type of settlement does not necessarily indicate racial differences (as Meitzen affirmed), but may result from the physical condition of the occupied district. It must, however, be remembered that *nucleated* villages occur in forest areas in Western Cambridgeshire and Eastern Huntingdonshire; some cause or causes other than the purely physical one must therefore have been in operation to produce diffuse settlement. The point is evidently worth investigating.

Finally, one may note that in the Cambridge Region, as elsewhere, the main Roman roads did not attract settlement; the distribution of the Domesday vills being evidently governed by factors independent of the existence of these roads, save at nodal points (river crossings). The villages of Great and Little Stukeley [Hunts.] may be held to present exceptions to the rule; but they are sited on the edge of the boulder-clay as are dozens of villages in our district and their relation to the Ermine Street is, I think, accidental.

Expansion of Settlement in the Roman and Anglo-Saxon Ages compared

It has been observed that the Roman Age presents the only parallel to the later Anglo-Saxon Age in respect to settlement in the forest areas; and we are now able to obtain a clearer idea as to the nature of such settlements as are known to exist in these districts in the former Age. Foci of settlement such as are represented by cemeteries at Kelshall and Sandon and Little Walden, by houses at Ashdon and Thaxted (see Map IV) may well indicate not only the transformation of forest into arable in their immediate neighbourhood but the existence of secondary clearings, the material traces of which (pottery, etc.) are too slight to have provoked recognition in modern days.

Again, if the distribution of finds of Roman date in the forest area west of Cambridge (north of Bourn Brook and east of Ermine Street), or in Huntingdonshire east of Ermine Street be compared with the distribution of Domesday vills in these areas, the parallelism will be apparent; and we may justifiably picture the processes of expansion of the arable in the I–IV centuries as identical with those operating in the VIII–XI centuries.

The extent to which this expansion was carried in the Roman Age cannot be definitely stated. That it proceeded even as far as in the Anglo-Saxon Age (at the close of which, as we know, immense tracts of woodland were still untouched) may be doubted. If settlement, for example, were in the former Age as close as in the later in the forest area south of the River Lark in Suffolk, I cannot believe that the recorded traces would be so slight as the map shows them to be. That the woodlands in the neighbourhood of Cambridge were entirely cleared is, however, possible.

CHAPTER VII
CONCLUSIONS

"The whole stage of things scarce serveth for our instruction."
SIR THOMAS BROWNE.

THE summaries contained in each chapter present the considered views of the writer on the archaeological evidence bearing on the history of each successive Age. Here the main results may be coördinated, their implications discussed, and the constant factors influencing our history emphasized.

A survey covering considerably more than three thousand years, from the Neolithic Age prior to 2000 B.C. to the close of the Anglo-Saxon Age, 1066 A.D., has demonstrated that the geological structure of our district is the dominant factor which has determined the position and range of Man's settlement and has controlled and limited his activities. Broadly speaking, the Cambridge Region can be divided into two areas, which have been described as of "primary settlement" and of "secondary settlement" respectively.

The area of "primary settlement" comprises those sites where abundant supplies of fresh water are adjacent to heathy warrens, wide stretches of upland pasture, or fertile cornlands; to wit, the valleys of the Little Ouse and Lark, the eastern borders of the fens (and, to some extent, the fen islands) and the Upper Cam[1] and Ivel (Upper Great Ouse) Valleys. The subsoil is for the most part chalk, greensand, or sands and gravels. Limited settlement has also been possible from the earliest times on the gravel terraces which border the streams in forest country.

The area of "secondary settlement" consists of densely forested country for the most part upland, the subsoil being mainly drift (chalky boulder-clay). It is coloured green on the maps.

The greater part of the former area can, as we have seen, be occupied or utilized by Man the stock-breeder; practically the whole of it by Man the tiller of the soil.

Evidence of continuity of settlement through 3000 years on sites within this area is abundant, as the period maps show. The valleys of the Lark and Little Ouse have been in occupation since Palaeolithic times, and present a most remarkable instance of continuity, every culture phase being represented. The neighbourhood of abundant chalk

---

[1] The lateral valleys of the Bourn River and the Essex Cam, as well as the main valley.

springs, as at Melbourn, Litlington, Wilbraham, and gravel terraces by the Cam, as at Barnwell, have probably never been entirely uninhabited since Neolithic times; while the fringes of the eastern fens, and the fen islands, such as Shippea, have, there can be little doubt, provided homes for fishers and fowlers without intermission for several thousand years. Continuity of occupation on such sites, so long as the land is inhabited, is indeed inevitable.

Effective occupation of the area of secondary settlement, on the other hand, is dependent on a certain standard of civilization being attained by an agricultural community. Development in forest districts involves much labour for which no adequate immediate return is possible; it therefore depends on security and a reasonable amount of political stability. The increase in the population which this brings about provides the necessary stimulus. Slight evidence of occupation of the forest area exists, it is important to note, in primitive culture phases, but in such must necessarily have been that of hunters—limited and non-progressive.

There are two periods within our survey which reveal a marked development of Man's activities in the area of secondary settlement; the Roman, and the Anglo-Saxon in its later phase. The interval, a period of invasion and conquest, accompanied by a sudden decline to barbarism, is marked significantly enough by the shrinkage of occupation to the area of primary settlement.

This view is based on the assumption that the area of occupation in the pagan Anglo-Saxon period can be deduced from an examination of the distribution of Anglo-Saxon cemeteries. The possibility of the survival of Romano-British elements in the less fertile districts is referred to on p. 282 and by implication on pp. 275 and 311.

A more detailed analysis of the area of primary settlement discloses interesting variations in the extent and range of occupation at different periods. In the Neolithic Age, when agriculture was of secondary importance, the sandy warrens of N.W. Suffolk and the eastern borders of the fens were the favoured districts, settlement being doubtless as to-day mainly in the river valleys and by the well-heads of the chalk.

The distribution of remains of the Neolithic and Bronze Ages in the eastern fens, especially those of the former Age, and their position in many cases on the marl or clay below the peat, has suggested that the ancient configuration of the country has been modified by subsidence and that areas such as Burnt Fen (see Map I) may originally have been dry land. Subsequently, shallow meres free from peat must have occupied large portions of the existing fenland.

CONCLUSIONS

The development of agriculture and of stock-breeding in the Bronze and Early Iron Ages caused a gradual extension of occupation—possibly an actual movement of population—from north-east to south-west along the chalk belt; from the warrens to the fertile alluvial plains of the main river valleys. The maps of the Neolithic, Bronze, and Early Iron Ages show how the change in the course of centuries—millennia it may be—worked itself out. With the effective occupation in the latter Age of the cornlands of the Ivel (Upper Great Ouse) Valley stability was attained. Though the Lark Valley within narrow limits is fertile and has always maintained a not inconsiderable population, the Upper Cam and the Ivel Valleys must always be the chief centres in our district of a people whose polity is based on agriculture[1].

The process by which, when a people has attained a certain measure of civilization, the areas of secondary settlement are developed has been discussed in Chapter VI (pp. 309–10) and need not be repeated here.

It should be noted that the results of the topographical analysis here summarized confirm the views on the distribution and movement of population in Britain in prehistoric times implicit or explicit in the work of Crawford, Fleure, Peake and others (see especially Fleure and James, 1916). Fleure and Whitehouse (1916, p. 123) point out that a population map of South England in the Stone Age would be very nearly the converse of a corresponding map for the present day. Comparison between the Neolithic map and (as representing a civilized period) the Roman map shows this to be true for the Cambridge Region.

The Cambridge Region is geographically part of the Fenland Basin, and is linked up by navigable rivers and by natural traffic routes to Lincolnshire and the north generally; on the other hand, direct contact with the south and south-east is hampered by the presence of a broad and continuous belt of forest, occupying the greater part of Suffolk, North Essex and North Hertfordshire.

From this it has followed that not only is there a tendency to unity of cultural character in our limited area, but also a tendency to unity embracing the east coastal district (the eastern plain of the geographers) as a whole from Yorkshire to Cambridgeshire, the southern boundary being the forest belt. The existence of this culture area was dimly visible to us in the Neolithic Age, and more clearly in the Early Bronze Age, while it is a marked feature of the pagan Anglo-Saxon period; and the well-defined southern limit, in Cam-

---

[1] I do not take into consideration the highly artificial conditions existing to-day in the fenlands.

bridgeshire, of the northern school of monumental art of X A.D. as worked out by C. Fox (1922) may justly be regarded as an expression of the same forces. To say that the situation of this natural culture area and the trend of the sea-coast which forms its eastern boundary lay it open to Continental influence from the north-east—Scandinavia, the Elbe region, Northern Holland—is to state a fact familiar to all, but the amplification which the results of the survey suggest may be less evident: namely, that those parts of England most open to Continental influence—the area south of the Thames, on the one hand, and the eastern plain on the other—always tend to form distinct culture areas, our region forming the natural southern boundary of the latter. This generalization requires further consideration.

It is evident that the cultural differentiation of the eastern plain may be in a given case due (i) to geographical isolation; (ii) to immigrants differing somewhat in culture from those who are at the same time occupying S.E. Britain; (iii) to the maintenance of commercial relations with N.E. Europe; or to a combination of these causes. History provides us with a fourth possibility— partial occupation of Britain by invading elements. This was seen in IX–X A.D. when the Danes failed to maintain their conquests in the southern Midlands beyond the natural boundaries of the eastern plain.

Their hold on Essex was slight. Edward the Elder in 911 advanced his frontier from London to Witham without opposition (*A.-S. C.* Parker MS. (Ā), 913).

With regard to (ii): we know that the Continental provenance of the Anglo-Saxon invaders was the region round and especially to the north of the lower Elbe, and can be certain that the portal of entry of this people into our district was the Wash and the fen rivers. Archaeological evidence renders it fairly certain that the beaker-folk entered by the same estuary, and the Peterborough finds are in favour of its having been employed by iron-using peoples about 500–400 B.C. Such a mode of entry suggests that those who in a given (pre-historic) migration period occupied our district embarked from Continental harbours further north than their contemporaries who invaded Kent and S.E. England, and may thus have been composed of different tribal or military groups; the grave-furniture and pottery of such might show differential individuality, but I have not yet gathered sufficient evidence to prove the point.

With reference to (iii): Maintenance of commercial relations with N.E. Europe may have helped, as we have seen, to differentiate our "Anglian" district in the pagan Anglo-Saxon period.

CONCLUSIONS

Geographical isolation has not only tended to differentiate the culture of the Cambridge Region; it has caused it normally to remain at a lower level than that of south England, for advances in culture are of southern origin and contact with the south is limited and hampered by the forest belt, the only convenient route being that from the south-west along the chalk escarpment. The disadvantage of our situation was very manifest in two periods, the Early Bronze and the pagan Anglo-Saxon; the analysis of the contents of 55 barrows in our district dating in the former period has shown that only 7·3 per cent. contained bronze, a percentage but little higher than that of Yorkshire, and very much lower than that of Wiltshire. In the latter period Kent was clearly at a higher stage of civilization than was East Anglia.

That in certain early periods, such as the Middle and the Late Bronze Age, the culture of the Cambridge Region was on the whole as high as in Britain south of the Thames is probable; but if our knowledge of such periods were more complete we should, I think, find that our culture, and still more that of districts further north, tended to lag behind that of South Britain. The remarkable wealth in gold and fine bronze implements of East Anglia in general and the Cambridge Region in particular in the Middle Bronze Age may be due partly to freedom of trade along the Icknield Way, partly to the utilization of east coast ports by gold traders from the Continent, consequent on that freedom. Our connections then were with Wiltshire, which was probably the economic centre of Britain.

At one interesting period within the range of our survey Southern Cambridgeshire was culturally part of South-east Britain. This was in the century which preceded the Roman conquest, the second phase of the Early Iron Age, when a highly organized civilization developed, chiefly in the cornlands of Kent, Essex and Hertfordshire; and I have shown by analysis of coin finds, pottery and cremation interments that the break in culture between north and south, the boundary, that is, between the Iceni and the Catuvellauni, was actually within our district.

It may here be noted that it is especially important that research should be directed to elucidating the history of the *first* phase of the Early Iron Age in Eastern England. An analysis of pottery presenting late Hallstatt features, discovered from time to time in Cambridgeshire (but hitherto neglected) has shown that the culture phase represented in Southern England on sites such as All Cannings Cross was present here. I do not know whether this culture is to be associated in our district with the first arrival of the Brythons, or whether it represents an earlier invasion; the date, moreover, cannot yet be fixed, but V B.C. seems probable.

It has been made clear in the course of this survey that we cannot obtain much assistance in defining successive racial movements from the Continent into the Cambridge Region from craniological data. It would, however, appear that—broadly speaking—the three main European types have played successive parts in our district as elsewhere in England; the Mediterranean ("Iberian") long-heads, mixed "Alpine" broad-heads, and the Nordic long-heads.

The rarity of long barrows in the Cambridge Region, and their complete absence from the populous Lark Valley area suggest that the "Iberian" folk having this culture may have been here but an intrusive dominant stratum, representing a very small minority of the population. The burial customs of the mass of the Neolithic population in our district are thus unknown, as is their racial type. About 2000 B.C. there arrived the broad-heads, this being, so far as is known, the only intrusion of the type *en masse* into England. The subsequent ethnological history of Eastern England, so far as our slender data permit generalization, would seem to be that of successive waves of invasion by peoples of Nordic type, and no doubt all from the Continental shores of the North Sea. At present I am inclined to the view that the chronological sequence was somewhat as follows: (*a*) *circa* 1000 B.C., Celtic-speaking peoples, introduce the leaf-shaped bronze sword; (*b*) *circa* 500–400 B.C., Celtic-speaking peoples, introduce iron; reinforced, (*c*) *circa* 150 B.C., by the closely related Belgae.

The latter were followed 600 years later by (*d*) the Anglo-Saxons, whose definite invasion was doubtless postponed for a century or two by the military power of the Roman Empire. It is, it seems, improbable that one could distinguish anatomically between any of these swarms from the ancient Nordic stock.

Certain of these invasions, that of the beaker-folk in the III millennium and of the iron-using Celtic-speaking peoples about 500–400 B.C., for example, seem to coincide with advances in culture. It is, however, probable that the effect of these invasions has generally been a temporary lowering of the standard of civilization in our district. Though the culture of the invaders may have had potentialities (*e.g.* knowledge of iron) superior to that of the natives, they were almost certainly less civilized, coming as they did from more backward regions bordering on the North Sea.

Whatever the movements of peoples in Europe may have been,

the cultural movements, as has already been pointed out, were mainly from south to north. In Eastern England in general, and in the Cambridge Region in particular the invaders from overseas have usually entered from the north and east, while the culture (trade) routes came from the south-west, south, or south-east. In the II millennium B.C. the Icknield Way was, I think, the main channel of entry; during the Early Iron Age the Lea Valley-Essex Cam Valley route from the lower Thames, and the Stour Valley route from Essex estuaries seem to have taken its place. These local changes are correlated with well-recognized changes in Continental trade-routes which tended to shorten the sea passage into Britain.

It is of course true that the most significant invasion of all, that of the Roman, entered Cambridgeshire from the south; and is thus an exception to the rule which we have formulated. This was an expansion of the Mediterranean civilization into Britain; an active phase of the ameliorative process by which directly or indirectly the standard of culture of northern peoples has been raised.

The expansion was temporary; but its results in the Cambridge Region, though less than might have been expected, were very definite.

The Roman civilization was swept away, and the Anglo-Saxon conquest resulted, apparently, in a return to the area of primary settlement; but the material achievements of that civilization profoundly modified the subsequent history of our Region. Metalled roads, causeways, paved fords such as the Roman made survive prolonged neglect, and while they survive they present routes for traffic, trade and war along alignments otherwise barred to a primitive people.

To this cause is due, among other results discussed in Chapter VI, the survival of Cambridge, a Roman creation.

Man in all Ages—Neolithic, Bronze, Early Iron—had dwelt on the gravel terraces by the river here; but the concentration of the Anglo-Saxons in the neighbourhood of Castle Hill is a novel phenomenon in the history of the settlement of primitive folk in our Region. It was imposed on them by circumstance, namely, the creation of an artificial centre of traffic routes by the Romans; the permanence of Roman road construction was such that the desertion of the site in late VII, attested by Bede, was necessarily temporary.

Study of the interrelation of successive culture phases in the Cambridge Region and of recurrent phenomena has yielded results of interest.

Much light, for example, has been thrown on the local Roman road system by an analysis of prehistoric trackways; the Romans are seen to have made extensive use of these earlier ways. An examination of the Roman roads in relation to the boundaries of Anglo-Saxon kingdoms, moreover, has suggested a solution in one important case at least, of their partial survival, and a promising line of enquiry has thus been opened up.

Comparison of the maps of the Early Iron, Roman, and Anglo-Saxon Ages has suggested (p. 219) a reason for the absence of Anglo-Saxon villages on Roman roads more consistent with the physiographical factors governing settlement in the Cambridge Region than that generally advanced. Examination of the distribution of finds attributable to the dawn of the Bronze Age and to the pagan Anglo-Saxon period respectively emphasizes the dominance of these factors; though separated by some two to three thousand years the beaker-folk and the Anglian settlers were, it is clear, similarly limited in their choice of sites for habitation (p. 274).

In the Cambridge Region the break in culture between the Middle and Late Bronze periods is very marked, practically no objects of the former period being found in association with those proper to the latter. So sharp a distinction does not seem to be present in Britain generally. Consideration of a similar phenomenon occurring 1400 years later suggests a possible explanation. In the Anglo-Saxon pagan period the influence of Romano-British art on the culture of the invaders (as represented by their grave-goods), very slight in East Anglia, becomes more marked as one proceeds westward across England. This fact is generally held to indicate that, broadly stated, while in Eastern Britain the Romanized inhabitants fled or were exterminated, in the less accessible parts they were (at a later date) absorbed. It is not improbable that similar fates overtook the men of the rapier-palstave-looped spear armature at the hands of the leaf-sword folk.

At the commencement of this analysis the tendency to unity of cultural character in the Cambridge Region in any given Age was held to be the natural consequence of the geographical unity which a river basin possesses. The peculiar configuration of the district—a narrow belt of open country bordered by fen and forest and forming a highway into Norfolk and North Suffolk—has, however, permitted this tendency at times to be modified by military or political action.

Evidence of cultural differences between the Lark Valley district of N.W. Suffolk and Southern Cambridgeshire is apparent in the later phase of the Early Iron Age, when the cremation culture of S.E. Britain was extending northward. Such differences necessarily disappear during the Roman Age when cultural unity was imposed on the greater part of Britain; and it is thus interesting to observe that after an interval of nearly 500 years (minor) divergencies of culture as between these two areas reappear in the pagan Anglo-Saxon period.

Now the earliest dateable objects found in our hill-forts are of the Early Iron Age; and the only one excavated, War Ditches, near Cherryhinton, is of this Age. It is possible that developed political and military organization, resulting in the construction all over the country of defensive earthworks on a grand scale, was the contribution of the Brythonic Celts to our social and economic history. There is some evidence that the defensible possibilities of the chalk escarpment were appreciated by this people; and the fact that differences in culture between the north-east and the south-west of our area are in the Early Iron Age first clearly demonstrable, is held to be not without significance in this connection.

The development, then, of political homogeneity in East Anglia, resulting in the construction of a military barrier or barriers on the vulnerable frontier between the Lark Valley and Cambridge, in the Early Iron Age by the Iceni, in the Anglo-Saxon Age by the "East Angles," is an hypothesis put forward to account for the cultural divergencies we are considering. The evidence provided by recent excavations suggests that the East Angles constructed the Fleam Dyke.

Many of the inductions arrived at in the course of this survey, and utilized in these conclusions, depend on the accuracy of the topographical pictures of distribution of finds and remains of each successive Age. These are all necessarily incomplete reflections of the life of the dwellers in our Region, both in scale and range; and in so far as they are incomplete my inductions are subject to correction. But the indications of human activity which they reveal are, on the whole, consistent one Age with another; the variations are evidently manifestations of secular change, which permit of reasonable explanation; and the history of three thousand years as thus depicted is, I think, sufficiently coherent to warrant the belief that future discoveries will not, in respect to the range of Man's activities, or to the distinction drawn between areas of primary and of secondary settlement, materially modify the conclusions here set down.

APPENDIX I

LIST OF BEAKERS OF THE "TRANSITION PERIOD" FOUND IN THE CAMBRIDGE REGION

Ref. no.	Parish	County	Height in inches	Present location	Abercromby type letter	Notes and references[1]
I	Barnwell	C.	7·3	Camb. Mus.	A	Abercromby (Pl. IX, fig. 69, and pp. 24, 88)
II	Barton Mills	S.	5·6	Colchester Mus.	C	Abercromby (Pl. X, fig. 93, and pp. 26, 88)
III	Berden	E.	7·5	Walden Mus.	A	Maynard and Benton (1920)
IV	Brandon	S.	3·8	Brit. Mus.	B	Associated. Abercromby (Pl. IX, figs. 82, 83, pp. 25, 88); Franks (1873); B.M.G. (1920, p. 68)
V	,,	S.	5	,,	B	
VI	Chesterford	E.	6	Audley End Mus.	A	Unpublished. "Found outside Boro' Field 1860"
VII	Chesterford?	E.	5·5	,, ,,	A	Closely resembles No. VI. Unpublished
VIII	Chesterton	C.	—	Camb. Mus.	—	Fragment.
IX	Doddington	C.	—	,,	A	Fragmentary. Unpublished
X	Ely?	C.	—	,,	—	Fragment. Domestic.
XI	Eriswell?[2]	S.	7·5	,,	A	Abercromby (Pl. VII, fig. 45, and pp. 23, 88)
XII	Fordham	C.	5·1	,,	—	Handled mug. My Pl. II
XIII	Hitchin?	H.	6·6	Brit. Mus.	A	Maynard and Benton (1920)
XIV	Icklingham	S.	5·7	Bury Mus.	C	Proc. S.I.A. (xi, p. 59)
XV	Lakenheath	S.	5·2	Camb. Mus.	B	My Pl. I
XVI	,,	S.	7·3	Brit. Mus.	A	Associated. For No. XVI see Abercromby (Pl. VIII, fig. 61, and pp. 24, 88)
XVII	,,	S.	5·3	,,	B	
XVIII	Methwold (S. of)	N.	5·5	,,	B	Abercromby (Pl. IX, fig. 80, and pp. 25, 88)
XIX	Ramsey St Mary's	Hunts.	—	Peterborough Mus.	A?	Fragmentary. Abbott (1910, p. 339)
XX	Shefford	B.	5·6	Huntingdon Inst.	A	Unpublished
XXI	Snailwell	C.	5·1	Camb. Mus.	A	Associated? Abercromby (Pl. VIII, fig. 65, Pl. X, fig. 89, and pp. 24, 26, 88)
XXII	,,	C.	7·5	,,	C	
XXIII	Somersham	Hunts.	10·8	,,	B	Abercromby (Pl. IX, fig. 76, and pp. 25, 88)
XXIV	Tuddenham	S.	5·7	Brit. Mus.	A	Abercromby (Pl. VIII, fig. 46, and pp. 23, 24, 88)
XXV	Wilburton	C.	6·1	Camb. Mus.	A	My Pl. I
XXVI	Worlington	S.	5	Brit. Mus.	AB	Abercromby (Pl. IX, fig. 70, and p. 25)
XXVII	Eriswell	S.	—	,,	—	Fragment. Domestic. W. G. Clarke (1915)
XXVIII	Santon	N.	—	,,	—	Fragment. ?Domestic. Penes W. G. Clarke
XXIX	Soham	C.	7·3	Ashmolean Mus.	C	Unpublished. Evans' Coll.
XXX	Somersham?	Hunts.	7·9	Camb. Mus.	B	Handled mug. Unpublished

Beakers from Great Barton [S] (Bury Mus.) and March (Camb. Mus.) are not included in the List or Map, being derived from sites just outside the limits of our Region, as defined in the Introduction. The provenance of the beaker in Bury Mus., figured on Pl. I, fig. 4, is uncertain, but it is certainly of local origin. For possible additions to my list see Barrows No. 15 and 19, p. 326.

[1] Abercromby = Abercromby, 1912, vol. i.
[2] A MS. note in C. M. gives Barton Hill, Barton Mills, as provenance.

APPENDIX II

BRONZE AGE

A. LIST OF HOARDS, OTHER THAN FOUNDERS'; AND SMALL GROUPS OF ASSOCIATED OBJECTS, SOME (?) VOTIVE

Ref. no.	Provenance	County	No. of objects	Chief types represented	Present location, principal references and notes
				(a) Early Bronze Period	
1	Grunty Fen	C.	2	Flanged axes	Alnwick Cas. Colln.
2	Mildenhall (Holywell Row)	S.	4	Flanged axes	St Albans Mus.
3	Postlingford (Hall Farm)	S.	21	Flanged axes, gold rings	Bury Mus. (four), Brit. Mus. (four), Evans (pp. 48, 389, and 464—further references)
				(b) Middle Bronze Period	
4	Stretham (Granta [*sic*] Fen)	C.	9	Rapier, gold torc and rings	Brit. Mus. Veasey (1853)
5	Grunty Fen	C.	4	Palstaves, gold armilla	C.M. Von Hügel (1908)
6	Grunty Fen	C.	3+x	Looped spear, palstaves, etc.	Alnwick Cas. (spear). "Found with palstaves and other bronzes"
				(c) Late Bronze Period	
7	Barrington	C.	3	Sock. axes, gouge	C.M. Evans (pp. 118, 462)
8	Burwell (Fen)	C.	2	Sock. axe, spear	Dr C. Lucas, Burwell
9	Bury (near)	S.	7	Sock. axes	Mr S. G. Fenton (seven, labelled "hoard found near Bury")
10	Chatteris (Langwood Fen)	C.	2	Looped spear, shield	C.M.
11	Coveney (Fen)	C.	2	Shields	C.M. Evans (p. 346, fig. 430)
12	Eriswell	S.	5	Sock. axe, palstaves	Bury Mus. (three), Brit. Mus. (two). Found in a barrow, 1837
13	Exning	S.	7+x	Sock. axes, spears, etc.	Brit. Mus. *Arch. Journ.* IX, 303; Evans (pp. 174, 461, 466)
14	Fulbourn (Common)	C.	5	Swords, spear, etc.	Brit. Mus. (two). E. D. Clarke (1821, figured); Evans (pp. 279, 282, 320, 340, 460, 464)
15	Hitchin (near Willbury Hill)	H.	4+x	Sock. axes, spear, etc.	St Albans Mus. *Soc. Antiq. Proc.* XXIV, pp. 133 ff. See also Buller (1913)
16	Melbourn	C.	7	Sock. axe, sword, gouge, etc.	*Arch. Journ.* XI, p. 294; Evans (pp. 174, 397, 461, 466)
17	Mildenhall	S.	2	Spears	Mr S. G. Fenton's Colln.
18	Pidley	Hunts.	2	Sock. axes	Huntingdon Inst. (one damaged). ? Part of Founder's hoard
19	Sawston	C.	5+x	Sock. axes, winged axe, spears	Walden Mus. (two). Maynard (19—, p. 2)
20	Wilburton (**Fen**)	C.	163	Sock. axes, palstave, swords, spears, etc.	C.M. J. Evans (1884)

NOTE. Evans = J. Evans (1881).

B. LIST OF HOARDS, PROBABLY OR CERTAINLY FOUNDERS'
(All of the Late Bronze Period)

Ref. no.	Provenance	County	No. of objects	Chief types represented	Present location, principal references and notes
21	Arkesden (Chardwell Farm)	E.	50*	Sock. and winged axes, palstave, spears, swords, mould, etc.	Some in Walden Mus. and Mayer Colln., Liverpool. J. Clark (1873)
22	Barrow (Old Hall)	S.	2	Swords	Bury Mus., Brit. Mus. Prigg (1888 b), Evans (p. 279, fig. 343)
23	Burwell (Churchyard)	C.	3*	Sock. axe, spear, tanged chisel	C.M. Found "near the tower." C.A.S. Rep. 22, 1862, p. 10
24	Burwell (Fen)	C.	3*	Sock. axe, spear, ring	C.M. Evans (pp. 112, 463, 467)
25	Chippenham	C.	3*	Swords	H. Prigg (1888 b)
26	Clavering (Clavering Bury)	E.	43+x	Sock. axes, spears	C.M. (two). MS. record in Mus. See Antiq. Journ. III, 65
27	Chrishall	E.	30+x*	Sock. axes, spears, sock. knife, swords, ring, etc.	Audley End Mus. (include those labelled Elmdon), Brit. Mus., Mayer Colln., Liverpool. Neville (1848, p. 2), J. Clark (1873, p. 280), Evans (pp. 117, 283, 462, 467)
28	Feltwell (Fen)	N.	13*	Sock. axes, spears, razor, gold leaf, etc.	Brit. Mus.
29	Furneaux Pelham	H.	4+x*	Sock. axes	Audley End Mus. (one). Neville MS.
30	Lakenheath	S.	3*	Sock. axe, palstave, sword	C.M.
31	Meldreth (Station)	C.	44*	Sock. axes, palstaves, spears, swords, etc.	Majority in Brit. Mus. Evans (pp. 172, 214, 411, 424, 462, 466)
32	Reach (Fen)	C.	53*	Sock. axes, spears, swords, gouges, etc.	C.M. (one, and metal). H. Prigg (1880), Evans (see his Index)
33	Rushden (Cumberlow Green)	H.	40*	Sock. axes, winged axes, swords, rapier?	C.M. (six), Brit. Mus. (many), Mr M. R. Pryor's Colln. (two). Bally (1877), Evans (pp. 94, 110, 424, 462, 467)
34	Therfield (near "Long Hill")	H.	1*	Axe	C.M. (metal only). Nunn's MS., p. 1
35	Wicken (Fen)	C.	9	Spears, swords, chape, etc.	Brit. Mus. (five). Evans (pp. 287, 460, 464)

* Indicates presence of founders' metal—jets or ingots of copper or bronze.
NOTE. Evans = J. Evans (1881).

APPENDIX III

LIST OF SIXTY-ONE BARROWS (Nos. 1–60 AND 22 A) IN THE CAMBRIDGE REGION, EXCAVATED, AND CONSIDERED TO BE OF THE BRONZE AGE[1]

[*Arranged alphabetically by Parishes*]

1. AMPTON [S], "Seven Hills." The most northerly barrow of the group on east side of Bury-Thetford road. Excavated (incompletely) in 1868. It contained many cremation interments. Greenwell (1869 a). One urn in British Museum.

The following nine barrows, at Balsham (Nos. 2–9), were excavated by Neville in 1848:

2–4. BALSHAM. Three barrows in Charterhouse Plantation, on the east side of the London-Newmarket road. For Nos. 2 and 3 see p. 34 of text. No. 4 contained a primary inhumation interment and bones of ox and sheep. A secondary interment, of Roman (?) date, was noted. These barrows are 20, 27 H and 21 B in Neville MS., Audley End Museum. The urn from 27 H is in the Museum.

5–7. BALSHAM. Three barrows in field adjacent to plantation mentioned above. No. 5 contained an inhumation interment. Two flint flakes were found, and plenty of charcoal in the mass of the barrow. No. 6 yielded a cinerary urn containing burnt human bones; there was a bronze pin within the ashes. No. 7 was composed of "greasy fatty ashes." "Human bones" are noted, and a "small fragment of rather finer pottery than usual." See p. 37 of text, and barrows Nos. 22 C, 23 D and 24 E in Neville MS. The urn from 23 D is in Audley End Museum.

8, 9. BALSHAM. "Summit of steep hill a short mile from preceding group." Two barrows within 50 yards of each other. No. 8 was composed of greasy fatty ashes mixed with soil. A "flint knife" and bones of the ox were found; together with a bronze object evidently of later date. No. 9 contained inhumation burials and an antler of the red deer only. Refer to barrows Nos. 25 F and 26 G in Neville MS.

10. BALSHAM. Barrow to the south of the Fleam Dyke (probably near Dungate Farm). The barrow contained three cinerary urns with burnt bones and ashes. Four flint flakes were found in the mound. Barrow No. 28 I in Neville MS. One urn is in Audley End Museum.

11. BARTON MILLS [S]. Barton Hill (Chalk Hill). One of four barrows. It contained inhumation and cremation interments. See p. 31 of text, and Greenwell (1869 a, p. 20).

12, 13. BOTTISHAM. Two barrows west of Bottisham Heath Farm. Marked on 6-inch O.S. XLVIII, N.E. Excavated in 1908. In one a burial

---

[1] Of the 61, two (Nos. 23 and 52) contained beaker burials. A supplementary list containing a further twenty excavated barrows (Nos. 61–80), probably or possibly of the Bronze Age, is appended.

by inhumation. Flint flakes and scrapers, tiny fragments of Bronze Age pottery, burnt human bones and charcoal were found in both. Finds in Cambridge Museum. Details from the late C. P. Allix, Esq., of Swaffham Prior House.

14. BOTTISHAM. Barrow, "near Street Way," "1½ miles from village." Excavated in 1852. See p. 35 of text, and barrow No. 29 in Neville MS. at Audley End.

15. BURWELL, Newmarket Heath. Ninescore Hill Barrow, 800 yards due east of Running Gap. Destroyed 1885. It contained two inhumation interments associated with beakers (?), and flint arrowheads, and a secondary interment, probably Saxon. Hughes (1885 b).

16. BURWELL. Newmarket Heath, "Tumulus on Exercise Ground." Destroyed in 1827. It contained a primary cremation interment. *Gent. Mag.* (1827); Babington (1883, 68).

17. BURWELL (?). Newmarket Heath, "Tumulus[1]." Exact site unknown. Contained a cremation interment. Burnt bones and sherds of Bronze Age type, also Roman sherds, in Camb. Mus. (Acc. List, 1892, 4).

18. CAVENHAM [S]. Barrow: site unknown. Contained a cremation interment, probably Bronze Age. *S.I.A. Proc.* II, 207.

19. CHRISHALL [E]. Barrow, Chrishall Grange; probably that on county boundary to the north-west of the steading. Excavated in 1847. Contained a primary inhumation interment possibly associated with a beaker, and secondary deposits of the Iron Age. Neville (1848, pp. 27–30).

20. GREAT WILBRAHAM. Mutlow Hill Barrow, close to Icknield Way-Fleam Dyke junction. Excavated by Neville. See p. 35 of text and Neville (1852 b, pp. 226 ff.). Six urns are in Audley End Museum (see Nos. 315–319 in MS. catalogue).

21. HOLWELL, near Hitchin [H]. One of three barrows just south of Willbury Hill. Opened in 1816. It contained a cremation interment, etc. Andrews (1904, p. 286).

22. ICKLINGHAM [S]. "The Cardle." Existence of barrow not certain. An inhumation interment in a stone cist. See p. 33 of text. The associated finds are in Cambridge Museum.

22 A. ICKLINGHAM. "How Hill." "Cinerary urn found and broken up." Letter from Mr W. G. Clarke, 18. 2. 23.

23. LAKENHEATH [S]. Site unknown. Two beakers were found together in a barrow. See Appendix I, Nos. XVI and XVII.

24, 25. MELBOURN. Two barrows in Five Barrow Field south-west of Heath Farm, close to Royston-Newmarket road. Excavated in 1848. No. 24 contained inhumation and cremation interments. No. 25 contained a cremation interment. Urns and incense cup from No. 24 are in Audley End Museum. See Neville (1848, pp. 17–25), and the Neville MS.

26. MELBOURN. Barrow (on Goffers Knoll?) "within ½ mile of Five Barrow Field." Excavated in 1847. See p. 34 and Neville (1848, p. 84).

---

[1] Three barrows are marked on the 1-inch O.S. (1836 edition) as being close to the Street Way, on the heath, and 1000 or more yards north-east of the Dyke; one of these may be No. 17 on my list, the others two of "several" destroyed in 1883 and of which no record survives.

APPENDIX III

27. MEPAL. "A very low and broad tumulus in Mepal Fen." See p. 37 of text and *C.A.S. Rep.* 20, 1860, p. 7.

28, 29. MILDENHALL [S], Warren Hill. "Three Hills" Barrows. In one (No. 28) an inhumation interment. See p. 32 of text and H. Prigg (1872). Food-vessel in Bury Museum. From a second (No. 29) a food-vessel, now in British Museum, was obtained.

30, 31. RISBY [S]. Two barrows on Risby Heath close to the Cavenham Road and to the "Black Ditches."

No. 30 contained inhumation interments and a cremation interment, also secondary Early Iron Age deposit; the other (No. 31, partly explored), cremation interments. See p. 33 of text and Greenwell (1869 *b*).

32. RISBY [S]. One of two barrows on Long Heath Field, 300 yards from Cuckoo Hill and ⅓ mile from Nos. 30 and 31. Contained two cremation interments. Greenwell (1869 *b*).

A large number of tumuli on the ridge adjacent to Upper Hare Park, in SWAFFHAM BULBECK parish, have at different times been examined. The majority are now destroyed. Thirteen (Nos. 33–45) are listed below.

33, 34. "The Beacons." Two barrows at "east end of 4-mile racecourse." An urn from No. 33, destroyed in 1815, is in Cambridge Museum. See *Archaeol.* XVIII, p. 436. The second barrow (No. 34) was opened in 1846 and, presumably, removed then or later. See p. 33 of text, Collings (1846), Babington (1883, p. 67). The urn is in Cambridge Museum.

35. Barrow on north-west side of Upper Hare Park, at "east end of 4-mile racecourse." Partially explored in 1883. Inhumation and cremation interments are recorded, and also a deposit of later date. A small pot and fragments of others in Cambridge Museum. Hughes (1885 *a*).

36. Barrow 300 yards N. 27° W. of Upper Hare Park. Excavated in 1884. It contained inhumation and cremation interments. See p. 66 of text. Finds in Cambridge Museum (Hughes Collection), but no published record of the excavation exists.

37. Round barrow ¼ mile N. 60° W. of Upper Hare Park. Excavated in 1906. Marked on 6-inch O.S. XLI, S.E., S.W. of B.M. 172. It contained inhumation and cremation interments. See p. 32 of text, and Allix and Hughes (1908). One of the urns is in Cambridge Museum (Allix Collection).

38. Barrow "In a field west of Upper Hare Park." Excavated in 1876. Contained three cremation interments. Three urns in Cambridge Museum. See Hughes (1876).

39, 40. "Barrows." Two at least, in Upper Hare Park. Excavated in 1880. Four small urns "discovered in tumuli in 1880" were presented to the Cambridge Museum in 1887 (Acc. List 1887, 19). Two contained burnt bone and charcoal; so also probably did the others; for burnt bones and charcoal from the same donor obtained during the excavations are also in the Museum.

41. Barrow "West of Hare Park." Excavated in 1875. A small vessel (4 inches high) is figured by Hughes and Allix (1908, p. 322).

42. Barrow "at Upper Hare Park," on crest of hill overlooking

Bottisham, near west entrance to Park. Opened in 1876. Contained cremation interments. See Hailstone (1878, Notes and Additions, p. 13). A small urn, with one lug, in Cambridge Museum is thought to be from this barrow.

43. Barrow "A little to the West of Upper Hare Park"; marked on 6-inch O.S. XLI, S.E., in field S.E. of B.M. 172. Excavated in 1882. Contained a cremation interment. The urn is in Allix Collection, Cambridge Museum. See also *C.A.S. Rep.* 44, 1884, p. cxxi.

44. Barrow. Upper Hare Park. Excavated in 1876. Apparently adjacent to No. 38. Contained two inhumation interments with red deer antlers, and secondary burials, Romano-British(?). See Hughes (1876).

45. Barrow 300 yards down south slope of Allington Hill. Excavated in 1846. Probably contained a primary cremation interment in an urn. See Collings (1846, p. 256).

46. THERFIELD [H]. Therfield Heath. "Money" or "Fylers Hill" Barrow. Examined and destroyed in 1855. See p. 36 of text, Beldam (1861, p. 306), and J. Evans (1881, p. 424). The objects found are in the Cambridge Museum.

47, 48. THERFIELD [H]. Therfield Heath. "Five Hills Barrows." Two opened in 1856 by E. B. Nunn. In one (No. 47) a cremated interment; the cinerary urn (height 5 inches) is in Cambridge Museum. The cist in which it lay was lined with large flints. For the other (No. 48) see p. 32 of text. Barrows 5 and 4 in Nunn's MS. in the Cambridge Museum Library, pp. 10 and 12.

49. THERFIELD. Therfield Heath. Barrow: apparently a third of the Five Hills group. Opened by E. B. Nunn in 1854. In the centre was a large cinerary urn (Plate III, No. 4, now in Cambridge Museum), and in the earth surrounding it, a "small bronze or copper pin." See p. 40 of text and Nunn's MS., Barrow No. 6, p. 15.

50. THERFIELD. Therfield Heath? A barrow on "Rumbolds Mount." Opened by E. B. Nunn in 1856. Contained a primary cremation interment without an urn. Nunn's MS., Barrow No. 13, p. 5.

51. THETFORD [N]. On site of cemetery. "Contained burnt human bones and flint flakes." Letter, W. G. Clarke, 18. 2. 23.

52. TUDDENHAM [S]. The beaker, No. XXIV, was derived from a barrow. See Appendix I.

53. WEETING [N]. Grimes Graves. Cremation interment in a barrow. *Rep. P.S.E.A.* (1915, p. 106).

54–59. WEETING. Grimes Graves (near). Cremation interments in seven barrows. Noted by Greenwell (1872, p. 372).

Six of these are identified by Mr W. G. Clarke, in a letter to me (20. 2. 23) as follows: two at Mount Ephraim; one by the Drove road north of Brandon Station; and three on the west side of Brandon-West Tofts road. The seventh is my No. 53, which had previously been trenched.

60. WESTLEY [S]. Barrow on Westley Heath. Large cinerary urn in Bury Museum. *S.I.A. Proc.* VII, 214.

APPENDIX III

LIST OF TWENTY EXCAVATED BARROWS, NOS. 61–80, PROBABLY OR POSSIBLY OF THE BRONZE AGE

61. LITLINGTON. Limlow Hill. Barrow. Destroyed 1888 or 1892. See p. 194 of text, and Nunn's MS., p. 22.

62. MELBOURN. Barrow in Five Barrow Field, west of Heath Farm. Six burials by inhumation. Excavated by Neville (1848, pp. 26–27).

63, 64. STAPLEFORD. The Twopenny Loaves; two barrows on the Gog-Magog Hills adjacent to Worstead Street. Destroyed. One was opened in 1778, and seven skeletons found. The other was destroyed in making the Golf Course; it had been turned up before and only a few broken human bones were found. See Babington (1883, p. 30), and Cooper (1842, p. 7). Information regarding the second barrow obtained from Dr G. S. Graham-Smith.

65–67. THERFIELD [H]. Three barrows probably on Therfield Heath. Opened by E. B. Nunn and described in his MS. (Camb. Mus. Lib.).

68, 69. TRIPLOW. Two barrows "between Heydon and Triplow, to the West of the Royston-Newmarket Road, two miles from Triplow." Excavated in 1846. In both cremation interments associated with bones of the horse. Possibly Early Iron Age. See p. 80 of text; Neville (1848, pp. 14–17, barrows 1 and 3) and (1847, pp. 27–29); also Neville MS. in Audley End Museum.

70. TRIPLOW. The "Twin Barrow." Like the others, apparently on Triplow Heath. Excavated in 1847. Contained an inhumation and a cremation interment, the latter possibly Early Iron Age. An urn of this period from one of these Triplow Barrows is in Audley End Museum. See p. 79 of text, Neville (1848, p. 17) and the Neville MS.

71. TRIPLOW. Barrow on the west side of the Royston-Newmarket road. Excavated by Neville (1848, p. 17). "Imperfectly examined."

72–80. TRIPLOW. Nine barrows on or near Triplow Heath. Excavated by Neville. In addition to the barrows already recorded from this area, a MS. note in Audley End Museum mentions nine in which either nothing was found or which "presented no feature worthy of remark."

REFERENCES TO AUTHORS QUOTED

Abbott, G. Wyman (1910). *Archaeologia*, LXII, p. 333.
Abercromby, Lord (1904). *Soc. Antiq. Scot. Proc.* XXXVIII, p. 323.
—— (1912). *A Study of the Bronze Age Pottery of Great Britain and Ireland.* 2 vols.
Acc. List, C.M. (1887–   ). Lists of Accessions to the Museum of Archaeology and of Ethnology, Cambridge, contained in the Annual Reports of the Antiquarian Committee to the Senate.
Akerman, J. Y. (1839). *Num. Chron.* I, p. 73.
Allcroft, A. Hadrian (1908). *Earthwork of England.*
Allen, J. Romilly (1898). *Archaeologia*, LVI, p. 39.
—— (1904). *The Reliquary*, N.S. X, p. 53.
Allix, C. P. and Hughes, T. McK. (1908). *C.A.S. Proc.* XII, p. 314.
Andrews, R. T. (1904). *East Herts. Arch. Soc. Trans.* II, p. 279.
Anglo-Saxon Chronicle. (See Earle and Plummer.)
Armitage, E. S. (1912). *The Early Norman Castles of the British Isles.*
Armstrong, A. L. (1921). *Antiq. Journ.* I, p. 81.
Artis, E. T. (1828). *The Durobrivae of Antoninus....*
Atkinson, T. D. (1894). *C.A.S. Proc.* VIII, p. 229.
Aylott, G. (1911). *East Herts. Arch. Soc. Trans.* IV, p. 269.
Babington, C. (1874). *S.I.A. Proc.* IV, p. 257.
Babington, Chas. Cardale[1] (1852). *C.A.S. Comm.* I, p. 43.
—— (1860). *Ibid.* II, p. 7.
—— (1863 a). *Ibid.* II, p. 285.
—— (1863 b). *Ibid.* II, p. 289.
—— (1883). *C.A.S.*, 8vo Series, XX; *Ancient Cambridgeshire*, 2nd ed.
Bally, E. F. (1877). *Journ. Anthrop. Inst.* VI, p. 195.
Barker, H. R. (1917). *S.I.A. Proc.* XVI, p. 181.
Battely, J. (1745). *Antiquitates Rutupinae...*
Beldam, J. (1859 a). *Soc. Antiq. Proc.* 1 S. IV, p. 5.
—— (1859 b). *Ibid.* IV, p. 285.
—— (1861). *Ibid.* 2 S. I, p. 306.
—— (1868). *Arch. Journ.* XXV, p. 21.
Belloc, H. (1913). *The Stane Street.*
Beloe, E. M. (1891). *C.A.S. Proc.* VII, p. 112.
—— (1896). *Ibid.* IX, p. 77.
Beltz, R. (1911). *Zeitschrift für Ethnologie*, XLIII, p. 664.
Birch, W. de G. (1893). *Cartularium Saxonicum*, vol. III.
Bowtell, T. MSS. in Downing College Library, Cambridge.
Braybrooke, Richard, 3rd Lord (1836). *History of Audley End.*
Braybrooke, Richard, 4th Lord[2] (1860). *Arch. Journ.* XVII, p. 117.
B.M.G. (1905). *British Museum Guide, Early Iron Age.*
—— (1920). *Ibid. Bronze Age*, 2nd ed.
—— (1922). *Ibid. Roman Britain.*
Brown, G. Baldwin (1915). *The Arts in Early England*, vols. III and IV.
Bull, A. (1904). *Cambs. and Hunts. Arch. Soc. Trans.* I, p. 49.
Buller, G. J. (1913). *East Herts. Arch. Soc. Trans.* V, p. 109.
Bullock-Hall, W. H. (1901). *C.A.S. Proc.* X, p. 69.
Bunbury, Sir H. (1834). *Archaeologia*, XXV, p. 609.
Bury, J. B. (1922). *Journ. Roman Studies*, X, p. 131.
Bushe-Fox, J. P. (1913). *Reports of Research Committee, Soc. Antiq.* No. I. *Excavations...at Wroxeter...in 1912.*
—— (1914). *Ibid.* No. II. *Excavations...at Wroxeter...in 1913.*
—— (1915). *Ibid.* No. III. *Excavations at Hengistbury Head, Hants. in 1911–1912.*
—— (1916). *Ibid.* No. IV. *Excavations...at Wroxeter...in 1914.*
Camden, William (1722). *Britannia*, revised by E. Gibson, 2nd ed.
Chadwick, H. M. (1907). *The Origin of the English Nation.*

[1] For "Babington" without date, in text, read "Babington C.C. 1883."
[2] See also Neville, Hon. R. C.

REFERENCES TO AUTHORS

Christy, Miller (1920). *Essex Arch. Soc. Trans.* N.S. XV, p. 190.
Clark, J. (1873). *Hist. Soc. Lancs. and Ches. Trans.* 3 S. I, p. 271.
Clarke, E. D. (1816). *Archaeologia*, XVIII, p. 340.
—— (1821). *Ibid.* XIX, p. 56.
Clarke, J. (1849). *Brit. Arch. Ass. Journ.* IV, p. 76.
Clarke, W. G. (1895). *Norf. and Norwich Nat. Soc. Trans.* VI, p. 23.
—— (1905). *Ibid.* VIII, p. 25.
—— (1907). *Ibid.* VIII, p. 393.
—— (1912). *P.S.E.A. Proc.* I, p. 240.
—— (1915). *Ibid.* II, p. 39.
—— (1918). *Ibid.* II, p. 539.
—— (1920). *Ibid.* III, p. 206.
Clarke, W. G. and Hewitt, H. D. (1914). *P.S.E.A. Proc.* I, p. 427.
Clinch, George (1901). *V.C.H. Norfolk*, I, p. 253.
—— (1911). *Ibid. Suffolk*, I, p. 263.
Codrington, T. (1918). *Roman Roads in Britain*, 3rd ed.
Collings, W. T. (1846). *Arch. Journ.* III, p. 255.
Conway, Sir Martin (1918). *Soc. Antiq. Proc.* XXX, p. 63.
Conybeare, J. W. E. (1884). *C.A.S. Rep.* XLIV, p. cxvi (In *Comm.* v).
—— (1904). *C.A.S. Proc.* X, p. 434.
Conybeare, E. (J. W. E.) (1911). *Roman Britain*, 2nd ed.
Cooper, C. H. (1842). *Annals of Cambridge*, vol. I.
Corbett, W. J. (1913). *Cambridge.Medieval History*, II, p. 543.
Crawford, O. G. S. (1912 a). *Soc. Antiq. Proc.* XXIV, p. 39.
—— (1912 b). *Geog. Journ.* XL. p. 304.
—— (1922). *Antiq. Journ.* II, p.27.
Cunningham, W. (1909). *C.A.S. Proc.* XIV, p. 74.
Cunnington, Mrs M. E. (1922). *Antiq. Journ.* II, p. 13.
Curle, James (1911). *A Roman Frontier Post and its People...* (Newstead).
Curwen, Eliot and Curwen, E. C. (1918). *Sussex Arch. Coll.* LIX, p. 35.
Dawkins, W. Boyd (1902). *Arch. Journ.* LIX, p. 211.
De Baye, Baron J. (1893). *The Industrial Arts of the Anglo-Saxons.*
Déchelette, Joseph (1901). *Revue Archéologique*, 3 S. XXXIX, p. 51.
—— (1904). *Les Vases céramiques ornés de la Gaule romaine.* 2 vols.
—— (1910). *Manuel d'archéologie prehistorique celtique et gallo-romaine*, II, première partie.
—— (1913). *Ibid.* II, deuxième partie.
—— (1914). *Ibid.* II, troisième partie.
Dixon, F. (1849). *Sussex Arch. Coll.* II, p. 260.
Dryden, Sir H. (1845). *C.A.S.* 4to Pub. No. VIII.
Du Chaillu, P. B. (1889). *The Viking Age.* 2 vols.
Duckworth, W. H. L. (1895). *C.A.S. Proc.* VIII, p. 322.
Dutt, W. A. (1911). *V.C.H. Suffolk*, I, p. 256.
Earle, J. and Plummer, C. (1892). *Two of the Saxon Chronicles Parallel*, vol. I.
Evans, Sir Arthur J.[1] (1890). *Archaeologia*, LII, p. 315.
—— (1908). *Soc. Antiq. Proc.* XXII, p. 121.
—— (1915). *Archaeologia*, LXVI, p. 569.
Evans, Sir John[2] (1864). *The Coins of the Ancient Britons.*
—— (1869). *Num. Chron.* 2 S. IX, p. 319.
—— (1881). *Ancient Bronze Implements....*
—— (1884). *Archaeologia*, XLVIII, p. 106.
—— (1890). *The Coins of the Ancient Britons. Supplement.*
—— (1892). *Archaeologia*, LIII, p. 245.
—— (1894). *Num. Chron.* 3 S. XIV, p. 18.
—— (1897). *Ancient Stone Implements....* 2nd ed.
—— (1902 a). *V.C.H. Hertfordshire*, I, p. 223.
—— (1902 b). *Num. Chron.* 4 S. II, p. 11.
—— (1902 c). *East Herts. Arch. Soc. Trans.* II, p. 6.
Evelyn-White, C. H. (1904). *Cambs. and Hunts. Arch. Soc. Trans.* I, p. 55.
Evelyn-White, C. H. and H. G. *Domesday Book. The Cambridgeshire portion....*
Fearnsides, W. G. (1904). In *Handbook to the Natural History of Cambridgeshire* (Marr and Shipley), p. 9.

[1] For Evans, without date, in Chapter III, read Evans, Sir A. J. (1890).
[2] For Evans, without date, in Chapter II, read Evans, Sir J. (1881).

332 REFERENCES TO AUTHORS

Fisher, Marshall (1862). *Arch. Journ.* XIX, p. 364.
Fleure, H. J. and James, T. C. (1916). *Journ. Roy. Anthrop. Inst.* XLVI, p. 35.
Fleure, H. J. and Whitehouse, W. E. (1916). *Arch. Camb.* XVI, p. 101.
Foster, W. K. (1883). *C.A.S. Comm.* V, p. 5.
Fox, Cyril (1922). *C.A.S. Proc.* XXIII, p. 15.
—— (1923). *Ibid.* XXIV, p. 21.
—— (1923 a). *Antiq. Journ.* III, p. 65.
Fox, Cyril and Palmer, W. M. (1923 b). *C.A.S. Proc.* XXIV, p. 28.
Fox, G. E. (1911). *V.C.H. Suffolk*, I, p. 279.
Fox, R. (1831). *History of Godmanchester....*
Franks, Sir A. Wollaston (1873). *Soc. Antiq. Proc.* 2 S. V, p. 270.
Gage, John (1834). *Archaeologia*, XXV, p. 1.
—— (1836). *Ibid.* XXVI, p. 300.
—— (1840). *Ibid.* XXVIII, p. 1.
—— (1842). *Ibid.* XXIX, p. 1.
Gent. Mag. (1766). *Gentleman's Magazine*, 36, p. 118.
—— (1819). *Ibid.* 89, i, p. 27.
—— (1827). *Ibid.* 97, ii, p. 265.
—— (1833). *Ibid.* 103, i, p. 453.
Goddard, A. R. (1899). *Essex Arch. Soc. Trans.* N.S. VII, p. 349.
—— (1904). *V.C.H. Bedfordshire*, I, p. 267.
Goodwin, C. W. (1848). *C.A.S. 4tos*, No. XIV, p. 7.
Gorham, G. C. (1820). *Hist. and Antiq. of Eynesbury and St Neots in Huntingdonshire....*
Gould, I. Chalkley (1903). *V.C.H. Essex*, I, p. 275.
—— (1904). *Essex Arch. Soc. Trans.* N.S. IX, p. 224.
Gray, Arthur (1896). *C.A.S. Proc.* IX, p. 61.
—— (1908). *C.A.S. 4tos.* N.S. No. I.
—— (1910). *C.A.S. Proc.* XIV, p. 126.
—— (1911). *Ibid.* XV, p. 42.
Greenwell, Canon (1869 a). *S.I. Quart. Journ.* Jan. 1869.
—— (1869 b). *Ibid.* June, 1869.
—— (1872). *Norf. Arch.* VII, p. 359.
—— (1874). *S.I.A. Proc.* IV, p. 208.
—— (1906). *Archaeologia*, LX, p. 251.
Greenwell, Canon and Rolleston, G. (1877). *British Barrows.*
Grundy, G. B. (1917). *Arch. Journ.* LXXIV, p. 79.
Hailstone, E. Jr. (1878). *C.A.S. 8vos*, No. XVI.
Haverfield, F. (1915). *The Romanization of Roman Britain*, 3rd ed.
—— (1916). *R.C.H.M. Essex*, I, p. xxi.
—— (1917). *C.A.S. Proc.* XX, p. 53.
Hoernes, M. (1905). *Archiv. für Anthropologie*, N.S. 3, XXXI, p. 233.
Hope, Sir W. H. St John (1907). *C.A.S. Proc.* XI, p. 324.
Hügel, Baron A. von (1908). *C.A.S. Proc.* XII, p. 96.
Hughes, T. McKenny (1876). *C.A.S. Rep.* XXXVI, p. 26 (in *Comm.* III).
—— (1879). *Ibid.* XXXIX, p. xiv (in *Comm.* IV).
—— (1885 a). *Ibid.* XLV, p. ix (in *Comm.* VI).
—— (1885 b). *Ibid.* XLV, p. xxii (in *Comm.* VI).
—— (1886). *Ibid.* XLVI, p. lx (in *Comm.* VI).
—— (1891 a). *C.A.S. Comm.* VI, p. 395.
—— (1891 b). *C.A.S. Proc.* VII, p. 24.
—— (1893). *Ibid.* VIII, p. 32.
—— (1894 a). *Ibid.* VIII, p. 87.
—— (1894 b). *Ibid.* VIII, p. 173.
—— (1899). *Brit. Arch. Ass. Journ.* N.S. V, p. 277.
—— (1902). *Arch. Journ.* LIX, p. 219.
—— (1903 a). *C.A.S. Proc.* X, p. 174.
—— (1903 b). *Ibid.* X, p. 194.
—— (1903 c). *Ibid.* X, p. 240.
—— (1904). *Ibid.* X, p. 452.
—— (1906 a). *Ibid.* XI, p. 210.
—— (1906 b). *Ibid.* XI, p. 211.
—— (1907 a). *Cambs. and Hunts. Arch. Soc. Trans.* II, p. 125.
—— (1907 b). *C.A.S. Proc.* XI, p. 393.
—— (1913). *Brit. Arch. Ass. Journ.* XIX, p. 135.

REFERENCES TO AUTHORS

Hughes, T. McKenny and Allix, C. P. (1908). *C.A.S. Proc.* XII, p. 314.
Hughes, T. McKenny and Hughes, M. C. (1909). *Cambridgeshire* (County Geographies).
Hughes, T. McKenny and Jenkinson, F. J. H. (1880). *C.A.S. Rep.* XL, p. xvi (in *Comm.* IV).
Inskip, T. (1845). *Arch. Journ.* I, p. 395.
—— (1851). *Assoc. Arch. Soc. Rep.* I, p. 165.
Jenkinson, F. J. H. (1881). *C.A.S. Rep.* XLI, p. xx (in *Comm.* v).
—— (1882). *Ibid.* XLII, p. li (in *Comm.* v).
—— (1884). *C.A.S. Comm.* v, p. 225.
—— MS. in Girton College Library.
Jenkinson, F. J. H. and Hughes, T. McK. See under Hughes, T. McK.
Johnson, C. (1906). *V.C.H. Norfolk*, II, p. 38.
Karslake, J. B. P. (1920). *Soc. Antiq. Proc.* XXXII, p. 185.
—— (1921). *Antiq. Journ.* I, p. 303.
Kempe, A. J. (1836). *Archaeologia*, XXVI, p. 368.
Kimmins, —. (1887). *C.A.S. Rep.* XLVII, p. cviii (in *Comm.* VI).
Ladds, S. I. (1915). *Cambs. and Hunts. Arch. Soc. Trans.* IV, p. 14.
Laver, Henry (1905). *Essex Arch. Soc. Trans.* N.S. IX, p. 348.
Leeds, E. Thurlow (1912). *Archaeologia*, LXIII, p. 159.
—— (1913). *The Archaeology of the Anglo-Saxon Settlements*.
—— (1915). *Soc. Antiq. Proc.* XXVII, p. 116.
—— (1922). *Antiq. Journ.* II, p. 220.
Lees, B. A. (1911). *V.C.H. Suffolk*, I, p. 357.
Lewis, S. S. (1881). *C.A.S. Comm.* IV, p. 337.
Lindenschmit, L. (1911). *Die Altertümer unserer heidnischen Vorzeit*, v (Mainz).
Loth, M. J. (1921). *Revue Celtique*, XXXVIII, 4, p. 259.
Lukis, W. C., ed. (1883). *Stukeley's Diaries and Letters*. Surtees Soc. LXXVI.
Lyell, A. H. (1912). *A Bibliographical List...of Romano-British Architectural Remains*....
Lysons, D. and S. (1808). *Magna Britannia*, II, Part I, *Cambridgeshire*.
Macalister, R. A. S. (1896). *C.A.S. Proc.* IX, p. 26.
Maitland, F. W. (1897). *Domesday Book and Beyond*.
Marshall, W. (1879). *C.A.S. Comm.* IV, p. 195.
May, Thomas (1916). *The Pottery found at Silchester*.
Maynard, G. (19—). *Saffron Walden Survey Soc.: Outline Survey of S.W. and its Region*: V, *Bronze and Iron Ages*.
—— (1916). *Guide to the Depts. of Archaeology and Ethnology in the Saffron Walden Museum*.
Maynard, G. and Benton, G. M. (1920). *Essex Arch. Soc. Trans.* N.S. XV, p. 282.
Mestorf, J. (1885). *Vorgeschichtliche Alterthümer aus Schleswig-Holstein* (Hamburg).
Miller, S. H. and Skertchly, S. B. J. (1878). *The Fenland, Past and Present*.
Montagu, H. (1886). *Num. Chron.* 3 S. VI, p. 23.
—— (1889). *Soc. Antiq. Proc.* XII, p. 83.
Montelius, Oscar (1908). *Archaeologia*, LXI, p. 97.
Montgomerie, D. H. (1908). *V.C.H. Hertfordshire*, II, p. 103
Morris, G. (1922). *Essex Naturalist*, XX, p. 49.
Mortimer, J. R. (1905). *Forty Years Researches in...Burial Mounds of East Yorkshire*.
Myers, C. S. (1896). *Journ. Anthrop. Inst.* XXVI, p. 113.
Neville, Hon. R. C.[1] (1847). *Antiqua Explorata*.
—— (1848). *Sepulchra Exposita*.
—— (1849). *Arch. Journ.* VI, p. 14.
—— (1849 b). *Brit. Arch. Ass. Journ.* IV, p. 356
—— (1850). *Arch. Journ.* VII, p. 139.
—— (1851). *Ibid.* VIII, p. 28.
—— (1852 a). *Saxon Obsequies*....
—— (1852 b). *Arch. Journ.* IX, p. 226.
—— (1853). *Ibid.* X, p. 14.
—— (1854 a). *Ibid.* XI, p. 77.
—— (1854 b). *Ibid.* XI, p. 95.
—— (1854 c). *Ibid.* XI, p. 207.

[1] See also Braybrooke, Richard, 4th Lord.

REFERENCES TO AUTHORS

Neville, Hon. R. C. (1855). *Arch. Journ.* XII, p. 109.
—— (1856). *Ibid.* XIII, p. 1.
—— (1857 a). *Ibid.* XIV, p. 63.
—— (1857 b). *Ibid.* XIV, p. 85.
—— (1857 c). *Ibid.* XIV, p. 357.
—— (1858). *Essex Arch. Soc. Trans.* I, p. 191.
—— MSS. in Audley End House Museum.
Noble, W. M. (1910). *Cambs. and Hunts. Arch. Soc. Trans.* III, p. 143.
Nunn, E. B. MS. in Library, Camb. Mus. Notes of Excavations, etc., Royston and neighbourhood, 1854–1884.
Oman, Sir Charles (1913). *A History of England.* Vol. I. *England before the Norman Conquest.* 3rd ed.
Oswald, F. and Pryce, T. D. (1920). *An Introduction to the Study of Terra Sigillata.*
Page, William and Keate (Miss) (1908). *V.C.H. Bedfordshire,* II, p. 1.
Parsons, F. G. (1921). *Journ. Roy. Anthrop. Inst.* LI, p. 55.
Peake, A. E. (1917). *P.S.E.A. Proc.* II, p. 409.
—— (1919). *Ibid.* III, p. 73.
Peake, Harold (1911). In *Memorials of Old Leicestershire.*
—— (1922 a). *The English Village.*
—— (1922 b). *The Bronze Age and the Celtic World.*
Pigott, G. F. (1888). *C.A.S. Proc.* VI, p. 309.
Pitt-Rivers, Lieut.-Gen. A. (1887). *Excavations in Cranborne Chase,* vol. I.
Porter, N. T. (1921). *C.A.S. Proc.* XXII, p. 124.
P.S.E.A. Rep. (1915). *Report on Excavations at Grimes Graves, Weeting, Norfolk,* Prehist. Soc. East Anglia.
Prigg, H. (1872). *S.I.A. Proc.* IV, p. 287.
—— (1878). *Brit. Arch. Ass. Journ.* XXXIV, p. 12.
—— (1880). *Ibid.* XXXVI, p. 56.
—— (1881). *Ibid.* XXXVII, p. 152.
—— (1888 a). *S.I.A. Proc.* VI, p. 57.
—— (1888 b). *Ibid.* VI, p. 184.
—— (1889). *Brit. Arch. Ass. Journ.* XLV, p. 81.
Ragg, F. W. (1904). *V.C.H. Bedfordshire,* I, p. 191.
Ransom, W. (1886). *Herts. Nat. Hist. Soc. Trans.* IV, p. 39.
—— (1890). *Soc. Antiq. Proc.* XIII, p. 16.
—— MS. notes on 1836 O.S. Map, 1 inch, now in Camb. Mus.
Reader, F. W. (1909). *Soc. Antiq. Proc.* XXII, p. 190.
Reid, Clement (1913). *Submerged Forests.*
Rice-Holmes, T. (1907). *Ancient Britain and the Invasions of Julius Caesar.*
Ridgeway, Sir William (1890). *Folk-Lore,* I, p. 82.
—— (1892). *C.A.S. Proc.* VII, p. 200.
—— (1901). *The Early Age of Greece,* vol. I.
—— (1905). *Origin and Influence of the Thoroughbred Horse.*
—— (1919). *Man,* No. 84.
Ridgeway, Sir William and Smith, R. A. (1906). *Soc. Antiq. Proc.* XXI, p. 97.
Ripley, W. Z. (1900). *The Races of Europe.*
Round, J. H. (1902). *V.C.H. Hertfordshire,* I, p. 300.
—— (1903). *V.C.H. Essex,* I, p. 333.
R.C.H.M. Essex (1916). *Roy. Comm. on Hist. Mon. (England); Inventory of... Essex,* vol. I.
—— (1921). *Ibid.* vol. II.
R.C.H.M. Herts. (1911). *Roy. Comm. on Hist. Mon. (England); Inventory of... Hertfordshire.*
Salin, Bernhard (1904). *Die altgermanische Thierornamentik.* Trs. J. Mestorf (Stockholm).
Schetelig, H. (1906). *The Cruciform Brooches of Norway.*
Seebohm, F. (1896). *The English Village Community,* 4th ed.
Skertchly, S. B. J. (1877). *Geology of the Fenland* (Memoirs of the Geological Survey).
Skertchly, S. B. J. and Miller, S. H. (1878). *The Fenland, Past and Present.*
Smith, C. Roach (1852). *Collectanea Antiqua,* II, p. 25.
—— (1856). *Inventorium Sepulchrale; an account of Antiquities dug up...by the Rev. Bryan Faussett.*
Smith, H. Ecroyd (1883). *Essex Arch. Soc. Trans.* N.S. II, p. 311.
Smith, Reginald A. (1901). *V.C.H. Norfolk,* I, p. 325.
—— (1902). *V.C.H. Hertfordshire,* I, p. 251.

REFERENCES TO AUTHORS

Smith, Reginald A. (1903). *V.C.H. Essex*, I, p. 315.
—— (1904). *V.C.H. Bedfordshire*, I, p. 175.
—— (1905). *Soc. Antiq. Proc.* XX, p. 344.
—— (1907). *Ibid.* XXI, p. 75.
—— (1909 a). *Ibid.* XXII, p. 56.
—— (1909 b). *Ibid.* XXII, p. 63.
—— (1909 c). *Ibid.* XXII, p. 333.
—— (1909 d). *Archaeologia*, LXI, p. 329.
—— (1909 e). *C.A.S. Proc.* XIII, p. 146.
—— (1911). *V.C.H. Suffolk*, I, p. 325.
—— (1912). *Archaeologia*, LXIII, p. 1.
—— (1913). *Soc. Antiq. Proc.* XXV, p. 185.
—— (1914). *Ibid.* XXVI, p. 238.
—— (1915 a). In *Rep. on Excav. at Grimes Graves (P.S.E.A.)*, p. 208.
—— (1915 b). *Soc. Antiq. Proc.* XXVII, p. 76.
—— (1915 c). *Ibid.* XXVIII, p. 87.
—— (1918). *P.S.E.A. Proc.* II, p. 479.
—— (1919 a). *Ibid.* III, p. 14.
—— (1919 b). *Soc. Antiq. Proc.* XXXI, p. 145.
—— (1920). *Archaeologia*, LXIX, p. 1.
Smith, Reginald A. and Ridgeway, Sir William (1906). *Soc. Antiq. Proc.* XXI, p. 97.
Smith, Urban A. (1913). *East Herts. Arch. Soc. Trans.* V. p. 117.
Stjerna, K. (1910). *L'Anthropologie*, XXI, p. 1.
Stukeley, Dr (1766). *Gent. Mag.* XXXVI, p. 118 (see also Lukis, W. C.).
Sturge, W. A. (1911). *V.C.H. Suffolk*, I, p. 248.
Tansley, A. G. (1911). *Types of British Vegetation*.
Taylor, M. V. (1914). *V.C.H. Hertfordshire*, IV, p. 147.
Thorpe, B. (1865). *Diplomatarium Anglicum aevi Saxonici*.
Tymms, S. (1853). *S.I.A. Proc.* I, p. 315.
Veasey, D. (1853). *Soc. Antiq. Proc.* I S. II, p. 103.
Walford, T. (1803 a). *Archaeologia*, XIV, p. 24.
—— (1803 b). *Ibid.* XIV, p. 61.
Walker, F. G.[1] (1908 a). *C.A.S. Proc.* XII, p. 267.
—— (1908 b). *Ibid.* XII, p. 273.
—— (1908 c). *Ibid.* XII, p. 296.
—— (1909). *Ibid.* XIII, p. 280.
—— (1910). *Ibid.* XIV, p. 141.
—— (1911 a). *Ibid.* XV, p. 64.
—— (1911 b). *Ibid.* XV, p. 166.
—— (1911 c). *Ibid.* XV, p. 178.
—— (1911 d). *Ibid.* XV, p. 192.
—— (1912). *Ibid.* XVI, p. 122.
—— (1913). *Ibid.* XVII, p. 14.
Walters, H. B. (1908 a). *Catalogue of Roman Pottery in the Brit. Mus.*
—— (1908 b). *C.A.S. Proc.* XII, p. 107.
Ward, John (1911 a). *Romano-British Buildings and Earthworks*.
—— (1911 b). *The Roman Era in Britain*.
Warren, S. Hazzledine (1912 a). *Journ. Roy. Anthrop. Inst.* N.S. XV, p. 91.
—— (1912 b). *Essex Naturalist*, XVI, p. 46.
—— (1912 c). *Ibid.* XVI, p. 265.
—— (1916). *Ibid.* XVIII, p. 145.
—— (1919). *P.S.E.A. Proc.* III, p. 94.
Watkin, W. T. (1882). *Arch. Journ.* XXXIX, p. 257.
Wheeler, W. H. (1897). *A History of the Fens of S. Lincolnshire*, 2nd ed.
—— (1906). *Fenland Notes and Queries*, VI, p. 362.
Wilkinson, J. (1868). *Collectanea Antiqua*, VI, p. 154.
Yorke, A. C. (1905). *C.A.S. Proc.* XI, p. 2.
—— (1908). *Ibid.* XII, p. 114.
—— (1911). *Ibid.* XV, p. 281.

[1] In text, for "Walker" without date, see Walker (1910).
NOTE. References to classical authors will be found in the Index.

INDEX: RULES OBSERVED

The following rules have been observed in indexing:

(a) Places referred to in the text, which are within the area covered by the Quarter-inch Ordnance Survey Map accompanying this book, are distinguished from those outside the area by the addition of the Square of Reference:

e.g. Chatteris [C] *A 3*; but March [C], Boyton [S].

(The letter in brackets indicates the County.)

The position of a River on the Map is indicated by recording the first and last squares which it traverses:

e.g. Nene, River, *A 1 to A 3*; Lark, River, *C 7 to B 4–5*.

(b) Sites and places in the Cambridge Region not marked on the Quarter-inch Map are distinguished by a Star *.

With certain exceptions the position of these is indicated by a *note in italics*. This note refers either (i) to a fixed point on the Map (*e.g.* Streetly End* *D 5* (*N. of first " e " of Horseheath*)); (ii) to a symbol placed on the site (*e.g.* Thetford, Barnham Common* *B 7* (*settlement, Map III*)), or (iii) to one of the text maps whereon it is marked (*e.g.* Fox Hill*, Orwell (*see Map E*)).

The exceptions referred to are (i) sites in the village or town (*e.g.* Melbourn, Melbournbury*, Cambridge, New Street*); (ii) certain Fens, which may be assumed to be adjacent to the villages the names of which they bear (*e.g.* Burwell Fen*); (iii) sites the positions of which are adequately described in the text, or (iv) sites the positions of which are unknown to me.

(c) The place-name following the name of a site (*e.g.* Chilford Hall*, Linton) is that of the parish (or town) in which it is situated. When the name of the parish is omitted the barrow, dyke or other object referred to may be assumed to be on a parish boundary.

(d) Sites or places discussed in the text without special reference to the parishes in which they occur are indexed under their own names (*e.g.* Chilford Hall*, Linton [C] *D 4*, Wandlebury, Stapleford [C] *D 4*). Other sites are indexed under the names of their parishes (*e.g.* Swaffham Prior [C] *C 4*, Middle Hill*).

For contractions employed in the Index, see List on p. xix.

INDEX

Abbott, G. Wyman, 15, 26 n, 85 n, 322; quoted, 102
Abercromby, Lord, on B.A. pottery, 21, 22, 23, 25, 26, 26 n, 38–41; burials, 42; invasion, 66; *see also* 35, 47–8, 51 n, 322
Abington, Great [C] *D 4*, 63
— Park* (1 m. S. of "o" of *Pampisford*), 126, 152
Abington Pigotts [C] *D 2–E 2*, 108, 110
Addedomaros, coins of, 88
Adze, iron, 261
Aelfric's Homilies, 300
Agricultural settlements, primitive, 231
Agriculture, 14, 64–5, 275; cultures based on, 219; in woodland areas, 224–5; results of development of, 116, 314–5; implements of, 252, 300
Akeman Street, *C 3 to C 4*, 165
Akerman, J. Y., 88
Alban, Saint, shrine of, 161 n
Alconbury [Hunts.] *B 1*, 103, 111, 170
— Hill, 171
Aldreth, Haddenham [C] *B 3*, 59, 141
— High Bridge* (*Map V*), 7, 141, 155
— Causeway* (*Map V*), 137, 155
Ale-vat, 300
Alfred, King, coins of, 298, 299
All Cannings Cross [Wilts.], finds at, 71, 82, 95 n, 317
Allcroft, A. Hadrian, 129
Allectus, 160
Allen, J. Romilly, 284, 298
Allington Hill*, Bottisham [C] *C 4* (*barrow*, *Map V*), 258, 264, 277 n, 294
Allix, C. P., 48 n; his collection, 48 n, 328
— and Hughes, T. McK., 32, 47, 327
Alnwick Castle [Northumberland], collection at, 323
"Alpine" Race, 318
"Alton" Hill [C], 264
Amber, 14, 42; beads, 51, 248
Amethyst, in A.-S. grave, 262
Amphorae, Italo-Greek, 98, 99, 100, 101, 205; Roman, 101, 192, 256
Ampton [S] *B 7*, Seven Hills* (*barrows*, *Map II*), 325
Anatomical Museum, Cambridge, 233
Andirons, *see* Fire-dogs
Andrews, R. T., 326
Angles and Saxons: one or two races? 238–9, 286–91; whence derived, 238
Anglesey Abbey* near Lode [C] *C 4* (*find, Map V*), 263
Anglian culture area, extent of, 295
Anglo-Saxon Chronicle, 287, 288; quoted, 301, 302 n, 304 n

Anglo-Saxon: *Grave-furniture*, 242–74; continental parallels to, 277; and regional variations in, 269
— *Pagan period*, chronology of, 240
— *Settlement*, pre-Roman analogies, 219, 274–5; raids preceding, 240; date of primary, 237, 240, 276–7; limited in pagan period, 307, 314; expansion of in Christian period, 307, 314; concentrated at Cambridge, 274, 319; *see also* Kingdoms, Interments, Pottery, etc.
Angrivarii, the, 293
Animals, domestic, bones of, 48, 110, 136; *see also* Ox, Sheep, Pig, Horse, etc.
Anstey [H] *E 3*, Hale's Farm* (*mound, Map IV*), 198
Antedrigus, coins of, 88
Antler-picks, 2
Antlers, red deer, 194; in B.A. barrows, 32, 32 n, 44, 325, 328; probable use as picks, 44; not found at Fleam Dyke, 131
Antoninus Pius, coins of, 229
Arable land, processes of extension of, 309–10, 312
Arbury*, near Histon [C] *C 3* (*earthwork, Map V*), 137, 141, 157
Arbury Banks*, Ashwell [H] *E 2* (*earthwork, Map III*), 109, 135–6; pit-dwellings in, 136; pottery from, 94; date of, 139
Arcadius, coins of, 226, 227, 228
Archaeological record, imperfect, 29, 158, 199, 200, 230, 241, 321
Arkesden [E] *E 4*, Chardwell Farm* (*hoard, Map II*), 49, 324; palstave in, 18 n; mould in, 58; axe in, 58; associations of, 60; in forest, 62
Arlesey [B] *E 1*, 90, 99
— Bury*, 304
Armillae, *see* Torcs
Arminius, 293
Armitage, E. S., 301
Armlets, *see* Bracelets
Armorica, source of culture elements, 94
Armour, Roman, 215
Arms Hills*, Bourn [C] *C 2–D 2* (*barrows, Map IV*), 194
Armstrong, A. L., 2, 48, 58; quoted, 63 n, 79
Arras [Yorks.], chariot burials at, 81, 86
Arretine platters, copies of, 101, 201, 211
— ware, 101, 201 n, 204, 226; stamps on, 201 n, 204

F A 22

338 INDEX

Arrington [C] *D 2*, 154
— Bridge* (*road junction, Map IV*), 164, 165, 172, 182
Arrowheads, of flint, types, 1; date, 4; provenance, 5–6; in a wolf's skull, 14; on living-floor, 15; in barrows, 12*n*, 44, 326
Art: *La Tène*: in Britain, 71, 104; recurrence of, 283–4
— *A.-S.*: excellence of, 248, 272; decline of, 272; provincial-Roman motives in, 256, 272, 280; influence of Roman civilization on, 280–2
Artis, E. T., 75, 84; his collection, 75
Arun, River [Sussex], 165
Ashdon [E] *E 4*, 172, 224; founders' metal at, 49*n*; Roman houses at, 186*n*, 188, 225, 312; kiln at, 211, 225
— parish, diffuse settlement in, 311
Ashes, vegetable, in a barrow, 35
Ashford [Msex], 41
Ashill [N], gold torc found at, 51
Ashley [C] *C 5*, 153
Ashmolean Museum, A.-S. objects in, 242, 245, 248, 248*n*, 251, 252, 256, 257, 258, 259, 264, 266, 294, 299, 301, 322. The majority of these are from the Evans' Collection
Ashwell [H] *E 2*, 147, 148; finds at, 92, 203, 205, 254*n*, 266
— End* (*coin hoard, Map IV*), 231
— The Bury*, 304
See also Arbury Banks
Ashwell Street, *E 2 to E 3*, 164, 167*n*, 181, 220; description, 147–50; partially Romanized, 149; trace, 148; antiquity of, 149–50; cemetery adjoining, 188; see also Street Way
"Assarts of the waste," 309
Astwick [B] *E 2*, 267
Audley End House*, Saffron Walden [E] *E 4* (1 m. W. of town), 153
— — Museum, objects in, 29, 35, 37, 40, 91, 92, 98, 105, 174, 197*n*, 206, 210, 217, 260, 261, 262, 269, 270, 322, 324, 325, 326, 329; Neville MSS. in, see Neville
Augustus, coins of, 177, 227, 228
Aulus Plautius, 160
Aurelianus, coin of, 177
Aureus, 228, 230
Avaricum, France, 132
Avebury [Wilts.], 146
Avon, River [Warwick.], 287, 288
Awls, flint, 1; bone, 136; bronze, 53; see also Pins
Axehammers: Stone, 1, 44; date, 3; with an urn, 3: Deer-antler, 53
Axes: *Stone*, 1, 2; abundance of, 5; hoard of, 6; types, 6, 9–11; in barrows, 12*n*; holed, 1, 2–3
— *Bronze*: classification according to Montelius, 17–18; his errors, 18; modifications suggested, 19, 20; associated with iron weapons, 70, 81. Flat, of copper or bronze, 53, 63–4. Flanged, 51, 54. Socketed, 57, 58. Winged, 20, 58
Axes: *Iron*, 243, 261, 264, 267, 292; double-horned, 247, 259; of Viking type, 299
Aylesford [Kent], La Tène cemetery at, 90, 91, 92, 93; flint flakes in, 4
"Aylesford" cremation culture, route of entry, 103, 118; limits of, 102–3, 118; pottery, 90–3, 110; burials, 97–9
Aylott, G., 135

Babington, C., 194
Babington, C. C., 78, 101, 125, 128, 142, 143*n*, 146, 149, 152*n*, 154, 176*n*, 178, 183*n*, 184, 185, 198*n*, 199, 201, 205, 221, 223, 226, 227, 228, 229, 230, 231, 250, 251, 263, 326, 327, 329; on Car Dyke, 179–80; on Roman roads, 162*n*, 164*n*, 165*n*, 168, 168*n*, 169, 170*n*; on Roman bronzes, 214, 215; on Roman earthworks, 175, 175*n*
Babraham [C] *D 4*, 145
Badlingham*, Chippenham [C] *B 5* (*Domesday vill, Map V*), 143, 149, 149*n*, 167
Baker's Map of Cambs., 165
Baldock [H] *E 2*, 143, 155, 164, 170, 171
Balks, 305–6
Bally, E. F., 324
Balsham [C] *D 4*, 153; Fleam Dyke ends near, 125
— Charterhouse Plantation* (*barrows near, Map II*), 34, 37, 197*n*, 325
— Dungate Farm* (*by "D" of Fleam Dyke*), 125, 129, 130, 130*n*
Baltic, the, 243
Bamborough [Northumberland], defences of, 304
Banassac, S. France, 206
Bangles, bronze, 62, 81, 253
Barker, H. R., 265; quoted, 94
Barkway, see Rokey Wood
Barnack Rag stone, 180, 194
Barnwell*, Cambridge [C] *C 3* (¾ m. S. of "n" of Chesterton), finds at, 25, 27, 37*n*, 86, 91, 92, 97, 99, 102, 203*n*, 205, 218, 244–5, 322, in Abbey Road, 93; settlement at, 64*n*, 99, 112, 120, 246, 314
Barrel-urns, 91
Barrington [C] *D 3*, finds at, 14, 58, 75, 86, 88, 89*n*, 92, 101, 107, 215, 228, 298, 301, 323; near a ford, 250*n*; at the Lower Mill, 186, 236; settlement at, 109–10, 231
— Edix Hill* (*cemetery, Map V*), 241, 250–1; see Barrington "A"
— Hooper's Field* (*cemetery, Map V*), 250, 251; see Barrington "B"

INDEX

Barrington "A," A.-S. cemetery, 251–2, 296; finds from, 248 n, 254 n, 269, 270, 271, 272, 273, 276, 283, 283 n, 294, 295

Barrington "B," A.-S. cemetery, 252–5, 296; finds from, 269, 270, 272, 273, 276, 278, 281, 295

Barrow [S] *C 6*, 59, 60, 63, 324
— Bottom* (*tumulus, Map III*), 76–7, 85, 265; dyke near, 124

Barrows: Long, 8, 11; distribution of, 12, 318
— Round, 149, 151, 152; with ditch and bank, 194; material not local, 194; pit with flints in, 194; relation to dykes, 128, to Icknield Way, 147, 147 n, to Street Way, 148, 149
  B.A., number, distribution, etc., 28–31, 325–9; inadequacy of record of, 29; destroyed, 29; relation to dykes, 31; secondary deposits in, 30, 34, 197, 197 n, 325, 326, 327, 328; absent from lowlands, 28; ditched, 32; objects found in, 42–4; analysis of, 43; in the Fens, 37; beakers rare in, 27; ring of chalk in, 31; as cemeteries, 35–6; enlarged for successive interments, 36; cessation of burial in, 46
  E.I.A., 76–80; on chalk escarpment, 30, 30 n, 116; pottery in, 77, 78, 79; double burials in, 78, 79; stone walls in, 78, 79; cremation in, 79, 80; of doubtful date, 197, 329; cessation of burial in, 76
  R., distribution of, 191, 197, 199, 235; numbers, 191; groups of, 191, 194, 197; bearings of, 197, 199; simple deposits in, 195; rich deposits in, 191–3; range of date of, 193, 199–200; brick tombs in, 191, 194, 198; wood coffers in, 191, 192, 197, 198; rites employed in, 193, 194, 198–9, 235; structural features of, 195, 199; profiles of, 199; sacrificial vessels in, 192–3; stone coffin in, 194, 199; probably Christian, 200; ditched, 194–5; floors of, 195–6; unexamined probably R., 169, 197, 198; by R. road, 101, 168, 169, 172; pre-R., R. burials in, 197, 197 n; R. with post-R. burials in, 195, 196
  A.-S., 264, 277 n; burials in a R. barrow, 196, 260, 277 n, in a B.A. barrow, 263, 265, 266, 277 n
  Post-R., 195

Barrows Corner*, Elveden [S] *B 6* (1 m. S. of "l" of Elveden), 146

Bartlow [C] *D 4*, finds at, 203, 207, 226; Roman house at, 185, 189, 225, 232, 283

Bartlow Hills*, Ashdon [E] *D 4* (*E. of Bartlow Station*), 197, 198, 199, 235, 236; described, 191–3; finds from, 201 n, 208, 213, 214, 216, 226; dwelling of builders undiscovered, 188

Barton [C] *D 3*, reputed finds at, 92, 241, 258–9, 284; settlements at, 110–11, 231, 303; R. road at, 165
— Deadman's Hill*, 172, 196
— Deadman's Way*, 154, 169, 196
— Lord's Bridge, *q.v.*

Barton, Great [S], 26, 39, 40, 322 n

Barton Mills [S] *B 5*, Barton Hill* (1¼ m. S.W. of village), 25, 31–2, 322, 322 n, 325

Baschurch [Shropshire], 104

Basins (bowls), bronze, with A.-S. burials, 247, 259–60, 261, 273; position of, 261; *see also* Bowls and Bronze Vessels

Basket-pattern, 107

Basket-work, 192

Bassingbourn [C] *E 2*, 57
— Springs* (*N. end of Mile Ditches, Map V*), 127

Battely, J., 267

Battle Ditches, *see* Paille Ditches

Beads: B.A., segmented, 35; of jet and bone, 55: R., 100: A.-S., 247, 251, 257, 262, 263, 266, 271; position of, 261; of crystal, 266; of blown glass, 248, 257; of Anglian type, 261: *see also* Amber

Beaker-folk, 22–3, 318; culture of, 15, 23, 28; route of invasion, 24, 316; distribution of, 24–5, compared with A.-S. settlers, 274–5, 320

Beaker-pottery, 15, 23–4; date of, 45; decoration of, 25–7; distribution of, 22, 24; typology of, 25–6; wide range of types, 27; influence of, 39–40; cause of elimination of, 65 n; on a living-floor, 48; list of finds, 322

Beane*, River *F 2*, 155

Beaver, tooth of, in A.-S. grave, 262

"Bedcanford," probably on Thames, 288

Bede, the Venerable, 221, 221 n, 245, 295 n

Bedford, 288
— Library, objects in, 99, 267 n

Bedfordshire, moated sites in, 302–3

Bedwell Hay Farm*, Ely St Mary [C] *B 4* (1¼ m. S. of "E" of Ely), 165 n

Beldam, J., 127, 142, 145 n; excavations by, 36, 128, 136, 328; quoted, 141, 175; collection of, 36, 36 n, 94, 206

Belgae, the, 71–2, 118–19, 318

"Belgic" culture and race, relations between, 102–4, 115, 118–9
— pottery, 90, 91, 92, 93; *see also* Pottery, Romano-Belgic
— tribes, craniological data, 114–5

22—2

INDEX

Belgium, mound-burial in, 199
Bell, of the A.-S. period, 266
Belloc, Hilaire, 165
Beloe, E. M., 142*n*, 165, 222
Belsar's Hill*, Willingham [C] *B 3–C 3* (*earthwork, Map V*), 137, 141, 155, 157
Belt-plates, 242, 243; sets of, 247–8, 248*n*, 256, 280, 295
Belt-tab, 266
Beltz, R., 75
Bennet, Bishop, 165, 165*n*
Benwick [C] *A 2–A 3*, xxiii, 179
Beowulf, 279, 301*n*
Berden [E] *F 4*, beaker from, 24, 27, 28, 322
Berkshire, mug from, 27
Beverley [Yorks.], axe from, 58
"Biedcanford," *see* Bedcanford
Bigbury Camp [Kent], finds at, 100, 101
Biggleswade [B] *D 1*, 164, 165, 170
— Furzenhall Farm* (*mound, Map IV*), 197, 198
Bill, iron, 252, 300
Billhook, iron, 252
Birch, W. de G., 130, 166
Birdbrook [E] *E 5*, 168, 190
Bishopric, East Anglian, 240
Bishop's Stortford [H], 161, 289
Black Ditches [S] *B 6–C 6* (*Map V*), 123–4, 132, 134, 146
Boar, wild, 225
Boar's head, in La Tène art, 105
Bodger, Mr J. W., 38; quoted, 212*n*, 223
Bodkin, bronze, 55, 62
Bokerly Dyke [Wilts.], 293*n*
Borgstedt, Slesvig, 268, 277
Boss, bronze-gilt, Irish, 298
Bottisham [C] *C 4*, finds at, 57, 64; barrows at, 35, 325–6; *see also* Allington Hill
— Fen*, 105
— Lode* (*canal, by "r" of Waterbeach*), 53, 54
— Anglesey Abbey, *q.v.*
Boulder-clay, xxii; settlements on, 308–9
Boundaries: County, mark ancient trackways, 145, 146, 147, 148
— Parish, along R. roads, 162, 164, 165, 168, 171, 180; mark ancient trackways, 142, 145, 146, 147, 148, 149, 150, 151, 154, 155; on crest-lines, 152; coincident with dykes, 127, 180; mark ford- or bridge-heads, 151; on modern roads, 167
— Political, become cultural, 102, 117, 118, 269, 320–1
Boundary ditch, under Devil's Dyke, 129
Bourn [C] *D 2*, 170, 194–5, 197, 209
Bourn Bridge* *D 4*, xxiii, 146
Bourn Brook, *C 2 to D 3*, xxiii, 185, 224
— — Valley, 154; R. road in, 164
Bourn River*, *E 5 to D 4*, xxiii, 8, 146, 224, 308

Bourn River Valley, 149; settlement in, 226, 276, 308
Bowcroft Wood*, Thaxted [E] *E 5* (*at angle of R. road, Map IV*), 172
Bowls, bronze, enamelled mounts from, 252, 258, 283–4, 297
Bowtell MS., 174, 175*n*, 214
Box, branches of, in a R. tomb, 193
Boyton [S], torc from, 51, 63
Bracelets, or Armlets, 251, 252, 253, 267; *see also* Torcs, Bangles
Bracer or wrist-guard, stone, 28, 44, 53
Brachycephaly, 32, 66; in Holland, 22; characteristic of beaker-folk, 23, 318
Bracteates, 282, 298
Brading [I. of W.], R. house at, 184, 184*n*
Bran Ditch, *see* Heydon Ditch
Brancaster [N], 182
Brandon [S] *A 6*, finds at, 6, 96; burials at, 25, 27, 53, 77, 114, 115*n*, 322
Braughing [H] *F 3*, finds at, 89, 89*n*, 214, 227; R. roads at, 161, 164, 166, 170, 173, 181, 289, 290; settlement at, 116, 173, 176, 220
Braybrooke, Richard, 3rd Lord, 135*n*
Braybrooke, Richard, 4th Lord, 190, 214, 231; *see also* Neville, Hon. R. C.
Breast ornaments, in A.-S. grave, 264
Breckland, *see* Heathland, East Anglian
Brent Ditch* [C] *D 4* (*Map V*), 123, 126, 128, 130*n*, 145, 146
Brent Pelham [H] *F 3*, Cole Green* (*mound, Map IV*), 198
Brick or tile, Roman, 181, 184, 185, 188, 196, 247; inscribed, 212; in tombs, 100, 189, 194, 198, 198*n*; *see also* Kilns, tile
Bridgham Heath [N], 146*n*
Brigg [Lincs.], food-vessel from, 38
British Museum, objects in, 6*n*, 15, 39*n*, 53, 55, 56, 62, 64, 74, 76, 77, 81, 91, 92, 94, 96, 99, 105, 108, 176, 176*n*, 192*n*, 214, 215, 216, 244, 245, 248, 251, 256, 263, 265, 267, 267*n*, 297, 298, 299, 301, 322, 323, 324, 325, 327
— — Guides, referred to, 57, 59, 74, 174, 176*n*, 180, 214, 215, 322
Britons, at Bedford in A.-S. period, 288
Brittany, trade with, 10, 14
Brocklebank, Mr C. G., quoted, 226
Bronze-Founding Industry, local evidence for, 18*n*, 49, 59–60, 62–3; significance of, 19, 51, 66, 67; the craftsmen, 51, 62, 63
Bronze Implements, finds of, analysed, 49–61; commonest types, 52; early, scarce N. of Thames, 42, 52
— Vessels, Roman: enamelled, 214; with interments, 100, 189–93, 213; incense-pan, 213–4; jugs or ewers, and patellae, 100, 104, 190, 191, 192, 192*n*, 213; strainer, 214; *see also* Basins, Bowls, Cauldrons, Situlae, Skillets

INDEX

Brooches, *see* Fibulae
Brown, Mr Chas., quoted, 265
Brown, G. Baldwin, on A.-S. grave-goods, 238, 240, 247, 248*n*, 254, 255, 257, 260, 263, 265, 266, 268, 269, 272, 273, 284, 288, 291, 299; quoted, 286
Broxbournebury [H], barrow at, 196*n*
Brussels, burial near, 70
Brythons, 71–2, 115, 118–9
Buckles, of bronze and bronze-gilt, 243, 247, 248, 253, 259, 263, 266; of iron, 265; of silver, 100; silvered, 295; *see also* Belt-plates
Bugle-shaped bronze objects, 61
Building, Roman, decline of, 232
Buildings, Roman, 185, 186, 187, 246–7; *see also* Houses, Temples
Bull, A., 179
Buller, G. J., 323
Bullock-Hall, W. H., 142*n*
"Bullock Way," 152*n*
Bunbury, Sir H., 265; quoted, 81
Burhred, coin of, 298
"Burhs," 302, 303–4
Burials of different periods, on same site, 98, 243, 247, 247*n*, 255–6, 263, 283; *see also* Barrows, Inhumation, Cremation, Interments
Burnt Fen, Littleport [C] *A* 4–5, 5, 7, 56, 229, 314
Burnt Mill Bridges* [C] *D 3* (*see Map E*), 150, 151
Burwell [C] *C 4*, finds at, 53, 54, 58, 64; A.-S. cemetery, 241, 262, 294; barrows near, 197*n*, 326
— Churchyard, hoard in, 324
— Fen*, finds in, 3, 10, 11, 14, abundance of, 6, position accounted for, 7; *see also* 54, 55, 61, 108, 263, 323, 324
Burwell Rock, *see* Totternhoe Stone, Clunch
"Bury," in compounds, 291, 291*n*, 303–4
Bury, J. B., 161*n*
Bury St Edmunds [S] *C 6*, finds at or near, 25, 26, 76, 82, 108, 323
— Abbey*, find at, 300
Bury Museum, *see* Moyses Hall Museum
Bushe-Fox, J. P., 82–3, 93, 107; quoted, 106
Bust, bronze, helmeted, 215
Buttons, bronze, 61
Bygrave [H] *E 2*, 88

Caesar, Julius, coins of, 177, 228; Commentaries, ref. to, 72, 103, 116, 131, 131*n*, 132, 140, 152
Caesar's Camp*, Sandy [B] *D 1* (*Map III*), 95, 109, 134, 135, 139, 140, 151, 154, 156, 176
Caldecote [C] *D 3*, 170
Caldecote [H] *E 2*, 165
Caligula, coins of, 227, 231

Cam, River, *E 2 to B 4*, xxii, xxiii; changes in course of, 179; lowest crossing-place, 169; finds in, 244, 278
Cam Valley, evidences of settlement in, 7, 62, 64, 65, 102, 116, 226–7, 230, 274, 276, 278, 296, 308, 315
Cambridge [C] *C 3*: N.A., find, 10; B.A., 64*n*; E.I.A., 112, 120
A R. creation, 112, 169–70, 182, 220–1; described, 174–5; causes of predominance, 221–2; of survival, 234, 319; temporarily deserted, 221; duration of R. occupation, 227–8; fortifications, 174–5, 183, 232–3, 236; ford or bridge at, 168, 221; R. roads at, 165–6, 168–70, 172, 181, 181*n*, 182, 228, 234, and Map H, 285
In A.-S. times, settlements at, 245–6, 281, 296; early date of, 243; cemeteries at, 242–6; importance of site, 275; historical evidence, 276; held by Redwald, 295; a "burgus," 302
Trackways at, 112–3, 141
Sites in the modern Borough: Barge Yard*, 203*n*, 205, 208; Barnwell*, *q.v.*; the Borough*, 203; Blackamore Piece*, 174; Cam, river, 244, 246; Castle St*, 93, 174, 212; Castle Hill*, 112, 166, 170, 210, 214, 221, 227–8, 294; Castle Yard*, 91; Chaucer Road*, 113*n*, 202, 203, 205; Chesterton, *q.v.*; Coldham*, 94, 96, 244; Grange Road*, 243, 278; Gravel Hill*, 168, 199, 244; Jesus Lane*, 101, 211, 228, 245; Hills Road*, 168; Lady Margaret Rd*, 205; Latham Rd*, 113*n*, 227; Madingley Rd*, 91, 112, 209, 210, 212*n*, 218, 243; Magdalene Coll.*, 175; Midsummer Common*, 38; Mill Rd*, 244–5; New Street*, 58; Newmarket Rd*, 244–5; Newnham*, *q.v.*; Northampton St*, 203*n*; Railway Station*, 176; River Farm*, 227; Rose Crescent*, 245, 246, 278; St John's Coll. cricket ground*, 242–3, 246, 248, 248*n*, 268, 269, 270, 273, 276, 278, 281, 294; St Sepulchre's*, 203*n*; Sidney St*, 245; Stourbridge Common*, 92, 208; Thoday St*, 203*n*; Trinity Hall*, 92, 96, 228, 245; Union Society's buildings*, 228; Vicar's Brook*, 227; Warkworth St*, 10
Finds in or "near" (sites unspecified), 54, 56, 57, 58, 64, 107, 108, 215, 218, 272, 281, 297, 298, 301
— Museum, *see* Museum of Arch. and Eth., Cambridge
Camden, William, quoted, 135, 300

INDEX

Camps, see Earthworks, Hill-forts, Ring-works
Camulodunum, 71–2, 88, 89n, 102, 153, 168, 170, 226; see also Colchester
Canals, 179–80; see also Car Dyke
Canoes, dug-out, 64, 65
Canterbury [Kent], finds at, 280n, 294
Car Dyke* [C] *C 4 to B 3 (Map IV)*, 173, 179–80, 222, 223, 234; in Lincs., 179, 180
Caskets, wooden, bronze-mounted, 100, 104
Cassivellaunus, 131n, 140
Castle Camps [C] *E 5*, 311
Castles, Norman, 146, 301
Castor [Northants.], fibulae from, 75, 84
"Castor ware," 209–10; see also 174, 177, 178, 180, 195, 213, 223, 230
Catuvellauni, racial type, 72, 86, 103, 114–5, 119; boundaries of, 88–90, 104, 119, 230, 317; coins of, 88, 89
Cauldrons, bronze, 62, 100, 104
Causeways, 137, 141, 155, 168, 180, 221
Cavenham [S] *C 6*, 58, 146, 153; barrows at, 147n, 326
— Heath* (*N. of village*), 128, 146
— Brook*, 124, 146
Caxton [C] *C 2*, 170
— Gibbet, 162n
Celtic deities, 215, 216
— village plan, survival of, 113
Celtic-speaking peoples, invasions of, 19, 47, 66–7, 68, 71–2, 86, 103, 115, 119, 318; survival of, 282
Cemeteries: B.A., 37, 41; E.I.A., 97–99; R., 188–90, and 168, 176, 177
— A.S., 241–68, 274; on earlier settlement site, 259; on earlier burial sites, 260, 277n, 283; by a trackway, 149; in cultural groups, 292, 294, 295; inadequacy of record of, 241
Cenimagni, 71
Chadwick, H. M., 240, 284; quoted, 119, 238–9, 279, 282, 300
Chadwick, Mrs H. M., 102
Chair, folding, in a barrow, 192
Chalk, position of spring-heads in the, 147; see Springs
Châlons, France, burials at, 79
Chapel Hill*, Haslingfield [C] *D 3*, 150, 151, 155, 157; cemeteries near, 241, 250, 294, 296
Chapes, bronze, 60, 107
Charcoal, in barrows, 32, 33, 34, 36, 325, 327
Chariot burials, 81, 118
Chariot-furniture, linchpin, 104; navebands, 104; boss, 108; see Horse trappings
Charters, Anglo-Saxon, 130, 145, 152, 166, 169n
Chatteris [C] *A 3*, 171; finds at, 38, 56, 64, 230, 241, 263, 276, 294

Chatteris, Langwood Fen*, finds in, 60, 63, 65, 323
Cherryhinton [C] *D 4*, 169, 203, 207; see War Ditches
Cherusci, the, 293
Chesterford, Great [E] *E 4*: In pre-Roman times: N.A., 3; B.A., 24, 27, 38, 46, 322; E.I.A., 98, 105, 110; see also 74, 88, 94, 96, 97, 103, 119, 120, 153
— In Roman times: finds at, 190, 206, 217, 231; town at, 140, 173–4, 225; duration of occupation, 227, 232; walls, 173, 183; R. roads, 161, 164, 166, 167, 181, 220; see also 91, 92, 188, 203, 208, 210, 211, 212n, 214, 215, 216, 218
— In A.-S. period: 246, 265, 276, 278, 291
Chesterton [C] *C 3*, 64n, 120, 218; finds at, 41, 58, 90, 92, 99, 203, 207, 244, 322
— Manor Farm* (¼ m. N. of second "e" of Chesterton), 165
Chesterton-on-Fossway [Warw.], 284
Chests, wooden, containing R. burials, 191, 192, 193, 195, 198
Cheveley [C] *C 5*, 153
Childerley [C] *C 3*, 309
— Dyke* (*Map V*), 305
— Gate* (*coin find, Map III*), 154
Chilford Hall*, Linton [C] *D 4* (¼ m. N. of "a" of Hildersham), 168
Chilford, Hundred of, 152
Chippenham [C] *B 5–C 5*, 59–60, 149n, 324
— Park*, 149
Chisels, flint, 1, 4, 6; bronze, 56, 61
Chishall, Great [C] *E 3*, 306
Chittering [C] *B 4*, 165
Chrishall [E] *E 3*, 9, 57, 60, 62, 324
— Bury*, 304
— Grange* (*see Map D*), 80, 145, 326
Christian symbol, on bronze bowls, 284; see Cross
Christy, Miller, 162n, 166n, 168, 172
Chronicle Hills*, Whittlesford [C] *D 3* (*see Map D*), 30n, 77–9, 149, 199
Chronology: N.A., 15; in Scandinavia, 10, 12: B.A., 67; basis of, 16; Montelius' system, 17–19; system adopted, 20–21: E.I.A., 70, 71, 86, 118: R., 160, 161, 161n, 234–6: A.-S., 237, 240, 276
Cinerary urns: B.A., *Overhanging-rim type*, 39–41, 66; date of, 33, 45–6; upright, 34; inverted, 33, 34; badly baked, 34, 40n; containing ashes of several persons, 32, of one only, 34; several in one barrow, 35; below ground level in a barrow, 36; in an urn-field, 37; with an incense cup, 37
Anomalous forms, 41; date, 45 bucket-shaped, 41, 46
— E.I.A., 90–2

Cinerary urns: *R.*, 188, 189, 191, 192, 197*n*
— *A.S.*, 247, 265, 273–4, 277–9, also 243, 244, 246, 256, 262; contents of, 247, also 243, 261
Cissbury [Sussex], mines at, 1, 2
Cists, of stone, burial in, 33; in floor of barrow, 34, 35, 36
Civilization, standard of, evidence for: *B.A.*, 19, 42, 47–8, 49–52, 67–8, 317: *E.I.A.*, 87–9, 111, 119–20, 317: *R.*, 235–6, see also 182, 187–8, 189–90, 218, 230–1; decline of, 232–3, 236: *A.S.*, 274–5, 280–2, 314, 317, 319
Clack, Rev. W., 183*n*; his collection, 206*n*
Clark, J., 324
Clarke, E. D., 259, 323
Clarke, J., 187
Clarke, W. G., 3, 5, 6*n*, 48, 111, 127, 142*n*, 146*n*, 229, 322; on Icknield Way, 146; quoted, 147, 326, 328
— and Hewitt, H. D., 6*n*, 155
Clarke's Hill*, Gt Shelford [C] *D 4* (1½ *m. N. of "o" of Shelford*), 112
Clasps, wrist, of developed types, 254–5; evolution of, 271–2; position of, 261; distribution of, 286; see also 243, 244, 247, 248, 251, 252, 253, 257, 260, 270, 280*n*, 285
Classical motives, in A.-S. art, 248*n*, 256, 271, 272, 280, 280*n*; in La Tène survivals, 284
Claudius, Emperor, 160, 230; coins of, 88, 177, 190, 227, 228
Clavering [E] *E 4*, 62, 301, 310
— Bury*, 324
Claybush Hill*, Ashwell [H] *E 2*, 135
Clayhithe*, Horningsea [C] *C 4* (1 *m. N.E. of village*), 223
Clifton [B] *E 1*, 197
Clinch, G., 6*n*, 107
Cloth, in B.A. barrows, 34, 35, 69; impression on pottery, 49, 69; in A.-S. grave, 255
Clothall [H] *E 2*, 155, 306
Club, bronze, symbolical, 215
Clunch (chalk marl; Burwell Rock), R. building material, 181, 184, 185, 187, 188; quarries, 181; carved frieze of, 185–6, 187, 236; balls of, in a barrow, 44
Cobbett, Dr L., 75*n*
Cockerell, Mr T. D. A., 86
Codrington, T., 142, 143*n*, 162*n*, 164*n*, 165*n*, 166, 166*n*, 168*n*, 169, 170*n*, 289; quoted, 162
Coenwulf, coins of, 298
Coffins, stone, Roman, 191, 194, 199
Coins, British, 87–9, also 71, 154, 176, 221, 227; in a hill-fort, 134; in a village, 110
— Gallic, 89*n*
— Ptolemaic, 86

Coins, Roman, 174, 175, 175*n*, 176, 177, 178, 226–33; hoards of, 214, 224, 226, 229–33; hoards of, reflect political instability, 160, 236; in barrows, 77, 196; in urns, 177, 188, 191–2, 192*n*; with burials, 190, 194, 213; in mouth of a skeleton, 189; in buildings, 184–8; ubiquity of, xxv; upper limit of date of, 161, 226, 229*n*, 233; with British, 88; in a hill-fort, 135; in A.-S. graves, 242, 271, 281; in an A.-S. jewel, 297; a late importation, 228
— Anglo-Saxon, 284, 298, 299, 300
Colchester [E], finds at, 41, 46, 201; a road centre, 153, 161, 168, 289; see also Camulodunum
— Museum, objects in, 85, 97, 103, 291*n*, 322
Cold Harbour Farm*, Southery [N] *A 4* (4*m. N.N.E. of Littleport*), 166
Cole Ambrose Collection, Cambridge Museum, 207, 299
Collings, W. T., 327, 328
Column, Roman Doric, 187
Comberton [C] *D 3*, 169, 198
— Fox's Bridge* (*R. house, Map IV*), 180, 185, 188
Combs, bone, unburnt, in urns, 247; comb-case, 247
Commercial relations influence cultural characters, 316; see Trade
Commodus, Emperor, 160; cult of, 215; coins of, 214, 231
Communications, see Roads, Trade-routes
Constantine I, 227, 229
Constantine family, coins of, 230
Constantine III, 161
Constantius II, coins of, 187, 228
Conway, Sir M., 260, 284
Conybeare, J. W. E., 186, 236, 253*n*, 298; his collection, 12, 12*n*, 86, 110*n*, 228, 252, 253, 298
Cook, Mr A. B., 207
Cooking, hearths, 48, 136; implements, 100
Coomb Grove Farm*, Wimpole [C] *D 2*, 150
Cooper, C. H., 329
Copley Hill*, Babraham [C] *D 4* (*at* "*u*" *of Vandlebury*), 148
Copper, Age, 16, 17; introduction of, 23; axes, 53, 63; armlet, 28, 52; "implement," 36; ingots, 36, 63; in founders' hoards, 49
Coprolite diggings, archaeological results of, 241, 253, 255–6
Corbett, W. J., 239; quoted, 306*n*, 310, 310*n*
Corbilo, on the Loire, 120
Corn, in B.A., 65; transport of, 180; forest area under, 225; ear of, on a gem, 192, on a coin, 192*n*
Coton [C] *C 3*, 7, 154

Cott Farm*, Babraham [C] *D 4*, 148
Cottenham [C] *C 3*, 7, 180, 215, 308
— Bullocks Haste Common* (*S.E. of Smithey Fen*), 223
— Setchel Fen* *B 3* (*E. of Smithey Fen*), 179
— Smithey Fen Farm *B 3*, 223
Coveney [C] *B 4*, 56, 59
— Fen*, shields from, 51, 60, 63, 65, 323
"Covered Ways," 126
Crawford, O. G. S., 20, 41, 52, 57 n, 61, 64, 315; quoted, 199
Cremation, introduction of, 45
Cremation interments: *B.A.*, distribution of, 31; in barrows, 32–6; multiple, 35–7; variety of primary, 33; burnt on site, 34; partial, 34; without urns, 32, 34, 37, 40–1; without barrows, 37
— *E.I.A.*, 79–80, 97–104, 139; partial, 80; with horses, 80, 81
— *R.*, 188–90, 233; in barrows, 191–7
— *A.-S.*, 277–80, see also 247, 248, 256, 261
Cressingham, Little [N], 51
Cross, an element of design, 271; of gold, 297
Crowland [Lincs.], 76, 118
Croydon [C] *D 2*, 55, 154, 309
Culford [S] *B 6*, 278
Cultivation, open-field system of, 305–6
Cultivation terraces, 119 n
Cultural relations, 14, 39, 52, 83, 85–6, 286–90, 295, 296, 317
— unity, in Fenland Basin, 11, 26–7, 38, 39, 41, 46–7, 119, 315; circumstances antagonistic to, 119, 292, 295, 320–1
Culture: of Southern origin, 319: *B.A.*, factors influencing, 317; diffusion by waterways, 64: *La Tène*, survival of, 119, 283–4: *R.*, influence on A.-S. settlers, 280–1, 296, 320; phases, successive, interrelation of, 117, 119, 319–20; routes, 16, 19, 70, 94, 147 (*see also* Trade): areas, 46–7, 295, 315–7
Cumberlow Green*, Rushden [H] *F 2* (*hoard, Map II*), 49 n, 57, 58, 60, 62, 155, 324
Cunningham, W., xxiv, 179
Cunnington, M. E., 82 n, 83, 85, 95 n
Cunobelinus, coins of, 88, 89, 154, 192 n
Curle, J., 107, 202 n
Currency, palstaves as, 18 n, 58
Curwen, E., and E. C., 126
Cynethryth, Queen, coin of, 298

Daggers, of flint, 1, 3–4, 6, 53, 147; of bone, 53; of bronze or copper, 44; of bronze, 22, 33, 48, 53, 54, 56; of iron, 70, 82
Damascening, 301, 301 n

Danish invasion, 287, 298–9, 302, 316
Dawkins, W. Boyd, 100, 101
Deadman's Way, see Barton
De Baye, Baron J., 274 n
Déchelette, J., 18 n, 59, 61, 70, 76, 77, 78, 79, 81, 94, 106, 202; on B.A. chronology, 16; criticized, 21; on early B.A. hoards, 54
Deck Collection, Cambridge Museum, 249
Decoration: *B.A.*, on pottery, 25–7, 32, 36, 38, 41–2, 47–8; on implements, etc., 53, 54, 55, 57, 58, 60
— *E.I.A.*, on pottery, 83, 90, 92, 93, 94, 94 n, 95, 96, 99; on bronzes, 74, 81, 99, 100, 104–9, 119, 214, 283–4
— *R.*, in houses, 184, 185, 186; on metal objects, 192, 213–7; on pottery, 201–13
— *A.-S.*, excellence of, 248; on pottery, 247, 267, 273–4; Carlovingian, 299; geometric, 248, 254, 257, 258, 271, 279; inlaid, 243, 297; interlaced, 297, 298, 300; naturalistic, 243, 259, 284; phyllomorphic, 272, 284, 299; spiral, 298; volute, 272; zoömorphic, 248, 254, 258, 271 (Salin, style I 279, style II 264); *see also* Cross, Classical, Damascening, Enamel, Garnets, Niello, Romanizing ornament, Shell, Swastika
— evolution of, on beakers, 26; on cinerary urns, 39–40; on axes, 55, 57–8; on Iron Age wares, 95–6; on A.-S. bronzes, 248, 258, 271–2
Deer, red, 225; on settlement sites, 47, 48; *see* Antlers
— roe, bones of, 36 n, 48
"Defended areas," 133, 156
Denmark, 51, 238 n, 252, 295; see Borgstedt, Slesvig
Denny Abbey, Waterbeach [C] *C 4*, 165 n, 223
Denver [N], Roman roads to, 165, 182, 222, 234
Derbyshire, beakers found in, 22
Desborough [Northants.], food-vessel from, 38
Deverel-Rimbury pottery types, 41, 46
Devil's Ditch, Beachamwell [N], 132–3, 133 n
— — West Harling [N], 132–3
Devil's Dyke [C] *C 4–C 5*, described, 124–5; date of, 90, 90 n, 128, 131, 156; covers a boundary ditch, 129; crossing point of Icknield Way, 145; a military frontier? 117–8; a culture boundary, 89–90, 235; used by the Iceni? 160; R. house near, 184; Lode at end of, 180; in A.-S. period, 128, 263, 292, 293; mentioned, 109, 121, 123, 132

INDEX

Dickins, Mr Bruce, quoted, 298, 300
Diocletian, coins of, 230, 232
Discs, bronze, X–XI cent., 299
Ditches, of slight profile, 127; at agricultural settlements, 231
Diviciacus, 103
Doddington [C] *A 3*, 229, 322
Dogs, 81
Dolichocephaly, in *B.A.*, 47, 66; in *E.I.A.*, 81, 114, 115, 119; *R.*, 233
Domesday Book, xxii, 151*n*, 303
Domesday vills, 306–10; relation to R. roads, 311
Domestic appliances, 108
Dorchester [Oxford.], finds at, 287
Dorset, pottery-type from, 47, 66
Downham Fen [N], finds in, 18, 56, 65
Drays Ditches [B], 127
Droveway* [N] *A 5–A 6* (*Map V*), 155
Dryden, Sir H., 80, 98, 99–100, 202*n*, 214; quoted, 100, 204
Du Chaillu, P. B., 260
Duckworth, W. H. L., 114, 115*n*; quoted, 66*n*
Dullingham [C] *C 5*, 310
Dunmow [E], 161
Dunstable [B], 11, 143, 147
Dunton [B] *E 2*, 309
Dunwich [S], 240, 295*n*
Durolipons, 173*n*
Durrow, Book of, 284, 298
Dutt, W. A., 5, 6*n*
Dux Britanniae, 160
Duxford [C] *D 4*, 64
Dykes, list of, 122 (see also 132, 179, 305); survey of, 123–4; weapons found at, 127–8, 292–3; relation of barrows to, 128, of Icknield Way to, 147; the builders, 134; gateways, 125, 128, 130; in A.-S. period, 292–4

Eagle, device of an, on a ring, 192*n*
Eanred, coin of, 298
Ear picks, 262, 263
Earith [Hunts.] *B 3*, 179, 214
Earle, J. and Plummer, C., 287, 288, 302*n*, 304*n*
Earrings, 251, 262
Earthwork, non-military, 223, 305–6
Earthworks, defensive: the result of military organization, 156–7, 321; pre-Roman, 109–10, 138–40; Roman, 112, 160, 173–6, 178, 179, 182–3, 232–3; occupied in R. times, 177–8; rectangular, date uncertain, 138; A.-S., 293; Danish, 301–2; post-Conquest, 194, 301, 303; manorial, 301; homestead moats, 303–5; moated and ramparted, 301, 302, 303; scarcity of finds near, xxv; *see also* Ditches, Dykes, Hill-forts, Ring-works

East Anglia, kingdom of, 239–40; problems of defence of, 292–4, 321; boundaries of, 239, 290, 292–4, 295; dominance of, 295
East Anglian heathlands, *see* Heathlands
East Saxons, 239; isolation of, 288; contact with Middle Angles, 291; cultural relations of, 290–1; *see* Essex
East Shefford [Berks.], finds at, 286
East Winch [N], 26
Eastbourne [Sussex], finds at, 71
Eastern Plain, a culture area, 315–6
Edward the Elder, 301, 302, 316
Edworth [B] *E 2*, 309
Elbe region, the, 238, 277, 316
Elmdon [E] *E 3*, 306
— Elmdonbury* (*see Map J*), 304
Eltisley [C] *C 2*, 154, 157
Elveden [S] *B 6*, 99, 102, 105, 308
— Hunwell Spring* (*near "n" of Elveden*), 6
Ely [C] *B 4*, finds at or near, 7, 54, 105, 203, 207, 210, 214, 229, 229*n*, 322; roads to, 161, 164, 165, 165*n*, 182, 234; ancient track to, 137, 141, 155
Emmanuel Knoll*, Godmanchester [Hunts.] *C 2* (barrow, *Map IV*), 168, 195, 197, 198, 228
Enamels: *E.I.A.*, 104, 105, 108; survivals, 109, 252, 283–4: *R.*, 192, 214, 247: *A.-S.*, 260, 262, 283, 294, 295
Engravings, on flint crust, 2
Eriswell [S] *B 5*, finds at, 18*n*, 25, 26, 91*n*, 107, 322, 323
— Foxhole Heath* (1 *m. E. of village*), 48
Ermine Street, *A 1–F 3*, 150, 161, 166, 177, 219, 221, 226, 228; described, 164–5; entirely R., 182; in A.-S. period, 289, 290
Escutcheons, bronze, 283–4
Essex, in R. times, 225; A.-S. kingdom of, 291; R. roads in, 289–91; boundaries of, 239, 290, 291; Danish occupation of, 316; woodland in, 225, 310
Essex Cam, river, *F 4* to *D 3*, defined, xxii; a political boundary, 295, 296
—— Valley, *see under* Trade-routes
Ethelbert, King, 239
Ethelred I, coins of, 299
Ethnology, 14, 23, 65–7, 114–5, 178, 233, 318
Evans, Sir Arthur J., 55, 82, 104*n*; criticizes Montelius, 17; on the Aylesford cemetery, 4, 90, 91, 92, 93, 100
Evans, Sir John, 3, 6*n*, 11, 196*n*, 197, 284; on bronze implements, 18*n*, 19, 54, 55, 56, 57, 59, 60, 61, 64, 323, 324, 328; on coins, 87, 88, 298; quoted, 266; his collection, *see* Ashmolean Museum

346 INDEX

Evelyn-White, C. H., 223, 306 n
Eversden, Great and Little [C] *D 3*, 154, 165
Everton [B] *D 1*, 154
Exning [S] *C 5*, 64, 147, 149, 212 n, 241, 264, 269, 323
— St Mindred's Well* (*by Street Way, Map III*), 149
Exports, 120
Eyebury [Northants.], food-vessel from, 38
Eynesbury [Hunts.] *C 1*, 267, 274, 276
Eyworth [B] *D 2*, 309

Fairford [Glouc.], 258
Faustina, coins of, 190
Fearnsides, W. G., 11
Feering [E], 291
— Feeringbury [E], 291 n
Felix, Saint, 295 n
Feltwell Fen [N] *A 5*, finds in, 55, 56, 61, 65, 324
Fen Ditton [C] *C 4*, 57, 125, 126
— — Wadloes Path* (*burial by, Map II*), 41
Fen Drayton [C] *C 2*, 198
Fen Stanton [Hunts.] *C 2*, 168
Fenland Basin, *see* Cultural unity in the Fenland Basin
Fens, the, topography of, xxii, xxiii–iv; subsidence in, 7, 65, 223, 314; drainage of, 179, 222–3; importance of waterways, 64, 223, 274, 276; settlement in, 64, 116–7, 229–30, 234, 235, 307, 313, 314; political orientation of, 239; Celtic-speaking element in, 282; R. roads in, 182, 222; sea-bank of, 222; finds in, 6, 7, 62, 64, 65, 214, 216, 222–3, 263
Fenton, Mr S. G., collection of, 323
Ferules, bronze, 61, 104, 264
Fibulae: *E.I.A.*, Hallstatt, 62, 72–5, 80–1; La Certosa, 74, 75, 84; La Tène I, 75–6, 83; La Tène II, 81; La Tène III–IV, 98, 100, 104, 105–7; of Gaulish type, 91; transitional, 106–7
— R., 187 n, 215–6, 229; in A.-S. graves, 242–3, 270, 281
— A.-S., position in burials, 251, 255, 261; of iron, 255, 262, 281; of R. types, 281; annular, 270, *also* 242, 243, 252, 253, 276, 282, 285; applied, 254, 287–8, 291, 292, *also* 243, 252, 253, 259, 260, 268, 296; disc, 262; equal-armed, 244, 256, 262, 276, 277; cruciform, 243, 248, 249, 252, 257, 262, 268–9, 286, 295, *also* 240, 244, 247, 251, 253, 255, 261, 262 n, 265, 270, 272, 274, 276, 280, 283, 287, 291, 294; penannular, 280; plate, 262, 270–1, 294, *also* 248, 251, 253, 256, 259, 282; radiating 240, 252, 260, 262, 294–5; "S"-shaped, 257, 259; saucer, 254, 279, 287, 292, *also* 243, 251, 252, 257, 260, 267, 268, 288, 296; "small long," 255, 257, 269–70, *also* 243, 245, 248, 251, 252, 253, 259, 266, 276, 285; square-headed, 252, 258, 260, 262, 271, 295; *also* 243, 251, 253, 255, 257, 279, 283, 285, 294; of Scandinavian types, 299
"Field" in compounds, 295
Finds, provenance of, inadequately recorded, 158
— and Remains, distribution of, 5–10, 24, 26–7, 30–1, 62–5, 86–7, 102–3, 115–7, 218–25, 274–5, 313–5, 319–21
Fire-dogs, iron, 99, 100, 101, 101 n, 193
Fisher, Marshall, 230
Fishhooks, bronze, 62
Fitzwilliam Museum, Cambridge, objects in, 168, 215, 298
Fleam Dyke [C] *D 4 and C 4 (Map V)*, described, 125–6; excavations at, 129–31; age of, 132, 292–4; origin of N.W. sector, 134; finds at, 4, 128, 131, 212, 293; barrows near, 30–1; relation to Icknield Way, 145, 166; *see also* 156, 160, 296, 321
Fletton [Hunts.], pottery from, 38, 41
Fleure, H. J. and James, T. C., 315
— and Whitehouse, W. E., 315
Flint flakes, in barrows, 31, 34, 35, 42, 325, 326, 328; trimmed, 1; range of date, 4
Flint mines, 1–2
Flints, in a long barrow, 11; in a round barrow, 194, 328; in R. building, 181, 184, 185, 188
Flute, bone, 100
Food, with a cremated burial, 193
"Food-vessels," 27, 32, 38, 39, 45
Fordham [C] *B 5*, finds at, 26, 27, 53, 57, 64, 66, 241, 264
Fords, relation to mills, 148 n; determine traffic lines, 142–3; of Cam River, 112, 113, 148, 150–1, 169, 175, 221, 221 n, 250 n; of Essex Cam, 111, 138, 143, 145, 150–1, 153, 259; of Bourn Brook, 182 n, 194; of Hiz, 143; of Great Ouse, 171 n; of Kennett, 149; of Lark, 146; of Little Ouse, 146; of Old West River, 155; of Rib, 176; of Stour, 178–9
Forest, area of, xxii; influence of, 290, 315–6; condition, extent and periods of occupation, 224–5, 234, 275, 307–10, 311, 312, 313–4; in N.A., 9; in B.A., 62; in E.I.A., 116; R. roads in, 219–20, 221; R. barrows in, 197
Fork, iron, 252
Foss Ditch* [N] *A 6 (Map V)*, 132

INDEX 347

Foss Dyke [Lincs.], 180
Foss Way, 94, 287
Foster, W. K., on Barrington excavations, 110, 250, 251 n, 252-3, 254, 255, 281
Foulsham [N], find at, 51
Founders' metal, 49
Fowlmere [C] *D 3*, 148; continuity of occupation of, 113
— Black Peak*, 127, 148
— Mill*, 148
— Round Moats*, q.v.
Fox, Cyril, 129, 237 n, 259, 300, 316
— and Palmer, W. M., 110, 129 n
Fox, G. E., 187 n, 194, 214, 229
Fox, R., 177, 228
Fox Hill*, Orwell [C] *D 3* (see Map E), 150 n, 155, 157, 165, 166
Foxton [C] *D 3*, finds at, 57, 91, 92, 101, 107, 108, 201, 241, 259
— The Bury*, 304
France, bronze implements in, 21, 54; Hallstatt finds in, 21; connections with, in *E.I.A.*, 86, 100, 103
Franks, the, 232; cultural connections with, 240, 245 n, 273, 274
Franks, Sir A. Wollaston, 322
Freckenham [S] *B 5*, 88, 95
Freestone, Northants., used in R. building, 180, 184, 185, 188, 247
Frettenham [N], find at, 58
Frisians, 240, 257, 295
Frontiers, *E.I.A.*, 103, 117, 230, 317, 321; *A.-S.*, 239, 285, 291, 292, 294-5, 296, 321
Fulbourn [C] *D 4*, 198, 198 n, 211, 323
— Fen*, 125, 135
— Lodge* (N. of "r" of Vandlebury), 148
Furneaux Pelham [H] *F 3*, 60, 62, 324

Gage, John, 191-2, 214
Gale, Roger, quoted, 191
Galley Hill*, Sandy [B] *D 1* (earthwork, Map V), 176
Gallienus, coins of, 175 n, 187, 228, 229, 230, 232
Gamlingay [C] *D 2*, 151, 154
Garnets, inlaid, 243, 262, 264, 294, 297; en cabochon, 252
Garrood, Dr, 9, 103 n, 177
Garrowby Wold [Yorks.], 38
Gazeley [S] *C 5*, 153
Geography, influence of, xxii, 275, 315, 317, 320
Geology, importance of, 275, 313
Germani, the, 293
Germanicus, coins of, 228
Germanus, Saint, 161 n
Girdle ornaments, 255
Girdle-hangers, 260, 261, 271, 282, 286; see also 243, 247, 248, 252, 253, 263, 280 n, 285
Gironde, River, 54
Girton [C] *C 3*, College, R. finds at, 168, 185, 187-8, 209, 228; A.-S. cemetery at, 246-9, 271, 272, 273, 278, 279-80; see also 256, 269, 270, 274 n, 276, 277, 281, 283
Girton College Library, objects in, 246, 247
Glass: *E.I.A.*, 100, 104; *R.*, 189, 213, 216-7, see also 174, 185, 191, 192, 192 n, 193, 198 n; *A.-S.*, 247, 260, 263, 294, see also 254, 256, 276
Glen, River [Lincs.], 179
Goat, bones of, in barrows, 35, 36 n
Goddard, A. R., 134, 176, 303; quoted, 192, 302
Godmanchester [Hunts.] *B 2-C 2*, R. town, 176-7, also 173 n, 222, 230; finds at, 188, 210, 228; roads at, 161, 164, 165, 168, 170, 171, 182, 221, 234
— King's Bush*, 164
— Lattenbury Hill*, 165
See also Emmanuel Knoll
Gog-Magog Hills [C] *D 4*, 139, 149, 150; importance of, 135; barrows on, 329; R. road on, 129, 168, 169, 181
Goidels, see Q-Celts
Gold: in B.A., 51, 52, 57, 63, 317, not found in barrows, 42: in later Periods, 81, 192, 226, 228, 252, 262, 297, 299, 300
Goodwin, C. W., 60
Gorham, G. C., quoted, 267-8
Gouges, 1, 4, 61
Gould, I. Chalkley, 135
Graffiti, 207-8
Graham-Smith, Dr G. S., quoted, 329
Granham Manor Camp*, Great Shelford [C] *D 4* (1½ m. N. of "l" of Shelford), 178
Gransden, Great [Hunts.] *D 2*, 154
Granta, River, a name not used, xxiii
"Granta" Fen, 51, 57, 323; see Grunty Fen
Grantchester [C] *D 3*, settlement at, 111-2; tracks to, 153, 154; roads through 169-70, 181-2; earthwork at, 169, 175, 183; R. house at, 185, 187, 188; finds at, 82-3, 92, 95, 96, 241, 249
Gratian, coins of, 185, 187, 227, 228, 229
Grave-covers, stone, 300
Gravel terraces, riverside, evidence of occupation of, 25, 31, 37, 38, 99, 120
Gray, Arthur, 168, 175 n, 245-6, 282, 295; quoted, 276-7
Greenwell, Canon, 2, 33, 42, 77, 265, 299, 325, 327, 328
Griffith, Mr A. F., quoted, 155, 249, 251 n, 256, 258
Grimes Graves*, Weeting [N] *A 6* (flint mines, Map I), 1, 2; B.A. finds, 48, 54, 61, 95, 110; banks near, 127; barrows near, 328
Grim's Ditch*, Saffron Walden [E] *E 4* (earthwork, Map V), 136

INDEX

Grundy, G. B., 152
Grunty Fen* [C] *B 4 (N.W. of Stretham)*, hoards in, 18, 51, 55, 57, 65, 323, significance of, 63
Guilden Morden [C] *E 2*, 165, 209
Guthlac, Saint, 282
Gyrwe, the, 239

Haddon, Dr A. C., quoted, 23
Hadrian, coins of, 184, 191, 192, 229
Hadstock [E] *D 4*, R. house at, 186, 188, 189, 232
Hailstone, E., *Jr.*, 328
Halberd, 54
Hallingbury, Little [E], finds at, 103, 139
Hallstatt, culture, 20, 21, 57, 61, 70, 71, 317; pottery, 82–3, 85, 112, 118; bronzes, 72–5, 76, 80–1, 84, 85, 118; *also* 59, 60, 61, 62
"Ham" in compounds, 295
Hammerheads, of stone, 47; of antler, 3; of bronze, 61
Hammerstones, 4, 33, 47
Hanover, grave-furniture found in, 243, 249, 259, 268, 269, 284, 296
Hardwick [C] *C 3*, 154, 171–2, 309
— Way*, 172
Hare Park* (Upper), Swaffham Bulbeck [C] *C 4* (*group of barrows, Map II*), 30, 30*n*, 32, 32*n*, 33, 41, 66, 149, 327–8
Harlton [C] *D 3*, 154, 186, 241, 257–8
Harrowden [B], 303
Harston [C] *D 3*, 151, 172
Hartford [Hunts.] *B 2*, 171*n*, 310
— Hill*, 171
Haslingfield [C] *D 3*: finds at, *N.A.*, 3; *E.I.A.*, 76, 91, 108; *R.*, 100, 203, 209, 210, 211, 256; *A.-S.*, 255–9, *also* 241, 242, 248*n*, 249, 250, 254*n*, 268–9, 270, 271, 272, 276, 278, 280, 283, 295, 296, 298: tracks near, 150, 151, 154–5
Hasps, iron, 300
Hauxton [C] *D 3*, Mill* (*see Map E*), ford at, 150–1, 157; settlement at, 111, 231, 259, 299; finds at, *B.A.*, 37*n*, 55; *E.I.A.*, 82, 83, 91, 91*n*, 93, 95, 96, 106, 108; *R.*, 212*n*, 216, 233; *A.-S.*, 241, 254*n*, 259, 278, 297, 298, 299–300
Hauxton parish, detached portion of, 151
Haverfield, F., 101, 160, 166*n*; on R. remains, 173, 174, 185, 186, 201, 208, 216, 225; on mound burial, 199
Haverhill [S] *D 5*, Roman road through, 157, 164, 166, 168, 172, 181
— Place Farm* (*hoard, Map III*), 89
Havocheston (Hauxton), 151*n*
Heathland, East Anglian, xxi, 5–6, 64, 155–6, 230, 308
Helmet, bronze, 215
Hemingford Abbots [Hunts.] *B 2*, 152
Hemingford Grey [Hunts.] *B 2*, 152
"Hendrica," 239

Hengistbury [Hants.], Hallstatt pottery from, 71, 82–3, 93, 95, 96
Henlow [B] *E 1*, 207, 267
Heraclius, coin of, 297
Hercules, statuettes of, 214
Herringfleet [S], 214
Herringswell [S] *B 5*, 265
Hertfordshire, in A.-S. times, 239, 290, 291, 291*n*
— County Museum, St Albans, 323
Heydon [C] *E 3*, Heydonbury*, 304
Heydon Ditch* [C] *E 3–D 3* (*Map V*), 123, 127, 140, 145; *also* 148, 156
— Grange* (*see Map D*), 145
Higham [S] *C 6*, 153
Hildersham [C] *D 4*, 195–6, 197, 199
Hill-forts, list of, 122; described, 134–6; topography of, 138–40; age and purpose of, 109, 120, 156–7, 321
Hill Lane* [B] *D 1* (*Map IV*), 164, 165, 170*n*
Hilly Wood [Northants.], 212*n*
Hinxton [C] *D 4*, 227
Histon [C] *C 3*, 7, 10, 155
Hitchin [H] *F 1*, 24, 91, 108, 298, 322, 323; *see also* Walsworth
Hithes, 223
Hoards: *N.A.*, 6: *B.A.*, list of, 323–4; distribution of, 62–3; importance of, 19; composition of, 18, 18*n*, 52, 61; analysis of, 49–51; Founders', 51, 62; Merchants', 51, 63; votive, 51, 63; of rough metal, 49, 63; of early date, 54; by a trackway, 149*n*, 155; in the fen, 65; in a barrow, 36: *E.I.A.*, 104, 119: *R.*, 231–33: *A.-S.*, 298, 300
Hod Hill [Dorset], 107
Hoernes, M., 80
Hones, 47
Honorius, coins of, 174, 226, 228, 229
Hope, Sir W. St John, 174, 175*n*
Hormead, Little [H] *F 3*, Bummers Hill* (*mound, Map IV*), 198
Horningsea [C] *C 4*, 57; kilns at, 210–11, 228; pottery from, 96, 177, 178, 212, 213, 281
— Biggin Abbey* (*settlement site, Map IV*), 203, 218
— Eye Hall* (*R. building, Map IV*), 185
Horse, in *B.A.*, 36*n*; in *E.I.A.*, 80, 81, 110; *R.*, 215; *A.-S.*, 261
— trappings: bits, 104, 107, 108, 215, 261; shoes, 108; harness, 81, 104, 108, 253, 261
Horseheath [C] *D 5*, 168, 226, 231
Houghton [Hunts.] *B 2*, 152, 171
Houses: *Roman*, types, 183–7; character, 187, 193, 236; distribution, 188; partly of wood, 186; architectural remains, 187–8; not found in towns, 175, 176, 177; not fortified, 235, 304*n*; desertion of, 227, 232, 236; fate of, 236; post-R. inhabitants of, 236; relation to A.-S. villages, 283

INDEX 349

Houses: *Roman* (cont.)
  Hypocausts in, 184, 185, 186; mosaics in, 184, 185, 186, 187; painted plaster in, 185; roofing-slabs of, 184; apse in, 184; building materials, *see* Freestone, Barnack Rag, Clunch, Brick
— *Anglo-Saxon*, defences of, 304–5
How House*, Impington [C] *C 3* (*barrow, Map IV*), 196
Hügel, Baron A. von, 57, 81, 206, 323; quoted, 214–5
Hughes, T. McKenny, xxiii, 11, 108, 111, 129, 326, 327, 328; on Limlow Hill, 194, 199; on mediaeval pottery, 281–2; on Devil's Dyke, 128; on R. occupation, 110, 173*n*, 175*n*, 185, 206, 210, 211, 218, 227, 231, 235; on A.-S. finds, 257–8, 259, 264, 300; on War Ditches, 114, 136, 177, 177*n*, 178, 190, 208; on Arbury, 137; *see also* Allix, C. P.
Hundreds, Anglo-Saxon, 146, 152
Hunsbury [Northants.], a hill-fort, 94, 96
Huntingdon [Hunts.] *B 2*, settlement at, 177, 222, 222*n*; roads at, 164, 171; earthwork at, 302; finds at, 228
— Institute, objects in, 322, 323
Huntingdonshire, 270; settlement of, 310
Hut-sites, 15, 110

Iberian race, *see* Mediterranean race
Iceni, the, 71–2; racial type, 86, 114, 118; burial rites of, 97, 102; boundary of, 90, 90*n*, 103, 230, 235, 290*n*, 317; construct Devil's Dyke? 156, 321; coins of, 87–9; history of, 132, 160; Romanization of, 230
Ickleford [H] *E 1–F 1*, 143
Ickleton [C] *E 4*, ford at, 143, 145; R. house at, 183–4, 188, 189, 208, 230*n*
— Coploe Hill* (*see Map D*), 306
— Granges* (*see Map D*), 145
Icklingham [S] *B 6*, finds at, 5, 6, 39*n*, 53, 63, 74, 92, 105, 107, 216, 217, 229, 248, 257, 322; R. house at, 187, 188, 232
— Farthing Bridge*, 146
— How Hill* (2 *m. N.N.W. of village*), 326
— Mitchell's Hill* (*cemetery, Map V*), 93–4, 97, 270, 271, 272
— Stonepit Hill*, 216
— The Cardle*, 33, 326
Icknield Way, *F 1–A 6*, described, 142, 142*n*, 143–7, 157; part of R. road system, 161, 166, 167, 181, 182; evidence of age, 8, 11, 14, 24, 147; in mediaeval record, 145*n*, 146; a trade and culture route, 8, 14, 52, 54, 63, 147, 317, 319; relation to barrows, 30, 30*n*; to dykes, 128, 130, 140; in A.-S. period, 277, 287, 288; *see also* 114, 121, 122, 125, 127, 135, 139, 148, 149, 153, 155, 174
Iliad, the, 33*n*
Incense-, cup, 36, 36*n*, 37, 41, 326; pan, 213; burner, 189, 208
Indulcius, 208
Ingham [N], 26
Inhumation interments: *N.A.*, 11, 12, 12*n*, 318
— *B.A.*, distribution of, 31; in barrows, 31, 32, 33; in a flat grave, 37; contracted, 31, 32, 33; with beakers, 27; disjointed before deposition, 32
— *E.I.A.*, 76–8, 97; contracted, 81; significance of, 118
— *R.*, 178, 231, 233; survival from E.I.A., 102, 190; in barrows, 191, 194; relation to cremation, 188–9; poverty of, 190
— *A.-S.*, 248, 259, 260, 261, 262, 264, 265, 266, 273, 274, 277, *also* 243, 245, 246, 247, 253, 256; relation to cremation, 242, 246, 278; vessels associated with, 273; early date of, 256, 277–8; orientation of, 253, 253*n*, 261
Inscriptions, 209, 300; *see* Graffiti
Inskip, T., 98, 99, 202*n*; quoted, 207*n*; his collection, 201, 202, 207*n*
Interments, customs connected with, evolution of, 100, 101, 192–3
— *N.A.*, *see* Inhumation
— *B.A.*, 27–37, 42–7; choice of sites for, 25, 30–1, 40; difficulty of dating, 21; of beaker-folk, 25, 27; of transition period, 31–2; of early B. period, 33; in flat graves, 37; on a dwelling site, 47
— *E.I.A.*, 76–81, 97–102; similarity to R., 101; in pits, 100; multiple, 78, 79
— *R.*, 188–200; secondary, 197; visible memorials of? 189; ritual, 189; the funeral piles, 189; objects deposited with, 189, 192–3
A.-S., 241–68, 299; absence of grave-goods in certain, 253; position and frequency of associated objects, 253, 261
See also Barrows, Inhumation, Cremation, Burials
Invasions, sequence of, 119, 318; effect of, 318; continental sources of, 318; route of entry of, 316; of beaker-folk, 15, 22, 24; of leaf-sword folk, 19–20, 46, 58, 61, 66–7, 68; of iron-using folk, 71, 85, 86, 118; of Romans, 160, 319; of Anglo-Saxons, 238, 274, 275, 277, 318; of Danes, *q.v.*
Ipswich [S], cemetery at, 245*n*, 290
— Museum, objects in, 6*n*

INDEX

Iron, introduction of, 71, 84; working, persistence of tradition in, 217; *see* Swords, iron, Spearheads, iron, etc., etc.
Irrigation works, 223
Isleham [C] *B 5*, Fen, finds in, 56, 209, 216, 223
Italy, source of certain finds, 84
Itineraries, East Anglian, 162, 173*n*
Ivel Valley, *F 1* and *E 2–C 1*, in B.A., 24; in E.I.A., 89, 102, 116, 156; in R. times, 205, 219, 226–7, 230; in A.-S. times, 276, 308; significance of occupation of, 315
Ivory, 255
Ixworth [S], finds at, 74, 75, 85–6, 266, 294, 298

Jenkinson, Mr F. J. H., 193, 206, 229–30, 232; on Girton finds, 185, 242*n*, 246–8, 248*n*, 272*n*, 279
Jewels, of gold, inlaid, 243, 262, 294, 295, 297
Johnson, C., 306*n*
Julian, coins of, 232
Jupiter, statuette of, 214
Jutes, 238; *see also* Kent

Karslake, J. B. P., 136
Kedington [S] *D 5*, 187
Kelshall [H] *E 2*, 224, 312
Kelvedon [E], 291
Kempe, A. J., describes a cemetery, 188–9; *see also* 184, 194, 199, 202*n*, 206*n*, 209
Kempston [B], cemetery at, 249, 254*n*, 256, 288
Kendrick, Mr T. D., 27*n*
Kennett, River*, *D 5* to *B 5*, 8, 63, 143, 146, 149
Kent, land route to, 139; cultural relations with, 290, 294–5; finds of objects of Kentish (or "Jutish") type, 254, 255, 262, 264, 265, 266, 274*n*, 294, 295, 297
Kentford [S] *C 5*, 63, 143, 146, 147*n*
Ketton Stone, *see* Freestone
Keys, 243, 255, 259, 282
Keysoe [B], 303
Kilns, pottery, 210–11; lime, 211; tile, 211, 225
Kimmeridge shale, vessels of, 96–7, 98; bangles of, 100, 247
Kimmins, Mr, 299
Kingdoms, Anglo-Saxon, 238–40, 285–95, 296
King's Hedges*, Chesterton [C] *C 3* (1 m. N. of "*r*" of *Chesterton*), 178
King's Ripton [Hunts.] *B 2*, 171
King's Walden [H] *F 1*, 266, 274*n*, 278
Kingston [Kent], 263
Kirtling [C] *C 5*, 311
Knapwell [C] *C 2*, 194
Kneesworth [C] *E 3*, 147

Knives, of flint, 5, 6; of bronze, 61; of iron, E.I.A., 98, 107, 110; R., 192; A.-S., 255, 261, *also* 247, 248, 249, 251, 253, 259, 262, 265, 266, 267
Knut's Delph, 179

La Graufesenque, potters of, 204, 205, 207, 229
Lackford [S] *B 6*, 123, 143, 146, 152, 265, 278
Ladds, S. Inskip, 195, 198
Lakenheath [S] *A 5–B 5*: N.A., 5, 6: B.A., beakers, 25, 26, 27, 322, 326; other finds, 18*n*, 31, 41, 46, 54, 55, 57, 324: E.I.A., finds, 74, 76, 82, 92, 95, 102, 105, 106, 107, 116: R., 203, 216: A.-S., 258, 270, 274, 283, *see also* 268, 269, 272, 273, 276, 284, 299
— Fen*, 105, 229*n*, 301
— Warren, *B 6*, 156, 299
Lamb's Cross* [C] *C 3* (by first "*w*" of *Westwick*), 155
Lamps, iron, 191, 192, 193; bronze, 192
Lanceheads, 5, 292; *see* Spearheads
Landbeach [C] *C 4*; Goosehall* (by "*n*" of *Akeman*), 165
Landwade [C] *C 5*, 185
Langenhoe [E], 94*n*
Langford [B] *E 1*, 267
Langley [E] *E 3*, 196
Lantilly, Côte-d'Or, burials at, 77
Lark Hall, Weston Colville [C] *D 4*, 166
Lark, River, *C 7* to *B 4–5*, 143, 146, 149
—— Valley of the, finds in, 5, 6, 24, 62, 63, 116, 229, 264, 274; settlement in, 276, 308, 313
Laver, Henry, 139
Leaden objects, 300
Leaf-sword folk, 19–20, 51, 66, 68, 318
Leather, 104, 104*n*; chair-seat, 192; headstall, 261
Leeds, E. Thurlow, on early pottery, 15, 38, 39, 40; on A.-S. period, 238, 239*n*, 243, 249, 252, 254, 257*n*, 258, 264, 269, 277, 279, 287–8
Lees, B. A., 306*n*
Legio IX, 212
Leicester, R. road to, 168, 170, 171
Leicestershire, finds in, 273
Letchworth [H] *E 2*, 90–1, 99, 143
Lewes [Sussex], pin from, 57*n*
Lewis, S. S., 185, 209; his collection, 209
Leys School Museum, Cambridge, 233
Lezoux, potters of, 204, 206, 207
Limlow Hill*, Litlington [C] *E 2* (barrow, Map II), 190, 194, 199, 329
Lincoln, 161, 179, 180, 221
Lincolnshire, 179, 270, 295
Lindenschmit, L., 76
Lindsell [E] *F 5*, 101, 116

INDEX

Linton [C] *D 4*, 153, 157
— Heath* (*cemetery, Map V*), 196–7, 255, 260, 283; *also* 241, 254*n*, 273, 277*n*, 294, 295
Liquids, deposited with interments, 192, 193
Litlington [C] *E 2*, 147, 314; R. cemetery, 167, 188–9, 199, 232; finds at, 92, 201, 202*n*, 203, 205–6, 208–9, 212, 212*n*, 216, 217, 227; houses at, 184–5, 188, 206, 236, 283; *see also* Limlow Hill
Littlebury, *see* Ring Hill
Littleport [C] *A 4*, xxiii, 64, 210; *see* Burnt Fen
— Old Croft River*, xxiii, 210, 223
Liverpool Museum, objects in, 265, 324
Living (or working) floors, 8, 47, 48, 110–11; *see* Hut-sites
Lockets, enamelled, 214
Lodes, the, xxiv
London [Msex.], 161, 316
"Long Barrow Race," 66*n*, 114
Long Melford [S] *D 7*, 103, 157
Long Stanton [C] *C 3*, 152
Loom, 69; -weights, 108
Looped tubes, bronze. *See* Bugle-shaped objects
Lord's Bridge, Barton [C] *D 3*, finds at, 95, 100–1, 102; barrow at, 101, 194, 197, 199
Loth, M. J., 67
Lucas, Dr Chas., 7; his collection, 3, 6, 58, 323
Lukis, W. C., 134, 168, 173*n*, 175*n*, 176*n*, 191, 195, 205, 227, 229, 263; *see also* Stukeley, Dr
Lyell, A. H., 173*n*, 183*n*, 184, 184*n*, 185
Lynchets, 305–6
Lysons, D. and S., quoted, 135*n*, 196, 304

Macalister, R. A. S., 205
Maceheads, of stone and antler, 1, 2, 3, 3*n*, 53
Madingley [C] *C 3*, 218
— Hill* (*S.E. of village*), 157
"Maerweg," 152
Magnentius, coin of, 227
Maitland, F. W., 303
Malaria, 9, 117
Malton*, Orwell [C] *D 3* (1 m. S. of "w" of Orwell), 61, 108, 241, 250, 251, 252
Manea [C] *A 4*, 229
— Fen* (*site find, Map V*), 7, 54, 263
Manningtree [E], finds at, 41
Manorial halls, antiquity of sites of, 303–4
Manors, settlements attached to, 310
Maps, described, xxiii, xxiv; employment of symbols on, xxiv, 9, 30, 162, 217–8, 224, 278; record provided by the, value of, 8–9
March [C], finds at, 26, 27, 88
Marcus Aurelius, coins of, 195, 226, 229, 231

Mare Way* [C] *D 2–D 3* (*see Map E*), 122, 150–2, 157
Marks Tey [E], 289, 297
Marmansgrave Wood*, Elveden [S] *B 6* (*by Icknield Way E.N.E. of Elveden*), 146
"Marne" ware, 83
Mars, statuette of, 214, 216
Mars Alator, figure of, 216
Mars Toutates, figure of, 216
Marshall, W., 64
Maximian, coins of, 227, 229
May, T., 91, 190*n*, 202, 202*n*, 204, 208, 209, 211, 212
Maynard, G., 323; quoted, 68–9, 139
— and Benton, G. M., 25, 322
Mecklenburg, 243, 268
Mediterranean, the, evidences of trade with, 84, 86, 101
Mediterranean (Iberian) race, 14, 318
Melbourn [C] *D 3–E 3*, 147, 148, 172, 314; finds at, 61, 202, 323; earthwork at, 175, 183
— Five Barrow Field* (*see Map D*), 34, 36*n*, 41, 199, 326, 329
— Goffers Knoll* (*see Map D*), 326
— Melbournbury*, 304
Melbourn Rock, 147
Meldreth [C] *D 3*, Station, hoard at, 18*n*, 19, 57, 324
Mepal [C] *B 3* Fen*, barrow in, 30*n*, 37, 40, 41, 263, 327
Mercia (and Mercians), 239, 245, 276–7, 290; coins of, 298
Mercury, statuette of, 214; bronze relief of, 214
"Mere" Ways, 152
Meres, in Southern Fens, xxii, 7, 65, 223, 314; *see under* Soham *and* Whittlesea
Mereway*, *C 4*, Roman road, 165, 178
Mestorf, J., 268, 270
Metal, introduction of, 17, 20; rarity of, in transition period, 42, 52
Methwold [N], near (*beaker, Map II, A 5*), 25, 322
Middle Angles, status, 239; cultural characters, 285, 291
Middle Anglia, boundaries, 239, 266, 285, 291–5; traffic routes, 290, 291
Mildenhall [S] *B 5*, finds at, 5, 6, 51, 60, 63, 75–6, 108, 109, 215, 265, 268, 276, 284, 298, 301; chariot? burial at, 81, 118; barrow at, 12*n*
— Warren Hill* (*barrows, Map II*), burials at, 32, 38, 66, 273, 277*n*, 327
— West Row, finds at, 216
— Holywell Row, finds at, 265, 323
— Fens, find in, 105
Mile Ditches* [H] and [C] *E 2* (*marked, Map V*), 127
Milestones, Roman, 168
Miller, S. H. and Skertchly, S. B. J., 179

INDEX

Millow, Dunton [B] *E 2*, 309
— Millowbury*, 304
Mills, at fords, 148*n*
Milton [C] *C 4*, Sewage Farm* (settlement site, Map *IV*), 91, 102, 110, 203, 207, 283
Mines, *see* Flint mines
Mirrors, bronze, 99, 108
Moat Way, 152*n*
Moated earthworks, 137, 141, 194, 301–5
Monceau-Laurent, Côte-d'Or, France, 79
Money Hill*, Haslingfield [C] *D 3* (*see* Map *E*), 151, 155
Money Hill*, Therfield [H] *E 3* (barrow, S.W. of Royston), 36, 40, 328
Mons Badonicus, 240
Montagu, H., 88, 95
Montelius, Oscar, 3, 10, 12, 57; system of chronology, 16–17, 70, criticized, 17–20
Montgomerie, D. H., 136
Monumental art, northern school of, 316
Morris, G., 8, 10*n*
Mortimer, J. R., 26*n*, 32, 32*n*, 34*n*, 38*n*, 42
Mortlake [Surrey], 15
Moulds, bronze, for axes, 58
Moulton [S] *C 5*, Bury Hill* (barrow, 2 *m. W. of village*), 147*n*
Mounds, dry-ditched, 194; moated, 194, 198
Mount Balk*, Haslingfield [C] *D 3* (*see* Map *E*), 151, 152
Mount Bures [E], finds at, 100, 202
Moyses Hall Museum, Bury St Edmunds, objects in, 12*n*, 24, 26, 74, 75, 76, 92, 94, 103*n*, 108, 211, 216, 229, 248, 265, 322, 323, 324, 327, 328
Mullers, stone, 108; *see* Pestles
Museum of Archaeology and of Ethnology, Cambridge, objects in, *N.A.*, 6*n*, 10; *B.A.*, 18, 18*n*, 25, 26, 32, 33, 53, 54, 55, 57, 58, 62, 64, 322, 323, 324, 326, 327, 328; *E.I.A.*, 74, 75*n*, 76, 81, 82, 82*n*, 90, 91, 92, 96, 97, 99, 100, 101, 104, 105, 107, 108, 109, 110*n*, 111, 134, 136; *R.*, 176, 178, 185, 188, 197, 201, 201*n*, 202, 203, 204, 208, 209, 210, 211, 212*n*, 213, 214, 216, 224, 228; *A.-S.*, 242, 243, 244, 245, 246, 247, 252, 253, 254, 255, 256, 257*n*, 259, 262, 263, 264, 265, 266, 267, 267*n*, 269, 270, 271, 272, 283, 284, 293, 294, 297, 298, 299, 301
— — Trinity College Loan Collection, 251, 253, 257–8; Allix, Beldam, Cole Ambrose, Deck, Ransom and Webb Collections, *q.v.*
Mussel-shells, in a barrow, 33
Mutlow Hill*, Great Wilbraham [C] *D 4* (1½ *m. S. of village*), barrow, 35, 40, 130, 147*n*, 194, 326; R.

settlement at, 94, 96, 110, 131, 212; building near, 187
Myers, C. S., quoted, 114, 115
Myres, Prof. J. L., quoted, 224

Nails, iron, 78, 189, 195, 196
Nar, River [N], 132
Needles, bone, 247
Nene, River, *A 1* to *A 3*, xxiii, 179, 290
— Valley, traffic from, 221; cultural relations with, 41, 287
Nero, coins of, 174, 177, 226, 228, 231
Nervii, the, 132
Neville, Hon. R. C., barrow excavations, 29, 30–1, 34, 35; *E.I.A.* finds, 98; Roman excavations, 174, 183, 184, 184*n*, 185, 186, 217, quoted, 225, 226, 227; on A.-S. excavations, 260–2, 270, 271, 272, 273; *see also* 74, 196, 198*n*, 199, 208, 211, 214, 232, 280, 324, 325, 326, 329
Neville MSS. in Audley End House, 60, 98, 195, 196–7, 197*n*, 324, 325, 326, 329
Newmarket [S] *C 5*, 143, 146, 166, 264
— Heath* (Burwell) (area S.W. of town), 6, 12*n*, 145, 326
Newnham*, Cambridge [C] *C 3* (*see* Map *G*), settlement at, 64*n*, 112, 120, 218, 245, 246; burial at, 81, 86, 107, 114, 115, 118
— Croft*, cemetery at, 244, 272, 276, 278
Newnham [H] *E 2*, 148
Newport [E] *E 4*, Shortgrove, 198
Newstead, Scotland, torc from, 107
Niedermendig lava, 198
Niello, 214, 248, 297
Noble, W. M., 64
Noon's Folly Farm*, Melbourn [C] *E 3* (½ *m. N.N.E. of "n" of Royston*), 145
"Nordic" race, 318
Norfolk, dyke-builders in, 132, 134; Icknield Way in, 146, 157
North Stow*, West Stow [S] *B 6* (2½ *m. N. of village*), 3, 147
Northumbria, coin of, 298
Norton [H] *E 2*, The Common*, 143
Norway, connections with, in A.-S. period, 240, 249, 269, 295
Norwich Castle Museum, 6*n*, 299
Notitia Dignitatum, 161
Nunn, E. B., his MS., 11, 77, 185, 324, 328, 329

Oakington [C] *C 3*, 7
Occupation, continuity of, *see under* Settlement
Oculist's stamp, Roman, 176*n*
Odsey*, Guilden Morden [C] *E 2* (near Ashwell Station), 92
Offa, coins of, 298; dyke, 293
Oil, olive, imported? 101

INDEX

Old Croft River*, *A 4 (N. of Littleport)*, xxiii
Old Hurst [Hunts.] *B 2*, 171
"Old Tillage*," the, Waterbeach [C] *C 4*, 180
Old Warden [B] *E 1*, 96, 97, 98–9, 108, 165
Old West River, *B 3 to B 4*, 7, 179; *see* Aldreth
Oman, Sir Charles, 72, 161, 288; quoted, 232
"Omphalos" base, on pottery, 83, 85, 85*n*; on bronze bowls, 105
Ordnance Survey Map, xxiii; 1836 ed., 28, 142, 148, 151, 153, 154, 169, 172, 198
Ornament, *see* Decoration
Orvieto, Etruscan tombs at, 79
Orwell [C] *D 3*, earthwork at, 137–8, 155; reputed finds at, 82, 241, 250, 251, 252
Ostorius Scapula, 132, 160, 230
Oswald, F. and Pryce, T. D., 101, 201*n*, 202, 202*n*, 206*n*
Ouse, Great, River, *D 1 to A 3 or A 4*, course of, xxiii; R. crossing-place, 164; find in, 59
— — Valley of the, absence of early occupation in, 7, 62; A.-S. settlement in, 310
Ouse, Little, River, *B 7 to A 5*, 132, 143
— — Valley of the, occupation of, 5, 116, 229, 308, 313
Over [C] *B 3*, 308
Ox, bones of the, on prehistoric sites, 34, 35, 47, 110, 325

P-Celts, 71
Page, W. and Keate, Miss, 176*n*, 202*n*, 214, 227
Paille Ditches*, Saffron Walden [E] *E 4 (Map V)*, 138, 153, 178
Palmer, W. M., *see* Fox and Palmer
Palstaves, 55–6, 58; as currency, 18*n*, 58; Montelius' classification of, 18; in hoards, 18*n*, 52
Pampisford [C] *D 4*, Dickman's Grove* (½ m. N.E. of village), 126; *see also* Brent Ditch
Pannage, 309
Parishes, settlement in forest, 310–11; detached portion of a, significance of, 151; *see* Boundaries, Parish
Parisii, 72, 86
Parsons, F. G., 66*n*
Patellae, bronze, *see* Bronze vessels
Paterae, of pottery, with burial, 189, 189*n*
Peada, 239; conversion of, 240
Peake, A. E., 2, 48, 54
Peake, Harold, 20, 59, 60, 224, 315
Peasantry, primitive life of, 48, 231
Peat, fen, finds beneath the, 7, 65, 223, 314
Peddars Way [N], 146*n*, 161, 182
Pedestalled urns, 90–1, 96, 99

Penda, 239
Pendant, in A.-S. grave, 262
"Penlowe Park," 207*n*
Pepperton Hill [C] *E 3–E 4 (see Map D)*, 145, 152
Personal names, Celtic, on Roman objects, 208, 214
Pestles, stone, of Bronze Age, 37, 37*n*, 44
Peterborough [Hunts.], 179, 180, 182; finds at, 15, 23, 26, 96, 118; importance of site, 24, 85; absence of Aylesford wares, 102
— Museum, objects in, 65, 75, 212, 216, 322
Pewter, Roman, 216, 235
Picks, flint, 1
Pidley [Hunts.] *B 2*, 63, 323
Pig, bones of, in pre-Roman deposits, 36*n*, 47, 110
Pigott, G. F., 110
Pilgrim's Path*, Icklingham [S] *B 6 (Map V)*, 146, 156
Pilgrim's Walk*, Weeting [N] *A 6 (Map V)*, 155
Pins: Bone, 136, 190; in barrows, 32, 35, 44, 80: Bronze, 57, 62, 76, 107, 248, 253, 271, 297–8; in barrows, 34, 37, 42, 325, 328
Pirton [H], 80, 85
Pit-dwellings, 109, 110, 111, 136
Pits, chalk, marking line of trackway, 153, 155; in chalk rock, 141
Pitt-Rivers, Lieut.-Gen. A., 2, 118*n*, 257
Place-names, indicative of R. buildings, 188–9, *see also* 183, 185; on R. roads, 168, 169, 169*n*; non-Teutonic, 282; "-bury" in com pounds, 291*n*, 303–4; indicative of political boundaries, 295; late date of certain, 275
Plough-share, iron, 300
Political organization, in E.I.A., 321
— relations, between Gaul and Britain, 103
Pompeii, finds at, 213, 214
Pool Street, Great Yeldham [E], 169
Population, distribution of, 7–8, 63–4, 116, 218–25, 233–4, 274–5, 306–12, 313–15
Porter, N. T., 112, 185
Portway*, at Hardwick [C] *C 3*, 162*n*, 171–2
— at Melbourn [C] *D 3*, 172, 175, 176, 183
Postlingford [S] *D 6*, 51, 54, 63, 323
Pot-boilers, 47, 48
Potters, Arretine, 101, 201*n*, 204, 226; Central Gaulish, 202, 204, 206, 207; East Gaulish, 202, 204, 206; Romano-Belgic, 201; South Gaulish, 202, 204, 205, 206, 207, 227, 229
— List of: Albvs, 204, 205; Albvcivs, 207; Albvcianvs, 206, 207; Ardacvs, 205; Asiaticvs, 207; Atili-

INDEX

Potters, List of (cont.):
  anvs, 207; Belliniccvs, 207; Bilicatvs, 204; Borillvs, 206; Calava, 206; Calvinvs, 205; Calvvs, 205; Celticvs, 206; Cocvs, 204; Cotto, 205; Cracisa, 205; Cracissa, 206; Criciro, 206; Cinnamvs, 206; Comitialis, 206; Constas, 206; Cvcalvs, 207; Damonvs, 205, 206; Divicatvs, 206; Elvillvs, 206; Germanvs, 205; Illiomarvs, 207; Licinvs, 205; Logirnvs, 204; Maccalvs, 207; Maccarvs, 205; Maccivs, 204, 206; Macrianvs, 206; Macrinvs, 207; Marcellinvs, 207; Mascvlvs, 205; Namilianvs, 207; Paternvs, 207; Pavllvs, 207; Pecvliaris, 206; Pisanvs, 201 n., 226; Primvlvs, 206, 207, 229; Rebvrrvs, 204, 207; Reginvs, 204; Sabinvs, 206; Satinvs, 206; Scottivs, 207, 229; Sennivs, 207; Sextvs, 206; Silvanvs, 204, 206; Tittivs, 206; Xanthvs, 101
Potters' marks, reproductions of, 191, 201, 201 n, 204
  See also Terra Sigillata, Terra Nigra
Pottery: N.A., 15, 26, 39
— B.A., 38–42; handled mugs, 26–7, 45; in barrows, 31–6; in flat graves, 37; domestic, 47, 48, 66, 138; see also Beakers, Cinerary urns, Food-vessels
— E.I.A., Hallstatt, q.v.; Aylesford, q.v.; domestic, 94–6, 110, 177; in hill-forts, 109, 134, 136; with pierced lugs, 96; with holes in base, 92; of "Marne" type, 78; with flowing decoration, 94, 94n; in a barrow, 30n; broken, in a barrow, 77, 79
— R., in barrows, 192–6; broken, with burials, 190, 194; by Car Dyke, 180; in R. house, 185; on settlement sites, 174, 177, 178; group finds not preserved, 200; late forms, 209, 213; amphorae, q.v.; Arretine, q.v.; biscuit ware, 208; Castor ware, q.v.; colour-coated wares, 209–10; glazed ware, 209; grain jars, 210; "gritted" ware, 212; "hunt cups," 209–10; local wares, 210–11; mortaria, 177, 206; New Forest wares, 210; painted wares, 209; Rhenish wares, 209; Romano-Belgic or Upchurch wares, 92, 178, 190, 191, 192, 208; "slip" ware, 177, 208, 209; terra nigra, q.v.; terra sigillata, q.v.
— A.-S., analysis of types, 273–4; narrow-necked vases, 265, 274; unusual decoration, 247, 265; "window-urns," q.v.; of Frankish type, 274; cinerary urns, q.v.; accessory vessels, 247, 249, 253, 267, position of, 247, 253, 260, 273; vessels with moulded feet, 273; small bowls, 273; domestic ware, 273: of Christian period, 299–300
Pottery: Survivals: R. showing La Tène influence, 208, 211, 212, 213; La Tène motives in A.-S. pottery, 94, 273; R. in A.-S. period, 281–2
Prehist. Soc. of East Anglia, 2, 6n
Pretan- for Britain, 71
Prickwillow [C] B 4, 3, 214
Prigg, H., 32, 60, 61, 97, 187 n, 273, 324, 327
Procopius, 240
"Promontory" fortresses, 132
Provenance of objects, errors in, 241; importance of exact, 158
Pryor, Mr M. R., his collection, 324
Ptolemy Soter, coins of, 86
Puddled clay, flooring a barrow, 196, 196n
Pulborough [Sussex], Stane Street at, 165
Punches, bronze, 61; iron, 300
Purwell Mill*, Great Wymondley [H] F 2 (house, Map IV), 186, 188, 227, 230n, 232, 236
Pyre, kindled at a barrow, 34
Pytheas, 71

Q-Celts (or Goidels), 19, 65
Quaveney (Ely Trinity) [C] B 4 (at "n" of Middle Fen), 56
Quays, Roman, 223
Quendon [E] F 4, 198
Querns, 108, 134
Quin, River, E 3 to F 3, 176, 224
Quy (Stow-cum-Quy) [C] C 4, finds at, 6, 53, 55, 64; reputed finds, 241, 264
— Fen*, 3, 56
— Water* (W. of village), 126

Radwell [H] E 2 Mill*, 148
Radwinter [E] E 5, 172
Ragg, F. W., 306n
Raids, pirate, in Roman Age, 160, 161
Rampton [C] C 3, 155, 301
Ramsey St Mary's [Hunts.] A 2, 26, 27, 322
Ransom, W., 99, 186, 193, 227, 232, 236, 267; his collection, 96, 210, 212, 254n, 266, 267; the majority of the objects are now in the Camb. Mus.
Rapier-folk, probable fate of, 52
Rapiers, bronze, 18, 52, 56, 59, 65; in a dug-out canoe, 64
Ravensburgh Castle [H], 127, 135
Razor, bronze, 61
Reach [C] C 4, 124, 181, 188, 218; finds at, 55, 58, 64, 96, 110
— Fen* (hoard), 60, 61, 65, 324
— Lode*, 173, 180–1, 223, 234

INDEX

Reader, F. W., 94n
Reading [Berks.], 286
Red Cross* [C] *D 3–D 4* (*road junction Map IV*), 150, 151; roads at, 167, 169, 170, 181, 182, 182n
Red Hill*, Sandon [H] *E 2* (*cemetery, S.W. of village, Map IV*), 224
Redwald, King of East Anglia, 239, 295, 295n
Regni, coin of the, 89n
Reid, Clement, 7
Repell Ditches, *see* Paille Ditches
Republic, Roman, coins of the, 228
Rheinzabern, potters of, 206
Rhine, River, 22, 83, 84
Rib*, River, *E 2 to F 3*, 176
Ridgeway, Sir William, 58, 60, 80, 84, 115n, 160; quoted, 126, 132; his collection, 53, 58, 96
— and Smith, R. A., 74, 75
Ridgeways, 150, 151, 154, 157; characteristics of, 141
Ridgewell [E] *E 6*, R. house at, 186, 188, 225, 226, 232; road at, 168, 169
Ring Hill* or Starbury*, Littlebury [E] *E 4* (*hill fort, Map III*), description of, 135; topography of, 120, 139, 156; importance of, 140; tracks near, 145, 153, 157; find at, 227
Rings, 62; finger, 192, 192n, 252, 262
Ring-works, rare in W. Norfolk, 132; lowland, 121, 122, 137–8, 141
Ripley, W. Z., 22
Risby [S] *C 6*, Heath* (*N.W. of village*), 33, 77, 85, 124, 128, 265, 327
River Farm*, Trumpington [C] *D 3* (*see Map G*), 172
River traffic in Roman times, evidence of, 223
Roads: modern, on ancient alignments, 113, 153, 157; woodland, 154; parallel, in a river valley, 153, 153n
— Pre-Roman, for wheeled vehicles, 112, 153, 167, 219; used by Romans, 113, 153, 155, 166–7, 168–9, 170, 181–2, 219–20, 234; *see* Trackways
— Roman, 161–72, 181–3; list of, 164; *also* 101, 113, 175, 220, 236; absence of settlement on, 219, 234; absent in fertile areas, 157, 220, 234; age of, 182, 228–9, 234; burials near, 168, 169, 194, 196, 197; causeway for, 168; churches on line of, 169; excavation of, 129, 165, 165n, 168, 176–7; fen and river crossings of, 164–5, 166; evidence for, 162; importance of, 221; method of setting-out, 164, 166; milestones on, 168; place-names on, 168; on pre-Roman dyke? 129; partial survival of, 167; parish boundaries along, 164, 168; difficulties of identification, 219; relation to pre-R. roads, 219–20, 319–20; supersession of earlier, 169–70, 171; preliminary survey of route, 166, 182
Roads: *Roman, in A.-S. period,* 288–91; break-down of system, 289; cemeteries by, 242, 243, 244, 245, 246; gaps in, causes of, 289–90; importance of, 275, 319; and boundaries of kingdoms, 297, 320; survival of, 290; relation to settlements, 311
"Robert's Castle," 301
Rokey Wood*, Barkway [H] *E 3* (*hoard, Map IV*), 216
Rolls Lode*, Stuntney [C] *B 4*, 223
Roman Age, comparison with XVIII century, 236; a period of expansion, 307, 312; hoard periods in, 231–3
— objects, in Anglo-Saxon graves, 242, 247, 255, 270, 271, 280n, 281
Romanization of La Tène Celts, 100, 104, 119, 178, 228, 230–31
Romanizing ornament, on Anglo-Saxon objects, 252, 256, 258, 276
Romano-Britons, survival of, 266, 282–3, 296–7, 314
Roof-tiles, covering interments, 189
Rostovtzeff, Professor, quoted, 215
Rothwell [Northants.], finds at, 26, 38, 272
Rougham [S], 193, 200
Round, J. H., 306n; quoted, 310
Round Moats*, Fowlmere [C] *D 3* (*see Map D*), 137, 141
Royal Commission on Historical Monuments, Inventories of the, 135, 136, 138, 139, 198; *see also* Haverfield, F.
Royston [H] *E 3*, 145, 164, 172; barrow at or near, 77; finds at or near, 58, 59, 93, 209; pits or caves near, 141; *see also* Therfield Heath
— Ditches, *see* Mile Ditches
"Rufi," coins inscribed, 88n
Rushden, *see* Cumberlow Green
Rushmore [Dorset], finds at, 118n
Rutland, objects from, 270, 273

Sacrificial utensils, accompanying interments, 101, 192–3
Saffron Walden [E] *E 4*, 153; Neolithic sites near, 8; finds at or near, 37, 54, 108, 203, 206, 209; cemetery at, 265–6, 282, 295, 299; woodland at, 310; *see also* Grim's Ditch *and* Paille Ditches
— — Museum, objects in, 3, 27, 38, 82, 98, 101, 107, 108, 192, 322, 323, 324
St Albans [H], 171; *see also* Verulamium
— Museum, *see* Hertfordshire County Museum

INDEX

St Ives [Hunts.] *B 2*, 171, 310
St Neots [Hunts.] *C 1*, 267-8
St Nicolas-lès-Arras, Artois, burials at, 100
St Remy en Rollat, 209
Salin, Bernhard, 241, 244, 268, 269, 270, 284; his "Style I," 279; his "Style II," 258, 264
Samian ware, *see* Terra Sigillata
Sampford, Great [E] *E 5*, 9
Sanctuaries, objects from, 215, 216
Sandon [H] *E 2*, 312; *see* Red Hill
Sandy [B] *D 1*: *B.A.*, finds, 53; *E.I.A.*, finds, 96, 103, 105, 107; *R.*, continuity of settlement at, 120; settlement at, 170, 176; roads at, 154, 170, 220; finds at, 192*n*, 214, 227; *A.-S.*, cemetery at, 267, 273, 278; *see also* Caesar's Camp, Galley Hill
Santon [N] *A 6*, 6, 299, 322
— Field* (*N.W. of village*), 48
Santon Downham [S] *A 6*, 5, 6; coin hoard, 88; bronze and iron hoard, 104, objects therein, 105, 106, 107, 108, 119, 192, 213, 215, 283
Saws, flint, 6
Sawston [C] *D 4*, 148, 149; hoard, 58, 323
— Huckeridge Hill* (¾ *m. N.N.W. of church*), 259-60
Sawtry Way, 171
Saxon Shore, Count of the, 160
Saxons, attacks of, 160-1, 232; a maritime people, 240
Scandinavia, 316; in N.A., 3, 4, 10, 12, 14; cultural connections with, in A.-S. period, 257, 258, 286, 295
Sceattas, finds of, 284, 298; decoration on, 284, 300
Schetelig, H., 241, 249, 257, 258, 262*n*, 268, 269, 295
Scramasax, 301
Scrapers, flint, 1, 5; date, 4; on settlement sites, 4, 15, 47; in barrows, 31, 326
Sculpture, Roman, 174, 185, 187-8, 236
Seal-boxes, 214
Seax, hilt-plates for, 259
Sedgwick Museum, Cambridge, 108
Seebohm, F., 306
Settlement, "primary," 307-8, 313-5; "secondary," 308-10, 313-5; factors controlling, 274-5; continuity of, 227-8, 299, 313-4; expansion of, in civilized periods, 218-31, 311-12; relation to R. roads, 219, 320; at Cambridge, 319; relation of E.I.A. to R., 219-20; *see also* 5-9, 24, 62-3, 68-9, 86-7, 116-7, 119-20, 183
Settlement sites, *N.A.*, 8, 15, 314; *B.A.*, 47-9, 138; *E.I.A.*, 85, 109-13, 182*n*; *R.*, 131, 169*n*, 218, 220-2, 225-8, 231, 234-5, 283; *A.-S.* (Christian period), 299, 306-11

Settlers, Anglo-Saxon, whence derived, 277, 296; segregation of, 278-9
Severus, coin of, 187
Shale, *see* Kimmeridge shale
Shapens*, Great Chishall [C] *E 3* (*see Map D*), 145
Shardelow's Well*, Fulbourn [C] *D 4*, 125, 148, 149
Shears, iron, 108, 247
Sheep bones, in barrows, 325; in a midden trench, 47
Shefford [B] *E 1*, beaker, 24, 26, 322; R. building, 186; R. cemetery, finds at, 192*n*, 201, 202-5, 210, 213-14, 216, 227, 232, 283; A.-S. burial, 267
Shelford, Great [C] *D 3* (*on right bank of river*), The Bury*, 304
Shell, *Concha Veneris*, 257; *Cypraea*, 260; used in decoration, 81, 262, 264, 294
Shelterhouse Corner* [S] *B 6* (2 *m. S. of Elveden church*), 146
Shepreth [C] *D 3*, 185
Shield bosses (umbos), of iron, A.-S., 243, 253, 259, 261, 263, 267, 293; position of, 261; of Kentish form, 265; with bronze button, 253
Shields, bronze, 60; strap-work of a, 107
Shillington [B], finds at, 99
Shingay [C] *D 2*, 165
Shoebury [E], find at, 94
Shudy Camps [C] *D 5*, 198
Sickles, bronze, 18, 56-7, 65
Silchester [Hants.], pottery from, 91, 118*n*, 201, 202, 204, 208
Silver: *E.I.A.*, fibulae and buckles, 100, 105: *R.*, votive objects, 216; inlay, on bronze fibula, 215: *A.-S.*, hoard of plates, 300; plaques on weapons and ornaments, 247, 257, 258, 293; inlay, on a buckle, 243; rings, 252, 262; spoon, 262; ear pick, 262; pendants, 262-3; fibulae, 252, 256; armlets or bracelets, 251, 252, 267
Silver Street*, Withersfield [S] *D 5*, 168
Situla, bronze, enamelled, 192
Situlae, wooden: *Iron-bound, E.I.A.*, 98; *A.-S.*, 253, 273
— *With bronze mounts*: *E.I.A.*, 99, 105: *A.-S.*, in graves, 247, 253, 273; position of, 251, 253, 255, 261
Skertchly, S. B. J., xxiv, 179
Skillets, bronze, 100, 192, 214
Slade Bottom*, Gazeley [S] *B 5*, 146
Slade, the*, Saffron Walden [E] *E 4*, 108, 138, 153
Slave chains, 101
Slesvig, 238, 270, 296; finds in, 240, 269; *see* Borgstedt
Sling-stones (?), 47
Slip End*, Ashwell [H] *E 2* (1¼ *m. S. of* "e" *of Ashwell*), 155
Smith, the, tools of, 217
Smith, C. Roach, 100, 202, 263

INDEX

Smith, H. Ecroyd, 266, 282, 299
Smith, Reginald A., on Neolithic problems, 10, 14; on E.I.A. pottery, 77; and burials, 90, 91, 100, 192-3; on a hoard, 104, 106, 119; on A.-S. cemeteries, 264, 290; on Christian antiquities, 298, 299, 300, 301; *see also* 2, 3, 60, 95, 99, 105, 107, 108, 213, 238, 240, 245*n*, 254, 256, 258, 273, 274*n*, 276, 284, 291*n*, 295*n*
— and Ridgeway, Sir William, 74, 75
Smith, Urban A., 142*n*, 170*n*, 171*n*
Snailwell [C] *C* 5, 25, 27*n*, 147, 149, 322
Soham [C] *B* 4, finds at, 81, 322
— Cemetery* (*cemetery, Map V*), 263
— Clipsel Field* (*burials at, Map II*), 31*n*, 37, 39, 40
— Fen* (*N.E. of town*), 54, 55, 56
— Mere, 7
Soissons, France, find at, 103
Sokemen, 303
Somersham [Hunts.] *B* 3, 308; beakers from, 25, 26, 27, 322; hoard, 230
— Ferry* (*S.S.W. of Chatteris*), 263
South Downs, "covered ways" of, 126
Spear- and lance-heads: *Bronze*: looped, 56; rare in hoards, 52; without loops, 60-1
— *Iron*: E.I.A., 76, 77, 78, 81, 82; copying bronze forms, 85, 117; with whole sockets, 107: A.-S., 243, 244, 247, 249, 253, 256, 260, 261, 263, 264, 265, 267, 293; position of, in grave, 261; of the Christian period, 300
Spear ferules, 61, 264
Spiennes, Belgium, 1
Spindle-whorls, 108, 110, 259, 265
Spits, of iron, 100
Spoon, perforated, 262, 263
Spoons or Scoops, of pottery, 96
Springs, chalk: determine alignment of trackways, 147, 148, 149, 155, and position of villages, 308; continuity of settlement by, 313-4
Stamford [Lincs.], finds at, 249
Stane Street* [E] and [H] *F* 3, 161, 289-91, 295, 297
Stane Street [Sussex], 165
Stanfordbury*, Southill [B] *E* 1 (*burials, Map III*), described, 99-100; objects from, 105, 119, 189-90, 192, 193, 200-1, 202-4, 213, 214, 216
Stanground [Hunts.], 223
Stansted Mountfitchet [E] *F* 4, 152; R. house at, 186*n*, 225, 283
Stapleford [C] *D* 4, 185
— The Bury*, 304
Starbury, *see* Ring Hill
Statuettes, bronze, Roman, 180, 214-15
Stature, of Anglo-Saxon settlers at Barrington, 252
"Stead" in compounds, 295
Steelyard, bronze, 104

Steeple Bumpstead [E] *E* 5, 298
— — Watsoe Bridge* (¼ *m. S. of "u" of Sturmer*), 178-9
Stetchworth [C] *C* 5, 153, 157
Stevenage [H] *F* 2, 171
— Six Hills* (*Map IV*), 197
Stilton [Hunts.] *A* 1, 164, 165
Stjerna, K., 27*n*
Stock-breeding, effect on distribution of population, 315
Stone implements, surface finds of, 1; distribution and abundance of, 5; below peat in fens, 7; post-Neolithic, 2-4, 53; *see also* Axes, Arrowheads, Hammerstones, etc.
Stonea*, Wimblington [C] *A* 3 (*E.N.E. of village*), finds at, 88, 203, 229, 229*n*, 230
Stort, River, *E* 3 to *F* 4, 224
— Valley, *see* Trade-routes
Stotfold [B] *E* 2, 99
Stour, River, *D* 5 to *E* 7, 224
— Valley, E.I.A. finds in, 88, 103, 116; R. settlement in, 222*n*, 226, 230; as a political boundary, 103, 289, 290, 290*n*; as a traffic line, *see* Trade-routes
Stow-cum-Quy, *see* Quy
Stowe MSS., 28
Strabo, 84, 116, 120*n*
"Straet," a, in a charter, 166, 169*n*
Strap-ends, bronze, 248, 297
Strap-link, bronze, 91
Street Way (with Ashwell Street), *E* 2-*B* 5, described, 147-50, 157; finds on line of, 59, 260; earthwork near, 135, 141, 176; barrows near, 77, 148, 149, 326*n*; passage of Dykes, 125, 148; *see also* 114, 121, 122, 183, 308
Streetly End*, West Wickham [C] *D* 5 (*N. of first "e" of Horseheath*), 168
Strethall [E] *E* 4, 145*n*, 166
Stretham [C] *B* 4, 165*n*
— Fen*, find in, 57, 65; *see also* Granta Fen
Strigils, 192
Studs, bronze, 248, 294; shoe-shaped, on a buckle, 255
Stukeley, Dr, 165, 173, 180; his Diaries and Letters, *see* Lukis, W. C.
Stukeley, Great [Hunts.] *B* 2, 164, 198, 311
Stump Cross* [C] *E* 4 (½ *m. S. of "i" of Hinxton*), 145, 146
Stuntney (Ely Trinity) [C] *B* 4, xxiii, 54, 223
Sturge, W. A., 5, 6*n*
Sturmer [E] *E* 5, 168, 198, 226
Stycas, 298
Subsidence, *see under* Fens
Sudbury [S], 103
— Institute, objects in, 103*n*
Suessiones, 103
Suetonius Paulinus, 160

INDEX

Suevi, the, 161
"Summer" Ways, 149, 167
Sussex, bronze bowl from, 260
Sutton [C] *B 3*, 92, 102, 216, 300
— The Burystead*, 304
Swaffham Bulbeck [C] *C 4*, see Hare Park, Upper
Swaffham Prior [C] *C 4*, 54; R. house at, 184, 210
— — Middle Hill* (*settlement site, Map II*), 3 n, 4, 47, 231
Swan Street, Sible Hedingham [E], 169
Swastika, in Anglo-Saxon art, 251, 270
Swavesey [C] *C 3*, 198
Sweden, finds in, 27, 269
Sword-sheath, bronze, 107; see also Chapes
Swords: Bronze, 20, 59–60, 61, 151; manufactured locally, 59
— Iron: E.I.A., 81, 107: A.-S., 253, 256, 259, 261, 263, 267, 301; position of, in grave, 261: Danish, 299
Symbols, on maps, see Maps

Tacitus, 131 n, 160, 179, 293
Tadlow [C] *D 2*, 165, 309
Tamworth [Staffs.], 290
Tankard, see Situla
Tansley, A. G., xxii
"Tascio-Ricon," on coins, 88 n
Tasciovanus, coins of, 88, 89
Taylor, M. V., 176 n, 207 n, 214 n, 216, 227, 231
Tazzas, of shale, 98; of pottery, 91–2, 98, 208
Temple, of Celtic type, 174; see also Votive objects
Tempsford [B] *D 1* (1 m. N. of "l" of Blunham), 302
— Gannock's Castle*, 301, 302
Terra Nigra (Belgic) ware, 101, 200–2, 227
Terra Sigillata (Samian) ware, 202–7; range of forms, 202; analysis, 203; in barrows, 191; with burials, 100, 189, 189 n, 193; see also 174, 176, 177, 178, 223, 227, 228, 229, 230, 235; see Potters
Tetricus, coins of, 175 n
Tetworth [Hunts.] *D 2*, 154
— Crane Hill* (*mound, Map IV*), 197, 198
Teutates, see Mars
Teversham [C] *C 4*, 56
— Fen*, 126
Thames estuary, a culture area, 290
— Upper, valley: beakers in, 22; route from, 24; route of raiders to, in A.-S. times, 287
Thanes Guild, 282
Thaxted [E] *F 5*, finds at, 101, 116, 120; R. road through, 172; R. house at, 186 n, 188, 225, 312; woodland at, 310
— Mill Hill Farm* (1 m. W.N.W. of town), 172 n

Thaxted, Monk Street* (1½ m. S. of town), 172
Theodosius, coins of, 226, 227, 228, 230
Therfield [H] *E 2*, Heath* (1½ m. N.N.W. of village), 30, 63, 324: barrows on—Five Hills*, 32, 40, 194, 266, 277, 328; Long Hill*, 8, 11, 147; Money Hill*, 36, 40, 328; other barrows, 328, 329: see also Royston
— Pen Hills*, 127
Thet, River*, *A 7* (*see Map C*), 132, 133
Thetford [N] *A 7*, 146, 167; finds at, 5, 56, 147, 264, 299; barrow at, 328; ford at, 143; Castle Hill, reason for position of, 146
— Barnham Common*, *B 7* (*settlement, Map III*), 111
Thetford, Little [C] *B 4*, 55
Thorn Hill*, Orwell [C] *D 3* (*see Map E*), 150
Thorpe, B., quoted, 283
Thriplow, see Triplow
Thurlow, Great [S] *D 5*, R. road to? 181; settlement at, 169 n, 187, 202, 203, 205, 226; A.-S. burial at, 265
Tiberius, coins of, 177, 227, 228
Tile, Roman, see Brick, Roman
Titchmarsh [Northants.], 170, 171
Titus, coin of, 190
Toft [C] *D 3*, 169, 170
Toilet, articles of the, 262–3
Tombs, brick-built, Roman, 191, 199
Tools, of iron, in hoards, 104, 300
Toppesfield [E], finds at, 190, 192, 213
Torcs, gold, 51, 52, 57, 63, 81
Tostock [S], 294
Totternhoe Stone, 147; see Clunch
Toutates, see Mars
Towns, Roman, open, 173, 176–7; fortified, 173–5; duration of occupation of, 232; fate of, 236, 240; reasons for survival of, 221–2, 234
Trackways, prehistoric, 141–57, also 137 and 221 n; identification of, 142; characters of, 141–2, 143; origin of certain, 152; hillside ways, 142, 147, 149, 154–5, 157; valley ways, 142, 152–3, 168–9; ridgeways, q.v.; across watersheds, 155; in forest, 154; along forest margin, 153; recorded in a charter, 166; utilized by Romans, 112–13, 157, 167, 170, 171, 172–3, 181, 220; post-Roman (?), 152, 157
Trade: restraint of, produces cultural divergence, 269, 320–1; with Brittany, 10; with Scandinavia, 14, 16; with Ireland, 51; with Gaul, 103, 116; with the Mediterranean area, 101, 119–20; across the North Sea, 240; with Kent and France, 294–5; see also 11, 54, 74, 84, 86, 257, 260, 262, 263, 274, 277, 317

INDEX 359

Trade-routes and traffic lines: control of, by tribes S. of Thames, 46; in Essex, 289–91; from the Continent, 54, 84, 120, 319; gold routes, 51, 52; waterways, 64, 179–80; in Lea-Stort-Essex Cam Valley, 24, 103, 112, 113, 120, 138, 139, 140, 152–3, 156, 166, 319; in Stour and Colne Valleys, 63, 103, 153, 226, 295, 319; along Icknield Way, q.v.
Transport, water, in Roman times, 180
Trent, River, 180
Tribal Hidage, the, 239
Trinity College Loan Collection, see Museum of Arch. and Eth.
Trinovantes, 71–2, 104, 140; race, 115, 118; boundaries, 103, 230
Triplow [C] D 3, 147, 148, 149, 311
— Heath* (see Map D), barrows on, 12n, 30n, 79–80, 116, 145, 197n, 329
Tripod, of iron, 100
Triquetrae, in A.-S. art, 248, 300
Troston Heath [S], urns from, 41, 46
Trumpet, bronze, 215
Trumpington [C] D 3, finds at, 74, 209; mound at, 194; tracks and roads at, 112–13, 152, 172
— Cemetery*, 111–12, also 83, 95, 96
— Anstey Hall*, 111–12
— Dam Hill* (River Farm), 91, 101, 112, 113n, 227, 249, 268, 269, 276; see also Cambridge, Latham and Chaucer Roads
— Drift* (1½ m. E.N.E. of village), 167
— Fen* (½ m. E. of village), 169
Tuddenham [S] B 6, beaker from, 25, 27, 322, 328; A.-S. finds, 258, 264, 265, 269, 273, 278, 294
Tumblers, glass, 263
Tumulus, see Barrow
Tweezers, bronze, 48, 61, 247, 248, 263, 265; iron, 248
Typology, notes on, in B.A., 26, 39–40, 53–4, 56, 59; in E.I.A., 93, 105, 106, 117; R., 213; A.-S., 249, 268–9, 271–2

Umbos, see Shield bosses
Undley* [S] B 5 (1½ m. S.W. of Lakenheath), 56, 75n, 207
Upper Hare Park, see Hare Park
Upware, Wicken [C] B 4, 223
Urus, horn of, with a burial, 28, 44

Valens, coin of, 229
Valentinian I, coin of, 187n
Valentinian II, coin of, 187
Valentinian III, coin of, 228
Vandals, the, 161
Vandlebury, see Wandlebury
Veasey, D., 57, 323
Veneti, the, 116
Verulamium, 72, 103; coins minted at, 87, 88, 89; roads from, 155, 171; see also St Albans

Vespasian, coins of, 185, 187n, 190, 213, 229, 232
Vevey, Switzerland, 78
Vicar's Brook* [C] D 3 (between Trumpington and Cambridge), 112, 172
Viking Period, remains of the, 298, 299
Villages, nucleated, 311; diffuse, 311; in forest, origin of, 275, 309–10; fortified, 109–10
Vitellius, coin of, 227
Votive objects and offerings, 51, 60, 63, 214, 215, 216
Vulcan, dedication to, on a silver plaque, 216

Walden, see Saffron Walden
Walden, Little* [E] E 4 (by "d" of Little Chesterford), 224
Walden Way*, E 3–E 4, 145n
Waldingfield, Great [S], 103
Walford, T., 89, 168, 192n, 226
Walker, F. G., 101, 110, 185, 190, 194, 198, 200, 211, 223, 228, 243; on Horningsea, 210, 212; on barrow excavation, 194, 195, 196; on R. roads, 162n, 164n, 165, 165n, 168n, 169, 171, 172, 172n; on R. Cambridge, 175, 175n, 176, 227; on Mare Way, 150, 151
Walkern [H] F 2, 155, 157
Wallbury [E], hill-fort, described, 139; see also 120, 140, 153, 156, 157
Walls, Roman, of a cemetery, 167n, 188; of Cambridge, 174; of Chesterford, 173, 173n, 183; see also Houses, Temples, Buildings
Walsworth [H] F 1, 90, 92, 99
Walters, H. B., 101, 176n, 202, 202n, 204, 206
Wandlebury, Stapleford [C] D 4, described, 134–5, 139; see also 108, 109, 140, 156
Wangford [S] A 6, 284
— Heath (Warren), 229
Wansdyke [Wilts.], 293n
War Ditches*, Cherryhinton [C] D 4 (marked on Map III), described, 109, 136, 177–8, 231; date, 139, 156, 178, 321; race occupying, 114, 233; burials at, 102, 178, 190, 194; pottery from, 83, 92, 95, 96, 208, 210; see also 93, 200
Warboys [Hunts.] B 2; Fen*, 64
Ward, John, 184n, 214, 216
Warfare, organized, introduction of, 156–7, 321
Warni, the, 240
Warren, S. Hazzledine, 7
Warrens, see Heathland
Wash, the, a route of invasion, 24, 87, 118, 274, 316
Waterbeach [C] C 4, 179, 301
Water-clocks, 105
Watkin, W. T., 170, 170n, 176n, 192n, 205
Watling Street, 290

INDEX

Wattle-work, 138
Weaving batten, 301
Weaving-combs, 108, 134
Webb Collection, Cambridge Museum, 202
Weeting [N] *A* 6, 1, 6, 79
Welney River*, *A* 4 (*N.W. of Littleport*), xxiii
Welwyn [H], 99, 155, 192
Wendens Ambo [E] *E* 4, 103, 153; B.A. burials, 31, 37; E.I.A. burials, 98; A.-S. burials, 265, 276, 295; R. house at, 186*n*, 225
Wereham [N], 38
Weser, River, 238, 240, 277
Wessex, coins of, 299
West Kennett barrow [Wilts.], 26
West Saxons, 286-8; N.E. boundary of, 285, 287; cultural elements derived from, 280
West Stow [S] *B* 6, 3
—— Heath* (*N.W. of village*), finds at, 97, 272, 278, 281, 299; kilns at, 211
West Water*, the, *B* 3–*A* 3, xxiii, 179
West Wratting [C] *D* 5, 145, 166, 169*n*, 181
Westley [S] *C* 6, 328
Westley Waterless [C] *D* 5, 300
Weston Colville [C] *D* 5, 169*n*
Wheeler, W. H., 179
Whittlesea Mere [Hunts.] *A* 1–*A* 2, finds in, 7, 62
—— Pond's (or Ponder's) Bridge, *A* 2, find at, 65
Whittlesford [C] *D* 4, 64, 148, 227
—— Bridge* (1 m. S.E. of village), find at, 90; ford at, 143, 145
—— Mill* (close to church), 148, 149
Wicken [C] *B* 4; Fen*, 6, 55, 217, 324
Wicklow Mountains, Ireland, 51
Wiesbaden, 263
Wilbraham, Great [C] *C* 4, 147, 149, 210, 314; see also Mutlow Hill
—— Temple, find at, 6
Wilbraham, Little [C] *C* 4, cemetery at, 260-2, 270, 271, 283, 294, 295; see also 253*n*, 269, 272, 273, 276, 278, 280
Wilburton [C] *B* 4, 198, 203, 207, 229
—— Fen*, beaker from, 25, 26, 27, 44, 322; hoard from, 18*n*, 58, 59, 60, 61, 65, 323
Wilkinson, J., 250, 251, 252
Willbury Hill* [H] *E* 1 (2 m. S. of "*l*" of Arlesey), 143, 148, 326; burial at, 266, 272, 277
Williams, Rev. J. F., 133*n*
Willingham [C] *B* 3–*C* 3, 152; see also Belsar's Hill

Willingham Fen*, finds in, 214-15, 217, 232
Wilsmere Down Farm*, Barrington [C] *D* 3 (see Map E), 154
Wilton (Hockwold-cum-Wilton) [N] *A* 5-6, 3, 297
Wiltshire, 22; cultural connections with, 26*n*, 39*n*, 47, 51, 317; entry of beaker-folk into, 24
Wimbish [E] *E* 4, woodland at, 310
Wimblington [C] *A* 3, 56
Wimpole [C] *D* 3; Hall, 154
Window-urns, 248, 248*n*, 249, 256, 276, 277
Wine, imports of, 101; flasks of, in R. burials, 193
Wine-jars, see Amphorae
Wisbech Museum, objects in, 38, 56
Wissey, River [N], 132
Witcham [C] *B* 3; Gravel* (*W. of Wardy Hill*), 215, 217
Witham [E], 316
Witham, River [Lincs.], 179, 180, 298
Wixoe [S] *E* 5, 203, 226
Wolf, skull of a, 14
Wood Ditton [C] *C* 5; Camois Hall* (*S.W. of village*), 125
Woodstone*, Ashdon [E] *E* 4 (see Map *J*), 152
Wool Street, see Worstead Street
Woolmer Green [H], 155
Working-floors, see Living-floors
Worlington [S] *B* 5, 27, 149, 167, 322
Wormwood Hill*, Stapleford [C] *D* 4 (by "*V*" of Vandlebury), 149
Worstead Street* [C] *D* 4, 149, 172; origin and purpose of, 129, 168
—— Lodge* (R. road junction, Map IV), 146, 167, 173, 181
Worts Causeway* [C] *D* 3–*D* 4 (by Red Cross, q.v.), 167
Wratting, see West Wratting
Wright, A. G., 25, 209*n*
Wrist-clasps, see Clasps
Wrist-guard, see Bracer
Wyboston [B], 303
Wymondley, Great [H] *F* 2, probable house site, 186, 283; cemetery at, 188, 193, 210; see also Purwell Mill
Wyton [Hunts.] *B* 2, 152

Yaxley [Hunts.] *A* 1, 64
Yorke, A. C., 113, 137, 162*n*, 173*n*; on trace of Street Way, 148
Yorkshire, cultural connections with, 22, 27, 38, 39, 76, 295; Brythonic invasion of, 71, 72; movement into fens from, 65*n*; iron-smelting in, 63*n*

Zosimus, 161

CAMBRIDGE: PRINTED BY W. LEWIS AT THE UNIVERSITY PRESS

MAP I. Finds and Remains attributed to the NEO
introduced abou

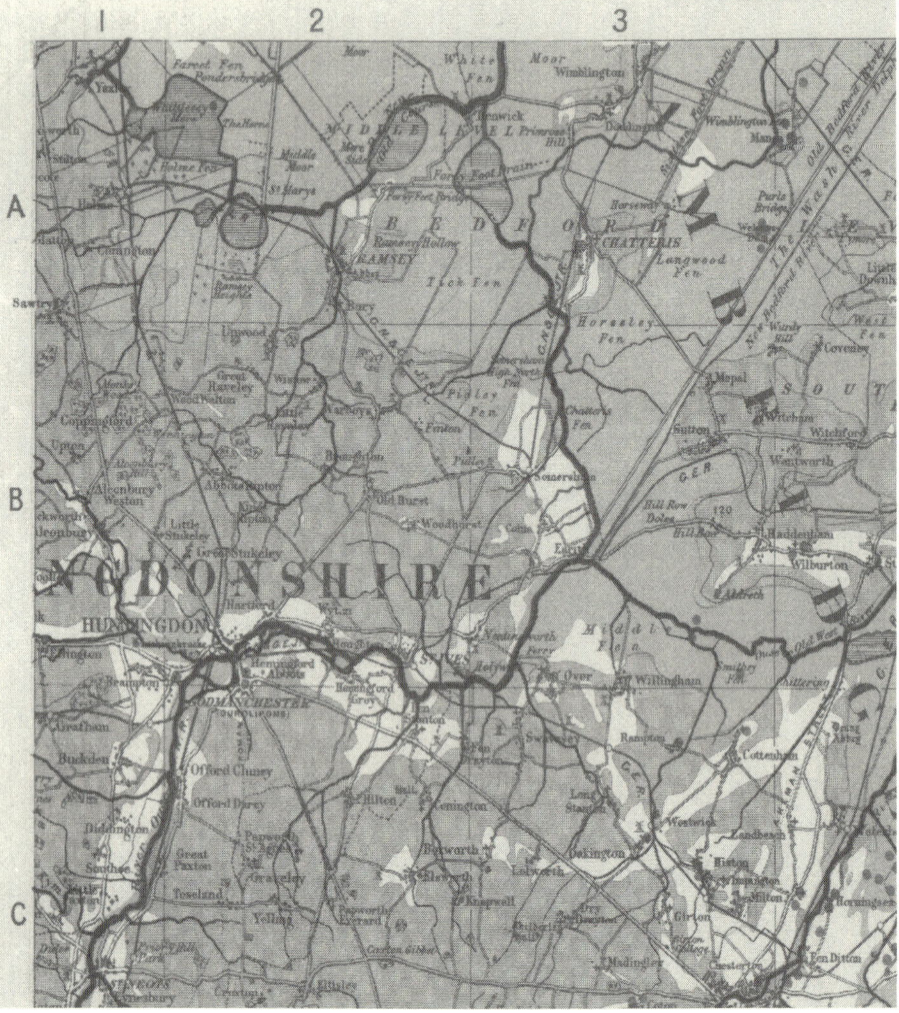

...OLITHIC AGE. Duration: unknown. [Metal was
...t 2,000 B.C.]

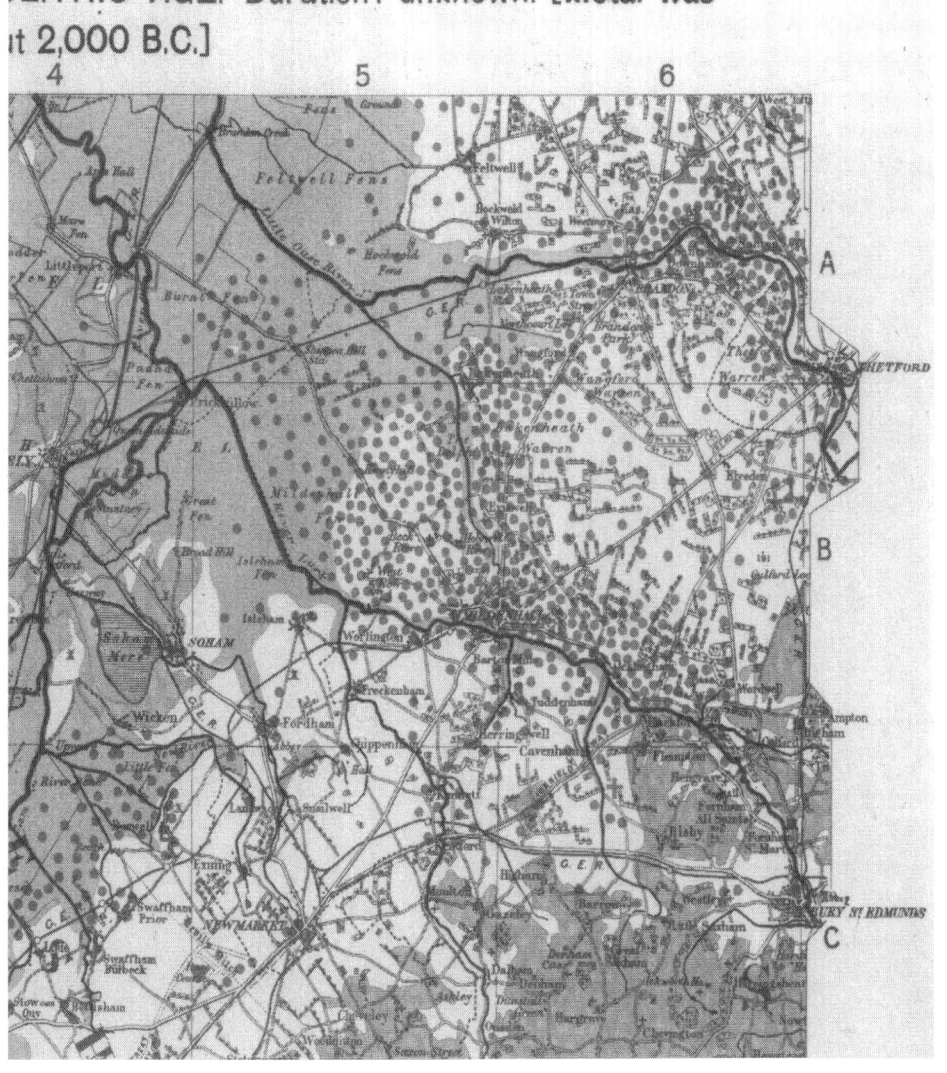

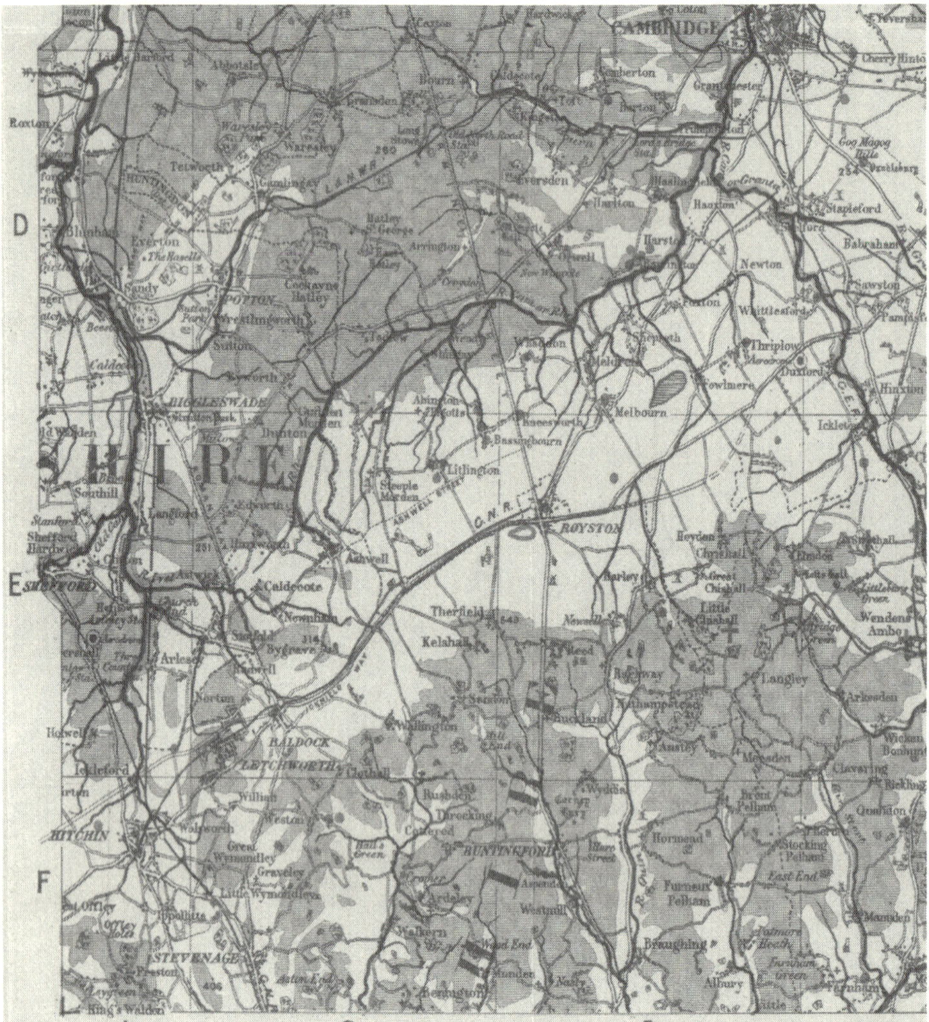

CAMBRIDGE
Grantchester
Barton
Comberton
Caldecote
Bourn
Gransden
Abbotsley
Waresley
Gamlingay
Tetworth
Everton
Sandy
POTTON
Wrestlingworth
Sutton
BIGGLESWADE
Dunton
Eversden
Harlton
Haslingfield
Hauxton
Stapleford
Babraham
Sawston
Newton
Whittlesford
Thriplow
Duxford
Fowlmere
Melbourn
Meldreth
Shepreth
Foxton
Harston
Whaddon
Arrington
Hatley George
Cockayne Hatley
Bassingbourn
Litlington
Steeple Morden
Ashwell
Caldecote
Newnham
ROYSTON
Therfield
Kelshall
Reed
Barkway
Nuthampstead
Barley
Great Chishall
Little Chishall
Langley
Arkesden
Wendens Ambo
Clavering
Meesden
Anstey
Buckland
Wyddial
Sandon
Wallington
Rushden
Clothall
Cottered
Throcking
BUNTINGFORD
Aspenden
Westmill
Hormead
Brent Pelham
Furneux Pelham
Stocking Pelham
Braughing
Albury
BALDOCK
LETCHWORTH
Willian
Weston
Walsworth
HITCHIN
Great Wymondley
Little Wymondley
Graveley
Ippollitts
STEVENAGE
Preston
King's Walden
Ardeley
Walkern
Benington
Ickleford
Holwell
Norton
Radwell
Bygrave
Arlesey
Stotfold
Langford
Southill
Roxton
Icknield Way
Ashwell Street
G.N.R.
SHIRE
D
E
F
1
2
3
Scale of 1inch to One M

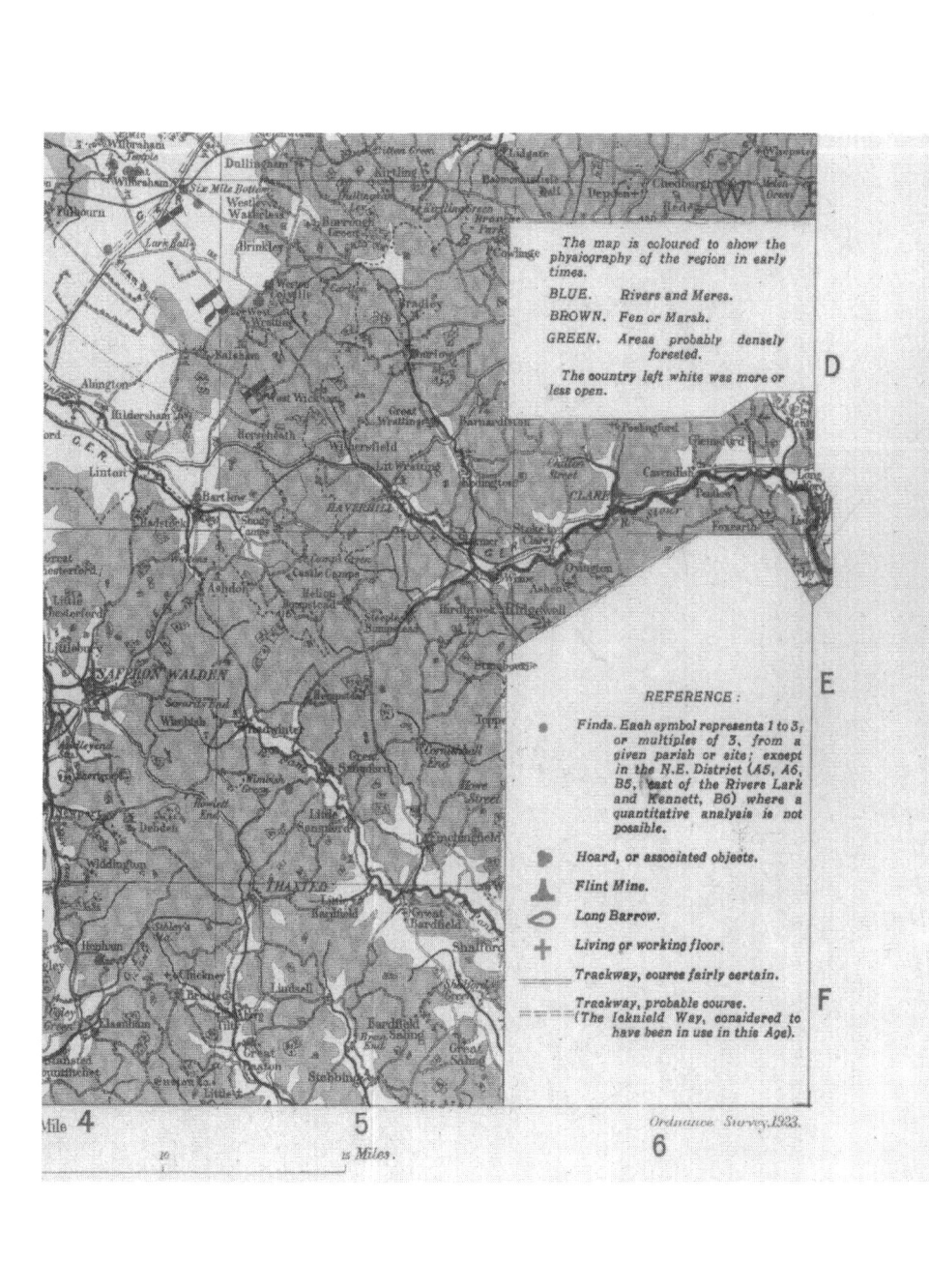

The map is coloured to show the physiography of the region in early times.

BLUE. Rivers and Meres.
BROWN. Fen or Marsh.
GREEN. Areas probably densely forested.

The country left white was more or less open.

REFERENCE:

● Finds. Each symbol represents 1 to 3, or multiples of 3, from a given parish or site; except in the N.E. District (A5, A6, B5, east of the Rivers Lark and Kennett, B6) where a quantitative analysis is not possible.

▲ Hoard, or associated objects.

⛏ Flint Mine.

⬭ Long Barrow.

+ Living or working floor.

⸻ Trackway, course fairly certain.

------ Trackway, probable course. (The Icknield Way, considered to have been in use in this Age).

Ordnance Survey, 1923.

MAP II. Finds and Remains attributed to the BRONZE
to metal]. Duration: from about

AGE [including the period of transition from stone
2,000 B.C. to 500-400 B.C.

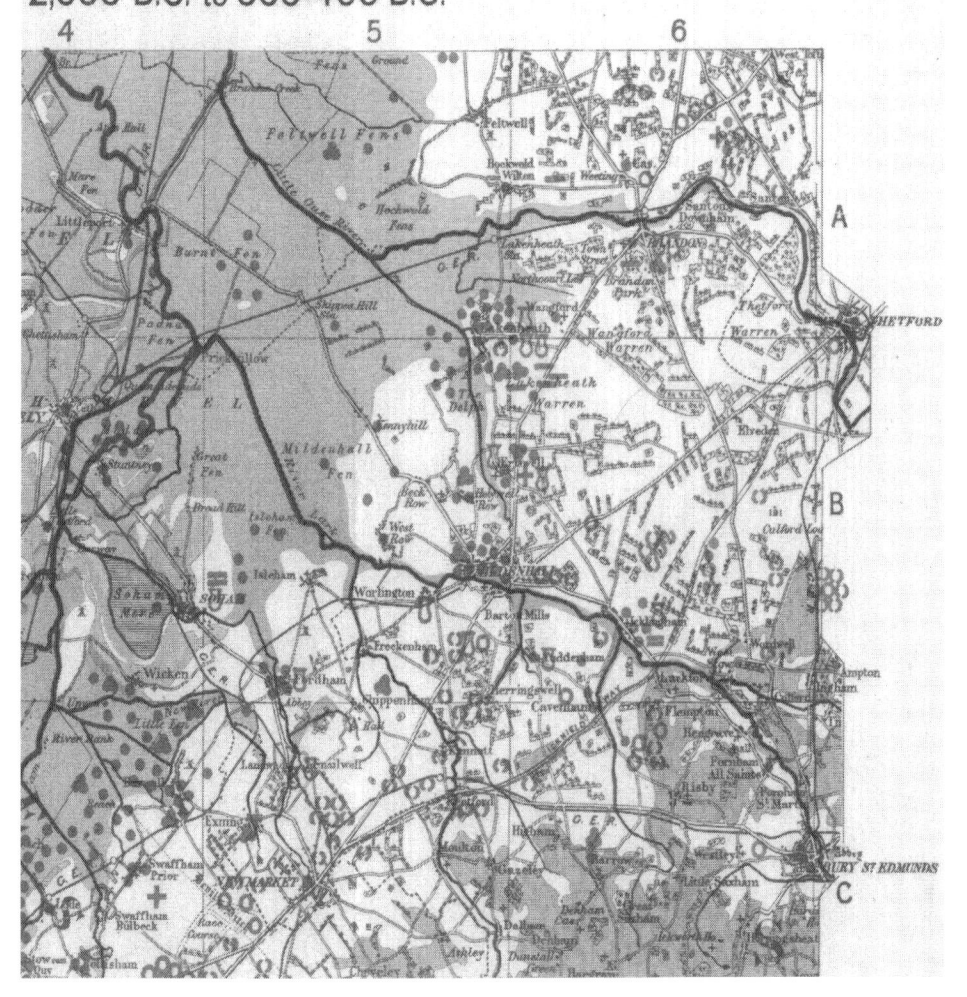

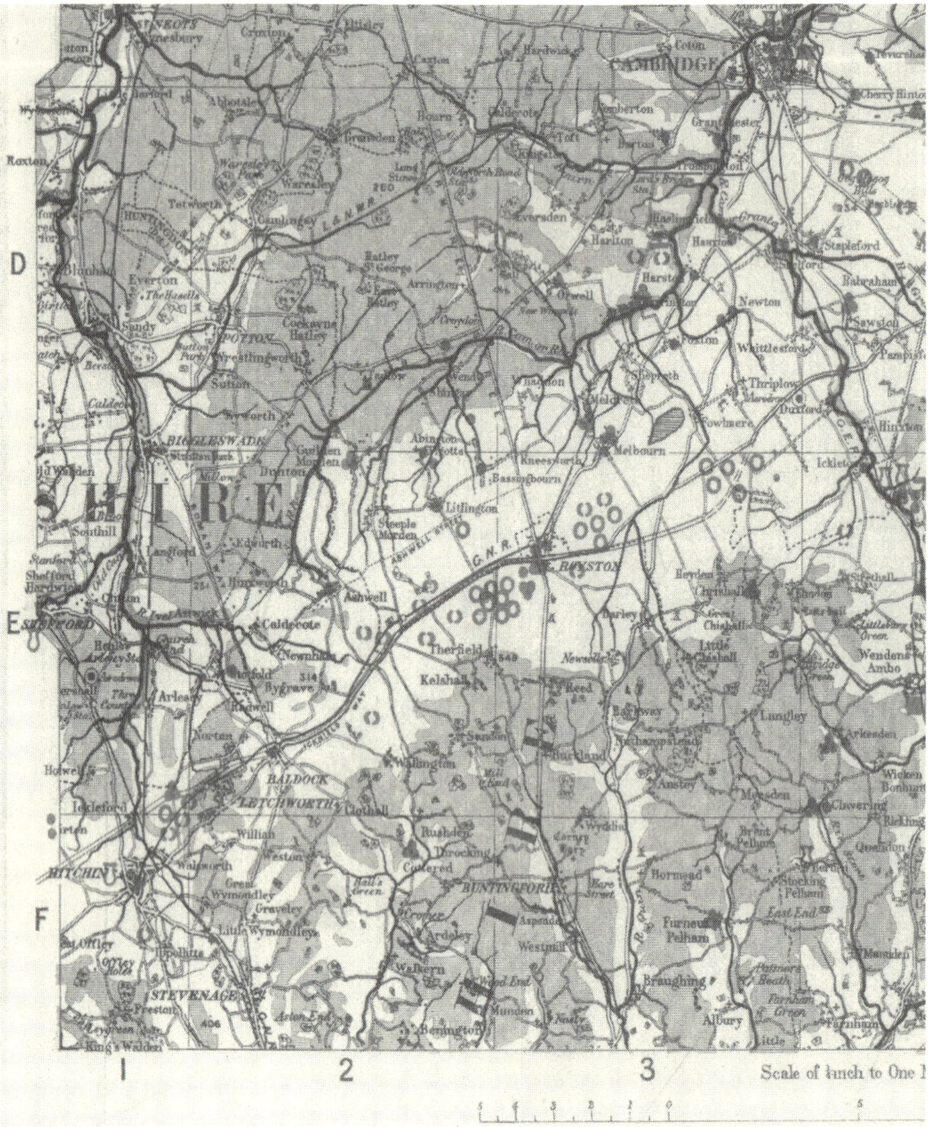

CAMBRIDGE
Coton
Hardwick
Grantchester
Cherry Hinton
Trumpington
Abbotsley
Gransden
Caldecote
Toft
Barton
Comberton
Roxton
Tetworth
Gamlingay
Eversden
Harlton
Haslingfield
Hauxton
Stapleford
Babraham
Sawston
Newton
Everton
Sandy
POTTON
Wrestlingworth
Hatley
Cockayne Hatley
Arrington
Orwell
Harston
Foxton
Whittlesford
Thriplow
Duxford
Fowlmere
Melbourn
Meldreth
Shepreth
Whaddon
Sutton
BIGGLESWADE
Dunton
Guilden Morden
Abington Pigotts
Bassingbourn
Kneesworth
Litlington
Steeple Morden
Ickleton
Hinxton
Southill
Langford
Edworth
Hinxworth
G.N.R.
ROYSTON
Ashwell
Caldecote
Newnham
Therfield
Kelshall
Heydon
Chishall
Little Chishall
Great Chishall
Elmdon
Strethall
Wendens Ambo
Langley
Arleasey
Bygrave
Radwell
Norton
Reed
Barkway
Nuthampstead
Anstey
Meesden
Clavering
Arkesden
Wicken Bonhunt
BALDOCK
LETCHWORTH
Clothall
Wallington
Sandon
Buckland
Wyddial
Rushden
Throcking
Cottered
BUNTINGFORD
Hormead
Brent Pelham
Stocking Pelham
Furneux Pelham
Quendon
Rickling
Holwell
Ickleford
Pirton
HITCHIN
Willian
Walsworth
Weston
Great Wymondley
Little Wymondley
Graveley
Ardeley
Walkern
Aspenden
Westmill
Braughing
Albury
East End
Patmore Heath
Farnham
Manuden
Wood End
STEVENAGE
Preston
King's Walden
Benington
Aston End
Munden
Little
Great Offley
Hexton
Beeston
Shefford
SHEFFORD
D
E
F
1
2
3
Scale of 1 inch to One M

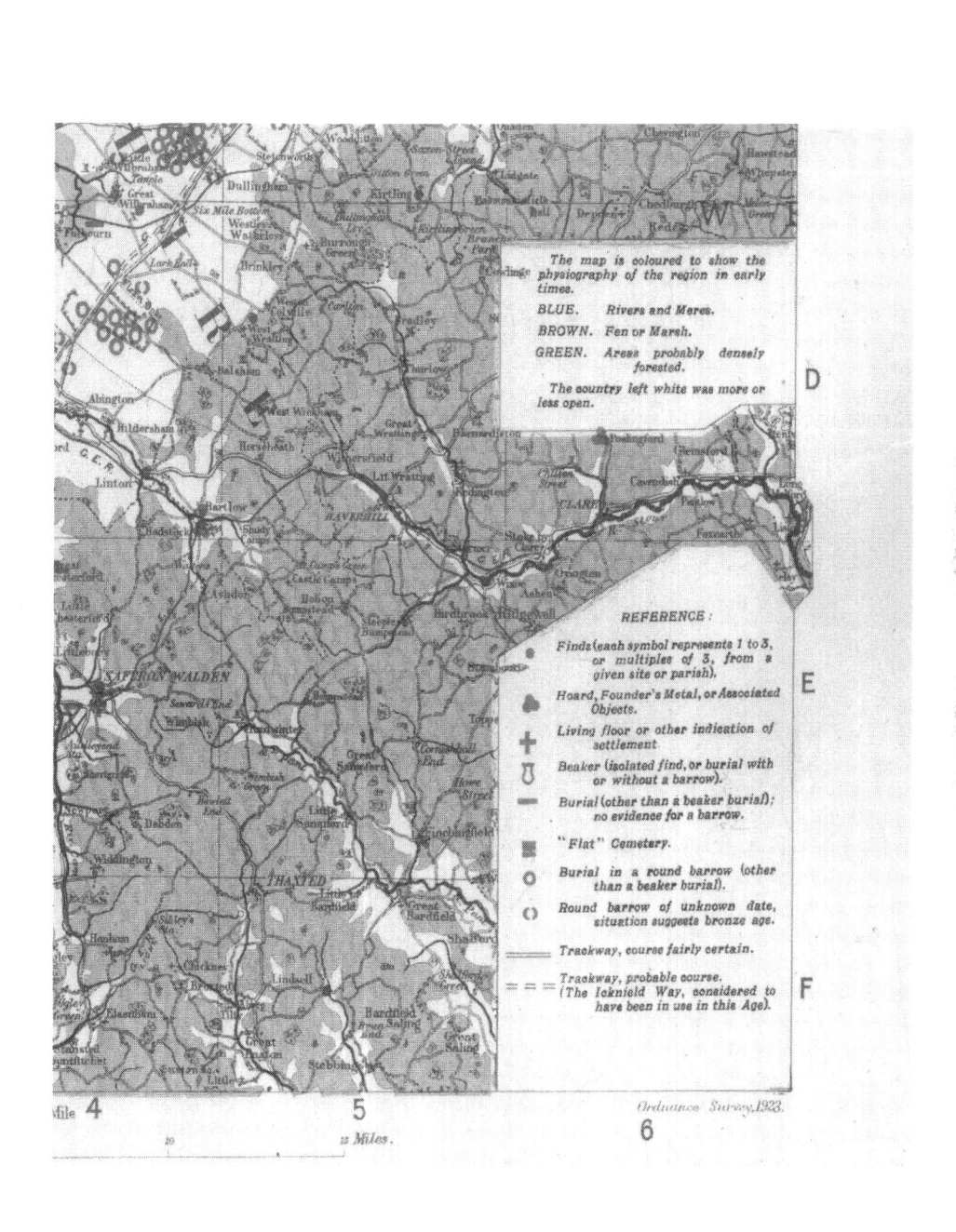

The map is coloured to show the physiography of the region in early times.

BLUE.   Rivers and Meres.
BROWN. Fen or Marsh.
GREEN. Areas probably densely forested.

The country left white was more or less open.

REFERENCE:

• Finds (each symbol represents 1 to 3, or multiples of 3, from a given site or parish).

♠ Hoard, Founder's Metal, or Associated Objects.

✚ Living floor or other indication of settlement

⛿ Beaker (isolated find, or burial with or without a barrow).

▬ Burial (other than a beaker burial); no evidence for a barrow.

▨ "Flat" Cemetery.

○ Burial in a round barrow (other than a beaker burial).

◌ Round barrow of unknown date, situation suggests bronze age.

══ Trackway, course fairly certain.

= = = Trackway, probable course. (The Icknield Way, considered to have been in use in this Age).

Ordnance Survey, 1923.

MAP III. Finds and Remains attributed to the EA
Middle of I. Ce

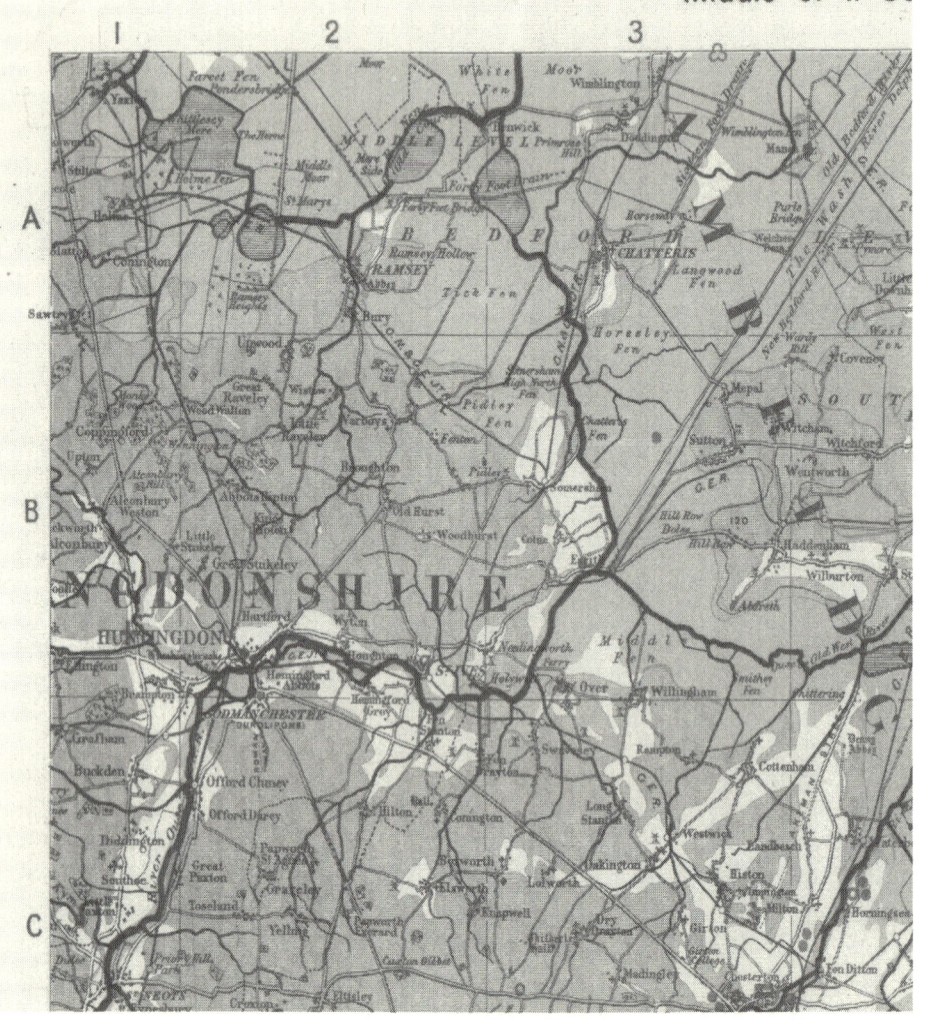

ARLY IRON AGE; from 500-400 B.C. to the
entury A.D.

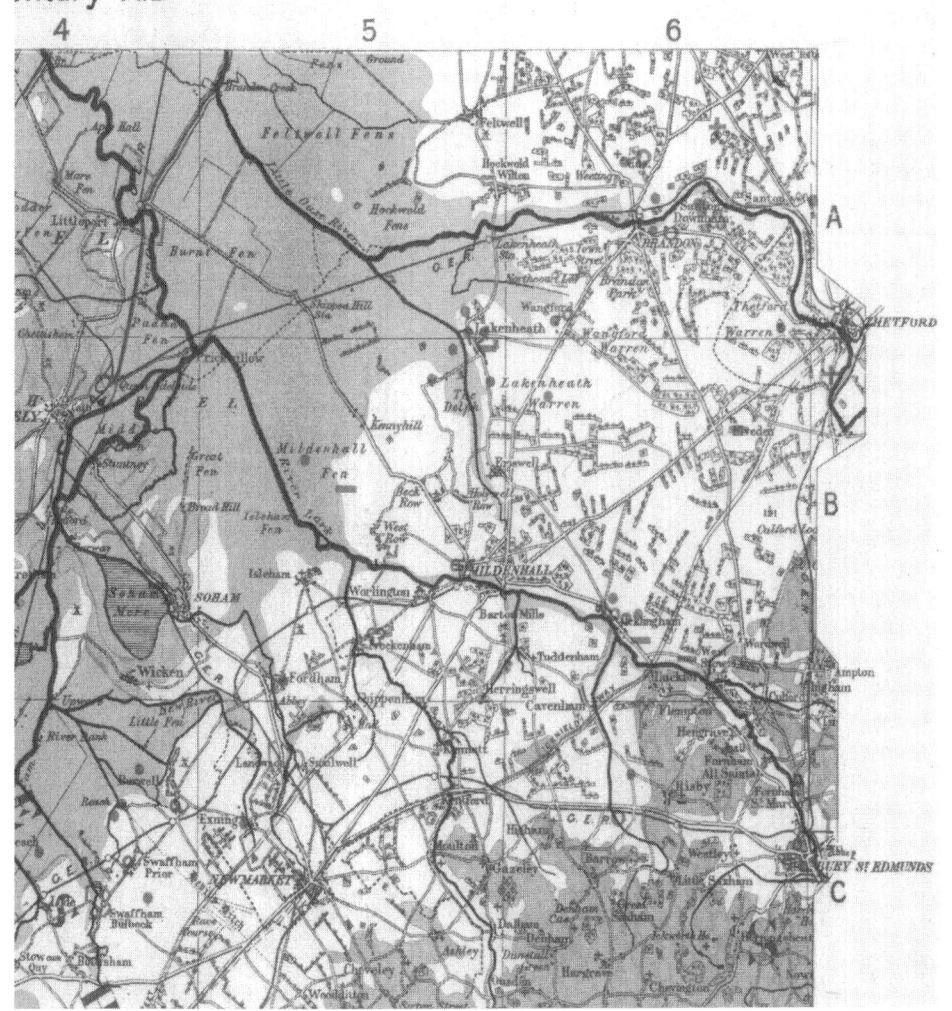

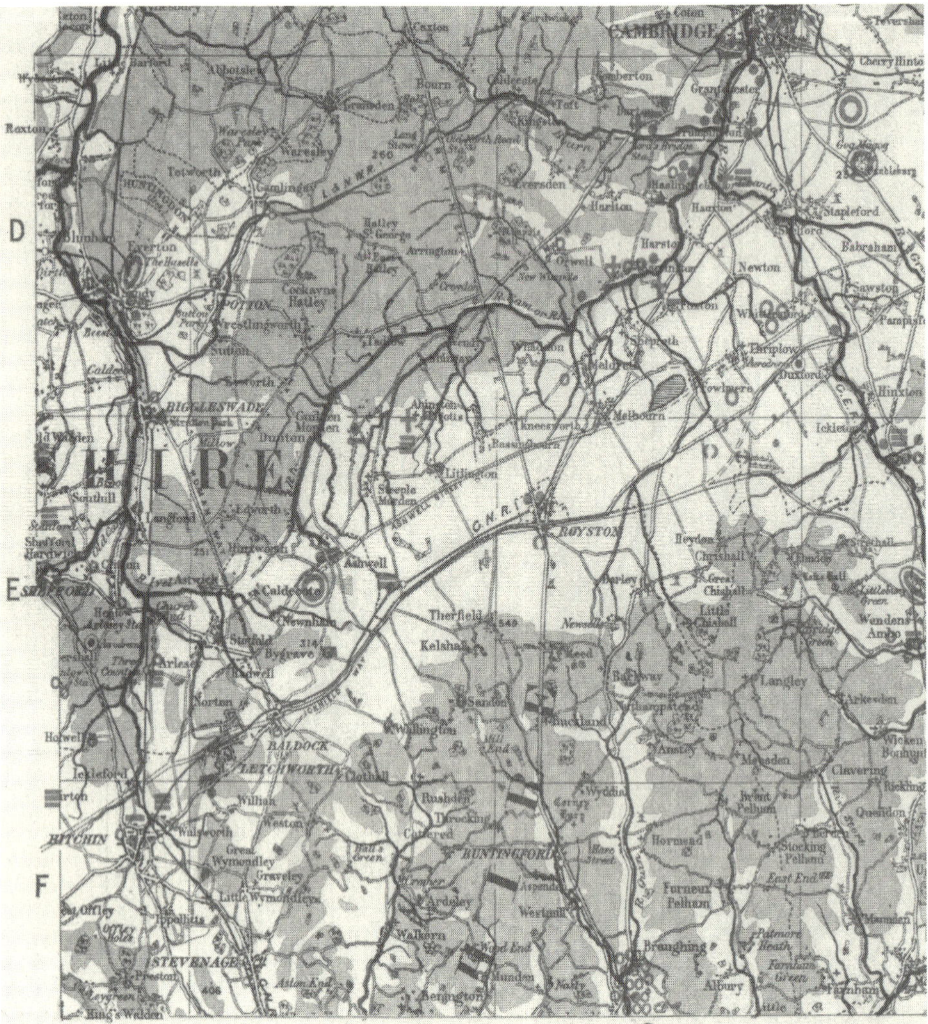

CAMBRIDGE
Caxton
Coton
Bourn
Gransden
Waresley
Abbotsley
Roxton
Gamlingay
Everton
POTTON
Wrestlingworth
Sutton
Cockayne Hatley
Hatley St. George
Arrington
Croydon
Orwell
Harlton
Haslingfield
Grantchester
Barton
Comberton
Toft
Kingston
Eversden
Hauxton
Stapleford
Babraham
Sawston
Newton
Harston
Whittlesford
Thriplow
Fowlmere
Duxford
Hinxton
Ickleton
Shepreth
Meldreth
Melbourn
Kneesworth
Bassingbourn
Whaddon
Litlington
Abington Pigotts
Steeple Morden
Guilden Morden
Dunton
BIGGLESWADE
Eyworth
Southill
Langford
Edworth
Hinxworth
Ashwell
Caldecote
Newnham
Stotfold
Bygrave
Radwell
Arlesey
Norton
BALDOCK
LETCHWORTH
Willian
Weston
Walsworth
HITCHIN
Ickleford
Great Wymondley
Little Wymondley
Graveley
Ippollitts
STEVENAGE
Preston
King's Walden
Aston End
Walkern
Ardeley
Cottered
Throcking
Rushden
Clothall
Wallington
Sandon
Kelshall
Therfield
ROYSTON
Barley
Reed
Barkway
Buckland
Nuthampstead
Anstey
Wyddial
BUNTINGFORD
Westmill
Aspenden
Hormead
Furneux Pelham
Brent Pelham
Stocking Pelham
Meesden
Langley
Clavering
Arkesden
Little Chishall
Great Chishall
Chishall
Heydon
Strethall
Wendens Ambo
Braughing
Albury
Farnham
Manuden
Patmore Heath
East End
Quendon
Wicken Bonhunt
SHEFFORD
Clifton
Henlow
Hardwick
Holwell
Blunham
Bourn
SHIRE
G.N.R.
ASHWELL STREET
ICKNIELD WAY
260
251
314
549
406
D
E
F
1
2
3
Scale of 1 inch to One M
5 4 3 2 1 0 5

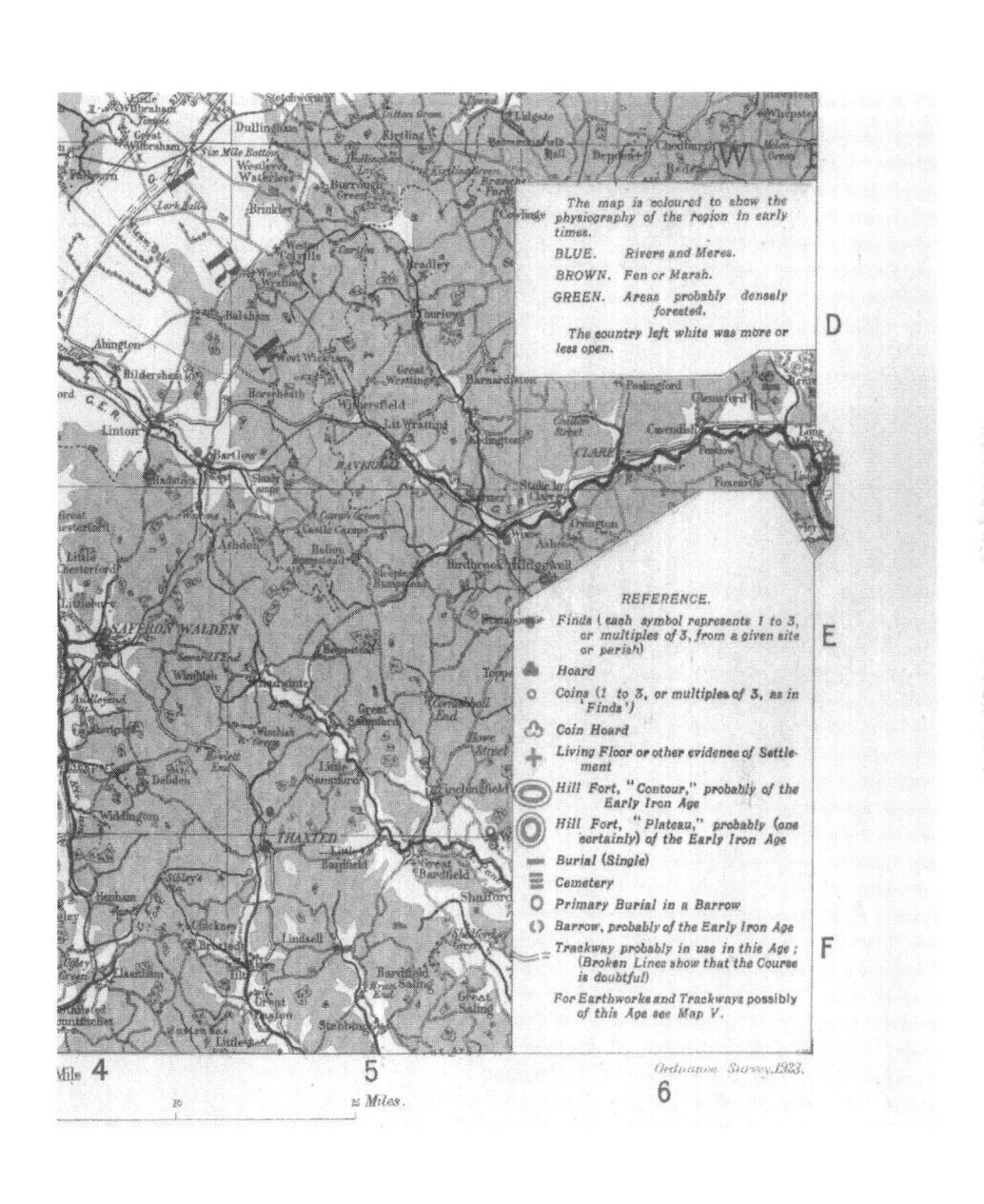

The map is coloured to show the physiography of the region in early times.

BLUE. Rivers and Meres.
BROWN. Fen or Marsh.
GREEN. Areas probably densely forested.

The country left white was more or less open.

REFERENCE.

Finds (each symbol represents 1 to 3, or multiples of 3, from a given site or parish)

Hoard

○ Coins (1 to 3, or multiples of 3, as in 'Finds')

Coin Hoard

+ Living Floor or other evidence of Settlement

Hill Fort, "Contour," probably of the Early Iron Age

Hill Fort, "Plateau," probably (one certainly) of the Early Iron Age

Burial (Single)

Cemetery

Primary Burial in a Barrow

() Barrow, probably of the Early Iron Age

Trackway probably in use in this Age; (Broken Lines show that the Course is doubtful)

For Earthworks and Trackways possibly of this Age see Map V.

Ordnance Survey, 1923.

MAP IV.—Finds and Remains attributed to the ROMA[N]

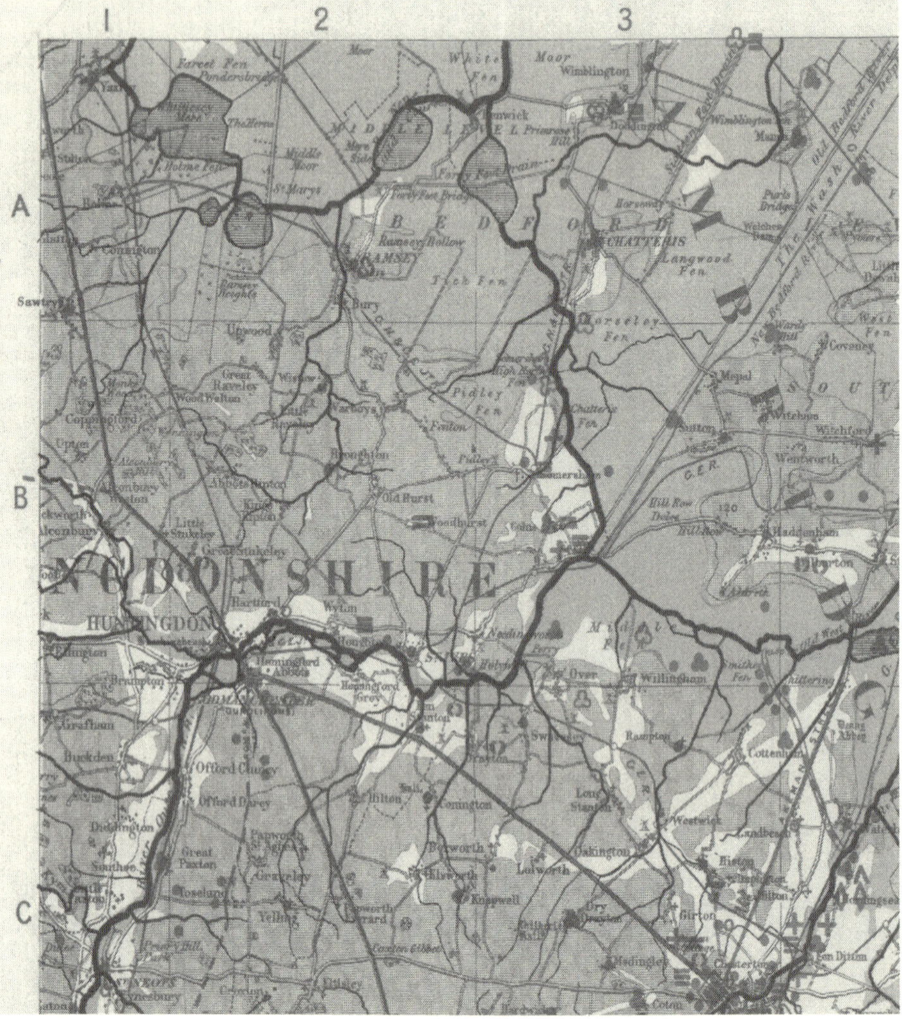

N AGE: from 43 A.D. to the early V. Century A.D.

CAMBRIDGE
Roxton
Abbotsley
Teworth
Gamlingay
Waresley
Bourn
Caldecote
Eversden
Barton
Grantchester
Trumpington
Cherry Hinton
Gog Magog Hills
Stapleford
Babraham
Sawston
Pampisford
Hauxton
Harston
Newton
Whittlesford
Thriplow
Duxford
Fowlmere
Hinxton
Ickleton
Foxton
Shepreth
Melbourn
Kneesworth
Bassingbourn
Abington Pigotts
Litlington
Steeple Morden
Guilden Morden
Dunton
Everton
Blunham
The Hasells
Cockayne Hatley
Potton
Wrestlingworth
Sutton
Eyworth
Biggleswade
Hatley St. George
East Hatley
Arrington
Croydon
Orwell
Wimpole
Southill
Langford
Hinxworth
Ashwell
Caldecote
Newnham
Bygrave
Stotfold
Arlesey
Norton
Baldock
Letchworth
Shefford
Holwell
Ickleford
Hitchin
William
Weston
Walsworth
Great Wymondley
Little Wymondley
Graveley
St. Ippolyts
Offley
Preston
Stevenage
Kings Walden
Aston End
Benington
Walkern
Ardeley
Cromer
Cottered
Throcking
Rushden
Clothall
Wallington
Sandon
Kelshall
Therfield
Royston
G.N.R.
Barley
Reed
Buckland
Wyddial
Buntingford
Aspenden
Westmill
Hormead
Braughing
Albury
Furneux Pelham
Brent Pelham
Meesden
Stocking Pelham
East End
Patmore Heath
Farnham
Manuden
Clavering
Arkesden
Langley
Nuthampstead
Anstey
Great Chishall
Little Chishall
Heydon
Chrishall
Elmdon
Littlebury Green
Wendens Ambo
Wicken Bonhunt
Berden
D
E
F
1
2
3
Scale of 1 inch to One M

For Explanation of Colouring, see Map I.

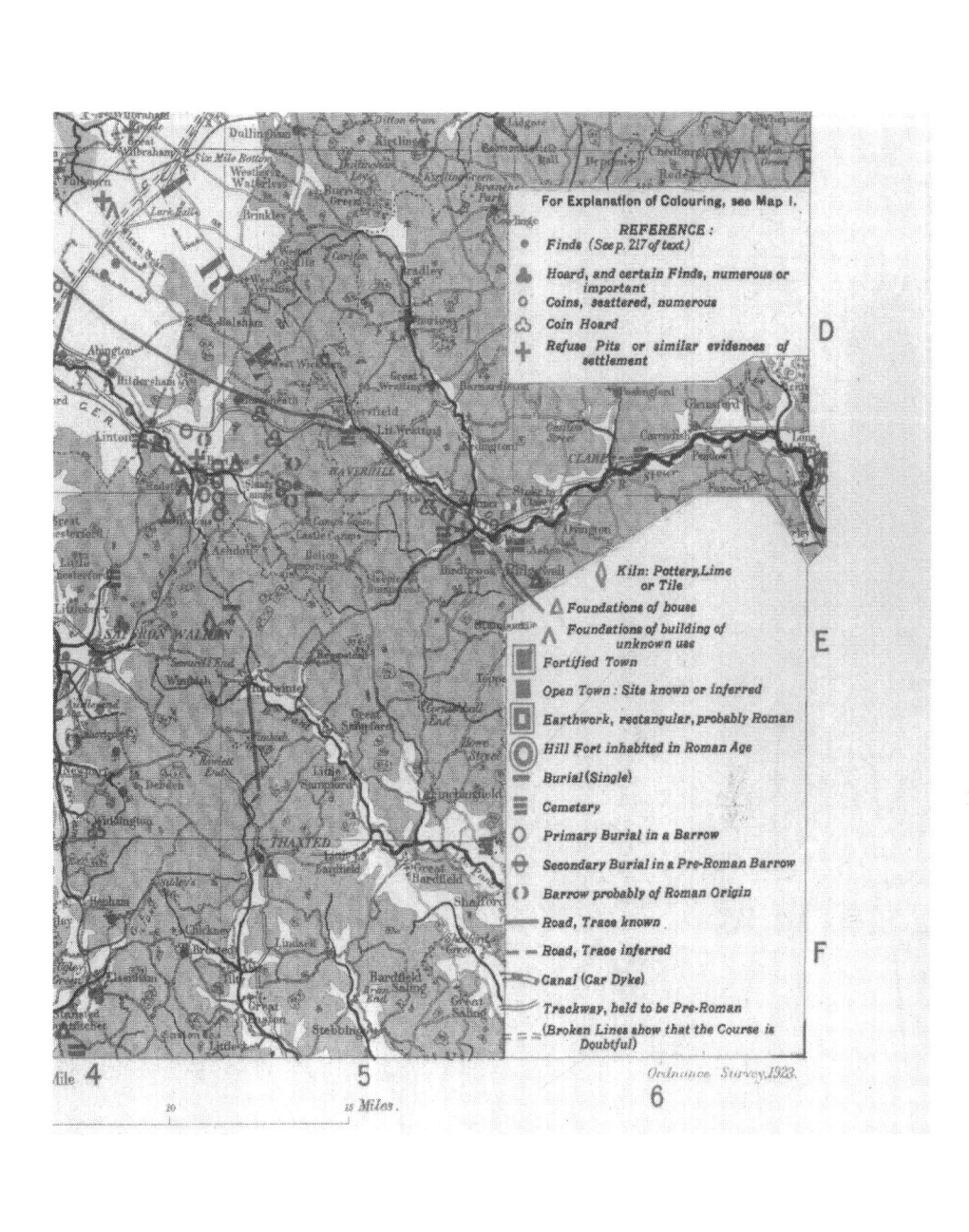

REFERENCE:
- • Finds (See p. 217 of text)
- ♣ Hoard, and certain Finds, numerous or important
- ○ Coins, scattered, numerous
- ⌂ Coin Hoard
- ✚ Refuse Pits or similar evidences of settlement
- ⬠ Kiln: Pottery, Lime or Tile
- △ Foundations of house
- ⌂ Foundations of building of unknown use
- ■ Fortified Town
- ▭ Open Town: Site known or inferred
- ▢ Earthwork, rectangular, probably Roman
- ◎ Hill Fort inhabited in Roman Age
- ▬ Burial (Single)
- ☰ Cemetery
- ○ Primary Burial in a Barrow
- ⊖ Secondary Burial in a Pre-Roman Barrow
- () Barrow probably of Roman Origin
- —— Road, Trace known
- – – Road, Trace inferred
- ≈≈≈ Canal (Car Dyke)
- ═══ Trackway, held to be Pre-Roman
- = = (Broken Lines show that the Course is Doubtful)

Ordnance Survey, 1923.

MAP V.—ANGLO-SAXON AGE, from

IN RED { (i) Finds and remains attributed to the Paga
(ii) Roman Roads, the survival of which indi

IN BLACK { (iii) Distribution of settlements at the close of
(iv) Trackways, Dykes and other Earthworks

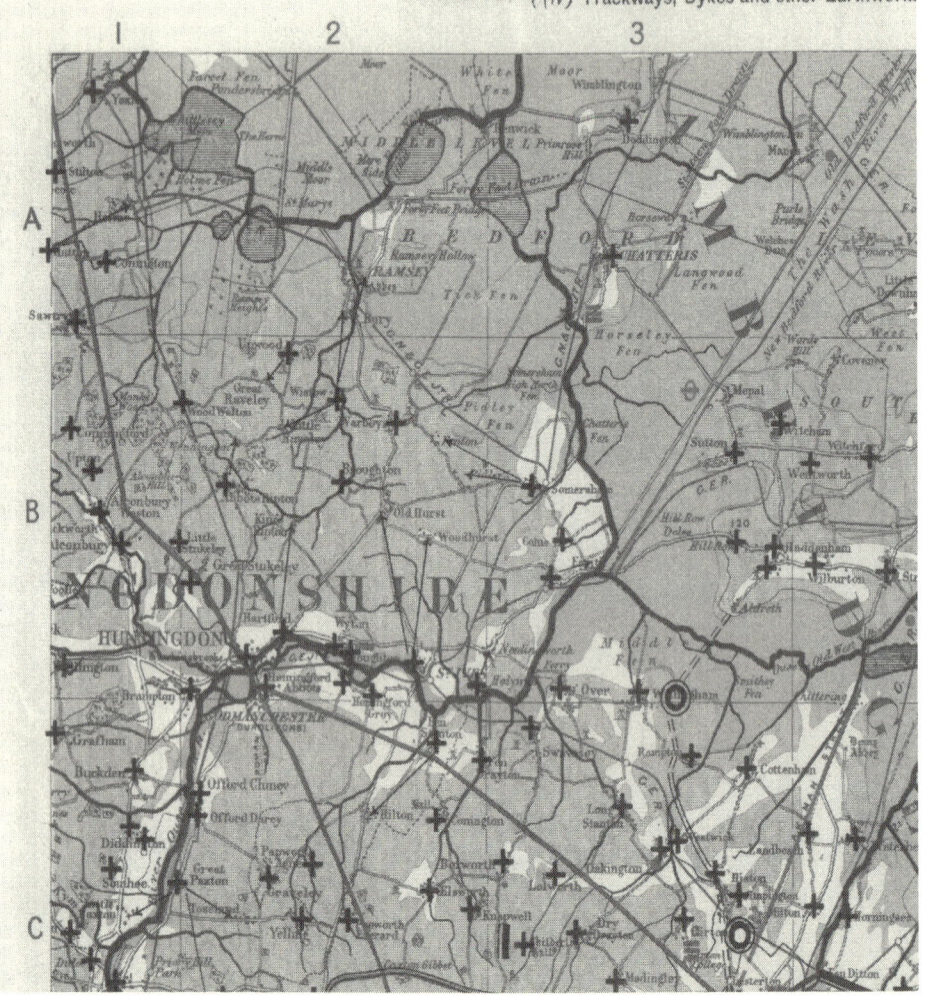

about 450 A.D. to 1066 A.D.

an Period, from about 450 A.D. to about 650 A.D.
icates use in the Pagan Period.
f the Anglo-Saxon Age as recorded in Domesday Book.
s, the majority of unknown date.

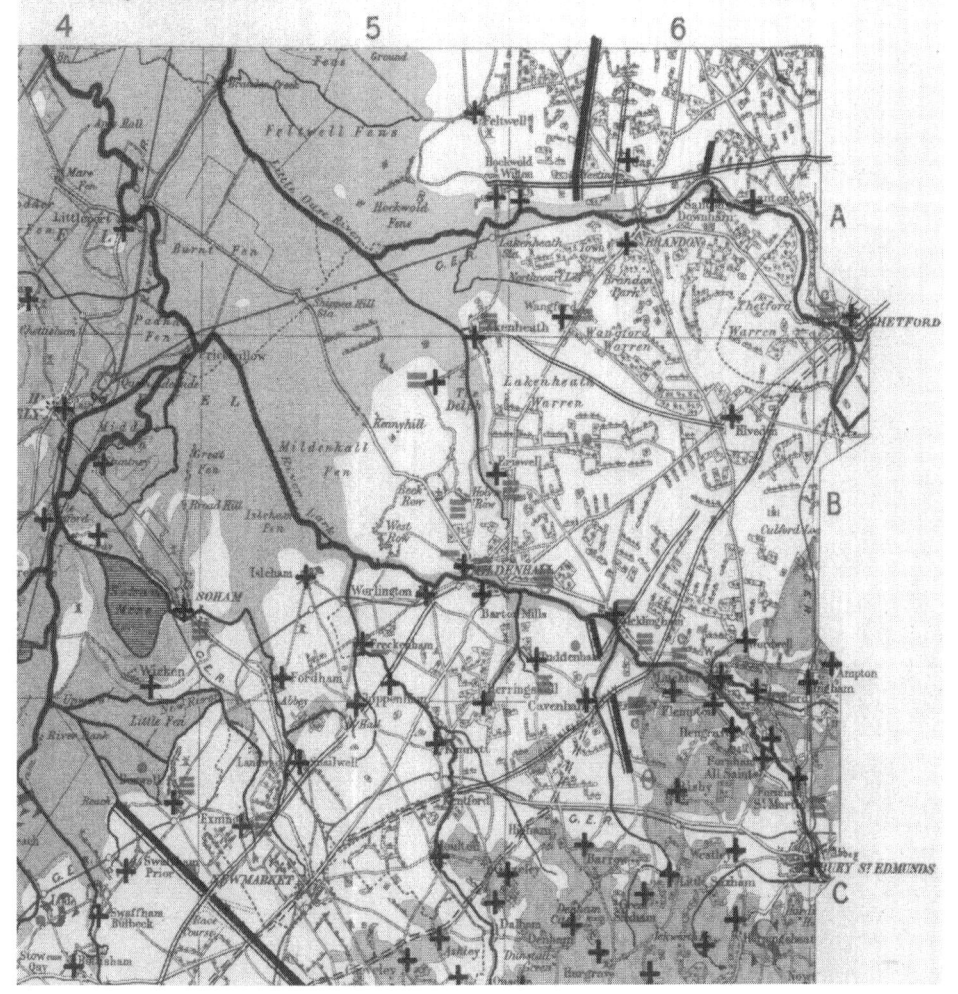

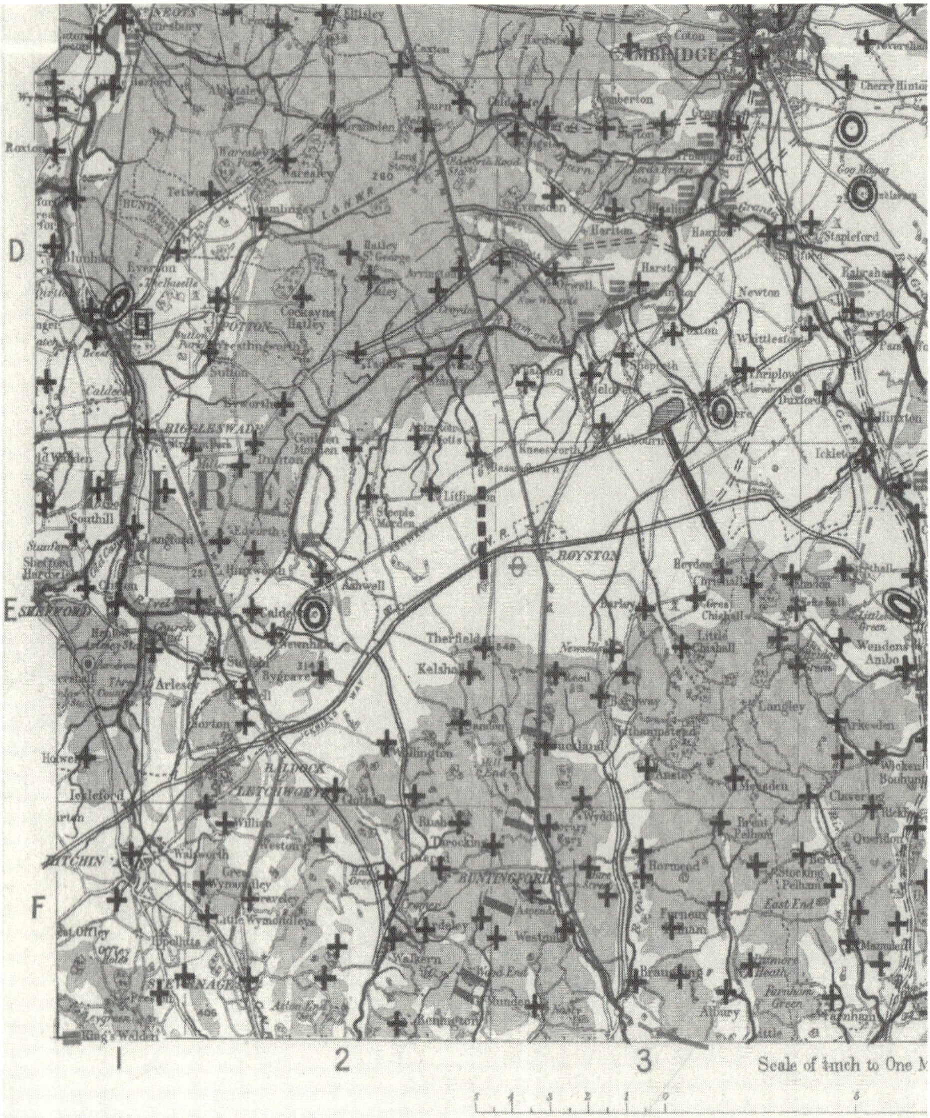

CAMBRIDGE
Coton
Caxton
Cherry Hinton
Stapleford
Harston
Newton
Whittlesford
Duxford
Thriplow
Melbourn
Kneesworth
Bassingbourn
Litlington
Steeple Morden
Guilden Morden
Ashwell
ROYSTON
Therfield
Kelshall
Sandon
Reed
Barkway
Barley
Heydon
Langley
Arkesden
Anstey
Meesden
Clavering
Brent Pelham
Stocking Pelham
East End
Furneux Pelham
Braughing
Albury
Manuden
Farnham Green
Westmill
Aspenden
BUNTINGFORD
Throcking
Rushden
Cottered
Wallington
Clothall
BALDOCK
LETCHWORTH
Willian
Weston
HITCHIN
Walsworth
Great Wymondley
Little Wymondley
Graveley
STEVENAGE
Walkern
Benington
Ickleford
Arlesey
Stotfold
Newnham
Caldecote
Bygrave
Norton
Southill
Langford
Edworth
Dunton
BIGGLESWADE
Sutton
Potton
Cockayne Hatley
Eversden
Haslingfield
Grantchester
Trumpington
Barton
Comberton
Bourn
Gransden
Waresley
Gamlingay
Everton
Wrestlingworth
Tempsford
Roxton
Wyboston
Hatley St George
Abbotsley
Eltisley
D
E
F
1
2
3
Scale of 1inch to One M

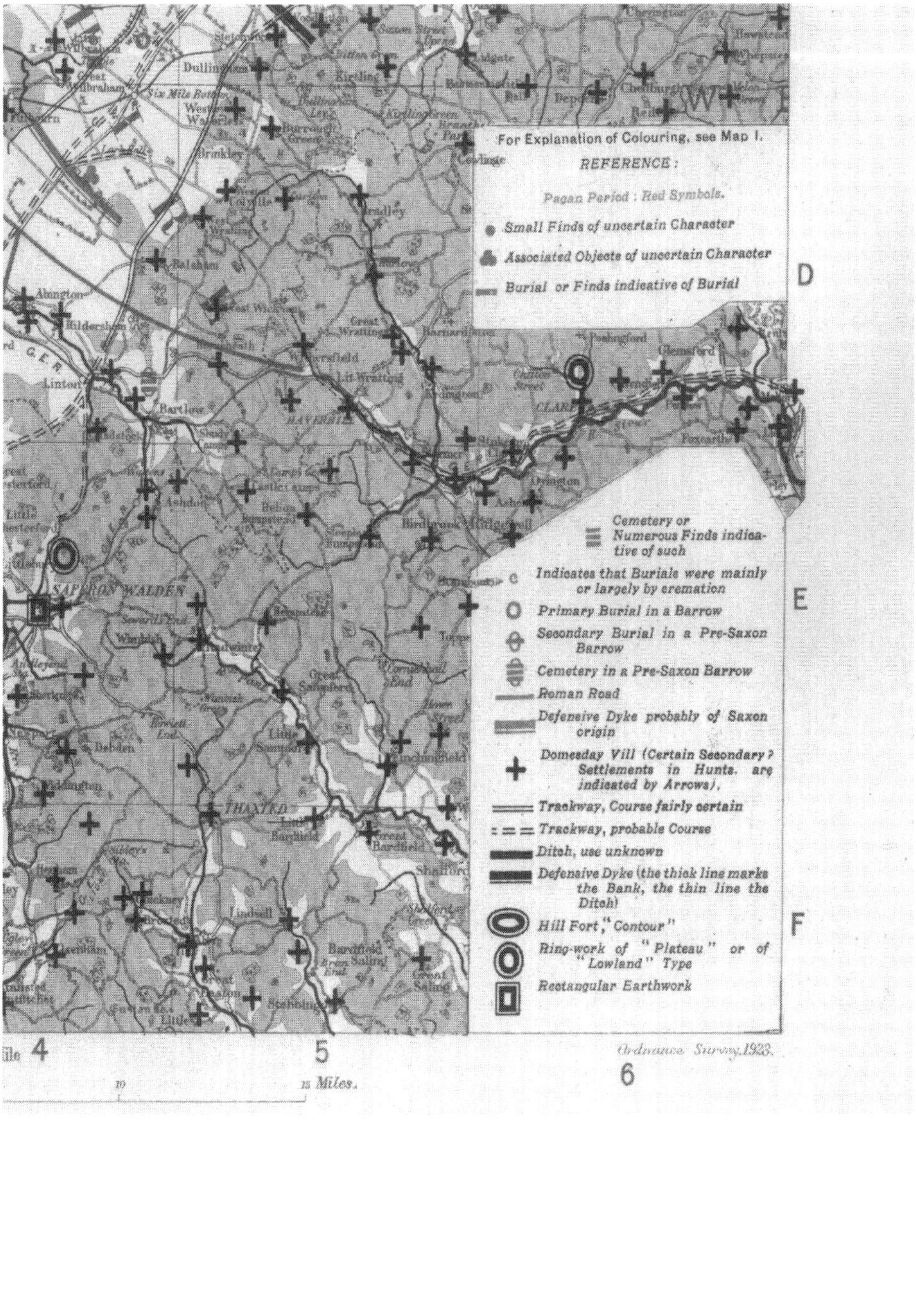
For Explanation of Colouring, see Map I.
REFERENCE:
Pagan Period: Red Symbols.
Small Finds of uncertain Character
Associated Objects of uncertain Character
Burial or Finds indicative of Burial
Cemetery or Numerous Finds indicative of such
Indicates that Burials were mainly or largely by cremation
Primary Burial in a Barrow
Secondary Burial in a Pre-Saxon Barrow
Cemetery in a Pre-Saxon Barrow
Roman Road
Defensive Dyke probably of Saxon origin
Domesday Vill (Certain Secondary? Settlements in Hunts. are indicated by Arrows).
Trackway, Course fairly certain
Trackway, probable Course
Ditch, use unknown
Defensive Dyke (the thick line marks the Bank, the thin line the Ditch)
Hill Fort, "Contour"
Ring-work of "Plateau" or of "Lowland" Type
Rectangular Earthwork
SAFFRON WALDEN
HAVERHILL
THAXTED
CLARE
D
E
F
4
5
6
15 Miles.
Ordnance Survey, 1923.

Printed in Great Britain
by Amazon.co.uk, Ltd.,
Marston Gate.